GREAT ISSUES IN WESTERN CIVILIZA-TION

VOLUME ONE

EDITED BY BRIAN TIERNEY,
DONALD KAGAN,
AND L. PEARCE WILLIAMS

CONSULTING EDITOR:
EUGENE RICE
Columbia University

GREAT ISSUES IN WESTERN CIVILIZA/ TION

VOLUME ONE

Second Edition

Random House · New York

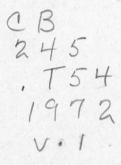

To Frederick G. Marcham

TEACHER—SCHOLAR—COLLEAGUE—FRIEND

NOTE ON THE SECOND EDITION

Many changes have been made in this new edition of *Great Issues* in response to the helpful suggestions we received from college teachers who have been using the volumes in their courses. In particular, the amount of introductory and explanatory material has been substantially increased. In the new, extended Preface we have tried to explain to the student the kinds of real historical problems that lie behind the questions posed in the title of each "great issue." In addition, the individual sections have been given more substantial introductions that explain the historical context of each issue considered and the significance of the particular documents cited.

Experience has shown that most instructors like to begin their courses with the topic "What Is History?" Accordingly, we have moved this section to the beginning of the book. Four sections that seem to have been little used have been omitted from this edition. The treatment of three topics has been radically revised; these are the sections on ancient science, Christianity, and the cold war. The whole work has been reedited in order to make the various sections more uniform in length.

For teachers who prefer to use *Great Issues* in alternative formats, the volume *Great Issues Since 1500* and the series of individual pamphlets are still available in their original editions.

BRIAN TIERNEY

DONALD KAGAN

L. PEARCE WILLIAMS

PREFACE

A major purpose of this two-volume work is to convince students in Western civilization courses that the essential task of a historian is not to collect dead facts but to confront live issues. The issues are alive because they arise out of the tensions that men have to face in every generation—tensions between freedom and authority, between reason and faith, between human free will and all the impersonal circumstances that help to shape our lives. Such issues concern scholars other than historians, of course—philosophers, sociologists, and theologians, for instance. But the historian thinks about them in a distinctive way. We have tried, therefore, to provide for the student not only a body of information about past events and ideas but also an introduction to the ways in which modern historians seek to interpret the record of the past.

In order to achieve any sophisticated understanding of such matters, a student needs to read the views of great modern historians as they are set out in their own words. He needs to develop a measure of critical historical insight by comparing these often conflicting views with the source material on which they are based. He needs, above all, to concern himself with the great issues that have shaped the course of Western civilization and not with historical "problems" that are mere artificially contrived conundrums.

This present volume is divided into ten parts. Each of them includes both original source material and a variety of modern interpretations, and each deals with a truly great issue in Western history. The questions that we have posed in the title of each section are real questions in the sense that they are issues that great historians have really argued about. But they are not questions of a simple "true-false" type. When two capable historians fall into a dispute it is possible, of course, that one is simply wrong and the other right. A historian may be ignorant of some of the source material relevant to the topic he is considering. He may misunderstand his sources. More reprehensibly, he may distort the meaning of the sources in order to make them fit in with his own political or religious prejudices. In all such cases he is likely to be challenged by another scholar.

But differences among historians often have more complex origins than simple error on the part of a particular writer. Sometimes they arise because different authors use the same words in different senses. Thus in considering the question "Periclean Athens—Democracy, Aristocracy, or Monarchy?" it is just as important to ask what the word "democracy" means to the different authors who use it as to ask how the Athenian state was organized in the time of Pericles.

Most typically, historical controversies arise when some historian brings a novel insight to bear on an old problem. The historian's enthusiasm for his new idea can lead to a deeper understanding of the problem he considers, but it can also encourage a one-sided approach to a complex issue. Other historians will point this out and emphasize different approaches—and so a controversy ensues. A good example is provided by the historians' classical problem concerning "the decline and fall of the Roman Empire." By the early twentieth century it was evident that social and economic factors were very important in historical causation. Accordingly, various historians produced social and economic explanations of the fall of Rome. But the fact that social and economic factors were important in the process of decline does not exclude the possibility that religious, moral, and military factors were important too. Hence when we consider a problem as broad as "The Roman Empire—Why Did It Fall?" our real task is not to identify one particular cause of disintegration but to explain how all the different causes of decay interacted to produce the final downfall.

When two historians disagree it is usually because each of them is stating a truth, but each is so preoccupied with his own truth that he regards the view of the other as simply an error. Historical understanding progresses when we come to see that the two truths are in fact compatible with one another and that both are necessary for the understanding of a given historical situation. Fifty years ago historians disagreed violently about the issues implied in the question "Renaissance Man—Medieval or Modern?" Nowadays virtually every sophisticated student of the problem would agree that some medieval ideas and institutions persisted as formative influences on the early modern world while others disappeared or survived only as unimportant anachronisms. In a sense, then, the historical argument that we have presented was a pseudoargument. But it led to a deeper understanding of a complex problem; for we can hardly hope to understand the course of Western history at all until we can determine what the ancient world and the Middle Ages contributed to the formation of modern civilization and what was distinctively new in the age of the Renaissance and the Scientific Revolution. This is a real problem and it is still far from settled.

In considering all the great issues in this book the reader has to ask himself not only what happened in the past but why historians disagree about what happened. Are they using the same words in different senses? Are they emphasizing one truth at the expense of another? Are they allowing their own prejudices to distort their interpretations of historical documents? Are the apparently conflicting opinions really incompatible with one another? If so, which view seems more persuasive? If not, how can the different opinions be reconciled with one another?

We believe that there are three major themes whose development and interplay have shaped the distinctive characteristics that set Western civilization apart from the other great historic cultures. They are the growth of a tradition of rational scientific inquiry, the persistence of a tension between Judaeo-Christian religious ideals and social realities, and the emergence of constitutional forms of government. These three themes are introduced in the first sections of Volume I. The reader will find them recurring in new forms and changing contexts throughout the rest of the work. We hope that in studying them he will come to a richer understanding of the heritage of Western civilization—and of the historian's approach to it.

Ithaca, 1971

BRIAN TIERNEY

DONALD KAGAN

L. PEARCE WILLIAMS

CONTENTS

WHAT IS
HISTORY

FACT OR
FANCY?

CONTENTS

3. *Ought the historian to make moral judgments about the past? Can he avoid doing so?*
4. *How far do you find the argument for relativism convincing?*
5. *Try to use Becker's theory of historical relativism to explain Marx's philosophy of history.*
6. *Does history have any use? If not, does it have any value?*

The first problem for a beginning student of history is to understand the kinds of tasks that historians set themselves and the different ways in which they approach the study of the past. During the past one hundred years men's ways of thinking about history have changed, just as their ways of thinking about science have. The great pioneers who laid the foundations of modern historical methodology in the nineteenth century could feel "assured of certain certainties." They believed that the past of the human race constituted a structure of fact that the historian could learn to understand through critical analysis of the surviving documents. Leopold von Ranke, for instance (pp. 5–6), simply took it for granted that, given sufficient skill and diligence, a historian could find out and set down without bias "what actually happened." Nowadays it is a platitude that a historian who professes total objectivity is likely to be merely ignorant of his own inherent prejudices. (We all have some.) Some historians, like Lord Acton (pp. 14–18) thought that a major part of their task was to judge the men of past ages in the light of their own moral principles, which they assumed to be eternally true. Other nineteenth-century scholars held that scientific "laws of history" could be educed that would not only explain the past but also predict the future. H. T. Buckle, for instance (pp. 6–9), called attention to certain statistical regularities in history and suggested that the whole life of the past might be explained in terms of such regularities. Karl Marx (pp. 9–13) enunciated a general law of "dialectical materialism," which, he thought, explained adequately the whole course of human history. (The three readings from Marx are excerpted from different works, but taken together they provide a brief, coherent statement of his central thesis.) A major difficulty in this "scientific" approach to history is that the historian is concerned not only with statistical regularities or with exemplifications of universal laws but also with unique human personalities and unique events. The history of England, for instance, was profoundly influenced by the Norman Conquest of 1066. But how could any body of statistics or any conceivable general law explain how William the Conqueror came to win the Battle of Hastings? (He very nearly lost it.)

The writers we have mentioned so far shared one presupposition in common. All were convinced of the objectivity of historical knowledge—the facts were objective; the standards of moral judgment were objective; the laws were objective. In the twentieth century all these assumptions were challenged and a theory of historical relativism grew up to complement the relativity of the physicists.

In 1912 J. H. Robinson (pp. 19–24) raised the problem of "relevance," which has become fashionable again sixty years later. Historical study, he argued, should not be mere aimless antiquarianism. It should be pursued in such a way as to serve the needs of the present. In a different spirit, Herbert Butterfield (pp. 24–29) maintained that historians ought not to approach the past with present-day considerations in mind. And, more radically, Carl Becker (pp. 30–43) held that they could not help doing so. Every historian, he argued, was conditioned by his own present. He saw the past, so to speak, through present-day spectacles. Therefore each new generation of historians would see a different past, and so there could be no permanent, objectively valid historical knowledge. Many historians in the 1930s found Becker's argument persuasive and irrefutable. But they continued to write history as though the argument did not exist at all, as though the historian could in fact establish objective truths about the past. Thus a gulf seemed to be opening up between the way historians actually worked and the theoretical explanations of their activity that they felt constrained to adopt.

The most recent movement of thought, presented in the last group of readings (pp. 44–59), has been characterized by a mixture of confidence, humility, and common sense. Many contemporary historians claim less for their craft than did the great system builders of the nineteenth century, but they remain happily convinced of the validity of historical knowledge, within due limits, and of its enduring value as a way of understanding the "condition of man."

1
THE SCIENCE OF HISTORY

Leopold von Ranke has been called the "father of modern historical scholarship." He was convinced that, if a historian studied the relevant documents with sufficient critical acumen, he could discover "what actually happened" in the past. The following extract is from his *Histories of the Latin and Germanic Nations,* published in 1832.

FROM Histories of the Latin and Germanic Nations from 1494–1514 BY LEOPOLD VON RANKE

. . . This book attempts to see these histories and the other, related histories of the Latin and Germanic nations in their unity. To history has been assigned the office of judging the past, of instructing the present for the benefit of future ages. To such high offices this work does not aspire: It wants only to show what actually happened (*wie es eigentlich gewesen*).

But whence the sources for such a new investigation? The basis of the present work, the sources of its material, are memoirs, diaries, letters, diplomatic reports, and original narratives of eyewitnesses; other writings were used only if they were immediately derived from the above mentioned or seemed to equal them because of some original information. These sources will be identified on every page; a second volume, to be published concurrently, will present the method of investigation and the critical conclusions.

Aim and subject mould the form of a book. The writing of history cannot be expected to possess the same free development of its subject which, in theory at least, is expected in a work of literature; I am not sure it was correct to ascribe this quality to the works of the great Greek and Roman masters.

The strict presentation of the facts, contingent and unattractive though they may be, is undoubtedly the supreme law. After this, it seems to me, comes the exposition of the unity and progress of events. Therefore, instead of starting as might have been expected with a general description of the political institutions of Europe—this would certainly have distracted, if not disrupted, our attention—I have preferred to discuss in detail each nation, each power, and each individual only when they assumed a preeminently active or dominant role. I have not been troubled by the fact that here and there they had to be mentioned beforehand, when their existence could not be ignored. In this way, we are better able to grasp the general line of their development, the direction they took, and the ideas by which they were motivated.

Finally, what will be said of my treatment of particulars, which is such an essential part of the writing of history? Will it not often seem harsh, disconnected, colorless, and tiring? There are, of course, noble models both ancient and—be it remembered—modern; I have not dared to emulate them: theirs was a different world. A sublime ideal does exist: the event in its human intelligibility, its unity, and its diversity; this should be within one's reach. I know to what extent I have fallen short of my aim. One tries, one strives, but in the end it is not attained. Let none be disheartened by this! The most important thing is always what we deal with, as Jakobi says, humanity as it is, explicable or inexplicable: the life of the individual, of generations, and of nations, and at times the hand of God above them.

Henry Thomas Buckle held that the proper task of a historian was to discover general laws of historical development that were closely analogous to the laws of physical science.

FROM History of Civilization in England
BY H. T. BUCKLE

Our acquaintance with history being so imperfect, while our materials are so numerous, it seems desirable that something should be done on a scale far larger than has hitherto been attempted, and that a strenuous effort should be made to bring up this great department of inquiry to a level with other de-

Henry Thomas Buckle, *History of Civilization in England*, 2nd ed. (1858), pp. 5–8, 22–23, 29–31.

partments, in order that we may maintain the balance and harmony of our knowledge. It is in this spirit that the present work has been conceived. To make the execution of it fully equal to the conception is impossible: still I hope to accomplish for the history of man something equivalent, or at all events analogous, to what has been effected by other inquirers for the different branches of natural science. In regard to nature, events apparently the most irregular and capricious have been explained, and have been shown to be in accordance with certain fixed and universal laws. This has been done because men of ability, and, above all, men of patient, untiring thought, have studied natural events with the view of discovering their regularity: and if human events were subjected to a similar treatment, we have every right to expect similar results. For it is clear that they who affirm that the facts of history are incapable of being generalized, take for granted the very question at issue. Indeed they do more than this. They not only assume what they cannot prove, but they assume what in the present state of knowledge is highly improbable. Whoever is at all acquainted with what has been done during the last two centuries, must be aware that every generation demonstrates some events to be regular and predictable, which the preceding generation had declared to be irregular and unpredictable: so that the marked tendency of advancing civilization is to strengthen our belief in the universality of order, of method, and of law. This being the case, it follows that if any facts, or class of facts, have not yet been reduced to order, we, so far from pronouncing them to be irreducible, should rather be guided by our experience of the past, and should admit the probability that what we now call inexplicable will at some future time be explained. This expectation of discovering regularity in the midst of confusion is so familiar to scientific men, that among the most eminent of them it becomes an article of faith: and if the same expectation is not generally found among historians, it must be ascribed partly to their being of inferior ability to the investigators of nature, and partly to the greater complexity of those social phenomena with which their studies are concerned.

Both these causes have retarded the creation of the science of history. The most celebrated historians are manifestly inferior to the most successful cultivators of physical science: no one having devoted himself to history who in point of intellect is at all to be compared with Kepler, Newton, or many others that might be named. And as to the greater complexity of the phenomena, the philosophic historian is opposed by difficulties far more formidable than is the student of nature; since, while on the one hand, his observations are more liable to those causes of error which arise from prejudice and passion, he, on the other hand, is unable to employ the great physical resource of experiment, by which we can often simplify even the most intricate problems in the external world.

It is not, therefore, surprising that the study of the movements of Man should be still in its infancy, as compared with the advanced state of the study of the movements of Nature. Indeed the difference between the progress of the two pursuits is so great, that while in physics the regularity of events, and the power of predicting them, are often taken for granted even in cases still unproved, a similar regularity is in history not only not taken for granted, but is actually denied. Hence it is that whoever wishes to raise history to a level with other branches of knowledge, is met by a preliminary obstacle; since he is told that in the affairs of men there is something mysterious and providential, which makes them impervious to our investigations, and which will always hide from us their future course. To this it might be sufficient to reply, that such an assertion is gratuitous; that it is by its nature incapable of proof; and that it is moreover opposed by the notorious fact that everywhere else increasing knowledge is accompanied by an increasing confidence in the uniformity with which, under the same circumstances, the same events must succeed each other. It will, however, be more satisfactory to probe the difficulty deeper, and inquire at once into the foundation of the common opinion that history must always remain in its present empirical state, and can never be raised to the rank of a science. We shall thus be led to one vast question, which indeed lies at the root of the whole subject, and is simply this: Are the actions of men, and therefore of societies, governed by fixed laws, or are they the result either of chance or of supernatural interference?

* * *

Of all offences, it might well be supposed that the crime of murder is one of the most arbitrary and irregular. . . . But now, how stands the fact? The fact is, that murder is committed with as much regularity, and bears as uniform a relation to certain known circumstances, as do the movements of the tides, and the rotations of the seasons. M. Quetelet, who has spent his life in collecting and methodizing the statistics of different countries, states, as the result of his laborious researches, that "in every thing which concerns crime, the same numbers re-occur with a constancy which cannot be mistaken: and that this is the case even with those crimes which seem quite independent of human foresight, such, for instance, as murders, which are generally committed after quarrels arising from circumstances apparently casual. Nevertheless, we know from experience that every year there not only take place nearly the same number of murders, but that even the instruments by which they are committed are employed in the same proportion." This was the language used in 1835 by confessedly the first statistician in Europe, and every subsequent investigation has confirmed its accuracy. For later inquiries have ascertained the extraordinary fact, that the uniform reproduction of crime is more clearly marked, and more capable of being predicted, than are the physical laws connected with the disease and destruction of our bodies.

* * *

Nor is it merely the crimes of men which are marked by this uniformity of sequence. Even the number of marriages annually contracted, is determined, not by the temper and wishes of individuals, but by large general facts, over which individuals can exercise no authority. It is now known that marriages bear a fixed and definite relation to the price of corn; and in England the experience of a century has proved that, instead of having any connexion with personal feelings, they are simply regulated by the average earnings of the great mass of the people, so that this immense social and religious institution is not only swayed, but is completely controlled, by the price of food and by the rate of wages. . . .

* * *

To those who have a steady conception of the regularity of events, and have firmly seized the great truth that the actions of men, being guided by their antecedents, are in reality never inconsistent, but, however capricious they may appear, only form part of one vast scheme of universal order, of which we in the present state of knowledge can barely see the outline,—to those who understand this, which is at once the key and the basis of history, the facts just adduced, so far from being strange, will be precisely what would have been expected, and ought long since to have been known. Indeed, the progress of inquiry is becoming so rapid and so earnest, that I entertain little doubt that before another century has elapsed, the chain of evidence will be complete, and it will be as rare to find an historian who denies the undeviating regularity of the moral world, as it now is to find a philosopher who denies the regularity of the material world.

The most famous attempt actually to construct a science of history in the nineteenth century was that of Karl Marx. The first extract given below is from a joint work of Marx and Engels published in 1846.

FROM The German Ideology
BY KARL MARX AND FRIEDRICH ENGELS

Men can be distinguished from animals by consciousness, by religion or anything else you like. They themselves begin to distinguish themselves from animals as soon as they begin to *produce* their means of subsistence, a step which is conditioned by their physical organization. By producing their means of subsistence men are indirectly producing their actual material life.

The way in which men produce their means of subsistence depends first of

Karl Marx and Frederick Engels, *The German Ideology* (1947), pp. 7–9, 14–15, edited with an Introduction by R. Pascal. Reprinted by permission of International Publishers Co., Inc.

all on the nature of the actual means they find in existence and have to reproduce. This mode of production must not be considered simply as being the reproduction of the physical existence of the individuals. Rather it is a definite form of activity of these individuals, a definite form of expressing their life, a definite *mode of life* on their part. As individuals express their life, so they are. What they are, therefore, coincides with their production, both with *what* they produce and with *how* they produce. The nature of individuals thus depends on the material conditions determining their production.

This production only makes its appearance with the increase of population. In its turn this presupposes the intercourse of individuals with one another. The form of this intercourse is again determined by production.

The relations of different nations among themselves depend upon the extent to which each has developed its productive forces, the division of labour and internal intercourse. This statement is generally recognized. But not only the relation of one nation to others, but also the whole internal structure of the nation itself depends on the stage of development reached by its production and its internal and external intercourse. How far the productive forces of a nation are developed is shown most manifestly by the degree to which the division of labour has been carried. Each new productive force, in so far as it is not merely a quantitative extension of productive forces already known, (for instance the bringing into cultivation of fresh land), brings about a further development of the division of labour.

The division of labour inside a nation leads at first to the separation of industrial and commercial from agricultural labour, and hence to the separation of town and country and a clash of interests between them. Its further development leads to the separation of commercial from industrial labour. At the same time through the division of labour there develop further, inside these various branches, various divisions among the individuals co-operating in definite kinds of labour. The relative position of these individual groups is determined by the methods employed in agriculture, industry and commerce (patriarchalism, slavery, estates, classes). These same conditions are to be seen (given a more developed intercourse) in the relations of different nations to one another.

The various stages of development in the division of labour are just so many different forms of ownership; i.e., the existing stage in the division of labour determines also the relations of individuals to one another with reference to the material, instrument, and product of the labour. . . .

In direct contrast to German philosophy which descends from heaven to earth, here we ascend from earth to heaven. That is to say, we do not set out from what men say, imagine, conceive, nor from men as narrated, thought of, imagined, conceived, in order to arrive at men in the flesh. We set out from real, active men, and on the basis of their real life-process we demonstrate the development of the ideological reflexes and echoes of this life-process. The phantoms formed in the human brain are also, necessarily, sublimates of their material life-process, which is empirically verifiable and bound to material premises. Morality, religion, metaphysics, all the rest of ideology and their corresponding forms of consciousness, thus no longer retain the semblance of independence. They have no history, no development; but men, developing their material production and their material intercourse, alter, along with this their real existence, their thinking and the products of their thinking. Life is not determined by consciousness, but consciousness by life. In the first method of approach the starting-point is consciousness taken as the living individual; in the second it is the real living individuals themselves, as they are in actual life, and consciousness is considered solely as *their* consciousness.

The following two extracts are from works of Marx that appeared in 1859 and 1867.

FROM Preface to A Contribution to the Critique of Political Economy BY KARL MARX

In the social production of their life, men enter into definite relations that are indispensable and independent of their will, relations of production which correspond to a definite stage of development of their material productive forces. The sum total of these relations of production constitutes the economic structure of society, the real foundation, on which rises a legal and political superstructure and to which correspond definite forms of social consciousness. The mode of production of material life conditions the social, political and intellectual life process in general. It is not the consciousness of men that determines their being, but, on the contrary, their social being that determines their consciousness. At a certain stage of their development, the material productive forces of society come in conflict with the existing relations of production, or—what is but a legal expression for the same thing—with the property relations within which they have been at work hitherto. From forms of development of the productive forces these relations turn into their fetters. Then begins an epoch of social revolution. With the change of the economic foundation the entire immense superstructure is more or less rapidly transformed. In considering such transformations a distinction should always be made between the material transformation of the economic conditions of production, which can be determined with the precision of natural

Karl Marx, "Preface to A Contribution to the Critique of Political Economy," in *Karl Marx and Frederick Engels: Selected Works,* I (1951), 328–329. Reprinted by permission of Lawrence and Wishart Ltd., London.

science, and the legal, political, religious, esthetic or philosophic—in short, ideological forms in which men become conscious of this conflict and fight it out. Just as our opinion of an individual is not based on what he thinks of himself, so can we not judge of such a period of transformation by its own consciousness; on the contrary, this consciousness must be explained rather from the contradictions of material life, from the existing conflict between the social productive forces and the relations of production. No social order ever perishes before all the productive forces for which there is room in it have developed; and new, higher relations of production never appear before the material conditions of their existence have matured in the womb of the old society itself. Therefore mankind always sets itself only such tasks as it can solve; since, looking at the matter more closely, it will always be found that the task itself arises only when the material conditions for its solution already exist or are at least in the process of formation. In broad outlines Asiatic, ancient, feudal, and modern bourgeois modes of production can be designated as progressive epochs in the economic formation of society. The bourgeois relations of production are the last antagonistic form of the social process of production—antagonistic not in the sense of individual antagonism, but of one arising from the social conditions of life of the individuals; at the same time the productive forces developing in the womb of bourgeois society create the material conditions for the solution of that antagonism. This social formation brings, therefore, the prehistory of human society to a close.

FROM Capital BY KARL MARX

As soon as this process of transformation has sufficiently decomposed the old society from top to bottom, as soon as the labourers are turned into proletarians, their means of labour into capital, as soon as the capitalist mode of production stands on its own feet, then the further socialisation of labour and further transformation of the land and other means of production into socially exploited and, therefore, common means of production, as well as the further expropriation of private proprietors, take a new form. That which is now to be expropriated is no longer the labourer working for himself, but the capitalist exploiting many labourers. This expropriation is accomplished by the action of the immanent laws of capitalistic production itself, by the centralisation of capital. One capitalist always kills many. Hand in hand with this centralisation, or this expropriation of many capitalists by few, develop, on an ever extending scale, the co-operative form of the labour-process, the conscious technical application of science, the methodical cultivation of the

Karl Marx, *Capital*, in *Karl Marx and Frederick Engels: Selected Works*, I (1951), 416–418. Reprinted by permission of Lawrence and Wishart Ltd., London.

soil, the transformation of the instruments of labour into instruments of labour only usable in common, the economising of all means of production by their use as the means of production of combined, socialised labour, the entanglement of all peoples in the net of the world market, and with this, the international character of the capitalistic régime. Along with the constantly diminishing number of the magnates of capital, who usurp and monopolise all advantages of this process of transformation, grows the mass of misery, oppression, slavery, degradation, exploitation; but with this too grows the revolt of the working-class, a class always increasing in numbers, and disciplined, united, organised by the very mechanism of the process of capitalist production itself. The monopoly of capital becomes a fetter upon the mode of production, which has sprung up and flourished along with, and under it. Centralisation of the means of production and socialisation of labour at last reach a point where they become incompatible with their capitalist integument. This integument is burst asunder. The knell of capitalist private property sounds. The expropriators are expropriated.

The capitalist mode of appropriation, the result of the capitalist mode of production, produces capitalist private property. This is the first negation of individual private property, as founded on the labour of the proprietor. But capitalist production begets, with the inexorability of a law of Nature, its own negation. It is the negation of negation. This does not re-establish private property for the producer, but gives him individual property based on the acquisitions of the capitalist era: i.e., on co-operation and the possession in common of the land and of the means of production.

The transformation of scattered private property, arising from individual labour, into capitalist private property is, naturally, a process, incomparably more protracted, violent, and difficult, than the transformation of capitalistic private property, already practically resting on socialised production, into socialised property. In the former case, we had the expropriation of the mass of the people by a few usurpers; in the latter, we have the expropriation of a few usurpers by the mass of the people.

2
THE
HISTORIAN
AS
JUDGE

Lord Acton urged the historian to analyze his sources scrupulously but not to stop there: he should proceed to sit in judgment on the deeds of the past.

FROM Inaugural Lecture on the Study of History
BY J. E. E. ACTON

For our purpose, the main thing to learn is not the art of accumulating material, but the sublimer art of investigating it, of discerning truth from falsehood and certainty from doubt. It is by solidity of criticism more than by the plenitude of erudition, that the study of history strengthens, and straightens, and extends the mind. And the accession of the critic in the place of the indefatigable compiler, of the artist in coloured narrative, the skilled limner of character, the persuasive advocate of good, or other, causes, amounts to a transfer of government, to a change of dynasty, in the historic realm. For the critic is one who, when he lights on an interesting statement, begins by suspecting it. He remains in suspense until he has subjected his authority to three operations. First, he asks whether he has read the passage as the author wrote it. For the transcriber, and the editor, and the official or officious censor on the top of the editor, have played strange tricks, and have much to answer for. And if they are not to blame, it may turn out that the author wrote his book twice over, that you can discover the first jet, the progressive variations, things added, and things struck out. Next is the question where the writer got his information. If from a previous writer, it can be ascertained, and the

John Edward Emerich Acton, "Inaugural Lecture on the Study of History," in *Lectures on Modern History* (1906), pp. 15–16, 23–24, 26–28.

inquiry has to be repeated. If from unpublished papers, they must be traced, and when the fountain-head is reached, or the track disappears, the question of veracity arises. The responsible writer's character, his position, antecedents, and probable motives have to be examined into; and this is what, in a different and adapted sense of the word, may be called the higher criticism, in comparison with the servile and often mechanical work of pursuing statements to their root. For a historian has to be treated as a witness, and not believed unless his sincerity is established. The maxim that a man must be presumed to be innocent until his guilt is proved, was not made for him.

* * *

I shall never again enjoy the opportunity of speaking my thoughts to such an audience as this, and on so privileged an occasion a lecturer may well be tempted to bethink himself whether he knows of any neglected truth, any cardinal proposition, that might serve as his selected epigraph, as a last signal, perhaps even as a target. I am not thinking of those shining precepts which are the registered property of every school; that is to say—Learn as much by writing as by reading; be not content with the best book; seek sidelights from the others; have no favourites; keep men and things apart; guard against the prestige of great names; see that your judgments are your own, and do not shrink from disagreement; no trusting without testing; be more severe to ideas than to actions; do not overlook the strength of the bad cause or the weakness of the good; never be surprised by the crumbling of an idol or the disclosure of a skeleton; judge talent at its best and character at its worst; suspect power more than vice, and study problems in preference to periods; for instance: the derivation of Luther, the scientific influence of Bacon, the predecessors of Adam Smith, the medieval masters of Rousseau, the consistency of Burke, the identity of the first Whig. Most of this, I suppose, is undisputed, and calls for no enlargement. But the weight of opinion is against me when I exhort you never to debase the moral currency or to lower the standard of rectitude, but to try others by the final maxim that governs your own lives, and to suffer no man and no cause to escape the undying penalty which history has the power to inflict on wrong. The plea in extenuation of guilt and mitigation of punishment is perpetual. At every step we are met by arguments which go to excuse, to palliate, to confound right and wrong, and reduce the just man to the level of the reprobate. The men who plot to baffle and resist us are, first of all, those who made history what it has become. They set up the principle that only a foolish Conservative judges the present time with the ideas of the past; that only a foolish Liberal judges the past with the ideas of the present.

The mission of that school was to make distant times, and especially the Middle Ages, then most distant of all, intelligible and acceptable to a society issuing from the eighteenth century. There were difficulties in the way; and among others this, that, in the first fervour of the Crusades the men who took the Cross, after receiving communion, heartily devoted the day to the extermination of Jews. To judge them by a fixed standard, to call them sacrilegious fanatics or furious hypocrites, was to yield a gratuitous victory to Voltaire. It became a rule of policy to praise the spirit when you could not defend the deed. So that we have no common code; our moral notions are always fluid; and you must consider the times, the class from which men sprang, the surrounding influences, the masters in their schools, the preachers in their pulpits, the movement they obscurely obeyed, and so on, until responsibility is merged in numbers, and not a culprit is left for execution. A murderer was no criminal if he followed local custom, if neighbours approved, if he was encouraged by official advisors or prompted by just authority, if he acted for the reason of state or the pure love of religion, or if he sheltered himself behind the complicity of the Law. The depression of morality was flagrant; but the motives were those which have enabled us to contemplate with distressing complacency the secret of unhallowed lives. The code that is greatly modified by time and place, will vary according to the cause. The amnesty is an artifice that enables us to make exceptions, to tamper with weights and measures, to deal unequal justice to friends and enemies.

It is associated with that philosophy which Cato attributes to the gods. For we have a theory which justifies Providence by the event, and holds nothing so deserving as success, to which there can be no victory in a bad cause; prescription and duration legitimate; and whatever exists is right and reasonable; and as God manifests His will by that which He tolerates, we must conform to the divine decree by living to shape the future after the ratified image of the past. Another theory, less confidently urged, regards History as our guide, as much by showing errors to evade as examples to pursue. It is suspicious of illusions in success, and, though there may be hope of ultimate triumph for what is true, if not by its own attraction, by the gradual exhaustion of error, it admits no corresponding promise for what is ethically right. It deems the canonisation of the historic past more perilous than ignorance or denial, because it would perpetuate the reign of sin and acknowledge the sovereignty of wrong, and conceives it the part of real greatness to know how to stand and fall alone, stemming, for a lifetime, the contemporary flood.

Ranke relates, without adornment, that William III ordered the extirpation of a Catholic clan, and scouts the faltering excuse of his defenders. But when he comes to the death and character of the international deliverer, Glencoe is forgotten, the imputation of murder drops, like a thing unworthy of notice. Johannes Mueller, a great Swiss celebrity, writes that the British Constitution occurred to somebody, perhaps to Halifax. This artless statement might not be approved by rigid lawyers as a faithful and felicitous indication of the manner of that mysterious growth of ages, from occult beginnings, that was never profaned by the invading wit of man; but it is less grotesque than it appears. Lord Halifax was the most original writer of political tracts in the pamphleteering crowd between Harrington and Bolingbroke; and in the Exclusion struggle he produced a scheme of limitations which, in substance, if not in form, foreshadowed the position of the monarchy in the later Hanoverian reigns. Although Halifax did not believe in the plot, he insisted that innocent victims should be sacrificed to content the multitude. Sir William Temple writes: "We only disagreed in one point, which was the leaving some priests to the law upon the accusation of being priests only, as the House of Commons had desired; which I thought wholly unjust. Upon this point Lord Halifax and I had so sharp a debate at Lord Sunderland's lodgings, that he told me, if I would not concur in points which were so necessary for the people's satisfaction, he would tell everybody I was a Papist. And upon his affirming that the plot must be handled as if it were true, whether it were so or no, in those points that were so generally believed." In spite of this accusing passage, Macaulay, who prefers Halifax to all the statesmen of his age, praises him for his mercy: "His dislike of extremes, and a forgiving and compassionate temper which seems to have been natural to him, preserved him from all participation in the worst crimes of his time."

If, in our uncertainty, we must often err, it may be sometimes better to risk excess in rigour than in indulgence, for then at least we do no injury by loss of principle. As Bayle has said, it is more probable that the secret motives of an indifferent action are bad than good; and this discouraging conclusion does not depend upon theology, for James Mozley supports the sceptic from the other flank, with all the artillery of Tractarian Oxford. "A Christian," he says, "is bound by his very creed to suspect evil, and cannot release himself. . . . He sees it where others do not; his instinct is divinely strengthened; his eye is supernaturally keen; he has a spiritual insight, and senses exercised to discern. . . . He owns the doctrine of original sin; that doctrine puts him necessarily on his guard against appearances, sustains his apprehension under perplexity, and prepares him for recognising anywhere what he knows to be everywhere." There is a popular saying of Madame de Staël, that we forgive whatever we really understand. The paradox has been judiciously pruned by her descendant, the Duke de Broglie, in the words: "Beware of too much explaining, lest we end by too much excusing." History, says Froude, does teach that right and wrong are real distinctions. Opinions alter, manners change, creeds rise and fall, but the moral law is written on the tablets of eternity. And if there are moments when we may resist the teaching of Froude, we have seldom the chance of resisting when he is supported by Mr. Goldwin Smith: "A sound historical morality will sanction strong measures in evil times; selfish ambition, treachery, murder, perjury, it will never sanction in the worst of times, for these are the things that make times evil.—Justice has been justice, mercy has been mercy, honour has been honour, good faith has been good faith, truthfulness has been truthfulness from the beginning." The doctrine that, as Sir Thomas Browne says, morality is not ambulatory, is expressed as follows by Burke, who, when true to himself, is the most intelligent of our instructors: "My principles enable me to form my judgment upon men and actions in history, just as they do in common life;

and are not formed out of events and characters, either present or past. History is a preceptor of prudence, not of principles. The principles of true politics are those of morality enlarged; and I neither now do, nor ever will admit of any other."

3
THE PAST
AND THE
PRESENT

In the early twentieth century a group of scholars in America wrote about the need for a "new history." They urged especially that the study of the past should be conducted in such a way as to illuminate the present and even to guide men's actions for the future.

FROM The New History BY J. H. ROBINSON

In its amplest meaning History includes every trace and vestige of everything that man has done or thought since first he appeared on the earth. It may aspire to follow the fate of nations or it may depict the habits and emotions of the most obscure individual. Its sources of information extend from the rude flint hatchets of Chelles to this morning's newspaper. It is the vague and comprehensive science of past human affairs. We are within its bounds whether we decipher a mortgage on an Assyrian tile, estimate the value of the Diamond Necklace, or describe the over-short pastry to which Charles V was addicted to his undoing. The tragic reflections of Eli's daughter-in-law, when she learned of the discomfiture of her people at Ebenezer, are history; so are the provisions of Magna Carta, the origin of the doctrine of transubstantiation, the fall of Santiago, the difference between a black friar and a white friar, and the certified circulation of the *New York World* upon February 1 of the current year. Each fact has its interest and importance; all have been carefully recorded.

James Harvey Robinson, *The New History* (1912), pp. 1–3, 17–24. Copyright 1912 by The Macmillan Company. Copyright renewed 1940 by The Bankers Trust Company. Reprinted by permission of The Macmillan Company.

Now, when a writer opens and begins to peruse the thick, closely written volume of human experience, with a view of making an abstract of it for those who have no time to study the original work, he is immediately forced to ask himself what he shall select to present to his reader's attention. He finds that the great book from which he gains his information is grotesquely out of perspective, for it was compiled by many different hands, and by those widely separated in time and in sentiment—by Herodotus, Machiavelli, Eusebius, St. Simon, Otto of Freising, Pepys, St. Luke, the Duchess of Abrantès, Sallust, Cotton Mather. The portentously serious alternates with the lightest gossip. A dissipated courtier may be allotted a chapter and the destruction of a race be left unrecorded. It is clear that in treating history for the general reader the question of selection and proportion is momentous. Yet when we turn to our more popular treatises on the subject, the obvious and pressing need of picking and choosing, of selecting, reselecting, and selecting again, would seem to have escaped most writers. They appear to be the victims of tradition in dealing with the past. They exhibit but little appreciation of the vast resources upon which they might draw, and unconsciously follow, for the most part, an established routine in their selection of facts. When we consider the vast range of human interests, our histories furnish us with a sadly inadequate and misleading review of the past, and it might almost seem as if historians had joined in a conspiracy to foster a narrow and relatively unedifying conception of the true scope and intent of historical study. This is apparent if we examine any of the older standard outlines or handbooks from which a great part of the public has derived its notions of the past, either in school or later in life.

The following is an extract from a compendium much used until recently in schools and colleges: "Robert the Wise (of Anjou) (1309–1343), the successor of Charles II of Naples, and the champion of the Guelphs, could not extend his power over Sicily where Frederick II (1296–1337), the son of Peter of Aragon, reigned. Robert's granddaughter, Joan I, after a career of crime and misfortune, was strangled in prison by Charles Durazzo, the last male descendant of the house of Anjou in Lower Italy (1382), who seized on the government. Joan II, the last heir of Durazzo (1414–1435), first adopted Alfonso V, of Aragon, and then Louis III, of Anjou, and his brother, René. Alfonso, who inherited the crown of Sicily, united both kingdoms (1435), after a war with René and the Visconti of Milan."

This is not, as we might be tempted to suspect, a mere collection of data for contingent reference, no more intended to be read than a table of logarithms. It is a characteristic passage from the six pages which a distinguished scholar devoted to the Italy of Dante, Petrarch, and Lorenzo the Magnificent.

* * *

History is doubtless

    An orchard bearing several trees
    And fruits of different tastes.

It may please our fancy, gratify our serious or idle curiosity, test our memories, and, as Bolingbroke says, contribute to "a creditable kind of ignorance." But the one thing that it ought to do, and has not yet effectively done, is to help us to understand ourselves and our fellows and the problems and prospects of mankind. It is this most significant form of history's usefulness that has been most commonly neglected.

It is true that it has long been held that certain lessons could be derived from the past—precedents for the statesman and the warrior, moral guidance and consoling instances of providential interference for the commonalty. But there is a growing suspicion, which has reached conviction in the minds of most modern historians, that this type of usefulness is purely illusory. The present writer is anxious to avoid any risk of being regarded as an advocate of these supposed advantages of historical study. Their value rests on the assumption that conditions remain sufficiently uniform to give precedents a perpetual value, while, as a matter of fact, conditions, at least in our own time, are so rapidly altering that for the most part it would be dangerous indeed to attempt to apply past experience to the solution of current problems. Moreover, we rarely have sufficient reliable information in regard to the supposed analogous situation in the past to enable us to apply it to present needs. Most of the appeals of inexpensive oratory to "what history teaches" belong to this class of assumed analogies which will not bear close scrutiny. When I speak of history enabling us to understand ourselves and the problems and prospects of mankind, I have something quite different in mind, which I will try to make plain by calling the reader's attention to the use that he makes of his own personal history.

We are almost entirely dependent upon our memory of our past thoughts and experiences for an understanding of the situation in which we find ourselves at any given moment. To take the nearest example, the reader will have to consult his own history to understand why his eyes are fixed upon this particular page. If he should fall into a sound sleep and be suddenly awakened, his memory might for the moment be paralyzed, and he would gaze in astonishment about the room, with no realization of his whereabouts. The fact that all the familiar objects about him presented themselves plainly to his view would not be sufficient to make him feel at home until his memory had come to his aid and enabled him to recall a certain portion of the past. The momentary suspension of memory's functions as one recovers from a fainting fit or emerges from the effects of an anaesthetic is sometimes so distressing as to amount to a sort of intellectual agony. In its normal state the mind selects automatically, from the almost infinite mass of memories, just those things in our past which make us feel at home in the present. It works so easily and efficiently that we are unconscious of what it is doing for us and of how dependent we are upon it. It supplies so promptly and so precisely what we need from the past in order to make the present intelligible that we are beguiled into the mistaken notion that the present is self-explanatory and quite able to take care of itself, and that the past is largely dead and irrelevant, except when we have to make a conscious effort to recall some elusive fact.

What we call history is not so different from our more intimate personal memories as at first sight it seems to be; for very many of the useful and essential elements in our recollections are not personal experiences at all, but include a multitude of things which we have been told or have read; and these play a very important part in our life. Should the reader of this page stop to reflect, he would perceive a long succession of historical antecedents leading up to his presence in a particular room, his ability to read the English language, his momentary freedom from pressing cares, and his inclination to center his attention upon a discussion of the nature and value of historical study. Were he not vaguely conscious of these historical antecedents, he would be in the bewildered condition spoken of above. Some of the memories necessary to save him from his bewilderment are parts of his own past experience, but many of them belong to the realm of history, namely, to what he has been told or what he has read of the past.

I could have no hope that this line of argument would make the slightest impression upon the reader, were he confined either to the immediate impressions of the moment, or to his personal experiences. It gives one something of a shock, indeed, to consider what a very small part of our guiding convictions are in any way connected with our personal experience. The date of our own birth is quite as strictly historical a fact as that of Artaphernes or of Innocent III; we are forced to a helpless reliance upon the evidence of others for both events.

So it comes about that our personal recollections insensibly merge into history in the ordinary sense of the word. History, from this point of view, may be regarded as an artificial extension and broadening of our memories and may be used to overcome the natural bewilderment of all unfamiliar situations. Could we suddenly be endowed with a Godlike and exhaustive knowledge of the whole history of mankind, far more complete than the combined knowledge of all the histories ever written, we should gain forthwith a Godlike appreciation of the world in which we live, and a Godlike insight into the evils which mankind now suffers, as well as into the most promising methods for alleviating them, *not because the past would furnish precedents of conduct, but because our conduct would be based upon a perfect comprehension of existing conditions founded upon a perfect knowledge of the past.* As yet we are not in a position to interrogate the past with a view to gaining light on great social, political, economic, religious, and educational questions in the manner in which we settle the personal problems which face us—for example, whether we should make such and such a visit or investment, or read such and such a book,—by unconsciously judging the situation in the light of our recollections. Historians have not as yet set themselves to furnish us with what lies behind our great contemporaneous task of human betterment. They have hitherto had other notions of their functions, and were they asked to furnish answers to the questions that a person *au courant* with the problems of the day would most naturally put to them, they would with one accord begin to make excuses. One would say that it had long been recognized that it was the historian's business to deal with kings, parliaments, constitutions, wars, treaties, and territorial changes; another would declare that recent history cannot be adequately written and that, therefore, we can never hope to bring the past into relation with the present, but must always leave a fitting interval between ourselves and the nearest point to which the historian should venture to extend his researches; a third will urge that to have a purpose in historical study is to endanger those principles of objectivity upon which all sound and scientific research must be based. So it comes about that our books are like very bad memories which insist upon recalling facts that have no assignable relation to our needs, and this is the reason why the practical value of history has so long been obscured.

In order to make still clearer our dependence upon history in dealing with the present, let the reader remember that we owe most of our institutions to a rather remote past, which alone can explain their origin. The conditions which produced the Holy Roman Apostolic Church, trial by jury, the Privy Council, the degree of LL.D., the Book of Common Prayer, "the liberal arts," were very different from those that exist to-day. Contemporaneous religious, educational, and legal ideals are not the immediate product of existing circumstances, but were developed in great part during periods when man knew far less than he now does. Curiously enough our habits of thought change much more slowly than our environment and are usually far in arrears. Our respect for a given institution or social convention may be purely traditional and have little relation to its value, as judged by existing conditions. We are, therefore, in constant danger of viewing present problems with obsolete emotions and of attempting to settle them by obsolete reasoning. This is one of the chief reasons why we are never by any means perfectly adjusted to our environment.

Our notions of a church and its proper function in society, of a capitalist, of a liberal education, of paying taxes, of Sunday observance, of poverty, of war, are determined only to a slight extent by what is happening to-day. The belief on which I was reared, that God ordained the observance of Sunday from the clouds of Sinai, is an anachronism which could not spontaneously have developed in the United States in the nineteenth century; nevertheless, it still continues to influence the conduct of many persons. We pay our taxes as grudgingly as if they were still the extortions of feudal barons or absolute monarchs for their personal gratification, although they are now a contribution to our common expenses fixed by our own representatives. Few have outgrown the emotions connected with war at a time when personal prowess played a much greater part than the Steel Trust. Conservative college presidents still feel obliged to defend the "liberal arts" and the "humanities" without any very clear understanding of how the task came to be imposed upon them. To do justice to the anachronisms in conservative economic and legal reasoning would require a whole volume.

Society is to-day engaged in a tremendous and unprecedented effort to better itself in manifold ways. Never has our knowledge of the world and of man been so great as it now is; never before has there been so much general good will and so much intelligent social activity as now prevails. The part that each of us can play in forwarding some phase of this reform will depend upon our understanding of existing conditions and opinion, and these can only be explained, as has been shown, by following more or less carefully the processes that produced them. We must develop historical-mindedness upon a far more generous scale than hitherto, for this will add a still deficient element in our intellectual equipment and will promote rational progress as nothing else can do. The present has hitherto been the willing victim of the past; the time has now come when it should turn on the past and exploit it in the interest of advance.

Herbert Butterfield was much more skeptical than Robinson about the results that could be achieved by approaching the past with present-day considerations in mind.

FROM The Whig Interpretation of History
BY HERBERT BUTTERFIELD

The primary assumption of all attempts to understand the men of the past must be the belief that we can in some degree enter into minds that are unlike our own. If this belief were unfounded it would seem that men must be for ever locked away from one another, and all generations must be regarded as a world and a law unto themselves. If we were unable to enter in any way into the mind of a present-day Roman Catholic priest, for example, and similarly into the mind of an atheistical orator in Hyde Park, it is difficult to see how we could know anything of the still stranger men of the 16th century, or pretend to understand the process of history-making which has moulded us into the world of to-day. In reality the historian postulates that the world is in some sense always the same world and that even the men most dissimilar are never absolutely unlike. And though a sentence from Aquinas may fall so strangely upon modern ears that it becomes plausible to dismiss the man as a fool or a mind utterly and absolutely alien, I take it that

Reprinted from The Whig Interpretation of History (1950), pp. 9–14, 16–18, 24–28, by Herbert Butterfield by permission of W. W. Norton & Company, Inc., and G. Bell & Sons Ltd., London, the original publisher. All Rights Reserved by W. W. Norton & Company, Inc.

to dismiss a man in this way is a method of blocking up the mind against him, and against something important in both human nature and its history; it is really the refusal to a historical personage of the effort of historical understanding. Precisely because of his unlikeness to ourselves Aquinas is the more enticing subject for the historical imagination; for the chief aim of the historian is the elucidation of the unlikenesses between past and present and his chief function is to act in this way as the mediator between other generations and our own. It is not for him to stress and magnify the similarities between one age and another, and he is riding after a whole flock of misapprehensions if he goes to hunt for the present in the past. Rather it is his work to destroy those very analogies which we imagined to exist. When he shows us that Magna Carta is a feudal document in a feudal setting, with implications different from those we had taken for granted, he is disillusioning us concerning something in the past which we had assumed to be too like something in the present. That whole process of specialised research which has in so many fields revised the previously accepted whig interpretation of history, has set out bearings afresh in one period after another, by referring matters in this way to their context, and so discovering their unlikeness to the world of the present-day.

It is part and parcel of the whig interpretation of history that it studies the past with reference to the present; and although there may be a sense in which this is unobjectionable if its implications are carefully considered, and there may be a sense in which it is inescapable, it has often been an obstruction to historical understanding because it has been taken to mean the study of the past with direct and perpetual reference to the present. Through this system of immediate reference to the present day, historical personages can easily and irresistibly be classed into the men who furthered progress and the men who tried to hinder it; so that a handy rule of thumb exists by which the historian can select and reject, and can make his points of emphasis. On this system the historian is bound to construe his function as demanding him to be vigilant for likenesses between past and present, instead of being vigilant for unlikenesses; so that he will find it easy to say that he has seen the present in the past, he will imagine that he has discovered a "root" or an "anticipation" of the 20th century, when in reality he is in a world of different connotations altogether, and he has merely tumbled upon what could be shown to be a misleading analogy. Working upon the same system the whig historian can draw lines through certain events, some such line as that which leads through Martin Luther and a long succession of whigs to modern liberty; and if he is not careful he begins to forget that this line is merely a mental trick of his; he comes to imagine that it represents something like a line of causation. The total result of this method is to impose a certain form upon the whole historical story, and to produce a scheme of general history which is bound to converge beautifully upon the present—all demonstrating throughout the ages the workings of an obvious principle of progress, of which the Protestants and whigs have been the perennial allies while Catholics and tories have perpetually formed obstruction. A caricature of this result is to be seen in a popular view that is still not quite eradicated: the view that the Middle Ages represented a period of darkness when man was kept tongue-tied by authority—a period against which the Renaissance was the reaction and the Reformation the great rebellion. It is illustrated to perfection in the argument of a man denouncing Roman Catholicism at a street corner, who said: "When the Pope ruled England them was called the Dark Ages."

The whig historian stands on the summit of the 20th century, and organises his scheme of history from the point of view of his own day; and he is a subtle man to overturn from his mountain-top where he can fortify himself with plausible argument. He can say that events take on their due proportions when observed through the lapse of time. He can say that events must be judged by their ultimate issues, which, since we can trace them no farther, we must at least follow down to the present. He can say that it is only in relation to the 20th century that one happening or another in the past has relevance or significance for us. He can use all the arguments that are so handy to men when discussion is dragged into the market place and philosophy is dethroned by common sense; so that it is no simple matter to demonstrate how the whig historian, from his mountain-top, sees the course of history only inverted and aslant. The fallacy lies in the fact that if the historian working on the 16th century keeps the 20th century in his mind, he makes direct reference across all the intervening period between Luther or the Popes and the world of our own day. And this immediate juxtaposition of past and present, though it makes everything easy and makes some inferences perilously obvious, is bound to lead to an over-simplification of the relations between events and a complete misapprehension of the relations between past and present.

*　*　*

There is an alternative line of assumption upon which the historian can base himself when he comes to his study of the past; and it is the one upon which he does seem more or less consciously to act and to direct his mind when he is engaged upon a piece of research. On this view he comes to his labours conscious of the fact that he is trying to understand the past for the sake of the past, and though it is true that he can never entirely abstract himself from his own age, it is none the less certain that this consciousness of his purpose is a very different one from that of the whig historian, who tells himself that he is studying the past for the sake of the present. Real historical understanding is not achieved by the subordination of the past to the present, but rather by our making the past our present and attempting to see life with the eyes of another century than our own. It is not reached by assuming that our own age is the absolute to which Luther and Calvin and their generation are only relative; it is only reached by fully accepting the fact that their generation was as valid as our generation, their issues as momentous as our issues and their day as full and as vital to them as our day is to us. The 20th century

which has its own hairs to split may have little patience with Arius and
Athanasius who burdened the world with a quarrel about a diphthong, but
the historian has not achieved historical understanding, has not reached that
kind of understanding in which the mind can find rest, until he has seen that
that diphthong was bound to be the most urgent matter in the universe to
those people. It is when the emphasis is laid in this way upon the historian's
attempt to understand the past, that it becomes clear how much he is concerned to elucidate the unlikenesses between past and present. Instead of
being moved to indignation by something in the past which at first seems
alien and perhaps even wicked to our own day, instead of leaving it in the
outer darkness, he makes the effort to bring this thing into the context where
it is natural, and he elucidates the matter by showing its relation to other
things which we do understand. Whereas the man who keeps his eye on the
present tends to ask some such question as, How did religious liberty arise?
while the whig historian by a subtle organisation of his sympathies tends to
read it as the question, To whom must we be grateful for our religious liberty? the historian who is engaged upon studying the 16th century at close
hand is more likely to find himself asking why men in those days were so
given to persecution. This is in a special sense the historian's question for it is
a question about the past rather than about the present, and in answering it
the historian is on his own ground and is making the kind of contribution
which he is most fitted to make. It is in this sense that he is always forgiving
sins by the mere fact that he is finding out why they happened. The things
which are most alien to ourselves are the very object of his exposition. And
until he has shown why men were persecuted in the 16th century one may
doubt whether he is competent to discuss the further question of how religious liberty has come down to the 20th.

* * *

The whig method of approach is closely connected with the question of the
abridgment of history; for both the method and the kind of history that
results from it would be impossible if all the facts were told in all their fullness. The theory that is behind the whig interpretation—the theory that we
study the past for the sake of the present—is one that is really introduced for
the purpose of facilitating the abridgment of history; and its effect is to provide us with a handy rule of thumb by which we can easily discover what
was important in the past, for the simple reason that, by definition, we mean
what is important "from our point of view." No one could mistake the aptness of this theory for a school of writers who might show the least inclination to undervalue one side of the historical story; and indeed there would be
no point in holding it if it were not for the fact that it serves to simplify the
study of history by providing an excuse for leaving things out. The theory is
important because it provides us in the long run with a path through the
complexity of history; it really gives us a short cut through that maze of
interactions by which the past was turned into our present; it helps us to

circumvent the real problem of historical study. If we can exclude certain things on the ground that they have no direct bearing on the present, we have removed the most troublesome elements in the complexity and the crooked is made straight. There is no doubt that the application of this principle must produce in history a bias in favour of the whigs and must fall unfavourably on Catholics and tories. Whig history in other words is not a genuine abridgment, for it is really based upon what is an implicit principle of selection. The adoption of this principle and this method commits us to a certain organisation of the whole historical story. A very different case arises when the historian, examining the 16th century, sets out to discover the things which were important to that age itself or were influential at that time. And if we could imagine a general survey of the centuries which should be an abridgment of all the works of historical research, and if we were then to compare this with a survey of the whole period which was compiled on the whig principle, that is to say, "from the point of view of the present," we should not only find that the complications had been greatly over-simplified in the whig version, but we should find the story recast and the most important valuations amended; in other words we should find an abridged history which tells a different story altogether. According to the consistency with which we have applied the principle of direct reference to the present, we are driven to that version of history which is called the whig interpretation.

Seeing Protestant fighting Catholic in the 16th century we remember our own feelings concerning liberty in the 20th, and we keep before our eyes the relative positions of Catholic and Protestant to-day. There is open to us a whole range of concealed inference based upon this mental juxtaposition of the 16th century with the present; and, even before we have examined the subject closely, our story will have assumed its general shape; Protestants will be seen to have been fighting for the future, while it will be obvious that the Catholics were fighting for the past. Given this original bias we can follow a technical procedure that is bound to confirm and imprison us in it; for when we come, say, to examine Martin Luther more closely, we have a magnet that can draw out of history the very things that we go to look for, and by a hundred quotations torn from their context and robbed of their relevance to a particular historical conjuncture we can prove that there is an analogy between the ideas of Luther and the world of the present day, we can see in Luther a foreshadowing of the present. History is subtle lore and it may lock us in the longest argument in a circle that one can imagine. It matters very much how we start upon our labours—whether for example we take the Protestants of the 16th century as men who were fighting to bring about our modern world, while the Catholics were struggling to keep the mediaeval, or whether we take the whole present as the child of the whole past and see rather the modern world emerging from the clash of both Catholic and Protestant. If we use the present as our perpetual touchstone, we can easily divide the men of the 16th century into progressive and reactionary; but we are likely to beg fewer questions, and we are better able to discover the way in which the past was turned into our present, if we adopt the outlook of the 16th century upon itself, or if we view the process of events as it appears to us when we look at the movements of our own generation; and in this case we shall tend to see not so much progressive fighting reactionary but rather two parties differing on the question of what the next step in progress is to be. Instead of seeing the modern world emerge as the victory of the children of light over the children of darkness in any generation, it is at least better to see it emerge as the result of a clash of wills, a result which often neither party wanted or even dreamed of, a result which indeed in some cases both parties would equally have hated, but a result for the achievement of which the existence of both and the clash of both were necessary.

4
HISTORICAL
RELATIVISM

Carl L. Becker, in a famous presidential address delivered to the American Historical Association, argued that every historian was so inescapably conditioned by the age in which he lived that he could never hope to establish permanently valid interpretations of the past. Historical truth was relative—it would always "vary with the time and place of the observer."

Everyman His Own Historian [1]
BY CARL L. BECKER

I

Once upon a time, long long ago, I learned how to reduce a fraction to its lowest terms. Whether I could still perform that operation is uncertain; but the discipline involved in early training had its uses, since it taught me that in order to understand the essential nature of anything it is well to strip it of all superficial and irrelevant accretions—in short, to reduce it to its lowest terms. That operation I now venture, with some apprehension and all due apologies, to perform on the subject of history.

I ought first of all to explain that when I use the term history I mean knowledge of history. No doubt throughout all past time there actually occurred a series of events which, whether we know what it was or not, constitutes history in some ultimate sense. Nevertheless, much the greater part of these events we can know nothing about, not even that they occurred; many

[1] Presidential Address delivered before the American Historical Association at Minneapolis, December 29, 1931.

Carl L. Becker, "Everyman His Own Historian," *American Historical Review*, XXXVII, 2 (January 1932), 221–236. By permission of the American Historical Association.

of them we can know only imperfectly; and even the few events that we think we know for sure we can never be absolutely certain of, since we can never revive them, never observe or test them directly. The event itself once occurred, but as an actual event it has disappeared; so that in dealing with it the only objective reality we can observe or test is some material trace which the event has left—usually a written document. With these traces of vanished events, these documents, we must be content since they are all we have; from them we infer what the event was, we affirm that it is a fact that the event was so and so. We do not say "Lincoln is assassinated"; we say "it is a fact that Lincoln was assassinated." The event *was,* but is no longer; it is only the affirmed fact about the event that *is,* that persists, and will persist until we discover that our affirmation is wrong or inadequate. Let us then admit that there are two histories: the actual series of events that once occurred; and the ideal series that we affirm and hold in memory. The first is absolute and unchanged—it was what it was whatever we do or say about it; the second is relative, always changing in response to the increase or refinement of knowledge. The two series correspond more or less, it is our aim to make the correspondence as exact as possible; but the actual series of events exists for us only in terms of the ideal series which we affirm and hold in memory. This is why I am forced to identify history with knowledge of history. For all practical purposes history is, for us and for the time being, what we know it to be.

It is history in this sense that I wish to reduce to its lowest terms. In order to do that I need a very simple definition. I once read that "History is the knowledge of events that have occurred in the past." That is a simple definition, but not simple enough. It contains three words that require examination. The first is knowledge. Knowledge is a formidable word. I alway think of knowledge as something that is stored up in the *Encylopaedia Britannica* or the *Summa Theologica;* something difficult to acquire, something at all events that I have not. Resenting a definition that denies me the title of historian, I therefore ask what is most essential to knowledge. Well, memory, I should think (and I mean memory in the broad sense, the memory of events inferred as well as the memory of events observed); other things are necessary too, but memory is fundamental: without memory no knowledge. So our definition becomes, "History is the memory of events that have occurred in the past." But events—the word carries an implication of something grand, like the taking of the Bastile or the Spanish-American War. An occurrence need not be spectacular to be an event. If I drive a motor car down the crooked streets of Ithaca, that is an event—something done; if the traffic cop bawls me out, that is an event—something said; if I have evil thoughts of him for so doing, that is an event—something thought. In truth anything done, said, or thought is an event, important or not as may turn out. But since we do not ordinarily speak without thinking, at least in some rudimentary way, and since the psychologists tell us that we can not think without speaking, or at least not without having anticipatory vibrations in the larynx, we may well combine thought events and speech events under one term; and so our definition becomes, "History is the memory of things said and done in the past." But the past—the word is both misleading and unnecessary: misleading, because the past, used in connection with history, seems to imply the distant past, as if history ceased before we were born; unnecessary, because after all everything said or done is already in the past as soon as it is said or done. Therefore I will omit that word, and our definition becomes, "History is the memory of things said and done." This is a definition that reduces history to its lowest terms, and yet includes everything that is essential to understanding what it really is.

If the essence of history is the memory of things said and done, then it is obvious that every normal person, Mr. Everyman, knows some history. Of course we do what we can to conceal this invidious truth. Assuming a professional manner, we say that so and so knows no history, when we mean no more than that he failed to pass the examinations set for a higher degree; and simple-minded persons, undergraduates and others, taken in by academic classifications of knowledge, think they know no history because they have never taken a course in history in college, or have never read Gibbon's *Decline and Fall of the Roman Empire*. No doubt the academic convention has its uses, but it is one of the superficial accretions that must be stripped off if we would understand history reduced to its lowest terms. Mr. Everyman, as well as you and I, remembers things said and done, and must do so at every waking moment. Suppose Mr. Everyman to have awakened this morning unable to remember anything said or done. He would be a lost soul indeed. This has happened, this sudden loss of all historical knowledge. But normally it does not happen. Normally the memory of Mr. Everyman, when he awakens in the morning, reaches out into the country of the past and of distant places and instantanously recreates his little world of endeavor, pulls together as it were things said and done in his yesterdays, and coödinates them with his present perceptions and with things to be said and done in his to-morrows. Without this historical knowledge, this memory of things said and done, his to-day would be aimless and his to-morrow without significance.

Since we are concerned with history in its lowest terms, we will suppose that Mr. Everyman is not a professor of history, but just an ordinary citizen without excess knowledge. Not having a lecture to prepare, his memory of things said and done, when he awakened this morning, presumably did not drag into consciousness any events connected with the Liman von Sanders mission or the Pseudo-Isidorian Decretals; it presumably dragged into consciousness an image of things said and done yesterday in the office, the highly significant fact that General Motors had dropped three points, a conference arranged for ten o'clock in the morning, a promise to play nine holes at four-thirty in the afternoon, and other historical events of similar import. Mr. Everyman knows more history than this, but at the moment of awakening this is sufficient: memory of things said and done, history functioning, at seven-thirty in the morning, in its very lowest terms, has effectively oriented Mr. Everyman in his little world of endeavor.

Yet not quite effectively after all perhaps; for unaided memory is notoriously fickle; and it may happen that Mr. Everyman, as he drinks his coffee, is uneasily aware of something said or done that he fails now to recall. A common enough occurrence, as we all know to our sorrow—this remembering, not the historical event, but only that there was an event which we ought to remember but can not. This is Mr. Everyman's difficulty, a bit of history lies dead and inert in the sources, unable to do any work for Mr. Everyman because his memory refuses to bring it alive in consciousness. What then does Mr. Everyman do? He does what any historian would do: he does a bit of historical research in the sources. From his little Private Record Office (I mean his vest pocket) he takes a book in MS, volume XXXV it may be, and turns to page 23, and there he reads: "December 29, pay Smith's coal bill, 20 tons, $1017.20." Instantaneously a series of historical events comes to life in Mr. Everyman's mind. He has an image of himself ordering twenty tons of coal from Smith last summer, of Smith's wagons driving up to his house, and of the precious coal sliding dustily through the cellar window. Historical events, these are, not so important as the forging of the Isidorian Decretals, but still important to Mr. Everyman: historical events which he was not present to observe, but which, by an artificial extension of memory, he can form a clear picture of, because he has done a little original research in the manuscripts preserved in his Private Record Office.

The picture Mr. Everyman forms of Smith's wagons delivering the coal at his house is a picture of things said and done in the past. But it does not stand alone, it is not a pure antiquarian image to be enjoyed for its own sake; on the contrary, it is associated with a picture of things to be said and done in the future; so that throughout the day Mr. Everyman intermittently holds in mind, together with a picture of Smith's coal wagons, a picture of himself going at four o'clock in the afternoon to Smith's office in order to pay his bill. At four o'clock Mr. Everyman is accordingly at Smith's office. "I wish to pay that coal bill," he says. Smith looks dubious and disappointed, takes down a ledger (or a filing case), does a bit of original research in his Private Record Office, and announces: "You don't owe me any money, Mr. Everyman. You ordered the coal here all right, but I didn't have the kind you wanted, and so turned the order over to Brown. It was Brown delivered your coal: he's the man you owe." Whereupon Mr. Everyman goes to Brown's office; and Brown takes down a ledger, does a bit of original research in his Private Record Office, which happily confirms the researches of Smith; and Mr. Everyman pays his bill, and in the evening, after returning from the Country Club, makes a further search in another collection of documents, where, sure enough, he finds a bill from Brown, properly drawn, for twenty tons of stove coal, $1017.20. The research is now completed. Since his mind rests satisfied, Mr. Everyman has found the explanation of the series of events that concerned him.

Mr. Everyman would be astonished to learn that he is an historian, yet it is obvious, isn't it, that he has performed all the essential operations involved in historical research. Needing or wanting to do something (which happened to be, not to deliver a lecture or write a book, but to pay a bill; and this is what misleads him and us as to what he is really doing), the first step was to recall things said and done. Unaided memory proving inadequate, a further step was essential—the examination of certain documents in order to discover the necessary but as yet unknown facts. Unhappily the documents were found to give conflicting reports, so that a critical comparison of the texts had to be instituted in order to eliminate error. All this having been satisfactorily accomplished, Mr. Everyman is ready for the final operation—the formation in his mind, by an artificial extension of memory, of a picture, a definitive picture let us hope, of a selected series of historical events—of himself ordering coal from Smith, of Smith turning the order over to Brown, and of Brown delivering the coal at his house. In the light of this picture Mr. Everyman could, and did, pay his bill. If Mr. Everyman had undertaken these researches in order to write a book instead of to pay a bill, no one would think of denying that he was an historian.

II

I have tried to reduce history to its lowest terms, first by defining it as the memory of things said and done, second by showing concretely how the memory of things said and done is essential to the performance of the simplest acts of daily life. I wish now to note the more general implications of Mr. Everyman's activities. In the realm of affairs Mr. Everyman has been paying his coal bill; in the realm of consciousness he has been doing that fundamental thing which enables man alone to have, properly speaking, a history: he has been reenforcing and enriching his immediate perceptions to the end that he may live in a world of semblance more spacious and satisfying than is to be found within the narrow confines of the fleeting present moment.

We are apt to think of the past as dead, the future as nonexistent, the present alone as real; and prematurely wise or disillusioned counselors have urged us to burn always with "a hard, gemlike flame" in order to give "the highest quality to the moments as they pass, and simply for those moments' sake." This no doubt is what the glowworm does; but I think that man, who alone is properly aware that the present moment passes, can for that very reason make no good use of the present moment simply for its own sake. Strictly speaking, the present doesn't exist for us, or is at best no more than an infinitesimal point in time, gone before we can note it as present. Nevertheless, we must have a present; and so we create one by robbing the past, by holding on to the most recent events and pretending that they all belong to our immediate perceptions. If, for example, I raise my arm, the total event is a series of occurrences of which the first are past before the last have taken place; and yet you perceive it as a single movement executed in one present

instant. This telescoping of successive events into a single instant philosophers call the "specious present." Doubtless they would assign rather narrow
limits to the specious present; but I will willfully make a free use of it, and
say that we can extend the specious present as much as we like. In common
speech we do so: we speak of the "present hour," the "present year," the
"present generation." Perhaps all living creatures have a specious present; but
man has this superiority, as Pascal says, that he is aware of himself and the
universe, can as it were hold himself at arm's length and with some measure
of objectivity watch himself and his fellows functioning in the world during
a brief span of allotted years. Of all the creatures, man alone has a specious
present that may be deliberately and purposefully enlarged and diversified
and enriched.

The extent to which the specious present may thus be enlarged and enriched will depend upon knowledge, the artificial extension of memory, the
memory of things said and done in the past and distant places. But not upon
knowledge alone; rather upon knowledge directed by purpose. The specious
present is an unstable pattern of thought, incessantly changing in response to
our immediate perceptions and the purposes that arise therefrom. At any
given moment each one of us (professional historian no less than Mr. Everyman) weaves into this unstable pattern such actual or artificial memories as
may be necessary to orient us in our little world of endeavor. But to be oriented in our little world of endeavor we must be prepared for what is coming
to us (the payment of a coal bill, the delivery of a presidential address, the
establishment of a League of Nations, or whatever); and to be prepared for
what is coming to us it is necessary, not only to recall certain past events, but
to anticipate (note I do not say predict) the future. Thus from the specious
present, which always includes more or less of the past, the future refuses to
be excluded; and the more of the past we drag into the specious present, the
more an hypothetical, patterned future is likely to crowd into it also. Which
comes first, which is cause and which effect, whether our memories construct
a pattern of past events at the behest of our desires and hopes, or whether our
desires and hopes spring from a pattern of past events imposed upon us by
experience and knowledge, I shall not attempt to say. What I suspect is that
memory of past and anticipation of future events work together, go hand in
hand as it were in a friendly way, without disputing over priority and leadership.

At all events they go together, so that in a very real sense it is impossible to
divorce history from life: Mr. Everyman can not do what he needs or desires
to do without recalling past events; he can not recall past events without in
some subtle fashion relating them to what he needs or desires to do. This is
the natural function of history, of history reduced to its lowest terms, of history conceived as the memory of things said and done: memory of things said
and done (whether in our immediate yesterdays or in the long past of mankind), running hand in hand with the anticipation of things to be said and
done, enables us, each to the extent of his knowledge and imagination, to be

intelligent, to push back the narrow confines of the fleeting present moment
so that what we are doing may be judged in the light of what we have done
and what we hope to do. In this sense all *living* history, as Croce says, is
contemporaneous: in so far as we think of the past (and otherwise the past,
however fully related in documents, is nothing to us) it becomes an integral
and living part of our present world of semblance.

It must then be obvious that living history, the ideal series of events that we
affirm and hold in memory, since it is so intimately associated with what we
are doing and with what we hope to do, can not be precisely the same for all
at any given time, or the same for one generation as for another. History in
this sense can not be reduced to a verifiable set of statistics or formulated in
terms of universally valid mathematical formulas. It is rather an imaginative
creation, a personal possession which each one of us, Mr. Everyman, fashions
out of his individual experience, adapts to his practical or emotional needs,
and adorns as well as may be to suit his aesthetic tastes. In thus creating his
own history, there are, nevertheless, limits which Mr. Everyman may not
overstep without incurring penalties. The limits are set by his fellows. If Mr.
Everyman lived quite alone in an unconditioned world he would be free to
affirm and hold in memory any ideal series of events that struck his fancy,
and thus create a world of semblance quite in accord with the heart's desire.
Unfortunately, Mr. Everyman has to live in a world of Browns and Smiths; a
sad experience, which has taught him the expediency of recalling certain
events with much exactness. In all the immediately practical affairs of life Mr.
Everyman is a good historian, as expert, in conducting the researches necessary for paying his coal bill, as need be. His expertness comes partly from
long practice, but chiefly from the circumstance that his researches are prescribed and guided by very definite and practical objects which concern him
intimately. The problem of what documents to consult, what facts to select,
troubles Mr. Everyman not at all. Since he is not writing a book on "Some
Aspects of the Coal Industry Objectively Considered," it does not occur to
him to collect all the facts and let them speak for themselves. Wishing merely
to pay his coal bill, he selects only such facts as may be relevant; and not
wishing to pay it twice, he is sufficiently aware, without ever having read
Bernheim's *Lehrbuch,* that the relevant facts must be clearly established by
the testimony of independent witnesses not self-deceived. He does not know,
or need to know, that his personal interest in the performance is a disturbing
bias which will prevent him from learning the whole truth or arriving at
ultimate causes. Mr. Everyman does not wish to learn the whole truth or to
arrive at ultimate causes. He wishes to pay his coal bill. That is to say, he
wishes to adjust himself to a practical situation, and on that low pragmatic
level he is a good historian precisely because he is not disinterested: he will
solve his problems, if he does solve them, by virtue of his intelligence and not
by virtue of his indifference.

Nevertheless, Mr. Everyman does not live by bread alone; and on all proper
occasions his memory of things said and done, easily enlarging his specious

present beyond the narrow circle of daily affairs, will, must inevitably, in mere compensation for the intolerable dullness and vexation of the fleeting present moment, fashion for him a more spacious world than that of the immediately practical. He can readily recall the days of his youth, the places he has lived in, the ventures he has made, the adventures he has had—all the crowded events of a lifetime; and beyond and around this central pattern of personally experienced events, there will be embroidered a more dimly seen pattern of artificial memories, memories of things reputed to have been said and done in past times which he has not known, in distant places which he has not seen. This outer pattern of remembered events that encloses and completes the central pattern of his personal experience, Mr. Everyman has woven, he could not tell you how, out of the most diverse threads of information, picked up in the most casual way, from the most unrelated sources—from things learned at home and in school, from knowledge gained in business or profession, from newspapers glanced at, from books (yes, even history books) read or heard of, from remembered scraps of newsreels or educational films or *ex cathedra* utterances of presidents and kings, from fifteen-minute discourses on the history of civilization broadcast by the courtesy (it may be) of Pepsodent, the Bulova Watch Company, or the Shepard Stores in Boston. Daily and hourly, from a thousand unnoted sources, there is lodged in Mr. Everyman's mind a mass of unrelated and related information and misinformation, of impressions and images, out of which he somehow manages, undeliberately for the most part, to fashion a history, a patterned picture of remembered things said and done in past times and distant places. It is not possible, it is not essential, that this picture should be complete or completely true: it is essential that it should be useful to Mr. Everyman; and that it may be useful to him he will hold in memory, of all the things he might hold in memory, those things only which can be related with some reasonable degree of relevance and harmony to his idea of himself and of what he is doing in the world and what he hopes to do.

In constructing this more remote and far-flung pattern of remembered things, Mr. Everyman works with something of the freedom of a creative artist; the history which he imaginatively recreates as an artificial extension of his personal experience will inevitably be an engaging blend of fact and fancy, a mythical adaptation of that which actually happened. In part it will be true, in part false; as a whole perhaps neither true nor false, but only the most convenient form of error. Not that Mr. Everyman wishes or intends to deceive himself or others. Mr. Everyman has a wholesome respect for cold, hard facts, never suspecting how malleable they are, how easy it is to coax and cajole them; but he necessarily takes the facts as they come to him, and is enamored of those that seem best suited to his interests or promise most in the way of emotional satisfaction. The exact truth of remembered events he has in any case no time, and no need, to curiously question or meticulously verify. No doubt he can, if he be an American, call up an image of the signing of the Declaration of Independence in 1776 as readily as he can call up an image of Smith's coal wagons creaking up the hill last summer. He suspects the one image no more than the other; but the signing of the Declaration, touching not his practical interests, calls for no careful historical research on his part. He may perhaps, without knowing why, affirm and hold in memory that the Declaration was signed by the members of the Continental Congress on the fourth of July. It is a vivid and sufficient image which Mr. Everyman may hold to the end of his days without incurring penalties. Neither Brown nor Smith has any interest in setting him right; nor will any court ever send him a summons for failing to recall that the Declaration, "being engrossed and compared at the table, was signed by the members" on the second of August. As an actual event, the signing of the Declaration was what it was; as a remembered event it will be, for Mr. Everyman, what Mr. Everyman contrives to make it: will have for him significance and magic, much or little or none at all, as it fits well or ill into his little world of interests and aspirations and emotional comforts.

III

What then of us, historians by profession? What have we to do with Mr. Everyman, or he with us? More, I venture to believe, than we are apt to think. For each of us is Mr. Everyman too. Each of us is subject to the limitations of time and place; and for each of us, no less than for the Browns and Smiths of the world, the pattern of remembered things said and done will be woven, safeguard the process how we may, at the behest of circumstance and purpose.

True it is that although each of us is Mr. Everyman, each is something more than his own historian. Mr. Everyman, being but an informal historian, is under no bond to remember what is irrelevant to his personal affairs. But we are historians by profession. Our profession, less intimately bound up with the practical activities, is to be directly concerned with the ideal series of events that is only of casual or occasional import to others; it is our business in life to be ever preoccupied with that far-flung pattern of artificial memories that encloses and completes the central pattern of individual experience. We are Mr. Everybody's historian as well as our own, since our histories serve the double purpose, which written histories have always served, of keeping alive the recollection of memorable men and events. We are thus of that ancient and honorable company of wise men of the tribe, of bards and story-tellers and minstrels, of soothsayers and priests, to whom in successive ages has been entrusted the keeping of the useful myths. Let not the harmless, necessary word "myth" put us out of countenance. In the history of history a myth is a once valid but now discarded version of the human story, as our now valid versions will in due course be relegated to the category of discarded myths. With our predecessors, the bards and story-tellers and priests, we have therefore this in common: that it is our function, as it was theirs, not to create, but to preserve and perpetuate the social tradition; to harmonize, as well as ignorance and prejudice permit, the actual and the remembered series of events; to enlarge and enrich the specious present common to us all to the end that "society" (the tribe, the nation, or all mankind) may judge of what it is doing in the light of what it has done and what it hopes to do.

History as the artificial extension of the social memory (and I willingly concede that there are other appropriate ways of apprehending human experience) is an art of long standing, necessarily so since it springs instinctively from the impulse to enlarge the range of immediate experience; and however camouflaged by the disfiguring jargon of science, it is still in essence what it has always been. History in this sense is story, in aim always a true story; a story that employs all the devices of literary art (statement and generalization, narration and description, comparison and comment and analogy) to present the succession of events in the life of man, and from the succession of events thus presented to derive a satisfactory meaning. The history written by historians, like the history informally fashioned by Mr. Everyman, is thus a convenient blend of truth and fancy, of what we commonly distinguish as "fact" and "interpretation." In primitive times, when tradition is orally transmitted, bards and story-tellers frankly embroider or improvise the facts to heighten the dramatic import of the story. With the use of written records, history, gradually differentiated from fiction, is understood as the story of events that actually occurred; and with the increase and refinement of knowledge the historian recognizes that his first duty is to be sure of his facts, let their meaning be what it may. Nevertheless, in every age history is taken to be a story of actual events from which a significant meaning may be derived; and in every age the illusion is that the present version is valid because the related facts are true, whereas former versions are invalid because based upon inaccurate or inadequate facts.

Never was this conviction more impressively displayed than in our own time—that age of erudition in which we live, or from which we are perhaps just emerging. Finding the course of history littered with the *débris* of exploded philosophies, the historians of the last century, unwilling to be forever duped, turned away (as they fondly hoped) from "interpretation" to the rigorous examination of the factual event, just as it occurred. Perfecting the technique of investigation, they laboriously collected and edited the sources of information, and with incredible persistence and ingenuity ran illusive error to earth, letting the significance of the Middle Ages wait until it was certainly known "whether Charles the Fat was at Ingelheim or Lustnau on July 1, 887," shedding their "life-blood," in many a hard fought battle, "for the sublime truths of Sac and Soc." I have no quarrel with this so great concern with hoti's business. One of the first duties of man is not to be duped, to be aware of his world; and to derive the significance of human experience from events that never occurred is surely an enterprise of doubtful value. To establish the facts is always in order, and is indeed the first duty of the historian; but to suppose that the facts, once established in all their fullness, will "speak for themselves" is an illusion. It was perhaps peculiarly the illusion of those historians of the last century who found some special magic in the word "scientific." The scientific historian, it seems, was one who set forth the facts without injecting any extraneous meaning into them. He was the objective man whom Nietzsche described—"a mirror: accustomed to prostration before something that wants to be known, . . . he waits until something comes, and then expands himself sensitively, so that even the light footsteps and gliding past of spiritual things may not be lost in his surface and film." [2] "It is not I who speak, but history which speaks through me," was Fustel's reproof to applauding students. "If a certain philosophy emerges from this scientific history, it must be permitted to emerge naturally, of its own accord, all but independently of the will of the historian." [3] Thus the scientific historian deliberately renounced philosophy only to submit to it without being aware. His philosophy was just this, that by not taking thought a cubit would be added to his stature. With no other preconception than the will to know, the historian would reflect in his surface and film the "order of events throughout past times in all places"; so that, in the fullness of time, when innumerable patient expert scholars, by "exhausting the sources," should have reflected without refracting the truth of all the facts, the definitive and impregnable meaning of human experience would emerge of its own accord to enlighten and emancipate mankind. Hoping to find something without looking for it, expecting to obtain final answers to life's riddle by resolutely refusing to ask questions—it was surely the most romantic species of realism yet invented, the oddest attempt ever made to get something for nothing!

That mood is passing. The fullness of time is not yet, overmuch learning proves a weariness to the flesh, and a younger generation that knows not Von Ranke is eager to believe that Fustel's counsel, if one of perfection, is equally one of futility. Even the most disinterested historian has at least one preconception, which is the fixed idea that he has none. The facts of history are already set forth, implicitly, in the sources; and the historian who could restate without reshaping them would, by submerging and suffocating the mind in diffuse existence, accomplish the superfluous task of depriving human experience of all significance. Left to themselves, the facts do not speak; left to themselves they do not exist, not really, since for all practical purposes there is no fact until some one affirms it. The least the historian can do with any historical fact is to select and affirm it. To select and affirm even the simplest complex of facts is to give them a certain place in a certain pattern of ideas, and this alone is sufficient to give them a special meaning. However "hard" or "cold" they may be, historical facts are after all not material substances which, like bricks or scantlings, possess definite shape and clear, persistent outline. To set forth historical facts is not comparable to dumping a barrow of bricks. A brick retains its form and pressure wherever placed; but

---

2 *Beyond Good and Evil*, p. 140.
3 Quoted in *English Historical Review*, V. 1.

the form and substance of historical facts, having a negotiable existence only in literary discourse, vary with the words employed to convey them. Since history is not part of the external material world, but an imaginative reconstruction of vanished events, its form and substance are inseparable: in the realm of literary discourse substance, being an idea, *is* form; and form, conveying the idea, *is* substance. It is thus not the undiscriminated fact, but the perceiving mind of the historian that speaks: the special meaning which the facts are made to convey emerges from the substance-form which the historian employs to recreate imaginatively a series of events not present to perception.

In constructing this substance-form of vanished events, the historian, like Mr. Everyman, like the bards and story-tellers of an earlier time, will be conditioned by the specious present in which alone he can be aware of his world. Being neither omniscient nor omnipresent, the historian is not the same person always and everywhere; and for him, as for Mr. Everyman, the form and significance of remembered events, like the extension and velocity of physical objects, will vary with the time and place of the observer. After fifty years we can clearly see that it was not history which spoke through Fustel, but Fustel who spoke through history. We see less clearly perhaps that the voice of Fustel was the voice, amplified and freed from static as one may say, of Mr. Everyman; what the admiring students applauded on that famous occasion was neither history nor Fustel, but a deftly colored pattern of selected events which Fustel fashioned, all the more skillfully for not being aware of doing so, in the service of Mr. Everyman's emotional needs—the emotional satisfaction, so essential to Frenchmen at that time, of perceiving that French institutions were not of German origin. And so it must always be. Played upon by all the diverse, unnoted influences of his own time, the historian will elicit history out of documents by the same principle, however more consciously and expertly applied, that Mr. Everyman employs to breed legends out of remembered episodes and oral tradition.

Berate him as we will for not reading our books, Mr. Everyman is stronger than we are, and sooner or later we must adapt our knowledge to his necessities. Otherwise he will leave us to our own devices, leave us it may be to cultivate a species of dry professional arrogance growing out of the thin soil of antiquarian research. Such research, valuable not in itself but for some ulterior purpose, will be of little import except in so far as it is transmuted into common knowledge. The history that lies inert in unread books does no work in the world. The history that does work in the world, the history that influences the course of history, is living history, that pattern of remembered events, whether true or false, that enlarges and enriches the collective specious present, the specious present of Mr. Everyman. It is for this reason that the history of history is a record of the "new history" that in every age rises to confound and supplant the old. It should be a relief to us to renounce omniscience, to recognize that every generation, our own included, will, must inevitably, understand the past and anticipate the future in the light of its own restricted experience, must inevitably play on the dead whatever tricks it finds necessary for its own peace of mind. The appropriate trick for any age is not a malicious invention designed to take anyone in, but an unconscious and necessary effort on the part of "society" to understand what it is doing in the light of what it has done and what it hopes to do. We, historians by profession, share in this necessary effort. But we do not impose our version of the human story on Mr. Everyman; in the end it is rather Mr. Everyman who imposes his version on us—compelling us, in an age of political revolution, to see that history is past politics, in an age of social stress and conflict, to search for the economic interpretation. If we remain too long recalcitrant Mr. Everyman will ignore us, shelving our recondite works behind glass doors rarely opened. Our proper function is not to repeat the past but to make use of it, to correct and rationalize for common use Mr. Everyman's mythological adaptation of what actually happened. We are surely under bond to be as honest and as intelligent as human frailty permits; but the secret of our success in the long run is in conforming to the temper of Mr. Everyman, which we seem to guide only because we are so sure, eventually, to follow it.

Neither the value nor the dignity of history need suffer by regarding it as a foreshortened and incomplete representation of the reality that once was, an unstable pattern of remembered things redesigned and newly colored to suit the convenience of those who make use of it. Nor need our labors be the less highly prized because our task is limited, our contributions of incidental and temporary significance. History is an indispensable even though not the highest form of intellectual endeavor, since it makes, as Santayana says, a gift of "great interests . . . to the heart. A barbarian is no less subject to the past than is the civic man who knows what the past is and means to be loyal to it; but the barbarian, for want of a transpersonal memory, crawls among superstitions which he cannot understand or revoke and among people whom he may hate or love, but whom he can never think of raising to a higher plane, to the level of a purer happiness. The whole dignity of human endeavor is thus bound up with historic issues, and as conscience needs to be controlled by experience if it is to become rational, so personal experience itself needs to be enlarged ideally if the failures and successes it reports are to touch impersonal interests." [4]

I do not present this view of history as one that is stable and must prevail. Whatever validity it may claim, it is certain, on its own premises, to be supplanted; for its premises, imposed upon us by the climate of opinion in which we live and think, predispose us to regard all things, and all principles of things, as no more than "inconstant modes or fashions," as but the "concurrence, renewed from moment to moment, of forces parting sooner or later on their way." It is the limitation of the genetic approach to human experience that it must be content to transform problems since it can never solve them. However accurately we may determine the "facts" of history, the facts them-

---

[4] *The Life of Reason,* V. 68.

selves and our interpretations of them, and our interpretation of our own interpretations, will be seen in a different perspective or a less vivid light as mankind moves into the unknown future. Regarded historically, as a process of becoming, man and his world can obviously be understood only tentatively, since it is by definition something still in the making, something as yet unfinished. Unfortunately for the "permanent contribution" and the universally valid philosophy, time passes; time, the enemy of man as the Greeks thought; to-morrow and to-morrow and to-morrow creeps in this petty pace, and all our yesterdays diminish and grow dim: so that, in the lengthening perspective of the centuries, even the most striking events (the Declaration of Independence, the French Revolution, the Great War itself; like the Diet of Worms before them, like the signing of the Magna Carta and the coronation of Charlemagne and the crossing of the Rubicon and the battle of Marathon) must inevitably, for posterity, fade away into pale replicas of the original picture, for each succeeding generation losing, as they recede into a more distant past, some significance that once was noted in them, some quality of enchantment that once was theirs.

5
REAPPRAISALS
OF THE
PROBLEM

If all our judgments about the past are necessarily conditioned by our experience of the present (Becker) and if judgments of this sort are obviously unsound (Butterfield), it might seem that the study of history is at best a futile occupation. The fact that it continues to attract fine minds suggests that there is more to be said.

Isaiah Berlin has argued that it is indeed possible to make objective judgments about the past and has attacked the relativist theory on logical grounds.

FROM Historical Inevitability BY ISAIAH BERLIN

When everything has been said in favor of attributing responsibility for character and action to natural and institutional causes; when everything possible has been done to correct blind or over-simple interpretations of conduct which fix too much blame on individuals and their free acts; when, in fact, there is strong evidence to show that it was difficult or impossible for men to do otherwise than they did, given their material environment or education or the influence upon them of various "social pressures"; when every relevant psychological and sociological consideration has been taken into account, every impersonal factor given due weight; after "hegemonist," nationalist, and other historical heresies have been exposed and refuted; after every effort has been made to induce history to aspire, so far as it can without open

Isaiah Berlin, *Historical Inevitability* (1954), pp. 58–62. Published by Oxford University Press under the auspices of the London School of Economics and Political Science, London.

absurdity, after the pure condition of a science; after all these severities, we continue to praise and to blame. We blame others as we blame ourselves; and the more we know, the more, it may be, we are disposed to blame. Certainly it will surprise us to be told that the better we understand our own actions— our own motives and the circumstances surrounding them—the freer from self-blame we shall inevitably feel. The contrary is surely often true. The more deeply we investigate the course of our own conduct, the more blame-worthy our behavior may seem to us to be, the more remorse we may be disposed to feel; and if this holds for ourselves, it is not reasonable to expect us necessarily, and in all cases, to withhold it from others. Our situations may differ from theirs, but not always so widely as to make all comparisons un-fair. We ourselves may be accused unjustly, and so become acutely sensitive to the dangers of unjustly blaming others. But because blame can be unjust and the temptation to utter it very strong, it does not follow that it is never just; and because judgments can be based on ignorance, can spring from violent, or perverse, or silly, or shallow, or unfair notions, it does not follow that the opposites of these qualities do not exist at all; that we are mysteri-ously doomed to a degree of relativism and subjectivism in history, from which we are no less mysteriously free, or at any rate more free, in our nor-mal daily thought and transactions with one another. Indeed, the major fal-lacy of this position must by now be too obvious to need pointing out. We are told that we are creatures of nature or environment, or of history, and that this colors our temperament, our judgments, our principles. Every judgment is relative, every evaluation subjective, made what and as it is by the interplay of the factors of its own time and place, individual or collective. But relative to what? Subjective in contrast with what? Involved in some ephemeral pat-tern as opposed to what conceivable, presumably timeless, independence of such distorting factors? Relative terms (especially pejoratives) need correla-tives, or else they turn out to be without meaning themselves, mere gibes, propagandist phrases designed to throw discredit, and not to describe or ana-lyze. We know what we mean by disparaging a judgment or a method as subjective or biased—we mean that proper methods of weighing evidence have been too far ignored: or that what are normally called facts have been overlooked or suppressed or perverted; or that evidence normally accepted as sufficient to account for the acts of one individual or society is, for no good reason, ignored in some other case similar in all relevant respects; or that canons of interpretation are arbitrarily altered from case to case, that is, with-out consistency or principle; or that we have reasons for thinking that the historian in question wished to establish certain conclusions for reasons other than those justified by the evidence according to canons of valid inference accepted as normal in his day or in ours, and that this has blinded him to the criteria and methods normal in his field for verifying facts and proving con-clusions; or all, or any, of these together; or other considerations like them. These are the kinds of ways in which superficiality is, in practice, distin-guished from depth, bias from objectivity, perversion of facts from honesty, stupidity from perspicacity, passion and confusion from detachment and lucidity. And if we grasp these rules correctly, we are fully justified in denouncing breaches of them on the part of anyone; why should we not? But, it may be objected, what of words such as we have used so liberally above—"valid," "normal," "proper," "relevant," "perverted," "suppression of facts," "interpretation"—what do they signify? Is the meaning and use of these crucial terms so very fixed and unambiguous? May not that which is thought relevant or convincing in one generation be regarded as irrelevant in the next? What are unquestioned facts to one historian may, often enough, seem merely a suspicious piece of theorizing to another. This is indeed so. Rules for the weighing of evidence do change. The accepted data of one age seem to its remote successors shot through with metaphysical presuppositions so queer as to be scarcely intelligible. All objectivity, we shall again be told, is subjective, is what it is relatively to its own time and place; all veracity, reliability, all the insights and gifts of an intellectually fertile period are such only relatively to their own "climate of opinion"; nothing is eternal, everything flows. Yet frequently as this kind of thing has been said, and plausible as it may seem it remains in this context mere rhetoric. We do distinguish facts, not indeed from the valuations which enter into their very texture, but from interpretations of them; the borderline may not be distinct, but if I say that Stalin is dead and General Franco still alive, my statement may be accurate or mistaken, but nobody in his senses could, as words are used, take me to be advancing a theory or an interpretation. But if I say that Stalin exterminated a great many peasant proprietors because in his infancy he had been swaddled by his nurse, and that this made him aggressive, while General Franco has not done so because he did not go through this kind of experience, no one but a very naive student of the social sciences would take me to be claiming to assert a fact, and that, no matter how many times I begin my sentences with the words "It is a fact." And I shall not readily believe you if you tell me that for Thucydides (or even for some Sumerian scribe) no fundamental distinction existed between relatively "hard" facts and relatively "disputable" interpretations. The borderline has, no doubt, always been wide and vague; it may be a shifting frontier, more distinct in some terrains than in others, but unless we know where, within certain limits, it lies, we fail to understand descriptive language altogether. The modes of thought of the ancients or of any cultures remote from our own are comprehensible to us only in the degree to which we share some, at any rate, of their basic categories; and the distinction between fact and theory is basic among these. I may dispute whether a given historian is profound or shallow, objective in his methods and impartial in his judgments, or borne on the wings of some obsessive hypothesis or overpowering emotion: but what I mean by these contrasted terms will not be utterly different for those who disagree with me, else there would be no argument; and will not, if I can claim to decipher texts at all correctly, be so widely different in different cultures and times and places as to make all communication systematically misleading and delusive. "Objective," "true," "fair," are words of large content, their uses are many, their edges often blurred. Ambiguities and confusions are always possible and often dangerous. Nevertheless such terms do possess meanings, which may, indeed, be fluid, but stay within limits recognized by normal usage, and refer to standards commonly accepted by those who work in relevant fields; and that not merely within one generation or society, but across large stretches of time and space. The mere claim that these crucial terms, these concepts or categories or standards, change in meaning or application, is to assume that such changes can to some degree be traced by methods which themselves are *pro tanto* not held liable to such change; for if these change in their turn, then, *ex hypothesi,* they do so in no way discoverable by us. And if not discoverable, then not discountable, and therefore of no use as a stick with which to beat us for our alleged subjectiveness or relativity, our delusions of grandeur and permanence, of the absoluteness of our standards in a world of ceaseless change.

J. H. Hexter has explained how the historian—even though he is formed by his own "day"—can still hope to attain to a true understanding of the past.

FROM The Historian and His Day BY J. H. HEXTER

The present-minded contend that in writing history no historian can free himself of his total experience and that that experience is inextricably involved not only in the limits of knowledge but also in the passions, prejudices, assumptions and prepossessions, in the events, crises and tensions of his own day. Therefore those passions, prejudices, assumptions, prepossessions, events, crises and tensions of the historian's own day inevitably permeate what he writes about the past. This is the crucial allegation of the present-minded, and if it is wholly correct, the issue must be settled in their favor and the history-minded pack up their apodictic and categorical-imperative baggage and depart in silence. Frequently discussions of this crucial issue have got bogged down because the history-minded keep trying to prove that the historian can counteract the influence of his own day, while the present-minded keep saying that this is utterly impossible. And of course on this question the latter are quite right. A historian has no day but his own, so what is he going to counteract it with? He is in the situation of Archimedes who could find no fulcrum for the lever with which to move the Earth. Clearly if the historian is to be history-minded rather than present-minded he

Reprinted from *Reappraisals in History* (1962), pp. 5–13, by J. H. Hexter, by permission of Northwestern University Press and Longmans, Green & Co., Ltd., Harlow, England.

must find the means of being so in his own day, not outside it. And thus at last we come up against the crucial question—what *is* the historian's own day?

As soon as we put the question this way we realize that there is no ideal Historian's Day; there are many days, all different, and each with a particular historian attached to it. Now since in actuality there is no such thing as The Historian's Day, no one can be qualified to say what it actually consists of. Indeed, although I know a good number of individual historians on terms of greater or less intimacy, I would feel ill-qualified to describe with certainty what any of their days are. There is, however, one historian about whose day I can speak with assurance. For I myself am a historian at least in the technical sense of the word; I have possessed for a considerable time the parchment inscribed with the appropriate phrases to indicate that I have served my apprenticeship and am out of my indentures. So I will describe as briefly as I can my own day. I do so out of no appetite for self-revelation or self-expression, but simply because the subject is germane to our inquiry and because it is the one matter on which I happen to be the world's leading authority. Let us then hurry through this dreary journal.

I rise early and have breakfast. While eating, I glance through the morning paper and read the editorial page. I then go to the college that employs me and teach for two to four hours five days a week. Most of the time the subject matter I deal with in class is cobwebbed with age. Three fourths of it dates back from a century and a quarter to three millennia; all of it happened at least thirty years ago. Then comes lunch with a few of my colleagues. Conversation at lunch ranges widely through professional shoptalk, politics, high and ghostly matters like religion, the nature of art or the universe, and the problems of child rearing, and finally academic scuttlebutt. At present there is considerable discussion of the peculiar incongruence between the social importance of the academic and his economic reward. This topic has the merit of revealing the profound like-mindedness, transcending all occasional conflicts, of our little community. From lunch to bedtime my day is grimly uniform. There are of course occasional and casual variations—preparation of the ancient material above mentioned for the next day's classes, a ride in the country with the family, a committee meeting at college, a movie, a play, a novel, or a book by some self-anointed Deep Thinker. Still by and large from one in the afternoon to midnight, with time out for dinner and domestic matters, I read things written between 1450 and 1650 or books written by historians on the basis of things written between 1450 and 1650. I vary the routine on certain days by writing about what I have read on the other days. On Saturdays and in the summer I start my reading or writing at nine instead of noon. It is only fair to add that most days I turn on a news broadcast or two at dinnertime, and that I spend an hour or two with the Sunday paper.

Now I am sure that many people will consider so many days so spent to be a frightful waste of precious time; and indeed, as most of the days of most men, it does seem a bit trivial. Be that as it may, it remains one historian's own day. It is his own day in the only sense in which that phrase can be used without its being pretentious, pompous and meaningless. For a man's own days are not everything that happens in the world while he lives and breathes. As I write, portentous and momentous things are no doubt being done in Peiping, Teheran, Bonn, and Jakarta. But these things are no part of my day; they are outside of my experience, and though one or two of them may faintly impinge on my consciousness tomorrow via the headlines in the morning paper, that is probably as far as they will get. At best they are likely to remain fluttering fragments on the fringe of my experience, not well-ordered parts of it. I must insist emphatically that the history I write is, as the present-minded say, intimately connected with my own day and inextricably linked with my own experience; but I must insist with even stronger emphasis that my day is not someone else's day, or the ideal Day of Contemporary Man; it is just the way I happen to dispose of twenty-four hours. By the same token the experience that is inextricably linked to any history I may happen to write is not the ideal Experience of Twentieth-Century Man in World Chaos, but just the way I happen to put in my time over the series of my days.

Now it may seem immodest or perhaps simply fantastic to take days spent as are mine—days so little attuned to the great harmonies, discords and issues of the present—and hold them up for contemplation. Yet I will dare to suggest that in this historian's own humdrum days there is one peculiarity that merits thought. The peculiarity lies in the curious relation that days so squandered seem to establish between the present and a rather remote sector of the past. I do not pretend that I am wholly unconcerned by the larger public issues and catastrophes of the present; nor am I without opinions on a large number of contemporary issues. On some of them I am vigorously dogmatic as, indeed, are most of the historians I know. Yet my knowledge about such issues, although occasionally fairly extensive, tends to be haphazard, vague, unsystematic and disorderly. And the brute fact of the matter is that even if I had the inclination, I do not have the time to straighten that knowledge out except at the cost of alterations in the ordering of my days that I am not in the least inclined to undertake.

So for a small part of my day I live under a comfortable rule of bland intellectual irresponsibility vis-à-vis the Great Issues of the Contemporary World, a rule that permits me to go off half-cocked with only slight and occasional compunction. But during most of my day—that portion of it that I spend in dealing with the Great and Not-So-Great Issues of the World between 1450 and 1650—I live under an altogether different rule. The commandments of that rule are:

1. Do not go off half-cocked.
2. Get the story straight.
3. Keep prejudices about present-day issues out of this area.

The commandments are counsels of perfection, but they are not merely that; they are enforced by sanctions, both external and internal. The serried array of historical trade journals equipped with extensive book-review columns provides the most powerful external sanction. The columns are often at the disposal of cantankerous cranks ever ready to expose to obloquy "pamphleteers" who think that Clio is an "easy bought mistress bound to suit her ways to the intellectual appetites of the current customer."[1] On more than one occasion I have been a cantankerous crank. When I write about the period between 1450 and 1650 I am well aware of a desire to give unto others no occasion to do unto me as I have done unto some of them.

The reviewing host seems largely to have lined up with the history-minded. This seems to be a consequence of their training. Whatever the theoretical biases of their individual members, the better departments of graduate study in history do not encourage those undergoing their novitiate to resolve research problems by reference to current ideological conflicts. Consequently most of us have been conditioned to feel that it is not quite proper to characterize John Pym as a liberal, or Thomas More as a socialist, or Niccolò Machiavelli as a proto-Fascist, and we tend to regard this sort of characterization as at best a risky pedagogic device. Not only the characterization but the thought process that leads to it lie under a psychological ban; and thus to the external sanction of the review columns is added the internal sanction of the still small voice that keeps saying, "One really shouldn't do it that way."[2]

The austere rule we live under as historians has some curious consequences. In my case one of the consequences is that my knowledge of the period around the sixteenth century in Europe is of a rather different order than my knowledge about current happenings. Those preponderant segments of my own day spent in the discussion, investigation and contemplation of that remote era may not be profitably spent but at least they are spent in an orderly, systematic, purposeful way. The contrast can be pointed up by a few details. I have never read the Social Security Act, but I have read the Elizabethan Poor Law in all its successive versions and moreover I have made some study of its application. I have never read the work of a single existentialist but I have read Calvin's *Institutes of the Christian Religion* from cover to cover. I know practically nothing for sure about the relation of the institutions of higher education in America to the social structure, but I know a fair bit about the relation between the two in France, England and the Netherlands in the fifteenth and sixteenth centuries. I have never studied the Economic Reports to the President that would enable me to appraise the state of

---

[1] *American Historical Review*, 51 (1946), 487.

[2] I do not for a moment intend to imply that current dilemmas have not suggested *problems* for historical investigation. It is obvious that such dilemmas are among the numerous and entirely legitimate points of origin of historical study. The actual issue, however, has nothing to do with the point of origin of historical studies, but with the mode of treatment of historical problems.

the American nation in the 1950s, but I have studied closely the *Discourse of the Commonwealth of England* and derived from it some reasonably coherent notions about the condition of England in the 1550s. Now the consequence of all this is inevitable. Instead of the passions, prejudices, assumptions and prepossessions, the events, crises and tensions of the present dominating my view of the past, *it is the other way about.* The passions, prejudices, assumptions and prepossessions, the events, crises and tensions of early modern Europe to a very considerable extent lend precision to my rather haphazard notions about the present. I make sense of present-day welfare-state policy by thinking of it in connection with the "commonwealth" policies of Elizabeth. I do the like with respect to the contemporary struggle for power and conflict of ideologies by throwing on them such light as I find in the Catholic-Calvinist struggle of the sixteenth century.

Teaching makes me aware of the peculiarities of my perspective. The days of my students are very different from mine. They have spent little time indeed in contemplating the events of the sixteenth century. So when I tell them that the Christian Humanists, in their optimistic aspiration to reform the world by means of education, were rather like our own progressive educators, I help them understand the Christian Humanists. But my teaching strategy moves in the opposite direction from my own intellectual experience. The comparison first suggested itself to me as a means for understanding not Christian Humanism but progressive education. There is no need to labor this point. After all, ordinarily the process of thought is from the better known to the worse known, and my knowledge of the sixteenth century is a good bit more precise than my knowledge of the twentieth. Perhaps there is nothing to be said for this peculiar way of thinking; it may be altogether silly; but in the immediate context I am not obliged to defend it. I present it simply as one of those brute facts of life dear to the heart of the present-minded. It is in fact one way that one historian's day affects his judgment.

In the controversy that provided the starting point of this rambling essay, the essential question is sometimes posed with respect to the relation of the historian to his own *day.* In other instances it is posed with respect to his relation to his own *time.* Having discovered how idiosyncratic was the day of one historian we may inquire whether his time is also peculiar. The answer is, "Yes, his time *is* a bit odd." And here it is possible to take a welcome leave of the first person singular. For, although my day is peculiar to me, my time, as a historian, is like the time of other historians.

For our purposes the crucial fact about the ordinary time of all men, even of historians in their personal as against their professional capacity, is that in no man's time is he *really* sure what is going to happen next. This is true, obviously, not only of men of the present time but also of all men of all past times. Of course there are large routine areas of existence in which we can make pretty good guesses; and if this were not so, life would be unbearable. Thus, my guess, five evenings a week in term time, that I will be getting up the following morning to teach classes at my place of employment provides me with a useful operating rule; yet it has been wrong occasionally, and will be wrong again. With respect to many matters more important, all is uncertain. Will there be war or peace next year? Will my children turn out well or ill? Will I be alive or dead thirty years hence? three years hence? tomorrow?

The saddest words of tongue or pen may be, "It might have been." The most human are, "If I had only known." But it is precisely characteristic of the historian that he does know. He is really sure what is going to happen next, not in his time as a pilgrim here below, but in his own time as a historian. The public servant Conyers Read, for example, when he worked high in the councils of the Office of Strategic Services did not know what the outcome of the maneuvers he helped plan would be. But for all the years from 1568 during which he painstakingly investigated the public career of Francis Walsingham, the eminent Tudor historian Conyers Read knew that the Spanish Armada would come against England and that the diplomatic maneuvers of Mr. Secretary Walsingham would assist in its defeat. Somewhat inaccurately we might say that while man's time ordinarily is oriented to the future, the historian's time is oriented to the past. It might be better to say that while men are ordinarily trying to connect the present with a future that is to be, the historian connects his present with a future that has already been.

The professional historian does not have a monopoly of his peculiar time, or rather, as Carl Becker once put it, every man is on occasion his own historian. But the historian alone lives systematically in the historian's own time. And from what we have been saying it is clear that this time has a unique dimension. Each man in his own time tries to discover the motives and the causes of the actions of those people he has to deal with; and the historian does the like with varying degrees of success. But, as other men do not and cannot, the historian knows something of the results of the acts of those he deals with: this is the unique dimension of the historian's time. If, in saying that the historian cannot escape his own time, the present-minded meant this peculiarly historical time—which they do not—they would be on solid ground. For the circumstances are rare indeed in which the historian has no notion whatever of the outcome of the events with which he is dealing. The very fact that he is a historian and that he has interested himself in a particular set of events fairly assures that at the outset he will have some knowledge of what happened afterward.

This knowledge makes it impossible for the historian to do merely what the history-minded say he should do—consider the past in its own terms, and envisage events as the men who lived through them did. Surely he should try to do that; just as certainly he must do more than that simply because he knows about those events what none of the men contemporary with them knew; he knows what their consequences were. To see the events surrounding the obscure monk Luther as Leo X saw them—as another "monks' quarrel" and a possible danger to the perquisites of the Curia—may help us understand the peculiar inefficacy of Papal policy at the time; but that does not preclude the historian from seeing the same events as the decisive step towards the final breach of the religious unity of Western Civilization. We may be quite sure however that nobody at the time, not even Luther himself, saw those events that way. The historian who resolutely refused to use the insight that his own peculiar time gave him would not be superior to his fellows; he would be merely foolish, betraying a singular failure to grasp what history is. For history is a becoming, an ongoing, and it is to be understood not only in terms of what comes before but also of what comes after.

What conclusions can we draw from our cursory examination of the historian's own time and his own day? What of the necessity, alleged by the present-minded, of rewriting history anew each generation? In some respects the estimate is over-generous, in one respect too niggardly. The necessity will in part be a function of the lapsed time between the events written about and the present. The history of the Treaty of Versailles of 1919 may indeed need to be written over a number of times in the next few generations as its consequences more completely unfold. But this is not true of the Treaty of Madrid of 1527. Its consequences for better or worse pretty well finished their unfolding a good while back. The need for rewriting history is also a function of the increase in actual data on the thing to be written about. Obviously any general estimate of the rate of increase of such data would be meaningless. History also must be rewritten as the relevant and usable knowledge about man, about his ways and his waywardness, increases. Here again there has been a tendency to exaggerate the speed with which that knowledge is increasing. The hosannahs that have greeted many master ideas about man during the past fifty years seem more often than not to be a reflection of an urge toward secular salvation in a shaky world rather than a precise estimate of the cognitive value of the ideas in question. Frequently such master ideas have turned out to be plain old notions in new fancy dress, or simply wrong. Perhaps the imperative, felt by the present-minded, to rewrite history every generation is less the fruit of a real necessity than of their own attempts to write it always in conformity with the latest intellectual mode. A little less haste might mean a little more speed. For the person engaged in the operation it is all too easy to mistake for progress a process that only involves skipping from recent to current errors.

If, instead of asking how often history *must* or ought to be rewritten we ask how often it *will* be rewritten, the answer is that it will be rewritten, as it always has been, from day to day. This is so because the rewriting of history is inescapably what each working historian in fact does in his own day. That is precisely how he puts in his time. We seek new data. We re-examine old data to discover in them relations and connections that our honored predecessors may have missed. On these data we seek to bring to bear whatever may seem enlightening and relevant out of our own day. And what may be relevant is as wide as the full range of our own daily experience, intellectual, aesthetic, political, social, personal. Some current event may, of course, afford a historian an understanding of what men meant five hundred years ago when they said that a prince must rule through *amour et crémeur*, love and fear. But then so might his perusal of a socio-psychological investigation into the ambivalence of authority in Papua. So might his reading of Shakespeare's *Richard II*. And so might his relations with his own children.

For each historian brings to the rewriting of history the full range of the remembered experience of his own days, that unique array that he alone possesses and is. For some historians that sector of their experience which impinges on the Great Crises of the Contemporary World sets up the vibrations that attune them to the part of the past that is the object of their professional attention. Some of us, however, vibrate less readily to those crises. We feel our way toward the goals of our historic quest by lines of experience having precious little to do with the Great Crises of the Contemporary World. He would be bold indeed who would insist that all historians should follow one and the same line of experience in their quest, or who would venture to say what this single line is that all should follow. He would not only be bold; he would almost certainly be wrong. History thrives in measure as the experience of each historian differs from that of his fellows. It is indeed the wide and varied range of experience covered by all the days of all historians that makes the rewriting of history—not in each generation but for each historian—at once necessary and inevitable.

One of the great historians of the twentieth century, Marc Bloch, held that knowledge about the past and knowledge about the present are mutually complementary and that both kinds of knowledge are essential for an understanding of the modern world. He wrote the following lines while working as a Resistance leader in France during World War II. The Nazis shot him in 1944.

FROM The Historian's Craft BY MARC BLOCH

[*Some scholars hold—B. T.*] that contemporary society is perfectly susceptible of scientific investigation. But they admit this only to reserve its study for branches of learning quite distinct from that which has the past for its object. They analyze, and they claim, for example, to understand the contemporary economic system on the basis of observations limited to a few decades. In a word, they consider the epoch in which we live as separated from its

Marc Bloch, *The Historian's Craft*, pp. 38–47, translated by Peter Putnam. Copyright 1953 by Alfred A. Knopf, Inc.

predecessors by contrasts so clear as to be self-explanatory. Such is also the instinctive attitude of a great many of the merely curious. The history of the remoter periods attracts them only as an innocuous intellectual luxury. On one hand, a small group of antiquarians taking a ghoulish delight in unwrapping the winding-sheets of the dead gods; on the other, sociologists, economists, and publicists, the only explorers of the living.

UNDERSTANDING THE PRESENT BY THE PAST

Under close scrutiny the prerogative of self-intelligibility thus attributed to present time is found to be based upon a set of strange postulates.

In the first place, it supposes that, within a generation or two, human affairs have undergone a change which is not merely rapid, but total, so that no institution of long standing, no traditional form of conduct, could have escaped the revolutions of the laboratory and the factory. It overlooks the force of inertia peculiar to so many social creations.

Man spends his time devising techniques of which he afterwards remains a more or less willing prisoner. What traveler in northern France has not been struck by the strange pattern of the fields? For centuries, changes in ownership have modified the original design; yet, even today, the sight of these inordinately long and narrow strips, dividing the arable land into a prodigious number of pieces, is something which baffles the scientific agriculturalist. The waste of effort which such a disposition entails and the problems which it imposes upon the cultivators are undeniable. How are we to account for it? Certain impatient publicists have replied: "By the Civil Code and its inevitable effects. Change the laws on inheritance and the evil will be removed." Had they known history better, or had they further questioned a peasant mentality shaped by centuries of experience, they would not have thought the cure so simple. Indeed, this pattern dates back to origins so distant that no scholar has yet succeeded in accounting for it satisfactorily. The settlers in the era of the dolmens have more to do with it than the lawyers of the First Empire. Perpetuating itself, as it were, of necessity, for want of correction, this ignorance of the past not only confuses contemporary science, but confounds contemporary action.

A society that could be completely molded by its immediately preceding period would have to have a structure so malleable as to be virtually invertebrate. It would also have to be a society in which communication between generations was conducted, so to speak, in "Indian file"—the children having contact with their ancestors only through the mediation of their parents.

Now, this is not true. It is not true even when the communication is purely oral. Take our villages, for example. Because working conditions keep the mother and father away almost all day, the young children are brought up chiefly by their grandparents. Consequently, with the molding of each new mind, there is a backward step, joining the most malleable to the most inflexible mentality, while skipping that generation which is the sponsor of change. There is small room for doubt that this is the source of that traditionalism inherent in so many peasant societies. The instance is particularly clear, but it is far from unique. Because the natural antagonism between age groups is always intensified between neighboring generations, more than one youth has learned at least as much from the aged as from those in their prime.

Still more strongly, between even widely scattered generations, the written word vastly facilitates those transfers of thought which supply the true continuity of a civilization. Take Luther, Calvin, Loyola, certainly men from another time—from the sixteenth century, in fact. The first duty of the historian who would understand and explain them will be to return them to their milieu, where they are immersed in the mental climate of their time and faced by problems of conscience rather different from our own. But who would dare to say that the understanding of the Protestant or the Catholic Reformation, several centuries removed, is not far more important for a proper grasp of the world today than a great many other movements of thought or feeling, which are certainly more recent, yet more ephemeral?

In a word, the fallacy is clear, and it is only necessary to formulate it in order to destroy it. It represents the course of human evolution as a series of short, violent jerks, no one of which exceeds the space of a few lifetimes. Observation proves, on the contrary, that the mighty convulsions of that vast, continuing development are perfectly capable of extending from the beginning of time to the present. What would we think of a geophysicist who, satisfied with having computed their remoteness to a fraction of an inch, would then conclude that the influence of the moon upon the earth is far greater than that of the sun? Neither in outer space, nor in time, can the potency of a force be measured by the single dimension of distance.

Finally, what of those things past which seem to have lost all authority over the present—faiths which have vanished without a trace, social forms which have miscarried, techniques which have perished? Would anyone think that, even among these, there is nothing useful for his understanding? That would be to forget that there is no true understanding without a certain range of comparison; provided, of course, that that comparison is based upon differing and, at the same time, related realities. One could scarcely deny that such is here the case.

Certainly, we no longer consider today, as Machiavelli wrote, and as Hume or Bonald thought, that there is, in time, "at least something which is changeless: that is man." We have learned that man, too, has changed a great deal in his mind and, no less certainly, in the most delicate organs of his body. How should it be otherwise? His mental climate has been greatly altered; and to no less an extent, so, too, have his hygiene and his diet. However, there must be a permanent foundation in human nature and in human society, or the very names of man or society become meaningless. How, then, are we to believe that we understand these men, if we study them only in their reactions to circumstances peculiar to a moment? It would be an inadequate test of them, even for that particular moment. A great many potentialities, which might at any instant emerge from concealment, a great many more or less unconscious drives behind individual or collective attitudes, would remain in the shadows. In a unique case the specific elements cannot be differentiated; hence an interpretation cannot be made.

UNDERSTANDING THE PAST BY THE PRESENT

This solidarity of the ages is so effective that the lines of connection work both ways. Misunderstanding of the present is the inevitable consequence of ignorance of the past. But a man may wear himself out just as fruitlessly in seeking to understand the past, if he is totally ignorant of the present. There is an anecdote which I have already recounted elsewhere: I had gone with Henri Pirenne to Stockholm; we had scarcely arrived, when he said to me: "What shall we go to see first? It seems that there is a new city hall here. Let's start there." Then, as if to ward off my surprise, he added: "If I were an antiquarian, I would have eyes only for old stuff, but I am a historian. Therefore, I love life." This faculty of understanding the living is, in very truth, the master quality of the historian. Despite their occasional frigidity of style, the greatest of our number have all possessed it. Fustel or Maitland, in their austere way, had it as much as Michelet. And, perhaps, it originates as a gift from the fairies, quite inaccessible to anyone who has not found it in his cradle. That does not lessen the obligation to exercise and develop it constantly. How? How better than by the example of Henri Pirenne—by keeping in constant touch with the present day?

For here, in the present, is immediately perceptible that vibrance of human life which only a great effort of the imagination can restore to the old texts. I have many times read, and I have often narrated, accounts of wars and battles. Did I truly know, in the full sense of that word, did I know from within, before I myself had suffered the terrible, sickening reality, what it meant for an army to be encircled, what it meant for a people to meet defeat? Before I myself had breathed the joy of victory in the summer and autumn of 1918 (and, although, alas! its perfume will not again be quite the same, I yearn to fill my lungs with it a second time) did I truly know all that was inherent in that beautiful word? In the last analysis, whether consciously or no, it is always by borrowing from our daily experiences and by shading them, where necessary, with new tints that we derive the elements which help us to restore the past. The very names we use to describe ancient ideas or vanished forms of social organization would be quite meaningless if we had not known living men. The value of these merely instinctive impressions will be increased a hundredfold if they are replaced by a ready and critical observation. A great mathematician would not, I suppose, be less great because blind to the world in which he lives. But the scholar who has no inclination to observe the men, the things, or the events around him will perhaps deserve the title, as Pirenne put it, of a useful antiquarian. He would be wise to renounce all claims to that of a historian.

Moreover, the cultivation of historical sensitivity is not always all that is involved. It may happen, in a given line, that the knowledge of the present bears even more immediately upon the understanding of the past.

It would be a grievous error, indeed, to think that the order which historians adopt for their inquiries must necessarily correspond to the sequence of events. Even though they restore its true direction afterwards, they have often benefited at the outset by reading history, as Maitland said, "backwards." For the natural progression of all research is from the best (or least badly) understood to the most obscure. Certainly, it is far from true that the light of documentation grows ever brighter as we pass down the corridor of the ages. For example, we are much less well-informed on the tenth century of our era than on the epoch of Caesar or Augustus. In the majority of cases, however, the nearest periods correspond better with the zones of relative clarity. We must add that, in proceeding mechanically from early to late, there is always the risk of wasting time in tracking down the beginning or causes of phenomena which, in the event, may turn out to be somewhat imaginary. The most illustrious among us have occasionally made strange mistakes through having neglected to pursue a prudently retrogressive method whenever and wherever it was indicated. Fustel de Coulanges devoted himself to the "origins" of feudal institutions of which he had formed, I fear, only a rather confused picture, and to the beginnings of a serfdom which, misled by secondhand descriptions, he conceived in entirely false colors.

Now, more often than is generally supposed, it happens that, in order to find daylight, the historian may have to pursue his subject right up to the present. In certain of its fundamental features, our rural landscape, as has been previously mentioned, dates from a very remote epoch. However, in order to interpret the rare documents which permit us to fathom its misty beginnings, in order to ask the right questions, even in order to know what we were talking about, it was necessary to fulfill a primary condition: that of observing and analyzing our present landscape. For it alone furnished those comprehensive vistas without which it was impossible to begin. Not, indeed, that there could be any question of imposing this forever-static picture, just as it is, at each stage of the journey upstream to the headwaters of the past. Here, as elsewhere, it is change which the historian is seeking to grasp. But in the film which he is examining, only the last picture remains quite clear. In order to reconstruct the faded features of the others, it behooves him first to unwind the spool in the opposite direction from that in which the pictures were taken.

There is, then, just one science of men in time. It requires us to join the study of the dead and the living. What shall we call it? I have already explained why the ancient name, "history," seemed to me the best. It is the most comprehensive, the least exclusive, the most electric with stirring reminders of a more than age-old endeavor. In proposing to extend history right down to the present (contrary to certain prejudices which are not so old as history itself), I have no desire to expand the claims of my own profession. Life is too short, and science too vast, to permit even the greatest genius a total experience of humanity. Some men will always specialize in the present, as others do in the Stone Age or in Egyptology. We simply ask both to bear in mind that historical research will tolerate no autarchy. Isolated, each will understand only by halves, even within his own field of study; for the only true history, which can advance only through mutual aid, is universal history.

PERICLEAN ATHENS

DEMOCRACY, ARISTOCRACY, OR MONARCHY?

CONTENTS

QUESTIONS FOR STUDY

1. *How does Pericles' picture of Athenian democracy differ from that of the "Old Oligarch"?*

2. *Which of the ancient authors believe(s) that Athens was not truly democratic?*

3. *In what sense does Beloch mean that Athens was aristocratic?*

4. *Is Van Hook's defense against the charge of aristocracy adequate?*

5. *How does McGregor try to refute the charge that Athens was a disguised monarchy?*

6. *If Athens may not be called "democratic," can you think of any state at any time that may?*

Athens in the time of Pericles is usually regarded as the perfect model of direct democracy. With its popular assembly, its law courts, its magistrates popularly elected or chosen by lot, it might seem, beyond any dispute, the most democratic of states. Yet to a contemporary observer, Thucydides, it was a "democracy in name but the rule of the first citizen in fact." Modern scholars have taken up the debate and added an element to it by arguing that a society that included slaves and despised labor can hardly be called "democratic." This section is an attempt to present a picture of Periclean Athens as it appeared to the ancients and to suggest the kinds of disputes that have engaged modern scholars.

The problem is compounded by the absence of any systematic statement of democratic theory written by a Greek democrat. Our understanding of Greek democracy, therefore, must be achieved by putting together scattered references in speeches by democratic statesmen—the funeral oration of Pericles, for instance (pp. 67–72), with the accounts of such enemies of democracy as Plato (pp. 81–84) and the "Old Oligarch" (pp. 77–81). Even less tendentious accounts such as those of Aristotle (pp. 75–76), Thucydides (pp. 73–74), and Plutarch (pp. 84–92) are tinged with antidemocratic bias.

We should remember that by the time of Pericles' acme (c. 443–429 B.C.) democracy was over half a century old in Athens. Cleisthenes had introduced what we may properly call a democratic regime in the last decade of the sixth century. Although the highest offices in the state were reserved for the upper classes, all male Athenians could vote, serve on the Council of Five Hundred, and on the juries. The reforms of Themistocles in the years between Marathon (490) and the Persian War (480–479 B.C.) opened all offices to the people and, in increasing the importance of the navy, gave increased political power to the lower classes, who rowed the ships. Ephialtes' successful attack on the Areopagus (462), the great bastion of aristocratic influence, cleared the way for even greater popular power.

Pericles continued the trend toward democracy by introducing payment for public service. It was possible, nevertheless, for ancient and modern writers to speak of Periclean Athens as undemocratic and even monarchical. To be sure, after the ostracism of Thucydides, son of Melesias, in 443 Pericles was never again faced with a serious political rival. It is also true that he seemed to determine Athenian policy without much hindrance. Yet none of this need be inconsistent with democratic government properly understood. Both Thucydides and Plutarch provide evidence by which modern scholars such as Larue Van Hook (pp. 93–110) and Malcolm McGregor (pp. 112–116) can challenge their interpretation. It soon becomes clear that the student must determine what constitutes a satisfactory definition of democracy and then test Periclean Athens against that definition.

1
THE DEMOCRATIC MONARCHY OF PERICLES

Georg Busolt argues that Periclean Athens was not a truly democratic state and makes clear the nature of the controversy.

FROM Griechische Geschichte BY GEORG BUSOLT

The extensive and glittering outfitting of the Panathenaic festival, the construction of a splendid new temple of Athena, the whole building activity in general were features of the Periclean leadership which it shared with the regime of the Peisistratids, a democratic monarchy to which, according to the judgment of Thucydides, it was really related. Both regimes were concerned with the relief of the lower classes, the attempt to give them employment, to provide a livelihood for them, and also with the acquisition of overseas possessions and the provision of landed property for many citizens. Pericles' colonization of the Chersonnese and his restoration of circuit judges join directly with the tradition of the time of the Peisistratids [who introduced similar popular measures].

* * *

[Busolt describes the ostracism of Thucydides, son of Melesias (not the historian), the leader of the faction opposed to Pericles—D.K.]
The oligarchic party lost, with its organizer, its firm coherence and its capacity for robust opposition. Pericles was thus without a rival, and therefore, in the eyes of the people, he became something other than what he had been

Georg Busolt, Griechische Geschichte, III (1893), Part I, 470, 497–499, translated by Donald Kagan.

before. If he had earlier felt himself compelled to be at the people's disposal and to yield to the wishes of the masses, he now began to behave independently and to take the bridle into his hand. By using the weight of his personality he ruled the state—on the one hand by means of the official authority given to him, on the other hand by means of his decisive influence on the decisions of the popular assembly. For fifteen years he would be elected to the generalship each year. In difficult times of war he received the supreme command, and at the beginning of the Peloponnesian War he also obtained extraordinarily full powers. Although he did not usually have greater official power than the other generals, he nevertheless held the authoritative position in the college of the generals and thereby collected into his own hand its conduct of the military, maritime, financial, and administrative affairs that were in its competence. The unbroken continuity of office, in fact, released him still further from the principle of accountability and gave him an exceptional position, which would nevertheless be held within bounds by the fact that the people, by means of the *epicheirotonia* that took place each prytany, could suspend him from office and place him before a court. In addition to the most important ordinary annual offices, Pericles quite regularly held the extraordinary office of *Epistates* (supervisor) of a public building. . . .

But, as the official power of Pericles was dependent on popular election and the mood of the people, he could only steer the entire ship of state in the direction he set if he could hold the leadership of the popular assembly in his hand. He succeeded by dint of his firmly based authority, his proven political insight, the integrity of his character, the dignity of his bearing, and the power of his speech. As he did not first need to acquire influence by improper means and was not accustomed to speak in order to please but, on the contrary, by virtue of the esteem in which he was already held, he could, under certain circumstances, even sharply oppose the people. He thus would not be led by the people, but instead he led them. As a result there developed a regime that was a popular government in name but one ruled by the first citizen in fact, a monarchical leadership on a democratic base, which frequently resumed the traditions of the democratic monarchy of the Peisistratids.

2
THE
GREATNESS
OF
ATHENS

In the winter following the first campaigns of the Peloponnesian War, Pericles was chosen to pronounce the customary eulogy over the fallen warriors. He turned it instead into an occasion to praise the Athenian state, its constitution, and its way of life. Thucydides, who was almost surely present, reported the speech in full.

FROM Pericles' Funeral Oration

Most of my predecessors in this place have commended him who made this speech part of the law, telling us that it is well that it should be delivered at the burial of those who fall in battle. For myself, I should have thought that the worth which had displayed itself in deeds, would be sufficiently rewarded by honours also shown by deeds; such as you now see in this funeral prepared at the people's cost. And I could have wished that the reputations of many brave men were not to be imperilled in the mouth of a single individual, to stand or fall according as he spoke well or ill. For it is hard to speak properly upon a subject where it is even difficult to convince your hearers that you are speaking the truth. On the one hand, the friend who is familiar with every fact of the story, may think that some point has not been set forth with that fulness which he wishes and knows it to deserve; on the other, he who is a stranger to the matter may be led by envy to suspect exaggeration if he hears anything above his own nature. For men can endure to hear others praised only so long as they can severally persuade themselves of their own ability to

Thucydides, *History of the Peloponnesian War* (1876), Book 2, Chapters 35–46, translated by Richard Crawley.

equal the actions recounted: when this point is passed, envy comes in and with it incredulity. However, since our ancestors have stamped this custom with their approval, it becomes my duty to obey the law and to try to satisfy your several wishes and opinions as best I may.

I shall begin with our ancestors: it is both just and proper that they should have the honour of the first mention on an occasion like the present. They dwelt in the country without break in the succession from generation to generation, and handed it down free to the present time by their valour. And if our more remote ancestors deserve praise, much more do our own fathers, who added to their inheritance the empire which we now possess, and spared no pains to be able to leave their acquisitions to us of the present generation. Lastly, there are few parts of our dominions that have not been augmented by those of us here, who are still more or less in the vigour of life; while the mother country has been furnished by us with everything that can enable her to depend on her own resources whether for war or for peace. That part of our history which tells of the military achievements which gave us our several possessions, or of the ready valour with which either we or our fathers stemmed the tide of Hellenic or foreign aggression, is a theme too familiar to my hearers for me to dilate on, and I shall therefore pass it by. But what was the road by which we reached our position, what the form of government under which our greatness grew, what the national habits out of which it sprang; these are questions which I may try to solve before I proceed to my panegyric upon these men; since I think this to be a subject upon which on the present occasion a speaker may properly dwell, and to which the whole assemblage, whether citizens or foreigners, may listen with advantage.

Our constitution does not copy the laws of neighbouring states; we are rather a pattern to others than imitators ourselves. Its administration favours the many instead of the few; this is why it is called a democracy. If we look to the laws, they afford equal justice to all in their private differences; if to social standing, advancement in public life falls to reputation for capacity, class considerations not being allowed to interfere with merit; nor again does poverty bar the way, if a man is able to serve the state, he is not hindered by the obscurity of his condition. The freedom which we enjoy in our government extends also to our ordinary life. There, far from exercising a jealous surveillance over each other, we do not feel called upon to be angry with our neighbour for doing what he likes, or even to indulge in those injurious looks which cannot fail to be offensive, although they inflict no positive penalty. But all this ease in our private relations does not make us lawless as citizens. Against this fear is our chief safeguard, teaching us to obey the magistrates and the laws, particularly such as regard the protection of the injured, whether they are actually on the statute book, or belong to that code which, although unwritten, yet cannot be broken without acknowledged disgrace.

Further, we provide plenty of means for the mind to refresh itself from business. We celebrate games and sacrifices all the year round, and the elegance of our private establishments forms a daily source of pleasure and helps to banish the spleen; while the magnitude of our city draws the produce of the world into our harbour, so that to the Athenian the fruits of other countries are as familiar a luxury as those of his own.

If we turn to our military policy, there also we differ from our antagonists. We throw open our city to the world, and never by alien acts exclude foreigners from any opportunity of learning or observing, although the eyes of an enemy may occasionally profit by our liberality; trusting less in system and policy than to the native spirit of our citizens; while in education, where our rivals from their very cradles by a painful discipline seek after manliness, at Athens we live exactly as we please, and yet are just as ready to encounter every legitimate danger. In proof of this it may be noticed that the Lacedaemonians do not invade our country alone, but bring with them all their confederates; while we Athenians advance unsupported into the territory of a neighbour, and fighting upon a foreign soil usually vanquish with ease men who are defending their homes. Our united force was never yet encountered by any enemy, because we have at once to attend to our marine and to despatch our citizens by land upon a hundred different services; so that, wherever they engage with some such fraction of our strength, a success against a detachment is magnified into a victory over the nation, and a defeat into a reverse suffered at the hands of our entire people. And yet if with habits not of labour but of ease, and courage not of art but of nature, we are still willing to encounter danger, we have the double advantage of escaping the experience of hardships in anticipation and of facing them in the hour of need as fearlessly as those who are never free from them.

Nor are these the only points in which our city is worthy of admiration. We cultivate refinement without extravagance and knowledge without effeminacy; wealth we employ more for use than for show, and place the real disgrace of poverty not in owning to the fact but in declining the struggle against it. Our public men have, besides politics, their private affairs to attend to, and our ordinary citizens, though occupied with the pursuits of industry, are still fair judges of public matters; for, unlike any other nation, regarding him who takes no part in these duties not as unambitious but as useless, we Athenians are able to judge at all events if we cannot originate, and instead of looking on discussion as a stumbling-block in the way of action, we think it an indispensable preliminary to any wise action at all. Again, in our enterprises we present the singular spectacle of daring and deliberation, each carried to its highest point, and both united in the same persons; although usually decision is the fruit of ignorance, hesitation of reflexion. But the palm of courage will surely be adjudged most justly to those who best know the difference between hardship and pleasure and yet are never tempted to shrink from danger. In generosity we are equally singular, acquiring our friends by conferring not by receiving favours. Yet, of course, the doer of the favour is the firmer friend of the two, in order by continued kindness to keep the recipient in his debt; while the debtor feels less keenly from the very consciousness that the return he makes will be a payment, not a free gift. And it is only the Athenians who, fearless of consequences, confer their benefits not from calculations of expediency, but in the confidence of liberality.

In short, I say that as a city we are the school of Hellas; while I doubt if the world can produce a man, who where he has only himself to depend upon, is equal to so many emergencies, and graced by so happy a versatility as the Athenian. And that this is no mere boast thrown out for the occasion, but plain matter of fact, the power of the state acquired by these habits proves. For Athens alone of her contemporaries is found when tested to be greater than her reputation, and alone gives no occasion to her assailants to blush at the antagonist by whom they have been worsted, or to her subjects to question her title by merit to rule. Rather, the admiration of the present and succeeding ages will be ours, since we have not left our power without witness, but have shown it by mighty proofs; and far from needing a Homer for our panegyrist, or other of his craft whose verses might charm for the moment only for the impression which they gave to melt at the touch of fact, we have forced every sea and land to be the highway of our daring, and everywhere, whether for evil or for good, have left imperishable monuments behind us. Such is the Athens for which these men, in the assertion of their resolve not to lose her, nobly fought and died; and well may every one of their survivors be ready to suffer in her cause.

Indeed if I have dwelt at some length upon the character of our country, it has been to show that our stake in the struggle is not the same as theirs who have no such blessings to lose, and also that the panegyric of the men over whom I am now speaking might be by definite proofs established. That panegyric is now in a great measure complete; for the Athens that I have celebrated is only what the heroism of these and their like have made her, men whose fame, unlike that of most Hellenes, will be found to be only commensurate with their deserts. And if a test of worth be wanted, it is to be found in their closing scene, and this not only in the cases in which it set the final seal upon their merit, but also in those in which it gave the first intimation of their having any. For there is justice in the claim that steadfastness in his country's battles should be as a cloak to cover a man's other imperfections; since the good action has blotted out the bad, and his merit as a citizen more than outweighed his demerits as an individual. But none of these allowed either wealth with its prospect of future enjoyment to unnerve his spirit, or poverty with its hope of a day of freedom and riches to tempt him to shrink from danger. No, holding that vengeance upon their enemies was more to be desired than any personal blessings, and reckoning this to be the most glorious of hazards, they joyfully determined to accept the risk, to make sure of their vengeance and to let their wishes wait; and while committing to hope the uncertainty of final success, in the business before them they thought fit to act boldly and trust in themselves. Thus choosing to die resisting, rather than to live submitting, they fled only from dishonour, but met danger face to face, and after one brief moment, while at the summit of their fortune, escaped, not from their fear, but from their glory.

So died these men as became Athenians. You, their survivors, must determine to have as unaltering a resolution in the field, though you may pray that it may have a happier issue. And not contented with ideas derived only from words of the advantages which are bound up with the defence of your country, though these would furnish a valuable text to a speaker even before an audience so alive to them as the present, you must yourselves realise the power of Athens, and feed your eyes upon her from day to day, till love of her fills your hearts; and then when all her greatness shall break upon you, you must reflect that it was by courage, sense of duty, and a keen feeling of honour in action that men were enabled to win all this, and that no personal failure in an enterprise could make them consent to deprive their country of their valour, but they laid it at her feet as the most glorious contribution that they could offer. For this offering of their lives made in common by them all they each of them individually received that renown which never grows old, and for a sepulchre, not so much that in which their bones have been deposited, but that noblest of shrines wherein their glory is laid up to be eternally remembered upon every occasion on which deed or story shall fall for its commemoration. For heroes have the whole earth for their tomb; and in lands far from their own, where the column with its epitaph declares it, there is enshrined in every breast a record unwritten with no tablet to preserve it, except that of the heart. These take as your model, and judging happiness to be the fruit of freedom and freedom of valour, never decline the dangers of war. For it is not the miserable that would most justly be unsparing of their lives; these have nothing to hope for: it is rather they to whom continued life may bring reverses as yet unknown, and to whom a fall, if it came, would be most tremendous in its consequences. And surely, to a man of spirit, the degradation of cowardice must be immeasurably more grievous than the unfelt death which strikes him in the midst of his strength and patriotism!

Comfort, therefore, not condolence, is what I have to offer to the parents of the dead who may be here. Numberless are the chances to which, as they know, the life of man is subject; but fortunate indeed are they who draw for their lot a death so glorious as that which has caused your mourning, and to whom life has been so exactly measured as to terminate in the happiness in which it has been passed. Still I know that this is a hard saying, especially when those are in question of whom you will constantly be reminded by seeing in the homes of others blessings of which once you also boasted: for grief is felt not so much for the want of what we have never known, as for the loss of that to which we have been long accustomed. Yet you who are still of an age to beget children must bear up in the hope of having others in their stead; not only will they help you to forget those whom you have lost, but will be to the state at once a reinforcement and a security; for never can a fair or just policy be expected of the citizen who does not, like his fellows, bring to the decision the interests and apprehensions of a father. While those of you who have passed your prime must congratulate yourselves with the thought that the best part of your life was fortunate, and that the brief span that remains will be cheered by the fame of the departed. For it is only the love of honour that never grows old; and honour it is, not gain, as some would have it, that rejoices the heart of age and helplessness.

Turning to the sons or brothers of the dead, I see an arduous struggle before you. When a man is gone, all are wont to praise him, and should your merit be ever so transcendent, you will still find it difficult not merely to overtake, but even to approach their renown. The living have envy to contend with, while those who are no longer in our path are honoured with a goodwill into which rivalry does not enter. On the other hand, if I must say anything on the subject of female excellence to those of you who will now be in widowhood, it will be all comprised in this brief exhortation. Great will be your glory in not falling short of your natural character; and greatest will be hers who is least talked of among the men whether for good or for bad.

My task is now finished. I have performed it to the best of my ability, and in words, at least, the requirements of the law are now satisfied. If deeds be in question, those who are here interred have received part of their honours already, and for the rest, their children will be brought up till manhood at the public expense: the state thus offers a valuable prize, as the garland of victory in this race of valour, for the reward both of those who have fallen and their survivors. And where the rewards for merit are greatest, there are found the best citizens.

And now that you have brought to a close your lamentations for your relatives, you may depart.

3

ANCIENT
AUTHORS ON
PERICLEAN
DEMOCRACY

Thucydides, the historian of the Peloponnesian War, experienced Athenian democracy in its glory under Pericles and at its nadir at the end of the war. His account deserves the most respectful attention, for he was an eyewitness of acute and discerning judgment. This selection follows an account of the response of the Athenians to the hardships of war; only the persuasiveness of Pericles had prevented them from seeking terms after a short period of fighting.

FROM History of the Peloponnesian War BY THUCYDIDES

They not only gave up all idea of sending to Lacedaemon, but applied themselves with increased energy to the war; still as private individuals they could not help smarting under their sufferings, the common people having been deprived of the little that they ever possessed, while the higher orders had lost fine properties with costly establishments and buildings in the country, and, worst of all, had war instead of peace. In fact, the public feeling against him [Pericles—D. K.] did not subside until he had been fined. Not long afterwards, however, according to the way of the multitude, they again elected him general and committed all their affairs to his hands, having now become less sensitive to their private and domestic afflictions, and understanding that

---

Thucydides, *History of the Peloponnesian War* (1876), Book 2, Chapter 65, translated by Richard Crawley.

he was the best man of all for the public necessities. For as long as he was at the head of the state during the peace, he pursued a moderate and conservative policy; and in his time its greatness was at its height. When the war broke out, here also he seems to have rightly gauged the power of his country. He outlived its commencement two years and six months, and the correctness of his previsions respecting it became better known by his death. He told them to wait quietly, to pay attention to their marine, to attempt no new conquests, and to expose the city to no hazards during the war, and doing this, promised them a favourable result. What they did was the very contrary, allowing private ambitions and private interests, in matters apparently quite foreign to the war, to lead them into projects unjust both to themselves and to their allies—projects whose success would only conduce to the honour and advantage of private persons, and whose failure entailed certain disaster on the country in the war. The causes of this are not far to seek. Pericles indeed, by his rank, ability, and known integrity, was enabled to exercise an independent control over the multitude—in short, to lead them instead of being led by them; for as he never sought power by improper means, he was never compelled to flatter them, but, on the contrary, enjoyed so high an estimation that he could afford to anger them by contradiction. Whenever he saw them unseasonably and insolently elated, he would with a word reduce them to alarm; on the other hand, if they fell victims to a panic, he could at once restore them to confidence. In short, what was nominally a democracy became in his hands government by the first citizen. With his successors it was different. More on a level with one another, and each grasping at supremacy, they ended by committing even the conduct of state affairs to the whims of the multitude. This, as might have been expected in a great and sovereign state, produced a host of blunders, and amongst them the Sicilian expedition; though this failed not so much through a miscalculation of the power of those against whom it was sent, as through a fault in the senders in not taking the best measures afterwards to assist those who had gone out, but choosing rather to occupy themselves with private cabals for the leadership of the commons, by which they not only paralysed operations in the field, but also first introduced civil discord at home. Yet after losing most of their fleet besides other forces in Sicily, and with faction already dominant in the city, they could still for three years make head against their original adversaries, joined not only by the Sicilians, but also by their own allies nearly all in revolt, and at last by the king's son, Cyrus, who furnished the funds for the Peloponnesian navy. Nor did they finally succumb till they fell the victims of their own intestine disorders. So superfluously abundant were the resources from which the genius of Pericles foresaw an easy triumph in the war over the unaided forces of the Peloponnesians.

The following selection is from the *Constitution of the Athenians,* probably written by Aristotle, although some scholars attribute it to one of his students. There is no doubt, however, that it was written about a century after the death of Pericles and represents the thinking of Aristotle and his school.

FROM Constitution of the Athenians BY ARISTOTLE

XXVI. . . . after this there came about an increased relaxation of the constitution, due to the eagerness of those who were the leaders of the People. For it so happened that during these periods the better classes had no leader at all, but the chief person among them, Cimon son of Miltiades, was a rather young man who had only lately entered public life; and in addition, that the multitude had suffered seriously in war, for in those days the expeditionary force was raised from a muster-roll, and was commanded by generals with no experience of war but promoted on account of their family reputations, so that it was always happening that the troops on an expedition suffered as many as two or three thousand casualties, making a drain on the numbers of the respectable members both of the people and of the wealthy. Thus in general all the administration was conducted without the same attention to the laws as had been given before, although no innovation was made in the election of the Nine Archons, except that five years after the death of Ephialtes they decided to extend to the Teamster class eligibility to the preliminary roll from which the Nine Archons were to be selected by lot; and the first of the Teamster class to hold the archonship was Mnesitheides. All the Archons hitherto had been from the Knights and Five-hundred-measure-men, while the Teamsters held the ordinary offices, unless some provision of the laws was ignored. Four years afterwards, in the archonship of Lysicrates, the thirty judges called the Local Justices were instituted again; and two years after Lysicrates, in the year of Antidotus, owing to the large number of the citizens an enactment was passed on the proposal of Pericles confining citizenship to persons of citizen birth on both sides.

XXVII. After this when Pericles advanced to the leadership of the people, having first distinguished himself when while still a young man he challenged the audits of Cimon who was a general, it came about that the constitution became still more democratic. For he took away some of the functions of the Areopagus, and he urged the state very strongly in the direction of

Aristotle, *Constitution of the Athenians* (1891), Sections XXVI–XXVIII, translated by F. G. Kenyon.

naval power, which resulted in emboldening the multitude, who brought all the government more into their own hands. Forty-eight years after the naval battle of Salamis, in the archonship of Pythodorus, the war against the Peloponnesians broke out, during which the people being locked up in the city, and becoming accustomed to earning pay on their military campaigns, came partly of their own will and partly against their will to the decision to administer the government themselves. Also Pericles first made service in the jury-courts a paid office, as a popular countermeasure against Cimon's wealth. For as Cimon had an estate large enough for a tyrant, in the first place he discharged the general public services in a brilliant manner, and moreover he supplied maintenance to a number of the members of his deme; for anyone of the Laciadae who liked could come to his house every day and have a moderate supply, and also all his farms were unfenced, to enable anyone who liked to avail himself of the harvest. So as Pericles' means were insufficient for this lavishness, he took the advice of Damonides of Oea (who was believed to suggest to Pericles most of his measures, owing to which they afterwards ostracized him), since he was getting the worst of it with his private resources, to give the multitude what was their own, and he instituted payment for the jury-courts; the result of which according to some critics was their deterioration, because ordinary persons always took more care than the respectable to cast lots for the duty. Also it was after this that the organized bribery of juries began, Anytus having first shown the way to it after his command at Pylos; for when he was brought to trial by certain persons for having lost Pylos he bribed the court and got off.

XXVIII. So long, then, as Pericles held the headship of the People, the affairs of the state went better, but when Pericles was dead they became much worse. For the People now for the first time adopted a head who was not in good repute with the respectable classes, whereas in former periods those always continued to lead the People.

The following selection is from a pamphlet on the Athenian constitution that has come down to us among the works of Xenophon. In the long debate concerning its authorship, the only fact generally agreed upon is that it could not have been written by Xenophon. Various authors have been proposed, among them Thucydides, son of Melesias, a political opponent of Pericles. None of these attributions has won wide acceptance, and the anonymous author is usually called the "Old Oligarch." Internal evidence places the date of the treatise toward the beginning of the Peloponnesian War. The author was thus, like Thucydides the historian, a contemporary of Pericles. His views, though contradictory to those of Thucydides, are not to be dismissed.

FROM Constitution of the Athenians
BY THE "OLD OLIGARCH"

Now, as for the constitution of the Athenians, and the type or manner of constitution which they have chosen, I praise it not, in so far as the very choice involves the welfare of the baser folk as opposed to that of the better class. I repeat, I withhold my praise so far; but, given the fact that this is the type agreed upon, I propose to show that they set about its preservation in the right way; and that those other transactions in connection with it, which are looked upon as blunders by the rest of the Hellenic world, are the reverse.

In the first place, I maintain, it is only just that the poorer classes and the common people of Athens should be better off than the men of birth and wealth, seeing that it is the people who man the fleet, and have brought the city her power. The steersman, the boatswain, the lieutenant, the lookoutman at the prow, the shipwright—these are the people who supply the city with power far rather than her heavy infantry and men of birth and quality. This being the case, it seems only just that offices of state should be thrown open to every one both in the ballot and the show of hands, and that the right of speech should belong to any one who likes, without restriction. For, observe, there are many of these offices which, according as they are in good or in bad hands, are a source of safety or of danger to the People, and in these the People prudently abstains from sharing; as, for instance, it does not think it incumbent on itself to share in the functions of the general or of the commander of cavalry. The commons recognises the fact that in forgoing the personal exercise of these offices, and leaving them to the control of the more powerful citizens, it secures the balance of advantage to itself. It is only those departments of government which bring pay and assist the private estate that the People cares to keep in its own hands.

In the next place, in regard to what some people are puzzled to explain—the fact that everywhere greater consideration is shown to the base, to poor people and to common folk, than to persons of good quality,—so far from being a matter of surprise, this, as can be shown, is the keystone of the preservation of the democracy. It is these poor people, this common folk, this worse element, whose prosperity, combined with the growth of their numbers, en-

Pseudo-Xenophon, *Constitution of the Athenians* (1942), Sections 1, 3, translated by H. G. Dakyns.

hances the democracy. Whereas, a shifting of fortune to the advantage of the wealthy and the better classes implies the establishment on the part of the commons of a strong power in opposition to itself. In fact, all the world over, the cream of society is in opposition to the democracy. Naturally, since the smallest amount of intemperance and injustice, together with the highest scrupulousness in the pursuit of excellence, is to be found in the ranks of the better class, while within the ranks of the People will be found the greatest amount of ignorance, disorderliness, rascality,—poverty acting as a stronger incentive to base conduct, not to speak of lack of education and ignorance, traceable to the lack of means which afflicts the average of mankind.

The objection may be raised that it was a mistake to allow the universal right of speech and a seat in council. These should have been reserved for the cleverest, the flower of the community. But here, again, it will be found that they are acting with wise deliberation in granting to even the baser sort the right of speech, for supposing only the better people might speak, or sit in council, blessings would fall to the lot of those like themselves, but to the commons the reverse of blessings. Whereas now, any one who likes, any base fellow, may get up and discover something to the advantage of himself and his equals. It may be retorted, "And what sort of advantage either for himself or for the People can such a fellow be expected to hit upon?" The answer to which is, that in their judgment the ignorance and the baseness of this fellow, together with his goodwill, are worth a great deal more to them than your superior person's virtue and wisdom, coupled with animosity. What it comes to, therefore, is that a state founded upon such institutions will not be the best state; but, given a democracy, these are the right means to secure its preservation. The People, it must be borne in mind, does not demand that the city should be well governed and itself a slave. It desires to be free and to be master. As to bad legislation it does not concern itself about that. In fact, what you belive to be bad legislation is the very source of the People's strength and freedom. But if you seek for good legislation, in the first place you will see the cleverest members of the community laying down the laws for the rest. And in the next place, the better class will curb and chastise the lower orders; the better class will deliberate in behalf of the state, and not suffer crack-brained fellows to sit in council, or to speak or vote in the assemblies. No doubt; but under the weight of such blessings the People will in a very short time be reduced to slavery.

Another point is the extraordinary amount of license granted to slaves and resident aliens at Athens, where a blow is illegal, and a slave will not step aside to let you pass him in the street. I will explain the reason of this peculiar custom. Supposing it were legal for a slave to be beaten by a free citizen, or for a resident alien or freedman to be beaten by a citizen, it would frequently happen that an Athenian might be mistaken for a slave or an alien and receive a beating; since the Athenian People is not better clothed than the slave or alien, nor in personal appearance is there any superiority. Or if the fact itself that slaves in Athens are allowed to indulge in luxury, and indeed in some cases to live magnificently, be found astonishing, this too, it can be shown, is done of set purpose. Where you have a naval power dependent upon wealth we must perforce be slaves to our slaves, in order that we may get in our slave-rents, and let the real slave go free. Where you have wealthy slaves it ceases to be advantageous that my slave should stand in awe of you. In Lacedaemon my slave stands in awe of you. But if your slave is in awe of me there will be a risk of his giving away his own moneys to avoid running a risk in his own person. It is for this reason then that we have established an equality between our slaves and free men; and again between our resident aliens and full citizens, because the city stands in need of her resident aliens to meet the requirements of such a multiplicity of arts and for the purposes of her navy. That is, I repeat, the justification of the equality conferred upon our resident aliens.

The common people put a stop to citizens devoting their time to athletics and to the cultivation of music, disbelieving in the beauty of such training, and recognising the fact that these are things the cultivation of which is beyond its power. On the same principle, in the case of the choregia, the management of athletics, and the command of ships, the fact is recognised that it is the rich man who trains the chorus, and the People for whom the chorus is trained; it is the rich man who is naval commander or superintendent of athletics, and the People that profits by their labours. In fact, what the People looks upon as its right is to pocket the money. To sing and run and dance and man the vessels is well enough, but only in order that the People may be the gainer, while the rich are made poorer. And so in the courts of justice, justice is not more an object of concern to the jurymen than what touches personal advantage.

To speak next of the allies, and in reference to the point that emissaries from Athens come out, and, according to common opinion, calumniate and vent their hatred upon the better sort of people, this is done on the principle that the ruler cannot help being hated by those whom he rules; but that if wealth and respectability are to wield power in the subject cities the empire of the Athenian People has but a short lease of existence. This explains why the better people are punished with infamy, robbed of their money, driven from their homes, and put to death, while the baser sort are promoted to honour. On the other hand, the better Athenians protect the better class in the allied cities. And why? Because they recognise that it is to the interest of their own class at all times to protect the best element in the cities. It may be urged that if it comes to strength and power the real strength of Athens lies in the capacity of her allies to contribute their money quota. But to the democratic mind it appears a higher advantage still for the individual Athenian to get hold of the wealth of the allies, leaving them only enough to live upon and to cultivate their estates, but powerless to harbour treacherous designs.

Again, it is looked upon as a mistaken policy on the part of the Athenian democracy to compel her allies to voyage to Athens in order to have their cases tried. On the other hand, it is easy to reckon up what a number of advantages the Athenian People derives from the practice impugned. In the first place, there is the steady receipt of salaries throughout the year derived from the court fees. Next, it enables them to manage the affairs of the allied states while seated at home without the expense of naval expeditions. Thirdly, they thus preserve the partisans of the democracy, and ruin her opponents in the law courts. Whereas, supposing the several allied states tried their cases at home, being inspired by hostility to Athens, they would destroy those of their own citizens whose friendship to the Athenian People was most marked. But besides all this the democracy derives the following advantages from hearing the cases of her allies in Athens. In the first place, the one per cent levied in Piraeus is increased to the profit of the state; again, the owner of a lodging-house does better, and so, too, the owner of a pair of beasts, or of slaves to be let out on hire; again, heralds and criers are a class of people who fare better owing to the sojourn of foreigners at Athens. Further still, supposing the allies had not to resort to Athens for the hearing of cases, only the official representative of the imperial state would be held in honour, such as the general, or trierarch, or ambassador. Whereas now every single individual among the allies is forced to pay flattery to the People of Athens because he knows that he must betake himself to Athens and win or lose his case at the bar, not of any stray set of judges, but of the sovereign People itself, such being the law and custom at Athens. He is compelled to behave as a suppliant in the courts of justice, and when some juryman comes into court, to grasp his hand. For this reason, therefore, the allies find themselves more and more in the position of slaves to the People of Athens.

Furthermore, owing to the possession of property beyond the limits of Attica, and the exercise of magistracies which take them into regions beyond the frontier, they and their attendants have insensibly acquired the art of navigation. A man who is perpetually voyaging is forced to handle the oar, he and his domestic alike, and to learn the terms familiar in seamanship. Hence a stock of skilful mariners is produced, bred upon a wide experience of voyaging and practice. They have learned their business, some in piloting a small craft, others a merchant vessel, while others have been drafted off from these for service on a ship-of-war. So that the majority of them are able to row the moment they set foot on board a vessel, having been in a state of preliminary practice all their lives.

* * *

I repeat that my position concerning the constitution of the Athenians is this: the type of constitution is not to my taste, but given that a democratic form of government has been agreed upon, they do seem to me to go the right way to preserve the democracy by the adoption of the particular type which I have set forth.

In the Gorgias dialogue Plato makes his view of Pericles' contribution to the Athenian constitution perfectly clear. Plato was little more than a generation removed from the time of Pericles and undoubtedly had good secondhand evidence of its character. It is possible, however, that his opinion was influenced by his own experience of the Athenian democracy of the fourth century, which he cordially disliked.

FROM Gorgias BY PLATO

soc. And now, my friend, as you are already beginning to be a public character, and are admonishing and reproaching me for not being one, suppose that we ask a few questions of one another. Tell me, then, Callicles, how about making any of the citizens better? Was there ever a man who was once vicious, or unjust, or intemperate, or foolish, and became by the help of Callicles good and noble? Was there ever such a man, whether citizen or stranger, slave or freeman? Tell me, Callicles, if a person were to ask these questions of you, what would you answer? Whom would you say that you had improved by your conversation? There may have been good deeds of this sort which were done by you as a private person, before you came forward in public. Why will you not answer?

cal. You are contentious, Socrates.

soc. Nay, I ask you, not from a love of contention, but because I really want to know in what way you think that affairs should be administered among us—whether, when you come to the administration of them, you have any other aim but the improvement of the citizens? Have we not already admitted many times over that such is the duty of a public man? Nay, we have surely said so; for if you will not answer for yourself I must answer for you. But if this is what the good man ought to effect for the benefit of his own state, allow me to recall to you the names of those whom you were just now mentioning, Pericles, and Cimon, and Miltiades, and Themistocles, and ask whether you still think that they were good citizens.

cal. I do.

soc. But if they were good, then clearly each of them must have made the citizens better instead of worse?

cal. Yes.

soc. And, therefore, when Pericles first began to speak in the assembly, the Athenians were not so good as when he spoke last?

Plato, *Gorgias* (1892), pp. 515–517 (Stephanus pagination), translated by Benjamin Jowett.

CAL. Very likely.

SOC. Nay, my friend, "likely" is not the word; for if he was a good citizen, the inference is certain.

CAL. And what difference does that make?

SOC. None; only I should like further to know whether the Athenians are supposed to have been made better by Pericles, or, on the contrary, to have been corrupted by him; for I hear that he was the first who gave the people pay, and made them idle and cowardly, and encouraged them in the love of talk and of money.

CAL. You heard that, Socrates, from the laconising set who bruise their ears.

SOC. But what I am going to tell you now is not mere hearsay, but well known both to you and me: that at first, Pericles was glorious and his character unimpeached by any verdict of the Athenians—this was during the time when they were not so good—yet afterwards, when they had been made good and gentle by him, at the very end of his life they convicted him of theft, and almost put him to death, clearly under the notion that he was a malefactor.

CAL. Well, but how does that prove Pericles' badness?

SOC. Why, surely you would say that he was a bad manager of asses or horses or oxen, who had received them originally neither kicking nor butting nor biting him, and implanted in them all these savage tricks? Would he not be a bad manager of any animals who received them gentle, and made them fiercer than they were when he received them? What do you say?

CAL. I will do you the favour of saying "yes."

SOC. And will you also do me the favour of saying whether man is an animal?

CAL. Certainly he is.

SOC. And was not Pericles a shepherd of men?

CAL. Yes.

SOC. And if he was a good political shepherd, ought not the animals who were his subjects, as we were just now acknowledging, to have become more just, and not more unjust?

CAL. Quite true.

SOC. And are not just men gentle, as Homer says?—or are you of another mind?

CAL. I agree.

SOC. And yet he really did make them more savage than he received them, and their savageness was shown towards himself; which he must have been very far from desiring.

CAL. Do you want me to agree with you?

SOC. Yes, if I seem to you to speak the truth.

CAL. Granted then.

SOC. And if they were more savage, must they not have been more unjust and inferior?

CAL. Granted again.

SOC. Then upon this view, Pericles was not a good statesman?

CAL. That is, upon your view.

SOC. Nay, the view is yours, after what you have admitted. Take the case of Cimon again. Did not the very persons whom he was serving ostracize him, in order that they might not hear his voice for ten years? and they did just the same to Themistocles, adding the penalty of exile; and they voted that Miltiades, the hero of Marathon, should be thrown into the pit of death, and he was only saved by the Prytanis. And yet, if they had been really good men, as you say, these things would never have happened to them. For the good charioteers are not those who at first keep their place, and then, when they have broken-in their horses, and themselves become better charioteers, are thrown out—that is not the way either in charioteering or in any profession. —What do you think?

CAL. I should think not.

SOC. Well, but if so, the truth is as I have said already, that in the Athenian State no one has ever shown himself to be a good statesman—you admitted that this was true of our present statesmen, but not true of former ones, and you preferred them to the others; yet they have turned out to be no better than our present ones; and therefore, if they were rhetoricians, they did not use the true art of rhetoric or of flattery, or they would not have fallen out of favour.

CAL. But surely, Socrates, no living man ever came near any one of them in his performances.

SOC. O, my dear friend, I say nothing against them regarded as the serving-men of the State; and I do think that they were certainly more serviceable than those who are living now, and better able to gratify the wishes of the State; but as to transforming those desires and not allowing them to have their way, and using the powers which they had, whether of persuasion or of force, in the improvement of their fellow-citizens, which is the prime object of the truly good citizen, I do not see that in these respects they were a whit superior to our present statesmen, although I do admit that they were more clever at providing ships and walls and docks, and all that.

Plutarch of Chaeronea was a Greek who lived in the second century of our era. Certainly the best known of his many works is the collection of biographies of illustrious Greeks and Romans. He was not a historian but a biographer, and he lacked the intellectual power of Thucydides, yet his *Lives* are peculiarly valuable. He used all the sources available to him almost indiscriminately. Many of these ancient sources are known to us only through his citation of them, so that his work often throws important light on the events he describes. His *Pericles* thus uses Thucydides but compares his views with those of other historians who may have employed reliable information not used by Thucydides. The first selection describes Pericles' rise to power and his early career.

FROM Pericles BY PLUTARCH

Since Thucydides describes the rule of Pericles as an aristocratical government, that went by the name of a democracy, but was, indeed, the supremacy of a single great man, while many others say, on the contrary, that by him the common people were first encouraged and led on to such evils as appropriations of subject territory, allowances for attending theatres, payments for performing public duties, and by these bad habits were, under the influence of his public measures, changed from a sober, thrifty people, that maintained themselves by their own labours, to lovers of expense, intemperance, and licence, let us examine the cause of this change by the actual matters of fact.

At the first, as has been said, when he set himself against Cimon's great authority, he did caress the people. Finding himself come short of his competitor in wealth and money, by which advantages the other was enabled to take care of the poor, inviting every day some one or other of the citizens that was in want to supper, and bestowing clothes on the aged people, and breaking down the hedges and enclosures of his grounds, that all that would might freely gather what fruit they pleased, Pericles, thus outdone in popular arts, by the advice of one Damonides of Oea, as Aristotle states, turned to the distribution of the public moneys; and in a short time having bought the people over, what with moneys allowed for shows and for service on juries, and what with other forms of pay and largess, he made use of them against the council of Areopagus of which he himself was no member, as having never been appointed by lot either chief archon, or lawgiver, or king, or captain. For from of old these offices were conferred on persons by lot, and they who had acquitted themselves duly in the discharge of them were advanced to the court of Areopagus. And so Pericles, having secured his power in interest with the populace, directed the exertions of his party against this council with such success, that most of these causes and matters which had been used to be tried there were, by the agency of Ephialtes, removed from its cognisance; Cimon, also, was banished by ostracism as a favourer of the Lacedaemonians and a hater of the people, though in wealth and noble birth he was among the first, and had won several most glorious victories over the barbarians, and had filled the city with money and spoils of war; as is recorded in the history of his life. So vast an authority had Pericles obtained among the people.

Plutarch, *Pericles* (abridged) (1683–1693), translated by John Dryden.

Cimon, while he was admiral, ended his days in the Isle of Cyprus. And the aristocratical party, seeing that Pericles was already before this grown to be the greatest and foremost man of all the city, but nevertheless wishing there should be somebody set up against him, to blunt and turn the edge of his power, that it might not altogether prove a monarchy, put forward Thucydides of Alopece [*the son of Melesias, not the historian—D. K.*], a discreet person, and a near kinsman of Cimon's, to conduct the opposition against him; who, indeed, though less skilled in warlike affairs than Cimon was, yet was better versed in speaking and political business and keeping close guard in the city, and, engaging with Pericles on the hustings, in a short time brought the government to an equality of parties. For he would not suffer those who were called the honest and good (persons of worth and distinction) to be scattered up and down and mix themselves and be lost among the populace, as formerly, diminishing and obscuring their superiority amongst the masses; but taking them apart by themselves and uniting them in one body, by their combined weight he was able, as it were upon the balance, to make a counterpoise to the other party.

For, indeed, there was from the beginning a sort of concealed split, or seam, as it might be in a piece of iron, marking the different popular and aristocratical tendencies; but the open rivalry and contention of these two opponents made the gash deep, and severed the city into the two parties of the people and the few. And so Pericles, at that time, more than at any other, let loose the reins to the people, and made his policy subservient to their pleasure, contriving continually to have some great public show or solemnity, some banquet, or some procession or other in the town to please them, coaxing his countrymen like children with such delights and pleasures as were not, however, unedifying. Besides that every year he sent out threescore galleys, on board of which there were numbers of the citizens, who were in pay eight months, learning at the same time and practising the art of seamanship.

He sent, moreover, a thousand of them into the Chersonese as planters, to share the land among them by lot, and five hundred more into the Isle of Naxos, and half that number to Andros, a thousand into Thrace to dwell among the Bisaltae, and others into Italy, when the city Sybaris, which now was called Thurii, was to be repeopled. And this he did to ease and discharge the city of an idle, and, by reason of their idleness, a busy meddling crowd of people; and at the same time to meet the necessities and restore the fortunes of the poor townsmen, and to intimidate, also, and check their allies from attempting any change, by posting such garrisons, as it were, in the midst of them.

That which gave most pleasure and ornament to the city of Athens, and the greatest admiration and even astonishment to all strangers, and that which now is Greece's only evidence that the power she boasts of and her ancient wealth are no romance or idle story, was his construction of the public and sacred buildings. Yet this was that of all his actions in the government which his enemies most looked askance upon and cavilled at in the

popular assemblies, crying out how that the commonwealth of Athens had
lost its reputation and was ill-spoken of abroad for removing the common
treasure of the Greeks from the Isle of Delos into their own custody; and
how that their fairest excuse for so doing, namely, that they took it away for
fear the barbarians should seize it, and on purpose to secure it in a safe place,
this Pericles had made unavailable and how that "Greece cannot but resent
it as an insufferable affront, and consider herself to be tyrannised over openly,
when she sees the treasure, which was contributed by her upon a necessity for
the war, wantonly lavished out by us upon our city, to gild her all over, and
to adorn and set her forth, as it were some vain woman, hung round with
precious stones and figures and temples, which cost a world of money."

Pericles, on the other hand, informed the people, that they were in no way
obliged to give any account of those moneys to their allies, so long as they
maintained their defence, and kept off the barbarians from attacking them;
while in the meantime they did not so much as supply one horse or man or
ship, but only found money for the service; "which money," said he, "is not
theirs that give it, but theirs that receive it, if so be they perform the conditions upon which they receive it." And that it was good reason, that, now the
city was sufficiently provided and stored with all things necessary for the war,
they should convert the overplus of its wealth to such undertakings as would
hereafter, when completed, give them eternal honour, and, for the present,
while in process, freely supply all the inhabitants with plenty. With their
variety of workmanship and of occasions for service, which summon all arts
and trades and require all hands to be employed about them, they do actually
put the whole city, in a manner, into state-pay; while at the same time she is
both beautiful and maintained by herself. For as those who are of age and
strength for war are provided for and maintained in the armaments abroad
by their pay out of the public stock, so, it being his desire and design that the
undisciplined mechanic multitude that stayed at home should not go without
their share of public salaries, and yet should not have them given them for
sitting still and doing nothing, to that end he thought fit to bring in among
them, with the approbation of the people, these vast projects of buildings and
designs of work, that would be of some continuance before they were finished, and would give employment to numerous arts, so that the part of the
people that stayed at home might, no less than those that were at sea or in
garrisons or on expeditions, have a fair and just occasion of receiving the
benefit and having their share of the public moneys.

When the orators, who sided with Thucydides and his party, were at one
time crying out, as their custom was, against Pericles, as one who squandered
away the public money, and made havoc of the state revenues, he rose in the
open assembly and put the question to the people, whether they thought that
he had laid out much; and they saying, "Too much, a great deal." "Then,"
said he, "since it is so, let the cost not go to your account, but to mine; and let
the inscription upon the buildings stand in my name." When they heard him
say thus, whether it were out of a surprise to see the greatness of his spirit or

out of emulation of the glory of the works, they cried aloud, bidding him to spend on, and lay out what he thought fit from the public purse, and to spare no cost, till all were finished.

At length, coming to a final contest with Thucydides which of the two should ostracise the other out of the country, and having gone through this peril, he threw his antagonist out, and broke up the confederacy that had been organised against him. So that now all schism and division being at an end, and the city brought to evenness and unity, he got all Athens and all affairs that pertained to the Athenians into his own hands, their tributes, their armies, and their galleys, the islands, the sea, and their wide-extended power, partly over other Greeks and partly over barbarians, and all that empire, which they possessed, founded and fortified upon subject nations and royal friendships and alliances.

After this he was no longer the same man he had been before, nor as tame and gentle and familiar as formerly with the populace, so as readily to yield to their pleasures and to comply with the desires of the multitude, as a steersman shifts with the winds. Quitting that loose, remiss, and, in some cases, licentious court of the popular will, he turned those soft and flowery modulations to the austerity of aristocratical and regal rule; and employing this uprightly and undeviatingly for the country's best interests, he was able generally to lead the people along, with their own wills and consents, by persuading and showing them what was to be done; and sometimes, too, urging and pressing them forward extremely against their will, he made them, whether they would or no, yield submission to what was for their advantage. In which, to say the truth, he did but like a skilful physician, who, in a complicated and chronic disease, as he sees occasion, at one while allows his patient the moderate use of such things as please him, at another while gives him keen pains and drug to work the cure. For there arising and growing up, as was natural, all manner of distempered feelings among a people which had so vast a command and dominion, he alone, as a great master, knowing how to handle and deal fitly with each one of them, and, in an especial manner, making that use of hopes and fears, as his two chief rudders, with the one to check the career of their confidence at any time, with the other to raise them up and cheer them when under any discouragement, plainly showed by this, that rhetoric, or the art of speaking, is, in Plato's language, the government of the souls of men, and that her chief business is to address the affections and passions, which are as it were the strings and keys to the soul, and require a skilful and careful touch to be played on as they should be. The source of this predominance was not barely his power of language, but, as Thucydides assures us, the reputation of his life, and the confidence felt in his character; his manifest freedom from every kind of corruption, and superiority to all considerations of money. Notwithstanding he had made the city of Athens, which was great of itself, as great and rich as can be imagined, and though he were himself in power and interest more than equal to many kings and absolute rulers, who some of them also bequeathed by will their power to their children, he, for his part, did not make the patrimony his father left him greater than it was by one drachma.

Thucydides, indeed, gives a plain statement of the greatness of his power; and the comic poets, in their spiteful manner, more than hint at it, styling his companions and friends the new Peisistratidae, and calling on him to abjure any intention of usurpation, as one whose eminence was too great to be any longer proportionable to and compatible with a democracy or popular government. And Teleclides says the Athenians had surrendered up to him—

The tribute of the cities, and with them, the cities too, to do with them as he pleases, and undo;
To build up, if he likes, stone walls around a town; and again, if so he likes, to pull them down;
Their treaties and alliances, power, empire, peace, and war, their wealth and their success forever more.

Nor was all this the luck of some happy occasion; nor was it the mere bloom and grace of a policy that flourished for a season; but having for forty years together maintained the first place among statesmen such as Ephialtes and Leocrates and Myronides and Cimon and Tolmides and Thucydides were, after the defeat and banishment of Thucydides, for no less than fifteen years longer, in the exercise of one continuous unintermitted command in the office, to which he was annually re-elected, of General, he preserved his integrity unspotted.

[*During the years just prior to the Peloponnesian War, Pericles' political control was threatened by attacks on his friends and collaborators, among them the sculptor Phidias—D. K.*]

Phidias then was carried away to prison, and there died of a disease; but, as some say, of poison, administered by the enemies of Pericles, to raise a slander, or a suspicion at least, as though he had procured it. The informer Menon, upon Glycon's proposal, the people made free from payment of taxes and customs, and ordered the generals to take care that nobody should do him any hurt. About the same time, Aspasia was indicted of impiety, upon the complaint of Hermippus the comedian, who also laid further to her charge that she received into her house freeborn women for the uses of Pericles. And Diopithes proposed a decree, that public accusations should be laid against persons who neglected religion, or taught new doctrines about things above, directing suspicion, by means of Anaxagoras, against Pericles himself. The people receiving and admitting these accusations and complaints, at length, by this means, they came to enact a decree, at the motion of Dracontides, that Pericles should bring in the accounts of the moneys he had expended, and lodge them with the Prytanes; and that the judges, carrying their suffrage from the altar in the Acropolis, should examine and determine the business in the city. This last clause Hagnon took out of the decree, and moved that the causes should be tried before fifteen hundred jurors, whether they should be styled prosecutions for robbery, or bribery, or any kind of malversation. Aspasia, Pericles begged off, shedding, as Aeschines says, many tears at the trial, and personally entreating the jurors. But fearing how it might go with Anaxagoras, he sent him out of the city. And finding that in Phidias's case he had miscarried with the people, being afraid of impeachment, he kindled the war, which hitherto had lingered and smothered, and blew it up into a flame; hoping, by that means, to disperse and scatter these complaints and charges, and to allay their jealousy; the city usually throwing herself upon him alone, and trusting to his sole conduct, upon the urgency of great affairs and public dangers, by reason of his authority and the sway he bore.

These are given out to have been the reasons which induced Pericles not to suffer the people of Athens to yield to the proposals of the Lacedaemonians; but their truth is uncertain.

The Lacedaemonians, for their part, feeling sure that if they could once remove him, they might be at what terms they pleased with the Athenians, sent them word that they should expel the "Pollution" with which Pericles on the mother's side was tainted, as Thucydides tells us. But the issue proved quite contrary to what those who sent the message expected; instead of bringing Pericles under suspicion and reproach, they raised him into yet greater credit and esteem with the citizens, as a man whom their enemies most hated and feared. In the same way, also, before Archidamus, who was at the head of the Peloponnesians, made his invasion into Attica, he told the Athenians beforehand, that if Archidamus, while he laid waste the rest of the country, should forbear and spare his estate, either on the ground of friendship or right of hospitality that was betwixt them, or on purpose to give his enemies an occasion of traducing him; that then he did freely bestow upon the state all his land and the buildings upon it for the public use. The Lacedaemonians, therefore, and their allies, with a great army, invaded the Athenian territories, under the conduct of King Archidamus, and laying waste the country, marched on as far as Acharnae, and there pitched their camp, presuming that the Athenians would never endure that, but would come out and fight them for their country's and their honour's sake. But Pericles looked upon it as dangerous to engage in battle, to the risk of the city itself, against sixty thousand men-at-arms of Peloponnesians and Boeotians; for so many they were in number that made the inroad at first; and he endeavoured to appease those who were desirous to fight, and were grieved and discontented to see how things went, and gave them good words, saying, that "trees, when they are lopped and cut, grow up again in a short time, but men, being once lost, cannot easily be recovered." He did not convene the people into an assembly, for fear lest they should force him to act against his judgment; but, like a skilful steersman or pilot of a ship, who, when a sudden squall comes on, out at sea, makes all his arrangements, sees that all is tight and fast, and then

follows the dictates of his skill, and minds the business of the ship, taking no
notice of the tears and entreaties of the sea-sick and fearful passengers, so he,
having shut up the city gates, and placed guards at all posts for security,
followed his own reason and judgment, little regarding those that cried out
against him and were angry at his management, although there were a great
many of his friends that urged him with requests, and many of his enemies
threatened and accused him for doing as he did, and many made songs and
lampoons upon him, which were sung about the town to his disgrace, reproaching him with the cowardly exercise of his office of General, and the
tame abandonment of everything to the enemy's hands.

Cleon, also, already was among his assailants, making use of the feeling
against him as a step to the leadership of the people, as appears in the ana-
paestic verses of Hermippus—

> Satyr-king, instead of swords,
> Will you always handle words?
> Very brave indeed we find them,
> But a Teles lurks behind them.
>
> Yet to gnash your teeth you're seen,
> When the little dagger keen,
> Whetted every day anew,
> Of sharp Cleon touches you.

Pericles, however, was not at all moved by any attacks, but took all patiently, and submitted in silence to the disgrace they threw upon him and the
ill-will they bore him; and, sending out a fleet of a hundred galleys to Pelop-
onnesus, he did not go along with it in person, but stayed behind, that he
might watch at home and keep the city under his own control, till the Peloponnesians broke up their camp and were gone. Yet to soothe the common
people, jaded and distressed with the war, he relieved them with distributions
of public moneys, and ordained new divisions of subject land. For having
turned out all the people of Aegina he parted the island among the Athenians according to lot. Some comfort, also, and ease in their miseries, they
might receive from what their enemies endured. For the fleet, sailing round
the Peloponnese, ravaged a great deal of the country, and pillaged and plundered the towns and smaller cities; and by land he himself entered with an
army the Megarian country, and made havoc of it all. Whence it is clear that
the Peloponnesians, though they did the Athenians much mischief by land,
yet suffering as much themselves from them by sea, would not have protracted the war to such a length, but would quickly have given it over, as
Pericles at first foretold they would, had not some divine power crossed human purposes.

In the first place, the pestilential disease, or plague, seized upon the city,
and ate up all the flower and prime of their youth and strength. Upon occasion of which, the people, distempered and afflicted in their souls, as well as in

their bodies, were utterly enraged like madmen against Pericles, and, like patients grown delirious, sought to lay violent hands on their physician, or, as it were, their father. They had been possessed, by his enemies, with the belief that the occasion of the plague was the crowding of the country people together into the town, forced as they were now, in the heat of the summer-weather, to dwell many of them together even as they could, in small tenements and stifling hovels, and to be tied to a lazy course of life within doors, whereas before they lived in a pure, open, and free air. The cause and author of all this, said they, is he who on account of the war has poured a multitude of people in upon us within the walls, and uses all these men that he has here upon no employ or service, but keeps them pent up like cattle, to be overrun with infection from one another, affording them neither shift of quarters nor any refreshment.

With the design to remedy these evils, and do the enemy some inconvenience, Pericles got a hundred and fifty galleys ready, and having embarked many tried soldiers, both foot and horse, was about to sail out, giving great hope to his citizens, and no less alarm to his enemies, upon the sight of so great a force. And now the vessels having their complement of men, and Pericles being gone aboard his own galley, it happened that the sun was eclipsed, and it grew dark on a sudden, to the affright of all, for this was looked upon as extremely ominous. Pericles, therefore, perceiving the steersman seized with fear and at a loss what to do, took his cloak and held it up before the man's face, and screening him with it so that he could not see, asked him whether he imagined there was any great hurt, or the sign of any great hurt in this, and he answering No, "Why," said he, "and what does that differ from this, only that what has caused that darkness there, is something greater than a cloak?" This is a story which philosophers tell their scholars. Pericles, however, after putting out to sea, seems not to have done any other exploit befitting such preparations, and when he had laid siege to the holy city Epidaurus, which gave him some hope of surrender, miscarried in his design by reason of the sickness. For it not only seized upon the Athenians, but upon all others, too, that held any sort of communication with the army. Finding after this the Athenians ill-affected and highly displeased with him, he tried and endeavoured what he could to appease and re-encourage them. But he could not pacify or allay their anger, nor persuade or prevail with them any way, till they freely passed their votes upon him, resumed their power, took away his command from him, and fined him in a sum of money; which by their account that say least, was fifteen talents, while they who reckon most, name fifty. The name prefixed to the accusation was Cleon, as Idomeneus tells us; Simmias, according to Theophrastus; and Heraclides Ponticus gives it as Lacratidas.

* * *

The city having made trial of other generals for the conduct of war, and orators for business of state, when they found there was no one who was of weight enough for such a charge, or of authority sufficient to be trusted with so great a command, regretted the loss of him, and invited him again to address and advise them, and to reassume the office of general. He, however, lay at home in dejection and mourning; but was persuaded by Alcibiades and others of his friends to come abroad and show himself to the people; who having, upon his appearance, made their acknowledgments, and apologised for their untowardly treatment of him, he undertook the public affairs once more.

4
MODERN
OPINIONS

In the following essay Larue Van Hook supports the view that Periclean Athens was a true democracy.

Was Athens in the Age of Pericles Aristocratic?
BY LARUE VAN HOOK

The majority of the numerous books which deal with Athenian political and social life in the latter part of the fifth century B.C. convey to student and to reader the general, but emphatic, impression that the *polis* Athens, while theoretically a democracy, was, generally speaking, an aristocracy. It is hardly an exaggeration to say that the composite picture of Athens under Pericles, as represented in the traditional view of the handbooks, reveals a society brilliant in its achievements, but quite selfishly constituted, and gravely defective, save from the viewpoint of the favored few. Profound social distinctions, even among the citizens themselves, are insisted upon. The conception still is widely prevalent that the *élite* of Athenian society, few but fit, led a life of glorious but intensely selfish leisure, which was their lordly prerogative as the result of the ruthless exploitation of all professional men, artists, producers, traders, artisans, workers, resident aliens, and slaves. Almost everywhere we find the time-honored assertion that in Athens all work was despised, labor was condemned, the workers were disdained, and, in fact, that *any* service for which financial remuneration was received was in disrepute and branded the doer with a humiliating social stigma. The free man is supposed to have done little or no work, for surely the aristocratic citizen must have a completely independent and carefree existence for his manifold political, social, and religious duties.

LaRue Van Hook, "Was Athens in the Age of Pericles Aristocratic?" *The Classical Journal*, XIV (1918–1919), 472–479.

Let me now present some typical quotations from some recent books on Athens which give this false, or exaggerated, as I think, impression of the nature of Athenian society in the second half of the fifth century b.c., in that they assert that it was essentially aristocratic. In the ninth edition (1915) of that very popular, widely influential, and, in many respects, admirable little book, *The Greek View of Life* by Mr. Lowes Dickinson, we read (italics are mine in every case): "In the Greek conception the citizen was an aristocrat. His excellence was thought to consist in public activity; and to the performance of public duties he ought therefore to be able to devote *the greater part of his time and energy*. But the existence of such a privileged class involved the existence of a class of producers to support them; and *the producers, by the nature of their calling,* be they slave *or free, were excluded from the life of the perfect citizen*. They had not the necessary leisure to devote to public business; neither had they the opportunity to acquire the mental and physical qualities which would enable them to transact it worthily. They were therefore regarded by the Greeks as an inferior class. . . . In Athens, the most democratic of all the Greek communities, though they were admitted to the citizenship and enjoyed considerable political influence, *they never appear to have lost the stigma of social inferiority*. And the distinction which was more or less definitely drawn in practice *between the citizens proper* and *the productive class* was even more emphatically affirmed in theory" (pp. 74-75). "The obverse of the Greek *citizen,* who realized in the state the highest life, was *an inferior class of producers who realized only the means to subsistence*" (p. 75). "The *inferiority* of the artisan and the trader was further emphasized by the fact that *they were excluded by their calling* from the cultivation of the higher personal qualities; from the training of the body by gymnastics and of the mind by philosophy; *from habitual conversance with public affairs;* from that perfect balance, in a word, of the physical, intellectual, and moral powers, which was only to be attained by a process of *self-culture, incompatible with the pursuance of a trade for bread*" (p. 82). "The existence of the Greek citizen depended upon that of an inferior class who were regarded, not as ends in themselves, but as means to his perfection." "The aim of modern societies is not to separate off a privileged class of citizens, set free by the labour of others to live the perfect life, but rather to distribute impartially to all the burdens and advantages of the state, so that every one shall be at once a labourer for himself and a citizen of the state. But this idea is clearly incompatible with the Greek conception of the citizen" (p. 130). "It is because labour with the hands or at the desk distorts or impairs the body, and the petty cares of a calling pursued for bread pervert the soul, that so *strong a contempt was felt by the Greeks for manual labour and trade.*" "If then the artisan . . . in Athens never altogether threw off *the stigma of inferiority attaching to his trade,* the reason was that the life he was compelled to lead was incompatible with the Greek conception of excellence" (p. 134). "The Greeks, on the whole, were quite content to sacrifice the majority to the minority. Their position was fundamentally aristocratic; they exaggerated rather than minimized the distinctions between men, the free-man and the slave, the gentleman and the artisan, regarding them as natural and fundamental, not as the casual product of circumstances. The 'equality' which they sought was proportional, not arithmetical, not of equal rights to all." "In a modern state it is different though class distinctions are clearly enough marked, yet the point of view from which they are regarded is funda-mentally different. They are attributed rather to accidents of fortune than to varieties of nature. The artisan, for example, ranks no doubt lower than the professional man; but no one maintains that he is a different kind of being incapable by nature, as Aristotle asserts, of the characteristic excellence of man" (p. 79).

In *Greek Ideals,* by Mr. C. Delisle Burns, a study of Athenian social life of the period under consideration, the Greek aristocratic conception of individ-ual liberty is likewise, I believe, overemphasized. Thus we find the state-ments: "It seemed essential that liberty and equality should only be the right of *a few* males. . . . Slaves and *workingmen had no time and no developed capacity for the 'good life'* " (p. 76). "Society was conceived only in terms . . . . of *a small social caste*" (p. 109). "The Athenian citizen might object to doing manual labour" (p. 112).

Similar assertions are common. Thus Mr. Edwards in Whibley's *Compan-ion to Greek Studies:* "The prejudice against trades and handicrafts was most pronounced in Sparta: elsewhere, though the political disabilities might be reduced or removed, the *social stigma was scarcely diminished*—indeed, even the fullest development of democracy at Athens did but stereotype the conventional horror of hard work, and proclaimed leisure, and not labour, to be the citizen's privilege. . . . The marvel is that, *amid all this depreciation,* mechanical skill and artistic taste should have attained so high a standard" (p. 437).

Gardner and Jevons, *Manual of Greek Antiquities* (p. 379), quote Aristotle and Plato to show the extreme *popular* prejudice against handiwork and the disesteem in which it was *universally* held—"only those too poor to buy slaves had to work themselves."

Gulick, in his excellent *Life of the Ancient Athenians,* says: "The class of artisans comprised callings which among us are regarded as the most digni-fied professions. Wherever one of these vocations *was in disrepute,* the cause is found in the fact that the person concerned *took money for his services,* and was to that extent not independent of others. Even the great artists, painters, and sculptors fell under *public contempt* simply because they earned money. A few artists, like Phidias, are said to have enjoyed the friendship of eminent men of aristocratic birth; but most of these stories of intimacy are later exaggerations which have not taken into account the conditions of an-cient industrial life. Schoolmasters, teachers of music and gymnastics, soph-ists and even physicians were not highly regarded" (p. 233). "To the *emporos* attached some of *the stigma of personal labor*." "Ancient communities (e.g., Athens) whose *citizens despised trade and manual labor*" (p. 65). "Art, letters, and politics, claimed the interest of the ordinary citizen far more than they do today, because it was the policy of Pericles *to render the democracy of Athens a leisure class, supported by their slaves and the revenues of the Empire"* (p. 118).

But enough of such representative quotations, they might be multiplied indefinitely. It is the aim of this paper to endeavor to correct, or, at least, to assist in the modification of this all too general conception of an essentially aristocratic Athenian society, a conception which is certainly false in some of its aspects and exaggerated or overemphasized in others.

Before a consideration of the subject proper it may well be asked, why is it that this view of Athenian society as aristocratic, if erroneous, is generally held? The reasons are, I believe, as follows: (1) Athens, like other Greek states, at an early period in its history, in fact, until after Solon and Cleisthenes, was, in large measure, oligarchic and aristocratic both politically and socially. Modern writers mistakenly assume that these early conditions, particularly in social life, continued. (2) Certain Greek states, e.g., Sparta, Thebes, and Crete, never suffered democratization. The strictly aristocratic conditions which were permanently characteristic of these states are sometimes thought of as necessarily existing also in Athens. (3) Modern writers have the tendency implicitly to follow Plato and Aristotle as authorities and imagine that actual fifth century Athenian conditions are accurately reflected in the pages of these philosophers even when the latter are discussing theoretical polities and imaginary and ideal societies. Caution must always be observed surely in the case of these "Laconizing" theorizers who, furthermore, were intense aristocrats and distrusted democracy. (4) It is true that Athens was conservative in the granting of full and technically legal citizenship to foreigners and slaves. (5) Slavery was, of course, a recognized institution from time immemorial throughout the ancient world and Athens as well. (6) Physical *drudgery* was not relished by the Athenians. The ground is now cleared for our discussion.

POLITICAL CONDITIONS

Was Athens in the Age of Pericles really a political democracy? We are fortunate in having no less an authority than Pericles himself to testify for us; Pericles, the aristocrat, as reported by Thucydides, the aristocrat. "Our government is *not copied* from those of our neighbors; we are an example to them rather than they to us. Our constitution is named a *democracy,* because it is in the hands not of the few but of *the many.* Our laws secure *equal* justice for *all* in their private disputes, and our *public opinion* welcomes and honors talent in *every branch of achievement,* not for any sectional reason, but on grounds of excellence alone. And as we give free play to *all* in our public life, so we carry the same spirit into our daily relations with one another. We are obedient to whomsoever is set in authority, and to the laws, more especially to those which offer protection to the oppressed and those unwritten ordinances whose transgression brings admitted shame. Wealth to us is not mere material for vainglory but an opportunity for achievement; and *poverty* we think is *no disgrace* to acknowledge but a real degradation to make no effort to overcome. *Our citizens attend both to public and private duties, and do not allow absorption in their own various affairs to interfere with their knowledge of the city's.* We differ from other states in regarding the man who *holds aloof from public life* not as quiet but as useless. In a word I claim that our city as a whole is an education to Greece, and that her members yield to none, man by man, for independence of spirit, manysidedness of attainment, and complete self-reliance in limbs and brain."

In Athens, then, if not in Sparta and Plato's *Republic,* the state existed for the individual and not the individual for the state. It is unnecessary to do more than briefly to cite the facts which reveal Athens as a political democracy. *All* citizens over eighteen years of age were members of the Assembly; *all* citizens over thirty were eligible to membership in the Council of Five Hundred, the members of which were elected annually *by lot; all* citizens over thirty were eligible to election *by lot* to serve as jurymen in the Heliastic law courts. As Warde Fowler says: "Every citizen had the right to hold all offices, with the doubtful exception in 450, of the archonship; to serve on the Council; to take part in the Assembly; to sit as judge. There was no privileged class, no skilled politicians, no bureaucracy. The whole Athenian people were identified with, actually were the state. All shared equally in the government, education, and pleasures." For this complete political equality we may let Mr. Dickinson himself eloquently testify. Although he tells us (p. 83) that the artisan and the trader were excluded by their calling from habitual conversance with public affairs, later he says (p. 112): "Among the free citizens, who included persons of every rank, no political distinction at all was drawn. All of them from the lowest to the highest had the right to speak and vote in the great assembly of the people which was ultimate authority; all were eligible to every administrative post; all sat in turn as jurors in the law courts. The disabilities of poverty were minimized by payment for attendance in the Assembly and courts. And what is more extraordinary, even distinctions of ability were levelled by the practice of filling all offices, except the highest, by lot. The citizenship was extended to every rank and calling; the poor man jostled the rich, the shopman the aristocrat, in the Assembly; cobblers, carpenters, smiths, farmers, merchants and retail dealers met together with the ancient landed gentry." "Politically the Athenian trader, and the Athenian artisan, was the equal of the aristocrat of purest blood" (p. 115).

We know that the power of the early Athenian aristocracy had been seriously curtailed by the legislation of Solon and Cleisthenes. After the Persian Wars its influence as an organized party became extremely small because of the democratic reforms of Ephialtes and Pericles through the blows dealt to the prestige of the Areopagus, the exile of Cimon, and the complete ascendency of Pericles. There was, then, in Athens in the Age of Pericles complete political equality among the citizens; poverty, wealth, station, family, occupation, and prestige all were of no consequence.

SOCIAL CONDITIONS

Social Status of Citizens in General

Let us now turn to an examination of the social conditions of Athenian life and scrutinize it for evidences of caste, class, snobbery, inequality, or injustice. In the city the house of the rich man and that of the poor man differed little in appearance. Private unostentation as contrasted with public magnificence was the rule. In fact, it was considered a breach of good taste to build and occupy a house of conspicuous cost or size. In the next place, simplicity in dress was general. Only the young (and, in particular, the Knights) dared to provoke possible derision or to invite popular prejudice by foppery of attire or appearance. Young Mantitheus apologizes to the Senate for his long hair and Strepsiades is disgusted with his son's "dandyism." Wearing the hair long might arouse suspicion of Spartan or aristocratic sympathies. An ancient witness testifies that "the Athenian people are not better clothed than the slave or alien, nor in personal appearance is there any superiority." Of course the nature of the employment might influence the quality and nature of the costume.

In all forms of social activity all the citizens articipated on a parity. All could attend the theater; all joined in the public festivals and in religious sacrifices and observances. In fact, if any element in Athens was favored it was the poor and lowly. Listen to the testimony of that unregenerate old Aristocrat (just quoted) who is bitterly opposed to Democracy as an institution but admits that it really exists in Athens. He says that if you *must* have Democracy Athens is a perfect example of it. "I do not praise the Polity of the Athenians, because the very choice involves the welfare of the *baser* folk as opposed to that of the *better* class. The poorer classes and the people of Athens should have the advantage over the men of birth and wealth because it is the people who row the vessels, and put around the city her girdle of power. Everywhere greater consideration is shown to the base, to poor people, and to common folk, than to persons of good quality—this should not surprise us, this is the keystone of the preservation of the democracy. It is these poor people, this common folk, this riff-raff, whose prosperity, combined with the growth of their numbers, enhance the democracy. All the world over the cream of society is in opposition to the democracy. The objection may be raised that it was a mistake to allow the universal right of speech and a seat in council; privileges which should have been reserved for the cleverest, the flower of the community. But if only the better people sat in council blessings would fall only to that class and the baser folk would get nothing.

Whereas it is the other way round. The people desire to be free and to be masters and their bad legislation is the very source of the people's strength and freedom." The happy lot of the common people in ancient Athens is further described by this contemporary witness: "The rich man trains the chorus; it is the people for whom the chorus is trained. The rich man is trierarch or gymnasiarch and the people profit by their labors. The whole state sacrifices at public cost a large number of victims; the Attic Democracy keeps holiday. They build at public cost a number of palaestras, dressing-rooms, bathing establishments; the mob gets the benefit of the majority of these luxuries rather than the select few or the well-to-do. In the theater the people do not like to be caricatured in comedy; it is the wealthy or well-born or influential man who is lampooned."

Enough has been said to show that the door of opportunity was open to all in Athens at this time. Worth, ability, character, not accident of birth or position counted. The rich did not grow richer while the poor grew poorer. Surplus wealth was not at the disposal of the few. It was expended for the good of all upon religious observances, the drama, gymnasia, the navy, public buildings and their adornment, and the state support of orphans and those physically incapacitated for earning a living. The wealthier classes were expected, and, in fact, were compelled, to contribute according to their means to the common welfare through the various liturgies and taxes.

The Social Status of the Producer, Artisan, etc.

We come next to a study of the social and economic position of the workers of various kinds. As we have seen, the handbooks in general tell us that all work was regarded as degrading, every activity for which one was paid was condemned, and producers, artisans, and all workers were branded by a humiliating social stigma. No adequate proof of such a condition of affairs is forthcoming; indeed, the actual situation seems to have been otherwise in democratic Athens at the time of Pericles. Why then is there this general mistaken notion? It is largely because of certain pronouncements in Plato and Aristotle. In the *Laws* and the *Republic* Plato insists on the gulf that should separate the citizen from the mechanic or trader. His ideal state rests upon agriculture and all the citizens are landed gentry forbidden to engage in trade. In this ideal *polis* trade and commerce are to be insignificant and the productive class is actually debarred from all political rights. A caste system is presupposed; governors and governed are sharply differentiated and each class is trained for its predestined position in the state. Aristotle, too, in his ideal state divides the population, on the one hand, into a ruling class of soldiers and judges and, on the other, into a subject class consisting of artisans and producers. As a mechanical trade renders the body and soul and intellect of free persons unfit for the exercise and practice of virtue Aristotle denies to the artisan the proper excellence of man on the ground that his occupation and status are unnatural. In an extreme democracy the mechanic and hired laborer must needs be citizens; this is impossible in an Aristocracy in which virtue and desert constitute the sole claim to the honors of state. Other radical statements of Aristotle are that the producer only differs from a slave in being subject to all instead of to one man and that the sedentary and within-door nature of the crafts unfitted the man who exercised them for war and the chase, the most dignified employments. Physical labor is condemned by him in that it is cheapening to work for another for pay or material profit as this reduces one to the rank of a slave. This would seem to be the chief source for the curious statement everywhere repeated that all Athenians who did anything for pay were condemned. That Aristotle did not represent Athenian opinion is conclusively shown by his condemnation of agriculture as preventing leisure which is at the basis of virtue. But no one doubts that agriculture was generally and highly esteemed by the Athenians. In Xeno-phon in a passage which is represented as spoken by Socrates those base mechanic arts are condemned which ruin the bodies of all those engaged in them, as those who are forced to remain in sitting postures and hug the gloom or crouch whole days confronting a furnace. This results in physical enervation and enfeebling of the soul and the victims have no leisure to de-vote to the claims of friendship and the state. Such will be sorry friends and ill-defenders of the fatherland.

It is absolutely wrong to accept these passages as conclusively proving that the Athenians regarded work as degrading and workers as social outcasts. (1) These writers do not claim to be describing actual Athenian conditions. (2) They are postulating an "ideal" society. (3) They are ever admirers of Spartan, and not their own Athenian polity. (4) They were intense aristocrats in sympathy and mistrusted democracy. (5) They despised the body and its needs. (6) They had particularly in mind soul-destroying drudgery, not rea-sonable labor and skilled work; corrupt and petty business, not necessary and honest trade and affairs. Frequently they were contrasting the philosopher-statesman set apart for ruling with the defective yokel. We can, indeed, if we wish, invoke the above-quoted writers in defense of work and the dignity of producing. Plato says in the *Laws:* "Retail trade in a city is not by nature intended to do any harm, but quite the contrary; for is not he a benefactor who reduces the inequalities and incommensurabilities of goods to equality and common measure? And this is what the power of money accomplishes, and the merchant may be said to be appointed for this purpose." Plato goes on to observe that many occupations have suffered ill-repute because of the inordinate love of gain and consequent corrupt practices on the part of the unscrupulous. He concludes: "If . . . we were to compel the best men everywhere to keep taverns for a time, or carry on retail trade, or do anything of that sort; or if, in consequence of some fate or necessity, the best women were compelled to follow similar callings, then we should know how agree-able and pleasant all these things are; and if all such occupations were man-aged on incorrupt principles, they would be honored as we honor a mother or nurse." Aristotle in the *Politics* condemns agriculture as we have seen, yet elsewhere he declares: "We honor the generous and brave and just. Such we conceive to be those who do not live upon others; and *such are they who live by labor* . . . chiefly agriculturalists, and chief among the agriculturalists, the small farmers." Now these small farmers tilled their own fields; in the remote districts of Attica slavery had scarcely penetrated. Xenophon tells the story of Eutherus, an old friend of Socrates, who, in poverty, as his property had been lost in the war, was gaining a livelihood by bodily toil. Socrates warns him that such employment in his case can be only temporary because of lack of necessary physical strength and urges him to secure a position as assistant to a large proprietor as manager of an estate. Eutherus fears the work may be servile. Socrates replies that heads of departments in a state who manage property are regarded not as performing undignified work but as having attained a higher dignity of freedom. Eutherus still demurs on the ground that he does not like to be accountable to anyone. Socrates replies that it is difficult to find work that is devoid of liability to account. It is difficult to avoid mistakes or unfriendly criticism. "Avoid captious critics," he says, "attach yourself to the considerate. Whatever you can do, do it heart and soul and make it your finest work." Another interesting and significant opinion of Socrates on this subject is reported by Xenophon which was expressed in a conversation between the philosopher and Aristarchus. The time was during the régime of the Thirty when economic and political conditions were very bad. Aristarchus' house was full of his indigent female relatives, fourteen in all. As these ladies are all expert needlewomen, skilled in the making of garments, Socrates advises his friend to put them to work; Ceramon, for example, with a few slaves, is very prosperous. Aristarchus objects to this proposal; the situations are not comparable; the members of his large household are not barbarian slaves but are kinswomen and free-born. Socrates replies: "Then, on the ground that they are free-born and relatives you think they ought to do nothing but eat and sleep? Or is it your opinion that free-born people who live in this way lead happier lives and are more to be congratulated than those who devote themselves to such useful arts of life as they are skilled in? Are work and study of no value? Did your relatives learn what they know merely for useless information or as a future asset? Is the well-tempered life and a juster one attained rather through idleness or the practice of the useful? If they were called upon to do some shameful work, let them choose death rather than that; but it is otherwise. It is suitable work for women. The things which we know are those we can best perform; it is a joy to do them, and the result is fair."

Plenty of evidence is available to show that work was esteemed, not only in the times portrayed by Homer in the *Iliad* and *Odyssey* and Hesiod in his *Works and Days,* but in Athens of the fifth century B.C. In Athens there was actually a law directed against idleness. That it was long in force is shown by the fact that Lysias wrote a speech in connection with a prosecution for ἀργία [*argia—D. K.*] for which the penalty on conviction was a fine of one hundred drachmas and ἀτιμία [*atimia—D. K.*] if the accused were thrice convicted. Plutarch tells us that a son who had not been taught a trade by his father was thereby released from the obligation to support his parent in old age. We have already quoted Pericles to the effect that not poverty but indolence is degrading.

Now the old-fashioned assumption that the Athenians found abundant leisure and opportunity for the *real life* (i.e., art, literature, politics, and philosophy) only because hirelings, slaves, and women did everything for them and the state treasury liberally supported them in *dolce far niente* is ridiculous. One thing is certain from all we know of the Athenians; they were not indolent; they were energetic in mind and body. Certainly in any state the wealthy are but a minority of the total population and even upon these rests the duty to manage their property and care for investments. Participation in public life and fulfilment of the demands and duties of good citizenship did not exact from the average Athenian anything like the major part of his waking hours. The Assembly met four times in each prytany (or tenth of a year period), i.e., less than once a week. As the attendance was voluntary only a fraction of all who were entitled to attend were ever present, as convenience or interest dictated. The Council was limited to five hundred citizens and no one might serve more than twice; furthermore, fifty only of the Council . . . (the standing committee) were continuously on duty so that the majority thus were free to attend to their private affairs. The Heliaea, or Courts of Justice, drew their dicasts or judges for jury service from a list of six thousand citizens. These were usually men of advanced years who had volunteered for such service. Universal military service at this time was not obligatory. Festivals and contests were generally attended but they occurred probably not oftener than once a week on the average. It has been estimated that a total of from two to three years of every citizen's life were required for deliberative and administrative duties. Many writers have emphasized the huge number of citizens who were supposedly pensioners luxuriously supported, apparently permanently and completely, by largess from the Periclean treasury. We have seen that public duties were not constant. As for the compensation it must be remembered that the daily living wage for the workman was from one drachma (about 18 cents), to one and a half. Now at the time under consideration Assemblymen received no compensation; jurymen received two obols (about six cents) daily for service; members of the Council of Five Hundred, elected annually by lot, were paid five obols (about fifteen cents). In the light of these facts how can it be claimed that Pericles *corrupted* the citizens generally by gifts of money, making them idle, cowardly, and greedy or to assume that these citizens were all dependent on public pay and could entirely support their households on these meager stipends. Mr. Grundy declares: "A condition of things in which a large proportion of a community is either practically or wholly dependent on the community for subsistence is unhealthy from both a social and political viewpoint." But only a minority of the fifty to sixty thousand adult male citizens received any state pay. The remuneration given was not a living wage; it was merely a contribution to support by which Pericles provided that *all,* and not merely the well-to-do, might participate, in turn, in civic affairs and obtain that benefit and culture from active personal public service to which he eloquently refers in the Funeral Oration. Nor was the remuneration intended as a sop to placate the discontented and starving proletariat. As Ferguson says: "Pericles did not intend to create a class of salaried officials; nor yet to make an advance toward communism. His ideal was political, not economic, equality—to enable all, irrespective of wealth or station, to use the opportunities and face the obligations which democracy brought in its train. Like all the great democratic leaders who preceded him, he was a nobleman by birth and breeding, and, like them, he did not doubt for a moment that the culture that ennobled the life of his class would dignify and uplift that of the masses also. His aim was to unite the whole people in a community of high ideas and emotions. It was to make them a nation of noblemen." If this were not the case, Pericles' noble speech, which stands in history by the side of Lincoln's Gettysburg Address, is the most hypocritical document preserved to us from the past.

Since the number of wealthy citizens was small how did the ordinary citizen gain his livelihood? It was by means of agriculture, handicrafts, trades, wholesale and retail business, and daily labor. No occupation was more respected and admired than agriculture. Farms were small, tenancy almost unknown. The small farmer tilled his fields with his own hands. In the arts and crafts and in labor no one needed to be idle, for the state policies of Pericles and the great building operations not only gave employment to all the residents of Athens, whether free men or slaves, but attracted workers from far and near. Thousands of citizens, perhaps a third of the whole, gained a livelihood by labor. While commerce was largely in the hands of the resident aliens, and the heaviest drudgery was performed by slaves, the mass of the skilled workers were free citizens. Stonecutters, masons, and sculptors had their shops or yards where they worked privately with their apprentices, or they might be engaged in public work, as the building operations on the Acropolis, working side by side with other citizens, with metics, and with slaves.

Modest means, even poverty (certainly *paupertas*), was the rule in Athens and was no bar to achievement and distinction. Life and its needs was simple, and money itself as an accumulation was not desired. A uniform wage was paid practically to all skilled workmen alike. Everyone who had skill or art was an artist, a term applied to sculptors, painters, physicians, and cobblers. Our handbooks generally assert that every occupation or profession which brought any financial return was despised and its practitioner was socially held in contempt. Slight reflection should show the absurdity of this thesis; there is no actual evidence to prove it. Plato, to be sure, who was wealthy and an aristocrat, sneers at those sophists and teachers who were compelled to take money for teaching. Of course there were some charlatans in this profession, but we may be certain that such sophists as Gorgias, Protagoras, Isocrates, and Alcidamas (all professors who accepted tuition from countless students who were only too glad to pay it) were held in high esteem in Athens. So were lawyers and speech-writers for pay, such as Antiphon, Lysias, and Isaeus. Literary men who accepted pay, poets who received purses for prizes, and actors who profited financially by their labors stood in the highest social esteem. The prestige of physicians depended on their skill and personality. The ignoramus and the charlatan were condemned; the skilled and public-spirited surgeon might be richly rewarded and given an honorary crown and public thanks. The elementary-school teacher, the music and gymnastic instructor, were not highly regarded, not because they received money for their services, but because most of them were ignorant men and often of inferior breeding. As for the great artists, sculptors, and painters it is simply impossible to believe such a statement as this: "Even the great artists, painters, and sculptors fell under public contempt simply because they earned money." Could this be true of a Phidias, a Polygnotus, an Ictinus, or a Mnesicles? But we know that Phidias was a warm and extremely intimate personal friend of Pericles. In fact, the statesman admired the sculptor so highly that the latter was entrusted with the greatest powers in superintending the ornamentation of the great temples. As for Polygnotus, a native of Thasos, he was the personal friend of Cimon, and was actually honored by the Athenians with citizenship. Expert potters and vase-painters were very numerous. While some of these were resident aliens (e.g., Amasis and Brygos), very many were citizens. Thus we find such names of prominent vase-makers as Klitias, Ergotimos, Nikosthenes, Epiktetes, Pamphaios, Euphronios, Hieron, and Megakles. A typical vase-making establishment would engage the services of some twelve persons who might be citizens, metics, and slaves all working side by side in equality. Citizen artists and artisans proclaim with pride, and do not conceal in shame, their occupations. Vase-painters and makers signed their wares. A scene (The Workshop of a Greek Vase-Painter) on a vase shows two Victories and Athena herself crowning the workmen, as Pottier says: "a poetic symbol to glorify the fame of Athenian industry." Indeed, artisans regarded themselves as under the special protection of Hephaestus, the smith, and of Athena, mistress of the arts and crafts, and were proud to claim descent from these deities. The potter, Euphronios, when making an offering to Athena calls himself in his dedication κεραμεύς [kerameus—D. K.], and the same procedure is followed by the fuller Simon, the tanner Smikros, and the potters, Mnesiades and Nearchus. On a funereal bas-relief a cobbler was represented in a heroic attitude holding the insignia of his trade. In the neighborhood of the Agora shops were especially numerous. These places served as centers of gossip and of news for Athenians generally, as we are told in a graphic passage in an informative speech of Lysias. It was among these craftsmen that Socrates, who had himself started in life as a stonecutter, spent much time in conversation. When he was, on an occasion, in search of a gentleman, he did not hesitate to go the round of various good carpenters, bronzeworkers, painters, and sculptors.

The comedies of Aristophanes are sometimes taken as proof of great social distinctions and inequalities existing among the citizens of Athens. Thus Mr. Dickinson, in an endeavor to maintain his thesis that Athens was politically democratic but socially intensely aristocratic, quotes at length the passage from the comedy of the *Knights* where the sausage-seller is assured that his crass ignorance, boorish vulgarity, and dense stupidity are the strongest possible recommendations and assets for the highest political distinction. We are apparently to infer that Aristophanes was himself a deep-dyed aristocrat who despised the people and their rule and that he was the spokesman for a large aristocratic section of Athenian society who were extremely hostile to democratic government. These views are unwarranted and, indeed, have been wholly discredited. Aristophanes was not a partisan; he was a conservative. He was not an opponent of democracy nor yet an aristocrat. It is true that he was a well-educated man of keen discernment, a friend of the Knights, and was doubtless on good terms with members of the aristocratic element in Athens. But he was friendly to the cause of democracy and sincerely wished to do it a favor by fearlessly revealing those defects to which a democratic form of government is especially liable and to give warning of possible dangers. This he constantly does in his plays with that exaggeration and caricature which are characteristic of the Old Comedy. In the opinion of the poet grave danger to the democracy might arise from unscrupulous demagogy as represented by such knaves as Cleon. In the case of Cleon, who is lampooned in the play of the *Knights,* Aristophanes is actuated by intense animus as a result of previous personal encounters. Thus Cleon is excoriated as a vulgar, coarse, and despicable individual, and the dramatist tries to discredit his influence and popularity. It is a great mistake to take Aristophanes' savage attacks on vulgar demagogues and criticisms of weaknesses in democratic government as proof that Aristophanes was an aristocrat who condemned and arraigned the people as a whole for vulgarity and incompetency. That he did not despair of the democracy and that he sympathized and fraternized with the "lower classes" is shown by those plays in which the chief personages, although of low degree, are "sympathetic characters," e.g., Dicaeopolis, the charcoal-burner of the *Acharnians,* and Strepsiades, the rough countryman of the *Clouds.*

In the opinion of Croiset, "the best Athenian society was the most open-hearted, most variously constituted, and most liberal society that has ever existed. The Athens that Plato shows us is a sort of talking place, where everybody is supposed to know everybody else, and where each person has a perfect right to make acquaintance with those he meets." As typical illustrations of this social democracy he refers to two social gatherings of which we have admirable accounts. In Xenophon's *Symposium* we have a description of a banquet held in 421 B.C., in the house of the wealthy Callias, son of Hipponicus, of a great and rich Athenian family. The guests include all sorts of people, rich, poor, philosophers and ignoramuses, and all converse familiarly on terms of equality and intimacy. In the same way, Plato, in his *Symposium,* an account of a dinner held at the house of Agathon in 416 B.C., reveals the same intermixture of classes and professions.

The Status of the Metics

We have now completed our discussion of the essentially democratic political and social status of Athenian citizens. It remains to consider briefly the other two classes of the inhabitants of Attica who are commonly regarded, along with the poorer citizens, as the exploited victims of the Athenian aristocracy. These elements are the metics (resident aliens) and the slaves.

The rapid commercial growth and naval expansion of Athens early caused a shortage of workers and helpers of all kinds. The citizen population was numerically inadequate to assume these new duties in addition to the performance of their regular occupations and the prosecution of agriculture. This demand was met by extending a welcome to foreigners and this policy was continued and encouraged by Pericles. Their exact number in the year 431 B.C. is unknown. Meyer's estimate is adult male metics 14,000 to about 55,000 adult male citizens; Clerc estimates them at 24,000, followed by Zimmern; Ferguson gives the number of adult male citizens as 50,000, and a total population of Attica of 300,000 of which one-sixth was foreign and one-third servile. There may have been, then, one adult male metic for every two citizens.

What was the lot of the metics? It has been asserted that their social position was humiliating and that they were disliked and even despised by the ordinary citizen. But contemporary evidence does not indicate this. Pericles says: "We open our city to all and never drive out foreigners." The scene of Plato's dialogue, *The Republic,* is the house of Cephalus, a prominent and influential man, but a metic who had been invited to Attica by Pericles himself. Another contemporary speaks of "the equality between the metics and the full citizens, because the city stands in need of her resident aliens to meet the requirements of such a multiplicity of arts and for the purposes of her navy." Thucydides has Nicias say to metic sailors that they and not any friends or allies outside were the "only free partners with the Athenians in the Empire." The metics participated fully in the social and religious life of the city. Neither in dress nor appearance could they be distinguished from the citizens. They attended the theater, they had a prominent place and dress in the Panathenaïc procession, they were demes-men and worshipped the same deities as the citizens. Like the citizens they defrayed the expenses of the liturgies and served in the army and the navy. When any list of Athenian inhabitants is given the metics are always named as an essential element of the population. They worked in large numbers side by side and for equal pay with the citizens in all kinds of work as, for example, the construction of the Erechtheum. They are found engaged in all the occupations, as workers and artisans of all kinds, as merchants at Peiraeus and at Athens, as bankers and capitalists, as painters, sculptors, and artists, as architects, and as philosophers and orators. Many of the famous pupils of Isocrates were metics, and no less than three of the celebrated Canon of the Ten Orators were resident aliens, namely, Isaeus of Chalcis, Lysias of Syracuse, and Deinarchus of Corinth.

The fee of twelve drachmas (about $2.16) required of metics was a petty matter, a legal formality of registration and license and not an onerous tax burden, as it is often regarded. The liability to taxes beyond those required of citizens was not great. Perhaps the most serious limitation imposed upon aliens was the inability legally to own real property. But metics might be placed on equal terms as to taxation and the owning of property with the citizens thereby becoming ἰσοτελεῖς [*isoteleis—D. K.*], and full citizenship might be conferred by vote of the Assembly. For example, an inscription is preserved which records the grant of full citizenship on those metics who participated in the return of the democrats from Phyle (in 404-3) and helped in the restoration. In the list occur some strangely sounding foreign names, e.g., Βενδιφάνης [*Bendiphanes—D. K.*] and Ψαμμίς [*Psammis—D. K.*], and their occupations as given are decidedly humble, such as cook, gardener, carpenter, fuller, etc.

The Athenians have been harshly criticized for not freely and generally granting citizenship to the metics. At first thought the criticism may seem valid and Athens illiberal. But the citizenship to the Athenian was not merely a political privilege; it was a sacred and usually an *inherited* possession. Loss of citizenship was to be feared more than death itself. Athens was a small and homogeneous community and the Athenians regarded themselves as autochthonous, like their favorite and symbolic cicada, sprung from the very soil of Attica itself. There is danger to a state in a too rapid influx of aliens who are given the powers of citizenship before real political and social assimilation has taken place. Even free America requires a term of years of probation before naturalization, and one of our greatest problems surely is this very one of the assimilation of the large number of our resident aliens. As Aristotle says: "Another cause for revolution is difference of races which do not acquire a common spirit; for the state is not the growth of a day, neither is it a multitude brought together by accident. Hence the reception of strangers in colonies has generally produced revolution." It is true that the metics of Athens were not on full terms of political equality with the citizens but it has been shown that the yawning social and economic gulf postulated by modern writers between citizen and resident foreigner did not really exist.

The Status of the Slaves

The institution of slavery existed throughout the ancient world from the earliest times. The Athenians, with but few exceptions, regarded slavery as natural and justifiable. It is again Aristotle, the fourth-century theorist and philosopher, who is made the starting-point for most modern discussions of slavery among the Greeks and the iniquity of the institution as maintained even by the cultured Athenians of the time of Pericles. In his treatment of this subject Aristotle characterizes in a cold-blooded legal fashion the slave as being merely "a breathing machine or tool, a piece of animated property" . . . and asserts that some men are so inferior that they may be regarded as slaves by nature. It is interesting to note, however, that Aristotle in another passage admits that there were some who protested against such a view. He says: "Others regard slave owning as doing violence to nature on the ground that the distinction of slave and free man is wholly conventional and has no place in nature, and therefore is void of justice, as resting on mere force." Plato, too, regards slavery as natural and justifiable but would forbid the enslavement of Greeks; he admits, however, that "a slave is an embarrassing possession, the distinction between man and slave being a difficult one and slaves should be well-treated and not abused or insulted." Aristotle, also, advises good treatment for the slave.

Recent writers have been very severe in their strictures on the Athenians for tolerating slavery. Professor Mahaffy writes: "Our real superiority lies in our moral ideals, in our philanthropy, our care of the poor and the sick. I do not know whether the existence and justification of slavery as a natural institution are not the main cause of this difference. Xenophon tells us of the callous and brutal attitude to slaves and prisoners. If it was true then it must have been true ten times more in the colder, harsher, and more selfish society of the preceding generation. The milk of human kindness seems to have run dry among them. . . . The association of the good with the beautiful and the true seems incomplete. The latter two are attained in no ordinary degree. The former, which is to us the most divine of the three, was but poorly represented." Mr. Dickinson goes so far as to say that Athenian slaves had *no political and social rights at all*. It is true that a minority of the slaves in Attica must have had an unenviable existence. These were the men who, in large numbers, slaved in the silver mines at Laurium. But what was the lot of the majority of the slaves in Attica? A contemporary testifies: "An extraordinary amount of license is granted to slaves . . . . where a blow is illegal, and slave will not step aside to let you pass him on the street. . . . The Athenian people is not better clothed than the slave or alien, nor in personal appearance is there any superiority. . . . Slaves in Athens are allowed to indulge in luxury, and indeed in some cases to live magnificently. . . . We have established an equality between our slaves and free men." Newly acquired slaves were received into the household with showers . . . of confections. They participated as members of the family in religious rites and sacrifices. They might attend the theater. They worked side by side with their masters in the workshop or might even be permitted to work on their own account exercising an independent profession . . . either paying a commission to their masters or actually purchasing their freedom and gaining thereby the status of metics. The law protected a slave from being the victim of ὕβρις [hybris—D. K.] and the aggressor was subject to find. The slave might not be put to death; a free man who had killed a slave was subject to prosecution for manslaughter. Refuge from a cruel master was afforded by flight to a temple as sanctuary, namely, to the Theseum, the Sanctuary of the Erinyes, and the altar of Athena Polias. Freedom might be granted outright by the master, while the state at times enfranchised slaves who had fought for Athens. In case of illness a slave might be affectionately cared for and at death mourned as a relative.

It is certainly a false assertion to claim that Athenian society *rested on slavery* and that slavery was the *dominant* factor in Athenian economic life. The slaves were in the minority in the total population at this period and the prosperity and greatness of the state was due to the industry, the initiative, and the efficiency of citizen and metic. Mr. Grundy says that "the ultimate controlling fact in Greek politics of the fifth and fourth centuries B.C. is the evil economic condition of the lower classes due to the competition of slave labour as competition with slave labour was impossible for the free proletariat." But this was not the case in the fifth century. There was no unemployment in Athens in the Age of Pericles. As we have seen the demand for labor was so great that extensive immigration was encouraged and there was a living wage for all. It is undoubtedly true, however, that in the fourth century and later the competition of slave with free labor gave rise to economic distress at a time when the citizens had decreased in number but the slaves had enormously increased. Mr. Grundy further declares that all hand-labor became associated with slavery and hence became incompatible with the dignity of the free man. The absolute falsity of this conception has already been established.

CONCLUSION

As a result of this study the following conclusions may be made:

1. Perhaps the greatest error and most unscientific procedure of many writers is to disregard or underestimate local conditions and, in particular, the chronological factor. Far too often authors indulge in generalizations regarding "the ancient Greek." It is no more possible to make general sweeping statements correctly characterizing the institutions of "the ancient Greek" than it would be accurately to estimate the civilization of "the modern European." Sparta and Athens were as far apart politically and socially in numerous respects as Germany and America, while Athens of the second half of the fifth century B.C. in its political, social, and economic conditions was by no means the Athens of the sixth or fourth centuries.

2. The ideal, aristocratic conceptions of Plato and Aristotle must not and cannot be taken literally to reflect actual Athenian conditions. Certainly Aristotle should not be taken as having "an average Greek mind" in his attitude toward society nor is he, or Plato, representative of fifth-century popular belief.

3. The time-honored tradition that Athenians despised all work and looked down upon all workers is false and our handbooks need revision in their treatment of this topic. It is true that in Athens, as with us, some occupations were thought less desirable and less dignified than others. In no land and at no time is the day laborer esteemed as highly as the statesman. Drudgery and menial employment the Athenians disliked and avoided; so do we. But the citizen who earned his living in some honest way and accepted money for his services was the rule and not the exception, nor was he as a result a social outcast but was a member, in good political and social standing, of the commonwealth.

4. The disabilities of the metics are generally exaggerated. Their position in Athenian society was not humiliating. While the resident aliens did not have full participation in political duties and privileges they did share, in a remarkable measure, the life of the citizens.

5. Slavery was, of course, an Athenian institution, and the right of owning slaves was, in general, not questioned. It is clear, however, that as a rule they were treated by their masters with humaneness and consideration, with the exception of the lowest class of public slaves who were employed in the mines.

6. It would be absurd to claim perfection for the Athenian democracy of the Age of Pericles, or to pretend that the Athenians had completely and happily solved the innumerable and complicated social, political, and economic problems which still vex the world and which still await solution even today. Athens was not, of course, at any time a perfect democracy. But that it was far more democratic and far less aristocratic in the time of Pericles than is generally assumed and asserted is certain.

Karl Beloch's view of Periclean "aristocracy" is quite different from that of Van Hook.

FROM Griechische Geschichte BY K. J. BELOCH

The leadership of the [democratic—D. K.] party, and in reality the leadership of the state with it, passed over to Pericles, the son of Xanthippus of Cholargus, the victor of Mycale. He was still a comparatively young man, perhaps at the beginning or middle of his thirties, and he had not yet had the

Karl Julius Beloch, *Griechische Geschichte,* 2nd ed., II, 154–156. Translated by Donald Kagan by permission of Walter de Gruyter & Co., Berlin.

opportunity to distinguish himself in war, since, in general, he did not possess an outstanding military talent. We may even doubt whether he was a great statesman. At least he was not able to preserve the Athenian empire at that height to which Themistocles and Cimon had brought it, and at his departure from the political stage he left behind as a legacy that war in which it finally came to ruin. But he was what we would call today a great parliamentarian. Like no other of his contemporaries he possessed the gift of leading the masses by the power of his speech and of drawing them along with him, and he had a very fine sense of what public opinion demanded. The road to power was opened to him by his family connections, and it was they, too, that determined his place in the party struggle. His mother was the niece of the great Cleisthenes, the founder of Athenian popular liberty. Pericles thus grew up in the tradition of the party of the Alcmaeonidae and in opposition to Cimon, which would necessarily have led him to an association with the reform party, even if he had not realized that the future belonged to it.

Pericles moved farther along the road Ephialtes had opened. If the democratization of the law courts were not to remain a dead letter, it was necessary to grant to the poorer classes of the citizenry the material capability to take up its share of the sessions of the Heliaea. So, on the proposal of Pericles, the jurors were granted a daily allowance of two obols per session, corresponding approximately to a minimal day's pay, as things stood in Athens in the mid-fifth century. This measure was all the more urgent as it would not otherwise have been possible to collect the required number of jurors, for the more important cases from the states of the empire were not yet being brought before the Athenian courts. This change soon resulted in a large part of the Athenian citizenry abstaining from productive labor and beginning to see its chief source of subsistence in the jury pay.

It was not far from this point to the demand that the state should provide the livelihood of its citizens altogether. Part of the purpose of the great public buildings that were completed under the Periclean regime in Athens was to offer pay to the poorer classes. Grain was also shared among the masses more often. Above all, the dominant position of Athens provided the possibility of assigning to thousands of Athenian citizens landed property outside Attica. If, for some, these so-called "cleruchies" were chiefly for the purpose of securing militarily important places by means of dependable garrisons, for others, nevertheless, the social-political purpose was of prime importance. Such was the case, for instance, with the assignments of land in the territories of Chalcis and Eretria after the conquest of Euboea in 446 or of Lesbos in 427. The recipients of these lots remained quietly living in Athens and allowed the property to be worked by native tenant farmers. Citizens capable of working were paid pensions from the state treasury, even if only in the amount of an obol a day, which just sufficed to pay for the support of the neediest. The children of citizens who had fallen in war were also supported at state expense until their majority.

But they went still further. If the tyrants had accepted it as their task to

offer the people the most splendid shows possible, the democracy did not lag
far behind this example. The festivals in Athens under the Periclean administration left behind in numbers as in the splendor of their outfitting all that
the Greek world had seen up to then, and, if that were not enough, money
payments were made to the citizens on such occasions.

We do not know how far other democracies at that time followed the
example given by Athens and even less whether the Periclean measures had
found their model already in other states. In any case, outside Athens the
more restricted sources of financial help drew narrower bounds to the intervention of the state in behalf of the "disinherited" classes. And we must not
forget that even in Athens itself it was still only the citizens, that is, at most
half the inhabitants of Attica, on whom the care of the state was bestowed,
not to mention the fact that the means for all this care was in large part taken
from the allies. Thus even this radical democracy really came out of the exploitation of the majority by a minority.

In the following selection Malcolm McGregor critically examines and rejects the Thucydidean assertion that Athens was a democracy in name only
during the Periclean age. What is more, he goes on to explain why Thucydides made such a claim. The problem is posed by the fact that although
Thucydides tells us that the oligarchic government installed by the Four
Hundred in 411 was the best in his time, he also has high praise for the
Athens of Pericles.

FROM The Politics of the Historian Thucydides
BY MALCOLM MCGREGOR

What we seek, ideally, is reconciliation of those comments by Thucydides on
government that seem to conflict. Our investigation commences with Perikles. From the ostracism of Kimon in 461 to his own death in 429 he was not
out of office for more than a year or two; for the last fifteen years consecu-
tively he was elected *strategos,* often, probably, *strategos autokrator.* Long
tenure of office, as we know, becomes in itself a ground for criticism and
Perikles did not escape. The Olympian figure in Aristophanes surely reflects a

Malcolm McGregor, "The Politics of the Historian Thucydides," *Phoenix,* X (1956), 97–98,
100–102. Published for the Classical Association of Canada by the University of Toronto Press,
Toronto.

phase of contemporary gossip. Today students are often told that Athens was not really a democracy at all; rather, it was a dictatorship. In more fashionable circles, we read of the principate of Perikles, a term which immediately summons Augustus Caesar from the shades. It must be granted that for this view there is weighty authority, Thucydides himself: "What was in theory democracy," he writes, "became in fact rule by the first citizen." The sentence has since been adopted by many as a fundamental text.

Perhaps the most quoted of Thucydides' opinions, it withstands analysis least; a cynic might remark that it is seldom subjected to analysis. Throughout Perikles' tenure of office the *ekklesia* met at least forty times a year. Each spring it elected the generals for the following year. Each year their fellow-citizens examined the qualifications of the generals before they took office. Ten times during the year the *ekklesia* heard reports from the generals. As they left office each year a jury of their fellow-citizens audited their records. One may employ other terms: during Perikles' political life the constitution functioned without interruption and Perikles had to retain the confidence of the sovereign and sensitive *demos* in order to remain in office. Not only was it possible for him to fail of re-election, as indeed he did in 444 B.C.; he might be removed from office, as indeed he was in 430 B.C. In the autumn of that year a disgruntled citizenry deposed and fined Perikles; more than that, they actually despatched a peace-mission to Sparta, *while he remained in office,* in direct contravention of his established policy. Now if democracy means and is government by the citizens, if the *ekklesia* decided policy by vote, if free elections persisted at their constitutional intervals, if Perikles was at all times responsible to the sovereign *demos,* and if an unoppressed political opposition survived, as it surely did,—if all this is so, then Athens was as democratic, not only in theory but in day-to-day practice, as government can conceivably be.* How such a system can be related to a dictatorship or to a principate is beyond my comprehension. The term principate is particularly unfortunate; for how does Augustus, the prototype, fit the conditions set out in this paragraph, which are not in dispute?

The principle of responsibility was paramount in the Athenian conception of democracy. The mere length of a responsible magistrate's tenure of office should not, by rational judges, be adopted at any time as a criterion of dictatorship. Within our own memories, however, a prolonged term has evoked the same indefensible protest in democratic countries, which should help us to understand, from our own experience, Perikles' position amidst his critics (and admirers) at the beginning of the Peloponnesian War. And nowhere in the modern world is the citizen's control over his representatives more direct and more constant than was the Athenian's. The truth is that Perikles had so won the confidence of his fellow-citizens that they elected him year after year and (wisely, I should say) allowed him, as their elder statesman, to guide them and shape their policies. But that they never surrendered, or diminished, their control of their own destinies is proved no more convincingly by Perikles' failure at the polls in 444 and his deposition in 430 than by his rapid re-election by a repentant *demos* a few months later. Athens remained a full and direct democracy.

* * *

We may find it simpler to understand Thucydides if we recognise that the democratic party at Athens itself developed two wings, one radical and one conservative. Perikles ended his life as a member of the latter. He had had his fling with the radical, aggressively imperialistic type of popular leadership and, by 446/5 B.C., had failed. His failure was remarkable in that he confessed it; he at once abandoned the aggressive policy by land and turned to the consolidation of the naval empire. He was thus able to guide Athens—and so most of the Aegean states—through what was probably the longest period of continuous prosperity and peace that Hellenes could remember. His thorough-going reversal I deem the surest evidence of his superior statecraft. This was the man who commanded the allegiance of Thucydides.

With the death of Perikles the restraining voice was gone and the way cleared for the imperialistic radicals, who offered to an avid *demos* a policy that was to prove as disastrous as Perikles had predicted. This transition allows Thucydides to give vent to his natural antipathy to democracy. His indictment of popular government, implied before the death of Perikles, is explicit in his treatment of Kleon, reaches a climax in the shameful words of the Athenian in the Melian Dialogue, and passes inexorably to the final collapse, which Thucydides, who lived to see it, attributes to the folly of the democracy. The state under Perikles, which we, unlike Thucydides, call democracy, Thucydides could endorse with enthusiasm; but Kleon and his kind, in a state in which the machinery and the system had undergone not the slightest change, the oligarchic Thucydides could not stomach. To him Kleon was democracy; we know that Perikles was too. Worse was to come. Alkibiades, that brilliant renegade, borrowed the foreign policies of Kleon; having greater ability and less sense of responsibility, he wrought greater harm.

Yet there were those upon whom the mantle of Perikles fell. Of these Nikias was most prominent. Sometimes considered an oligarch, he was in truth, with his loyalty to Periklean tradition and policy, a conservative, or Periklean, democrat. Of him Thucydides, not surprisingly, writes with a nice appreciation, and in the increasingly grim pages one can detect a real sympathy for Nikias, so honest, so loyal, and, at the last, so ineffective.

The situation after Perikles has been neatly described by John Finley: "Pericles . . . had four characteristics: he could see and expound what was necessary, he was patriotic and above money. Athens' misfortune and the essential cause of her ruin was that none of his successors combined all these traits. Nicias, who was honest but inactive, had the last two; Alcibiades, who was able but utterly self-interested, had the first two. . . ."

This was Athens' tragedy, that she produced no successor who combined all the qualities of Perikles. I have heard it argued that Perikles was culpable for not having left a political heir, that is, that he did not brook rivalry. This, to be sure, is the charge that is commonly levelled at the great man. Apart from the fact that this assumes a principate that never existed and that Nikias *was* his heir, though not his intellectual peer, it is a formidable undertaking to show how one man could suppress others of comparable talent within his own party in a system in which an office-holder was ever subject to discipline and in which a popular assembly provided the ideal arena for the potential statesman to acquire education, training, and reputation. When we bewail the quality of those who received the reins from Perikles, we perhaps fail sufficiently to emphasize the surpassing genius of one who so excelled his contemporaries. "Perikles," Thucydides points out, "influential because of his reputation and intelligence and obvious integrity, was able freely to restrain the people; he led them rather than was led by them. . . . His successors were more evenly matched with one another, striving, each one of them, to be first."

Perikles commanded the respect and the loyalty of men of various political persuasions. Thucydides was one of those to whom the man was more significant than their own partly inherited political convictions. It is a truism that the inspired leader draws support from the state as a whole, irrespective of party-lines. To Thucydides the events that followed the death of Perikles must have come as a bitter, if not entirely unexpected, disappointment; not unexpected, because he had no real faith in democracy and the death of Perikles removed the source of his self-deception. Steadily, as he saw it, the Periklean state was being destroyed. When Theramnes' moderate oligarchy of Five Thousand, with its unrestricted citizenship but restricted privilege, emerged from the revolution of 411/0, Thucydides, reverting easily to his tradition, could follow the dictates of his intellect and pronounce this the best government enjoyed by the Athenians in his time. It is his only categorical judgement on government; it is the key to his political convictions.

One might draw a parallel between Thucydides and the Old Oligarch. The Old Oligarch, it will be recalled, is so named for the nature of his anti-democratic essay written about 425 B.C. He writes, in effect, "I do not approve of democracy, but, if you *must* have it, I admit that the Athenians make a fine job of it." Thucydides, the oligarch born, might have said, "I do not approve of democracy, I see no strength or wisdom in the rabble; but I do admire and will support the Periklean state, which of course is not democracy at all."

We are ready to summarise. Thucydides was reared in the conservative anti-democratic tradition. His orderly and impartial mind was impressed by the genius of Perikles, and so he became a Periklean, though not a democrat; nor could he admit that by so doing he was, in essence, approving of democracy. Later, the oligarchic tradition of his family that had never been abandoned, reasserted itself, as he saw Periklean ideals forgotten, Periklean warnings ignored. He witnessed, with a brutally piercing eye, what seemed to him the evils of a democracy run to seed, its moral fibre weakening. He ended his life as he had begun it, a confirmed oligarch who had never renounced the creed of his fathers.

ANCIENT
SCIENCE

OBSERVED FACTS,
MATHEMATICAL
SYSTEMS, OR
PHILOSOPHICAL
FANCIES?

CONTENTS

QUESTIONS FOR STUDY

1. *Compare the approaches of Hippocrates and Plato to the problem of epistemology (the knowledge of how we know anything).*

2. *How does Aristotle's approach differ from both Plato's and Hippocrates'?*

3. *What are the Aristotelian "four causes"? How do they influence Aristotle's scientific method?*

4. *On what basic points would Farrington and Santillana disagree?*

5. *What is Farrington's definition of science? Would Aristotle have agreed with it? would Plato? would Archimedes?*

6. *How do Archimedes and Hippocrates differ in their approaches to science?*

7. *What is the role of fact in ancient science? What is the role of mathematics?*

8. *What would an ancient philosopher have considered a scientific theory to be? How would he have judged whether or not it was a valid one?*

The desire to know is a common attribute of the entire human species. Modern science, however, is a unique product of Western civilization and its origin is to be found in ancient Greece. Why this should be so has baffled generations of scholars. All we can do is to point to some conditions that obtained in Greece and suggest that these conditions helped to stimulate the growth of a scientific approach to nature.

One of the characteristics of Greek civilization that immediately strikes the historian of science is the relative intellectual puerility of Greek religion. The Greek gods were powerful but they were also arbitrary, childish, and often petulant. Zeus was to be feared, for his penchant for hurling thunderbolts was well known. But could Zeus, who seemingly spent most of his time seducing mortals, be seriously considered as the author of the awesome observable universe? The contrast here with Babylonia and Egypt is instructive. The Babylonians lived in an area of almost constant and catastrophic natural upheavals. Violent storms, flash floods, and earthquakes threatened life, limb, and crops. To the Babylonian, the gods were omnipresent and evil, to be propitiated if possible. Both nature and man were divine playthings, to be manipulated at will by Marduk and his divine followers. The Egyptians, on the other hand, experienced almost complete regularity and beneficence from their environment. The Nile flooded regularly every year, the sun brought forth abundance from the alluvial mud, and even the wind blew constantly from the north, permitting Egyptians to sail effortlessly up the Nile and coast down it with the current. Here the gods obviously smiled on the land and its inhabitants. The Egyptians responded with gratitude. In neither case was there much stimulus for the understanding of the natural environment. It was accepted as part of the divine plan, and that was that.

In Greece nature was something else. In the early myths nature and natural forces appear before the gods—Earth, the Heavens, and the Pit are the original creations out of Chaos. Even the gods are subject to fate, and very early in Greek thought there appears the dim concept of law regulating the activities of nature, men, and gods. The very word "cosmos" is Greek and it means order. The cosmos was ordered by law, and implicit in this statement is the idea that men can come to know and understand both the cosmic order and the regulatory laws.

Men too are ordered by law, and the second aspect of Greek civilization that contributed to the birth of science is the *polis*. Here, for the first time, men were forced to think about the means of providing laws that would guarantee order in the city-state. They could not rely upon Pharaoh, himself a god, to provide the requisite order. Nor could they, like Hammurabi, really expect a god to take time off from his philandering to dictate a code of laws. Instead, they had to think about what man was, what a well-ordered city was, and what laws should properly be devised for the government of the *polis*. They also had to convince their fellow citizens, and this meant having to present their views in convincing guise. Logic and dialectic—the means of argumentation—are Greek inventions and they have an obvious application to science.

Weakness of theology and concern for rational government may contribute to the growth of science, but they cannot account for its birth. Nor can anyone. We can simply report that, sometime in the sixth century before Christ, something like science made its appearance in Greek-speaking lands. The traditional name associated with this birth of science is Thales of Miletus, who flourished in the second half of the sixth century. His fame rests upon two innovations. He was the first to invent a geometric proof, in this case proving by irrefutable logic that a triangle inscribed in a semicircle must be a right triangle. In addition, he was the first to attempt to give an answer to the question, still haunting physicists: Of what is the world composed? Both of these achievements were to have momentous consequences. The invention of geometry as a branch of mathematics, rather than of surveying, was to provide a model of scientific discourse for centuries. There was something elegant and starkly beautiful about geometric reasoning. One started from a few basic, indisputable axioms and then, by the use of rigorous logic, deduced consequences that were both unexpected and unassailable. The Greeks loved certainty and found it in geometry.

The question of the nature of the world, however, was to prove even more fruitful in the production of scientific theories and hypotheses. There are a number of things to be noted about it. In the first place, it has played a role of fundamental importance in the development of Western thought. The question assumes that there is a reality *behind* everyday appearances, for it is clear that Thales and his successors would never have accepted as an answer that the world is made of wood and grass and flesh and stones and air and clouds and water and all the myriad of individual substances of which the world is obviously made. The reason they would not have accepted such an answer is that these objects were constantly changing into one another. A man drinks wine and water, eats grain and meat, and somehow transmutes these substances into "man." This could not happen if the world (and man) were really made of the objects he ingested. Thus the different objects of sense experience must conceal a basic unity of matter common to all objects.

For Thales this common element was water; for later philosophers it was other substances—or even nonsubstantial "things" like number. But what is of importance is that reality was *not* what the senses presented to the mind but something hidden behind these appearances. The task of science was to discover what these ultimate elements were and, from them, to reconstitute the world by human reason. It is worth noting that this is what scientists are still attempting to do today.

The second question raised by Thales is this: If reality is hidden by appearances, how does the human mind penetrate these appearances to arrive at the ultimate reality? This was to stimulate philosophers from antiquity to the present day. The problem in the following section is really centered around this: How can we know about a world that is constantly changing. The answers given by the Greeks were often wrong, but the methods they devised and the theories they constructed served as starting points for later investigators. One has learned something even when he has learned that he is wrong. As Sir Francis Bacon later put it, "Truth is more likely to emerge from error than from confusion." The Greeks were the first to attempt seriously to clear up the confusion created by the contemplation of nature.

1
THE SEARCH FOR KNOWLEDGE IN GREEK ANTIQUITY

The greatest physician of antiquity was the almost legendary Hippocrates of Cos (c. 460–375 B.C.), whose effect on medicine is still visible in the Hippocratic oath. The treatise *On Ancient Medicine* laid out the basic medical ideas of the Hippocratic school.

FROM On Ancient Medicine BY HIPPOCRATES

Whoever having undertaken to speak or write on Medicine, have first laid down for themselves some hypothesis to their argument, such as hot, or cold, or moist, or dry, or whatever else they choose, (thus reducing their subject within a narrow compass, and supposing only one or two original causes of diseases or of death among mankind,) are all clearly mistaken in much that they say; and this is the more reprehensible as relating to an art which all men avail themselves of on the most important occasions, and the good operators and practitioners in which they hold in especial honour. . . . Wherefore I have not thought that it stood in need of an empty hypothesis, like those subjects which are occult and dubious, in attempting to handle which it is necessary to use some hypothesis; as, for example, with regard to things above us and things below the earth; if any one should treat of these and undertake to declare how they are constituted, the reader or hearer could not find out, whether what is delivered be true or false; for there is nothing which can be referred to in order to discover the truth.

The Genuine Works of Hippocrates, I (1849), 161–162, 168–173, 174–176, translated by Francis Adams.

belong of old to Medicine, and an origin and way
⎼hich many and elegant discoveries have been made,
and others will yet be found out, if a person pos-
⎼y, and knowing those discoveries which have been
⎼m them to prosecute his investigations. But who-
⎼g all these, attempts to pursue another course and
⎼e has discovered anything, is deceived himself and
⎼g is impossible. And for what reasons it is impos-
⎼r to explain, by stating and showing what the Art

* * *

to revert to the new method of those who prose-
⎼rt by hypothesis. For if hot, or cold, or moist, or
⎼injurious to man, and if the person who would
⎼ply cold to the hot, hot to the cold, moist to the
⎼et me be presented with a man, not indeed one of
⎼e of the weaker, and let him eat wheat, such as it
⎼g-floor, raw and unprepared, with raw meat, and
⎼ng such a diet I know that he will suffer much
⎼rience pains, his body will become weak, and his
bowels deranged, and he will not subsist long. What remedy, then, is to be
provided for one so situated? Hot? or cold? or moist? or dry? For it is clear
that it must be one or other of these. For, according to this principle, if it is
one of these which is injuring the patient, it is to be removed by its contrary.
But the surest and most obvious remedy is to change the diet which the
person used, and instead of wheat to give bread, and instead of raw flesh,
boiled, and to drink wine in addition to these: for by making these changes it
is impossible but that he must get better, unless completely disorganised by
time and diet. What, then, shall we say? whether that, as he suffered from
cold, these hot things being applied were of use to him, or the contrary? I
should think this question must prove a puzzler to whomsoever it is put. For
whether did he who prepared bread out of wheat remove the hot, the cold,
the moist, or the dry principle in it?—for the bread is consigned both to fire
and to water, and is wrought with many things, each of which has its peculiar property and nature, some of which it loses and with others it is diluted
and mixed.

And this I know, moreover, that to the human body it makes a great
difference whether the bread be fine or coarse; of wheat with or without the
hull, whether mixed with much or little water, strongly wrought or scarcely
at all, baked or raw—and a multitude of similar differences; and so, in like
manner, with the cake (maza); the powers of each, too, are great, and the
one nowise like the other. Whoever pays no attention to these things, or,
paying attention, does not comprehend them, how can he understand the
diseases which befall a man? For, by every one of these things, a man is

affected and changed this way or that, and the whole of his life is subjected to them, whether in health, convalescence, or disease. Nothing else, then, can be more important or more necessary to know than these things. So that the first inventors, pursuing their investigations properly, and by suitable train of reasoning, according to the nature of man, made their discoveries, and thought the Art worthy of being ascribed to a god, as is the established belief. For they did not suppose that the dry or the moist, the hot or cold, or any of these, are either injurious to man, or that man stands in need of them; but whatever in each was strong, and more than a match for a man's constitution, whatever he could not manage, that they held to be hurtful, and sought to remove. Now, of the sweet, the strongest is that which is intensely sweet; of the bitter, that which is intensely bitter; of the acid, that which is intensely acid; and of all things that which is extreme, for these things they saw both existing in man, and proving injurious to him. For there is in man the bitter and the salt, the sweet and the acid, the sour and the insipid, and a multitude of other things having all sorts of powers, both as regards quantity and strength. These, when all mixed and mingled up with one another, are not apparent, neither do they hurt a man; but when any of them is separate, and stands by itself, then it becomes perceptible, and hurts a man. And thus, of articles of food, those which are unsuitable and hurtful to man when administered, every one is either bitter, or intensely so, or saltish or acid, or something else intense and strong, and therefore we are disordered by them in like manner as we are by the secretions in the body. But all those things of which a man eats and drinks are devoid of any such intense and well-marked quality, such as bread, cake, and many other things of a similar nature which man is accustomed to use for food, with the exception of condiments and confectionaries, which are made to gratify the palate and for luxury. And from those things, when received into the body abundantly, there is no disorder nor dissolution of the powers belonging to the body; but strength, growth, and nourishment result from them, and this for no other reason than because they are well mixed, have nothing in them of an immoderate character, nor anything strong, but the whole forms one simple and not strong substance.

I cannot think in what manner they who advance this doctrine, and transfer the Art from the cause I have described to hypothesis, will cure men according to the principle which they have laid down. For, as far as I know, neither the hot nor the cold, nor the dry, nor the moist, has ever been found unmixed with any other quality; but I suppose they use the same articles of meat and drink as all we other men do. But to this substance they give the attribute of being hot, to that cold, to that dry, and to that moist. Since it would be absurd to advise the patient to take something hot, for he would straightway ask what it is? so that he must either play the fool, or have recourse to some one of the well-known substances: and if this hot thing happen to be sour, and that hot thing insipid, and this hot thing has the power of raising a disturbance in the body (and there are many other kinds of heat, possessing many opposite powers), he will be obliged to administer some one of them, either the hot and the sour, or the hot and the insipid, or that which, at the same time, is cold and sour (for there is such a substance), or the cold and the insipid. For, as I think, the very opposite effects will result from either of these, not only in man, but also in a bladder, a vessel of wood, and in many other things possessed of far less sensibility than man; for it is not the heat which is possessed of great efficacy, but the sour and the insipid, and other qualities as described by me, both in man and out of man, and that whether eaten or drunk, rubbed in externally, and otherwise applied.

* * *

Certain sophists and physicians say that it is not possible for any one to know medicine who does not know what man is [and how he was made and how constructed], and that whoever would cure men properly, must learn this in the first place. But this saying rather appertains to philosophy, as Empedocles and certain others have described what man in his origin is, and how he first was made and constructed. But I think whatever such has been said or written by sophist or physician concerning nature has less connexion with the art of medicine than with the art of painting. And I think that one cannot know anything certain respecting nature from any other quarter than from medicine; and that this knowledge is to be attained when one comprehends the whole subject of medicine properly, but not until then; and I say that this history shows what man is, by what causes he was made, and other things accurately. Wherefore it appears to me necessary to every physician to be skilled in nature, and strive to know, if he would wish to perform his duties, what man is in relation to the articles of food and drink, and to his other occupations, and what are the effects of each of them to every one. And it is not enough to know simply that cheese is a bad article of food, as disagreeing with whoever eats of it to satiety, but what sort of disturbance it creates, and wherefore, and with what principle in man it disagrees; for there are many other articles of food and drink naturally bad which affect man in a different manner. Thus, to illustrate my meaning by an example, undiluted wine drunk in large quantity renders a man feeble; and everybody seeing this knows that such is the power of wine, and the cause thereof; and we know, moreover, on what parts of a man's body it principally exerts its action; and I wish the same certainty to appear in other cases. For cheese (since we used it as an example) does not prove equally injurious to all men, for there are some who can take it to satiety without being hurt by it in the least, but, on the contrary, it is wonderful what strength it imparts to those it agrees with; but there are some who do not bear it well, their constitutions are different, and they differ in this respect, that what in their body is incompatible with cheese, is roused and put in commotion by such a thing; and those in whose bodies such a humour happens to prevail in greater quantity and intensity, are likely to suffer the more from it. But if the thing had been pernicious to the whole nature of man, it would have hurt all. Whoever knows these things will not suffer from it.

Plato (429–347 B.C.) was one of the greatest philosophers of all time. In *The Republic,* Plato was intent upon examining the requirements of the perfect political state. Science entered in as part of the training of those who were to guide the state. In the extract that follows the main speaker is Socrates; his audience is Glaucon.

FROM The Republic BY PLATO

And now, I said, let me show in a figure how far our nature is enlightened or unenlightened:—Behold! human beings living in an underground den, which has a mouth open towards the light and reaching all along the den; here they have been from their childhood, and have their legs and necks chained so that they cannot move, and can only see before them, being prevented by the chains from turning round their heads. Above and behind them a fire is blazing at a distance, and between the fire and the prisoners there is a raised way; and you will see, if you look, a low wall built along the way, like the screen which marionette players have in front of them, over which they show the puppets.

I see.

And do you see, I said, men passing along the wall carrying all sorts of vessels, and statues and figures of animals made of wood and stone and various materials, which appear over the wall? Some of them are talking, others silent.

You have shown me a strange image, and they are strange prisoners.

Like ourselves, I replied; and they see only their own shadows, or the shadows of one another, which the fire throws on the opposite wall of the cave?

True, he said; how could they see anything but the shadows if they were never allowed to move their heads?

And of the objects which are being carried in like manner they would only see the shadows?

Yes, he said.

And if they were able to converse with one another, would they not suppose that they were naming what was actually before them?

Very true.

And suppose further that the prison had an echo which came from the other side, would they not be sure to fancy when one of the passers-by spoke that the voice which they heard came from the passing shadow?

The Dialogues of Plato, I (1937), 773–776; translated by Benjamin Jowett.

No question, he replied.

To them, I said, the truth would be literally nothing but the shadows of the images.

That is certain.

And now look again, and see what will naturally follow if the prisoners are released and disabused of their error. At first, when any of them is liberated and compelled suddenly to stand up and turn his neck round and walk and look towards the light, he will suffer sharp pains; the glare will distress him, and he will be unable to see the realities of which in his former state he had seen the shadows; and then conceive some one saying to him, that what he saw before was an illusion, but that now, when he is approaching nearer to being and his eye is turned towards more real existence, he has a clearer vision,—what will be his reply? And you may further imagine that his instructor is pointing to the objects as they pass and requiring him to name them,—will he not be perplexed? Will he not fancy that the shadows which he formerly saw are truer than the objects which are now shown to him?

Far truer.

And if he is compelled to look straight at the light, will he not have a pain in his eyes which will make him turn away to take refuge in the objects of vision which he can see, and which he will conceive to be in reality clearer than the things which are now being shown to him?

True, he said.

And suppose once more, that he is reluctantly dragged up a steep and rugged ascent, and held fast until he is forced into the presence of the sun himself, is he not likely to be pained and irritated? When he approaches the light his eyes will be dazzled, and he will not be able to see anything at all of what are now called realities.

Not all in a moment, he said.

He will require to grow accustomed to the sight of the upper world. And first he will see the shadows best, next the reflections of men and other objects in the water, and then the objects themselves; then he will gaze upon the light of the moon and the stars and the spangled heaven; and he will see the sky and the stars by night better than the sun or the light of the sun by day?

Certainly.

Last of all he will be able to see the sun, and not mere reflections of him in the water, but he will see him in his own proper place, and not in another; and he will contemplate him as he is.

Certainly.

He will then proceed to argue that this is he who gives the season and the years, and is the guardian of all that is in the visible world, and in a certain way the cause of all things which he and his fellows have been accustomed to behold?

Clearly, he said, he would first see the sun and then reason about him.

And when he remembered his old habitation, and the wisdom of the den and his fellow-prisoners, do you not suppose that he would felicitate himself on the change, and pity them?

Certainly, he would.

And if they were in the habit of conferring honours among themselves on those who were quickest to observe the passing shadows and to remark which of them went before, and which followed after, and which were together; and who were therefore best able to draw conclusions as to the future, do you think that he would care for such honours and glories, or envy the possessors of them? Would he not say with Homer,

Better to be the poor servant of a poor master,

and to endure anything, rather than think as they do and live after their manner?

Yes, he said, I think that he would rather suffer anything than entertain these false notions and live in this miserable manner.

Imagine once more, I said, such an one coming suddenly out of the sun to be replaced in his old situation; would he not be certain to have his eyes full of darkness?

To be sure, he said.

And if there were a contest, and he had to compete in measuring the shadows with the prisoners who had never moved out of the den, while his sight was still weak, and before his eyes had become steady (and the time which would be needed to acquire this new habit of sight might be very considerable), would he not be ridiculous? Men would say of him that up he went and down he came without his eyes; and that it was better not even to think of ascending; and if any one tried to loose another and lead him up to the light, let them only catch the offender, and they would put him to death.

No question, he said.

This entire allegory, I said, you may now append, dear Glaucon, to the previous argument; the prison-house is the world of sight, the light of the fire is the sun, and you will not misapprehend me if you interpret the journey upwards to be the ascent of the soul into the intellectual world according to my poor belief, which, at your desire, I have expressed—whether rightly or wrongly God knows. But, whether true or false, my opinion is that in the world of knowledge the idea of good appears last of all, and is seen only with an effort; and, when seen, is also inferred to be the universal author of all things beautiful and right, parent of light and of the lord of light in this visible world, and the immediate source of reason and truth in the intellectual; and that this is the power upon which he who would act rationally either in public or private life must have his eye fixed.

Plato's greatest pupil was Aristotle (384–322 B.C.). After some twenty years of close association with Plato, he broke with Platonism and created his own system. Like his master, Aristotle felt it essential to ask what knowledge was and how it could be attained. In the *Posterior Analytics* he examined this question with the cold logic of the expert dialectician that he was. This difference in approach from Plato is worth noting, for it helps to explain the relative popularity of the two philosophers in later ages. Aristotle was the strict logician who appealed to the no-nonsense professional philosopher; Plato was the superb dramatist of the dialogues, the mythmaker, to whom artists instinctively turned.

FROM Posterior Analytics BY ARISTOTLE

We suppose ourselves to possess unqualified scientific knowledge of a thing, as opposed to knowing it in the accidental way in which the sophist knows, when we think that we know the cause on which the fact depends, as the cause of that fact and of no other, and, further, that the fact could not be other than it is. Now that scientific knowing is something of this sort is evident—witness both those who falsely claim it and those who actually possess it, since the former merely imagine themselves to be, while the latter are also actually, in the condition described. Consequently the proper object of unqualified scientific knowledge is something which cannot be other than it is.

There may be another manner of knowing as well—that will be discussed later. What I now assert is that at all events we do know by demonstration. By demonstration I mean a syllogism productive of scientific knowledge, a syllogism, that is, the grasp of which is *eo ipso* such knowledge. Assuming then that my thesis as to the nature of scientific knowing is correct, the premisses of demonstrated knowledge must be true, primary, immediate, better known than and prior to the conclusion, which is further related to them as effect to cause. Unless these conditions are satisfied, the basic truths will not be "appropriate" to the conclusion. Syllogism there may indeed be without these conditions, but such syllogism, not being productive of scientific knowledge, will not be demonstration. The premisses must be true: for that which is non-existent cannot be known—we cannot know, e.g. that the diagonal of a square is commensurate with its side. The premisses must be primary and

---

W. D. Ross, ed., *The Works of Aristotle*, I (1928), 71b–73b, 88a, 99b–100a, translated by G. R. G. Mure.

indemonstrable; otherwise they will require demonstration in order to be known, since to have knowledge, if it be not accidental knowledge, of things which are demonstrable, means precisely to have a demonstration of them. The premisses must be the causes of the conclusion, better known than it, and prior to it; its causes, since we possess scientific knowledge of a thing only when we know its cause; prior, in order to be causes; antecedently known, this antecedent knowledge being not our mere understanding of the meaning, but knowledge of the fact as well. Now "prior" and "better known" are ambiguous terms, for there is a difference between what is prior and better known in the order of being and what is prior and better known to man. I mean that objects nearer to sense are prior and better known to man; objects without qualification prior and better known are those further from sense. Now the most universal causes are furthest from sense and particular causes are nearest to sense, and they are thus exactly opposed to one another. . . . I call an immediate basic truth of syllogism a "thesis" when, though it is not susceptible of proof by the teacher, yet ignorance of it does not constitute a total bar to progress on the part of the pupil: one which the pupil must know if he is to learn anything whatever is an axiom. I call it an axiom because there are such truths and we give them the name of axioms *par excellence*. If a thesis assumes one part or the other of an enunciation, i.e. asserts either the existence or the non-existence of a subject, it is a hypothesis; if it does not so assert, it is a definition. Definition *is* a "thesis" or a "laying something down," since the arithmetician lays it down that to be a unit is to be quantitatively indivisible; but it is not a hypothesis, for to define what a unit is is not the same as to affirm its existence.

Now since the required ground of our knowledge—i.e. of our conviction— of a fact is the possession of such a syllogism as we call demonstration, and the ground of the syllogism is the facts constituting its premisses, we must not only know the primary premisses—some if not all of them—beforehand, but know them better than the conclusion: for the cause of an attribute's inherence in a subject always itself inheres in the subject more firmly than that attribute; e.g. the cause of our loving anything is dearer to us than the object of our love. So since the primary premisses are the cause of our knowledge—i.e. of our conviction—it follows that we know them better—that is, are more convinced of them—than their consequences, precisely because our knowledge of the latter is the effect of our knowledge of the premisses. Now a man cannot believe in anything more than in the things he knows, unless he has either actual knowledge of it or something better than actual knowledge. But we are faced with this paradox if a student whose belief rests on demonstration has not prior knowledge; a man must believe in some, if not in all, of the basic truths more than in the conclusion. Moreover, if a man sets out to acquire the scientific knowledge that comes through demonstration, he must not only have a better knowledge of the basic truths and a firmer conviction of them than of the connexion which is being demonstrated: more than this, nothing must be more certain or better known to him than these basic truths in their character as contradicting the fundamental premises which lead to the opposed and erroneous conclusion. For indeed the conviction of pure science must be unshakable.

Some hold that, owing to the necessity of knowing the primary premises, there is no scientific knowledge. Others think there is, but that all truths are demonstrable. Neither doctrine is either true or a necessary deduction from the premises. The first school, assuming that there is no way of knowing other than by demonstration, maintains that an infinite regress is involved, on the ground that if behind the prior stands no primary, we could not know the posterior through the prior (wherein they are right, for one cannot traverse an infinite series): if on the other hand—they say—the series terminates and there are primary premises, yet these are unknowable because incapable of demonstration, which according to them is the only form of knowledge. And since thus one cannot know the primary premises, knowledge of the conclusions which follow from them is not pure scientific knowledge nor properly knowing at all, but rests on the mere supposition that the premises are true. The other party agree with them as regards knowing, holding that it is only possible by demonstration, but they see no difficulty in holding that all truths are demonstrated, on the ground that demonstration may be circular and reciprocal.

Our own doctrine is that not all knowledge is demonstrative: on the contrary, knowledge of the immediate premises is independent of demonstration. (The necessity of this is obvious; for since we must know the prior premises from which the demonstration is drawn, and since the regress must end in immediate truths, those truths must be indemonstrable.) Such, then, is our doctrine, and in addition we maintain that besides scientific knowledge there is its originative source which enables us to recognize the definitions.

Now demonstration must be based on premises prior to and better known than the conclusion; and the same things cannot simultaneously be both prior and posterior to one another: so circular demonstration is clearly not possible in the unqualified sense of "demonstration," but only possible if "demonstration" be extended to include that other method of argument which rests on a distinction between truths prior to us and truths without qualification prior, i.e. the method by which induction produces knowledge. But if we accept this extension of its meaning, our definition of unqualified knowledge will prove faulty; for there seem to be two kinds of it. Perhaps, however, the second form of demonstration, that which proceeds from truths better known to us, is not demonstration in the unqualified sense of the term.

* * *

Since the object of pure scientific knowledge cannot be other than it is, the truth obtained by demonstrative knowledge will be necessary. And since demonstrative knowledge is only present when we have a demonstration, it follows that demonstration is an inference from necessary premises. So we must consider what are the premisses of demonstration—i.e. what is their character: and as a preliminary, let us define what we mean by an attribute "true in every instance of its subject," an "essential" attribute, and a "commensurate and universal" attribute. I call "true in every instance" what is truly predicable of all instances—not of one to the exclusion of others—and at all times, not at this or that time only; e.g. if animal is truly predicable of every instance of man, then if it be true to say "this is a man," "this is an animal" is also true, and if the one be true now the other is true now. A corresponding account holds if point is in every instance predicable as contained in line. There is evidence for this in the fact that the objection we raise against a proposition put to us as true in every instance is either an instance in which, or an occasion on which, it is not true. Essential attributes are (1) such as belong to their subject as elements in its essential nature (e.g. line thus belongs to triangle, point to line; for the very being or "substance" of triangle and line is composed of these elements, which are contained in the formulae defining triangle and line): (2) such that, while they belong to certain subjects, the subjects to which they belong are contained in the attribute's own defining formula. Thus straight and curved belong to line, odd and even, prime and compound, square and oblong, to number; and also the formula defining any one of these attributes contains its subject—e.g. line or number as the case may be.

Extending this classification to all other attributes, I distinguish those that answer the above description as belonging essentially to their respective subjects; whereas attributes related in neither of these two ways to their subjects I call accidents or "coincidents"; e.g. musical or white is a "coincident" of animal.

Further (a) that is essential which is not predicated of a subject other than itself: e.g. "the walking [thing]" walks and is white in virtue of being something else besides; whereas substance, in the sense of whatever signifies a "this somewhat," is not what it is in virtue of being something else besides. Things, then, not predicated of a subject I call essential; things predicated of a subject I call accidental or "coincidental."

In another sense again (b) a thing consequentially connected with anything is essential; one not so connected is "coincidental." An example of the latter is "While he was walking it lightened": the lightning was not due to his walking; it was, we should say, a coincidence. If, on the other hand, there is a consequential connexion, the predication is essential; e.g. if a beast dies when its throat is being cut, then its death is also essentially connected with the cutting, because the cutting was the cause of death, not death a "coincident" of the cutting.

So far then as concerns the sphere of connexions scientifically known in the unqualified sense of that term, all attributes which (within that sphere) are essential either in the sense that their subjects are contained in them, or in the sense that they are contained in their subjects, are necessary as well as consequentially connected with their subjects. For it is impossible for them not to inhere in their subjects—either simply or in the qualified sense that one or other of a pair of opposites must inhere in the subject; e.g. in line must be either straightness or curvature, in number either oddness or evenness. For within a single identical genus the contrary of a given attribute is either its privative or its contradictory; e.g. within number what is not odd is even, inasmuch as within this sphere even is a necessary consequent of not-odd. So, since any given predicate must be either affirmed or denied of any subject, essential attributes must inhere in their subjects of necessity.

Thus, then, we have established the distinction between the attribute which is "true in every instance" and the "essential" attribute.

I term "commensurately universal" an attribute which belongs to every instance of its subject, and to every instance essentially and as such; from which it clearly follows that all commensurate universals inhere *necessarily* in their subjects. The essential attribute, and the attribute that belongs to its subject as such, are identical. E.g. point and straight belong to line essentially, for they belong to line as such; and triangle as such has two right angles, for it is *essentially* equal to two right angles.

An attribute belongs commensurately and universally to a subject when it can be shown to belong to any random instance of that subject and when the subject is the first thing to which it can be shown to belong. Thus, e.g., (1) the equality of its angles to two right angles is not a commensurately universal attribute of figure. For though it is possible to show that a figure has its angles equal to two right angles, this attribute cannot be demonstrated of any figure selected at haphazard, nor in demonstrating does one take a figure at random—a square is a figure but its angles are not equal to two right angles. On the other hand, any isosceles triangle has its angles equal to two right angles, yet isosceles triangle is not the primary subject of this attribute but triangle is prior. So whatever can be shown to have its angles equal to two right angles, or to possess any other attribute, in any random instance of itself and primarily—that is the first subject to which the predicate in question belongs commensurately and universally, and the demonstration, in the essential sense, of any predicate is the proof of it as belonging to this first subject commensurately and universally: while the proof of it as belonging to the other subjects to which it attaches is demonstration only in a secondary and unessential sense. Nor again (2) is equality to two right angles a commensurately universal attribute of isosceles; it is of wider application.

* * *

Scientific knowledge is not possible through the act of perception. Even if perception as a faculty is of "the such" and not merely of a "this somewhat," yet one must at any rate actually perceive a "this somewhat," and at a definite present place and time: but that which is commensurately universal and true in all cases one cannot perceive, since it is not "this" and it is not "now"; if it were, it would not be commensurately universal—the term we apply to what is always and everywhere. Seeing, therefore, that demonstrations are commensurately universal and universals imperceptible, we clearly cannot obtain scientific knowledge by the act of perception: nay, it is obvious that even if it were possible to perceive that a triangle has its angles equal to two right angles, we should still be looking for a demonstration—we should not (as some say) possess knowledge of it; for perception must be of a particular, whereas scientific knowledge involves the recognition of the commensurate universal. So if we were on the moon, and saw the earth shutting out the sun's light, we should not know the cause of the eclipse: we should perceive the present fact of the eclipse, but not the reasoned fact at all, since the act of perception is not of the commensurate universal. I do not, of course, deny that by watching the frequent recurrence of this event we might, after tracking the commensurate universal, possess a demonstration, for the commensurate universal is elicited from the several groups of singulars.

The commensurate universal is precious because it makes clear the cause; so that in the case of facts like these which have a cause other than themselves universal knowledge is more precious than sense-perceptions and than intuition. (As regards primary truths there is of course a different account to be given.) Hence it is clear that knowledge of things demonstrable cannot be acquired by perception, unless the term perception is applied to the possession of scientific knowledge through demonstration. Nevertheless certain points do arise with regard to connexions to be proved which are referred for their explanation to a failure in sense-perception: there are cases when an act of vision would terminate our inquiry, not because in seeing we should be knowing, but because we should have elicited the universal from seeing; if, for example, we saw the pores in the glass and the light passing through, the reason of the kindling would be clear to us because we should at the same time see it in each instance and intuit that it must be so in all instances.

* * *

As regards syllogism and demonstration, the definition of, and the conditions required to produce each of them, are now clear, and with that also the definition of, and the conditions required to produce, demonstrative knowledge, since it is the same as demonstration. As to the basic premisses, how they become known and what is the developed state of knowledge of them is made clear by raising some preliminary problems.

We have already said that scientific knowledge through demonstration is impossible unless a man knows the primary immediate premisses. But there are questions which might be raised in respect of the apprehension of these immediate premisses: one might not only ask whether it is of the same kind as the apprehension of the conclusions, but also whether there is or is not scientific knowledge of both; or scientific knowledge of the latter, and of the former a different kind of knowledge; and, further, whether the developed states of knowledge are not innate but come to be in us, or are innate but at first unnoticed. Now it is strange if we possess them from birth; for it means that we possess apprehensions more accurate than demonstration and fail to notice them. If on the other hand we acquire them and do not previously possess them, how could we apprehend and learn without a basis of pre-existent knowledge? For that is impossible, as we used to find in the case of demonstration. So it emerges that neither can we possess them from birth, nor can they come to be in us if we are without knowledge of them to the extent of having no such developed state at all. Therefore we must possess a capacity of some sort, but not such as to rank higher in accuracy than these developed states. And this at least is an obvious characteristic of all animals, for they possess a congenital discriminative capacity which is called sense-perception. But though sense-perception is innate in all animals, in some the sense-impression comes to persist, in others it does not. So animals in which this persistence does not come to be have either no knowledge at all outside the act of perceiving, or no knowledge of objects of which no impression persists; animals in which it does come into being have perception and can continue to retain the sense-impression in the soul: and when such persistence is frequently repeated a further distinction at once arises between those which out of the persistence of such sense-impressions develop a power of systematising them and those which do not. So out of sense-perception comes to be what we call memory, and out of frequently repeated memories of the same thing develops experience; for a number of memories constitute a single experience. From experience again—i.e. from the universal now stabilized in its entirety within the soul, the one beside the many which is a single identity within them all—originate the skill of the craftsman and the knowledge of the man of science, skill in the sphere of coming to be and science in the sphere of being.

We conclude that these states of knowledge are neither innate in a determinate form, nor developed from other higher states of knowledge, but from sense-perception. It is like a rout in battle stopped by first one man making a stand and then another, until the original formation has been restored. The soul is so constituted as to be capable of this process.

Let us now restate the account given already, though with insufficient clearness. When one of a number of logically indiscriminable particulars has made a stand, the earliest universal is present in the soul: for though the act of sense-perception is of the particular, its content is universal—is man, for example, not the man Callias. A fresh stand is made among these rudimentary universals, and the process does not cease until the indivisible concepts, the true universals, are established: e.g. such and such a species of animal is a step towards the genus animal, which by the same process is a step towards a further generalization.

Thus it is clear that we must get to know the primary premises by induction; for the method by which even sense-perception implants the universal is inductive. Now of the thinking states by which we grasp truth, some are unfailingly true, others admit of error—opinion, for instance, and calculation, whereas scientific knowing and intuition are always true: further, no other kind of thought except intuition is more accurate than scientific knowledge, whereas primary premisses are more knowable than demonstrations, and all scientific knowledge is discursive. From these considerations it follows that there will be no scientific knowledge of the primary premisses, and since except intuition nothing can be truer than scientific knowledge, it will be intuition that apprehends the primary premisses—a result which also follows from the fact that demonstration cannot be the originative source of demonstration, nor, consequently, scientific knowledge of scientific knowledge. If, therefore, it is the only other kind of true thinking except scientific knowing, intuition will be the originative source of scientific knowledge. And the originative source of science grasps the original basic premiss, while science as a whole is similarly related as originative source to the whole body of fact.

FROM The Physics BY ARISTOTLE

Now that we have established these distinctions, we must proceed to consider causes, their character and number. Knowledge is the object of our inquiry, and men do not think they know a thing till they have grasped the "why" of it (which is to grasp its primary cause). So clearly we too must do this as regards both coming to be and passing away and every kind of physical change, in order that, knowing their principles, we may try to refer to these principles each of our problems.

In one sense, then, (1) that out of which a thing comes to be and which persists, is called "cause," e.g. the bronze of the statue, the silver of the bowl, and the genera of which the bronze and the silver are species.

In another sense (2) the form or the archetype, i.e. the statement of the essence, and its genera, are called "causes" (e.g. of the octave the relation of 2:1, and generally number), and the parts in the definition.

Again (3) the primary source of the change or coming to rest; e.g. the man who gave advice is a cause, the father is cause of the child, and generally what makes of what is made and what causes change of what is changed.

Again (4) in the sense of end or "that for the sake of which" a thing is done, e.g. health is the cause of walking about. ("Why is he walking about?" we say. "To be healthy," and, having said that, we think we have assigned the cause.) The same is true also of all the intermediate steps which are brought about through the action of something else as means towards the end, e.g. reduction of flesh, purging, drugs, or surgical instruments are means towards health. All these things are "for the sake of" the end, though they differ from one another in that some are activities, others instruments.

This then perhaps exhausts the number of ways in which the term "cause" is used.

W. D. Ross, ed., The Works of Aristotle, II (1930), 194b–195a, translated by R. P. Hardie and R. K. Gaye. Reprinted by permission of The Clarendon Press, Oxford.

As the word has several senses, it follows that there are several causes of the same thing (not merely in virtue of a concomitant attribute), e.g. both the art of the sculptor and the bronze are causes of the statue. These are causes of the statue *qua* statue, not in virtue of anything else that it may be—only not in the same way, the one being the material cause, the other the cause whence the motion comes. Some things cause each other reciprocally, e.g. hard work causes fitness and *vice versa,* but again not in the same way, but the one as end, the other as the origin of change. Further the same thing is the cause of contrary results. For that which by its presence brings about one result is sometimes blamed for bringing about the contrary by its absence. Thus we ascribe the wreck of a ship to the absence of the pilot whose presence was the cause of its safety.

There were other ways in antiquity to account for the physical world than through recourse to Platonic ideas or Aristotelian forms. Might not reality consist of atoms, themselves not capable of being perceived but constituting the bodies around us? The atomic theory was to have a most successful future, but in antiquity it was regarded as atheistic and subversive of public order. One of the philosophical problems the atomic theory had to confront was how, if atoms were imperceptible, we could know anything of them. And could we know enough to use them to explain things? These were the questions that Epicurus (341–270 B.C.) set out to answer in his letter to Herodotus.

Epicurus' Letter to Herodotus

Having made these points clear, we must now consider things imperceptible to the senses. First of all, that nothing is created out of that which does not exist: for if it were, everything would be created out of everything with no need of seeds. And again, if that which disappears were destroyed into that which did not exist, all things would have perished, since that into which they were dissolved would not exist. Furthermore, the universe always was such as it is now, and always will be the same. For there is nothing into which it changes: for outside the universe there is nothing which could come into it and bring about the change.

C. Bailey, *Epicurus: The Extant Remains* (1926), pp. 21, 23, 25, 27, 29, 31, 33, 49, 51, 53. Reprinted by permission of The Clarendon Press, Oxford.

Moreover, the universe is (bodies and space): for that bodies exist, sense itself witnesses in the experience of all men, and in accordance with the evidence of sense we must of necessity judge of the imperceptible by reasoning, as I have already said. And if there were not that which we term void and place and intangible existence, bodies would have nowhere to exist and nothing through which to move, as they are seen to move. And besides these two nothing can even be thought of either by conception or on the analogy of things conceivable such as could be grasped as whole existences and not spoken of as the accidents or properties of such existences. Furthermore, among bodies some are compounds, and others those of which compounds are formed. And these latter are indivisible and unalterable (if, that is, all things are not to be destroyed into the non-existent, but something permanent is to remain behind at the dissolution of compounds): they are completely solid in nature, and can by no means be dissolved in any part. So it must needs be that the first-beginnings are indivisible corporeal existences.

Moreover, the universe is boundless. For that which is bounded has an extreme point: and the extreme point is seen against something else. So that as it has no extreme point, it has no limit; and as it has no limit, it must be boundless and not bounded. Furthermore, the infinite is boundless both in the number of the bodies and in the extent of the void. For if on the one hand the void were boundless, and the bodies limited in number, the bodies could not stay anywhere, but would be carried about and scattered through the infinite void, not having other bodies to support them and keep them in place by means of collisions. But if, on the other hand, the void were limited, the infinite bodies would not have room wherein to take their place.

Besides this the indivisible and solid bodies, out of which too the compounds are created and into which they are dissolved, have an incomprehensible number of varieties in shape: for it is not possible that such great varieties of things should arise from the same (atomic) shapes, if they are limited in number. And so in each shape the atoms are quite infinite in number, but their differences of shape are not quite infinite, but only incomprehensible in number.

And the atoms move continuously for all time, some of them falling straight down, others swerving, and others recoiling from their collisions. And of the latter, some are borne on separating to a long distance from one another, while others again recoil and recoil, whenever they chance to be checked by the interlacing with others, or else shut in by atoms interlaced around them. For on the one hand the nature of the void which separates each atom by itself brings this about, as it is not able to afford resistance, and on the other hand the hardness which belongs to the atoms makes them recoil after collision to as great a distance as the interlacing permits separation after the collision. And these motions have no beginning, since the atoms and the void are the cause.

These brief sayings, if all these points are borne in mind, afford a sufficient outline for our understanding of the nature of existing things.

Furthermore, there are infinite worlds both like and unlike this world of ours. For the atoms being infinite in number, as was proved already, are borne on far out into space. For those atoms, which are of such nature that a world could be created out of them or made by them, have not been used up either on one world or on a limited number of worlds, nor again on all the worlds which are alike, or on those which are different from these. So that there nowhere exists an obstacle to the infinite number of the worlds.

* * *

Now we must suppose too that it is when something enters us from external objects that we not only see but think of their shapes. For external objects could not make on us an impression of the nature of their own colour and shape by means of the air which lies between us and them, nor again by means of the rays or effluences of any sort which pass from us to them— nearly so well as if models, similar in colour and shape, leave the objects and enter according to their respective size either into our sight or into our mind; moving along swiftly, and so by this means reproducing the image of a single continuous thing and preserving the corresponding sequence of qualities and movements from the original object as the result of their uniform contact with us, kept up by the vibration of the atoms deep in the interior of the concrete body.

* * *

Moreover, we must suppose that the atoms do not possess any of the qualities belonging to perceptible things, except shape, weight, and size, and all that necessarily goes with shape. For every quality changes; but the atoms do not change at all, since there must needs be something which remains solid and indissoluble at the dissolution of compounds, which can cause changes; not changes into the non-existent or from the non-existent, but changes effected by the shifting of position of some particles, and by the addition or departure of others. For this reason it is essential that the bodies which shift their position should be imperishable and should not possess the nature of what changes, but parts and configuration of their own. For thus much must needs remain constant. For even in things perceptible to us which change their shape by the withdrawal of matter it is seen that shape remains to them, whereas the qualities do not remain in the changing object, in the way in which shape is left behind, but are lost from the entire body. Now these particles which are left behind are sufficient to cause the differences in compound bodies, since it is essential that some things should be left behind and not be destroyed into the non-existent.

* * *

Furthermore, the motions of the heavenly bodies and their turnings and eclipses and risings and settings, and kindred phenomena to these, must not be thought to be due to any being who controls and ordains or has ordained them and at the same time enjoys perfect bliss together with immortality (for trouble and care and anger and kindness are not consistent with a life of blessedness, but these things come to pass where there is weakness and fear and dependence on neighbours). Nor again must we believe that they, which are but fire agglomerated in a mass, possess blessedness, and voluntarily take upon themselves these movements. But we must preserve their full majestic significance in all expressions which we apply to such conceptions, in order that there may not arise out of them opinions contrary to this notion of majesty. Otherwise this very contradiction will cause the greatest disturbance in men's souls. Therefore we must believe that it is due to the original inclusion of matter in such agglomerations during the birth-process of the world that this law of regular succession is also brought about.

Furthermore, we must believe that to discover accurately the cause of the most essential facts is the function of the science of nature, and that blessedness for us in the knowledge of celestial phenomena lies in this and in the understanding of the nature of the existences seen in these celestial phenomena, and of all else that is akin to the exact knowledge requisite for our happiness: in knowing too that what occurs in several ways or is capable of being otherwise has no place here, but that nothing which suggests doubt or alarm can be included at all in that which is naturally immortal and blessed. Now this we can ascertain by our mind is absolutely the case. But what falls within the investigation of risings and settings and turnings and eclipses, and all that is akin to this, is no longer of any value for the happiness which knowledge brings, but persons who have perceived all this, but yet do not know what are the natures of these things and what are the essential causes, are still in fear, just as if they did not know these things at all: indeed, their fear may be even greater, since the wonder which arises out of the observation of these things cannot discover any solution or realize the regulation of the essentials. And for this very reason, even if we discover several causes for turnings and settings and risings and eclipses and the like, as has been the case already in our investigation of detail, we must not suppose that our inquiry into these things has not reached sufficient accuracy to contribute to our peace of mind and happiness. So we must carefully consider in how many ways a similar phenomenon is produced on earth, when we reason about the causes of celestial phenomena and all that is imperceptible to the senses; and we must despise those persons who do not recognize either what exists or comes into being in one way only, or that which may occur in several ways in the case of things which can only be seen by us from a distance, and further are not aware under what conditions it is impossible to have peace of mind. If, therefore, we think that a phenomenon probably occurs in some such particular way, and that in circumstances under which it is equally possible for us to be at peace, when we realize that it may occur in several ways, we shall be just as little disturbed as if we know that it occurs in some such particular way.

And besides all these matters in general we must grasp this point, that the principal disturbance in the minds of men arises because they think that these celestial bodies are blessed and immortal, and yet have wills and actions and motives inconsistent with these attributes; and because they are always expecting or imagining some everlasting misery, such as is depicted in legends, or even fear the loss of feeling in death as though it would concern them themselves; and, again, because they are brought to this pass not by reasoned opinion, but rather by some irrational presentiment, and therefore, as they do not know the limits of pain, they suffer a disturbance equally great or even more extensive than if they had reached this belief by opinion. But peace of mind is being delivered from all this, and having a constant memory of the general and most essential principles.

Wherefore we must pay attention to internal feelings and to external sensations in general and in particular, according as the subject is general or particular, and to every immediate intuition in accordance with each of the standards of judgement. For if we pay attention to these, we shall rightly trace the causes whence arose our mental disturbance and fear, and, by learning the true causes of celestial phenomena and all other occurrences that come to pass from time to time, we shall free ourselves from all which produces the utmost fear in other men.

2

THE
ACHIEVEMENT
OF ANCIENT
SCIENCE

The physician's main task is to cure the sick. To do this, or to recognize that cure is impossible, the physician must first know what the sickness is. Most illnesses have a cluster of symptoms that permit them to be diagnosed and, once diagnosed, either to be cured or to have their course predicted. The "case history" is as old as medicine itself. The question is: Is it science?

FROM The Book of Prognostics BY HIPPOCRATES

1. It appears to me a most excellent thing for the physician to cultivate Prognosis; for by foreseeing and foretelling, in the presence of the sick, the present, the past, and the future, and explaining the omissions which patients have been guilty of, he will be the more readily believed to be acquainted with the circumstances of the sick; so that men will have confidence to intrust themselves to such a physician. And he will manage the cure best who has foreseen what is to happen from the present state of matters. For it is impossible to make all the sick well; this, indeed, would have been better than to be able to foretell what is going to happen; but since men die, some even before calling the physician, from the violence of the disease, and some die immediately after calling him, having lived, perhaps, only one day or a little longer, and before the physician could bring his art to counteract the disease; it therefore becomes necessary to know the nature of such affections, how far

The Genuine Works of Hippocrates, I (1869), 234–237, 374–377, translated by Francis Adams.

they are above the powers of the constitution; and, moreover, if there be anything divine in the diseases, and to learn a foreknowledge of this also. Thus a man will be the more esteemed to be a good physician, for he will be the better able to treat those aright who can be saved, from having long anticipated everything; and by seeing and announcing beforehand those who will live and those who will die, he will thus escape censure.

2. He should observe thus in acute diseases: first, the countenance of the patient, if it be like those of persons in health, and more so, if like itself, for this is the best of all; whereas the most opposite to it is the worst, such as the following: *a sharp nose, hollow eyes, collapsed temples; the ears cold, contracted, and their lobes turned out; the skin about the forehead being rough, distended, and parched; the colour of the whole face being green, black, livid, or lead-coloured.* If the countenance be such at the commencement of the disease, and if this cannot be accounted for from the other symptoms, inquiry must be made whether the patient has long wanted sleep; whether his bowels have been very loose; and whether he has suffered from want of food; and if any of these causes be confessed to, the danger is to be reckoned so far less; and it becomes obvious, in the course of a day and a night, whether or not the appearance of the countenance proceed from these causes. But if none of these be said to exist, and if the symptoms do not subside in the aforesaid time, it is to be known for certain that death is at hand. And, also, if the disease be in a more advanced stage either on the third or fourth day, and the countenance be such, the same inquiries as formerly directed are to be made, and the other symptoms are to be noted, those in the whole countenance, those on the body, and those in the eyes; for if they shun the light, or weep involuntarily, or squint, or if the one be less than the other, or if the white of them be red, livid, or has black veins in it; if there be a gum upon the eyes, if they are restless, protruding, or are become very hollow; and if the countenance be squalid and dark, or the colour of the whole face be changed—all these are to be reckoned bad and fatal symptoms. The physician should also observe the appearance of the eyes from below the eyelids in sleep; for when a portion of the white appears, owing to the eyelids not being closed together, and when this is not connected with diarrhoea or purgation from medicine, or when the patient does not sleep thus from habit, it is to be reckoned an unfavorable and very deadly symptom; but if the eyelid be contracted, livid, or pale, or also the lip, or nose, along with some of the other symptoms, one may know for certain that death is close at hand. It is a mortal symptom, also, when the lips are relaxed, pendent, cold, and blanched.

* * *

CASE V.—The wife of Epicrates, who was lodged at the house of Archigetes, being near the term of delivery, was seized with a violent rigor, and, as was said, she did not become heated; next day the same. On the third, she was delivered of a daughter, and everything went on properly. On the day following her delivery, she was seized with acute fever, pain in the cardiac region of the stomach, and in the genital parts. Having had a suppository, was in so far relieved; pain in the head, neck, and loins; no sleep; alvine discharges scanty, bilious, thin, and unmixed; urine thin, and blackish. Towards the night of the sixth day from the time she was seized with the fever, became delirious. On the seventh, all the symptoms exacerbated; insomnolency, delirium, thirst; stools bilious, and high coloured. On the eighth, had a rigor; slept more. On the ninth, the same. On the tenth, her limbs painfully affected; pain again of the cardiac region of the stomach; heaviness of the head; no delirium; slept more; bowels constipated. On the eleventh, passed urine of a better colour, and having an abundant sediment, felt lighter. On the fourteenth, had a rigor; acute fever. On the fifteenth, had a copious vomiting of bilious and yellow matters; sweated; fever gone; at night acute fever; urine thick, sediment white. On the seventeenth, an exacerbation; night uncomfortable; no sleep; delirium. On the eighteenth, thirsty; tongue parched; no sleep; much delirium; legs painfully affected. About the twentieth, in the morning, had a slight rigor; was comatose; slept tranquilly; had slight vomiting of bilious and black matters; towards night deafness. About the twenty-first, weight generally in the left side, with pain; slight cough; urine thick, muddy, and reddish; when allowed to stand, had no sediment; in other respects felt lighter; fever not gone; fauces painful from the commencement, and red; uvula retracted; defluxion remained acrid, pungent, and saltish throughout. About the twenty-seventh, free of fever; sediment in the urine; pain in the side. About the thirty-first, was attacked with fever, bilious diarrhoea; slight bilious vomiting on the fortieth. Had a complete crisis, and was freed from the fever on the eightieth day.

CASE VI.—Cleonactides, who was lodged above the Temple of Hercules, was seized with a fever in an irregular form; was pained in the head and left side from the commencement, and had other pains resembling those produced by fatigue; paroxysms of the fevers inconstant and irregular; occasional sweats; the paroxysms generally attacked on the critical days. About the twenty-fourth was cold in the extremities of the hands, vomitings bilious, yellow, and frequent, soon turning to a verdigris-green colour; general relief. About the thirtieth, began to have hemorrhage from both nostrils, and this continued in an irregular manner until near the crisis; did not loathe food, and had no thirst throughout, nor was troubled with insomnolency; urine thin, and not devoid of colour. When about the thirtieth day, passed reddish urine, having a copious red sediment; was relieved; but afterwards the characters of the urine varied, sometimes having sediment, and sometimes not. On the sixtieth, the sediment in the urine copious, white, and smooth; all the symptoms ameliorated; intermission of the fever; urine thin, and well coloured. On the seventieth, fever gone for ten days. On the eightieth had a rigor, was seized with acute fever, sweated much; a red, smooth sediment in the urine; had a perfect crisis.

CASE VII.—Meton was seized with fever; there was a painful weight in the loins. Next day, after drinking water pretty copiously, had proper evacuations from the bowels. On the third, heaviness of the head, stools thin, bilious, and reddish. On the fourth, all the symptoms exacerbated; had twice a scanty trickling of blood from the right nostril; passed an uncomfortable night; alvine discharges like those on the third day; urine darkish, had a darkish cloud floating in it, of a scattered form, which did not subside. On the fifth, a copious hemorrhage of pure blood from the left nostril; he sweated, and had a crisis. After the fever restless, and had some delirium; urine thin, and darkish; had an affusion of warm water on the head; slept, and recovered his senses. In this case there was no relapse, but there were frequent hemorrhages after the crisis.

CASE VIII.—Erasinus, who lived near the Canal of Bootes, was seized with fever after supper; passed the night in an agitated state. During the first day quiet, but in pain at night. On the second, symptoms all exacerbated; at night delirious. On the third, was in a painful condition; great incoherence. On the fourth, in a most uncomfortable state; had no sound sleep at night, but dreaming and talking; then all the appearances worse, of a formidable and alarming character; fear, impatience. On the morning of the fifth, was composed, and quite coherent, but long before noon was furiously mad, so that he could not constrain himself; extremities cold, and somewhat livid; urine without sediment; died about sunset. The fever in this case was accompanied by sweats throughout; the hypochondria were in a state of meteorism, with distension and pain; the urine was black, had round substances floating in it, which did not subside; the alvine evacuations were not stopped; thirst throughout not great; much spasms with sweats about the time of death.

CASE IX.—Criton, in Thasus, while still on foot, and going about, was seized with a violent pain in the great toe; he took to bed the same day, had rigors and nausea, recovered his heat slightly, at night was delirious. On the second, swelling of the whole foot, and about the ankle erythema, with distension, and small bullae (phlyctaenae); acute fever; he became furiously deranged; alvine discharges bilious, unmixed, and rather frequent. He died on the second day from the commencement.

Aristotle was not only a great philosopher but a practicing scientist. His works include treatises on the heavens, meteorology, psychology, physics, and physiology, as well as on natural history and political science. Everything he wrote was expressed in terms of his philosophical system and his keen and exact observations were interpreted in philosophical terms. The result was one of the great syntheses of the history of science, not to be superseded until modern times.

FROM De Caelo (On the Heavens) BY ARISTOTLE

The question as to the nature of the whole, whether it is infinite in size or limited in its total mass, is a matter for subsequent inquiry. We will now speak of those parts of the whole which are specifically distinct. Let us take this as our starting-point. All natural bodies and magnitudes we hold to be, as such, capable of locomotion; for nature, we say, is their principle of movement. But all movement that is in place, all locomotion, as we term it, is either straight or circular or a combination of these two, which are the only simple movements. And the reason of this is that these two, the straight and the circular line, are the only simple magnitudes. Now revolution about the centre is circular motion, while the upward and downward movements are in a straight line, "upward" meaning motion away from the centre, and "downward" motion towards it. All simple motion, then, must be motion either away from or towards or about the centre. This seems to be in exact accord with what we said above: as body found its completion in three dimensions, so its movement completes itself in three forms.

Bodies are either simple or compounded of such; and by simple bodies I mean those which possess a principle of movement in their own nature, such as fire and earth with their kinds, and whatever is akin to them. Necessarily, then, movements also will be either simple or in some sort compound—simple in the case of the simple bodies, compound in that of the composite—and in the latter case the motion will be that of the simple body which prevails in the composition. Supposing, then, that there is such a thing as simple movement, and that circular movement is an instance of it, and that both movement of a simple body is simple and simple movement is of a simple body (for if it is movement of a compound it will be in virtue of a prevailing simple element), then there must necessarily be some simple body which revolves naturally and in virtue of its own nature with a circular movement. By constraint, of course, it may be brought to move with the motion of something else different from itself, but it cannot so move naturally, since there is one sort of movement natural to each of the simple bodies. Again, if the unnatural movement is the contrary of the natural and a thing can have no more than one contrary, it will follow that circular movement, being a simple motion, must be unnatural, if it is not natural, to the body moved. If then (1) the body, whose movement is circular, is fire or some other element, its natu-

---

W. D. Ross, ed., *The Works of Aristotle*, II (1930), 268b–270b, 286a–286b, 289a–290a, 291a–291b, translated by J. L. Stocks.

ral motion must be the contrary of the circular motion. But a single thing has a single contrary; and upward and downward motion are the contraries of one another. If, on the other hand, (2) the body moving with this circular motion which is unnatural to it is something different from the elements, there will be some other motion which is natural to it. But this cannot be. For if the natural motion is upward, it will be fire or air, and if downward, water or earth. Further, this circular motion is necessarily primary. For the perfect is naturally prior to the imperfect, and the circle is a perfect thing. This cannot be said of any straight line: —nor of an infinite line; for, if it were perfect, it would have a limit and an end: nor of any finite line; for in every case there is something beyond it, since any finite line can be extended. And so, since the prior movement belongs to the body which is naturally prior, and circular movement is prior to straight, and movement in a straight line belongs to simple bodies—fire moving straight upward and earthy bodies straight downward towards the centre—since this is so, it follows that circular movement also must be the movement of some simple body. For the movement of composite bodies is, as we said, determined by that simple body which preponderates in the composition. These premises clearly give the conclusion that there is in nature some bodily substance other than the formations we know, prior to them all and more divine than they. But it may also be proved as follows. We may take it that all movement is either natural or unnatural, and that the movement which is unnatural to one body is natural to another—as, for instance, is the case with the upward and downward movements, which are natural and unnatural to fire and earth respectively. It necessarily follows that circular movement, being unnatural to these bodies, is the natural movement of some other. Further, if, on the one hand, circular movement is *natural* to something, it must surely be some simple and primary body which is ordained to move with a natural circular motion, as fire is ordained to fly up and earth down. If, on the other hand, the movement of the rotating bodies about the centre is *unnatural,* it would be remarkable and indeed quite inconceivable that this movement alone should be continuous and eternal, being nevertheless contrary to nature. At any rate the evidence of all other cases goes to show that it is the unnatural which quickest passes away. And so, if, as some say, the body so moved is fire, this movement is just as unnatural to it as downward movement; for any one can see that fire moves in a straight line away from the centre. On all these grounds, therefore, we may infer with confidence that there is something beyond the bodies that are about us on this earth, different and separate from them; and that the superior glory of its nature is proportionate to its distance from this world of ours.

*   *   *

It is equally reasonable to assume that this body will be ungenerated and indestructible and exempt from increase and alteration, since everything that comes to be comes into being from its contrary and in some substrate, and passes away likewise in a substrate by the action of the contrary into the contrary, as we explained in our opening discussions. Now the motions of contraries are contrary. If then this body can have no contrary, because there can be no contrary motion to the circular, nature seems justly to have exempted from contraries the body which was to be ungenerated and indestructible. For it is in contraries that generation and decay subsist. Again, that which is subject to increase increases upon contact with a kindred body, which is resolved into its matter. But there is nothing out of which this body can have been generated. And if it is exempt from increase and diminution, the same reasoning leads us to suppose that it is also unalterable. For alteration is movement in respect of quality; and qualitative states and dispositions, such as health and disease, do not come into being without changes of properties. But all natural bodies which change their properties we see to be subject without exception to increase and diminution. This is the case, for instance, with the bodies of animals and their parts and with vegetable bodies, and similarly also with those of the elements. And so, if the body which moves with a circular motion cannot admit of increase or diminution, it is reasonable to suppose that it is also unalterable.

The reasons why the primary body is eternal and not subject to increase or diminution, but unaging and unalterable and unmodified, will be clear from what has been said to any one who believes in our assumptions. Our theory seems to confirm experience and to be confirmed by it. For all men have some conception of the nature of the gods, and all who believe in the existence of gods at all, whether barbarian or Greek, agree in allotting the highest place to the deity, surely because they suppose that immortal is linked with immortal and regard any other supposition as inconceivable. If then there is, as there certainly is, anything divine, what we have just said about the primary bodily substance was well said. The mere evidence of the senses is enough to convince us of this, at least with human certainty. For in the whole range of time past, so far as our inherited records reach, no change appears to have taken place either in the whole scheme of the outermost heaven or in any of its proper parts. The common name, too, which has been handed down from our distant ancestors even to our own day, seems to show that they conceived of it in the fashion which we have been expressing. The same ideas, one must believe, recur in men's minds not once or twice but again and again. And so, implying that the primary body is something else beyond earth, fire, air, and water, they gave the highest place a name of its own, *aither,* derived from the fact that it "runs always" for an eternity of time. Anaxagoras, however, scandalously misuses this name, taking *aither* as equivalent to fire.

It is also clear from what has been said why the number of what we call simple bodies cannot be greater than it is. The motion of a simple body must itself be simple, and we assert that there are only these two simple motions, the circular and the straight, the latter being subdivided into motion away from and motion towards the centre.

* * *

Since circular motion is not the contrary of the reverse circular motion, we must consider why there is more than one motion, though we have to pursue our inquiries at a distance—a distance created not so much by our spatial position as by the fact that our senses enable us to perceive very few of the attributes of the heavenly bodies. But let not that deter us. The reason must be sought in the following facts. Everything which has a function exists for its function. The activity of God is immortality, i.e. eternal life. Therefore the movement of that which is divine must be eternal. But such is the heaven, viz. a divine body, and for that reason to it is given the circular body whose nature it is to move always in a circle. Why, then, is not the whole body of the heaven of the same character as that part? Because there must be something at rest at the centre of the revolving body; and of that body no part can be at rest, either elsewhere or at the center. It could do so only if the body's natural movement were towards the centre. But the circular movement is natural, since otherwise it could not be eternal: for nothing unnatural is eternal. The unnatural is subsequent to the natural, being a derangement of the natural which occurs in the course of its generation. Earth then has to exist; for it is earth which is at rest at the centre. (At present we may take this for granted: it shall be explained later.) But if earth must exist, so must fire. For, if one of a pair of contraries naturally exists, the other, if it is really contrary, exists also naturally. In some form it must be present, since the matter of contraries is the same. Also, the positive is prior to its privation (warm, for instance, to cold), and rest and heaviness stand for the privation of lightness and movement. But further, if fire and earth exist, the intermediate bodies must exist also: for each element stands in a contrary relation to every other. (This, again, we will here take for granted and try later to explain.) With these four elements generation clearly is involved, since none of them can be eternal: for contraries interact with one another and destroy one another. Further, it is inconceivable that a movable body should be eternal, if its movement cannot be regarded as naturally eternal: and these bodies we know to possess movement. Thus we see that generation is necessarily involved. But if so, there must be at least one other circular motion: for a single movement of the whole heaven would necessitate an identical relation of the elements of bodies to one another. This matter also shall be cleared up in what follows: but for the present so much is clear, that the reason why there is more than one circular body is the necessity of generation, which follows on the presence of fire, which, with that of the other bodies, follows on that of earth; and earth is required because eternal movement in one body necessitates eternal rest in another.

The shape of the heaven is of necessity spherical; for that is the shape most appropriate to its substance and also by nature primary.

* * *

We have next to speak of the stars, as they are called, of their composition, shape, and movements. It would be most natural and consequent upon what has been said that each of the stars should be composed of that substance in which their path lies, since, as we said, there is an element whose natural movement is circular. In so saying we are only following the same line of thought as those who say that the stars are fiery because they believe the upper body to be fire, the presumption being that a thing is composed of the same stuff as that in which it is situated. The warmth and light which proceed from them are caused by the friction set up in the air by their motion. Movement tends to create fire in wood, stone, and iron; and with even more reason should it have that effect on air, a substance which is closer to fire than these. An example is that of missiles, which as they move are themselves fired so strongly that leaden balls are melted; and if they are fired the surrounding air must be similarly affected. Now while the missiles are heated by reason of their motion in air, which is turned into fire by the agitation produced by their movement, the upper bodies are carried on a moving sphere, so that, though they are not themselves fired, yet the air underneath the sphere of the revolving body is necessarily heated by its motion, and particularly in that part where the sun is attached to it. Hence warmth increases as the sun gets nearer or higher or overhead. Of the fact, then, that the stars are neither fiery nor move in fire, enough has been said.

Since changes evidently occur not only in the position of the stars but also in that of the whole heaven, there are three possibilities. Either (1) both are at rest, or (2) both are in motion, or (3) the one is at rest and the other in motion.

(1) That both should be at rest is impossible; for, if the earth is at rest, the hypothesis does not account for the observations; and we take it as granted that the earth is at rest. It remains either that both are moved, or that the one is moved and the other at rest.

(2) On the view, first, that both are in motion, we have the absurdity that the stars and the circles move with the same speed, i.e. that the pace of every star is that of the circle in which it moves. For star and circle are seen to come back to the same place at the same moment; from which it follows that the star has traversed the circle and the circle has completed its own movement, i.e. traversed its own circumference, at one and the same moment. But it is difficult to conceive that the pace of each star should be exactly proportioned to the size of its circle. That the pace of each circle should be proportionate to its size is not absurd but inevitable: but that the same should be true of the movement of the stars contained in the circles is quite incredible. For if, on the one hand, we suppose that the star which moves on the greater circle is necessarily swifter, clearly we also admit that if stars shifted their position so as to exchange circles, the slower would become swifter and the swifter slower. But this would show that their movement was not their own, but due to the circles. If, on the other hand, the arrangement was a chance combina-

tion, the coincidence in every case of a greater circle with a swifter movement of the star contained in it is too much to believe. In one or two cases it might not inconceivably fall out so, but to imagine it in every case alike is a mere fiction. Besides, chance has no place in that which is natural, and what happens everywhere and in every case is no matter of chance.

(3) The same absurdity is equally plain if it is supposed that the circles stand still and that it is the stars themselves which move. For it will follow that the outer stars are the swifter, and that the pace of the stars corresponds to the size of their circles.

Since, then, we cannot reasonably suppose either that both are in motion or that the star alone moves, the remaining alternative is that the circles should move, while the stars are at rest and move with the circles to which they are attached. Only on this supposition are we involved in no absurd consequence. For, in the first place, the quicker movement of the larger circle is natural when all the circles are attached to the same centre. Whenever bodies are moving with their proper motion, the larger moves quicker. It is the same here with the revolving bodies: for the arc intercepted by two radii will be larger in the larger circle, and hence it is not surprising that the revolution of the larger circle should take the same time as that of the smaller. And secondly, the fact that the heavens do not break in pieces follows not only from this but also from the proof already given of the continuity of the whole.

Again, since the stars are spherical, as our opponents assert and we may consistently admit, inasmuch as we construct them out of the spherical body, and since the spherical body has two movements proper to itself, namely rolling and spinning, it follows that if the stars have a movement of their own, it will be one of these. But neither is observed. (1) Suppose them to *spin*. They would then stay where they were, and not change their place, as, by observation and general consent, they do. Further, one would expect them all to exhibit the same movement: but the only star which appears to possess this movement is the sun, at sunrise or sunset, and this appearance is due not to the sun itself but to the distance from which we observe it. The visual ray being excessively prolonged becomes weak and wavering. The same reason probably accounts for the apparent twinkling of the fixed stars and the absence of twinkling in the planets. The planets are near, so that the visual ray reaches them in its full vigour, but when it comes to the fixed stars it is quivering because of the distance and its excessive extension; and its tremor produces an appearance of movement in the star: for it makes no difference whether movement is set up in the ray or in the object of vision.

(2) On the other hand, it is also clear that the stars do not *roll*. For rolling involves rotation: but the "face," as it is called, of the moon is always seen. Therefore, since any movement of their own which the stars possessed would presumably be one proper to themselves, and no such movement is observed in them, clearly they have no movement of their own.

There is, further, the absurdity that nature has bestowed upon them no organ appropriate to such movement. For nature leaves nothing to chance, and would not, while caring for animals, overlook things so precious. Indeed, nature seems deliberately to have stripped them of everything which makes self-originated progression possible, and to have removed them as far as possible from things which have organs of movement. This is just why it seems proper that the whole heaven and every star should be spherical. For while of all shapes the sphere is the most convenient for movement in one place, making possible, as it does, the swiftest and most self-contained motion, for forward movement it is the most unsuitable, least of all resembling shapes which are self-moved, in that it has no dependent or projecting part, as a rectilinear figure has, and is in fact as far as possible removed in shape from ambulatory bodies. Since, therefore, the heavens have to move in one place, and the stars are not required to move themselves forward, it is natural that both should be spherical—a shape which best suits the movement of the one and the immobility of the other.

* * *

That the stars are spherical and are not self-moved, has now been explained.

With their order—I mean the position of each, as involving the priority of some and the posteriority of others, and their respective distances from the extremity—with this astronomy may be left to deal, since the astronomical discussion is adequate. This discussion shows that the movements of the several stars depend, as regards the varieties of speed which they exhibit, on the distance of each from the extremity. It is established that the outermost revolution of the heavens is a simple movement and the swiftest of all, and that the movement of all other bodies is composite and relatively slow, for the reason that each is moving on its own circle with the reverse motion to that of the heavens. This at once leads us to expect that the body which is nearest to that first simple revolution should take the longest time to complete its circle, and that which is farthest from it the shortest, the others taking a longer time the nearer they are and a shorter time the farther away they are. For it is the nearest body which is most strongly influenced, and the most remote, by reason of its distance, which is least affected, the influence on the intermediate bodies varying, as the mathematicians show, with their distance.

With regard to the shape of each star, the most reasonable view is that they are spherical. It has been shown that it is not in their nature to move themselves, and, since nature is no wanton or random creator, clearly she will have given things which possess no movement a shape particularly unadapted to movement. Such a shape is the sphere, since it possesses no instrument of movement. Clearly then their mass will have the form of a sphere. Again, what holds of one holds of all, and the evidence of our eyes shows us that the moon is spherical. For how else should the moon as it waxes and wanes show for the most part a crescent-shaped or gibbous figure, and only at one moment a half-moon? And astronomical arguments give further confirmation; for no other hypothesis accounts for the crescent shape of the sun's eclipses. One, then, of the heavenly bodies being spherical, clearly the rest will be spherical also.

Aristotle was the son of a physician and an excellent observer of animal life. In his *History of Animals* he described what he had seen; in the *Parts of Animals* he explained why his observations were as they were.

FROM De Partibus Animalium (Parts of Animals)
BY ARISTOTLE

Of things constituted by nature some are ungenerated, imperishable, and eternal, while others are subject to generation and decay. The former are excellent beyond compare and divine, but less accessible to knowledge. The evidence that might throw light on them, and on the problems which we long to solve respecting them, is furnished but scantily by sensation; whereas respecting perishable plants and animals we have abundant information, living as we do in their midst, and ample data may be collected concerning all their various kinds, if only we are willing to take sufficient pains. Both departments, however, have their special charm. The scanty conceptions to which we can attain of celestial things give us, from their excellence, more pleasure than all our knowledge of the world in which we live; just as a half-glimpse of persons that we love is more delightful than a leisurely view of other things, whatever their number and dimensions. On the other hand, in certitude and in completeness our knowledge of terrestrial things has the advantage. Moreover, their greater nearness and affinity to us balances somewhat the loftier interest of the heavenly things that are the objects of the higher philosophy. Having already treated of the celestial world, as far as our conjectures could reach, we proceed to treat of animals, without omitting, to the best of our ability, any member of the kingdom, however ignoble. For if some have no graces to charm the sense, yet even these, by disclosing to intellectual perception the artistic spirit that designed them, give immense pleasure to all who can trace links of causation, and are inclined to philosophy. Indeed, it would be strange if mimic representations of them were attractive, because they disclose the mimetic skill of the painter or sculptor, and the

W. D. Ross, ed., *The Works of Aristotle*, V (1912), 644b–645b, 658b–660a, translated by William Ogle.

original realities themselves were not more interesting, to all at any rate who have eyes to discern the reasons that determine their formation. We therefore must not recoil with childish aversion from the examination of the humbler animals. Every realm of nature is marvellous: and as Heraclitus, when the strangers who came to visit him found him warming himself at the furnace in the kitchen and hesitated to go in, is reported to have bidden them not to be afraid to enter, as even in that kitchen divinities were present, so we should venture on the study of every kind of animal without distaste; for each and all will reveal to us something natural and something beautiful. Absence of haphazard and conduciveness of everything to an end are to be found in nature's works in the highest degree, and the resultant end of her generations and combinations is a form of the beautiful.

* * *

The course of exposition must be first to state the attributes common to whole groups of animals, and then to attempt to give their explanation. Many groups, as already noticed, present common attributes, that is to say, in some cases absolutely identical affections, and absolutely identical organs,—feet, feathers, scales, and the like; while in other groups the affections and organs are only so far identical as that they are analogous. For instance, some groups have lungs, others have no lung, but an organ analogous to a lung in its place; some have blood, others have no blood, but a fluid analogous to blood, and with the same office. To treat of the common attributes in connexion with each individual group would involve, as already suggested, useless iteration. For many groups have common attributes. So much for this topic.

As every instrument and every bodily member subserves some partial end, that is to say, some special action, so the whole body must be destined to minister to some plenary sphere of action. Thus the saw is made for sawing, for sawing is a function, and not sawing for the saw. Similarly, the body too must somehow or other be made for the soul, and each part of it for some subordinate function, to which it is adapted.

We have, then, first to describe the common functions, common, that is, to the whole animal kingdom, or to certain large groups, or to the members of a species. In other words, we have to describe the attributes common to all animals, or to assemblages, like the class of Birds, of closely allied groups differentiated by gradation, or to groups like Man not differentiated into subordinate groups. In the first case the common attributes may be called analogous, in the second generic, in the third specific.

When a function is ancillary to another, a like relation manifestly obtains between the organs which discharge these functions; and similarly, if one function is prior to and the end of another, their respective organs will stand to each other in the same relation. Thirdly, the existence of these parts involves that of other things as their necessary consequents.

Instances of what I mean by functions and affections are Reproduction, Growth, Copulation, Waking, Sleep, Locomotion, and other similar vital actions. Instances of what I mean by parts are Nose, Eye, Face, and other so-called members or limbs, and also the more elementary parts of which these are made. So much for the method to be pursued. Let us now try to set forth the causes of all vital phenomena, whether universal or particular, and in so doing let us follow that order of exposition which conforms, as we have indicated, to the order of nature.

* * *

Both eyebrows and eyelashes exist for the protection of the eyes; the former that they may shelter them, like the eaves of a house, from any fluids that trickle down from the head; the latter to act like the palisades which are sometimes placed in front of enclosures, and keep out any objects which might otherwise get in. The brows are placed over the junction of two bones, which is the reason that in old age they often become so bushy as to require cutting. The lashes are set at the terminations of small blood-vessels. For the vessels come to an end where the skin itself terminates; and, in all places where these endings occur, the exudation of moisture of a corporeal character necessitates the growth of hairs, unless there be some operation of nature which interferes, by diverting the moisture to another purpose.

Viviparous quadrupeds, as a rule, present no great variety of form in the organ of smell. In those of them, however, whose jaws project forwards and taper to a narrow end, so as to form what is called a snout, the nostrils are placed in this projection, there being no other available plan; while, in the rest, there is a more definite demarcation between nostrils and jaws. But in no animal is this part so peculiar as in the elephant, where it attains an extraordinary size and strength. For the elephant uses its nostril as a hand; this being the instrument with which it conveys food, fluid and solid alike, to its mouth. With it, too, it tears up trees, coiling it round their stems. In fact it applies it generally to the purposes of a hand. For the elephant has the double character of a land animal, and of one that lives in swamps. Seeing then that it has to get its food from the water, and yet must necessarily breathe, inasmuch as it is a land animal and has blood; seeing, also, that its excessive weight prevents it from passing rapidly from water to land, as some other sanguineous vivipara that breathe can do, it becomes necessary that it shall be suited alike for life in the water and for life on dry land. Just then as divers are sometimes provided with instruments for respiration, through which they can draw air from above the water, and thus may remain for a long time under the sea, so also have elephants been furnished by nature with their lengthened nostril; and, whenever they have to traverse the water, they lift this up above the surface and breathe through it. For the elephant's proboscis, as already said, is a nostril. Now it would have been impossible for this nostril to have the form of a proboscis, had it been hard and incapable of bending. For its very length would then have prevented the animal from supplying itself with food, being as great an impediment as the horns of certain oxen, that are said to be obliged to walk backwards while they are grazing. It is therefore soft and flexible, and, being such, is made, in addition to its own proper functions, to serve the office of the fore-feet; nature in this following her wonted plan of using one and the same part for several purposes. For in polydactylous quadrupeds the fore-feet are intended not merely to support the weight of the body, but to serve as hands. But in elephants, though they must be reckoned polydactylous, as their foot has neither cloven nor solid hoof, the fore-feet, owing to the great size and weight of the body, are reduced to the condition of mere supports; and indeed their slow motion and unfitness for bending make them useless for any other purpose. A nostril, then, is given to the elephant for respiration, as to every other animal that has a lung, and is lengthened out and endowed with its power of coiling because the animal has to remain for considerable periods of time in the water, and is unable to pass thence to dry ground with any rapidity. But as the feet are shorn of their full office, this same part is also, as already said, made by nature to supply their place, and give such help as otherwise would be rendered by them.

As to other sanguineous animals, the Birds, the Serpents, and the oviparous quadrupeds, in all of them there are the nostril-holes, placed in front of the mouth; but in none are there any distinctly formed nostrils, nothing in fact which can be called nostrils except from a functional point of view. A bird at any rate has nothing which can properly be called a nose. For its so-called beak is a substitute for jaws. The reason for this is to be found in the natural conformation of birds. For they are winged bipeds; and this makes it necessary that their head and neck shall be of light weight; just as it makes it necessary that their breast shall be narrow. The beak therefore with which they are provided is formed of a bone-like substance, in order that it may serve as a weapon as well as for nutritive purposes, but is made of narrow dimensions to suit the small size of the head. In this beak are placed the olfactory passages. But there are no nostrils; for such could not possibly be placed there.

As for those animals that have no respiration, it has already been explained why it is that they are without nostrils, and perceive odours either through gills, or through a blow-hole, or, if they are insects, by the hypozoma; and how the power of smelling depends, like their motion, upon the innate spirit of their bodies, which in all of them is implanted by nature and not introduced from without.

Under the nostrils are the lips, in such sanguineous animals, that is, as have teeth. For in birds, as already has been said, the purposes of nutrition and defence are fulfilled by a bone-like beak, which forms a compound substitute for teeth and lips. For supposing that one were to cut off a man's lips, unite his upper teeth together, and similarly his under ones, and then were to lengthen out the two separate pieces thus formed, narrowing them on either side and making them project forwards, supposing, I say, this to be done, we should at once have a bird-like beak.

The use of the lips in all animals except man is to preserve and guard the teeth; and thus it is that the distinctness with which the lips are formed is in direct proportion to the degree of nicety and perfection with which the teeth are fashioned. In man the lips are soft and flesh-like and capable of separating from each other. Their purpose, as in other animals, is to guard the teeth, but they are more especially intended to serve a higher office, contributing in common with other parts to man's faculty of speech. For just as nature has made man's tongue unlike that of other animals, and, in accordance with what I have said is her not uncommon practice, has used it for two distinct operations, namely for the perception of savours and for speech, so also has she acted with regard to the lips, and made them serve both for speech and for the protection of the teeth. For vocal speech consists of combinations of the letters, and most of these it would be impossible to pronounce, were the lips not moist, nor the tongue such as it is. For some letters are formed by closures of the lips and others by applications of the tongue. But what are the differences presented by these and what the nature and extent of such differences, are questions to which answers must be sought from those who are versed in metrical science. It was necessary that the two parts which we are discussing should, in conformity with the requirements, be severally adapted to fulfill the office mentioned above, and be of appropriate character. Therefore are they made of flesh, and flesh is softer in man than in any other animal, the reason for this being that of all animals man has the most delicate sense of touch.

The tongue is placed under the vaulted roof of the mouth. In land animals it presents but little diversity. But in other animals it is variable, and this whether we compare them as a class with such as live on land, or compare their several species with each other. It is in man that the tongue attains its greatest degree of freedom, of softness, and of breadth; the object of this being to render it suitable for its double function. For its softness fits it for the perception of savours, a sense which is more delicate in man than in any other animal, softness being most impressionable by touch, of which sense taste is but a variety. This same softness again, together with its breadth, adapts it for the articulation of letters and for speech. For these qualities, combined with its freedom from attachment, are those which suit it best for advancing and retiring in every direction. That this is so is plain, if we consider the case of those who are tongue-tied in however slight a degree. For their speech is indistinct and lisping; that is to say, there are certain letters which they cannot pronounce. In being broad is comprised the possibility of becoming narrow; for in the great the small is included, but not the great in the small.

Hero of Alexandria, who flourished in the early Christian era, was not a professional philosopher but an engineer. Nevertheless, he was acquainted with the philosophical writings of the earlier Greeks and was particularly attracted by the doctrine of Epicurus. His work on pneumatics was a treatise on gadgets run by steam, but it was founded upon the atomic theory and reveals one of the fruits of the union of theory and practice.

FROM The Pneumatics BY HERO OF ALEXANDRIA

A TREATISE ON PNEUMATICS

The investigation of the properties of Atmospheric Air having been deemed worthy of close attention by the ancient philosophers and mechanists, the former deducing them theoretically, the latter from the action of sensible bodies, we also have thought proper to arrange in order what has been handed down by former writers, and to add thereto our own discoveries: a task from which much advantage will result to those who shall hereafter devote themselves to the study of mathematics. We are further led to write this work from the consideration that it is fitting that the treatment of this subject should correspond with the method given by us in our treatise, in four books, on water-clocks. For, by the union of air, earth, fire and water, and the concurrence of three, or four, elementary principles, various combinations are effected, some of which supply the most pressing wants of human life, while others produce amazement and alarm.

But, before proceeding to our proper subject, we must treat of the vacuum. Some assert that there is absolutely no vacuum; others that, while no continuous vacuum is exhibited in nature, it is to be found distributed in minute portions through air, water, fire and all other substances: and this latter opinion, which we will presently demonstrate to be true from sensible phenomena, we adopt. Vessels which seem to most men empty are not empty, as they suppose, but full of air. Now the air, as those who have treated of physics are agreed, is composed of particles minute and light, and for the most part invisible. If, then, we pour water into an apparently empty vessel, air will leave the vessel proportioned in quantity to the water which enters it. This may be seen from the following experiment. Let the vessel which seems to be empty be inverted, and, being carefully kept upright, pressed down into water; the water will not enter it even though it be entirely immersed: so that it is

The Pneumatics by Hero of Alexandria (1851), pp. 1–10, translated and edited by Bennet Woodcroft.

manifest that the air, being matter, and having itself filled all the space in the vessel, does not allow the water to enter. Now, if we bore the bottom of the vessel, the water will enter through the mouth, but the air will escape through the hole. Again, if, before perforating the bottom, we raise the vessel vertically, and turn it up, we shall find the inner surface of the vessel entirely free from moisture, exactly as it was before immersion. Hence it must be assumed that the air is matter. The air when set in motion becomes wind, (for wind is nothing else but air in motion), and if, when the bottom of the vessel has been pierced and the water is entering, we place the hand over the hole, we shall feel the wind escaping from the vessel; and this is nothing else but the air which is being driven out by the water. It is not then to be supposed that there exists in nature a distinct and continuous vacuum, but that it is distributed in small measures through air and liquid and all other bodies. Adamant alone might be thought not to partake of this quality, as it does not admit of fusion or fracture, and, when beaten against anvils or hammers, buries itself in them entire. This peculiarity however is due to its excessive density: for the particles of fire, being coarser than the void spaces in the stone, do not pass through them, but only touch the outer surface; consequently, as they do not penetrate into this, as into other substances, no heat results. The particles of the air are in contact with each other, yet they do not fit closely in every part, but void spaces are left between them, as in the sand on the sea shore: the grains of sand must be imagined to correspond to the particles of air, and the air between the grains of sand to the void spaces between the particles of air. Hence, when any force is applied to it, the air is compressed, and, contrary to its nature, falls into the vacant spaces from the pressure exerted on its particles: but when the force is withdrawn, the air returns again to its former position from the elasticity of its particles, as is the case with horn shavings and sponge, which, when compressed and set free again, return to the same position and exhibit the same bulk. Similarly, if from the application of force the particles of air be divided and a vacuum be produced larger than is natural, the particles unite again afterwards; for bodies will have a rapid motion through a vacuum, where there is nothing to obstruct or repel them, until they are in contact. Thus, if a light vessel with a narrow mouth be taken and applied to the lips, and the air be sucked out and discharged, the vessel will be suspended from the lips, the vacuum drawing the flesh towards it that the exhausted space may be filled. It is manifest from this that there was a continuous vacuum in the vessel. The same may be shown by means of the egg-shaped cups used by physicians, which are of glass, and have narrow mouths. When they wish to fill these with liquid, after sucking out the contained air, they place the finger on the vessel's mouth and invert them into the liquid; then, the finger being withdrawn, the water is drawn up into the exhausted space, though the upward motion is against its nature. Very similar is the operation of cupping-glasses, which, when applied to the body, not only do not fall though of considerable weight, but even draw the contiguous matter towards them through the apertures of the body. The explanation is that the fire placed in them consumes and rarefies the air they contain, just as other substances, water, air or earth, are consumed and pass over into more subtle substances.

That something is consumed by the action of fire is manifest from coalcinders, which, preserving the same bulk as they had before combustion, or nearly so, differ very much in weight. The consumed parts pass away with the smoke into a substance of fire or air or earth: the subtlest parts pass into the highest region where fire is; the parts somewhat coarser than these into air, and those coarser still, having been borne with the others a certain space by the current, descend again into the lower regions and mingle with earthy substances. Water also, when consumed by the action of fire, is transformed into air; for the vapour arising from cauldrons placed upon flames is nothing but the evaporation from the liquid passing into air. That fire, then, dissolves and transforms all bodies grosser than itself is evident from the above facts. Again, in the exhalations that rise from the earth the grosser kinds of matter are changed into subtler substances; for dew is sent up from the evaporation of the water contained in the earth by exhalation; and this exhalation is produced by some igneous substance, when the sun is under the earth and warms the ground below, especially if the soil be sulphureous or bituminous, and the ground thus warmed increases the exhalation. The warm springs found in the earth are due to the same cause. The lighter portions of the dew, then, pass into air; the grosser, after being borne upwards for a certain space from the force of the exhalation, when this has cooled at the return of the sun, descend again to the surface.

Winds are produced from excessive exhalation, whereby the air is disturbed and rarefied, and sets in motion the air in immediate contact with it. This movement of the air, however, is not everywhere of uniform velocity: it is more violent in the neighbourhood of the exhalation, where the motion began; fainter at a greater distance from it: just as heavy bodies, when rising, move more rapidly in the lower region where the propelling force is, and more slowly in the higher; and when the force which originally propelled them no longer acts upon them, they return to their natural position, that is, to the surface of the earth. If the propelling force continued to urge them onward with equal velocity, they would never have stopped; but now the force gradually ceases, being as it were expended, and the speed of the motion ceases with it.

Water, again, is transformed into an earthy substance: if we pour water into an earthy and hollow place, after a short time the water disappears, being absorbed by the earthy substance, so that it mingles with, and is actually transformed into, earth. And if any one says that it is not transformed or absorbed by the earth, but is drawn out by heat, either of the sun or some other body, he shall be shewn to be mistaken: for if the same water be put into a vessel of glass, or bronze, or any other solid material, and placed in the sun, for a considerable time it is not diminished except in a very small degree.

Water, therefore, is transformed into an earthy substance: indeed, slime and mud are transformations of water into earth.

Moreover, the more subtle substance is transformed into the grosser; as in the case of the flame of a lamp dying out for want of oil,—we see it for a time borne upwards and, as it were, striving to reach its proper region, that is, the highest of all above the atmosphere, till, overpowered by the mass of intervening air, it no longer tends to its kindred place, but, as though mixed and interwoven with the particles of air, becomes air itself. The same may be observed with air. For, if a small vessel containing air and carefully closed be placed in water with the mouth uppermost, and then, the vessel being uncovered, the water be allowed to rush in, the air escapes from the vessel; but, being overpowered by the mass of water, it mingles with it again and is transformed so as to become water.

When, therefore, the air in the cupping-glasses, being in like manner consumed and rarefied by fire, issues through the pores in the sides of the glass, the space within is exhausted and draws towards it the matter adjacent, of whatever kind it may be. But, if the cupping-glass be slightly raised, the air will enter the exhausted space and no more matter will be drawn up.

They, then, who assert that there is absolutely no vacuum may invent many arguments on this subject, and perhaps seem to discourse most plausibly though they offer no tangible proof. If, however, it be shewn by an appeal to sensible phenomena that there is such a thing as a continuous vacuum, but artificially produced; that a vacuum exists also naturally, but scattered in minute portions; and that by compression bodies fill up these scattered vacua, those who bring forward such plausible arguments in this matter will no longer be able to make good their ground.

Provide a spherical vessel, of the thickness of metal plate so as not to be easily crushed, containing about 8 cotylae (2 quarts). When this has been tightly closed on every side, pierce a hole in it, and insert a siphon, or slender tube, of bronze, so as not to touch the part diametrically opposite to the point of perforation, that a passage may be left for water. The other end of the siphon must project about 3 fingers' breadth (2 in.) above the globe, and the circumference of the aperture through which the siphon is inserted must be closed with tin applied both to the siphon and to the outer surface of the globe, so that when it is desired to breathe through the siphon no air may possibly escape from the vessel. Let us watch the result. The globe, like other vessels commonly said to be empty, contains air, and as this air fills all the space within it and presses uniformly against the inner surface of the vessel, if there is no vacuum, as some suppose, we can neither introduce water nor more air, unless the air contained before make way for it; and if by the application of force we make the attempt, the vessel, being full, will burst sooner than admit it. For the particles of air cannot be condensed, as there must in that case be interstices between them, by compression into which their bulk may become less; but this is not credible if there is no vacuum: nor

again, as the particles press against one another throughout their whole surface and likewise against the sides of the vessel, can they be pushed away so as
to make room if there is no vacuum. Thus in no way can anything from
without be introduced into the globe unless some portion of the previously
contained air escape; if, that is to say, the whole space is closely and uniformly filled, as the objectors suppose. And yet, if any one, inserting the
siphon in his mouth, shall blow into the globe, he will introduce much wind
without any of the previously contained air giving way. And, this being the
uniform result, it is clearly shewn that a condensation takes place of the particles contained in the globe into the interspersed vacua. The condensation
however is effected artificially by the forcible introduction of air. Now if,
after blowing into the vessel, we bring the hand close to the mouth, and
quickly cover the siphon with the finger, the air remains the whole time pent
up in the globe; and on the removal of the finger the introduced air will rush
out again with a loud noise, being thrust out, as we stated, by the expansion
of the original air which takes place from its elasticity. Again, if we draw out
the air in the globe by suction through the siphon, it will follow abundantly,
though no other substance take its place in the vessel, as has been said in the
case of the egg. By this experiment it is completely proved that an accumulation of vacuum goes on in the globe; for the particles of air left behind cannot
grow larger in the interval so as to occupy the space left by the particles
driven out. For if they increase in magnitude when no foreign substance can
be added, it must be supposed that this increase arises from expansion, which
is equivalent to a re-arrangement of the particles through the production of a
vacuum. But it is maintained that there is no vacuum; the particles therefore
will not become larger, for it is not possible to imagine for them any other
mode of increase. It is clear, then, from what has been said that certain void
spaces are interspersed between the particles of the air, into which, when
force is applied, they fall contrary to their natural action.

The air contained in the vessel inverted in water does not undergo much
compression, for the compressing force is not considerable, seeing that water,
in its own nature, possesses neither weight nor power of excessive pressure.
Whence it is that, though divers to the bottom of the sea support an immense
weight of water on their backs, respiration is not compelled by the water,
though the air contained in their nostrils is extremely little. It is worth while
here to examine what reason is given why those who dive deep, supporting
on their backs an immense weight of water, are not crushed. Some say that it
is because water is of uniform weight: but these give no reason why divers
are not crushed by the water above. The true reason may be shewn as follows.
Let us imagine the column of liquid which is directly over the surface of the
object under pressure, (in immediate contact with which the water is), to be
a body of same weight and form as the superincumbent liquid, and that
this is so placed in the water that its under surface coincides with the surface
of the body pressed, resting upon it in the same manner as the previously

superincumbent liquid, with which it exactly corresponds. It is clear, then, that this body does not project above the liquid in which it is immersed, and will not sink beneath its surface. For Archimedes has shewn, in his work on "Floating Bodies," that bodies of equal weight with any liquid, when immersed in it, will neither project above nor sink beneath its surface: therefore they will not exert pressure on objects beneath. Again, such a body, if all objects which exert pressure from above be removed, remains in the same place; how then can a body which has no tendency downward exert pressure? Similarly, the liquid displaced by the body will not exert pressure on objects beneath; for, as regards rest and motion, the body in question does [not] differ from the liquid which occupies the same space.

Again, that void spaces exist may be seen from the following considerations: for, if there were not such spaces, neither light, nor heat, nor any other material force could penetrate through water, or air, or any body whatever. How could the rays of the sun, for example, penetrate through water to the bottom of the vessel? If there were no pores in the fluid, and the rays thrust the water aside by force, the consequence would be that full vessels would overflow, which however does not take place. Again, if the rays thrust the water aside by force, it would not be found that some were reflected while others penetrated below; but now all those rays that impinge upon the particles of the water are driven back, as it were, and reflected, while those that come in contact with the void spaces, meeting with but few particles, penetrate to the bottom of the vessel. It is clear, too, that void spaces exist in water from this, that, when wine is poured into water, it is seen to spread itself through every part of the water, which it would not do if there were no vacua in the water. Again, one light traverses another; for, when several lamps are lighted, all objects are brilliantly illuminated, the rays passing in every direction through each other. And indeed it is possible to penetrate through bronze, iron, and all other bodies, as is seen in the instance of the marine torpedo.

That a continuous vacuum can be artificially produced has been shewn by the application of a light vessel to the mouth, and by the egg of physicians. With regard, then, to the nature of the vacuum, though other proofs exist, we deem those that have been given, and which are founded on sensible phenomena, to be sufficient. It may, therefore, be affirmed in this matter that every body is composed of minute particles, between which are empty spaces less than the particles of the body, (so that we erroneously say that there is no vacuum except by the application of force, and that every place is full either of air, or water, or some other substance), and, in proportion as any one of these particles recedes, some other follows it and fills the vacant space: that there is no continuous vacuum except by the application of some force: and again, that the absolute vacuum is never found, but is produced artificially.

Archimedes (c. 287–212 B.C.) would probably be most modern scientists' candidate for the greatest physicist of antiquity. His works on floating bodies and on the lever have that spare elegance that marks the best treatises in theoretical physics. His method is that of the mathematical physicist who keeps his fundamental assumptions to the very minimum and from them deduces, with rigorous mathematical logic, important and unimpeachable physical truths.

FROM On Floating Bodies BY ARCHIMEDES

POSTULATE 1

"Let it be supposed that a fluid is of such a character that, its parts lying evenly and being continuous, that part which is thrust the less is driven along by that which is thrust the more; and that each of its parts is thrust by the fluid which is above it in a perpendicular direction if the fluid be sunk in anything and compressed by anything else."

Proposition 1

If a surface be cut by a plane always passing through a certain point, and if the section be always a circumference [of a circle] whose centre is the aforesaid point, the surface is that of a sphere.

For, if not, there will be some two lines drawn from the point to the surface which are not equal.

Suppose O to be the fixed point, and A, B to be two points on the surface such that OA, OB are unequal. Let the surface be cut by a plane passing through OA, OB. Then the section is, by hypothesis, a circle whose centre is O.

Thus $OA = OB$; which is contrary to the assumption. Therefore the surface cannot but be a sphere.

Proposition 2

The surface of any fluid at rest is the surface of a sphere whose centre is the same as that of the earth.

Suppose the surface of the fluid cut by a plane through O, the centre of the earth, in the curve $ABCD$.

T. L. Heath, ed., *The Works of Archimedes*, New York, Dover Publications, pp. 253–261.

ABCD shall be the circumference of a circle.

For, if not, some of the lines drawn from *O* to the curve will be unequal. Take one of them, *OB*, such that *OB* is greater than some of the lines from *O* to the curve and less than others. Draw a circle with *OB* as radius. Let it be *EBF*, which will therefore fall partly within and partly without the surface of the fluid.

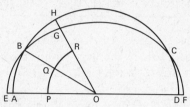

Draw *OGH* making with *OB* an angle equal to the angle *EOB*, and meeting the surface in *H* and the circle in *G*. Draw also in the plane an arc of a circle *PQR* with centre *O* and within the fluid.

Then the parts of the fluid along *PQR* are uniform and continuous, and the part *PQ* is compressed by the part between it and *AB*, while the part *QR* is compressed by the part between *QR* and *BH*. Therefore the parts along *PQ*, *QR* will be unequally compressed, and the part which is compressed the less will be set in motion by that which is compressed the more.

Therefore there will not be rest; which is contrary to the hypothesis.

Hence the section of the surface will be the circumference of a circle whose centre is *O;* and so will all other sections by planes through *O*.

Therefore the surface is that of sphere with centre *O*.

Proposition 3

Of solids those which, size for size, are of equal weight with a fluid will, if let down into the fluid, be immersed so that they do not project above the surface but do not sink lower.

If possible, let a certain solid *EFHG* of equal weight, volume for volume, with the fluid remain immersed in it so that part of it, *EBCF*, projects above the surface.

Draw through *O*, the centre of the earth, and through the solid a plane cutting the surface of the fluid in the circle *ABCD*.

Conceive a pyramid with vertex *O* and base a parallelogram at the surface of the fluid, such that it includes the immersed portion of the solid. Let this pyramid be cut by the plane of *ABCD* in *OL*, *OM*. Also let a sphere within the fluid and below *GH* be described with centre *O*, and let the plane of *ABCD* cut this sphere in *PQR*.

Conceive also another pyramid in the fluid with vertex *O*, continuous with the former pyramid and equal and similar to it. Let the pyramid so described be cut in *OM*, *ON* by the plane of *ABCD*.

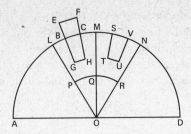

Lastly, let *STUV* be a part of the fluid within the second pyramid equal and similar to the part *BGHC* of the solid, and let *SV* be at the surface of the fluid.

Then the pressures on *PQ*, *QR* are unequal, that on *PQ* being the greater. Hence the part at *QR* will be set in motion by that at *PQ*, and the fluid will not be at rest; which is contrary to the hypothesis.

Therefore the solid will not stand out above the surface.

Nor will it sink further, because all the parts of the fluid will be under the same pressure.

Proposition 4

A solid lighter than a fluid will, if immersed in it, not be completely submerged, but part of it will project above the surface.

In this case, after the manner of the previous proposition, we assume the solid, if possible, to be completely submerged and the fluid to be at rest in that position, and we conceive (1) a pyramid with its vertex at *O*, the centre of the earth, including the solid, (2) another pyramid continuous with the former and equal and similar to it, with the same vertex *O*, (3) a portion of the fluid within this latter pyramid equal to the immersed solid in the other pyramid, (4) a sphere with centre *O* whose surface is below the immersed solid and the part of the fluid in the second pyramid corresponding thereto. We suppose a plane to be drawn through the centre *O* cutting the surface of the fluid in the circle *ABC*, the solid in *S*, the first pyramid in *OA*, *OB*, the second pyramid in *OB*, *OC*, the portion of the fluid in the second pyramid in *K*, and the inner sphere in *PQR*.

Then the pressures on the parts of the fluid at *PQ*, *QR* are unequal, since *S* is lighter than *K*. Hence there will not be rest; which is contrary to the hypothesis.

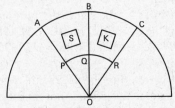

Therefore the solid *S* cannot, in a condition of rest, be completely sub-merged.

Proposition 5

Any solid lighter than a fluid will, if placed in the fluid, be so far immersed that the weight of the solid will be equal to the weight of the fluid displaced.

For let the solid be *EGHF*, and let *BGHC* be the portion of it immersed when the fluid is at rest. As in Prop. 3, conceive a pyramid with vertex *O* including the solid, and another pyramid with the same vertex continuous with the former and equal and similar to it. Suppose a portion of the fluid *STUV* at the base of the second pyramid to be equal and similar to the immersed portion of the solid; and let the construction be the same as in Prop. 3.

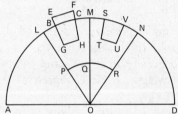

Then, since the pressure on the parts of the fluid at *PQ*, *QR* must be equal in order that the fluid may be at rest, it follows that the weight of the portion *STUV* of the fluid must be equal to the weight of the solid *EGHF*. And the former is equal to the weight of the fluid displaced by the immersed portion of the solid *BGHC*.

Proposition 6

If a solid lighter than a fluid be forcibly immersed in it, the solid will be driven upwards by a force equal to the difference between its weight and the weight of the fluid displaced.

For let *A* be completely immersed in the fluid, and let *G* represent the weight of *A*, and (*G* + *H*) the weight of an equal volume of the fluid. Take a solid *D*, whose weight is *H*, and add it to *A*. Then the weight of (*A* + *D*) is less than that of an equal volume of the fluid; and, if (*A* + *D*) is immersed in the fluid, it will project so that its weight will be equal to the weight of the fluid displaced. But its weight is (*G* + *H*).

Therefore the weight of the fluid displaced is (*G* + *H*), and hence the volume of the fluid displaced is the volume of the solid *A*. There will accordingly be rest with *A* immersed and *D* projecting.

Thus the weight of *D* balances the upward force exerted by the fluid on *A*, and therefore the latter force is equal to *H*, which is the difference between the weight of *A* and the weight of the fluid which *A* displaces.

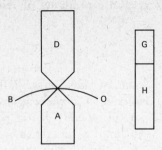

Proposition 7

A solid heavier than a fluid will, if placed in it, descend to the bottom of the fluid, and the solid will, when weighed in the fluid, be lighter than its true weight by the weight of the fluid displaced.

(1) The first part of the proposition is obvious, since the part of the fluid under the solid will be under greater pressure, and therefore the other parts will give way until the solid reaches the bottom.

(2) Let A be a solid heavier than the same volume of the fluid, and let $(G+H)$ represent its weight, while G represents the weight of the same volume of the fluid.

Take a solid B lighter than the same volume of the fluid, and such that the weight of B is G, while the weight of the same volume of the fluid is $(G+H)$.

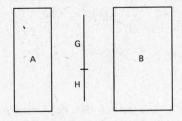

Let A and B be now combined into one solid and immersed. Then, since $(A+B)$ will be of the same weight as the same volume of fluid, both weights being equal to $(G+H)+G$, it follows that $(A+B)$ will remain stationary in the fluid.

Therefore the force which causes A by itself to sink must be equal to the upward force exerted by the fluid on B by itself. This latter is equal to the difference between $(G+H)$ and G [Prop. 6]. Hence A is depressed by a force equal to H, i.e. its weight in the fluid is H, or the difference between $(G+H)$ and G.

[This proposition may, I think, safely be regarded as decisive of the question how Archimedes determined the proportions of gold and silver contained in the famous crown. The proposition suggests in fact the following method.

Let W represent the weight of the crown, w_1 and w_2 the weights of the gold and silver in it respectively, so that $W = w_1 + w_2$.

(1) Take a weight W of pure gold and weigh it in a fluid. The apparent loss of weight is then equal to the weight of the fluid displaced. If F_1 denote this weight, F_1 is thus known as the result of the operation of weighing.

It follows that the weight of fluid displaced by a weight w_1 of gold is $\frac{w_1}{W} \cdot F_1$.

(2) Take a weight W of pure silver and perform the same operation. If F_2 be the loss of weight when the silver is weighed in the fluid we find in like manner that the weight of fluid displaced by w_2 is $\frac{w_2}{W} \cdot F_2$.

(3) Lastly, weigh the crown itself in the fluid, and let F be the loss of weight. Therefore the weight of fluid displaced by the crown is F.

It follows that
$$\frac{w_1}{W} \cdot F_1 + \frac{w_2}{W} \cdot F_2 = F,$$

or
$$w_1 F_1 + w_2 F_2 = (w_1 + w_2) F,$$

whence
$$\frac{w_1}{w_2} = \frac{F_2 - F}{F - F_1}.$$

This procedure corresponds pretty closely to that described in the poem *de ponderibus et mensuris* (written probably about 500 A.D.) purporting to explain Archimedes' method. According to the author of this poem, we first take two equal weights of pure gold and pure silver respectively and weigh them against each other when both immersed in water; this gives the relation between their weights in water and therefore between their loss of weight in water. Next we take the mixture of gold and silver and an equal weight of pure silver and weigh them against each other in water in the same manner.

The other version of the method used by Archimedes is that given by Vitruvius, according to which he measured successively the *volumes* of fluid displaced by three equal weights, (1) the crown, (2) the same weight of gold, (3) the same weight of silver, respectively. Thus, if as before the weight of the crown is W, and it contains weights w_1 and w_2 of gold and silver respectively,

(1) the crown displaces a certain quantity of fluid, V say;

(2) the weight W of gold displaces a certain volume of fluid, V_1 say; therefore a weight w_1 of gold displaces a volume $\frac{w_1}{W} \cdot V_1$ of fluid;

(3) the weight W of silver displaces a certain volume of fluid, say V_2; therefore a weight w_2 of silver displaces a volume $\frac{w_2}{W} \cdot V_2$ of fluid.

It follows that $$V = \frac{w_1}{W} \cdot V_1 + \frac{w_2}{W} \cdot V_2,$$

whence, since $$W = w_1 + w_2,$$

$$\frac{w_1}{w_2} = \frac{V_2 - V}{V - V_1};$$

and this ratio is obviously equal to that before obtained, viz. $\dfrac{F_2 - F}{F - F_1}$.

3
THE ASSESSMENT OF ANCIENT SCIENCE

Benjamin Farrington is a leading exponent of that school of thought that finds the origins of science in ordinary practice and daily life. It is from this point of view that he describes and evaluates the contributions of the various schools of ancient science.

FROM Greek Science BY BENJAMIN FARRINGTON

Science, whatever be its ultimate developments, has its origin in techniques, in arts and crafts, in the various activities by which man keeps soul and body together. Its source is experience, its aims practical, its only test that it works. Science arises in contact with things; it is dependent on the evidence of the senses, and however far it seems to move from them, must always come back to them. It requires logic and the elaboration of theory, but its strictest logic and choicest theory must be proved in practice. Science in the practical sense is the necessary basis for abstract and speculative science.

As thus conceived, science develops in close correspondence with the stages of man's social progress and becomes progressively more self-conscious as man's whole way of life becomes more purposive. A food-gatherer has one kind of knowledge of his environment, a food-producer another. The latter is more active and purposive in his relation to mother earth. Increased mastery of the environment brings increased productivity, which, in its turn, brings

Benjamin Farrington, *Greek Science* (1949), pp. 14–15, 24–25, 66, 67, 68–71, 91–92, 95–96, 98, 102–104. Reprinted by permission of Penguin Books Ltd., Harmondsworth.

social change. The science of gentile or tribal society cannot be the same as the science of political society. The division of labour has an influence on the development of science. The emergence of a leisured class gives opportunity for reflection and elaboration of theory. It also gives opportunity for theorizing without relation to facts. Furthermore, with the development of classes, the need for a new kind of "science" arises which might be defined as "the system of behaviour by which man acquires mastery over man." When the task of mastering men becomes the preoccupation of the ruling class and the task of mastering nature becomes the forced labour of another class, science takes a new and dangerous turn. Fully to understand the science of any society, we must be acquainted with the degree of its material advancement and with its political structure. There is no such thing as science *in vacuo*. There is only the science of a particular society at a particular place and time. The history of science can only be understood as a function of the total life of society. . . .

These considerations will be found applicable to the whole development of science in antiquity. They are still even to some degree operative to-day. The history of Greek science, which is our main concern, is unintelligible unless they are constantly borne in mind. To borrow the mechanical arts from Egypt or elsewhere was to borrow also the social consequences, at least to some extent. "What are called the mechanical arts," says Xenophon, "carry a social stigma and are rightly dishonoured in our cities. For these arts damage the bodies of those who work at them or who act as overseers, by compelling them to a sedentary life and to an indoor life, and, in some cases, to spend the whole day by the fire. This physical degeneration results also in deterioration of the soul. Furthermore, the workers at these trades simply have not got the time to perform the offices of friendship or citizenship. Consequently they are looked upon as bad friends and bad patriots, and in some cities, especially the warlike ones, it is not legal for a citizen to ply a mechanical trade." (*Oeconomicus*, iv, 203.)

This contempt of the mechanical arts hindered in Greece, as it did in Egypt, the development of the chemical sciences. Greek science represents an enormous advance on Egyptian science, but it shows the same great limitation. Mathematics, surgery, medicine, and astronomy are not only the main divisions of Egyptian science, but of Greek. Physics, chemistry, mechanics were dishonoured and therefore weak. . . .

Medicine, no doubt, like other practices, first became scientific in Ionia. But now, in the fifth century, there were rival medical schools in the West which did not possess the same understanding of medicine as originating in a technique, but sought to deduce the rules of medical practice from *a priori* cosmological opinions.

* * *

It was in the school of Empedocles at Agrigentum that cosmology produced its worst effects on the healing art. There man, like everything else, was supposed to consist of the four elements. The doctrine of the elements included a theory as to their characteristic qualities. Earth was said to be Cold and Dry; Air, Hot and Wet; Water, Cold and Wet; Fire, Hot and Dry. The distemperature of man's body, like the distemperature of nature, was ascribed to the excess of defect of one or other of these qualities. Fever was to be interpreted as an excess of the Hot, a chill as an excess of Cold. This being so, what remedies would a physician who was also a philosopher suggest? Would he not recommend a dose of the Hot to cure a chill and of the Cold to cure a fever?

When the new-fangled doctrines of the western philosophical schools began to be spoken of in his beloved Ionia, anger seized the heart of the author of *Ancient Medicine*. In his opening sentence he leaps to the attack. "All who attempt to discuss the art of healing on the basis of a postulate— heat, cold, moisture, dryness, or anything else they fancy—thus narrowing down the causes of disease and death among men to one or two postulates, are not only obviously wrong, but are especially to be blamed because they are wrong in what is an art or technique (*technè*), and one moreover which all men use at the crises of life, highly honouring the practitioners and crafts- men in this art, if they are good."

Into this first sentence our author has managed to pack four separate objec- tions to the new trend in medicine. As they are all of great significance in the history of science, it will be well for us to pick them out and discuss them one by one.

First he objects to the basing of medicine on postulates. The effect of this objection is to separate medicine as a positive science, depending on observa- tion and experiment, from cosmology, where experimental control was not possible in antiquity. . . .

Secondly, he protests that the new-fangled doctors are "narrowing down the causes of death and disease." This is most remarkable. It is a protest by a practising technician, conscious of the richness of his positive science, against the barrenness of metaphysics. The historical significance of this is very great. The technician is appalled at the ignorance of the philosophers. Art had not yet been made tongue-tied by authority. For the Hippocratic doctor the quali- ties of things which affect a man's health were not three or four. They were infinitely various. . . .

Then he proceeds to supplement the handful of Empedoclean concepts with a list of others more relevant to medical science—in foods, such qualities as sweetness, bitterness, acidity, saltness, insipidity, astringency; in human anatomy, the shapes of the organs; in human physiology, the capacity of the organism to react to an external stimulus. Thus does the cook rebuke the cosmologist.

The third reason for his anger is, not that the philosopher should be wrong, but that he should be wrong in a technique or art (*technè*). The reason why ignorance in respect of a *technè* is inexcusable is, that no knowledge was worthy to be called a *technè* unless it gave results. Here the justifiable pride of the craftsman is noticeable; and it admonishes us that the test of early science was, not the laboratory, but practice. We must not overlook this fact when we debate the point, whether Greek science knew experiment or not. A technique was a mode of imitating nature. If it worked, that was proof that the technician understood nature.

The fourth reason for his anger with the doctor who possesses only philosophical postulates but is ignorant of the art is that it is the patient who suffers. This concern for the patient is specially characteristic of the Hippocratic doctors. They were severely scientific at their best, but at their best they also maintained that the first duty of the doctor is to heal the sick rather than to study disease. In this there was a certain measure of disagreement between them and the neighbouring school at Cnidus. We might express the difference by saying that the ideal of the men of Cnidus was science, that of the men of Cos science in the service of humanity.

We have now listed the four chief objections of our practising physician to the medical innovations of the philosophers. At this early date, before much positive knowledge had accumulated, and before specialization had in consequence become necessary, it was natural that a philosopher should embrace every branch of knowledge. There is nothing therefore surprising in Empedocles turning his attention to medicine. But his doing so brought sharply into view the fact that there was a kind of speculation that was admissible in cosmology but inadmissible in medicine. Cosmologists tended to start from some observation, or some few observations (change of water into ice or steam; the mathematical relation between the lengths of vibrating strings; the transmutation of food into flesh), and then elaborate on this slender foundation a theory of the universe, satisfied if the system they evolved hung together with reasonable logic. But this could not satisfy the doctor, whose theories were continually tested in practice, proved right or wrong by their effect on the patient. A stricter conception of the scientific method was formed. It can truly be said that the Hippocratic doctors at their best advanced fully to the idea of a positive science. What differentiated their science from ours was less the failure to realize the importance of experiment than the absence of instruments of exact measurement and of any technique of chemical analysis. They were as scientific as the material conditions of their time permitted.

* * *

The Platonic writings have long attracted, and still attract, a degree of attention which the earlier philosophers and sophists cannot claim. But the great prestige of his writings constitutes a difficulty for the historian of science. Plato wrote much about those problems of epistemology which lie on the border between philosophy and science. There is no doubt about his eminence as a philosopher. His contribution to science is, however, open to question. Does he deserve the same place in the history of science which by universal accord he holds in philosophy?

Science before Plato had achieved remarkable advances which we may roughly classify under three heads. The first and decisive step, which we associate especially with the Milesians, was the new attitude of attempting to explain the phenomena of nature, including human nature, without supernatural intervention. Secondly, we find that a rudimentary technique of interrogating nature by means of experiments had begun. There was a growing practice of observation and experiments, in Ionia, in Italy, in Sicily, in Athens itself, accompanied, as its philosophical implications became more clearly understood, by a lively debate on the validity of sense-evidence. Thirdly, although the importance of this has been little recognized and the fact has been denied by some, there was the vital connection between natural philosophy and techniques, which determined the character of the early philosophy of nature. In developing his attack on the Ionian philosophers, Plato accords their recognition of this connection an important place in their general world-outlook. The following are the words in which he describes their point of view: "The arts which make the most serious contribution to human life are those which blend their own power with that of nature, like medicine, agriculture, and gymnastics" (*Laws,* X, 889d). This plainly implies a philosophy of the techniques, an attempt to define their essential character and to assign them their very important place in the development of civilized society. . . . Plato was the author, or propagator, of an astral theology in which the stars were cast for the rôle of patterns of divine regularity. He found it incompatible with this requirement that, conspicuous among the hosts of heaven, where

> Round the ancient track marched rank on rank
> The army of unalterable law,

should be a parcel of five disorderly vagabonds (the word planet means vagabond in Greek). The inconvenience was especially great inasmuch as the problem of human vagabondage had reached a crisis at this time in Greece.

Plato's contemporary, Isocrates, had made a special study of the problem of these sturdy beggars. The remedy he proposed was not increased production and better distribution of this world's goods. Faced with an ever-increasing throng of roving outcasts, his idea was to enlist them, drill them, and hurl them against the Persian Empire. If they could not conquer it outright, they could at least tear enough off its territory to provide living-space for themselves. The alternative was revolution at home. "If we cannot check the growing strength of these vagabonds," wrote Isocrates, "by providing them with a satisfactory life, before we know where we are they will be so numerous that they will constitute as great a danger to the Greeks as to the barbarians" (*Philip,* 121). Under these circumstances it is not surprising that, as a contribution to the liquidation of vagabondage on earth, Plato should have determined to liquidate it in heaven. He "set it as a problem to all earnest students to find 'what are the uniform and ordered movements by the assumption of which the apparent movements of the planets can be accounted for.'" Until this problem could be solved, his astral theology, by which he set much store in his proposed reconstruction of society, risked total failure. Why worship the stars if these divine beings could do no better than set a conspicuous example of irregularity and disorder? It is altogether false to regard Plato's challenge to the mathematicians to reduce the planets to order as proof of a disinterested love of science. It was not an attempt to find out the facts, but to conjure away socially inconvenient appearances on the basis of any plausible hypothesis.

* * *

This kind of astronomy, in which natural laws were subordinated to divine principles, and in which more regard was paid to the heavenly bodies as objects of worship than subjects of scientific study, was further developed by Aristotle. Systematizing the doctrines of Plato and the Pythagoreans, he taught, not only that the circular motions of the heavenly bodies are proof of their being under the control of divine intelligence, but that the very substance of which they are made—what he called "the fifth element," to distinguish it from Earth, Air, Fire, and Water—is different from any that exists below the circle of the moon. The astronomy which he taught in his theological mood (it must be stressed that it is not characteristic of his scientific outlook) is that inherited by the Middle Ages.

Aristotle's account was that the universe consists of fifty-nine concentric spheres, with the earth at the centre. To the earth were allowed four spheres, one for each of the four elements. Outside the four terrestrial spheres were fifty-five celestial spheres, that of the moon being the lowest and that of the fixed stars the highest. The spheres were supposed to revolve round a stationary earth and carry with them, in their revolutions, the heavenly bodies. Only below the moon, in Aristotle's scheme of the universe, was change possible. There the four elements, whose "natural" movements were up and down, might mingle and be transformed into one another. But above the moon, in the ethereal spheres, whose "natural" movement was in circles, no change occurred. In this scheme, as the substance of heaven is different from that of earth, so are the laws of motion different. There is a celestial mechanics and a terrestrial mechanics, and the rules of one are not valid for the other. Not till Newton did terrestrial mechanics regain control of heaven.

* * *

Plato added nothing to science in the observational and experimental sense. It is extremely doubtful whether he added anything to mathematics. Heath's judgment on his mathematical attainment is that "he does not appear to have been more than up to date." . . . But he did contribute to the philosophy of mathematics. What fascinated him was the meaning of those mathematical truths which seem to be independent of experience. In *Republic,* vi, 510, he says of the geometers: "You know that they make use of visible figures and argue about them, but in doing so they are not thinking of these figures but of the things which they represent; thus it is the absolute square and the absolute diameter which is the object of their argument, not the diameter which they draw." In distinguishing this type of knowledge from the knowledge which appears to be wholly dependent on sensuous impressions, Plato made a fundamental contribution to epistemology. It is his concern for this that must excuse, if anything can excuse, a hostility to practical geometry so great that he regarded the mere construction of figures as essentially antagonistic to a true study of the subject.

When we come to the third point, the connection between philosophy and the techniques, which had proved so fruitful in an earlier period, we find that Plato has nothing to contribute. Preoccupied with theological, metaphysical, or political problems, and disbelieving in the possibility of a science of nature, Plato has little appreciation of the connections between Greek thought and Greek practice which were clear to an earlier age. These connections are many. Astronomy was, of course, not studied out of mere curiosity. It was studied in order to solve those very problems concern with which Plato deprecates—the exact relations of the lengths of day and night, of both to the month, and of the month to the year. On the solution of these problems depended the improvement of the calendar. On the improvement of the calendar depended improvements in agriculture, navigation, and the general conduct of public affairs. Neither was geometry studied, outside the Academy, purely for the good of the soul. It was studied in connection with land-surveying, navigation, architecture, and engineering. Mechanical science was applied in the theatre, the field of battle, the docks and dockyards, the quarries, and wherever building was afoot. Medicine was a conspicuous example of applied science. It was a scientific study of man in his environment with a view to promoting his well-being. But the political programme put forward by Plato in the *Republic* and the *Laws* is all but barren of understanding of the rôle of applied science in the improvement of the lot of humanity. In his *Republic* and *Laws* Plato is wholly occupied with the problem of managing men, not at all with the problem of the control of the material environment. Accordingly the works, if full of political ingenuity, are devoid of natural science.

Giorgio de Santillana was professor of the history of science at the Massachusetts Institute of Technology until his recent retirement. He sees ancient science through more philosophically tinted glasses than does Farrington.

FROM The Origins of Scientific Thought
BY GIORGIO DE SANTILLANA

SOCRATIC THOUGHT

Socratic thought, such as we have tried to characterize, is the foundation on which Plato (428–348 B.C.) raises his vast cathedral of the Theory of Ideas. As Socrates had seen it, the real assemblage of the world, whatever it may be, is of little relevance, compared to its "true" constitution, which must show the mark of the good which rules over all being. This is also the way in which Plato sees physical reality, which he describes in a famous simile as the impenetrable dark wall of the Cave in which souls are imprisoned until they break the shackles and turn toward the contemplation of truth. Plato is far too profound a philosopher and far too great a writer for us to want to analyze his "contributions to science," that is, cut out from the context of his opus the fragments of physical theory and the flashes of half-understood archaic knowledge that he deals out "not quite seriously," as he is willing to admit, in the guise of myth or "plausible story" intended as a help to the imagination where reason cannot give a true account. For indeed, as Plato insists to the end of his life, there cannot be a "true physics." There is one whole dialogue of his, the *Timaeus,* which gives us a detailed cosmology in the Pythagorean manner, and is usually quoted as his physical theory. Yet the *Timaeus* is nothing but one myth or allegory meant to adumbrate the workings of the World Soul, and its physics is a shadow play.

The center of gravity of Plato's thought lies entirely elsewhere, in the realm of Ideas which are supposed to exist somehow beyond the world, to be contemplated only by the eye of the mind. In the *Theaetetus,* a dialogue which tackles the problem of knowledge, Socrates helps Theaetetus, the great young mathematician, to discard the current definition of knowledge as "true opinion." He examines the possible sources of knowledge. It cannot come from sensation because sensation is change and movement, both outside and in us. Or is it in thought? But we should consider the process of thought. It is "the discourse that the soul holds with itself," until it has formed an "opinion." The opinion may be true. But then how do we happen to form often puzzlingly wrong opinions? How do we know when they are true? This does not give true science (*epistēme*). Theaetetus suggests shyly that we might have "true opinion accompanied by a rational account of itself." But this, too, is found insufficient, for on what are we to found that rational account? The argument has come to a dead end. But, meanwhile, the possibility of what *we* would call the scientific approach to reality has been written off. Along that way, we meet only the "likely."

The very inconclusiveness of the dialogue—which starts out in search of a theory of true knowledge and admittedly fails in its quest—shows up the intellectual predicament. There is a gulf between abstraction and reality, between theory and things, which can be overflown upward, creatively, by Eros, downward, imaginatively, by the myth, but remains impassable to any effort at bringing them together. It is this gulf, this gap (*chorismos*) which makes nature insoluble, not through any fault of our intellect, but because she *is* essentially darkness and inchoate approximation. We cannot hope to find in matter any precise consequences of the logical connections of the world above, but only reminders, fumbling attempts to "imitate" it, doomed to remain halfway between being and nonbeing; it is, in fact, the World of Becoming. It would be even better to say that it is "trying to become." How? Why? What is it that causes it even to try, lost in the darkness below? Plato suggests it does so by some kind of "participation"—a notion still wrapped in the mists of magic. As Aristotle will remark rather acidly, it is saying no more than the Pythagoreans meant already when they spoke of things "imitating" numbers. But Plato is prevented from finding a better answer by the very width of the gap that he places between reality and Ideas. The separation is far more drastic than between Parmenides's "Truth" and "Opinion," for the substrate of Becoming is for Parmenides the diamond-like firmness of Being, which is geometrical space; whereas in Plato space itself seems to lose all geometrical properties; it is the "receptacle" or "matrix" of the inchoate effort of matter to become. Situated even below matter, it is close to the absolute zero of "nonbeing." The way in which the Matrix of Becoming, as the cosmogonic story is told us in the *Timaeus,* "was filled with powers not alike nor evenly balanced, and was swayed unevenly and shaken like the winnower's basket," and thus brought forth the diversity of things, may prompt a modern to think of Schrödinger's atom, seen as a system of standing waves in *psi*-space, a space surely not geometrical. But even if it reveals some strange kinship of minds, the analogy is unwarranted. Plato is, like Timaeus himself, a Pythagorean in cosmology—but then he makes it clear that the physics of it is only a metaphor. His atoms are stereometric formations in empty space, brought forth by "participation." The mixing together of ingredients by the Demiurge or Manufacturing God, the subsequent distribution of the product in accord with the intervals of a musical scale to form different substances, this is again the Pythagorean idea of Empedocles, but presented this time not as science, only as "plausible myth" inside a vaster metaphysical theory.

As a matter of historic fact, this lofty point of view was reactionary; it deflected Pythagorean thought from the patient endeavor at finding numeric data inside the actual phenomena, that is, at discovering inductively where it is that number rules matter exactly. Even astronomy, the divine science, cannot be said to retain its previous status. Plato does not think that astronomy "lifts one's eyes upward" in any other way than if one were to look up at the ceiling.

Looking up with your mouth open, or down with your mouth closed, is about the same so long as we investigate any kind of sensible object. . . . The only true way of looking "up" is to investigate pure Being, which cannot be seen at all.

This is an important passage, in that it shows vividly how Plato's conception of science has nothing to do with anything happening in time and space.

Truth may come down, however, from the world of Ideas where it lives, to make some sense of reality, to "save" it or to "guide" it. So it may come down by way of the mind to "guide" the city, or to "save" the appearances in Heaven, that is, invest them with the ideal structures that they try stumblingly and half senselessly to imitate. So we may have astronomy after all, but down from the Ideas, not up from the facts. And it surely *is* a mathematical physics as Plato understood it, but that is because the stars, in their close-to-divine nature, know how to respond exactly to the Idea which informs their motion, viz., the circle. This has to be spelled out in order to give the proper meaning to the enterprise of Eudoxus, the great mathematician, in his theory of homocentric spheres. As he formalized astronomy and detached it from the physical imaginations of the Pythagoreans, he accepted Plato's program of "saving the phenomena." The theory was intended to give a strictly mathematical model on this level. Put in Platonic terms, it intended to establish the relation between the actual planetary shifts and an abstract *Eidos* or Form—uniform circular motion compounded. The appearances ("phenomena") were "saved"—but not in any physically translatable way. This was the mathematizing ideal which allowed science to be reborn later; for indeed Platonism remains for twenty centuries the framework in which mathematics is seen to be important; it not only hallows with its "golden eloquence" and preserves for the future all the Pythagorean speculations, it also established the ideal of a thoroughgoing rationality, the will to "follow the argument wherever it will lead us," as Socrates says. It would indeed have led quite naturally to a science of the modern type—if it had not been for the gap.

* * *

It is said that Plato agreed once, on insistent request, to deliver a public lecture on the Good. The lecturer, remarks Whitehead, was competent; the lecture was a failure. The Athenians, who must have come expecting some clever Sophistic teaching, were dismayed when Plato proceeded to draw geo-metrical diagrams and to build up propositions. Most of them left unceremo-niously. The text of that lecture is lost. We have, however, what was probably the first part of it, decked in shining literary form, in the *Republic* (end of Book VI and beginning of Book VII). In this section, Plato reveals what seems to have been his ideas of the central role of mathematics in the Science of the Good. The Pythagorean Harmonic proportion which also expresses itself in the cube appears as the key to the structure of knowledge as well as to that of the cosmos itself. The argument moves on three successive levels: dialectical, systematic, and allegorical. The famous myth of the Cave turns out to be not a mere literary analogy, but a true allegoric parable, a synthesis of the doctrine. . . .

* * *

ARISTOTLE

Aristotle (384–323 B.C.), "the Master of those who know" as Dante calls him reverently, was the son of a doctor from the Ionian colony of Stagira in Thrace. He came to Athens at the age of eighteen, proceeded, says a tradition, to waste most of his fortune on dancing girls, then entered Plato's Academy, where he remained until his master's death. Being then about thirty-five, he moved to the city of Atarneus in Asia Minor, whose self-made ruler, Her-mias, was his friend. When Hermias was captured and crucified by the Per-sians, Aristotle sailed to Mytilene, taking with him Hermias's orphaned daughter, whom he married. He settled with his little princess on the island of Lesbos, where he seems to have done much of his work on natural history during the two years that followed. In 342, Philip of Macedon invited him to his court as the tutor of his son, who was to become Alexander the Great and to bring to an end all that Aristotle knew and taught in his *Politics*.

When Alexander came to the throne, Aristotle settled in Athens and founded a university of his own, the Lyceum (which also became known as the "Peripatos" or "promenade" because discussion took place in its shaded walks). Alexander, it is said, put emissaries at his disposal to collect material on natural history from all over his empire. Thus was born the first great scientific project. After Alexander's death, the Athenians with Demosthenes rose against Macedonian rule. Aristotle left "lest they be tempted to commit another crime against philosophy," and withdrew to the island of Euboea, where he died at the age of sixty-three.

Aristotle's enterprise started from Plato's research into the classification of Ideas. It was aimed at encompassing all the knowledge of his times, and at organizing it philosophically into one coherent whole. He had first, therefore, to forge the "Instrument" (*Organon*) of Formal Logic. As the Master of the Syllogism, he provided the foundations of liberal education for the next two thousand years. But this for him was only the premise to a system which moved from the First Philosophy (later called Metaphysics) to his Treatise on the Soul and then to Physics, i.e., cosmology, and on to Natural History, which concluded the theoretical part, while the "productive" and "practical" part embraced Poetics, Ethics, Economics, and Politics.

Aristotle, like the Presocratics, again focuses his attention on nature. But he has a way of making all his predecessors look archaic, and himself as the first representative of the full maturity of thought. Those who come before stand there, as we said earlier, like prophets in the wilderness, each voicing his lone unsupported revelation. It is his patient concern to show how each of them discovered some one aspect of the truth, in his own singular way, and how good "method" (the word is his) will fit these facets together in the true construction. Aristotle turns out thus to be the earliest historian of thought, even if, in order to fit the various thinkers in their proper place, he has to distort their ideas at times most unfairly. But it is revealing of the man who has so often been accused of haughtiness that he has turned the Socratic inquiry into an openminded procedure almost similar to that of a modern anthropologist exploring a new culture. Let us see, he suggests, what people can mean when they use certain terms; then let us clean it up and put it all together with good method. There is no denying the scientific aspect of this exploration; but it yields essentially a verbal machinery, a "science" of coherent discourse about all that is already known. In this way Aristotle stabilized knowledge. Greece had after him many thinkers more appealing, more profound, or more effective, but none greater than he for amplitude of scope and organizing power: he remains the Teacher over the centuries. With him, in fact, is born a figure which, for better or worse, will have an important role in the Western world, that of the Professor.

The Choices Involved

"There is no science except of the general." Such is Aristotle's firm principle. But instead of beginning from Ideas, he takes his start from things. This shows that excellent trait called curiosity, which is often lacking in philosophers. The actual starting point of philosophical attention is, in his own engagingly simple language, *to de ti*, literally "this thing here," and the basic question about it is *to ti en einai*, "the what it is to be."

Right here, without further ado, a modern scientist might challenge the question as pointless and ask instead: What is it made of and how does it work? That is, he would focus on certain properties of the thing, mathematical, chemical, or what not, and try to tie those up into a system of universal relations. He would have reached thus another science of the general, and one which yields high results, but he would have by-passed the question of what that particular thing *is*. This is what was done even by Aristotle's elder contemporary, Democritus. To the question: What is this cat here? Democritus would have answered: "In reality nothing but atoms and the void." A penetrating answer, no doubt, but it would have taken a whole, and as yet non-existent, body of science to give the quantitative composition of the cat; and this would have left us still immeasurably far from the cat itself. It must be admitted that the founders of modern science left the question of the cat beyond the horizon, and decided to find what quantitative cosmic laws could be deduced from the fall of stones, the orbiting of planets, or the oxidation of mercury.

Greek thought may then be excused for trying to make sense of the universe in a more direct way than ours, and one which should do justice to its manifold diversity. It might be called the search for a nondeforming perspective. And this is exactly what Aristotle stands for. There were two ways open: artistic intuition, which does not lead to the general, and coherent discourse, which does. He had therefore to choose the latter, and with it he chose inevitably the logico-verbal approach. A cat is a being in its own right, its catness part of the scheme of universals.

It is in the name of things as they are that Aristotle builds up his distinctions and categorizations, ever more subtly and elaborately knit to do justice to the innumerable "modes" of being, in the manner of a jurist seeing things from many angles. From this, in time, and with the help of Christianity, will come our concept of the uniqueness of the individual. Without question, it is the truly civilized attitude, for is not the richness of civilization tantamount to knowing how to see and name distinctions, shades of meaning, varieties of situations? What is definition but difference clearly determined? The intuitive and the formal mind will meet in this desire to enrich our capacity to discern the varieties of being, instead of throwing them back into the caldron of reduction.

But this is just what causes Aristotle to swerve away from mathematics. The tendency to reduce, to simplify, the same which has given the modern physicist his power over nature, renders that physicist helpless when it comes to complex living reality. Aristotle feels that he has to make a choice of instruments. He, too, if algebra has been invented in his time, would have described it as some type of "low cunning." There is, he suggests, a more natural and sensible way than mathematics to build up understanding of organic and "architectonic" cosmos of which there is a *gnōsis,* in which man has a true and significant place.

But since science has to be universal, he takes to legislating over mathematics itself, and bringing in, there too, the proper distinctions. It is wrong to say, he teaches for instance, that curved and straight lines are in any way commensurable, or even comparable. They are different species and must be kept distinct. And so, too, must earthly and heavenly motions be utterly distinct and noncomparable. He goes even further; he eschews geometric words for real situations. We say, he remarks, of a nose that it is "snub," of a hoop that it is "bent"; we do not use the word "curved," which is abstract and inappropriate. In this way mathematics is relegated to pure and inoperant abstraction.

It is an utterly different road from that of Plato which Aristotle has taken. But when it comes to organizing, the Platonism which has become to him a second nature reasserts itself.

The Primacy of the Mind

This second nature is a tendency to explain in terms of the mind. It is absolutely obvious to Aristotle that the mind, comprehender of essences, comes first, and that nothing can be explained if we do not begin with that beginning. He remarks somewhere that by introducing the mind as an active factor throughout the universe, Anaxagoras looked like the only sane man among the early thinkers. This is not a good historical point of view but it is revealing.

To the fact-minded modern, this primacy of the mind may seem stranger than it is. Galileo, when he said that the book of nature is written in mathematical characters, was stating, too, one kind of idealism, the objective kind. He approached reality by one of its ideal properties, and tried to see where it would lead. Aristotle logicalizes reality from all possible aspects, which is what makes him the master of the *distinguo* and the fountainhead of much quibbling (he is able to do this methodically, in that he is sure of where he is going, for he has the Platonic model of a universal science, whereas our time is still trying to discover a particular one). But whichever way it is handled, idealism is a necessary component of all science; it *is* the search for a central perspective; hence we should make an effort to understand. Any evidence of orderly process is, for Aristotle, evidence of some kind of analogous relationship between the observer's mind and what he is looking at. The components of reality appear to fit together as the components of a thought would do. Supposing that conscious thought were to devise an apparatus for seeing, it would come up with something very similar to the eye. This, for the true idealist and transcendental philosopher, may mean that we recognize a conscious super-mind behind the universe, who thought it all out to the least detail. But even at the other pole, that supreme skeptic Mr. Hume concluded that we have evidence of something analogous to a mind—a vague footprint in the sands of time, too little to go on, as far as he was concerned, so he suggested we let it go at that. Taken in 1750, such an attitude was the essence of good sense.

Now, for Aristotle the analogy does hold; the footprint must be followed up. But he is no absolute idealist. He decides that the categories of mind are a conscious version of what takes place in nature in the first place. The form of each thing is a kind of pre-mental component (moderns would call it an "intentionality") inherent in the very process of reality, and it comes to being in the actual thing by realizing its "potency." It is through this analogy between thought and its object that we can understand.

If we do not try to *understand*, then of course we need not try any such scheme. For us inside modern physics, who want only to *explain*, the direction of thought is another. But it is far from being the natural one. We mentioned the eye as a prime example of what can be possibly understood, but hardly "explained," as we stand now. If we show a man a watch, he will not tend to explain it in terms of its machinery, unless he is a watchmaker or a very curious person. He will simply understand it as a timepiece. A watch is defined by its purpose, which is telling time, and that is also the "good" of a watch. Our understanding tends thus to be formulated in terms of the "good."

And so back to the Good, which is a dangerously simple idea. Everyone thinks he knows about his own good—at least until he finds a Socrates to paralyze him like an electric eel. But here we are beyond Socrates and man's motives. What is a flower good for, or a cockroach for that matter, or, as Franklin said, what good is a baby? Faced with the world as a whole, once we have outgrown the simple desire to say it is good for our convenience (and before we have reached the mechanistic phase), there is only one way of speaking about it and that is in terms at once rational and esthetic. For, whatever reconciliation we achieve, the thinking being can come to terms with it only on the esthetic level. A flower or a baby is simply meant to become what it is, its own "what it is to be." Its complete achievement is its own "good." And what is the total "good"? The universe makes sense as something eternal and diverse and eternally well-ordered. On this Aristotle claims to find himself in complete agreement both with Plato and with the Pythagoreans. It is in "the best tradition." Notice how careful he always is of putting back of him consensus and the best results of the thinking of all ages.

If we try to define the curve that goes from, say, Parmenides to Aristotle, a way to describe it would be this: science rejoins again the needs of society. The Eleatic and atomistic attempt was grandiose enough, but it must be admitted that it looked both stern and inconclusive. Modern science has made itself acceptable by delivering results. That science only set problems: ever new problems more and more difficult and profound, which lead ever farther away from our social and worldly perspectives. Socrates had come to discard natural philosophy. Aristotle tries to bring it back, but it has to be in another garb. Instead of the universe of rigor and necessity, of symmetry and sufficient reason, we have a universe of variety, neatness, distinction, of aptness and of plausible reason; the universe of the biologist and the jurist.

A Biological Physics

Aristotle is averse to reduction. As for material principles, they explain, in his eyes, nothing of what is essential. Parmenides was surely right, he says, in seeing that the kind of principle we need has properties of eternity and perfection which cannot belong to matter itself. That is why, in fact, Heraclitus had brought in the *logos,* why the Pythagoreans had believed in Numbers, why Parmenides has become the "inventor of metaphysics." But we must go farther. Parmenides had been tied to a curious presentation of primal substance, or rather substrate, which he had in some way tried to intellectualize into Being. But if, as he said, the only truth is that which is obtained by legitimate thinking itself, we must take the full consequences of his statement and say that truth about Being can be had only through the mind.

It is through the mind and its creative and esthetic motives that we are in most immediate contact with the reality of process in the universe. But in what sense can one think of mind as reflecting the scheme of eternity? It can, forever, project the consistency and the variety, and the delight in the union of both. To understand a tree from the point of view of Nature is to understand that apparently Nature wants that type of tree to be there forever, and to be there beside all other types that she has been pleased to bring forth. The pleasure that we find in naming and in distinguishing the variety of things in the world will be in some way creatively, if only intellectually, akin to the pleasure that Nature herself has had in bringing them forth. Nature clearly does not care much for the individual; nor does Science. Science is of the universal, that is, of what is meaningful to Nature. We can make a wooden bed and be pleased with it, but Nature does not register its existence. If we bury the bed in the earth, "it is not beds that shall spring forth from it, but wood." Where does this lead us?

To the substances. The cat, like the wood, is not made of plain atoms. It is one, continuous, specific substance called "cat," unique in the scheme; the knowable aspect of its essence is "catness," which applies to all cats. We can distinguish between "attributes" which are inherent to it (such as its shape and behavior) and "accidents" (such as its color and size). It is related to other substances in many different ways, in which the universals become evident. We have been led again to description, distinction, organization, generality, as the proper goal of science. It is natural history leading to a system of ideas, thanks to the power of classification which can rise in less than ten steps without confusion from a million individual species to a general concept. To contemplate an eternal well-organized order is to partake in some way of the mind of Nature herself. There is no possibility of evolution here, only the unchanging firmness of Design.

To know, it has been said, is to know by causes. How can we figure out a cause in this system if not by analogy with ours? Let us define a cause in the most ample and general sense as answering the question "Why?": that antecedent without which something would not be. Then let us consider, "for instance," says Aristotle, the house which is our own creation. A house would not be without (a) the material to build it, (b) a builder, (c) plans, and (d) the decision to build a house. Clearly the decision comes first, not only in time but in significance, because the decision contains implicitly in it all that the house will really be, since it is taken with a definite intention related to definite circumstances. As we go down in the order of causes, the definiteness decreases. The plan must be such as to correspond to the intention; but a certain measure of invention is allowed. The builder has only one requirement: that he be expert in building. As for the material, it is absolutely a matter of circumstances and local choices. Any material will do that corresponds to the general requirements. Now these four levels are what Aristotle calls the four types of cause: in ascending order, they are (a) the material, (b) the efficient, (c) the formal, and (d) the final. Here we have Aristotle's own kind of sufficient reason.

If we take now, instead of the analogy of the house, the anaology of the statue, the parallel comes closer. For the artist is at the same time the efficient, formal, and final cause of his work. He has conceived it out of his own esthetic decision and he carries it through with esthetic choice in complete freedom. The only thing still outside him is the material. Then we see that Nature herself is nothing but an unconscious artist who has in addition to all the other causes the material cause in herself, that is, who gets the material of her work out of herself. In this case the form that she impresses on the material goes throughout the material. Quite naturally, we have reached an important definition of life: Form actualizing itself. It has remained inside our culture to this day.

The definition is no doubt striking and ample, but that is just the trouble: it is, so to say, complete in itself. We need not search further for the nature of life, because we have already expressed it. It is Form intrinsic to the living substance. The idea works because each being in the course of its life acts exactly *as if* it were realizing a complete form of itself out of an amorphous beginning. It is the change of the seed into the bud, of the bud into the flower. It is as if an unconscious will and projected pattern were urging the Form to manifest itself by commanding the growth of the being. The will is directed to an end—the completion of the being is full Form. This is what Aristotle called *change* and *motion*. Beings attain their full Form and at the same time begin to decay. The process of things on earth is held between these two terms: generation and corruption, coming-into-being and passing-away. It is as it were the heartbeat of life; everything that exists will go to completion and death, but also it will have generated another thing which in turn undergoes the same cycle.

The same creativeness which is the secret of God's Active Intellect in the universe is also the secret of Nature; it manifests itself forever again in the pulse of individual life coming into being. No mechanical doctrine could have achieved this. We hope this has been made clear already. The mechanical world models produced under the Newtonian aegis through the eighteenth century do look childish in the face of the full problem. Aristotle had to go his own way. Since he agreed that nature is motion, he had to work out an entirely different conception of that key term itself.

Here we are at the heart of what he calls *physics*.

What we call "motion" is only one type of motion for Aristotle, who calls it "local motion" as distinct from quantitative and qualitative. This must be understood in terms of what Aristotle was trying to do, viz., organize a "science of nature" (the *Physics*) which should comprehend what we call today cosmology, physics, chemistry, and biology into a single frame of explanation, and starting from the most familiar characteristics and regularities. Nature is change. All change between "contraries" is what Aristotle calls motion. Change has to take place inside an order, or chaos would supervene. Moreover, in that order there seem to be "natures" which go on notwithstanding change, e.g., the living species, and they are a clue to the principle of order whereby things are kept or restored to their function in the order of Nature. Since there is, clearly, such an order, we can think only of two sorts of change or movement: that whereby something becomes what it really is (growth); and that whereby it becomes the material for the growth of something else (decay). Hence the famous definition that Descartes rather unfairly said made no sense in any language: movement is the act of being in potency in so far as it has not reached its full actualization or unfolding. The fulfillment must be there as a goal, potentially and directly, before it is realized; it may be a place (up, down) or a form (the grown animal); in any case it implies a *real* change, in no way relativistic. The existence of an order implies a direction and a goal. And in fact we see fire striving toward heaven, stones toward the center of the earth, as the seed strives toward the full-grown form. This leads to the idea of a place or "natural locus" as the goal of "natural movement." Any "violent movement" which would tend to break the balance is soon checked, and order restored. As to rest, it means the thing has reached its locus or has been temporarily checked on its way there. It must needs be, then, that each singular movement on earth is transitory, as it disturbs or restores the balance; but, as it needs another movement for its cause, the chain of causes is eternal. It is clear at this point that Aristotle is thinking all along of what we call *process* in general. If we translate him thus, the argument falls into place. Thus, "movement" takes place always against a resistance (here, again, the appeal is to familiar things) and comes to an end by the re-establishment of equilibrium; it is a passage between contraries; it needs an exterior cause, removing which it comes to a stop. It will be seen also why to Aristotle inertial motion—that is, motion undirected, unprompted, in a nonpatterned space—must appear as an unreal and perverse abstraction. The void cannot exist, for things would not know which way to go in it. The conflict with the strictly mechanical conception is unreconcilable. In the realm of astronomy it will lead to a system again unreconcilable with mechanics.

What is cause in all this? It is certainly not the "material" cause which is pure amorphous possibility; it is Reason in action in the other three causes—a *logos* that goes from thought to action, or, more generally still, from plan to realization. It is never, at any point, the Principle of Sufficient Reason of the scientists, which we have also called the Principle of Uniformly Distributed Ignorance—a principle which operates in terms of openness, symmetry, and continuity, not to mention discovery. Understanding is teleological. It always involves a principle of Specific Reason: "This item should be thus, and unique, because such is its place in the pattern." It leads to variety and formal discontinuity. It leads also to saying more than we know about things.

Addressing himself to the same ultimate questions as Farrington, the late Professor Edelstein of Johns Hopkins University brings the argument full circle.

FROM Motives and Incentives for Science in Antiquity
BY LUDWIG EDELSTEIN

So far I have considered science merely as theoretical understanding and have left out of consideration its usefulness for practical ends. Of the applicability of their findings the scientists were of course quite conscious, as the testimony shows. Archytas's studies in the the theory of mechanics led him to construct instruments and machines, and even a rattle, "a good invention," Aristotle says, "which people give to children in order that while occupied with this they may not break any furniture, for young things cannot keep still." Archimedes, the "geometrical Briareus" as the Roman aggressors called him, invented weapons for the defence of his native city. Astronomers and geographers applied their knowledge to drawing maps that could be used by sailors and travellers. It is true, scientists did not undertake their research with practical purposes in mind, they did not feel that their labours were more valuable or justifiable on account of the practical fruits they bore. The latter rather were by-products, so to say. Yet science did not shy away from technology, as is often assumed.

On the other hand, one cannot deny that applied science, as all ancient technology, did not advance as far as it could conceivably have done. During the thousand years of scientific studies in which the intellect of its "flight through the universe" revolutionized man's understanding of nature and achieved ever greater triumphs, the forms of daily existence changed relatively little, less perhaps than during the later Middle Ages, surely much less than in some of the decades since the middle of the nineteenth century. That the usefulness of science in Graeco-Roman times was comparatively unexploited, that it was, strictly speaking, no motive for developing scientific knowledge, is due I think mainly to three factors.

First, the "empirical" scientists, who considered speculation and theory of less importance, if of importance at all, and who on account of their prevalent concern with reality might have taken a special interest in applying their knowledge, were the ones to curtail research and thereby to curtail also the

Ludwig Edelstein, "Motives and Incentives for Science in Antiquity," in A. C. Crombie, ed., *Scientific Change*, pp. 22–27, 28–32. Reprinted by permission of Heinemann Educational Books Ltd., London; published by Basic Books, Inc., New York, 1963.

chances of mastering the phenomena. For in the Hellenistic theory of empiricism, the possibility of comprehending nature is severely narrowed down. Everything inaccessible to the senses is regarded as hidden from exploration and thus closed to scientific study. It was the empirical physician who denied that anatomy and physiology could become sciences and rendered useful for medical treatment. Also, reading of books—the treasured-up experience of the past—for him took precedence over making new experiments and accumulating more data. Extension of knowledge, the opening-up of new opportunities for applied science, was therefore left almost exclusively to the "theoretical" scientists—the "dogmatists" as they were derisively called by their opponents, and yet in fact the only ones to venture beyond the already known. But with them, of course, knowledge for the sake of knowledge was the prime motive and the prime concern.

Second, one must not forget that ancient sciences have by their very nature so to say a slant towards the theoretical rather than the practical. Some, physics and psychology for instance, were really "philosophical" sciences. For they remained in the domain of the philosopher and were studied by him as part of his analysis of the physical world and of human nature. When the original unity of philosophy and all the sciences, obtaining in the pre-Socratic period, dissolved, and independent, particular sciences were established—sciences pursued by specialists—they still kept in close touch with philosophy. Their first principles, their methodology rested on philosophical grounds. The issue between mechanism and teleology, the controversy about the respective values of empirical observation and theoretical reasoning were fought not with scientific but with philosophical arguments, and these discussions occupied a much larger part of scientific writing than they would in later science. Not that the scientist slavishly followed the dictates of a philosophic law-giver. Rather he took an active interest in philosophy, he became himself a philosopher. The title of Galen's essay "That the best physician is also a philosopher" epitomizes the prevailing attitude. On the other hand, there was a feeling that men of experience, as Aristotle says, are better in practical matters, better equipped to handle particulars, than is the scientist who knows the universals. Thus the improvement of the technical apparatus remained largely in the hands of artisans and craftsmen, who changed things slowly and cautiously in their traditional conservative manner.

Last though not least, the relative neglect of the practical must I think be viewed against the background of the ancients' general attitude towards life, of which it seems characteristic that they acknowledged and respected boundaries set to their actions. They would, to be sure, aim at perfection in rational insight and in right conduct; they would fashion their cities or states in accordance with political ideals; they would above all civilize human existence so that it became truly human. They did not feel that it was their business to take the world over altogether. Men no more claimed than did their gods to be creators out of nothing, to act with a free will that imposes its law on things that have no nature of their own. Rather did they feel called upon to shape matter that was given and, here below at any rate, refractory to reason. The gods but mould, or to use a Platonic phrase, persuade the physical universe to accommodate itself to their wishes as far as possible. It does not stand otherwise with that universe which men build. Having accomplished what appeared possible and essential, the pagans were satisfied to use knowledge mostly for taking care of their daily wants which were modest, for defending their country when there was need, for adorning temple services and festivals, for increasing pleasure through play and amusement.

It is mainly for such reasons, I think, that ancient science remained relatively useless, that changes which in principle were within reach were actually not made. But to a certain extent the ineffectiveness of science in altering conditions depended also on social factors, as should become clear from the discussion of the incentives for science, to which I shall now turn.

The new venture of science which started in the pre-Socratic centuries was a venture undertaken by individuals; it lacked the support of society. In the opinion of the citizens of the Greek communities, the scientist's "activity" was "idleness"—indeed withdrawal from the realities of life. They neither cared to be like him nor had they any use for him. Why then should they have given support to science? Far from supporting it, they did not even pay homage to it, as they did honour and reward poets or athletes. One who wished to engage in scientific studies had to be a man of independent means, free to indulge his fancies. At most he might maintain himself by teaching converts to the new cause. He certainly had no other hope of making a living. There were no schools with which one could be associated, no careers that one could follow as a scientist. The few who favoured the scientific movement advocated redress of the situation, for they were well aware of the fact that what society does not pay for or prize does not flourish. No one listened to their remonstrances. Throughout the classical age science remained beyond the pale of society.

Why did science fail to secure more recognition and encouragement? The responsibility certainly does not lie with distrust of science, with political schemes of any class of society designed to prevent science from becoming a weapon in the fight for freedom and enlightenment. If fear was felt regarding the relationship of society and science, it was the scientists who were suspicious. For they were well aware of the fact that royal support or support from any outside quarters was potentially a danger to the objectivity of their research, because favours might be expected in return, favours that could necessitate distortions of the truth or actions irreconcilable with their ideals. The true explanation for the reaction of society is I think to be found first of all in the scientific situation as it had taken shape by the time of Hellenism.

It was a situation not dissimilar to that of modern philosophy. Rival systems of science were competing with one another, rival systems which were in fact rival sciences. For there was nothing one could call science in the modern sense of the term, a body of knowledge valid everywhere, a system of principles, of rules of procedure and of theories, well defined and generally accepted. With the exception perhaps of mathematics, there were but "sciences," the adherence to which was optional. A science of mathematical astronomy. faced a science of empirical astronomy. Empirical medicine, discarding anatomy and physiology, opposed dogmatic medicine based on anatomy and physiology. Descriptive geography rejecting quantitative analysis stood against a highly mathematized geography. Each of these sciences of course in the opinion of its proponents was true, but their claim to this effect clashed with counter-claims. This "dissension" as the ancients called it—a dissension not concerning particular results but concerning the basic presuppositions and aims of the scientific enterprise as such—made it almost impossible for anyone not a partisan to say what science was and what it was about, let alone to decide which of the existing systems of science should be encouraged and rewarded.

That science in general or science as the Greeks knew it begins one day, and that, after the liberating word has been spoken, everyone knows the right course to follow, seems an ineradicable historical prejudice. In fact, the history of Greek science, in addition to being the story of the discovery of true and false data—true and false from the modern point of view—is also the story of the gradual discovery of the meaning of science. The concept of science itself has a history. It took almost eight hundred years to work out the implications of the enterprise on which the ancients had ventured and to create general agreement on it. . . . The last step was only taken in the second century A.D., when largely through the work of Galen and of Ptolemy— theoreticians of science no less than scientists—a *scientia aeterna* began to be built up, science as it was to be understood from then on.

Yet, one may object, if men had been wiser, if they had recognized the value of science, if they had encouraged it as so many of the ancients themselves desired, the "dissension" of which I spoke could have been resolved earlier, and science would then have become integrated into civilization in Antiquity as it was later on. In such an objection there is I think a kernel of truth. The neglect of science on the part of society was undoubtedly due also to the predominance of other intellectual and emotional concerns.

Even those friendly to science often did not accept it altogether. The pre-Socratics and most of the classical philosophers to be sure were its fervent devotees. But among the minor Socratics emphasis on ethics began to grow, not to mention the fact that with Cynicism a conscious revolt of the civilized against civilization set in, which, though never spectacularly successful, left its mark on subsequent thought. Primitivism, the dream of a Golden Age of the past or future, a Rousseauesque admiration for the "noble savage" who has not eaten from the tree of knowledge, was the shadow of ancient rationalism and progressionism. Hellenistic philosophies, Stoicism as well as Epicureanism, were interested in science; in their last phases they even showed a strong appreciation of the significance of science. But they were given to the study of moral values at least as much as to the study of brute facts; if to them God was visible in nature, he was even more manifest in man and his actions. Rhetorical training, whose hold was probably greater than that of philosophical education, never included more than the rudiments of science, for everything beyond them was considered useless. The so-called liberal arts led to the threshold of science but no farther. And education in general, being a matter of the individual's free choice, continued to consist mainly in the study of poetry and music. Centuries after the eclipse of the sun had been proved to be a natural, recurrent phenomenon, such an event was still taken even by men in prominent positions as a divine omen, without their incurring the least censure except from the *avant garde* of intellectuals. For not everybody was willing to resign himself to the disenchantment of the world which followed from the attempt to comprehend nature in rational terms. Without the pressure of a general school system through which the results of science would be filtered down to the people, they did not feel obliged to believe in the results of science and preferred to cling to the mythos, to live in it, to think in its categories. Science never succeeded in breaking the power of mythology. No less an achievement than art and poetry, it was in contrast to them but a thin layer over ancient civilization and not at all as important to the Greeks and Romans as it was destined to become to the future.

It goes without saying that the lack of institutionalization of ancient science accounts for many of its shortcomings. Without adequate prestige and recognition, without promise of financial security, it did not attract many people, not as many at any rate as could profitably have worked on securing the terrain which had been laid out. On the other hand, what was accomplished seems even more impressive because it was done with so little outside assistance. Considering why "men originally instituted a prize for competitions of the body, but none for wisdom," a pupil of Aristotle considers it a satisfactory answer to the puzzle that "the prize must be more desirable than the competition"; and he adds that though in the case of athletic contests such a prize can be found, "what prize could be better than wisdom?" It would be carrying flattery to extremes if one believed that ancient society failed to pay scientists because kings and citizens admiringly realized that wisdom is its own reward. But one may fairly say, I think, that in a world in which science was not a career, the overwhelming majority of those who studied science must have done so for the sake of science. This is perhaps not the least of the reasons for the strength and the survival of the ideal of the theoretical life in all periods of ancient history. For motives rather than incentives, desire for the truth rather than outward allurement, had to persuade men to enter the service of science.

CHRISTIANITY
A NEW WORLD VIEW?

CONTENTS

QUESTIONS FOR STUDY

1. *How do Gibbon and Ladner differ in their evaluations of the novelty of the Christian religion?*

2. *How did this novelty contribute to the success of Christianity?*

3. *What does the correspondence of Pliny and Trajan show us about the Roman attitude toward Christianity?*

4. *Are all the theological doctrines set out in the Nicene Creed to be found in the excerpts from the New Testament given in this section?*

5. *Compare the observations of Gibbon, Dawson, and Ladner on the organization of the primitive church. How do they differ in their attitudes? What can you find out about the organization of the church from the early sources?*

6. *What do you consider to be the most convincing explanation for the success of Christianity?*

Christianity, which conquered the Roman Empire, was to provide the religious basis of Western civilization. This religion, originating among poor fishermen in an insignificant oriental province of the empire, competed not only against the official pagan cults of Rome but also against such popular mystery cults as those of Isis and Osiris, Mithra, and many others. It came into a world educated by the philosophies of Plato, Aristotle, the Stoa, and Epicurus. Without armies it resisted the force and oppression of emperors. In spite of all it won out, first gaining tolerance, then absolute control. The problem in this section is to understand what was new in the teaching of the Christian church and why the new religion achieved such astonishing success.

The most important sources for the origins of Christianity are the Gospel narratives concerning the life and death of Jesus (pp. 212–226). But they are difficult sources that have given rise to endless controversy among modern scholars. The essential problem is that none of the Gospels was written during the lifetime of Christ or in the years immediately after his death. The earliest one (Mark) is commonly dated A.D. 65–75 and the latest (John) A.D. 90–110. The Gospels are based on earlier written sources that themselves record a still earlier oral tradition. It is very hard to determine how far this oral tradition preserved a reliable account of actual historical facts. It is also hard to determine just how each of the four Evangelists selected or adapted elements of the existing tradition in the light of his own theological convictions.

These are problems for theologians as much as for historians. For the historian one very important fact is that the Gospels (whether they are literally true or not) do preserve for us the beliefs of the early Christian church. From this point of view they are entirely trustworthy historical documents. They tell us what the primitive Christian church believed. And since our problem is to understand the teaching of this church and to explain its success, the Gospels form our necessary starting point. Subsequent readings from early Christian sources given below illustrate the growth of church doctrine and organization and the reaction of the Roman state to the new religion (pp. 227–232, 235–242).

Among the modern authors who have sought to explain the extraordinary success of Christianity, Edward Gibbon (pp. 199–211) approached the problem from the standpoint of an eighteenth-century rationalist. He evidently felt it necessary to set out the conventional view that the Christian religion triumphed because of the miracles worked by its first leaders and because of the superior virtue of the Christian community. Yet he could not resist the inclination to make fun of the very arguments that he was advancing. The result is elegant and witty but highly paradoxical. Christopher Dawson (pp. 233–234) emphasized the importance of the church's organizational structure in preserving a distinctive Christian tradition. The final reading presents a reconsideration of various problems raised by Gibbon from the standpoint of a contemporary church historian (pp. 243–256). Gerhart Ladner is concerned especially with explaining the "innovating power" of Christianity through a discussion of the ways in which the new faith differed from the existing religions of the ancient world.

1
GIBBON ON THE VICTORY OF CHRISTIANITY

FROM The History of the Decline and Fall of the Roman Empire BY EDWARD GIBBON

A candid but rational inquiry into the progress and establishment of Christianity may be considered as a very essential part of the history of the Roman empire. While that great body was invaded by open violence, or undermined by slow decay, a pure and humble religion gently insinuated itself into the minds of men, grew up in silence and obscurity, derived new vigour from opposition, and finally erected the triumphant banner of the Cross on the ruins of the Capitol. Nor was the influence of Christianity confined to the period or to the limits of the Roman empire. After a revolution of thirteen or fourteen centuries, that religion is still professed by the nations of Europe, the most distinguished portion of human-kind in arts and learning as well as in arms. By the industry and zeal of the Europeans it has been widely diffused to the most distant shores of Asia and Africa; and by the means of their colonies has been firmly established from Canada to Chili, in a world unknown to the ancients.

But this inquiry, however useful or entertaining, is attended with two peculiar difficulties. The scanty and suspicious materials of ecclesiastical history seldom enable us to dispel the dark cloud that hangs over the first age of the church. The great law of impartiality too often obliges us to reveal the imperfections of the uninspired teachers and believers of the Gospel; and, to a careless observer, *their* faults may seem to cast a shade on the faith which they professed. But the scandal of the pious Christian, and the fallacious triumph of the Infidel, should cease as soon as they recollect not only *by whom,*

Edward Gibbon, *The History of the Decline and Fall of the Roman Empire*, William Smith, ed., II (1854), 151–190, 197, 204.

but likewise *to whom,* the Divine Revelation was given. The theologian may indulge the pleasing task of describing Religion as she descended from Heaven, arrayed in her native purity. A more melancholy duty is imposed on the historian. He must discover the inevitable mixture of error and corruption which she contracted in a long residence upon earth, among a weak and degenerate race of beings.

Our curiosity is naturally prompted to inquire by what means the Christian faith obtained so remarkable a victory over the established religions of the earth. To this inquiry an obvious but satisfactory answer may be returned; that it was owing to the convincing evidence of the doctrine itself, and to the ruling providence of its great Author. But as truth and reason seldom find so favourable a reception in the world, and as the wisdom of Providence frequently condescends to use the passions of the human heart, and the general circumstances of mankind, as instruments to execute its purpose, we may still be permitted, though with becoming submission, to ask, not indeed what were the first, but what were the secondary causes of the rapid growth of the Christian church? It will, perhaps, appear that it was most effectually favoured and assisted by the five following causes:—I. The inflexible, and, if we may use the expression, the intolerant zeal of the Christians, derived, it is true, from the Jewish religion, but purified from the narrow and unsocial spirit which, instead of inviting, had deterred the Gentiles from embracing the law of Moses. II. The doctrine of a future life, improved by every additional circumstance which could give weight and efficacy to that important truth. III. The miraculous powers ascribed to the primitive church. IV. The pure and austere morals of the Christians. V. The union and discipline of the Christian republic, which gradually formed an independent and increasing state in the heart of the Roman empire.

I. THE FIRST CAUSE

We have already described the religious harmony of the ancient world, and the facility with which the most different and even hostile nations embraced, or at least respected, each other's superstitions. A single people refused to join in the common intercourse of mankind. The Jews, who, under the Assyrian and Persian monarchies, had languished for many ages the most despised portion of their slaves, emerged from obscurity under the successors of Alexander; and as they multiplied to a surprising degree in the East, and afterwards in the West, they soon excited the curiosity and wonder of other nations. The sullen obstinacy with which they maintained their peculiar rites and unsocial manners seemed to mark them out a distinct species of men, who boldly professed, or who faintly disguised, their implacable hatred to the rest of human-kind. Neither the violence of Antiochus, nor the arts of Herod, nor the example of the circumjacent nations, could ever persuade the Jews to associate with the institutions of Moses the elegant mythology of the Greeks.

According to the maxims of universal toleration, the Romans protected a superstition which they despised. The polite Augustus condescended to give orders that sacrifices should be offered for his prosperity in the temple of Jerusalem; while the meanest of the posterity of Abraham, who should have paid the same homage to the Jupiter of the Capitol, would have been an object of abhorrence to himself and to his brethren. But the moderation of the conquerors was insufficient to appease the jealous prejudices of their subjects, who were alarmed and scandalised at the ensigns of paganism, which necessarily introduced themselves into a Roman province. The mad attempt of Caligula to place his own statue in the temple of Jerusalem was defeated by the unanimous resolution of a people who dreaded death much less than such an idolatrous profanation. Their attachment to the law of Moses was equal to their detestation of foreign religions. The current of zeal and devotion, as it was contracted into a narrow channel, ran with the strength, and sometimes with the fury, of a torrent.

* * *

In the admission of new citizens that unsocial people was actuated by the selfish vanity of the Greeks, rather than by the generous policy of Rome. The descendants of Abraham were flattered by the opinion that they alone were the heirs of the covenant, and they were apprehensive of diminishing the value of their inheritance by sharing it too easily with the strangers of the earth. A larger acquaintance with mankind extended their knowledge without correcting their prejudices; and whenever the God of Israel acquired any new votaries, he was much more indebted to the inconstant humour of polytheism than to the active zeal of his own missionaries. The religion of Moses seems to be instituted for a particular country as well as for a single nation; and if a strict obedience had been paid to the order that every male, three times in the year, should present himself before the Lord Jehovah, it would have been impossible that the Jews could ever have spread themselves beyond the narrow limits of the promised land. That obstacle was indeed removed by the destruction of the temple of Jerusalem; but the most considerable part of the Jewish religion was involved in its destruction; and the Pagans, who had long wondered at the strange report of an empty sanctuary, were at a loss to discover what could be the object, or what could be the instruments, of a worship which was destitute of temples and of altars, of priests and of sacrifices. Yet even in their fallen state, the Jews, still asserting their lofty and exclusive privileges, shunned, instead of courting, the society of strangers. They still insisted with inflexible rigour on those parts of the law which it was in their power to practise. Their peculiar distinctions of days, of meats, and a variety of trivial though burdensome observances, were so many objects of disgust and aversion for the other nations, to whose habits and prejudices they were diametrically opposite. The painful and even dangerous rite of circumcision was alone capable of repelling a willing proselyte from the door of the synagogue.

Under these circumstances, Christianity offered itself to the world, armed with the strength of the Mosaic law, and delivered from the weight of its fetters. An exclusive zeal for the truth of religion and the unity of God was as carefully inculcated in the new as in the ancient system: and whatever was now revealed to mankind concerning the nature and designs of the Supreme Being was fitted to increase their reverence for that mysterious doctrine. The divine authority of Moses and the prophets was admitted, and even established, as the firmest basis of Christianity. From the beginning of the world an uninterrupted series of predictions had announced and prepared the long-expected coming of the Messiah, who, in compliance with the gross apprehensions of the Jews, had been more frequently represented under the character of a King and Conqueror, than under that of a Prophet, a Martyr, and the Son of God. By his expiatory sacrifice the imperfect sacrifices of the temple were at once consummated and abolished. The ceremonial law, which consisted only of types and figures, was succeeded by a pure and spiritual worship, equally adapted to all climates, as well as to every condition of mankind; and to the initiation of blood, was substituted a more harmless initiation of water. The promise of divine favour, instead of being partially confined to the posterity of Abraham, was universally proposed to the freeman and the slave, to the Greek and to the barbarian, to the Jew and to the Gentile. Every privilege that could raise the proselyte from earth to heaven, that could exalt his devotion, secure his happiness, or even gratify that secret pride which, under the semblance of devotion, insinuates itself into the human heart, was still reserved for the members of the Christian church; but at the same time all mankind was permitted, and even solicited, to accept the glorious distinction, which was not only proffered as a favour, but imposed as an obligation. It became the most sacred duty of a new convert to diffuse among his friends and relations the inestimable blessing which he had received, and to warn them against a refusal that would be severely punished as a criminal disobedience to the will of a benevolent but all-powerful Deity.

. . . The philosopher, who considered the system of polytheism as a composition of human fraud and error, could disguise a smile of contempt under the mask of devotion, without apprehending that either the mockery or the compliance would expose him to the resentment of any invisible, or, as he conceived them, imaginary powers. But the established religions of Paganism were seen by the primitive Christians in a much more odious and formidable light. It was the universal sentiment both of the church and of heretics, that the daemons were the authors, the patrons, and the objects of idolatry. Those rebellious spirits who had been degraded from the rank of angels, and cast down into the infernal pit, were still permitted to roam upon earth, to torment the bodies and to seduce the minds of sinful men. The daemons soon discovered and abused the natural propensity of the human heart towards devotion, and, artfully withdrawing the adoration of mankind from their Creator, they usurped the place and honours of the Supreme Deity. By the success of their malicious contrivances, they at once gratified their own vanity and revenge, and obtained the only comfort of which they were yet susceptible, the hope of involving the human species in the participation of their guilt and misery. It was confessed, or at least it was imagined, that they had distributed among themselves the most important characters of polytheism, one daemon assuming the name and attributes of Jupiter, another of Aesculapius, a third of Venus, and a fourth perhaps of Apollo; and that, by the advantage of their long experience and aërial nature, they were enabled to execute, with sufficient skill and dignity, the parts which they had undertaken. They lurked in the temples, instituted festivals and sacrifices, invented fables, pronounced oracles, and were frequently allowed to perform miracles. The Christians, who, by the interposition of evil spirits, could so readily explain every preternatural appearance, were disposed and even desirous to admit the most extravagant fictions of the Pagan mythology. But the belief of the Christian was accompanied with horror. The most trifling mark of respect to the national worship he considered as a direct homage yielded to the daemon, and as an act of rebellion against the majesty of God.

II. THE SECOND CAUSE

The writings of Cicero represent in the most lively colours the ignorance, the errors, and the uncertainty of the ancient philosophers with regard to the immortality of the soul. When they are desirous of arming their disciples against the fear of death, they inculcate, as an obvious, though melancholy position, that the fatal stroke of our dissolution releases us from the calamities of life; and that those can no longer suffer who no longer exist . . . We are sufficiently acquainted with the eminent persons who flourished in the age of Cicero and of the first Caesars, with their actions, their characters, and their motives, to be assured that their conduct in this life was never regulated by any serious conviction of the rewards or punishments of a future state. At the bar and in the senate of Rome the ablest orators were not apprehensive of giving offence to their hearers by exposing that doctrine as an idle and extravagant opinion, which was rejected with contempt by every man of a liberal education and understanding.

* * *

When the promise of eternal happiness was proposed to mankind on condition of adopting the faith, and of observing the precepts, of the Gospel, it is no wonder that so advantageous an offer should have been accepted by great numbers of every religion, of every rank, and of every province in the Roman empire. The ancient Christians were animated by a contempt for their present existence, and by a just confidence of immortality, of which the doubtful and imperfect faith of modern ages cannot give us any adequate notion. In the primitive church the influence of truth was very powerfully strengthened by an opinion which, however it may deserve respect for its usefulness and antiquity, has not been found agreeable to experience. It was universally believed that the end of the world, and the kingdom of heaven, were at hand. The near approach of this wonderful event had been predicted by the apostles; the tradition of it was preserved by their earliest disciples, and those who understood in their literal sense the discourses of Christ himself were obliged to expect the second and glorious coming of the Son of Man in the clouds, before that generation was totally extinguished which had beheld his humble condition upon earth, and which might still be witness of the calamities of the Jews under Vespasian or Hadrian. The revolution of seventeen centuries has instructed us not to press too closely the mysterious language of prophecy and revelation; but as long as, for wise purposes, this error was permitted to subsist in the church, it was productive of the most salutary effects on the faith and practice of Christians, who lived in the awful expectation of that moment when the globe itself, and all the various race of mankind, should tremble at the appearance of their divine Judge.

Whilst the happiness and glory of a temporal reign were promised to the disciples of Christ, the most dreadful calamities were denounced against an unbelieving world. . . .

The condemnation of the wisest and most virtuous of the Pagans, on account of their ignorance or disbelief of the divine truth, seems to offend the reason and the humanity of the present age. But the primitive church, whose faith was of a much firmer consistence, delivered over, without hesitation, to eternal torture, the far greater part of the human species. A charitable hope might perhaps be indulged in favour of Socrates, or some other sages of antiquity, who had consulted the light of reason before that of the Gospel had arisen. But it was unanimously affirmed that those who, since the birth or the death of Christ, had obstinately persisted in the worship of the daemons, neither deserved nor could expect a pardon from the irritated justice of the Deity. These rigid sentiments, which had been unknown to the ancient world, appear to have infused a spirit of bitterness into a system of love and harmony. The ties of blood and friendship were frequently torn asunder by the difference of religious faith; and the Christians, who, in this world, found themselves oppressed by the power of the Pagans, were sometimes seduced by resentment and spiritual pride to delight in the prospect of their future triumph. "You are fond of spectacles," exclaims the stern Tertullian, "expect the greatest of all spectacles, the last and eternal judgment of the universe. How shall I admire, how laugh, how rejoice, how exult, when I behold so many proud monarchs, and fancied gods, groaning in the lowest abyss of darkness; so many magistrates, who persecuted the name of the Lord, liquefying in fiercer fires than they ever kindled against the Christians; so many sage philosophers blushing in red-hot flames with their deluded scholars; so many celebrated poets trembling before the tribunal, not of Minos, but of Christ; so many tragedians, more tuneful in the expression of their own sufferings; so many dancers—" But the humanity of the reader will permit me to draw a veil over the rest of this infernal description, which the zealous African pursues in a long variety of affected and unfeeling witticisms.

Doubtless there were many among the primitive Christians of a temper more suitable to the meekness and charity of their profession. There were many who felt a sincere compassion for the danger of their friends and countrymen, and who exerted the most benevolent zeal to save them from the impending destruction. The careless Polytheist, assailed by new and unexpected terrors, against which neither his priests nor his philosophers could afford him any certain protection, was very frequently terrified and subdued by the menace of eternal tortures. His fears might assist the progress of his faith and reason; and if he could once persuade himself to suspect that the Christian religion might possibly be true, it became an easy task to convince him that it was the safest and most prudent party that he could possibly embrace.

III. THE THIRD CAUSE

The supernatural gifts, which even in this life were ascribed to the Christians above the rest of mankind, must have conduced to their own comfort, and very frequently to the conviction of infidels. Besides the occasional prodigies, which might sometimes be effected by the immediate interposition of the Deity when he suspended the laws of Nature for the service of religion, the Christian church, from the time of the apostles and their first disciples, has claimed an uninterrupted succession of miraculous powers, the gift of tongues, of vision, and of prophecy, the power of expelling daemons, of healing the sick, and of raising the dead. The knowledge of foreign languages was frequently communicated to the contemporaries of Irenaeus, though Irenaeus himself was left to struggle with the difficulties of a barbarous dialect whilst he preached the Gospel to the natives of Gaul. The divine inspiration, whether it was conveyed in the form of a waking or of a sleeping vision, is described as a favour very liberally bestowed on all ranks of the faithful, on women as on elders, on boys as well as upon bishops. When their devout minds were sufficiently prepared by a course of prayer, of fasting, and of vigils, to receive the extraordinary impulse, they were transported out of their senses, and delivered in extasy what was inspired, being mere organs of the Holy Spirit, just as a pipe or flute is of him who blows into it. We may add that the design of these visions was, for the most part, either to disclose the future history, or to guide the present administration, of the church. The expulsion of the daemons from the bodies of those unhappy persons whom they had been permitted to torment was considered as a signal though ordinary triumph of religion, and is repeatedly alleged by the ancient apologists as the most convincing evidence of the truth of Christianity. The awful ceremony was usually performed in a public manner, and in the presence of a great number of spectators; the patient was relieved by the power or skill of the exorcist, and the vanquished daemon was heard to confess that he was one of the fabled gods of antiquity, who had impiously usurped the adoration of mankind. But the miraculous cure of diseases of the most inveterate or even preternatural kind can no longer occasion any surprise, when we recollect that in the days of Irenaeus, about the end of the second century, the resurrection of the dead was very far from being esteemed an uncommon event; that the miracle was frequently performed on necessary occasions, by great fasting and the joint supplication of the church of the place, and that the persons thus restored to their prayers had lived afterwards among them many years. At such a period, when faith could boast of so many wonderful victories over death, it seems difficult to account for the scepticism of those philosophers who still rejected and derided the doctrine of the resurrection. A noble Grecian had rested on this important ground the whole controversy, and promised Theophilus, bishop of Antioch, that, if he could be gratified with the sight of a single person who had been actually raised from the dead, he would immediately embrace the Christian religion. It is somewhat remarkable that the prelate of the first eastern church, however anxious for the conversion of his friend, thought proper to decline this fair and reasonable challenge.

* * *

IV. THE FOURTH CAUSE

But the primitive Christian demonstrated his faith by his virtues; and it was very justly supposed that the Divine persuasion, which enlightened or subdued the understanding, must at the same time purify the heart and direct the actions of the believer. The first apologists of Christianity who justify the innocence of their brethen, and the writers of a later period who celebrate the sanctity of their ancestors, display, in the most lively colours, the reformation of manners which was introduced into the world by the preaching of the Gospel. As it is my intention to remark only such human causes as were permitted to second the influence of revelation, I shall slightly mention two motives which might naturally render the lives of the primitive Christians much purer and more austere than those of their Pagan contemporaries or their degenerate successors—repentance for their past sins, and the laudable desire of supporting the reputation of the society in which they were engaged.

It is a very ancient reproach, suggested by the ignorance or the malice of infidelity, that the Christians allured into their party the most atrocious criminals, who, as soon as they were touched by a sense of remorse, were easily persuaded to wash away, in the water of baptism, the guilt of their past conduct, for which the temples of the gods refused to grant them any expiation. But this reproach, when it is cleared from misrepresentation, contributes as much to the honour as it did to the increase of the church. The friends of

Christianity may acknowledge without a blush that many of the most eminent saints had been before their baptism the most abandoned sinners. Those persons who in the world had followed, though in an imperfect manner, the dictates of benevolence and propriety, derived such a calm satisfaction from the opinion of their own rectitude as rendered them much less susceptible of the sudden emotions of shame, of grief, and of terror, which have given birth to so many wonderful conversions. After the example of their Divine Master, the missionaries of the Gospel disdained not the society of men, and especially of women, oppressed by the consciousness, and very often by the effects, of their vices. As they emerged from sin and superstition to the glorious hope of immortality, they resolved to devote themselves to a life, not only of virtue, but of penitence. The desire of perfection became the ruling passion of their soul; and it is well known that, while reason embraces a cold mediocrity, our passions hurry us with rapid violence over the space which lies between the most opposite extremes.

* * *

It is a very honourable circumstance for the morals of the primitive Christians, that even their faults, or rather errors, were derived from an excess of virtue. The bishops and doctors of the church, whose evidence attests, and whose authority might influence, the professions, the principles, and even the practice of their contemporaries, had studied the Scriptures with less skill than devotion; and they often received in the most literal sense those rigid precepts of Christ and the apostles to which the prudence of succeeding commentators has applied a looser and more figurative mode of interpretation. Ambitious to exalt the perfection of the Gospel above the wisdom of philosophy, the zealous fathers have carried the duties of self-mortification, of purity, and of patience, to a height which it is scarcely possible to attain, and much less to preserve, in our present state of weakness and corruption. A doctrine so extraordinary and so sublime must inevitably command the veneration of the people; but it was ill calculated to obtain the suffrage of those worldly philosophers who, in the conduct of this transitory life, consult only the feelings of nature and the interest of society.

There are two very natural propensities which we may distinguish in the most virtuous and liberal dispositions, the love of pleasure and the love of action. If the former is refined by art and learning, improved by the charms of social intercourse, and corrected by a just regard to economy, to health, and to reputation, it is productive of the greatest part of the happiness of private life. The love of action is a principle of a much stronger and more doubtful nature. It often leads to anger, to ambition, and to revenge; but when it is guided by the sense of propriety and benevolence, it becomes the parent of every virtue, and, if those virtues are accompanied with equal abilities, a family, a state, or an empire, may be indebted for their safety and prosperity to the undaunted courage of a single man. To the love of pleasure we may therefore ascribe most of the agreeable, to the love of action we may attribute most of the useful and respectable, qualifications. The character in which both the one and the other should be united and harmonised would seem to constitute the most perfect idea of human nature. The insensible and inactive disposition, which should be supposed alike destitute of both, would be rejected, by the common consent of mankind, as utterly incapable of procuring any happiness to the individual, or any public benefit to the world. But it was not in *this* world that the primitive Christians were desirous of making themselves either agreeable or useful.

The acquisition of knowledge, the exercise of our reason of fancy, and the cheerful flow of unguarded conversation, may employ the leisure of a liberal mind. Such amusements, however, were rejected with abhorrence, or admitted with the utmost caution, by the severity of the fathers, who despised all knowledge that was not useful to salvation, and who considered all levity of discourse as a criminal abuse of the gift of speech. In our present state of existence the body is so inseparably connected with the soul, that it seems to be our interest to taste, with innocence and moderation, the enjoyments of which that faithful companion is susceptible. Very different was the reasoning of our devout predecessors; vainly aspiring to imitate the perfection of angels, they disdained, or they affected to disdain, every earthly and corporeal delight. Some of our senses indeed are necessary for our preservation, others for our subsistence, and others again for our information; and thus far it was impossible to reject the use of them. The first sensation of pleasure was marked as the first moment of their abuse. The unfeeling candidate for heaven was instructed, not only to resist the grosser allurements of the taste or smell, but even to shut his ears against the profane harmony of sounds, and to view with indifference the most finished productions of human art. Gay apparel, magnificent houses, and elegant furniture, were supposed to unite the double guilt of pride and of sensuality: a simple and mortified appearance was more suitable to the Christian who was certain of his sins and doubtful of his salvation. In their censures of luxury the fathers are extremely minute and circumstantial; and among the various articles which excite their pious indignation we may enumerate false hair, garments of any colour except white, instruments of music, vases of gold or silver, downy pillows (as Jacob reposed his head on a stone), white bread, foreign wines, public salutations, the use of warm baths, and the practice of shaving the beard, which, according to the expression of Tertullian, is a lie against our own faces, and an impious attempt to improve the works of the Creator. When Christianity was introduced among the rich and the polite, the observation of these singular laws was left, as it would be at present, to the few who were ambitious of superior sanctity. But it is always easy, as well as agreeable, for the inferior ranks of mankind to claim a merit from the contempt of that pomp and pleasure which fortune has placed beyond their reach. The virtue of the primitive Christians, like that of the first Romans, was very frequently guarded by poverty and ignorance.

The chaste severity of the fathers in whatever related to the commerce of the two sexes flowed from the same principle—their abhorrence of every en-joyment which might gratify the sensual, and degrade the spiritual nature of man. It was their favourite opinion, that if Adam had preserved his obedience to the Creator, he would have lived for ever in a state of virgin purity, and that some harmless mode of vegetation might have peopled paradise with a race of innocent and immortal beings. The use of marriage was permitted only to his fallen posterity, as a necessary expedient to continue the human species, and as a restraint, however imperfect, on the natural licentiousness of desire. The hesitation of the orthodox casuists on this interesting subject be-trays the perplexity of men unwilling to approve an institution which they were compelled to tolerate. The enumeration of the very whimsical laws which they most circumstantially imposed on the marriage-bed would force a smile from the young and a blush from the fair. It was their unanimous sentiment that a first marriage was adequate to all the purposes of nature and of society. The sensual connection was refined into a resemblance of the mystic union of Christ with his church, and was pronounced to be indissol-uble either by divorce or by death. The practice of second nuptials was branded with the name of a legal adultery; and the persons who were guilty of so scandalous an offence against Christian purity were soon excluded from the honours, and even from the arms, of the church. Since desire was im-puted as a crime, and marriage was tolerated as a defect, it was consistent with the same principles to consider a state of celibacy as the nearest ap-proach to the Divine perfection. It was with the utmost difficulty that ancient Rome could support the institution of six vestals; but the primitive church was filled with a great number of persons of either sex who had devoted them-selves to the profession of perpetual chastity. A few of these, among whom we may reckon the learned Origen, judged it the most prudent to disarm the tempter. Some were insensible and some were invincible against the assaults of the flesh. Disdaining an ignominious flight, the virgins of the warm cli-mate of Africa encountered the enemy in the closest engagement; they per-mitted priests and deacons to share their bed, and gloried amidst the flames in their unsullied purity. But insulted Nature sometimes vindicated her rights, and this new species of martyrdom served only to introduce a new scandal into the church. Among the Christian ascetics, however (a name which they soon acquired from their painful exercise), many, as they were less presump-tuous, were probably more successful. The loss of sensual pleasure was sup-plied and compensated by spiritual pride. Even the multitude of Pagans were inclined to estimate the merit of the sacrifice by its apparent difficulty; and it was in the praise of these chaste spouses of Christ that the fathers have poured forth the troubled stream of their eloquence. Such are the early traces of monastic principles and institutions, which, in a subsequent age, have counterbalanced all the temporal advantages of Christianity.

* * *

V. THE FIFTH CAUSE

But the human character, however it may be exalted or depressed by a temporary enthusiasm, will return by degrees to its proper and natural level, and will resume those passions that seem the most adapted to its present condition. The primitive Christians were dead to the business and pleasures of the world; but their love of action, which could never be entirely extinguished, soon revived, and found a new occupation in the government of the church. A separate society, which attacked the established religion of the empire, was obliged to adopt some form of internal policy, and to appoint a sufficient number of ministers, intrusted not only with the spiritual functions, but even with the temporal direction of the Christian commonwealth. The safety of that society, its honour, its aggrandisement, were productive, even in the most pious minds, of a spirit of patriotism, such as the first of the Romans had felt for the republic, and sometimes of a similar indifference in the use of whatever means might probably conduce to so desirable an end. The ambition of raising themselves or their friends to the honours and offices of the church was disguised by the laudable intention of devoting to the public benefit the power and consideration which, for that purpose only, it became their duty to solicit. In the exercise of their functions they were frequently called upon to detect the errors of heresy or the arts of faction, to oppose the designs of perfidious brethren, to stigmatise their characters with deserved infamy, and to expel them from the bosom of a society whose peace and happiness they had attempted to disturb. The ecclesiastical governors of the Christians were taught to unite the wisdom of the serpent with the innocence of the dove; but as the former was refined, so the latter was insensibly corrupted, by the habits of government. In the church as well as in the world, the persons who were placed in any public station rendered themselves considerable by their eloquence and firmness, by their knowledge of mankind, and by their dexterity in business; and while they concealed from others, and perhaps from themselves, the secret motives of their conduct, they too frequently relapsed into all the turbulent passions of active life, which were tinctured with an additional degree of bitterness and obstinacy from the infusion of spiritual zeal.

* * *

The progress of the ecclesiastical authority gave birth to the memorable distinction of the laity and of the clergy, which had been unknown to the Greeks and Romans. The former of these appellations comprehended the body of the Christian people; the latter, according to the signification of the word, was appropriated to the chosen portion that had been set apart for the service of religion; a celebrated order of men which has furnished the most important, though not always the most edifying, subjects for modern history. Their mutual hostilities sometimes disturbed the peace of the infant church, but their zeal and activity were united in the common cause, and the love of power, which (under the most artful disguises) could insinuate itself into the breasts of bishops and martyrs, animated them to increase the number of their subjects, and to enlarge the limits of the Christian empire. They were destitute of any temporal force, and they were for a long time discouraged and oppressed, rather than assisted, by the civil magistrate; but they had acquired, and they employed within their own society, the two most efficacious instruments of government, rewards and punishments; the former derived from the pious liberality, the latter from the devout apprehensions, of the faithful.

* * *

In the course of this important, though perhaps tedious, inquiry, I have attempted to display the secondary causes which so efficaciously assisted the truth of the Christian religion. If among these causes we have discovered any artificial ornaments, any accidental circumstances, or any mixture of error and passion, it cannot appear surprising that mankind should be the most sensibly affected by such motives as were suited to their imperfect nature. It was by the aid of these causes—exclusive zeal, the immediate expectation of another world, the claim of miracles, the practice of rigid virtue, and the constitution of the primitive church—that Christianity spread itself with so much success in the Roman empire. To the first of these the Christians were indebted for their invincible valour, which disdained to capitulate with the enemy whom they were resolved to vanquish. The three succeeding causes supplied their valour with the most formidable arms. The last of these causes united their courage, directed their arms, and gave their efforts that irresistible weight which even a small band of well-trained and intrepid volunteers has so often possessed over an undisciplined multitude, ignorant of the subject and careless of the event of the war. . . .

2
THE
EVIDENCE OF
THE BIBLE

This account of the birth of Christ is given in the Gospel of Luke.

FROM The Gospel According to Luke

1 . . . [26]In the sixth month the angel Gabriel was sent from God to a city of Galilee named Nazareth, [27]to a virgin betrothed to a man whose name was Joseph, of the house of David; and the virgin's name was Mary. [28]And he came to her and said, "Hail, O favored one, the Lord is with you!" [29]But she was greatly troubled at the saying, and considered in her mind what sort of greeting this might be. [30]And the angel said to her, "Do not be afraid, Mary, for you have found favor with God. [31]And behold, you will conceive in your womb and bear a son, and you shall call his name Jesus.
[32]He will be great, and will be called the Son of the Most High;
 and the Lord God will give him the throne of his father David,
[39]and he will reign over the house of Jacob for'ever;
 and of his kingdom there will be no end."
[34]And Mary said to the angel, "How can this be, since I have no husband?"
[35]And the angel said to her,
 "The Holy Spirit will come upon you,
 and the power of the Most High will overshadow you;
 therefore the child to be born will be called holy,
 the Son of God."

* * *

2 ¹In those days a decree went out from Caesar Augustus that all the world should be enrolled. ²This was the first enrollment, when Quirin'i-us was governor of Syria. ³And all went to be enrolled, each to his own city. ⁴And Joseph also went up from Galilee, from the city of Nazareth, to Judea, to the city of David, which is called Bethlehem, because he was of the house and lineage of David, ⁵to be enrolled with Mary, his betrothed, who was with child. ⁶And while they were there, the time came for her to be delivered. ⁷And she gave birth to her first-born son and wrapped him in swaddling cloths, and laid him in a manger, because there was no place for them in the inn.

⁸And in that region there were shepherds out in the field, keeping watch over their flock by night. ⁹And an angel of the Lord appeared to them, and the glory of the Lord shone around them, and they were filled with fear. ¹⁰And the angel said to them, "Be not afraid; for behold, I bring you good news of a great joy which will come to all the people; ¹¹for to you is born this day in the city of David a Savior, who is Christ the Lord. ¹²And this will be a sign for you: you will find a babe wrapped in swaddling cloths and lying in a manger." ¹³ And suddenly there was with the angel a multitude of the heavenly host praising God and saying,

¹⁴"Glory to God in the highest,
   and on earth peace among men with whom he is pleased!"

¹⁵When the angels went away from them into heaven, the shepherds said to one another, "Let us go over to Bethlehem and see this thing that has happened, which the Lord has made known to us." ¹⁶And they went with haste, and found Mary and Joseph, and the babe lying in a manger. ¹⁷And when they saw it they made known the saying which had been told them concerning this child; ¹⁸and all who heard it wondered at what the shepherds told them. ¹⁹But Mary kept all these things, pondering them in her heart. ²⁰And the shepherds returned, glorifying and praising God for all they had heard and seen, as it had been told them.

²¹And at the end of eight days, when he was circumcised, he was called Jesus, the name given by the angel before he was conceived in the womb.

Luke's account should be compared with the more "theological" version of Christ's coming given by John.

FROM The Gospel According to John

1 ¹In the beginning was the Word, and the Word was with God, and the Word was God. ²He was in the beginning with God; ³all things were made through him, and without him was not anything made that was made. ⁴In him was life, and the life was the light of men. ⁵The light shines in the darkness, and the darkness has not overcome it.

⁶There was a man sent from God, whose name was John. ⁷He came for testimony, to bear witness to the light, that all might believe through him. ⁸He was not the light, but came to bear witness to the light.

⁹The true light that enlightens every man was coming into the world. ¹⁰He was in the world, and the world was made through him, yet the world knew him not. ¹¹He came to his own home, and his own people received him not. ¹²But to all who received him, who believed in his name, he gave power to become children of God; ¹³who were born, not of blood nor of the will of the flesh nor of the will of man, but of God.

¹⁴And the Word became flesh and dwelt among us, full of grace and truth; we have beheld his glory, glory as of the only Son from the Father. (¹⁵John bore witness to him, and cried, "This was he of whom I said, 'He who comes after me ranks before me, for he was before me.'") ¹⁶And from his fullness have we all received, grace upon grace. ¹⁷For the law was given through Moses; grace and truth came through Jesus Christ. ¹⁸No one has ever seen God; the only Son, who is in the bosom of the Father, he has made him known.

The tradition of miracles performed by Jesus and his disciples played a powerful part in attracting heathens to the Christian faith. The story of Lazarus is a striking example of the miraculous tradition.

FROM The Gospel According to John

11 [1]Now a certain man was ill, Laz'arus of Bethany, the village of Mary and her sister Martha. [2]It was Mary who anointed the Lord with ointment and wiped his feet with her hair, whose brother Laz'arus was ill. [3]So the sisters sent to him, saying, "Lord, he whom you love is ill." [4]But when Jesus heard it he said, "This illness is not unto death; it is for the glory of God, so that the Son of God may be glorified by means of it."

[5]Now Jesus loved Martha and her sister and Laz'arus. [6]So when he heard that he was ill, he stayed two days longer in the place where he was. [7]Then after this he said to the disciples, "Let us go into Judea again." [8]The disciples said to him, "Rabbi, the Jews were but now seeking to stone you, and are you going there again?" [9]Jesus answered, "Are there not twelve hours in the day? If any one walks in the day, he does not stumble, because he sees the light of this world. [10]But if any one walks in the night, he stumbles, because the light is not in him." [11]Thus he spoke, and then he said to them, "Our friend Laz'arus has fallen asleep, but I go to awake him out of sleep." [12]The disciples said to him, "Lord, if he has fallen asleep, he will recover." [13]Now Jesus had spoken of his death, but they thought that he meant taking rest in sleep. [14]Then Jesus told them plainly, "Laz'arus is dead; [15]and for your sake I am glad that I was not there, so that you may believe. But let us go to him." [16]Thomas, called the Twin, said to his fellow disciples, "Let us also go, that we may die with him."

[17]Now when Jesus came, he found that Laz'arus had already been in the tomb four days. [18]Bethany was near Jerusalem, about two miles off, [19]and many of the Jews had come to Martha and Mary to console them concerning their brother. [20]When Martha heard that Jesus was coming, she went and met him, while Mary sat in the house. [21]Martha said to Jesus, "Lord, if you had been here, my brother would not have died. [22]And even now I know that whatever you ask from God, God will give you." [23]Jesus said to her, "Your brother will rise again." [24]Martha said to him, "I know that he will rise again in the resurrection at the last day." [25]Jesus said to her, "I am the resurrection and the life; he who believes in me, though he die, yet shall he live, [26]and whoever lives and believes in me shall never die. Do you believe this?" [27]She

---

John 11:1–44, The Revised Standard Version of the Bible, copyrighted 1946, 1952.

said to him, "Yes, Lord; I believe that you are the Christ, the Son of God, he who is coming into the world."

²⁸When she had said this, she went and called her sister Mary, saying quietly, "The Teacher is here and is calling for you." ²⁹And when she heard it, she rose quickly and went to him. ³⁰Now Jesus had not yet come to the village, but was still in the place where Martha had met him. ³¹When the Jews who were with her in the house, consoling her, saw Mary rise quickly and go out, they followed her, supposing that she was going to the tomb to weep there. ³²Then Mary, when she came where Jesus was and saw him, fell at his feet, saying to him, "Lord, if you had been here, my brother would not have died." ³³When Jesus saw her weeping, and the Jews who came with her also weeping, he was deeply moved in spirit and troubled; ³⁴and he said, "Where have you laid him?" They said to him, "Lord, come and see." ³⁵Jesus wept. ³⁶So the Jews said, "See how he loved him!" ³⁷But some of them said, "Could not he who opened the eyes of the blind man have kept this man from dying?"

³⁸ Then Jesus, deeply moved again, came to the tomb; it was a cave, and a stone lay upon it. ³⁹Jesus said, "Take away the stone." Martha, the sister of the dead man, said to him, "Lord, by this time there will be an odor, for he has been dead four days." ⁴⁰Jesus said to her, "Did I not tell you that if you would believe you would see the glory of God?" ⁴¹So they took away the stone. And Jesus lifted up his eyes and said, "Father, I thank thee that thou hast heard me. ⁴²I knew that thou hearest me always, but I have said this on account of the people standing by, that they may believe that thou didst send me." ⁴³When he had said this, he cried with a loud voice, "Laz'arus, come out." ⁴⁴The dead man came out, his hands and feet bound with bandages, and his face wrapped with a cloth. Jesus said to them, "Unbind him, and let him go."

One of the most attractive features of Christianity has always been the high standard of morality preached by its founder. Much of the moral message of Christianity is contained in the Sermon on the Mount.

FROM The Gospel According to Matthew

5 [1]Seeing the crowds, he went up on the mountain, and when he sat down his disciples came to him. [2]And he opened his mouth and taught them, saying:

[3] "Blessed are the poor in spirit, for theirs is the kingdom of heaven.

[4] "Blessed are those who mourn, for they shall be comforted.

[5] "Blessed are the meek, for they shall inherit the earth.

[6] "Blessed are those who hunger and thirst for righteousness, for they shall be satisfied.

[7] "Blessed are the merciful, for they shall obtain mercy.

[8] "Blessed are the pure in heart, for they shall see God.

[9] "Blessed are the peacemakers, for they shall be called sons of God.

[10] "Blessed are those who are persecuted for righteousness' sake, for theirs is the kingdom of heaven.

[11] "Blessed are you when men revile you and persecute you and utter all kinds of evil against you falsely on my account. [12]Rejoice and be glad, for your reward is great in heaven, for so men persecuted the prophets who were before you.

[13] "You are the salt of the earth; but if salt has lost its taste, how shall its saltness be restored? It is no longer good for anything except to be thrown out and trodden under foot by men.

[14] "You are the light of the world. A city set on a hill cannot be hid. [15]Nor do men light a lamp and put it under a bushel, but on a stand, and it gives light to all in the house. [16]Let your light so shine before men, that they may see your good works and give glory to your Father who is in heaven.

[17] "Think not that I have come to abolish the law and the prophets; I have come not to abolish them but to fulfil them. [18]For truly, I say to you, till heaven and earth pass away, not an iota, not a dot, will pass from the law until all is accomplished. [19]Whoever then relaxes one of the least of these commandments and teaches men so, shall be called least in the kingdom of heaven; but he who does them and teaches them shall be called great in the kingdom of heaven. [20]For I tell you, unless your righteousness exceeds that of the scribes and Pharisees, you will never enter the kingdom of heaven.

[21] "You have heard that it was said to the men of old, 'You shall not kill; and whoever kills shall be liable to judgment.' [22]But I say to you that every one who is angry with his brother shall be liable to judgment; whoever insults his brother shall be liable to the council, and whoever says, 'You fool!' shall be liable to the hell of fire. [23]So if you are offering your gift at the altar, and there remember that your brother has something against you, [24]leave your gift there before the altar and go; first be reconciled to your brother, and then come and offer your gift. [25]Make friends quickly with your accuser, while you are going with him to court, lest your accuser hand you over to the judge, and the judge to the guard, and you be put in prison; [26]truly, I say to you, you will never get out till you have paid the last penny.

[27] "You have heard that it was said, 'You shall not commit adultery.' [28]But I say to you that every one who looks at a woman lustfully has already committed adultery with her in his heart. [29]If your right eye causes you to sin, pluck it out and throw it away; it is better that you lose one of your members than that your whole body be thrown into hell. [30]And if your right hand causes you to sin, cut it off and throw it away; it is better that you lose one of your members than that your whole body go into hell.

[31] "It was also said, 'Whoever divorces his wife, let him give her a certificate of divorce.' [32]But I say to you that every one who divorces his wife, except on the ground of unchastity, makes her an adultress; and whoever marries a divorced woman commits adultery.

[33] "Again you have heard that it was said to the men of old, 'You shall not swear falsely, but shall perform to the Lord what you have sworn.' [34]But I say to you, Do not swear at all, either by heaven, for it is the throne of God, [35]or by the earth, for it is his footstool, or by Jerusalem, for it is the city of the great King. [36]And do not swear by your head, for you cannot make one hair white or black. [37]Let what you say be simply 'Yes' or 'No'; anything more than this comes from evil.

[38] "You have heard that it was said, 'An eye for an eye and a tooth for a tooth.' [39]But I say to you, Do not resist one who is evil. But if any one strikes you on the right cheek, turn to him the other also; [40]and if any one would sue you and take your coat, let him have your cloak as well; [41]and if any one forces you to go one mile, go with him two miles. [42]Give to him who begs from you, and do not refuse him who would borrow from you.

[43] "You have heard that it was said, 'You shall love your neighbor and hate your enemy.' [44]But I say to you, Love your enemies and pray for those who persecute you, [45]so that you may be sons of your Father who is in heaven; for he makes his sun rise on the evil and on the good, and sends rain on the just and on the unjust. [46]For if you love those who love you, what reward have you? Do not even the tax collectors do the same? [47]And if you salute only your brethren, what more are you doing than others? Do not even the Gentiles do the same? [48]You, therefore, must be perfect, as your heavenly Father is perfect.

6 ¹ "Beware of practicing your piety before men in order to be seen by them; for then you will have no reward from your Father who is in heaven.

² "Thus, when you give alms, sound no trumpet before you, as the hypocrites do in the synagogues and in the streets, that they may be praised by men. Truly, I say to you, they have their reward. ³But when you give alms, do not let your left hand know what your right hand is doing, ⁴so that your alms may be in secret; and your Father who sees in secret will reward you.

⁵ "And when you pray, you must not be like the hypocrites; for they love to stand and pray in the synagogues and at the street corners, that they may be seen by men. Truly, I say to you, they have their reward. ⁶But when you pray, go into your room and shut the door and pray to your Father who is in secret; and your Father who sees in secret will reward you.

⁷ "And in praying do not heap up empty phrases as the Gentiles do; for they think that they will be heard for their many words. ⁸Do not be like them, for your Father knows what you need before you ask him. ⁹Pray then like this:

> Our Father who art in heaven,
> Hallowed be thy name.
> ¹⁰ Thy kingdom come,
> Thy will be done,
>   On earth as it is in heaven.
> ¹¹ Give us this day our daily bread;
> ¹² And forgive us our debts,
>   As we also have forgiven our debtors;
> ¹³ And lead us not into temptation,
>   But deliver us from evil.

¹⁴ For if you forgive men their trespasses, your heavenly Father also will forgive you; ¹⁵but if you do not forgive men their trespasses, neither will your Father forgive your trespasses.

¹⁶ "And when you fast, do not look dismal, like the hypocrites, for they disfigure their faces that their fasting may be seen by men. Truly, I say to you, they have their reward. ¹⁷But when you fast, anoint your head and wash your face, ¹⁸that your fasting may not be seen by men but by your Father who is in secret; and your Father who sees in secret will reward you.

¹⁹ "Do not lay up for yourselves treasures on earth, where moth and rust consume and where thieves break in and steal, ²⁰but lay up for yourselves treasures in heaven, where neither moth nor rust consumes and where thieves do not break in and steal. ²For where your treasure is, there will your heart be also.

²² "The eye is the lamp of the body. So, if your eye is sound, your whole body will be full of light; ²³but if your eye is not sound, your whole body will be full of darkness. If then the light in you is darkness, how great is the darkness!

²⁴ "No one can serve two masters; for either he will hate the one and love the other, or he will be devoted to the one and despise the other. You cannot serve God and mammon.

²⁵ "Therefore I tell you, do not be anxious about your life, what you shall eat or what you shall drink, nor about your body, what you shall put on. Is not life more than food, and the body more than clothing? ²⁶Look at the birds of the air; they neither sow nor reap nor gather into barns, and yet your heavenly Father feeds them. Are you not of more value than they? ²⁷And which of you by being anxious can add one cubit to his span of life? ²⁸And why are you anxious about clothing? Consider the lilies of the field, how they grow; they neither toil nor spin; ²⁹yet I tell you, even Solomon in all his glory was not arrayed like one of these. ³⁰But if God so clothes the grass of the field, which today is alive and tomorrow is thrown into the oven, will he not much more clothe you, O men of little faith? ³¹Therefore do not be anxious, saying, 'What shall we eat?' or 'What shall we drink?' or 'What shall we wear?' ³²For the Gentiles seek all these things; and your heavenly Father knows that you need them all. ³³But seek first his kingdom and his righteousness, and all these things shall be yours as well.

³⁴ "Therefore do not be anxious about tomorrow, for tomorrow will be anxious for itself. Let the day's own trouble be sufficient for the day.

7 ¹ "Judge not, that you be not judged. ²For with the judgment you pronounce you will be judged, and the measure you give will be the measure you get. ³Why do you see the speck that is in your brother's eye, but do not notice the log that is in your own eye? ⁴Or how can you say to your brother, 'Let me take the speck out of your eye,' when there is the log in your own eye? ⁵You hypocrite, first take the log out of your own eye, and then you will see clearly to take the speck out of your brother's eye.

⁶ "Do not give dogs what is holy; and do not throw your pearls before swine; lest they trample them under foot and turn to attack you.

⁷ "Ask, and it will be given you; seek, and you will find; knock, and it will be opened to you. ⁸ For every one who asks receives, and he who seeks finds, and to him who knocks it will be opened. ⁹Or what man of you, if his son asks him for a loaf, will give him a stone? ¹⁰Or if he asks for a fish, will give him a serpent? ¹¹If you then, who are evil, know how to give good gifts to your children, how much more will your Father who is in heaven give good things to those who ask him? ¹²So whatever you wish that men would do to you, do so to them; for this is the law and the prophets.

¹³ "Enter by the narrow gate; for the gate is wide and the way is easy, that leads to destruction, and those who enter by it are many. ¹⁴For the gate is narrow and the way is hard, that leads to life, and those who find it are few.

¹⁵ "Beware of false prophets, who come to you in sheep's clothing but inwardly are ravenous wolves. ¹⁶You will know them by their fruits. Are grapes gathered from thorns, or figs from thistles? ¹⁷So, every sound tree

bears good fruit, but the bad tree bears evil fruit. [18]A sound tree cannot bear evil fruit, nor can a bad tree bear good fruit. [19]Every tree that does not bear good fruit is cut down and thrown into the fire. [20]Thus you will know them by their fruits.

[21] "Not every one who says to me, 'Lord, Lord,' shall enter the kingdom of heaven, but he who does the will of my Father who is in heaven. [22]On that day many will say to me, 'Lord, Lord, did we not prophesy in your name, and cast out demons in your name, and do many mighty works in your name?' [23]and then will I declare to them, 'I never knew you; depart from me, you evildoers.'

[24] "Every one then who hears these words of mine and does them will be like a wise man who built his house upon the rock; [25]and the rain fell, and the floods came, and the winds blew and beat upon that house, but it did not fall, because it had been founded on the rock. [26]And every one who hears these words of mine and does not do them will be like a foolish man who built his house upon the sand; [27]and the rain fell, and the floods came, and the winds blew and beat against that house, and it fell; and great was the fall of it."

[28]And when Jesus finished these sayings, the crowds were astonished at his teaching, [29]for he taught them as one who had authority, and not as their scribes.

At the center of Christianity is the belief in the resurrection of Christ. The earliest surviving account of the Crucifixion and the Resurrection is that of Mark.

FROM The Gospel According to Mark

15 [1]And as soon as it was morning the chief priests, with the elders and scribes, and the whole council held a consultation; and they bound Jesus and led him away and delivered him to Pilate. [2]And Pilate asked him, "Are you the King of the Jews?" And he answered him, "You have said so." [3]And the chief priests accused him of many things. [4]And Pilate again asked him, "Have you no answer to make? See how many charges they bring against you." [5]But Jesus made no further answer, so that Pilate wondered.

[6]Now at the feast he used to release for them any one prisoner whom they

---

asked. [7]And among the rebels in prison, who had committed murder in the insurrection, there was a man called Barab′bas. [8]And the crowd came up and began to ask Pilate to do as he was wont to do for them. [9]And he answered them, "Do you want me to release for you the King of the Jews?" [10]For he perceived that it was out of envy that the chief priests had delivered him up. [11]But the chief priests stirred up the crowd to have him release for them Barab′bas instead. [12]And Pilate again said to them, "Then what shall I do with the man whom you call the King of the Jews?" [13]And they cried out again, "Crucify him." [14]And Pilate said to them, "Why, what evil has he done?" But they shouted all the more, "Crucify him." [15]So Pilate, wishing to satisfy the crowd, released for them Barab′bas; and having scourged Jesus, he delivered him to be crucified.

[16]And the soldiers led him away inside the palace (that is, the praetorium); and they called together the whole battalion. [17]And they clothed him in a purple cloak, and plaiting a crown of thorns they put it on him. [18]And they began to salute him, "Hail, King of the Jews!" [19]And they struck his head with a reed, and spat upon him, and they knelt down in homage to him. [20]And when they had mocked him, they stripped him of the purple cloak, and put his own clothes on him. And they led him out to crucify him.

[21]And they compelled a passer-by, Simon of Cyre′ne, who was coming in from the country, the father of Alexander and Rufus, to carry his cross. [22]And they brought him to the place called Gol′gotha (which means the place of a skull). [23]And they offered him wine mingled with myrrh; but he did not take it. [24]And they crucified him, and divided his garments among them, casting lots for them, to decide what each should take. [25]And it was the third hour, when they crucified him. [26]And the inscription of the charge against him read, "The King of the Jews." [27]And with him they crucified two robbers, one on his right and one on his left. [29]And those who passed by derided him, wagging their heads, and saying, "Aha! You who would destroy the temple and build it in three days, [30]save yourself, and come down from the cross!" [31]So also the chief priests mocked him to one another with the scribes, saying, "He saved others; he cannot save himself. [32]Let the Christ, the King of Israel, come down now from the cross, that we may see and believe." Those who were crucified with him also reviled him.

[33]And when the sixth hour had come, there was darkness over the whole land until the ninth hour. [34]And at the ninth hour Jesus cried with a loud voice, "E′lo-i, E′lo-i, la′ ma sabach-tha′ni?" which means, "My God, my God, why hast thou forsaken me?" [35]And some of the bystanders hearing it said, "Behold, he is calling Eli′jah." [36]And one ran and, filling a sponge full of vinegar, put it on a reed and gave it to him to drink, saying, "Wait, let us see whether Eli′jah will come to take him down." [37]And Jesus uttered a loud cry, and breathed his last. [38]And the curtain of the temple was torn in two, from top to bottom. [39]And when the centurion, who stood facing him, saw that he thus breathed his last, he said, "Truly this man was a son of God!"

[40]There were also women looking on from afar, among whom were Mary

Mag'dalene, and Mary the mother of James the younger and of Joses, and Salo'me, [41]who, when he was in Galilee, followed him, and ministered to him; and also many other women who came up with him to Jerusalem.

[42]And when evening had come, since it was the day of Preparation, that is, the day before the sabbath, Joseph of Arimathe'a, a respected member of the council, who was also himself looking for the kingdom of God, took courage and went to Pilate, and asked for the body of Jesus. [44]And Pilate wondered if he were already dead; and summoning the centurion, he asked him whether he was already dead. [45]And when he learned from the centurion that he was dead, he granted the body to Joseph. [46]And he bought a linen shroud, and taking him down, wrapped him in the linen shroud, and laid him in a tomb which had been hewn out of the rock; and he rolled a stone against the door of the tomb. [47]Mary Mag'dalene and Mary the mother of Joses saw where he was laid.

16 [1]And when the sabbath was past, Mary Mag'dalene, and Mary the mother of James, and Salo'me, bought spices, so that they might go and anoint him. [2]And very early on the first day of the week they went to the tomb when the sun had risen. [3]And they were saying to one another, "Who will roll away the stone for us from the door of the tomb?" [4]And looking up, they saw that the stone was rolled back; for it was very large. [5]And entering the tomb, they saw a young man sitting on the right side, dressed in a white robe; and they were amazed. [6]And he said to them, "Do not be amazed; you seek Jesus of Nazareth, who was crucified. He has risen, he is not here, see the place where they laid him. [7]But go, tell his disciples and Peter that he is going before you to Galilee; there you will see him, as he told you." [8]And they went out and fled from the tomb; for trembling and astonishment had come upon them; and they said nothing to any one, for they were afraid.

Paul was the greatest of the missionaries who spread Christianity to non-Jewish peoples. The following passage illustrates the significance that Christ's resurrection had for the first generation of Christians.

FROM Paul's First Epistle to the Corinthians

15 [1]Now I would remind you, brethren, in what terms I preached to you the gospel, which you received, in which you stand, [2]by which you are saved, if you hold it fast—unless you believed in vain.

[3]For I delivered to you as of first importance what I also received, that Christ died for our sins in accordance with the scriptures, [4]that he was buried, that he was raised on the third day in accordance with the scriptures, [5]and that he appeared to Cephas, then to the twelve. [6]Then he appeared to more than five hundred brethren at one time, most of whom are still alive, though some have fallen asleep. [7]Then he appeared to James, then to all the apostles. [8]Last of all, as to one untimely born, he appeared also to me. [9]For I am the least of the apostles, unfit to be called an apostle, because I persecuted the church of God. [10]But by the grace of God I am what I am, and his grace toward me was not in vain. On the contrary, I worked harder than any of them, though it was not I, but the grace of God which is with me. [11]Whether then it was I or they, so we preach and so you believed.

[12]Now if Christ is preached as raised from the dead, how can some of you say that there is no resurrection of the dead? [13]But if there is no resurrection of the dead, then Christ has not been raised; [14]if Christ has not been raised, then our preaching is in vain and your faith is in vain. [15]We are even found to be misrepresenting God, because we testified of God that he raised Christ, whom he did not raise if it is true that the dead are not raised. [16]For if the dead are not raised, then Christ has not been raised. [17]If Christ has not been raised, your faith is futile and you are still in your sins. [18]Then those also who have fallen asleep in Christ have perished. [19]If in this life we who are in Christ have only hope, we are of all men most to be pitied.

[20]But in fact Christ has been raised from the dead, the first fruits of those who have fallen asleep. [21]For as by a man came death, by a man has come also the resurrection of the dead. [22]For as in Adam all die, so also in Christ shall all be made alive. [23]But each in his own order: Christ the first fruits, then at his coming those who belong to Christ. [24]Then comes the end, when he delivers the kingdom to God the Father after destroying every rule and every authority and power. [25]For he must reign until he has put all his enemies under his feet. [26]The last enemy to be destroyed is death. [27]"For God has put all things in subjection under his feet." But when it says, "All things

I Corinthians 15, The Revised Standard Version of the Bible, copyrighted 1946, 1952, and used by permission.

are put in subjection under him," it is plain that he is excepted who put all things under him. [28]When all things are subjected to him, then the Son himself will also be subjected to him who put all things under him, that God may be everything to every one.

[29]Otherwise, what do people mean by being baptized on behalf of the dead? If the dead are not raised at all, why are people baptized on their behalf? [30]Why am I in peril every hour? [31]I protest, brethren, by my pride in you which I have in Christ Jesus our Lord, I die every day! [32]What do I gain if, humanly speaking, I fought with beasts at Ephesus? If the dead are not raised, "Let us eat and drink, for tomorrow we die." [33]Do not be deceived: "Bad company ruins good morals." [34]Come to your right mind, and sin no more. For some have no knowledge of God. I say this to your shame.

[35]But some one will ask, "How are the dead raised? With what kind of body do they come?" [36]You foolish man! What you sow does not come to life unless it dies. [37]And what you sow is not the body which is to be but a bare kernel, perhaps of wheat or of some other grain. [38]But God gives it a body as he has chosen, and to each kind of seed its own body. [39]For not all flesh is alike, but there is one kind for men, another for animals, another for birds, and another for fish. [40]There are celestial bodies and there are terrestrial bodies; but the glory of the celestial is one, and the glory of the terrestrial is another. [41]There is one glory of the sun, and another glory of the moon, and another glory of the stars; for star differs from star in glory.

[42]So is it with the resurrection of the dead. What is sown is perishable, what is raised is imperishable. [43]It is sown in dishonor, it is raised in glory. It is sown in weakness, it is raised in power. [44]It is sown a physical body, it is raised a spiritual body. If there is a physical body, there is also a spiritual body. [45]Thus it is written, "The first man Adam became a living being"; the last Adam became a life-giving spirit. [46]But it is not the spiritual which is first but the physical, and then the spiritual. [47]The first man was from the earth, a man of dust; the second man is from heaven. [48]As was the man of dust, so are those who are of the dust; and as is the man of heaven, so are those who are of heaven. [49]Just as we have borne the image of the man of dust, we shall also bear the image of the man of heaven. [50]I tell you this, brethren: flesh and blood cannot inherit the kingdom of God, nor does the perishable inherit the imperishable.

[51]Lo! I tell you a mystery. We shall not all sleep, but we shall all be changed, [52]in a moment, in the twinkling of an eye, at the last trumpet. For the trumpet will sound, and the dead will be raised imperishable, and we shall be changed. [53]For this perishable nature must put on the imperishable, and this mortal nature must put on immortality. [54]When the perishable puts on the imperishable, and the mortal puts on immortality, then shall come to pass the saying that is written:

"Death is swallowed up in victory."
[55] "O death, where is thy victory?
O death, where is thy sting?"

[56]The sting of death is sin, and the power of sin is the law. [57]But thanks be to God, who gives us the victory through our Lord Jesus Christ.

[58]Therefore, my beloved brethren, be steadfast, immovable, always abounding in the work of the Lord, knowing that in the Lord your labor is not in vain.

3
THE SPREAD
OF CHRISTIANITY
AND THE
ROMAN
RESPONSE

In the first century after Christ the religion of the Cross spread rapidly throughout the Roman Empire, especially in the eastern provinces. Pliny the Younger was an intimate of the Emperor Trajan (A.D. 98–117) and governor of the province of Bithynia in Asia Minor. His letter to the emperor and Trajan's answer give us evidence of the attitude of Rome toward the new religion at the end of the first century.

FROM Pliny's Letters

EP. 96. It is my custom, my lord, to refer to you all questions about which I have doubts. Who, indeed, can better direct me in hesitation, or enlighten me in ignorance? In the examination of Christians I have never taken part; therefore I do not know what crime is usually punished or investigated or to what extent. So I have no little uncertainty whether there is any distinction of age, or whether the weaker offenders fare in no respect otherwise than the stronger; whether pardon is granted on repentance, or whether when one has been a Christian there is no gain to him in that he has ceased to be such; whether the mere name, if it is without crimes, or crimes connected with the

Reprinted with the permission of Charles Scribner's Sons from *A Source Book for Ancient Church History*, pp. 20–22, by Joseph Cullen Ayer. Copyright 1913 Charles Scribner's Sons; renewal copyright 1941 Joseph Cullen Ayer, Jr.

name are punished. Meanwhile I have taken this course with those who were accused before me as Christians: I have asked them whether they were Christians. Those who confessed I asked a second and a third time, threatening punishment. Those who persisted I ordered led away to execution. For I did not doubt that, whatever it was they admitted, obstinacy and unbending perversity certainly deserve to be punished. There were others of the like insanity, but because they were Roman citizens I noted them down to be sent to Rome. Soon after this, as it often happens, because the matter was taken notice of, the crime became wide-spread and many cases arose. An unsigned paper was presented containing the names of many. But these denied that they were or had been Christians, and I thought it right to let them go, since at my dictation they prayed to the gods and made supplication with incense and wine to your statue, which I had ordered to be brought into the court for the purpose, together with the images of the gods, and in addition to this they cursed Christ, none of which things, it is said, those who are really Christians can be made to do. Others who were named by an informer said that they were Christians, and soon afterward denied it, saying, indeed, that they had been, but had ceased to be Christians, some three years ago, some many years, and one even twenty years ago. All these also not only worshipped your statue and the images of the gods, but also cursed Christ. They asserted, however, that the amount of their fault or error was this: that they had been accustomed to assemble on a fixed day before daylight and sing by turns [i.e., antiphonally] a hymn to Christ as a god; and that they bound themselves with an oath, not for any crime, but to commit neither theft, nor robbery, nor adultery, not to break their word and not to deny a deposit when demanded; after these things were done, it was their custom to depart and meet together again to take food, but ordinary and harmless food; and they said that even this had ceased after my edict was issued, by which, according to your commands, I had forbidden the existence of clubs. On this account I believed it the more necessary to find out from two maid-servants, who were called deaconesses [ministrae], and that by torture, what was the truth. I found nothing else than a perverse and excessive superstition. I therefore adjourned the examination and hastened to consult you. The matter seemed to me to be worth deliberation, especially on account of the number of those in danger. For many of every age, every rank, and even of both sexes, are brought into danger; and will be in the future. The contagion of that superstition has penetrated not only the cities but also the villages and country places; and yet it seems possible to stop it and set it right. At any rate, it is certain enough that the temples, deserted until quite recently, begin to be frequented, that the ceremonies of religion, long disused, are restored, and that fodder for the victims comes to market, whereas buyers of it were until now very few. From this it may easily be supposed what a multitude of men can be reclaimed if there be a place of repentance.

EP. 97 (*Trajan to Pliny*). You have followed, my dear Secundus, the proper course of procedure in examining the cases of those who were accused to you as Christians. For, indeed, nothing can be laid down as a general law which contains anything like a definite rule of action. They are not to be sought out. If they are accused and convicted, they are to be punished, yet on this condition, that he who denies that he is a Christian and makes the fact evident by an act, that is, by worshipping our gods, shall obtain pardon on his repentance, however much suspected as to the past. Papers, however, which are presented anonymously ought not to be admitted in any accusation. For they are a very bad example and unworthy of our times.

Not all the emperors were as humane as Trajan, and there were several persecutions of various degrees of severity. It is not too much to say that the persecutions were ultimately helpful to the Christian cause, for they were too sporadic and inefficient to destroy the sect yet enabled the Christians to win sympathy for their faith and courage.

FROM Acts of the Scillitan Martyrs

When Praesens, for the second time, and Claudianus were the consuls, on the seventeenth day of July, at Carthage, there were set in the judgment-hall Speratus, Nartzalus, Cittinus, Donata, Secunda and Vestia.

Saturninus the proconsul said: Ye can win the indulgence of our lord the Emperor, if ye return to a sound mind.

Speratus said: We have never done ill, we have not lent ourselves to wrong, we have never spoken ill, but when ill-treated we have given thanks; because we pay heed to OUR EMPEROR.

Saturninus the proconsul said: We too are religious, and our religion is simple, and we swear by the genius of our lord the Emperor, and pray for his welfare, as ye also ought to do.

Speratus said: If thou wilt peaceably lend me thine ears, I can tell thee the mystery of simplicity.

Saturninus said: I will not lend mine ears to thee, when thou beginnest to speak evil things of our sacred rites; but rather swear thou by the genius of our lord the Emperor.

"Acts of the Scillitan Martyrs," in *Selections from Early Writers Illustrative of Church History to the Time of Constantine* (1961), pp. 79–83, translated by H. M. Gwatkin. Reprinted by permission of James Clarke & Co., Ltd., London.

Speratus said: The empire of this world I know not; but rather I serve that God, *whom no man hath seen, nor* with these eyes *can see*. I have committed no theft; but if I have bought anything I pay the tax; because I know my Lord, the King of kings and Emperor of all nations.

Saturninus the proconsul said to the rest: Cease to be of this persuasion.

Speratus said: It is an ill persuasion to do murder, to speak false witness.

Saturninus the proconsul said: Be not partakers of this folly.

Cittinus said: We have none other to fear, save only our Lord God, who is in heaven.

Donata said: Honour to Caesar as Caesar: but fear to God.

Vestia said: I am a Christian.

Secunda said: What I am, that I wish to be.

Saturninus the proconsul said to Speratus: Dost thou persist in being a Christian?

Speratus said: I am a Christian. And with him they all agreed.

Saturninus the proconsul said: Will ye have a space to consider?

Speratus said: In a matter so straightforward there is no considering.

Saturninus the proconsul said: What are the things in your chest?

Speratus said: Books and epistles of Paul, a just man.

Saturninus the proconsul said: Have a delay of thirty days and bethink yourselves.

Speratus said a second time: I am a Christian. And with him they all agreed.

Saturninus the proconsul read out the decree from the tablet: Speratus, Nartzalus, Cittinus, Donata, Vestia, Secunda and the rest having confessed that they live according to the Christian rite, since after opportunity offered them of returning to the custom of the Romans they have obstinately persisted, it is determined that they be put to the sword.

Speratus said: We give thanks to God.

Nartzalus said: To-day we are martyrs in heaven; thanks be to God.

Saturninus the proconsul ordered it to be declared by the herald: Speratus, Nartzalus, Cittinus, Veturius, Felix, Aquilinus, Leatantius, Januaria, Generosa, Vestia, Donata and Secunda, I have ordered to be executed.

They all said: Thanks be to God.

And so they all together were crowned with martyrdom; and they reign with the Father and the Son and the Holy Ghost, for ever and ever. Amen.

In 313 Constantine and Licinius, joint emperors, granted toleration to the Christians. The following document is not the actual edict but a letter to a prefect referring to the edict.

FROM De Mortibus Persecutorum BY LACTANTIUS

When I, Constantine Augustus, and I, Licinius Augustus, had happily met together at Milan, and were having under consideration all things which concern the advantage and security of the State, we thought that, among other things which seemed likely to profit men generally, we ought, in the very first place, to set in order the conditions of the reverence paid to the Divinity by giving to the Christians and all others full permission to follow whatever worship any man had chosen; whereby whatever divinity there is in heaven may be benevolent and propitious to us, and to all placed under our authority. Therefore we thought we ought, with sound counsel and very right reason, to lay down this law, that we should in no way refuse to any man any legal right who had given up his mind either to the observance of Christianity or to that worship which he personally feels best suited to himself; to the end that the Supreme Divinity, whose worship we freely follow, may continue in all things to grant us his accustomed favor and good-will. Wherefore your devotion should know that it is our pleasure that all provisions whatsoever which have appeared in documents hitherto directed to your office regarding Christians and which appeared utterly improper and opposed to our clemency should be abolished, and that every one of those men who have the same wish to observe Christian worship may now freely and unconditionally endeavor to observe the same without any annoyance or molestation. These things we thought it well to signify in the fullest manner to your carefulness, that you might know that we have given free and absolute permission to the said Christians to practice their worship. And when you perceive that we have granted this to the said Christians, your devotion understands that to others also a similarly full and free permission for their own worship and observance is granted, for the quiet of our times, so that every man may have freedom in the practice of whatever worship he has chosen. And these things were done by us that nothing be taken away from any honor or form of worship. Moreover, in regard to the Christians, we have thought fit to ordain this also, that if any appear to have bought, either from

Reprinted with the permission of Charles Scribner's Sons from *A Source Book for Ancient Church History*, pp. 263–265, by Joseph Cullen Ayer. Copyright 1913 Charles Scribner's Sons; renewal copyright 1941 Joseph Cullen Ayer, Jr.

our exchequer or from others, the places in which they were accustomed formerly to assemble, and concerning which definite orders have been given before now, and that by letters sent to your office, the same be restored to the Christians, setting aside all delay and dispute, without payment or demand of price. Those also who have obtained them by gift shall restore them in like manner without delay to the said Christians; and those, moreover, who have bought them, as well as those who have obtained them by gift, if they request anything of our benevolence, they shall apply to the deputy that order may be taken for them too by our clemency. All these must be delivered over at once and without delay by your intervention to the corporation of the Christians. And since the same Christians are known to have possessed not only the places where they are accustomed to assemble, but also others belonging to their corporation, namely, to the churches and not to individuals, all these by the law which we have described above you will order to be restored without any doubtfulness or dispute to the said Christians—that is, to their said corporations and assemblies; provided always, as aforesaid, that those who restore them without price, as we said, shall expect a compensation from our benevolence. In all these things you must give the aforesaid Christians your most effective intervention, that our command may be fulfilled as soon as may be, and that in this matter also order may be taken by our clemency for the public quiet. And may it be, as already said, that the divine favor which we have already experienced in so many affairs, shall continue for all time to give us prosperity and successes, together with happiness for the State. But that it may be possible for the nature of this decree and of our benevolence to come to the knowledge of all men, it will be your duty by a proclamation of your own to publish everywhere and bring to the notice of all men this present document when it reaches you, that the decree of this our benevolence may not be hidden.

4
ORGANIZATION
AND DOCTRINE
IN THE EARLY
CHURCH

Whatever weight one gives to the several reasons for the success of Christian teaching, there is no denying the important role of the church organization. This was emphasized by Christopher Dawson.

FROM The Making of Europe BY CHRISTOPHER DAWSON

If Christianity had been merely one among the oriental sects and mystery religions of the Roman Empire it must inevitably have been drawn into this oriental syncretism. It survived because it possessed a system of ecclesiastical organisation and a principle of social authority that distinguished it from all the other religious bodies of the age. From the first, as we have seen, the Church regarded itself as the New Israel, "an elect race, a royal priesthood, a holy nation, a people set apart." This holy society was a theocracy inspired and governed by the Holy Spirit, and its rulers, the apostles, were the representatives not of the community but of the Christ, who had chosen them and transmitted to them His divine authority. This conception of a divine apostolic authority remained as the foundation of ecclesiastical order in the post-apostolic period. The "overseers" and elders, who were the rulers of the local churches, were regarded as the successors of the apostles, and the churches that were of direct apostolic origin enjoyed a peculiar prestige and authority among the rest.

From *The Making of Europe* by Christopher Dawson, pp. 24–27, published by Sheed & Ward Inc., New York. Reprinted by permission of The Society of Authors, London.

This was the case above all with the Roman Church, for, as Peter had possessed a unique position among the Twelve, so the Roman Church, which traced its origins to St. Peter, possessed an exceptional position among the churches. Even in the first century, almost before the close of the apostolic age, we see an instance of this in the authoritative intervention of Rome in the affairs of the Church of Corinth. The First Epistle of Clement to the Corinthians (c. A.D. 96) gives the clearest possible expression to the ideal of hierarchic order which was the principle of the new society. The author argues that order is the law of the universe. And as it is the principle of external nature so, too, is it the principle of the Christian society. The faithful must preserve the same discipline and subordination of rank that marked the Roman army. As Christ is from God, so the apostles are from Christ, and the apostles, in turn, "appointed their first converts, testing them by the spirit, to be the bishops and deacons of the future believers. And, knowing there would be strife for the title of bishop, they afterwards added the codicil that if they should fall asleep other approved men should succeed to their ministry." Therefore it is essential that the Church of Corinth should put aside strife and envy and submit to the lawfully appointed presbyters, who represent the apostolic principle of divine authority.

The doctrine of St. Clement is characteristically Roman in its insistence on social order and moral discipline, but it has much in common with the teaching of the Pastoral Epistles, and there can be no doubt that it represents the traditional spirit of the primitive Church. It was this spirit that saved Christianity from sinking in the morass of oriental syncretism.

In his polemic against the Gnostics in the following century St. Irenaeus appeals again and again to the social authority of the apostolic tradition against the wild speculations of Eastern theosophy. "The true Gnosis is the teaching of the apostles and the primitive constitution of the Church throughout the world." And with him also it is the Roman Church that is the centre of unity and the guarantee of orthodox belief.

In this way the primitive Church survived both the perils of heresy and schism and the persecution of the imperial power and organised itself as a universal hierarchical society over against the pagan world-state. Thence it was but a step to the conquest of the Empire itself, and to its establishment as the official religion of the reorganised Constantinian state. . . .

The following selection illustrates the organization and beliefs of the early church.

FROM A Source Book for Ancient Church History
BY J. C. AYER

No subject in Church history has been more hotly discussed than the organization of the primitive Christian Church. Each of several Christian confessions have attempted to justify a polity which it regarded as *de fide* by appeal to the organization of the Church of the primitive ages. Since it has been seen that the admission of the principle of development does not invalidate claims for divine warrant for a polity, the acrimonious debate has been somewhat stilled. There seems to have been in the Church several forms of organization, and to some extent the various contentions of conflicting creeds and polities have been therein justified. The ultimately universal form, episcopacy, may in some parts of the Church be traced to the end of the apostolic age, but it seems not to have been universally diffused at that time. Since Christian communities sprang up without official propaganda, at least in many instances, and were due to the work of independent Christian believers moving about in the Empire, this variety of organization was what might have been expected, especially as the significance of the organization was first felt chiefly in connection with the danger from heresy. That various external influences affected the development is also highly probable.

CLEMENT OF ROME, EP. AD CORINTHIOS, I, 42, 44 [C. A.D. 96].

CH. 42. The Apostles have preached the Gospel to us from the Lord Jesus Christ; Jesus Christ was sent forth from God. Christ, therefore, was from God, and the Apostles from Christ. Both these appointments, then, came about in an orderly way, by the will of God. Having, therefore, received their orders, and being fully assured by the resurrection of our Lord Jesus Christ, and established in the word of God, with full assurance of the Holy Ghost, they went forth proclaiming that the kingdom of God was at hand. And thus preaching through countries and cities, they appointed their first-fruits, having proved them by the Spirit, to be bishops and deacons of those who should afterward believe. Nor was this a new thing; for, indeed, many ages before it

Reprinted with the permission of Charles Scribner's Sons from *A Source Book for Ancient Church History*, pp. 36–42, 112–113, by Joseph Cullen Ayer. Copyright 1913 Charles Scribner's Sons; renewal copyright 1941 Joseph Cullen Ayer, Jr.

was written concerning bishops and deacons. For thus saith the Scripture in a certain place: "I will appoint their bishops in righteousness, and their deacons in faith."

* * *

CH. 44. Our Apostles also knew, through our Lord Jesus Christ, that there would be strife on account of the office of the episcopate. For this cause, therefore, inasmuch as they had obtained a perfect foreknowledge of this, they appointed those already mentioned, and afterward gave instructions that when these should fall asleep other approved men should succeed them in their ministry. We are of the opinion, therefore, that those appointed by them, or afterward by other eminent men, with the consent of the whole Church, and who have blamelessly served the flock of Christ in lowliness of mind, peaceably, and with all modesty, and for a long time have borne a good report with all—these men we consider to be unjustly thrust out of their ministrations. For it will be no light sin for us, if we thrust out those who have offered the gifts of the bishop's office blamelessly and holily. Blessed are those presbyters who have gone before seeing their departure was fruitful and ripe; for they have no fear lest any one should remove them from their appointed place. For we see that ye have displaced certain persons, though they were living honorably, from the ministration which had been honored by them blamelessly.

DIDACHE, 11–15.

The *Didache* is a very early manual of the instruction for Christian converts. It consists of two quite distinct parts, viz., a brief account of the moral law (chapters 1–6), which appears to be based upon a Jewish original to which the name of *The Two Ways* has been given, and a somewhat longer account of the various rites of the Church and the regulations governing its organization. Its date is in the first half of the second century and belongs more probably to the first quarter than to the second. It is a document of first-class importance, especially in the part bearing on the organization of the Church, which is here given.

CH. 11. Whosoever, therefore, shall come and teach you all these things that have been said receive him; bit if the teacher himself be perverted and teach a different doctrine to the destruction thereof, hear him not; but if to the increase of righteousness and knowledge of the Lord, receive him as the Lord.

But concerning the apostles and prophets, so do ye according to the ordinance of the Gospel: Let every apostle coming to you be received as the Lord; but he shall not abide more than a single day, or if there be need, a second likewise; but if he abide three days, he is a false prophet. And when he departs, let not the apostle receive anything save bread until he find shelter; but if he ask money, he is a false prophet. And any prophet speaking in the Spirit ye shall not try, neither discern; for every sin shall be forgiven, but this sin shall not be forgiven. Yet not every one that speaketh in the Spirit is a prophet, but only if he have the ways of the Lord. From his ways, therefore, the false prophet and the [true] prophet shall be recognized. And no prophet when he ordereth a table in the Spirit shall eat of it; otherwise he is a false prophet. And every prophet teaching the truth, if he doeth not what he teacheth, is a false prophet. And every prophet approved and found true, working unto a worldly mystery of the Church, and yet teacheth not to do what he himself doeth, shall not be judged before you; he hath his judgment in the presence of God; for in like manner also did the ancient prophets. And whosoever shall say in the Spirit, Give me silver or anything else, do not listen to him; but if he say to give on behalf of others who are in want, let no one judge him.

CH. 12. But let every one coming in the name of the Lord be received; and when ye have tested him ye shall know him, for ye shall have understanding on the right hand and on the left. If the comer is a traveller, assist him as ye are able; but let him not stay with you but for two or three days, if it be necessary. But if he wishes to settle with you, being a craftsman, let him work and eat. But if he has no craft, according to your wisdom provide how without idleness he shall live as a Christian among you. If he will not do this, he is trafficking upon Christ. Beware of such men.

CH. 13. But every true prophet desiring to settle among you is worthy of his food. In like manner, a true teacher is also worthy, like the workman, of his food. Every first-fruit, then, of the produce of the wine-vat and of the thresh-ing-floor, of thy oxen and of thy sheep, thou shalt take and give as the first-fruit to the prophets; for they are your chief priests. But if ye have not a prophet, give them to the poor. If thou makest bread, take the first-fruit and give according to the commandment. In like manner, when thou openest a jar of wine or oil, take the first-fruit and give to the prophets; yea, and of money and raiment and every possession take the first-fruit, as shall seem good to thee, and give according to the commandment.

CH. 14. And on the Lord's day gather yourselves together and break bread and give thanks, first confessing your transgressions, that your sacrifice may be pure. And let no man having a dispute with his fellow join your assembly until they have been reconciled, that your sacrifice may not be defiled; for this is the sacrifice spoken of by the Lord: In every place and at every time offer me a pure sacrifice; for I am a great king, saith the Lord, and my name is wonderful among the nations. [Mal. 1:11, 14.]

CH. 15. Appoint [i.e., lay hands on], therefore, for yourselves bishops and deacons worthy of the Lord, men meek, not lovers of money, truthful, and approved; for they also render you the service of prophets and teachers. Despise them not, therefore, for they are your honored ones together with the prophets and teachers.

IRENAEUS, *ADVERSUS HAERESES,* III, 3:1–2.

The first appearance of the appeal to apostolic tradition as preserved in apostolic sees is the following passage from Irenaeus, written about 175. The reference to the church of Rome, beginning, "For with this Church, on account of its more powerful leadership," has been a famous point of discussion. While it is obscure in detail, the application of its general purport to the argument of Irenaeus is clear. Since for this passage we have not the original Greek of Irenaeus, but only the Latin translation, there seems to be no way of clearing up the obscurities and apparently contradictory statements.

CH. 1. The tradition, therefore, of the Apostles, manifested throughout the world, is a thing which all who wish to see the facts can clearly perceive in every church; and we are able to count up those who were appointed bishops by the Apostles, and to show their successors to our own time, who neither taught nor knew anything resembling these men's ravings. For if the Apostles had known hidden mysteries which they used to teach the perfect, apart from and without the knowledge of the rest, they would have delivered them especially to those to whom they were also committing the churches themselves. For they desired them to be very perfect and blameless in all things, and were also leaving them as their successors, delivering over to them their own proper place of teaching; for if these should act rightly great advantage would result, but if they fell away the most disastrous calamity would occur.
CH. 2. But since it would be very long in such a volume as this to count up the successions [*i.e.,* series of bishops] in all the churches, we confound all those who in any way, whether through self-pleasing or vainglory, or through blindness and evil opinion, gather together otherwise than they ought, by pointing out the tradition derived from the Apostles of the greatest, most ancient, and universally known Church, founded and established by the two most glorious Apostles, Peter and Paul, and also the faith declared to men which through the succession of bishops comes down to our times. For with this Church, on account of its more powerful leadership [*potiorem principalitatem*], every church, that is, the faithful, who are from everywhere, must needs agree; since in it that tradition which is from the Apostles has always been preserved by those who are from everywhere.

The first general council of the church met at Nicea in 325. The following fourth-century formulation of Christian doctrine was based on the dogmatic definitions of this council.

The Nicene Creed

We believe in one God, the Father Almighty, maker of all things visible and invisible; and in one Lord Jesus Christ, the Son of God, the only-begotten of his Father, of the substance of the Father, God of God, Light of Light, very God of very God, begotten not made, being of one substance with the Father, By whom all things were made, both which be in heaven and in earth. Who for us men and for our salvation came down [from heaven] and was incarnate and was made man. He suffered and the third day he rose again, and ascended into heaven. And he shall come again to judge both the quick and the dead. And [we believe] in the Holy Ghost. And whosoever shall say that there was time when the Son of God was not, or that before he was begotten he was not, or that he was made of things that were not, or that he is of a different substance or essence [from the Father] or that he is a creature, or subject to change or conversion—all that so say, the Catholic and Apostolic Church anathematizes them.

The canons of Nicea illustrate the growing complexity of church organization.

FROM Canons of the Council of Nicea

CANON II

Forasmuch as, either from necessity, or through the urgency of individuals, many things have been done contrary to the Ecclesiastical canon, so that men just converted from heathenism to the faith, and who have been instructed but a little while, are straightway brought to the spiritual laver, and as soon as

---

The Seven Ecumenical Councils, in Library of the Nicene and Post-Nicene Fathers, 2nd Series XIV (1900), 3, 10, 13, 15, translated by A. C. McGiffert and E. C. Richardson.

they have been baptized, are advanced to the episcopate or the presbyterate, it has seemed right to us that for the time to come no such thing shall be done. For to the catechumen himself there is need of time and of a longer trial after baptism. For the apostolical saying is clear, "Not a novice; lest, being lifted up with pride, he fall into condemnation and the snare of the devil." But if, as time goes on, any sensual sin should be found out about the person, and he should be convicted by two or three witnesses, let him cease from the clerical office. And whoso shall transgress these [enactments] will imperil his own clerical position, as a person who presumes to disobey the great Synod.

CANON V

Concerning those, whether of the clergy or of the laity, who have been excommunicated in the several provinces, let the provision of the canon be observed by the bishops which provides that persons cast out by some be not readmitted by others. Nevertheless, inquiry should be made whether they have been excommunicatd through captiousness, or contentiousness, or any such like ungracious disposition in the bishop. And, that this matter may have due investigation, it is decreed that in every province synods shall be held twice a year, in order that when all the bishops of the province are assembled together, such questions may by them be thoroughly examined, that so those who have confessedly offended against their bishop, may be seen by all to be for just cause excommunicated, until it shall seem fit to a general meeting of the bishops to pronounce a milder sentence upon them. And let these synods be held, the one before Lent (that the pure Gift may be offered to God after all bitterness has been put away), and let the second be held about autumn.

CANON VI

Let the ancient customs in Egypt, Libya and Pentapolis prevail, that the Bishop of Alexandria have jurisdiction in all these, since the like is customary for the Bishop of Rome also. Likewise in Antioch and the other provinces, let the Churches retain their privileges. And this is to be universally understood, that if any one be made bishop without the consent of the Metropolitan, the great Synod has declared that such a man ought not to be a bishop. If, however, two or three bishops shall from natural love of contradiction, oppose the common suffrage of the rest, it being reasonable and in accordance with the Ecclesiastical law, then let the choice of the majority prevail.

In his *City of God,* Augustine (354–430) provided a famous explanation of the proper relationship between Christian believers and the secular world in which Christianity developed.

FROM The City of God BY AUGUSTINE

But the families which do not live by faith seek their peace in the earthly advantages of this life; while the families which live by faith look for those eternal blessings which are promised, and use as pilgrims such advantages of time and of earth as do not fascinate and divert them from God, but rather aid them to endure with greater ease, and to keep down the number of those burdens of the corruptible body which weigh upon the soul. Thus the things necessary for this mortal life are used by both kinds of men and families alike, but each has its own peculiar and widely different aim in using them. The earthly city, which does not live by faith, seeks an earthly peace, and the end it proposes, in the well-ordered concord of civic obedience and rule, is the combination of men's wills to attain the things which are helpful to this life. The heavenly city, or rather the part of it which sojourns on earth and lives by faith, makes use of this peace only because it must, until this mortal condition which necessitates it shall pass away. Consequently, so long as it lives like a captive and a stranger in the earthly city, though it has already received the promise of redemption, and the gift of the Spirit as the earnest of it, it makes no scruple to obey the laws of the earthly city, whereby the things necessary for the maintenance of this mortal life are administered; and thus, as this life is common to both cities, so there is a harmony between them in regard to what belongs to it. But, as the earthly city has had some philosophers whose doctrine is condemned by the divine teaching . . . it has come to pass that the two cities could not have common laws of religion, and that the heavenly city has been compelled in this matter to dissent, and to become obnoxious to those who think differently, and to stand the brunt of their anger and hatred and persecutions, except in so far as the minds of their enemies have been alarmed by the multitude of the Christians and quelled by the manifest protection of God accorded to them. This heavenly city, then, while it sojourns on earth, calls citizens out of all nations, and gathers together a society of pilgrims of all languages, not scrupling about diversities in the manners, laws, and institutions whereby earthly peace is secured and maintained, but recognizing that, however various these are, they all tend to one and the same end of earthly peace. It therefore is so far from rescinding and abolish-

Augustine, *The City of God II* (1871), pp. 326–328 translated by Marcus Dodds.

ing these diversities, that it even preserves and adopts them, so long only as no hindrance to the worship of the one supreme and true God is thus introduced. Even the heavenly city, therefore, while in its state of pilgrimage, avails itself of the peace of earth, and, so far as it can without injuring faith and godliness, desires and maintains a common agreement among men regarding the acquisition of the necessaries of life, and makes this earthly peace bear upon the peace of heaven; for this alone can be truly called and esteemed the peace of the reasonable creatures, consisting as it does in the perfectly ordered and harmonious enjoyment of God and of one another in God. When we shall have reached that peace, this mortal life shall give place to one that is eternal, and our body shall be no more this animal body which by its corruption weighs down the soul, but a spiritual body feeling no want, and in all its members subjected to the will. In its pilgrim state the heavenly city possesses this peace by faith; and by this faith it lives righteously when it refers to the attainment of that peace every good action towards God and man; for the life of the city is a social life.

5
THE VICTORY OF CHRISTIANITY— A MODERN VIEW

In the following selection Gerhart Ladner reconsiders Gibbon's interpretation of the rise of Christianity.

FROM The Impact of Christianity BY GERHART B. LADNER

I believe then that Gibbon really understood the tragic spirit of Greece and Rome, not only as expressed in literature, but also as manifest in historical events, and that when he speaks of the "melancholy" character of this or that phase of the decline and fall of Rome he is, if not always consciously mindful of tragedy, at least subtly influenced by his realization of it.

But when a historian of the Roman Empire reaches the moment in which the effect of Christianity upon the course of events cannot be overlooked, he is confronted by an altogether new problem with regard to the tragic or melancholy character of history, and it is part of Gibbon's greatness that he did not shirk the problem, though he did not do it full justice.

On the one hand, in the Christian view of things, the coming of Christ had once and for all overcome the tragic course of human history by lifting the destiny of man out of the range of those suprahuman or infrahuman forces

Gerhart B. Ladner, "The Impact of Christianity," in Lynn White, ed., *The Transformation of the Roman World* (1966), pp. 63–91. Originally published by the University of California Press; reprinted by permission of the Regents of the University of California.

symbolised or represented by the gods or by fate or by hybris, forces with which he could no longer cope by himself. On the other hand, even those who had responded to the new chance given to mankind, that is to say, the Christians, had not lastingly or not fully responded to it and had thus caused a new and, in a sense, worse tragedy than that of pre-Christian history. To Gibbon, and not to him alone, the tragedy of Christian history is that of a great promise only partially fulfilled.

Let us listen to Gibbon himself at the beginning of his famous fifteenth chapter on "The Progress of the Christian Religion":

A candid but rational inquiry into the progress and establishment of Christianity may be considered as a very essential part of the history of the Roman Empire. While that great body was invaded by open violence, or undermined by slow decay, a pure and humble religion gently insinuated itself into the minds of men, grew up in silence and obscurity, derived new vigour from opposition, and finally erected the triumphant banner of the Cross on the ruins of the Capitol. . . .

But this inquiry, however useful or entertaining, is attended with two peculiar difficulties. The scanty and suspicious materials of ecclesiastical history seldom enable us to dispel the dark cloud that hangs over the first age of the Church. The great law of impartiality too often obliges us to reveal the imperfections of the uninspired teachers and believers of the Gospel; and, to a careless observer, their faults may seem to cast a shade on the faith which they professed. But the scandal of the pious Christian, and the fallacious triumph of the infidel, should ease as soon as they recollect not only by whom, but likewise to whom, the divine revelation was given. The theologian may indulge the pleasing task of describing religion as she descended from heaven, arrayed in her native purity. A more melancholy duty is imposed on the historian. He must discover the inevitable mixture of error and corruption, which she contracted in a long residence upon earth, among a weak and degenerate race of beings.

To this text one of Gibbon's editors, the well-known Anglican divine H. H. Millman, adds the following comment: "Divest this whole passage of the latent sarcasm betrayed by the subsequent tone of the whole disquisition, and it might commence a Christian history, written in the most Christian spirit of candour."

I must say that I do not find much latent sarcasm here, nor do I believe that Gibbon, out of prudence or fear of ecclesiastical persecution, dissembled his true feelings about the Christian religion when he remarked on the lofty character of early Christianity or on its later contributions to civilization. Had he been afraid or prudent, he would never have affected the ironical, sarcastic, even hostile tone that he did indeed use toward Christianity and Christians on many occasions.

The main problem, then, confronting the historian who wants to understand the innovating power of Christianity in ancient and later history can be stated in terms that I think are not alien to Gibbon: If the essence of Christianity was tragically diminished by events of Christian history, what was its lasting newness, its actual greatness?

Gibbon himself discusses five characteristics of early Christianity which, according to him, made up the newness and the greatness that led to its success: the zeal of the Christians, their doctrine of a future life, their miracles, their pure and austere morality, and, finally, the development of hierarchical government in the Church concurrently with the decline of political government in the state, or to use Gibbon's own words, "the union and discipline of the Christian republic, which gradually formed an independent and increasing state in the heart of the Roman Empire." Obviously, these five points, in spite of their significance, do not suffice to define the tremendous and truly decisive change that Christianity brought about in the world.

Among the foremost idiosyncrasies that caused Gibbon to slight essential aspects of Christianity were his contempt for theology and his hatred of monasticism. As a result, he did not see that the meaning of Christianity for the late Roman Empire cannot be intellectually grasped if there is no clear understanding of who and what Christians of that time believed Christ was; he therefore underestimated the religious and intellectual importance of the trinitarian and Christological disputes of the first four general councils. Nor did he recognize that the monks were the greatest fighters against that recurrent contamination of Christianity by the worldliness he so deplored: he failed to appreciate that monasticism was an attempt to establish a purer form of the Christian life than that which could be expected from the whole Church once it had become very large and very mixed. One might go even further and assert that Gibbon, great historian though he was, did not fully understand the new dimensions that the concepts of time and history had received in Christian thought through the coming of Christ and the phenomenon of the Church.

In the following discussion of Christianity I omit two of the elements Gibbon considered essential: the belief in a future life and the belief in miracles. It is true that the Christians developed these beliefs in a very special way, but, even though Gibbon is right in assuming that they greatly contributed to the success of the Christian religion, they were and are to be found also in various forms outside Christianity. It is different with Gibbon's three remaining reasons for the victory of the Christians over the pagans. We may use them as starting points for the investigation of the innovating force of Christianity if we somewhat widen their scope. What Gibbon calls zeal—and his feeling about zeal and zealots was, to say the least, ambivalent—was really a new attitude to truth based on the event of the Incarnation; what he calls pure and austere morality involved a new approach both to ethics and to asceticism, culminating in the triumph of the monastic ideal; and what he considers the growth of an ecclesiastical state within the political state was, in fact, only one aspect of the life of the Christian Church which saw itself peculiarly suspended between heaven and earth, between eternity and time, and thus, among other things, produced a new conception of history.

Let us then first look at Christianity's new attitude toward truth. It was, above all, an exclusive attitude; it was an exact opposite of the pluralistic conception of religion prevalent in the Greco-Roman-oriental milieu of late Antiquity into which Christ was born. I need hardly recall how amicably Isis, Mithras, the Great Mother, the Invincible Sun, and other deities were associated in the Pantheon of the Roman Empire with the Olympian gods and the cult of Roma and the Emperor and how amazed and indignant the Romans were when they discovered that the Christians did not recognize any god except their own. But Christians had no choice in the matter if they wanted to be faithful to their Master, who, according to the Gospel of St. John, had said: "I am the Way, and the Truth, and the Life" (John 14:6).

There seem to be three important exceptions, however, to the novelty and uniqueness of the Christian attitude toward truth. These are the Greek, the Jewish, and the Buddhist attitudes. A very brief discussion of each will help us to understand Christianity better.

First, the deep and admirable search for supreme and even divine truth in Greek philosophical thought from Socrates to Plotinus, while it had never revoked its dedication to reason, had nevertheless not been lacking in religious elements. Yet, the ultimate quasi-religious realities of the classical conception of truth had remained in the realm of poetic myth as in Plato, or of cosmic intuition as in Aristotle, or of mystic speculation as in Plotinus, whereas the Christians believed and claimed that the truly divine had entered into experienced history, into verifiable reality. This, according to Christianity, was what happened in the Incarnation.

As Professor Harry Wolfson has so clearly shown in his books on Philo and on the philosophy of the Church Fathers, the meeting of the Judeo-Christian religious revelation with the Greco-Roman habits of rational thought produced a new kind of theological philosophy or philosophical theology, which is one of the great achievements of the human mind, though this achievement carries with it great problems of its own. The historical, as well as metahistorical, character of the New Testament religion forced the mind of Christians to come to terms that were rational and at the same time "binding" with events and phenomena, such as the Incarnation and the Church, which to them were both actual and transcendent. For the Greeks to learn how to *know* truly had been a sure way to become good or even godlike. For the Christians, the situation was somewhat different: Christ himself was the ultimate truth, and he had entrusted it to his Church. Not to know, or not to accept, this truth seemed incompatible with true goodness. Heresy was considered a moral defect because it was a lack of love for the Church of Christ, a Christ who had become incarnate and a Church in which he continued to live on mysteriously. The certainty of possessing the truth eclipsed the religious pluralism of late Antiquity, and only very slowly was this Christian certainty to learn how to respect religious dissent.

It is because of the Jewish refusal to accept the Christian view of Christ Incarnate that the second apparent exception to the novelty and uniqueness of the Christian attitude toward religious truth is no real exception either. On Christian premises, Jewish faith in the one true God was incomplete if compared with the corresponding Christian belief, except in so far as it prophesied and foreshadowed the coming of a God-Man and His universal role as the bringer of supreme truth to all men. And it radically differed from the Christian faith in so far as it wanted to keep the one God and the Messiah the property of the Jewish people alone. Moreover, Christ himself had strongly asserted his divine sonship, whereas the Jews thought of the Messiah as a God-sent but otherwise merely human being.

How much the Christian attitude to truth is centered in the person of a divine Christ can be seen if we compare the two accounts of creation found in the first chapter of the Book of Genesis and in the prologue to the Gospel of St. John, respectively. The Book of Genesis begins with the words: "In the beginning God created heaven and earth. And the earth was void and empty, and darkness was upon the face of the deep; and the Spirit of God moved over the waters" (Gen. 1:1 f.). This means that God created both heaven, which is spiritual, and earth, which is material. This conception was an advance over those old oriental, and especially Babylonian, dualistic creation accounts, according to which the spiritual powers of heaven had to overcome pre-existent material and chaotic forces, so that the cosmos, an ordered universe, could emerge. In the Gospel of St. John, however, the traces of the old dualism have become even more subordinate: "In the beginning was the Word, and the Word was with God, and the Word was God. . . . All things were made by Him: and without Him was made nothing that was made. In Him was life and the life was the light of men. . . . That was the true light, which enlighteneth every man that cometh into this world." Here creation is clearly from nothing and the spiritual and unique character of the creational act has become even more explicit through the fact that creation is carried out by God's own Word, the Logos, Christ, who is also His Divine Son.

The Christian conception of truth then is rooted in a God who is both a Creator-God and God Incarnate. And this brings us to the last of the three attitudes to truth which at first glance seem to compete with the Christian one, the Buddhist attitude. The Buddha certainly came to teach religious truth, above all the four holy truths of his Sermon of Benares, which are concerned with suffering and the overcoming of suffering. Yet the content of Buddhist truth taken as a whole is quite different from that of Christian truth taken as a whole. The Buddha himself never claimed that he was in any way connected with the creation of this world or that he was the Son of God, God Incarnate. Even when Mahayana Buddhism conceived of a succession of Buddhas, in all of whom an ultimate divine reality or truth was embodied, this belief was not so much one of Incarnation in the Christian sense of the term as one of reincarnation. The Buddhas have passed through many deaths and reincarnations before achieving Buddhahood. Bodhisattvas or future Buddhas may stand at the threshold of Buddhahood, capable of entering Nirvana if they so choose, but may nevertheless submit to further reincarnation for the benefit of mankind.

Such pluralistic views of reincarnation differ greatly from basic Christian assertions of incarnational and redemptional belief such as St. Augustine's statement in his *City of God:* "Christ died once and for all for our sins." Here everything is centered on the uniqueness of the deity's entry into our world; furthermore, in the radically sacrificial character of this divine intervention, the effectiveness of which could be real, however, only if Christ was in truth God and Man.

The novel Christian conception of truth is therefore based on the belief that a man, Jesus, was himself the Supreme Truth, in other words, that he was truly God. How exactly could this be possible? The two general councils of Ephesus and Chalcedon in 431 and 451 attempted to answer this question in their debates and decisions against heretics who stressed either the humanity of Christ at the expense of his divinity, or his divinity at the cost of his humanity. The first of these two councils was directed against Nestorius of Constantinople's teaching about the Incarnation, in which according to his opponents, he overemphasized Christ's humanity. It may hold our attention for a moment, for, among all general councils of the Church, it is one of the most "melancholy" in Gibbon's sense of the term, and nevertheless it succeeded in defending one of the most essential tenets of Christianity. Nestorius' chief antagonist, the Patriarch Cyril of Alexandria, is the crucial figure in both respects. He used dubious and perhaps reprehensible means to reach his goal, the condemnation of Nestorius, who had good reasons for writing a book entitled *Tragedy* about his experiences. Gibbon is rightly indignant about the way in which Nestorius and his Antiochene friends were treated and rightly censures the intrigues, briberies, and violence of Cyril and his followers. He allows that "humanity may drop a tear on the fate of Nestorius" (in spite of the latter's own inhumanity in the prosecution of heretics). Yet even though we may well be repelled by Cyril's methods and even if Nestorius really was condemned unjustly or for the wrong reasons, such considerations cannot, I think, alter the fact that it was Cyril and not Nestorius who asserted and saved the core of Christian religiousness. This core was the belief that the divine Logos, the Word of God, had become flesh and that therefore in the union between the divine and the human nature which exists in Christ Incarnate, the divine Logos Himself had remained the unifying subject, as it were, rather than being only one of the two natures present in the union.

The safeguarding of the doctrine of Christ's full divinity by Cyril corresponded to one of the deepest concerns of the Christian, and especially of the Greek Christian, soul: the desire for deification, for godlikeness even in this life. Only if the Christ who walked on this earth as a man was at the same time truly a divine being could man hope to be deified to the extent of his capacity.

Western Christendom was to express assimilation to God, imitation of Christ, more in terms of sanctification than of divinization; the idea of holiness as well as that of godlikeness had been inherited by Christianity from Judaism, but the former idea seems to have remained less susceptible to Greek philosophical influence than the latter. However this may be, in terms of sanctity, too, only the fullest conceivable, that is to say, truly divine, holiness of Christ could form the presupposition for the achievement of sainthood by man, which again is ultimately his union with God.

Cyril's mystical theology certainly continued the best tradition of the spirituality of the Greek Christian East. It is all the more distressing for us, as it was for Gibbon, to see that high mystical thought could be joined to an unscrupulous ecclesiastical policy, which was largely governed by the longstanding rivalries between the patriarchal sees of Alexandria and Constantinople and, combined with monastic fanaticism, could, after Cyril's death, lead to the regrettable events of the so-called Robber Synod of Ephesus of 449. Yet the melancholy moral deficiencies of some mystics and monks must not make one forget that mysticism and monasticism were in many ways the most sublime products of that great renewal of morality which was brought about by Christianity and which, according to Gibbon, was one of the reasons for its success.

"The pure and austere morality of the Christians," "the reformation of manners which was introduced into the world by the preaching of the Gospels," were inseparable in Gibbon's eyes "from the divine persuasion which enlightened or subdued the understanding."

And, indeed, in Christianity the link between the religious and moral sphere was unprecedented in closeness. That a man must strive for moral goodness in order to worship God effectively is not a commonplace in the history of religions. Christian morality was all the more novel in the late ancient milieu as it included sexual purity centered around virginity or around strict fidelity in monogamous marriage. In the ethical sphere, too, the New Testament message amounted to a great religious innovation, though the Old Testament had prepared the way.

In classical Antiquity, morality had, on the whole, been the domain of philosophy rather than of religion. The doings of the Olympian and non-Olympian gods were certainly no model of pure morals. On the other hand, Judaism, governed by legal as well as by ethical postulates, had not so consistently set morality and its culmination in love above the law as Christ was to do.

Gibbon touches upon a very important point when he links the Christian reformation of morality to repentance, for repentance (*metanoia*), a complete change of mind or heart, was exactly what Jesus demanded of those who wanted to enter the Kingdom of God. Yet Gibbon rationalistically underestimates the range of the phenomenon of penitence. He has little more to say about it other than that many a saint was first a sinner. But there was considerably more to it. Gibbon does not sufficiently analyze, because he does not sufficiently understand, Christian ethics, which is an ethic of spiritual perfection modeled after a mediator between God and man, who was morally, and in every other respect, a perfect man and the divine Son of a perfect God. In Christianity the best way, perhaps the only way, not to be a sinner is to strive to be a saint, is to imitate Christ and thus to be united with God, to be deified.

In the greatest document of Christian ethics, the Sermon on the Mount, Christ said to all men, "Be you therefore perfect, as also your Heavenly Father is perfect" (Matt. 5:48). To be a true Christian means to follow the commandments of this perfect God: "By their fruits you will know them" (Matt. 7:16) and "Not everyone that saith to Me, Lord, Lord, shall enter into the Kingdom of Heaven; but he that doth the will of my Father, who is in Heaven, he shall enter into the Kingdom of Heaven" (Matt. 7:21). Other scriptural texts, both in the Old and the New Testament, indicate, however, that perfection is not merely justice or righteousness; it is, above all, altruistic love as described in St. Paul's great hymn on charity in the First Letter to the Corinthians (ch. 13). Such love begins and ends with the love of God and includes depreciation of self-love in one's love for others. "Thou shalt love the Lord thy God with thy whole heart and with thy whole soul and with thy whole mind," and "Thou shalt love thy neighbour as thyself" (Matt. 22:37, 39; cf. Mark 12:31, Deut. 6:5, Levit, 19:18).

It is difficult to conceive of a higher goal of ethical perfection. Nevertheless, the qualms of a wealthy young man elicited from Christ an even more specific statement on what perfection is. This statement is known by an almost technical term as the counsels of perfection: "If thou wilt be perfect, go, sell what thou hast, and give to the poor . . . and come follow me." This text from Matthew 19:21 played a great role in that concentration of Christian virtue called monasticism.

The origins of monasticism in the strict sense coincided approximately with the moment in the history of the Church in which she was confronted by the new tasks and dangers resulting from her having become a power, not only in the spiritual but also in the material order; and, from that time onward, those who in one manner or another followed the monastic way of life were the principal agents of reform in the Christian world. The monks, however, went to the desert not only because they sought a moral perfection that was hard to attain in the world; this to them was only a stepping-stone to higher things. Their greatest desire was to anticipate on earth by their prayers the perpetual praise of God by the angels and saints in Heaven.

As a group, the monks were the most spiritual Christians. They were the foremost witnesses for the so-called eschatological aspect of Christian existence, that is to say, through their constant prayers they prepared themselves and others for whom they prayed for the "eschata," the last things, the return of Christ as judge of the world. Wealth and sexual love therefore meant nothing to them; some, in fact, overreacted against the luxury and sexual excesses of late ancient society by practising eccentric forms of asceticism. No doubt monasticism in general tended to emphasize those relatively moderate dualistic and puritanical strains present in Christianity since its early days, especially with regard to sexuality. Yet the monks, in spite of their spiritualism, never went so far as the rigorously dualistic Gnostics and Manichaeans in rejecting and opposing the material and corporeal world: they supplemented rather than denied the validity of the latter.

Significantly, it was the liturgical worship of God in the monastic community which made the spiritual and eschatological mentality of the monks manifest first in chanted prayer and religious poetry and art and then in the transference of the monastic principle of ordered peace under spiritual guidance to ecclesiastical life at large and more generally to the life of Christian society.

The early history of monasticism was at times marred, especially in the Christian East, by tragically un-Christian narrow-mindedness and militancy, whether the monks merely defended their own ideals or supported hierarchic faction leaders. Yet Gibbon and like-minded critics were greatly mistaken in seeing all asceticism and monasticism as escapism or as fanaticism. On the contrary, the constructive contributions of monasticism were many and varied, and the underlying ascetic spirit gave to the monastic and quasi-monastic communities a dynamic impulse that did not remain limited to the search for individual perfection, but enabled them to assume reforming and innovating leadership in almost all crucial phases of late ancient, medieval, and early modern Church history. The monastic and religious orders were the spiritual avant-garde in the Church's periodically repeated renewal.

It is impossible to enumerate or discuss all monastic accomplishments on this occasion. Let me mention only two points. One is the combination of ascetic God-seeking and of intellectual labor which one of the great Benedictine scholars of our own age, Dom Jean Leclercq, in the title of a famous book, has characterized as "The Love of Learning and the Desire for God." We all owe very much to the medieval monks' conviction that the pursuit of both secular and sacred knowledge is a God-pleasing enterprise. On such grounds they not only preserved in their manuscript copies the Christian and pagan classics, but also, between the sixth and the twelfth century, developed a literature and art of their own which, in an intellectually and aesthetically inspiring way, blended mystical and humanistic elements.

The second point is the emergence of a new ethos of work even in occupations of a physical and menial kind. This new attitude was by no means exclusively Benedictine; it was part and parcel of the monastic outlook from the times of St. Pachomius, St. Basil, and St. Augustine to those of St. Bernard of Clairvaux and of St. Francis of Assisi. The conception of work well done, a conception not altogether extinct in our civilization, is much indebted to this monastic ethos.

We now finally must fix our attention on that new and peculiarly Christian phenomenon known as the Church, whose constitution and government Gibbon both appreciates as a historian and dislikes as a devotee of the Enlightenment. His much discussed contention that Christianity, and especially the emergence of an organized Church, had a great share in the decline and fall of the Roman Empire, because loyalty to the Church replaced loyalty to the state, is to a large extent refuted by the long continued existence of the Byzantine Empire and of its flourishing Greco-Roman-oriental Christian culture, of which Gibbon had only a dim conception. From this point of view, perhaps more than from any other, the grand formula he uses to summarize the conception of his work, "I have described the triumph of barbarism and religion," appears as false as it seems seductive. Whether in the West, too, the Empire could have survived, in spite of the more violent onslaught of the barbarians and the more serious socio-economic situation, if such great Christian leaders as St. Ambrose of Milan or St. Leo the Great had wholeheartedly served the state rather than the Church, is perhaps not an idle question, but one that hardly permits a sure answer. And even if an affirmative answer could be given to this question, it would only lead to another problem that involves a value judgment: whether an integral preservation of the Roman Empire and its culture would have been more desirable than the new way of life of Christianity, the new world of the Church.

The novelty of the Christian Church was not absolute, but, nevertheless, it was very real. Even the most closely comparable pre-Christian religious community, the *sangha* of the followers of the Buddha, lacks not a few of the significant connotations of the Christian Church. In the Mediterranean world, at any rate, the emergence of the Church was in many ways unprecedented.

In Near Eastern and Greco-Roman Antiquity, religion had been primarily an affair of the state. Personal and sectarian religiousness had not been lacking, but they did not form a comprehensive socio-religious community outside and beyond the political or ethical sphere. Aristotle's postulate in the first book of his *Politics* was still valid at the end of classical Antiquity: ". . . the state or political community, which is the highest of all and which embraces all the rest, aims at good in a greater degree than any other." In contrast with this, consider a famous statement by St. Augustine: "Two loves have made two cities, love of self unto contempt of God the earthly city, love of God unto contempt of self the heavenly city." For Augustine, the community that pursues the highest good, that is, God, is not a state but a suprapolitical, supranational, and supranatural society, mixed on this earth with the earthly or worldly society, but nevertheless extending beyond to embrace its members in heaven. This is the Augustinian City of God, which very largely overlaps with the concept of the Church; there does remain a distinctness between the two concepts which does not, however, concern us here.

All great social concepts of Christianity, be it the Kingdom of God or the Communion of Saints, the Church or the City of God, were conceived as immanent in this world, as visible, struggling, and timebound, and, at the same time, as transcendent, as invisible, as triumphant, and as eternal in the world to come. There was, then, a Church as the community of the faithful on earth and a Church as the congregation of the heavenly city consisting of its citizens, that is to say, the saints and the angels. It is one of the great paradoxes of Christianity that such a concept as the Church can appear under these two aspects and nevertheless be ultimately one. For even though the many evil men who are part of the visible Church will never be found in its heavenly counterpart, the terrestrial and the celestial Church are seen as identical because only the good and the reformable are believed to make up the *true* Church, either in this life or the next, either now or at the end of history.

The general tension between the divine and the human element in the organism of the Church repeats itself in different forms on two more particularized levels: in the tension between the clergy and laity, or, to be more exact, between the hierarchy and the community of the faithful, and in the tension between the spiritual and the temporal concerns of the Church.

The Church, according to the developed doctrine of the Middle Ages, is, on the one hand, the community of all believers who, in a mysterious way, have, according to St. Paul (I Cor. 12:12 f.), become the body of Christ on earth and all of whom possess, according to St. Peter (I Peter 2:5, 9), a certain priestly character. On the other hand, the Church is in a very special way represented by the corporation of the hierarchy, that is to say, by the ordained bishops and priests who alone are able, again in a mysterious, though real, way, to call the celestial body of Christ down upon the altar in the great sacramental act of worship called the eucharistic sacrifice or the Mass.

The hierarchical aspect of the Church had been decisive for the relationship between Church and state since the time of Constantine the Great, if not earlier. Since Pope Gregory VII in the eleventh century, the clerical hierarchy, explicitly concentrated toward the papal office, became even more important in political-ecclesiastical relations. In Catholic countries this has remained so, at least in principle, through early modern times. Not surprisingly, such a development was accompanied by a corresponding rise of hierarchical power, and it is easy enough for Gibbon to present the history of the ecclesiastical hierarchy as the history of ecclesiastical power politics. It was that, but it was not only that. It is hardly necessary to recall how hierarchs such as St. Athanasius, St. Basil, and St. Ambrose defended the liberty of the Church and through it the freedom of the spirit against the brute political power of the state, which, though Christianized, had nevertheless not quite given up the ancient and ever-tempting fusion and confusion of the religious and political spheres. It was probably unavoidable that the supremacy of the spiritual order which the Church claimed against the material order of the world, would gradually come to mean that the Church itself could exercise its, by then considerable, material power, and even coercive material power. It would do so in the Middle Ages and early modern times whenever its own spiritual mission in the world with regard to Christian doctrine and morals was directly or even indirectly involved.

A temptation to transgress limits, a temptation different but hardly less dangerous than that inherited from Antiquity by the state, did in certain periods lead the hierarchical Church toward an undifferentiated spiritualism that could become a pretext for the overextension of the exercise of material power. At the same time and despite the warnings of far-seeing hierarchs such as Pope Gregory the Great, the hierarchy, while claiming material power on spiritual grounds, would rarely attempt to improve fundamentally those depressed material conditions of the majority of mankind which made a healthy spiritual life difficult. Simplistic spiritualism of this kind was altogether harmful to the dignity of the full human person when it placed the whole field of manual work, including all economic and technological activity, on a low level in the scale of values. Such attitudes, on the whole, were not shared by the monks, but rather were characteristic of certain hierarchs. The hierarchical office had been founded as a ministerial office, above all for the sake of the humble and the poor, above all for those who toiled and suffered under the material pressures of this world. Yet the record of the hierarchical Church with regard to the practical aspects of social-economic justice, though great at certain times and in certain places, has been far from coherent.

For instance, the ancient and medieval Church, while treating individual slaves and serfs in a spirit of brotherly love and while considering their freeing as a work of Christian charity, rarely challenged the institutions of slavery and serfdom. Patristic-scholastic thought saw them as a consequence of original sin, on the same level as other consequences, such as coercive government and just or defensive war, equally regrettable and equally irremediable in this world. It is true that a thorough reversal of the ancient and medieval attitude toward slavery and serfdom, and of the socially and economically depressed condition of slaves and serfs, on grounds of Christian morality would have been exceedingly difficult, and probably impossible, before economic and social conditions had begun to change radically in the later Middle Ages under secular rather than ecclesiastical pressures and under the impact of technological and organizational innovations. But even then the dead weight of tradition in matters of servitude and economic subservience continued for a long time to influence the attitude of the Church. Christianity's relative lack of sensibility in matters of social-economic justice was a melancholy, a tragic aspect of Christian history which remained more or less hidden until more recent times when excesses and remedies matured, as it were, as a result of industrial and political revolutions. In this respect, even today Christian renewal urgently needs to be further developed and completed.

The tension between the spiritual and the material power of the Church, and especially of the papacy, was and is often conceptualized in the terms "direct power in spiritual things" and "indirect (spiritual) power in temporal things." The term "temporal" in this antithetical formula is not so obvious as it might seem. It is connected with the development in the ecclesiastical and political theory of the Middle Ages of the metaphor of the spiritual sword and the material sword, the latter concept often being widened to that of the secular or temporal sword from the early thirteenth century onward. The term "temporal" was substituted in this area of thought for the term "material" at a relatively late date. Nevertheless, this substitution is highly significant, for it is a logical consequence of the Christian view of time which was not only a *novum* in the world into which Christianity entered, but also continued to be of great importance for the civilization shaped by the Christian religion, and quite especially for Western civilization.

In pre-Christian Antiquity, speculation on time had been based on the belief in the perpetual cyclical recurrence of identical or similar situations and events. This belief is rooted in a widespread archaic mentality that attempts to deny the relentless deathbound course of time by the assumption of ever new cosmic or, at least, ever new biological beginnings. With Christianity, all this changed or received a new meaning. Past and future, extending from Creation to the Last Judgment, were seen with reference to the one principal historical fact of the coming of Christ. All past history led up to this event; all future history would be deeply influenced by it. The Christian view of time and history, then, is unilinear rather than cyclical. Moreover, this linear extension has not only a beginning and an end, but also a privileged focal point along the line, the event of Christ's coming, whereas eternally recurrent cycles have no meaningful center.

On Christian terms, unilinear time is for man the necessary, the one and only, road to eternity. Thus, for instance, in St. Augustine's profound philosophy of time and history, time, it is true, dissolves the unity of God's eternity into multiple succession, but it also instills a first element of order into the otherwise directionless and chaotic flux of all things. In conjunction with man's memory of the past and anticipation of the future, time gives him leeway and guidance to reform himself and the times—ransoming the time, St. Paul called it (Eph. 5:15 f.)—and through this effort to win eternity.

It has often been observed that Christians, and especially Western Christians and those influenced by them, are much more involved in time and history than, for instance, the ancient Greeks or Indians had been. The Christian position on time, like so many other Christian positions, was ambivalent and even paradoxical. On the one hand, Christians must not become too involved in temporal events; on the other hand, the latter are not without value or purpose. The temporal sphere is not a mere Indian *sansara,* no mere seductive and deceptive illusion. Once more we are brought back to the crucial fact that Christ himself has entered the temporal and historical world.

No doubt the relatively affirmative Christian conception of time is one of the reasons why the Church, especially in the West, felt entitled and constrained to apply its spiritual and, in one sense, timeless principles so energetically to the existential and temporal realities of the world, an attitude that brought about, among other things, the papal hegemony of the central part of the Middle Ages. That the tension between the spiritual and the temporal spheres could lead to confusion, to some abuse of wealth and power on the part of the Church, and to a fierce and ultimately successful struggle of the political against the ecclesiastical order, is undeniable. But this need not lead the historian to Gibbon's conclusion that all ecclesiastical and hierarchical interventions in the temporal sphere were in themselves necessarily evil. In the actual history of the Church in time there have been deformations, but there also has come into operation the typically Christian temporal and historical category of reform. Reform avoids the automatism of eternal recurrence, be it cosmological or biological, and asserts the intentionality of the human spirit and its unique position in a world which is seen as both temporal and on the way to eternity.

To conclude, Gibbon, who wanted to be a philosophical historian in the spirit of Montesquieu, tried to establish the secondary causes and effects of Christianity as of other facts of history. His understanding of the Christian religion remained fragmentary, owing not so much to his dismissal of the first cause—this was, in part, the methodically sound bracketing of divine providence in a strictly historical inquiry—but instead to his failure to realize the full range of the religious motives of men and their results in history. Nevertheless, Gibbon did not lack all perceptiveness for the history of Christianity, especially not for its "melancholy" aspects. Church historians could learn from him to take seriously the many human imperfections, corruptions, and tragedies that are interwoven with the history of the Church. There are, it seems to me, far too few modern Church historians who have accepted and presented such facts in all their starkness and harshness. At the same time, there have been too many who have presented them with a hostile bias. A truly integral view of the complexities of Church history and of history in general would certainly not be satisfied merely with Gibbon's melancholy and skeptical resignation or with his scornful and cynical irony. For in such a wider view, which had been that of Giambattista Vico a generation before Gibbon, there is no fatal tragedy, no final decline; there are *corsi*, but there are also *ricorsi*. Continual rebirth, reform, renewal are of the essence of the Christian religion and therefore also of Christian civilization and of its history.

THE
ROMAN
EMPIRE

WHY DID
IT FALL?

CONTENTS

QUESTIONS FOR STUDY

1. *Does the evidence fully support Gibbon's estimate of Rome in the second century? What light does Pliny shed on that estimate?*
2. *What is the relationship among the evidence of Justinian, Herodian, and Salvian?*
3. *Both Walbank and Rostovtzeff emphasize economic and social elements. How do their interpretations differ?*
4. *How does the interpretation of Piganiol compare with that of Gibbon?*
5. *Was the fall of Rome inevitable?*

The problem of the causes of the decline and fall of the classical world as represented by the Roman Empire in the West is at least as old as the Renaissance and was posed in definitive form by Edward Gibbon in the eighteenth century. It has not yet lost its fascination, for in the twentieth century historians and philosophers of history have continued to use it as the focal point for speculations on the nature of historical change. The Roman Empire is admirably suited as a subject for such speculations, for it represents a complete cycle of civilization. At the same time it is of special interest to students of Western civilization, for the classical heritage is a vital component of that civilization.

The difficulties presented by the problem of the decline and fall are enormous. The passage of time and the vagaries of fortune have destroyed many of the sources we should like to have as evidence and have preselected the rest; but beyond the problem of sources is the difficult methodological problem of distinguishing cause from effect and assigning the proper weight to each contributing factor. In light of these difficulties it is not surprising that there seem to be as many interpretations as there are scholars and that each age has seen the problem from a different perspective.

The concept of the fall of the Roman Empire was invented by such Renaissance figures as Petrarch, who blamed internal problems, and Machiavelli, who emphasized the role of barbarian attacks. Thus the two fundamental modes of explanation were set quite early. It remained for Gibbon, an eighteenth-century *philosophe,* to deal with the problem in a magisterial way in his great history. Gibbon's own answer to the question of why Rome fell is more ambiguous than is generally recognized. To be sure, the common view that he blames the rise of Christianity on Rome's decline is partly true (pp. 264–265), but he also took a more fatalistic approach: "The decline of Rome was the natural and inevitable effect of immoderate greatness" (p. 263).

Before we can speak of decline we must decide when Rome reached the peak of peace, prosperity, and civilization from which it fell. Gibbon selected the second half of the second century, the age of the Antonines, as "the period in the history of the world during which the condition of the human race was most happy and prosperous" (p. 266). Modern scholars have shown that the problems that were later to cause so much trouble—economic strain, decline of public spirit, reluctance of citizens to serve the state, and pressures of barbarians on the frontier—all eixsted at least in embryonic form in the second century. It is generally agreed, however, that these difficulties were managed and controlled rather well until the death of Marcus Aurelius in A.D. 180. Thereafter came a period in which the rule of Rome showed itself unequal to the trials of government. Emperors were overthrown by rebellious armies. The land was ravaged by marauding bands of soldiers, often indistinguishable from bandits. Members of the old governing class chose to flee rather than pay exorbitant taxes or serve the state in burdensome and dangerous offices. The barbarians pressed ever harder, defeating Roman armies or being bought off by bribes. In the late third and early fourth centuries the Emperors Diocletian and Constantine made valiant attempts, with some success, to shore up the tottering empire. But in 410 the barbarians sacked Rome, and in 476 the last Roman emperor in the West was deposed.

Modern students of the problem of Rome's fall have not been satisfied with Gibbon's fatalistic explanation but have sought a more active cause for the collapse of ancient civilization. Like Petrarch and Machiavelli, they have been divided for the most part into those who blame internal causes and those who look outside Rome's borders for the trouble. Explorations into internal failures have been the most popular and the most various. They have included explanations based on agricultural failures caused by climatic changes and on manpower shortage due to various causes. A recent, not very persuasive, version blames this manpower shortage on lead poisoning from the pipes used to carry water to Roman houses. A second category of explanation might be called the bio-political. One version of this explains the decline of Rome as a result of the destruction of the best class of people by imperial executions and civil war, leaving the state without a competent ruling class.

Another version blames race mixture, which diluted the old Roman stock with Semitic and Germanic elements (p. 296). A third important category of explanation has been the economic. Some scholars have blamed the drain of gold and silver, and they have seen this decline as the true source of Rome's troubles. Still others have thought that the economic measures taken by Diocletian and Constantine stifled free enterprise and brought about the deadly economic paralysis that destroyed Rome.

The most influential of the interpretations that stress internal problems, however, have been more sophisticated formulations that take into account economic, social, and political factors. Of these, the explanations of F. W. Walbank (pp. 283-285) and M. I. Rostovtzeff (pp. 286-294) are excellent, if contradictory, examples. Walbank's somewhat Marxian version derives the causes of Rome's fall "from the premises upon which classical civilisation arose, namely an absolutely low technique and, to compensate for this, the institution of slavery." Rostovtzeff, on the other hand, stands Marx on his head. He blames Rome's fall on the class war waged by the army of peasant soldiers against the bourgeoisie, the bearers of classical culture: "The main phenomenon which underlines the process of decline is the gradual absorption of the educated classes by the masses and the consequent simplification of all the functions of political, social, economic, and intellectual life, which we call the barbarization of the ancient world."

Explanations emphasizing external causes have been fewer and less popular. They are not, however, to be disregarded. A particularly vigorous formulation is that of André Piganiol (pp. 295-302), who sees no reason why Rome could not have emerged from her period of troubles renewed and invigorated had it not been for the hostility of the barbarian Germanic tribes. The following selections give some idea of the nature of the debate.

1
GIBBON ON
THE DECLINE
AND FALL

Edward Gibbon framed the question we are considering in this section in the eighteenth century. His formulation remains the basis for modern discussion.

FROM The History of the Decline and Fall of the Roman Empire BY EDWARD GIBBON

The Greeks, after their country had been reduced into a province, imputed the triumphs of Rome, not to the merit, but to the FORTUNE of the republic. The inconstant goddess, who so blindly distributes and resumes her favours, had *now* consented (such was the language of envious flattery) to resign her wings, to descend from her globe, and to fix her firm and immutable throne on the banks of the Tiber. A wiser Greek, who has composed, with a philosophic spirit, the memorable history of his own times, deprived his countrymen of this vain and delusive comfort by opening to their view the deep foundations of the greatness of Rome. The fidelity of the citizens to each other, and to the state, was confirmed by the habits of education and the prejudices of religion. Honour, as well as virtue, was the principle of the republic; the ambitious citizens laboured to deserve the solemn glories of a triumph; and the ardour of the Roman youth was kindled into active emulation, as often as they beheld the domestic images of their ancestors. The temperate struggles of the patricians and plebeians had finally established the

Edward Gibbon, *The History of the Decline and Fall of the Roman Empire*, J. B. Bury, ed., IV (1901), 160–163.

firm and equal balance of the constitution; which united the freedom of popular assemblies with the authority and wisdom of a senate and the executive powers of a regal magistrate. When the consul displayed the standard of the republic, each citizen bound himself, by the obligation of an oath, to draw his sword in the cause of his country, till he had discharged the sacred duty by a military service of ten years. This wise institution continually poured into the field the rising generations of freemen and soldiers; and their numbers were reinforced by the warlike and populous states of Italy, who, after a brave resistance, had yielded to the valour, and embraced the alliance, of the Romans. The sage historian, who excited the virtue of the younger Scipio and beheld the ruin of Carthage, has accurately described their military system; their levies, arms, exercises, subordination, marches, encampments; and the invincible legion, superior in active strength to the Macedonian phalanx of Philip and Alexander. From these institutions of peace and war, Polybius has deduced the spirit and success of a people incapable of fear and impatient of repose. The ambitious design of conquest, which might have been defeated by the seasonable conspiracy of mankind, was attempted and achieved; and the perpetual violation of justice was maintained by the political virtues of prudence and courage. The arms of the republic, sometimes vanquished in battle, always victorious in war, advanced with rapid steps to the Euphrates, the Danube, the Rhine, and the Ocean; and the images of gold, or silver, or brass, that might serve to represent the nations and their kings, were successively broken by the *iron* monarchy of Rome.

The rise of a city, which swelled into an empire, may deserve, as a singular prodigy, the reflection of a philosophic mind. But the decline of Rome was the natural and inevitable effect of immoderate greatness. Prosperity ripened the principle of decay; the causes of destruction multiplied with the extent of conquest; and, as soon as time or accident had removed the artificial supports, the stupendous fabric yielded to the pressure of its own weight. The story of its ruin is simple and obvious; and, instead of inquiring why the Roman empire was destroyed, we should rather be surprised that it had subsisted so long. The victorious legions, who, in distant wars, acquired the vices of strangers and mercenaries, first oppressed the freedom of the republic, and afterwards violated the majesty of the purple. The emperors, anxious for their personal safety and the public peace, were reduced to the base expedient of corrupting the discipline which rendered them alike formidable to their sovereign and to the enemy; the vigour of the military government was relaxed, and finally dissolved, by the partial institutions of Constantine; and the Roman world was overwhelmed by a deluge of Barbarians.

The decay of Rome has been frequently ascribed to the translation of the seat of empire; but this history has already shewn that the powers of government were *divided* rather than *removed*. The throne of Constantinople was erected in the East; while the West was still possessed by a series of emperors who held their residence in Italy and claimed their equal inheritance of the legions and provinces. This dangerous novelty impaired the strength, and fomented the vices, of a double reign; the instruments of an oppressive and arbitrary system were multiplied; and a vain emulation of luxury, not of merit, was introduced and supported between the degenerate successors of Theodosius. Extreme distress, which unites the virtue of a free people, embitters the factions of a declining monarchy. The hostile favourites of Arcadius and Honorius betrayed the republic to its common enemies; and the Byzantine court beheld with indifference, perhaps with pleasure, the disgrace of Rome, the misfortunes of Italy, and the loss of the West. Under the succeeding reigns, the alliance of the two empires was restored; but the aid of the Oriental Romans was tardy, doubtful, and ineffectual; and the national schism of the Greeks and Latins was enlarged by the perpetual difference of language and manners, of interest, and even of religion. Yet the salutary event approved in some measure the judgment of Constantine. During a long period of decay, his impregnable city repelled the victorious armies of Barbarians, protected the wealth of Asia, and commanded, both in peace and war, the important straits which connect the Euxine and Mediterranean seas. The foundation of Constantinople more essentially contributed to the preservation of the East than to the ruin of the West.

As the happiness of a *future* life is the great object of religion, we may hear, without surprise or scandal, that the introduction, or at least the abuse, of Christianity had some influence on the decline and fall of the Roman empire. The clergy successfully preached the doctrines of patience and pusillanimity; the active virtues of society were discouraged; and the last remains of the military spirit were buried in the cloister; a large portion of public and private wealth was consecrated to the specious demands of charity and devotion; and the soldiers' pay was lavished on the useless multitudes of both sexes, who could only plead the merits of abstinence and chastity. Faith, zeal, curiosity, and the more earthly passions of malice and ambition kindled the flame of theological discord; the church, and even the state, were distracted by religious factions, whose conflicts were sometimes bloody, and always implacable; the attention of the emperors was diverted from camps to synods; the Roman world was oppressed by a new species of tyranny; and the persecuted sects became the secret enemies of their country. Yet party-spirit, however pernicious or absurd, is a principle of union as well as of dissension. The bishops, from eighteen hundred pulpits, inculcated the duty of passive obedience to a lawful and orthodox sovereign; their frequent assemblies, and perpetual correspondence, maintained the communion of distant churches: and the benevolent temper of the gospel was strengthened, though confined, by the spiritual alliance of the Catholics. The sacred indolence of the monks was devoutly embraced by a servile and effeminate age; but, if superstition had not afforded a decent retreat, the same vices would have tempted the unworthy Romans to desert, from baser motives, the standard of the republic. Religious precepts are easily obeyed, which indulge and sanctify the natural inclinations of their votaries; but the pure and genuine influence of Christianity may be traced in its beneficial, though imperfect, effects on the Barbarian proselytes of the North. If the decline of the Roman empire was hastened by the conversion of Constantine, his victorious religion broke the violence of the fall, and mollified the ferocious temper of the conquerors.

2
THE EMPIRE
AT ITS
HEIGHT

For Gibbon the empire reached its peak in the age of the Antonines.

FROM The History of the Decline and Fall
of the Roman Empire BY EDWARD GIBBON

In the second century of the Christian era, the empire of Rome comprehended the fairest part of the earth, and the most civilized portion of mankind. The frontiers of that extensive monarchy were guarded by ancient
renown and disciplined valour. The gentle, but powerful, influence of laws
and manners had gradually cemented the union of the provinces. Their
peaceful inhabitants enjoyed and abused the advantages of wealth and luxury.
The image of a free constitution was preserved with decent reverence. The
Roman senate appeared to possess the sovereign authority, and devolved on
the emperors all the executive powers of government. During a happy period
of more than fourscore years, the public administration was conducted by
the virtue and abilities of Nerva, Trajan, Hadrian, and the two Antonines. It
is the design of this and of the two succeeding chapters, to describe the
prosperous condition of their empire; and afterwards, from the death of
Marcus Antoninus, to deduce the most important circumstances of its decline
and fall: a revolution which will ever be remembered, and is still felt by the
nations of the earth.

* * *

Edward Gibbon, *The History of the Decline and Fall of the Roman Empire*, J. B. Bury, ed.,
I (1897), 1, 56, 78.

Notwithstanding the propensity of mankind to exalt the past, and to depreciate the present, the tranquil and prosperous state of the empire was warmly felt, and honestly confessed, by the provincials as well as Romans. "They acknowledged that the true principles of social life, laws, agriculture, and science, which had been first invented by the wisdom of Athens, were now firmly established by the power of Rome, under whose auspicious influence the fiercest barbarians were united by an equal government and common language. They affirm that, with the improvement of arts, the human species was visibly multiplied. They celebrate the increasing splendour of the cities, the beautiful face of the country, cultivated and adorned like an immense garden; and the long festival of peace, which was enjoyed by so many nations, forgetful of their ancient animosities, and delivered from the apprehension of future danger." Whatever suspicions may be suggested by the air of rhetoric and declamation which seems to prevail in these passages, the substance of them is perfectly agreeable to historic truth.

* * *

If a man were called to fix the period in the history of the world during which the condition of the human race was most happy and prosperous, he would, without hesitation, name that which elapsed from the death of Domitian to the accession of Commodus. The vast extent of the Roman empire was governed by absolute power, under the guidance of virtue and wisdom. The armies were restrained by the firm but gentle hand of four successive emperors, whose characters and authority commanded involuntary respect. The forms of the civil administration were carefully preserved by Nerva, Trajan, Hadrian, and the Antonines, who delighted in the image of liberty, and were pleased with considering themselves as the accountable ministers of the laws. Such princes deserved the honour of restoring the republic, had the Romans of their days been capable of enjoying a rational freedom.

3
THE
EVIDENCE OF
DECLINE

Dio Cassius, a historian of the third century, considered the death of Marcus Aurelius (A.D. 180) and the accession of his son Commodus as the beginning of troubles for Rome. "Our history," he wrote, "now descends from a kingdom of gold to one of iron and rust." Although Gibbon and others have accepted this date as a starting point, there is good evidence that many of the problems that were to trouble Rome later were already present in the "golden age" of the second century.

The greatness of classical antiquity was based on urban life. Wherever Roman power reached, municipalities sprang up to provide a prosperous and educated class of citizens, soldiers, and administrators. In the first century participation in municipal duties was lively and desirable, as the following document shows.

Pompeii was destroyed by volcanic eruption in A.D. 79. These notices were painted on the walls of buildings in the city.

Election Posters in Pompeii

I

The fruit dealers together with Helvius Vestalis unanimously urge the election of Marcus Holconius Priscus as duovir with judicial power.

Roman Civilization, I (1955), 326–327, translated by Naphtali Lewis and Meyer Reinhold. Reprinted by permission of Columbia University Press, New York.

II

The goldsmiths unanimously urge the election of Gaius Cuspius Pansa as aedile.

III

I ask you to elect Gaius Julius Polybius aedile. He gets good bread.

IV

The muleteers urge the election of Gaius Julius Polybius as duovir.

V

The worshippers of Isis unanimously urge the election of Gnaeus Helvius Sabinus as aedile.

VI

Proculus, make Sabinus aedile and he will do as much for you.

VII

His neighbors urge you to elect Lucius Statius Receptus duovir with judicial power; he is worthy. Aemilius Celer, a neighbor, wrote this. May you take sick if you maliciously erase this!

VIII

Satia and Petronia support and ask you to elect Marcus Casellius and Lucius Albucius aediles. May we always have such citizens in our colony!

IX

I ask you to elect Epidius Sabinus duovir with judicial power. He is worthy, a defender of the colony, and in the opinion of the respected judge Suedius Clemens and by agreement of the council, because of his services and uprightness, worthy of the municipality. Elect him!

X

If upright living is considered any recommendation, Lucretius Fronto is well worthy of the office.

XI

Genialis urges the election of Bruttius Balbus as duovir. He will protect the treasury.

XII

I ask you to elect Marcus Cerrinius Vatia to the aedileship. All the late drinkers support him. Florus and Fructus wrote this.

XIII

The petty thieves support Vatia for the aedileship.

XIV

I ask you to elect Aulus Vettius Firmus aedile. He is worthy of the municipality. I ask you to elect him, ballplayers. Elect him!

XV

I wonder, O wall, that you have not fallen in ruins from supporting the stupidities of so many scribblers.

The Emperor Trajan (A.D. 98–117) found it necessary to send special agents to deal with problems in the provinces. One of them was Pliny the Younger, who was sent to the province of Bithynia in Asia Minor. The following exchange of letters shows how burdensome public service could become, even in the "golden age."

FROM Pliny's Letters

LETTER CXIII. TO THE EMPEROR TRAJAN

The Pompeian law, Sir, which is observed in Pontus and Bithynia, does not direct that any money should be given by those who are elected into the public council by the Censors. It has however been usual for such members as have been admitted into those assemblies, in pursuance of the privilege which you were pleased to grant to some particular cities, of receiving above their legal number, to pay one or two thousand denarii. Subsequent to this, the Proconsul Anicius Maximus ordained (tho' indeed his edict extended to some few cities only) that those who were elected by the Censors should also pay into the treasury a certain sum, which varied in different places. It remains therefore for your consideration, whether it would not be proper to settle a certain fixed sum for each member, who is elected into the council, to pay upon his entrance; for it well becomes you, whose every word and action deserves immortality, to give laws that shall for ever be permanent.

LETTER CXIV. TRAJAN TO PLINY

I can give no general directions applicable to all the cities of Bithynia, whether those who are made members of their respective councils shall pay an honorary fee upon their admittance, or not. It seems best therefore, in this case (what indeed upon all occasions is the safest way), to leave each city to its respective laws. But I think, however, that the Censors ought to set the sum lower to those who are chosen into the senate contrary to their inclinations, than to the rest.

Pliny's Letters (1789), translated by William Melmoth.

By the third and fourth centuries the troubles of the empire were such that necessary public services could be guaranteed only by the regular use of compulsion. The upper classes who had vied for positions as municipal councillors (decuriones or curiales) in the first century now became a hereditary caste and were compelled to serve. Their chief and sometimes only function was the collection of taxes, ever more burdensome. The emperors made the curiales personally liable for the taxes due. Little wonder that they made every effort to escape service, but gradually the imperial jurists closed all avenues of evasion.

FROM Justinian's Digest

The governor of the province shall see to it that decurions who are proved to have left the area of the municipality to which they belong and to have moved to other places are recalled to their native soil and perform the appropriate public services. . . .

Persons over fifty-five are forbidden by imperial enactments to be called to the position of decurion against their will, but if they do consent to this they ought to perform the duties, although if they are over seventy they are not compelled to assume compulsory municipal services. . . .

Municipal duties of a personal character are: representation of a municipality, that is, becoming a public advocate; assignment to taking the census or registering property; secretaryships; camel transport; commissioner of food supply and the like, of public lands, of grain procurement, of water supply; horse races in the circus; paving of public streets; grain storehouse; heating of public baths; distribution of food supply; and other duties similar to these. From the above-mentioned, other duties can be deduced in accordance with the laws and long-established custom of each municipality. . . .

The governor of the province shall see to it that the compulsory public services and offices in the municipalities are imposed fairly and in rotation according to age and rank, in accordance with the gradation of public services and offices long ago established, so that the men and resources of municipalities are not inconsiderately ruined by frequent oppression of the same persons. If two sons are under parental power, the father is not compelled to support their public services at the same time. . . .

The care of constructing or rebuilding a public work in a municipality is a

Justinian's Digest, in *Roman Civilization*, II (1955), 446–447, translated by Naphtali Lewis and Meyer Reinhold. Reprinted by permission of Columbia University Press, New York.

compulsory public service from which a father of five living children is excused; and if this service is forcibly imposed, this fact does not deprive him of the exemption that he has from other public services. The excusing of those with insufficient resources who are nominated to public services or offices is not permanent but temporary. For if a hoped-for increase comes to one's property by honorable means, when his turn comes an evaluation is to be made to determine whether he is suitable for the services for which he was chosen. . . . A person who is responsible for public services to his municipality and submits his name for military service for the purpose of avoiding the municipal burden cannot make the condition of his community worse.

In the third century the Roman Empire's capacity to maintain order and security broke down. The army made and unmade emperors; the upper classes were terrorized and plundered by rapacious armies of peasant soldiers, increasingly led by peasant generals. Private and public property were fair game, farmland was ravaged, and cities were destroyed. A good example of this chaotic period is provided by the reign of Gaius Julius Maximinus (235–238). A Thracian peasant, a barbarian of Gothic and Alan stock, he was the first emperor to rise from the ranks. He waged a war against the propertied classes and the prosperous cities of Italy. Previous emperors had attacked elements of the nobility, but Maximinus instituted a systematic terror against the entire bourgeoisie. In 238 he marched against the city of Aquileia.

FROM History of the Roman Empire BY HERODIAN

Before these events occurred, Aquileia was already a huge city, with a large permanent population. Situated on the sea and with all the provinces of Illyricum behind it, Aquileia served as a port of entry for Italy. The city thus made it possible for goods transported from the interior by land or by the rivers to be traded to the merchant mariners and also for the necessities brought by sea to the mainland, goods not produced there because of the cold climate, to be sent to the upland areas. Since the inland people farm a region that produces much wine, they export this in quantity to those who do not cultivate grapes. A huge number of people lived permanently in Aquileia, not only the native residents but also foreigners and merchants. At this time the

Herodian, *History of the Roman Empire* (1961), pp. 199–207, translated by Edward C. Echols. Reprinted by permission of University of California Press.

city was even more crowded than usual; all the people from the surrounding area had left the small towns and villages and sought refuge there. They put their hope of safety in the city's great size and its defensive wall; this ancient wall, however, had for the most part collapsed. Under Roman rule the cities of Italy no longer had need of walls or arms; they had substituted permanent peace for war and had also gained a participating share in the Roman government. Now, however, necessity forced the Aquileians to repair the wall, rebuild the fallen sections, and erect towers and battlements. After fortifying the city with a rampart as quickly as possible, they closed the gates and remained together on the wall day and night, beating off their assailants. Two senators named Crispinus and Meniphilus, former consuls, were appointed generals. These two had seen to everything with careful attention. With great foresight they had brought into the city supplies of every kind in quantities sufficient to enable it to withstand a long siege. An ample supply of water was available from the many wells in the city, and a river flowing at the foot of the city wall provided both a defensive moat and an abundance of water.

These are the preparations which had been made in the city. When it was reported to Maximinus that Aquileia was well defended and tightly shut, he thought it wise to send envoys to discuss the situation with the townspeople from the foot of the wall and try to persuade them to open the gates. There was in the besieging army a tribune who was a native of Aquileia, and whose wife, children, and relatives were inside the city. Maximinus sent this man to the wall accompanied by several centurions, expecting their fellow citizen to win them over easily. The envoys told the Aquileians that Maximinus, their mutual emperor, ordered them to lay down their arms in peace, to receive him as a friend, not as an enemy, and to turn from killing to libations and sacrifices. Their emperor directed them not to overlook the fact that their native city was in danger of being razed to its very foundations, whereas it was in their power to save themselves and to preserve their city when their merciful emperor pardoned them for their offenses. Others, not they, were the guilty ones. The envoys shouted their message from the foot of the wall so that those above might understand it. Most of the city's population was on the walls and in the towers; only those standing guard at other posts were absent. They all listened quietly to what the envoys were saying. Fearing that the people, convinced by these lying promises, might choose peace instead of war and throw open the gates, Crispinus ran along the parapet, pleading with the Aquileians to hold out bravely and offer stout resistance; he begged them not to break faith with the senate and the Roman people, but to win a place in history as the saviors and defenders of all Italy.

* * *

When the envoys returned unsuccessful, Maximinus, in a towering rage, pressed on toward the city with increased speed. But when he came to a large river sixteen miles from Aquileia, he found it flowing very wide and very deep. The warmth at that season of the year had melted the mountain snow that had been frozen all winter, and a vast, snow-swollen flood had resulted. It was impossible for Maximinus' army to cross this river because the Aquileians had destroyed the bridge, a huge structure of imposing proportions built, by earlier emperors, of squared stones and supported on tapering piers. Since neither bridges nor boats were available, the army halted in confusion. Some of the Germans, unfamiliar with the swift, violent rivers of Italy and thinking that these flowed down to the plains as lazily as their own streams (it is the slow current of the German rivers which causes them to freeze over), entered the river with their horses, which are trained to swim, and were carried away and drowned.

After a ditch had been dug around the camp to prevent attacks, Maximinus halted for two or three days beside the river, considering how it might be bridged. Timber was scarce, and there were no boats which could be fastened together to span the river. Some of his engineers, however, called attention to the many empty wooden kegs scattered about the deserted fields, the barrels which the natives use to ship wine safely to those forced to import it. The kegs are hollow, like boats; when fastened together and anchored to the shore by cables, they float like pontoons, and the current cannot carry them off. Planks are laid on top of these pontoons, and with great skill and speed a bank of earth is piled up evenly on the platform thus fashioned. After the bridge had been completed, the army crossed over and marched to Aquileia, where they found the buildings on the outskirts deserted. The soldiers cut down all the trees and grapevines and burned them, and destroyed the crops which had already begun to appear in those regions. Since the trees were planted in even rows and the interwoven vines linked them together everywhere, the countryside had a festive air; one might even say that it wore a garland of green. All these trees and vines Maximinus' soldiers cut down to the very roots before they hurried up to the walls of Aquileia. The army was exhausted, however, and it seemed wiser not to launch an immediate attack. The soldiers therefore remained out of range of the arrows and took up stations around the entire circuit of the wall by cohorts and legions, each unit investing the section it was ordered to hold. After a single day's rest, the soldiers kept the city under continuous siege for the remaining time.

They brought up every type of siege machinery and attacked the wall with all the power they could muster, leaving untried nothing of the art of siege warfare. They launched numerous assaults virtually every day, and the entire army held the city encircled as if in a net, but the Aquileians fought back determinedly, showing real enthusiasm for war. They had closed their houses and temples and were fighting in a body, together with the women and children, from their advantageous position on the parapet and in the towers. In this way they held off their attackers, and no one was too young or too old to take part in the battle to preserve his native city. All the buildings in the suburbs and outside the city gates were demolished by Maximinus' men, and the wood from the houses was used to build the siege engines. The soldiers made every effort to destroy a part of the wall, so that the army might break in, seize everything, and, after leveling the city, leave the area a deserted pasture land. The journey to Rome would not be fittingly glorious if Maximinus failed to capture the first city in Italy to oppose him. By pleading and promising gifts, Maximinus and his son, whom he had appointed his Caesar, spurred the army to action; they rode about on horseback, encouraging the soldiers to fight with resolution. The Aquileians hurled down stones on the besiegers; combining pitch and olive oil with asphalt and brimstone, they ignited this mixture and poured it over their attackers from hollow vessels fitted with long handles. Bringing the flaming liquid to the walls, they scattered it over the soldiers like a heavy downpour of rain. Carried along with the other ingredients, the pitch oozed onto the unprotected parts of the soldiers' bodies and spread everywhere. Then the soldiers ripped off their blazing corselets and the rest of their armor too, for the iron grew red hot, and the leather and wooden parts caught fire and burned. As a result, soldiers were seen everywhere stripping themselves, and the discarded armor appeared like the spoils of war, but these were taken by cunning and treachery, not by courage on the field of battle. In this tragedy, most of the soldiers suffered scarred and disfigured faces and lost eyes and hands, while every unprotected part of the body was severely injured. The Aquileians hurled down torches on the siege engines which had been dragged up to the walls. These torches, sharpened at the end like a javelin, were soaked in pitch and resin and then ignited; the firebrands, still blazing, stuck fast in the machines, which easily caught fire and were consumed by the flames.

During the opening days, then, the fortunes of war were almost equal. As time passed, however, the army of Maximinus grew depressed and, cheated in its expectations, fell into despair when the soldiers found that those whom they had not expected to hold out against a single assault were not only offering stout resistance but were even beating them back. The Aquileians, on the other hand, were greatly encouraged and highly enthusiastic, and, as the battle continued, their skill and daring increased. Contemptuous of the soldiers now, they hurled taunts at them. As Maximinus rode about, they shouted insults and indecent blasphemies at him and his son. The emperor became increasingly angry because he was powerless to retaliate. Unable to vent his wrath upon the enemy, he was enraged at most of his troop commanders because they were pressing the siege in cowardly and halfhearted fashion. Consequently, the hatred of his supporters increased, and his enemies grew more contemptuous of him each day.

As it happened, the Aquileians had everything they needed in abundant quantities. With great foresight they had stored in the city all the food and drink required for men and animals. The soldiers of the emperor, by contrast, lacked every necessity, since they had cut down the fruit trees and devastated the countryside. Some of the soldiers had built temporary huts, but the majority were living in the open air, exposed to sun and rain. And now many died of starvation; no food was brought in from the outside, as the Romans had blocked all the roads of Italy by erecting walls provided with narrow gates. The senate dispatched former consuls and picked men from all Italy to guard the beaches and harbors and prevent anyone from sailing. Their intent was to keep Maximinus in ignorance of what was happening at Rome; thus the main roads and all the bypaths were closely watched to prevent anyone's passing. The result was that the army which appeared to be maintaining the siege was itself under siege, for it was unable to capture Aquileia or leave the city and proceed to Rome; all the boats and wagons had been hidden, and no vehicles of any kind were available to the soldiers. Exaggerated rumors were circulated, based only on suspicion, to the effect that the entire Roman people were under arms; that all Italy was united; that the provinces of Illyricum and the barbarian nations in the East and South had gathered an army; and that everywhere men were solidly united in hatred of Maximinus. The emperor's soldiers were in despair and in need of everything. There was scarcely even sufficient water for them. The only source of water was the nearby river, which was fouled by blood and bodies. Lacking any means of burying those who died in the city, the Aquileians threw the bodies into the river; both those who fell in the fighting and those who died of disease were dropped into the stream, as the city had no facilities for burial.

And so the completely confused army was in the depths of despair. Then one day, during a lull in the fighting, when most of the soldiers had gone to their quarters or their stations, Maximinus was resting in his tent. Without warning, the soldiers whose camp was near Rome at the foot of Mount Alba, where they had left their wives and children, decided that the best solution was to kill Maximinus and end the interminable siege. They resolved no longer to ravage Italy for an emperor they now knew to be a despicable tyrant. Taking courage, therefore, the conspirators went to Maximinus' tent about noon. The imperial bodyguard, which was involved in the plot, ripped Maximinus' pictures from the standards; when he came out of his tent with his son to talk to them, they refused to listen and killed them both [A.D. 238]. They killed the army's commanding general also, and the emperor's close friends. Their bodies were handed over to those who wished to trample and mutilate them, after which the corpses were exposed to the birds and dogs. The heads of Maximinus and his son were sent to Rome. Such was the fate suffered by Maximinus and his son, who paid the penalty for their savage rule.

The obvious and immediate cause of Rome's fall was the invasion of the barbarians. The following selection illustrates the Romans' attitude toward the tribes who pressed on their frontiers.

FROM Res Gestae BY AMMIANUS MARCELLINUS

The people called Huns, barely mentioned in ancient records, live beyond the sea of Azof, on the border of the Frozen Ocean, and are a race savage beyond all parallel. At the very moment of birth the cheeks of their infant children are deeply marked by an iron, in order that the hair, instead of growing at the proper season on their faces, may be hindered by the scars; accordingly the Huns grow up without beards, and without any beauty. They all have closely knit and strong limbs and plump necks; they are of great size, and low legged, so that you might fancy them two-legged beasts or the stout figures which are hewn out in a rude manner with an ax on the posts at the end of bridges.

They are certainly in the shape of men, however uncouth, and are so hardy that they neither require fire nor well-flavored food, but live on the roots of such herbs as they get in the fields, or on the half-raw flesh of any animal, which they merely warm rapidly by placing it between their own thighs and the backs of their horses.

They never shelter themselves under roofed houses, but avoid them, as people ordinarily avoid sepulchers as things not fit for common use. Nor is there even to be found among them a cabin thatched with reeds; but they wander about, roaming over the mountains and the woods, and accustom themselves to bear frost and hunger and thirst from their very cradles. . . .

There is not a person in the whole nation who cannot remain on his horse day and night. On horseback they buy and sell, they take their meat and drink, and there they recline on the narrow neck of their steed, and yield to sleep so deep as to indulge in every variety of dream.

And when any deliberation is to take place on any weighty matter, they all hold their common council on horseback. They are not under kingly authority, but are contented with the irregular government of their chiefs, and under their lead they force their way through all obstacles. . . .

None of them plow, or even touch a plow handle, for they have no settled abode, but are homeless and lawless, perpetually wandering with their wagons, which they make their homes; in fact, they seem to be people always in flight. . . .

Ammianus Marcellinus, *Res Gestae* (1862), 3.1, 2–4, 13, translated by C. D. Yonge.

This active and indomitable race, being excited by an unrestrained desire of plundering the possessions of others, went on ravaging and slaughtering all the nations in their neighborhood till they reached the Alani. . . .

[After having harassed the territory of the Alani and having slain many of them and acquired much plunder, the Huns made a treaty of friendship and alliance with those who survived. The allies then attacked the German people to the west.] In the meantime a report spread far and wide through the nations of the Goths, that a race of men, hitherto unknown, had suddenly descended like a whirlwind from the lofty mountains, as if they had risen from some secret recess of the earth, and were ravaging and destroying everything which came in their way.

And then the greater part of the population resolved to flee and seek a home remote from all knowledge of the new barbarians; and after long deliberation as to where to fix their abode, they resolved that a retreat into Thrace was the most suitable for these two reasons: first of all, because it is a district most fertile in grass; and secondly, because, owing to the great breadth of the Danube, it is wholly separated from the districts exposed to the impending attacks of the invaders.

Accordingly, under the command of their leader Alavivus, they occupied the banks of the Danube, and sent ambassadors to the emperor Valens, humbly entreating to be received by him as his subjects. They promised to live quietly, and to furnish a body of auxiliary troops if necessary.

While these events were taking place abroad, the terrifying rumor reached us that the tribes of the north were planning new and unprecedented attacks upon us; and that over the whole region which extends from the country of the Marcomanni and Quadi to Pontus, hosts of barbarians composed of various nations, which had suddenly been driven by force from their own countries, were now, with all their families, wandering about in different directions on the banks of the river Danube.

At first this intelligence was lightly treated by our people, because they were not in the habit of hearing of any wars in those remote districts till they were terminated either by victory or by treaty.

But presently the belief in these occurrences grew stronger and was confirmed by the arrival of ambassadors, who, with prayers and earnest entreaties, begged that their people, thus driven from their homes and now encamped on the other side of the river, might be kindly received by us.

The affair now seemed a cause of joy rather than of fear, according to the skillful flatterers who were always extolling and exaggerating the good fortune of the emperor. They congratulated him that an embassy had come from the farthest corners of the earth, unexpectedly offering him a large body of recruits; and that, by combining the strength of his own people with these foreign forces, he would have an army absolutely invincible. They observed further that the payment for military reënforcements, which came in every year from the provinces, might now be saved and accumulated in his coffers and form a vast treasure of gold.

Full of this hope, he sent forth several officers to bring this ferocious people and their carts into our territory. And such great pains were taken to gratify this nation which was destined to overthrow the Empire of Rome, that not one was left behind, not even of those who were stricken with mortal disease. Moreover, so soon as they had obtained permission of the emperor to cross the Danube and to cultivate some districts in Thrace, they poured across the stream day and night, without ceasing, embarking in troops on board ships and rafts and on canoes made of the hollow trunks of trees. . . .

In this way, through the turbulent zeal of violent people, the ruin of the Roman Empire was brought about. This, at all events, is neither obscure nor uncertain, that the unhappy officers who were intrusted with the charge of conducting the multitude of the barbarians across the river, though they repeatedly endeavored to calculate their numbers, at last abandoned the attempt as hopeless. The man who would wish to ascertain the number might as well (as the most illustrious of poets says) attempt to count the waves in the African sea, or the grains of sand tossed about by the zephyrs. . . .

Salvian the Presbyter wrote in the middle of the fifth century. His book *On the Governance of God* contrasted the excellence of the barbarians with the decadence and corruption of the Roman Empire. In the following selection he indicates how serious the effect of taxation was.

FROM On the Governance of God BY SALVIAN

But what else can these wretched people wish for, they who suffer the incessant and even continuous destruction of public tax levies. To them there is always imminent a heavy and relentless proscription. They desert their homes, lest they be tortured in their very homes. They seek exile, lest they suffer torture. The enemy is more lenient to them than the tax collectors. This is proved by this very fact, that they flee to the enemy in order to avoid the full force of the heavy tax levy. This very tax levying, although hard and inhuman, would nevertheless be less heavy and harsh if all would bear it equally and in common. Taxation is made more shameful and burdensome because all do not bear the burden of all. They extort tribute from the poor man for the taxes of the rich, and the weaker carry the load for the stronger.

The Writings of Salvian, the Presbyter (1947), pp. 138–141, translated by J. F. O'Sullivan. Reprinted by permission of The Catholic University of America Press.

There is no other reason that they cannot bear all the taxation except that the burden imposed on the wretched is greater than their resources.

They suffer from envy and want, which are misfortunes most diverse and unlike. Envy is bound up with payment of the tax; need, with the ability to pay. If you look at what they pay, you will think them abundant in riches, but if you look at what they actually possess, you will find them poverty stricken. Who can judge an affair of this wretchedness? They bear the payment of the rich and endure the poverty of beggars. Much more serious is the following: the rich themselves occasionally make tributary levies which the poor pay.

But, you say, when the assessment due from the rich is very heavy and the taxes due from them are very heavy, how does it happen that they wish to increase their own debt? I do not say that they increase the taxes for themselves. They increase them because they do not increase them for themselves. I will tell you how this is done. Commonly, new envoys, new bearers of letters, come from the imperial offices and those men are recommended to a few well-known men for the mischief of many. For them new gifts are decreed, new taxes are decreed. The powerful levy what the poor are to pay, the courtesy of the rich decrees what the multitude of the wretched are to lose. They themselves in no way feel what they levy.

You say they who were sent by our superiors cannot be honored and generously entertained otherwise. Therefore, you rich men, you who are the first to levy, be the first to give. Be the first in generosity of goods, you who are the first in profusion of words. You who give of mine, give of thine. Most justly, whoever you are, you who alone wish to receive favor, you alone should bear the expense. But to your will, O rich men, we the poor accede. What you, the few, order, we all pay. What is so just, so humane? Your decrees burden us with new debts; at least make your debt common to us all. What is more wicked and more unworthy than that you alone are free from debt, you who make us all debtors?

Indeed, the most wretched poor thus pay all that I have mentioned, but for what cause or for what reason they pay, they are completely ignorant. For, to whom is it lawful to discuss why they pay; to whom is permitted to find out what is owed? Then it is given out most publicly when the rich get angry with each other, when some of them get indignant because some levies are made without their advice and handling.

Then you may hear it said by some of them, "What an unworthy crime! Two or three decree what kills many; what is paid by many wretched men is decreed by a few powerful men." Each rich man maintains his honor by being unwilling that anything is decreed in his absence, yet he does not maintain justice by being unwilling that evil things be done when he is present. Lastly, what these very men consider base in others they themselves later legalize, either in punishment of a past contempt or in proof of their power. Therefore, the most unfortunate poor are, as it were, in the midst of the sea, between conflicting, violent winds. They are swamped by the waves rolling now from one side, now from the other.

But, surely, those who are wicked in one way are found moderate and just in another, and compensate for their baseness in one thing by goodness in another. For, just as they weigh down the poor with the burden of new tax levies, so they sustain them by the assistance of new tax reliefs; just as the lower classes are oppressed by new taxes, so they are equally relieved by tax mitigations. Indeed, the injustice is equal in taxes and reliefs, for, as the poor are the first to be burdened, so they are the last to be relieved.

For when, as has happened lately, the highest powers thought it would be advisable that taxation should be lessened somewhat for the cities which were in arrears in their payments, the rich alone instantly divided among themselves the remedy given for all. Who, then, remembers the poor? Who calls the poor and needy to share in the common benefit? Who permits him who is first in bearing the burden even to stand in the last place for receiving redress? What more is there to say? In no way are the poor regarded as taxpayers, unless when the mass of taxes is imposed upon them; they are not reckoned among the number of taxpayers when the tax-reliefs are portioned.

Do we think we are unworthy of the punishment of divine severity when we thus constantly punish the poor? Do we think, when we are constantly wicked, that God should not exercise His justice against all of us? Where or in whom are evils so great, except among the Romans? Whose injustice so great except our own? The Franks are ignorant of this crime of injustice. The Huns are immune to these crimes. There are no wrongs among the Vandals and none among the Goths. So far are the barbarians from tolerating these injustices among the Goths, that not even the Romans who live among them suffer them.

Therefore, in the districts taken over by the barbarians, there is one desire among all the Romans, that they should never again find it necessary to pass under Roman jurisdiction. In those regions, it is the one and general prayer of the Roman people that they be allowed to carry on the life they lead with the barbarians. And we wonder why the Goths are not conquered by our portion of the population, when the Romans prefer to live among them rather than with us. Our brothers, therefore, are not only altogether unwilling to flee to us from them, but they even cast us aside in order to flee to them.

4
THE SOCIAL PROBLEM

F. W. Walbank takes the view that the rigidity of Roman society was a major cause of Rome's fall.

FROM The Decline of the Roman Empire in the West BY F. W. WALBANK

The cause of the decline of the Roman Empire is not to be sought in any one feature—in the climate, the soil, the health of the population, or indeed in any of those social and political factors which played so important a part in the actual process of decay—but rather in the whole structure of ancient society. The date at which the contradictions, which were ultimately to prove fatal, first began to appear is not A.D. 200 nor yet the setting-up of the Principate by Augustus Caesar in 27 B.C., but rather the fifth century B.C. when Athens revealed her inability to keep and broaden the middle-class democracy she had created. The failure of Athens epitomised the failure of the City-State. Built on a foundation of slave labour, or on the exploitation of similar groups, including the peasantry, the City-State yielded a brilliant minority civilisation. But from the start it was top-heavy. Through no fault of its citizens, but as a result of the time and place when it arose, it was supported by a woefully low level of technique. To say this is to repeat a truism. The paradoxical contrast between the spiritual achievements of Athens and her scanty material goods has long been held up to the admiration of generations who had found that a rich material inheritance did not automatically ensure richness of cultural life. But it was precisely this low level of technique, relative to

F. W. Walbank, *The Decline of the Roman Empire in the West* (1953), pp. 3–7. Reprinted by permission of Lawrence and Wishart Ltd., London.

the tasks Greek and Roman society set itself, that made it impossible even to consider dispensing with slavery and led to its extension from the harmless sphere of domestic labour to the mines and workshops, where it grew stronger as the contradictions of society became more apparent.

As so often, we find ourselves discussing as cause and effect factors which were constantly interacting, so that in reality the distinction between the effective agent and the result it brought about is often quite arbitrary. But roughly speaking, the City-State, precisely because it was a minority culture, tended to be aggressive and predatory, its claim to autonomy sliding over insensibly, at every opportunity, into a claim to dominate others. This led to wars, which in turn took their place among the many sources of fresh slaves. Slavery grew, and as it invaded the various branches of production it led inevitably to the damping down of scientific interest, to the cleavage, already mentioned, between the classes that used their hands and the superior class that used—and later ceased using—its mind. This ideological cleavage thus reflects a genuine separation of the community into classes; and henceforward it becomes the supreme task of even the wisest sons of the City-State—a Plato and an Aristotle—to maintain this class society, whatsoever the cost.

That cost was indeed heavy. It says much for Plato's singlemindedness that he was willing to meet it. In the *Laws*, his last attempt to plan the just city, he produces a blue-print for implanting beliefs and attitudes convenient to authority through the medium of suggestion, by a strict and ruthless censorship, the substitution of myths and emotional ceremonies for factual knowledge, the isolation of the citizen from the outside world, the creation of types with standardised reactions, and, as a final guarantee, by the sanctions of the police-state, to be invoked against all who cannot or will not conform.

Such was the intellectual and spiritual fruit of this tree, whose roots had split upon the hard rock of technical inadequacy. Materially, the result of increasing slavery was the certainty that new productive forces would not be released on any scale sufficient for a radical transformation of society. Extremes of wealth and poverty became more marked, the internal market flagged, and ancient society suffered a decline of trade and population and, finally, the wastage of class warfare. Into this sequence the rise of the Roman Empire brought the new factor of a parasitical capital; and it spread the Hellenistic system to Italy, where agrarian pauperism went side by side with imperial expansion and domination on an unparalleled scale.

From all this arose the typical developments of the social life of the Empire —industrial dispersion and a reversion to agrarian self-sufficiency—and the final attempt to retrieve the crisis, or at least to salvage whatever could be salvaged from the ruins, by the unflinching use of oppression and the machinery of the bureaucratic State. These tendencies we have already analysed, and need not repeat them here. The important point is that they fall together into a sequence with its own logic, and that they follow—not of course in the specific details, which were determined by a thousand personal or fortuitous factors, but in their general outlines—from the premises upon which classical civilisation arose, namely an absolutely low technique and, to compensate for this, the institution of slavery. Herein lie the real causes of the decline and fall of the Roman Empire.

5
THE ROSTOVTZEFF THESIS

Like Walbank, M. I. Rostovtzeff sees the chief problem to be the organization of Roman society, but his analysis is different from Walbank's, as are his conclusions.

FROM Social and Economic History of the Roman Empire BY M. I. ROSTOVTZEFF

Incomplete as it is, the picture which we have drawn shows very clearly the chaos and misery that reigned throughout the Roman Empire in the third century and especially in the second half of it. We have endeavoured to show how the Empire gradually reached this pitiful state. It was due to a combination of constant civil war and fierce attacks by external foes. The situation was aggravated by the policy of terror and compulsion which the government adopted towards the population, using the army as its instrument. The key to the situation lies, therefore, in the civil strife which provoked and made possible the onslaughts of neighbouring enemies, weakened the Empire's powers of resistance, and forced the emperors, in dealing with the population, to have constant recourse to methods of terror and compulsion, which gradually developed into a more or less logically organized system of administration. In the policy of the emperors we failed to discover any systematic plan. It was a gradual yielding to the aspirations of the army and to the necessity of maintaining the existence of the Empire and preserving its unity. Most of the emperors of this troubled period were not ambitious men who

Michael I. Rostóvtzeff, *Social and Economic History of the Roman Empire,* 2nd ed., I (1957), 491–501. Reprinted by permission of The Clarendon Press, Oxford.

were ready to sacrifice the interests of the community to their personal aspirations: they did not seek power for the sake of power. The best of them were forced to assume power, and they did it partly from a natural sense of self-preservation, partly as a conscious sacrifice of their own lives to the noble task of maintaining and safeguarding the Empire. If the state was transformed by the emperors on the lines described above, on the lines of a general levelling, by destroying the part played in the life of the Empire by the privileged and educated classes, by subjecting the people to a cruel and foolish system of administration based on terror and compulsion, and by creating a new aristocracy which sprang up from the rank and file of the army, and if this policy gradually produced a slave state with a small ruling minority headed by an autocratic monarch, who was commander of an army of mercenaries and of a militia compulsorily levied, it was not because such was the ideal of the emperors but because it was the easiest way of keeping the state going and preventing a final breakdown. But this goal could be achieved only if the army provided the necessary support: and the emperors clearly believed they could get its help by the policy they pursued.

If it was not the ambition of the emperors that drew the state ever deeper into the gulf of ruin, and threatened to destroy the very foundations of the Empire, what was the immanent cause which induced the army constantly to change the emperors, to slay those whom they had just proclaimed, and to fight their brothers with a fury that hardly finds a parallel in the history of mankind? Was it a "mass psychosis" that seized the soldiers and drove them forward on the path of destruction? Would it not be strange that such a mental disease should last for at least half a century? The usual explanation given by modern scholars suggests that the violent convulsions of the third century were the accompaniment of the natural and necessary transformation of the Roman state into an absolute monarchy. The crisis (it is said) was a political one; it was created by the endeavour of the emperors to eliminate the senate politically and to transform the Augustan diarchy into a pure monarchy; in striving towards this goal the emperors leaned on the army, corrupted it, and provoked the state of anarchy, which formed a transitional phase that led to the establishment of the Oriental despotism of the fourth century. We have endeavoured to show that such an explanation does not stand the test of facts. The senate, as such, had no political importance whatsoever in the time of the enlightened monarchy. Its social prestige was high, for it represented the educated and propertied classes of the Empire, but its direct political participation in state affairs was very small. In order to establish the autocratic system of government there was not the slightest necessity to pass through a period of destruction and anarchy. Monarchy was established in actual fact by the Antonines without shedding a drop of blood. The real fight was not between the emperor and the senate.

The theory that a bloody struggle developed in the third century between the emperors and the senate must therefore be rejected as not fitting the facts. Certainly, the transformation of the principate into a military monarchy did not agree with the wishes of the senate, but that body had no political force to oppose the emperors. Recognizing this fact, some leading modern scholars have attempted to explain the crisis in another way, but still in terms of political causes; on the assumption that the crisis of the third century arose not so much from the active opposition of the senate as from the relations between the emperors and the army. The new army of the second part of the third century was no longer the army of Roman citizens recruited from Italy and the romanized provinces; the elements of which it was composed were provinces of little or no romanization and warlike tribes recruited beyond its frontiers. No sooner had this army recognized its own power at the end of the Antonine age, than it was corrupted by the emperors with gifts and flattery, and familiarized with bribery; it felt itself master of the state and gave orders to the emperors. The conditions imposed by it were partly of a material, and partly, up to a certain point, of a political, nature: for example, that the privileges enjoyed by the ruling classes should be extended to the army. As the emperors had not succeeded in giving their power a juridical or religious basis which was sufficiently clear to convince the masses and the army without delay, it became increasingly clear that they governed only by the grace of the soldiers; each body of troops chose its own emperor and regarded him as the instrument for the satisfaction of its wishes.

This theory, which I hope I have summarized exactly, is undoubtedly nearer the truth and coincides in the main with the views set forth in this book. I have shown how the Roman emperors tried hard to find a legal basis for their power. Emperors like Vespasian and, even more, Domitian saw clearly that the dynastic principle of hereditary succession, founded upon the Oriental conception of the divine nature of imperial power, and therefore upon the apotheosis of the living emperor, was much more intelligible to the masses than the subtle and complex theory of the principate as formulated by Augustus and applied by the majority of his successors, particularly the Antonines. Yet the simplification proposed by Domitian could not be accepted by the leading classes of the Roman Empire, since it implied the complete negation of the idea of liberty, which they cherished so dearly. These classes fought against the transformation of the principate into an unconcealed monarchy, and in their tenacious struggle they had, if not as an ally, at least not as an enemy, the army composed of citizens who held to a great extent the same opinions as themselves. The result was a compromise between the imperial power on one side, and the educated classes and the senate which represented them, on the other. This compromise was affected by the Antonines. When, at the end of the second century A.D., the barbarization of the army was complete, that body was no longer able to understand the delicate theory of the principate. It was instead prepared to accept the hereditary monarchy established by Septimius Severus, and the emperor, with the army's help, was able to suppress without difficulty the opposition aroused by his action. So far I am in the fullest agreement with the theory described above.

But at this point difficulties begin. Why did the dynasty of the Severi not last, after it had been established, and accepted willingly by the army and unwillingly by the educated classes? How are we to explain the fact that the soldiers murdered Severus Alexander, and later even killed and betrayed the emperors they had themselves elected, thereby creating that political chaos which exposed the Empire to the greatest dangers? The continuous upheavals must have had a deeper cause than the struggle for the hereditary monarchy of divine right. This goal had been reached from the first moment; why did the struggle continue for another fifty years?

Perhaps the wisest course would be to be satisfied with his partial explanation, in the company of the majority of scholars. Our evidence is scanty, and the most comfortable way is always that of *non liquet* and *ignoramus*. In the first edition of this work I dared to offer a theory which is to some extent supported by our inadequate evidence, and which, if it proved acceptable, would enable us to understand the nature of the crisis of the Roman Empire. The five pages devoted to this explanation attracted the attention of the majority of my critics, and much has been written against my "theory," though without a single fact being adduced against it. The chief argument invoked against my "theory" is that the trend of my thoughts was influenced by events in modern Russia. Without entering upon an argument on this topic, I see no reason to abandon my previous explanation simply because I may, or may not, have been led to it by the study of similar events in later history. It still satisfies me and agrees with the facts in so far as I know them.

In my opinion, when the political struggle which had been fought around the hereditary monarchy between the emperors, supported by the army, and the upper classes, came to an end, the same struggle was repeated in a different form. Now, no political aim was at stake: the issue between the army and the educated classes was the leadership of the state. The emperors were not always on the side of the army; many of them tried to preserve the system of government which the enlightened monarchy had based upon the upper classes. These efforts were, however, fruitless, since all concessions made by the emperors, any act which might mean a return to the conditions of the Antonine age, met the half-unconscious resistance of the army. In addition, the *bourgeoisie* was no longer able to give the emperors effective aid.

Such was the real meaning of the civil war of the third century. The army fought the privileged classes, and did not cease fighting until these classes had lost all their social prestige and lay powerless and prostrate under the feet of the half-barbarian soldiery. Can we, however, say that the soldiery fought out this fight for its own sake, with the definite plan of creating a sort of tyranny or dictatorship of the army over the rest of the population? There is not the slightest evidence in support of such a view. An elemental upheaval was taking place and developing. Its final goal may be comprehensible to us, but was not understood even by contemporaries and still less by the actors in the terrible tragedy. The driving forces were envy and hatred, and those who sought to destroy the rule of the bourgeois class had no positive programme.

The constructive work was gradually done by the emperors, who built on the ruins of a destroyed social order as well, or as badly, as it could be done and not in the least in the spirit of destroyers. The old privileged class was replaced by another, and the masses, far from being better off than they had been before, became much poorer and much more miserable. The only difference was that the ranks of the sufferers were swelled, and that the ancient civilized condition of the Empire had vanished for ever.

If the army acted as the destroyer of the existing social order, it was not because as an army it hated that order. The position of the army was not bad even from the social point of view, since it was the natural source of recruits for the municipal *bourgeoisie*. It acted as a powerful destructive and levelling agent because it represented, at the end of the second century and during the third, those large masses of the population that had little share in the brilliant civilized life of the Empire. We have shown that the army of M. Aurelius and of Commodus was almost wholly an army of peasants, a class excluded from the advantages of urban civilization, and that this rural class formed the majority of the population of the Empire. Some of these peasants were small landowners, some were tenants or serfs of the great landlords or of the state; as a mass they were the subjects, while the members of the city aristocracy were the rulers; they formed the class of *humiliores* as contrasted with the *honestiores* of the towns, the class of *dediticii* as compared with the burgesses of the cities. In short, they were a special caste separated by a deep gulf from the privileged classes, a caste whose duty it was to support the high civilization of the cities by their toil and work, by their taxes and rents. The endeavours of the enlightened monarchy and of the Severi to raise this class, to elevate it into a village *bourgeoisie,* to assimilate as large a portion of it as possible to the privileged classes, and to treat the rest as well as possible, awakened in the minds of the *humiliores* the consciousness of their humble position and strengthened their allegiance to the emperors, but they failed to achieve their main aim. In truth, the power of the enlightened monarchy was based on the city *bourgeoisie,* and it was not the aim of the *bourgeoisie* to enlarge their ranks indefinitely and to share their priviliges with large numbers of newcomers.

The result was that the dull submissiveness which had for centuries been the typical mood of the *humiliores* was gradually transformed into a sharp feeling of hatred and envy towards the privileged classes. These feelings were naturally reflected in the rank and file of the army, which now consisted exclusively of peasants. When, after the usurpation of Septimius, the army became gradually aware of its power and influence with the emperors, and when the emperors of his dynasty repeatedly emphasized their allegiance to it and their sympathy with the peasants, and treated the city *bourgeoisie* harshly, it gradually yielded to its feelings and began to exert a half-conscious pressure on the emperors, reacting violently against the concessions made by some of them to the hated class. The *bourgeoisie* attempted to assert its influence and to save its privileges, and the result was open war from time to time and a ruthless extermination of the privileged class. Violent outbreaks took place after the reign of Alexander, whose ideals were those of the enlightened monarchy, and more especially after the short period of restoration which followed the reaction of Maximinus. It was this restoration that was ultimately responsible for the dreadful experiences of the reign of Gallienus; and the policy consequently adopted by that emperor and most of his successors finally set aside the plan of restoring the rule of the cities, and met the wishes of the peasant army. This policy, although it was a policy of despair, at least saved the fabric of the Empire. The victory of the peasants over the city *bourgeoisie* was thus complete, and the period of the domination of city over country seemed to have ended. A new state based on a new foundation was built up by the successors of Gallienus, with only occasional reversions to the ideals of the enlightened monarchy.

It is, of course, not easy to prove our thesis that the antagonism between the city and the country was the main driving force of the social revolution of the third century. But the reader will recollect the picture we have drawn of Maximinus' policy, of his extermination of the city *bourgeoisie,* of the support given him by the African army of peasants against the city landowners; and he will bear in mind the violent outbreaks of military anarchy after the reign of Pupienus and Balbinus, of Gordian III, and of Philip. Many other facts testify to the same antagonism between country and city. It is remarkable how easily the soldiers could be induced to pillage and murder in the cities of the Roman Empire. We have already spoken of the destruction of Lyons by the soldiery after the victory of Septimius over Albinus, of the Alexandrian massacre of Caracalla, of the demand of the soldiers of Elagabal to loot the city of Antioch. We have alluded to the repeated outbreaks of civil war between the population of Rome and the soldiers. The fate of Byzantium, pillaged by its own garrison in the time of Gallienus, is typical. Still more characteristic of the mood both of the peasants and of the soldiers is the destruction of Augustodunum (Autun) in the time of Tetricus and Claudius in A.D. 269. When the city recognized Claudius, Tetricus sent a detachment of his army against the "rebels." It was joined by gangs of robbers and peasants. They cut off the water supply and finally took the flourishing city and destroyed it so utterly that it never revived. The two greatest creations of the period of urbanization in Gaul—Lyons and Autun—were thus laid in ruins by enraged soldiers and peasants. One of the richest cities of Asia Minor, Tyana, was in danger of suffering the same fate in the time of Aurelian. It was saved by the emperor, and the words he used to persuade the soldiers not to destroy it are interesting: "We are carrying on war to free these cities; if we are to pillage them, they will trust us no more. Let us seek the spoil of the barbarians and spare these men as our own people." It was evidently not easy to convince the soldiers that the cities of the Empire were not their chief enemies. The attitude of the soldiers towards them was like that of the plundering Goths, as described by Petrus Patricius. His words certainly expressed the feelings of many Roman soldiers. "The Scythians jeered at those who

were shut up in the cities, saying, They live a life not of men but of birds
sitting in their nests aloft; they leave the earth which nourishes them and
choose barren cities; they put their trust in lifeless things rather than in themselves."

We have frequently noted also the close relations existing between the
peasants and the soldiers. It was through soldiers that the peasants forwarded
their petitions to the emperor in the time of Commodus and Septimius as
well as in that of Philip and Gordian. In fact, most of the soldiers had no
knowledge or understanding of the cities, but they kept up their relations
with their native villages, and the villagers regarded their soldiers as their
natural patrons and protectors, and looked on the emperor as their emperor
and not as the emperor of the cities. In the sixth and seventh chapters we
described the important part played during the third century by soldiers and
ex-soldiers in the life of the villages of the Balkan peninsula and Syria, the
lands of free peasant *possessores,* as contrasted with the lands of tenants or
coloni, and we pointed out that they formed the real aristocracy of the villages and served as intermediaries between the village and the administrative
authorities. We showed how large was the infiltration of former soldiers into
the country parts of Africa in the same century; and in describing the conditions of Egypt during that period we repeatedly drew attention to the large
part played in the economic life of the land by active and retired soldiers. All
this serves to show that the ties between the villages and the army were never
broken, and that it was natural that the army should share the aspirations of
the villages and regard the dwellers in the cities as aliens and enemies.

Despite the changed conditions at the end of the fourth century, the relations between the army and the villages remained exactly as they had been in
the third. The cities still existed, and the municipal aristocracy was still used
by the government to collect the taxes and exact compulsory work from the
inhabitants of the villages. It was no wonder that, even after the cities almost
completely lost their political and social influence, the feelings of the peasants
towards them did not change. For the villages the cities were still the oppres-
sors and exploiters. Occasionally such feelings are expressed by writers of the
fourth century, both Western (chiefly African) and Eastern, especially the latter. Our information is unusually good for Syria, and particularly for the
neighbourhood of Antioch, thanks to Libanius and John Chrysostom. One of
the leading themes which we find in both writers is the antagonism between
city and country. In this constant strife the government had no definite
policy, but the soldiers sided with the peasants against the great men
from the cities. The sympathies of the soldiers are sufficiently shown by the
famous passage in Libanius' speech *De patrociniis,* where he describes the
support which they gave to certain large villages inhabited by free peasants,
the excesses in which the villagers indulged, and the miserable situation of
the city aristocracy, which was unable to collect any taxes from the peasants
and was maltreated both by them and by the soldiers. Libanius, being himself
a civilian and a large landowner, experienced all the discomfort of this

entente cordiale between soldiery and peasants. The tenants on one of his own estates, perhaps in Judaea, who for four generations had not shown any sign of insubordination, became restless and tried, with the help of a higher officer, who was their patron, to dictate their own conditions of work to the landowner. Naturally Libanius is full of resentment and bitterness towards the soldiers and the officers. On the other hand, the support given by the troops to the villages cannot be explained merely by greed. The soldiers in the provinces were still themselves peasants, and their officers were of the same origin. They were therefore in real sympathy with the peasants and were ready to help them against the despised inhabitants of the cities.

Some scattered evidence on the sharp antagonism between the peasants and the landowners of the cities may be found also in Egypt. In a typical document of the year A.D. 320 a magnate of the city of Hermupolis, a gymnasiarch and a member of the municipal council, Aurelius Adelphius, makes a complaint to the strategus of the nome. He was a hereditary lessee . . . of γῆ οὐσιακή [*gê ousiakê—D. K.*], a man who had inherited his estate from his father and had cultivated it all his life long. He had invested money in the land and improved its cultivation. When harvest-time arrived, the peasants of the village to the territory of which the estate belonged, "with the usual insolence of villagers" . . . tried to prevent him from gathering in the crop. The expression quoted shows how deep was the antagonism between city and country. It is not improbable that the "insolence" of the peasants is to be explained by their hopes of some support from outside. They may have been justified: the proprietor may have been a land-grabber who had deprived them of plots of land which they used to cultivate; but the point is the deep-rooted mutual hostility between the peasants and the landowners which the story reveals.

I feel no doubt, therefore, that the crisis of the third century was not political but definitely social in character. The city *bourgeoisie* had gradually replaced the aristocracy of Roman citizens, and the senatorial and the equestrian class was mostly recruited from its ranks. It was now attacked in turn by the masses of the peasants. In both cases the process was carried out by the army under the leadership of the emperors. The first act ended with the short but bloody revolution of A.D. 69–70, but it did not affect the foundations of the prosperity of the Empire, since the change was not a radical one. The second act, which had a much wider bearing, started the prolonged and calamitous crisis of the third century. Did this crisis end in a complete victory of the peasants over the city *bourgeoisie* and in the creation of a brand-new state? There is no question that the city *bourgeoisie,* as such, was crushed and lost the indirect influence on state affairs which it had exerted through the senate in the second century. Yet it did not disappear. The new ruling bureaucracy very soon established close social relations with the surviving remnant of this class, and the strongest and richest section of it still formed an important element of the imperial aristocracy. The class which was disappearing was the middle class, the active and thrifty citizens of the thousands of cities in the Empire, who formed the link between the lower and the upper classes. Of this class we hear very little after the catastrophe of the third century, save for the part which it played, as *curiales* of the cities, in the collection of taxes by the imperial government. It became more and more oppressed and steadily reduced in numbers.

While the *bourgeoisie* underwent the change we have described, can it be said that the situation of the peasants improved in consequence of their temporary victory? There is no shadow of doubt that in the end there were no victors in the terrible class war of this century. If the *bourgeoisie* suffered heavily, the peasants gained nothing. Any one who reads the complaints of the peasants of Asia Minor and Thrace which have been quoted above, or the speeches of Libanius and the sermons of John Chrysostom and Salvian, or even the "constitutions" of the Codices of Theodosius and Justinian, will realize that in the fourth century the peasants were much worse off than they had been in the second. A movement which was started by envy and hatred, and carried on by murder and destruction, ended in such depression of spirit that any stable conditions seemed to the people preferable to unending anarchy. They therefore willingly accepted the stabilization brought about by Diocletian, regardless of the fact that it meant no improvement in the condition of the mass of the population of the Roman Empire.

6

THE BARBARIANS AND THE RUIN OF THE ROMAN EMPIRE

The interpretation of André Piganiol is the simplest and most direct of any recent attempt at an explanation.

FROM L'Empire Chrétien BY ANDRÉ PIGANIOL

The Late Empire is usually considered as the very model of an epoch of decadence. A useful and happy decadence from the point of view of Augustine and his modern emulators because it liberated new forces, since the fall of Rome permitted the shaking off of the oppression of the past.

Nevertheless, this notion of decadence is quite confused. If one wishes to say that Roman civilization went through a critical period, no one will deny it. The problem is to know if it could not renew itself, transform itself, without going through the catastrophe which was followed, not at all by a miraculous rise, but by the dark age of the beginning of the Middle Ages.

To explain the decadence, the ancient Greek philosophers taught that it was tied to a certain periodicity of the course of the stars. Moderns have not altogether renounced these cosmological explanations.

According to Ellsworth Huntington, periods of decadence coincide with

André Piganiol, *L'Empire Chrétien* (1947), pp. 411–422. Translated by Donald Kagan by permission of Presses Universitaires de France, Paris. Reprinted from Donald Kagan, ed., *Decline and fall of the Roman Empire* (1962), by permission of D. C. Heath and Company.

world periods of drought. There would have been a constant decrease in rainfall from 200 to 400, whence the pressure of the barbarians, themselves pressed by others who were dying of hunger. "Thus Rome perished, and its fall was followed by that period of unfavorable climate which is called the dark age of the Middle Ages."

Unfortunately, we possess no statistics of rainfall during Mediterranean antiquity, and we doubt that they can be supplied by determining the periods of growth of old trees in California.

Oliganthropy, Malthusianism, ruined Greece according to Polybius. The apogee of the population of the Roman Empire seems to be placed toward the time of Caracalla and a decline, doubtless very sharp, followed in the course of the catastrophes of the third century. The evil was aggravated in the 4th century when one sees cultivated lands return to wasteland, as well in Italy as in North Africa or in Egypt, and the cities shrank to very small enclaves. In addition, Christianity aggravated Malthusianism; if Eusebius does not attest to it expressly, the Life of St. Melanie would prove it.

Not only did the population decline, but its very composition was changed. According to the pseudo-biological theory of Seeck, the Romans practiced a reverse selection (*Ausrottung der Besten*): the emperors on the one hand, the popular revolts on the other, worked toward the destruction of men of character, the elite. For the imperial period as a whole must be defined as a period of terror. One would also like to pose the problem of knowing to what degree the mixing of peoples favored cross-breeding, the diffusion of Germanic or Semitic elements; but, without statistics this inquiry will come to naught. Besides, it is useless, since in order to condemn the theory of Seeck it is enough to observe that the fourth century produced some very fine human types and that in this respect the century of the Antonines is far from being able to rival it. When all has been reckoned, moreover, the diminution of the population did not return its number, to what it was at the beginning of the Christian era, and was, in fact, far from it.

G. Ferrero informs us that the fall of Rome had as its cause a crisis of authority. The principal cause of this crisis was the equivocal and badly defined character of the imperial power. What was its source, the people or the senatorial aristocracy? Did the army have the title to speak in the name of the people? Did the imperial power, born of an acclamation, have the right to perpetuate itself in a dynasty? From these uncertainties resulted revolutions, massacres of the elite and anarchy.

But did not the system of Diocletian remedy these evils? It does not appear that the absolutist regime of the late empire was seriously contested. At most one may say that, in the circle of Roman nobles, the dynastic principle was discussed. The theory of the divine character of the prince was susceptible to interpretations which made it acceptable even to the Christians.

G. Ferrero adds that in the late empire the destruction of the elite handed over power to a new oligarchy of the newly wealthy and of high officials who came from barbarous elements of the population. He thus agrees with

M. Rostovtzeff, according to whom the revolution of the third century, the victory of the masses, the physical destruction of the cultivated class, had as a consequence a fatal "bolshevization" of civilization.

But when we read Marcus Aurelius we find in his *Meditations* harsher judgments on the incomprehension and incapacity of the ruling class; to save the empire an appeal had to be made to new men. It is not at all proved that the governmental personnel of the late empire could not bear comparison with that of the second century. What debased spirits and broke their *élan* was the deprivation of liberty. Not only had the masses taken no part in government since the republic, but the municipal aristocracy itself was put into tutelage under the empire. It would, however, be rash to assert that the Roman Empire died because liberty died, for it had been dead for centuries.

At the heart of the Roman Empire the conquered nationalities had in no way lost consciousness of their origin and many were the means of resistance to the unifying will of Rome. In the fourth century there was a rebirth of indigenous languages. In the artistic realm one sees very old popular traditions revive. In Africa under cover of the donatist schism, it was the Berbers who rose up against Rome. Egypt had always been like a foreign body in the empire. What is especially new and serious is the growth of a feeling of opposition in Gaul; it is certain that the emperors of the fourth century were preoccupied with it and it is doubtless to overcome it that Valentinian had to consent to take up his home at Trèves. It is not easy to know what elements made up the feeling of opposition of the Gauls. Did they blame Rome for not defending the Rhine attentively enough? Or rather, on the other hand, were the Germanic elements which had infiltrated Gaul during the third century plotting treason? It is quite probable that both parties existed in Gaul and that neither was satisfied with Rome.

But this resistance of nationalities would have been serious only if it was opposed to a Roman nationalism which would try to maintain them in a state of inferiority or slavery. There was none of that, all the people of the empire were equal; the rebirth and multiplication of local diets allowed them to express their wishes.

The nationalities which awoke, moreover, were conscious of the profound tie which united them to one another. A little later than the terms *Francia, Alamannia, Gothia* appeared *Romania*. The wisdom of the imperial policy permitted all nationalities to live fraternally in the bosom of this great family which had only barbarians for enemies.

The Roman state went bankrupt in the third century. It was incapable of continuing to pay its officials and its armies without recourse to confiscations, monetary falsifications, requisition in kind, and unpaid services (*munera*).

Diocletian tried to put order into these improvisations; nevertheless the fiscal system of the fourth century is full of survivals which recall the great crisis of the third. In the time of great distress men supposed that burdens would no longer be placed on individuals but on interdependent groups. In the fourth century they did not succeed in freeing themselves from this con-

venient and perilous method. It was this fiscal system which led to the transformation of the class of municipal councillors into an army of tax collectors
unpaid by the state and the class of free peasants into serfs of the great lords.
It is above all because of its financial policies that the Roman state provoked
the hatred of the masses. In vain did a pamphleteer in the time of Valentinian
demand "fiscal relaxation."

But why did the state have to face these crushing expenses? Because of the
squandering of the court, because of the increase of the bureaucracy, but
above all, because of the needs of the army. It is easy to discern a series of
important events which overturned the ancient economic order:

1. The decline of slavery. "The possessor of slaves," wrote M. Weber, "became the support of ancient culture." But the slave system is a consumer of
men as the blast furnace is of coal; it is necessary constantly to supply a
complement of slaves. Under the empire this supply dried up, and what happened is what would happen to our industrial civilization if there were no
coal.

But may one not object to Weber that this crisis could be the instigator of a
renewal? The homage rendered by the Fathers to the labor of the worker is a
pleasing thing and so too is the great progress of the construction of the
individual house of the peasant succeeding the barracks of the slaves.

2. The decline of the cities and the progress of the autarchy of the estate.
The great estate was self-sufficient and allowed the city to die of starvation.
Now, says Weber, the estate is the cell of the feudal regime, while the city
was the birth-place of liberty.

3. The destruction of capital and the progress of a natural economy. Endemic war since the time of Marcus Aurelius was the cause of this destruction
of wealth. The restoration of devastated regions had to absorb a great part of
the public revenue; still it was never accomplished; Gaul in the fourth century was strewn with ruins. The state, overwhelmed by expenses, became a
counterfeiter.

Is it correct to say, however, that in the fourth century there was a return to
a natural economy? It seems to us that in reality two systems of exchange and
two price systems had coexisted since the third century. On the one hand,
there was the public market, where prices were controlled by the state, where
provisions were, in part, on a quota basis; they were furnished by requisi-
tions, the state undertaking their collection. They were bought with those
dreadful pieces of debased coinage whose perpetual devaluations the numis-
matists have disentangled with such difficulty. But there was, on the other
hand, a market for the rich. There, gold circulated not secretly, but under the
control of the state, which took a large percentage for itself. For the price of
gold one could obtain objects of the greatest luxury. When Ausonius retired
he returned to live on his lands and sent his men into the country, provision-
ing himself, as we say, "on the black market." It was this coexistence of a
public market, anemic and badly supplied, and a clandestine and abundant
market which was probably the most disquieting feature of the late empire.

4. The removal of the routes of commerce to central Europe. A great continental route connecting the valleys of the Rhine and the Danube tended to
compete with Mediterranean commerce at the time of Trajan's death. We
pick out the string of new imperial capitals, Trèves, Milan, Sirmium, Serdica,
Constantinople. The emperors no longer had any occasion to pass through
Rome. It was on both sides of this Rhine–Danube axis that the Celtic empire
was based and on it would one day be founded the new Europe.

Nevertheless, we do not have the right to speak of a decline of Mediterranean commerce. Maritime relations remained active from Narbonne to
Alexandria, from Carthage to Constantinople. If the Roman peace had lasted,
we might have seen a civilization of central Europe prosper in the radiance of
the Mediterranean civilization.

5. The abuse of interventionism. State socialism, says H. M. R. Leopold,
made the empire a workshop of forced labor; thus the state committed sui-
cide; it provoked the discontent of the lower classes and ruined economic
prosperity.

To this view is opposed that of F. Heichelheim, who believes, on the contrary, that the state had the duty of intervening to save the economy threatened by the crisis and that its intervention was effective. The state, according
to him, struggled heroically to save civilization, to arrest tendencies toward
feudalism, to maintain circulation.

From all these observations it follows that a new economic system was
being born, characterized by associations of free workers, control exercised by
the state on the circulation and allotment of provisions, more scientific exploitation of the great estates. But progress was hindered by monetary instability,
insecurity, excessive taxation, and all these evils had a single cause, war.

The extraordinary luxury of the mighty was brutally opposed to the
wretchedness of the poor who were at the point of abject mendicity. Gaius
Gracchus had already asked why should the poor, living in holes, take up
arms for the defense of their country. It is not in doubt that the poor of the
late empire sometimes appealed to the barbarians in order to avenge themselves on the rich. It was in the wake of the invasions of the third century that
the countryside was depopulated and that the nobles extended their properties without limit: at the source of their scandalous fortunes were all the
abuses which made the state of war possible. English scholars, studying the
dispossession of the peasants in the fourth century, conclude that in Britain
none of the conditions leading to a social revolution were absent.

Rome had been saved formerly, says Ammianus, by its austerity, by the
solidarity between rich and poor, by the disregard of death; it was now lost
because of its luxury and cupidity. Innumerable are the evidences of the
Church Fathers, who stigmatized the immorality of both rich and poor. Sal-
vienus confirms Ammianus in affirming that the cupidity (*avaritia*) was a
vice common to almost all Romans.

But this is the common language of moralists which Sallust used in his
beautiful gardens; to these black pictures the history of the fourth century

would oppose how many examples of heroism, candor, and charity! The social transformation since the time of the Severi favored the progress of a morality which was brutal, simplistic, and fraternal.

The conflicts between pagans and Christians were a serious cause of disintegration; we have said that they often served to mask ethnic conflicts.

Christianity did not declare war on Roman society, but it condemned it. It impatiently awaited the fall of the new Babylon which would be the first episode of the end of the world. That is why, before the accession of Constantine, the Christian went on strike, fled the burdens of the state, refused to fight for Rome. The heroic remedy of Constantine, to call in the Christians to govern, is comparable to the one a statesman would apply who gave power to revolutionaries, in the hope that the experience would moderate them. The Catholics in power were enriched and occupied the highest positions; they undertook the defense of property and allowed the hope that the fall of Rome would not take place tomorrow. But when Rome came to the supreme crisis the Christians, seeing it lost, treated it as the city of the devil, and betrayed it once more. The Roman nation had much to complain of these bad citizens.

Nevertheless, if Rome could have overcome this ordeal, is it not evident that Christianity by imposing the unity of faith on the whole empire would have contributed to a political solidification of this great body? Is it not under the form of the unity of Christianity that the empire perpetuated itself after its collapse? One may not say, therefore, that Christianity was responsible for the dissolution of the empire, since it was capable, on the contrary, had there been time, to confirm its moral unity.

M. Rostovtzeff believes that the decadence of Rome is explained by "the gradual absorption of the educated classes by the masses, and in consequence, the simplification of all the functions of political, social, economic and intellectual life which we call the barbarization of the ancient world." Has one really the right to speak of barbarization in the fourth century?

In the same way as, in economic life, gold was reserved for the wealthy while a dreadful bronze coinage was sufficient for the poor, so too did the Romanic languages, sprung from the vulgar language, begin to undermine the beautiful artistic language which was that of the late Latin writers and of polite society. The diversity of these languages will soon correspond to those of the nationalities, and this evolution was doubtless inevitable.

But it is not true that the intellectual was in regression. Certainly the rulers were afraid of books and one cannot think without horror of the *autos da fé* ordered by Constantine on Valens. Certainly the Christians regarded scientific culture with suspicion and St. Augustine held to a theory of obscurantism. It does not alter the fact that the plan of education which he himself traced derives from Hellenistic programs. What is important is the fact that the modern book at last made its appearance in the form of the *codex,* which took the place of the *volumen* and which became a marvelous instrument of culture. What is important is that the Roman nobles by editing the ancient texts showed the way to Byzantium, which was the librarian of the world.

What is important is that slavery, which for so long was an obstacle to technological progress, declined, for at once it seems that a period of scientific invention was going to open up. The new art was quite clumsy and did not respect the classical formulas and certain works provoke horror: but what is important is that to the old rhetorical and narrative style there succeeded a moving and impressionistic style, that the architects invested new models with disconcerting prodigality, that the miniature was born.

The philosophy and theology of these times discourage us. But let us remember those men whom a text of Filastrius lets us get a glimpse of, who meditated on the innumerable centuries of human prehistory and on the infinity of worlds. The truth seems to be that an admirable blossoming was in preparation if a catastrophe had not occurred. The catastrophe arrived in the form of the barbarian invasions.

The Germans lived in a dreadful land whose sterile soil they were too lazy to clear. They preferred war to ordered work and invaded neighboring states *fame urgente*. Neither the influence of Greece nor of Rome had succeeded in civilizing them after so many centuries. They had a primitive economy, they were ignorant of coinage, they had a rudimentary alphabet. But they were born soldiers. Their social organization was a form of their army; the tribe was divided into hundreds, and the centurion was at the same time leader for agriculture and war. The chief was surrounded by faithful men who wanted to die bravely for him. "The struggle was between the Roman Empire and the rule of the warrior band." These cruel people, according to a contemporary German historian, experienced a kind of ecstasy. Now the pressure of nomads from Asia drove them toward the West.

Against so evident and grave a danger the Romans needed a strong army. Yet the Roman emperors from fear of liberty, since the time of Augustus, had systematically disarmed the citizens and trusted the defense of the empire to mercenaries. They resorted first to the populations of the barbarous regions of the empire, then to foreign barbarians. In the fourth century Rome dared to confide the defense of the frontiers to barbarian tribes which it received into its bosom: it installed the Franks in Toxandria, charging them with the defense of the Rhine. In Pannonia they placed the Vandals and Ostrogoths, in Moesia the Visigoths, charging them with the defense of the Danube. In the reserve army itself the most highly regarded bodies were the barbarian *auxilia*, and barbarian officers occupied the highest ranks up to that of master of the militia. Synesius, addressing Arcadius a short time after the death of Theodosius, denounced the evil in these terms: "We are protected by armies composed of men who are of the same race as our slaves," and he recommends the remedy: obligatory military service. It is chiefly because Rome relinquished compulsory military service for citizens that she perished.

It is false to say that Rome was in decay. Pillaged, disfigured by the barbarian invaders of the third century, it restored its ruins. At the same time, at the price of a serious crisis, a work of internal metamorphosis was accomplished: a new concept of imperial power was formed which is that of Byzantium, a new concept of truth and beauty which is that of the Middle Ages, a new concept of collective and mutually responsible labor in the service of the social interest. And all the evils from which the empire suffered, crushing taxation, overthrow of fortunes and social classes, had as their origin not at all this fecund work of metamorphosis, but the perpetual war carried on by unorganized bands of those Germans who had succeeded in living on the frontiers of the empire for centuries without being civilized.

It is too convenient to assert that at the arrival of the barbarians into the empire "all was dead, it was a worn out body, a corpse stretched out in its own blood," or, again, that the Roman Empire in the West was not destroyed by a brutal shock, but that it had "fallen asleep."

Roman civilization did not die a natural death.

It was murdered.

CHARLEMAGNE
THE MAKER OF EUROPE?

CONTENTS

QUESTIONS FOR STUDY

1. *What impressions of Charlemagne's ideals of government do you get from reading Dawson? Burns? the General Capitulary of 802?*

2. *What is the major difference between Einhard's account of the coronation and those of other contemporary writers? How can the discrepancy be explained?*

3. *What evidence can you find in the sources that Charlemagne felt either attraction toward or aversion to the imperial title?*

4. *Who do you think took the initiative in planning the imperial coronation?*

5. *What were the motives of the principal participants in the coronation ceremony?*

6. *Why are the politics of Byzantium relevant to an understanding of the events at Rome?*

Many historians have seen in the age of Charlemagne the beginnings of a distinctively Western civilization. The Roman Empire had been essentially a Mediterranean state, with its greatest centers of population and wealth located in the East. And even after the breakdown of the empire it seemed likely for centuries that Italy would continue to be dominated by Byzantium. There was nothing inevitable in the emergence of the civilization we call "European" or "Western." That civilization was formed by a fusion between the Latin culture of the Mediterranean and the Teutonic culture of the north. But Italy might well have remained a satellite of Greek culture and northern Europe merely barbarian. There would then have been no Western European civilization as later ages would know it.

In fact, events took a different turn during the course of the eighth century. The Roman popes quarreled bitterly with the Byzantine emperors over the issue of iconoclasm (p. 338) and then entered into an alliance with the Franks, the most powerful Teutonic people of the north. The importance of this alliance for the future of European culture is emphasized by Christopher Dawson (pp. 308–312), and the events leading up to it are outlined by Delisle Burns (pp. 325–331).

Two factors made the alliance possible—the spread of Roman religious influence in the north and the penetration of Frankish political influence into Italy. The principal agent of the first movement was St. Boniface (c. 680–755). An Anglo-Saxon by birth, he journeyed to Rome in 722 and was sent by the pope to evangelize the still heathen peoples of central Germany. During the next twenty years he made many converts and organized them in a series of dioceses closely dependent on Rome. Then, in 742, Boniface was sent on a new mission as papal legate to the kingdom of the Franks.

During Boniface's mission it became clear to the pope and the Frankish king that they could render useful services to one another. The pope needed a strong ally to defend Rome against marauding Lombards. The Frankish leader, Pepin, who had seized the throne of the Franks in 750, wanted papal approval to legitimize his action. Accordingly, in 752 Pope Stephen II crossed the Alps and crowned Pepin king. In return Pepin invaded Italy, defeated the Lombards, and conferred on the papacy the lands that he seized from them. This was the beginning of papal temporal power in central Italy.

Pepin's son Charlemagne, a great conqueror, made himself ruler of France, western Germany, and northern Italy; and on Christmas Day, 800, Pope Leo III crowned him "emperor and Augustus" in Rome. The readings in the following section are devoted largely to the circumstances surrounding this imperial coronation, and the reader may well wonder why modern historians are still fascinated by an apparently obscure event that took place nearly twelve hundred years ago. There are two main reasons for their interest. The coronation of Charlemagne was an enormously important event in European history. And to explain how it came about offers a major challenge to the skill and ingenuity of a historian.

Charlemagne's coronation symbolized perfectly the mingling of the Christian, classical, and Teutonic influences that flowed together in the newly emerging Western, medieval civilization. (The official who crowned Charlemagne was the most exalted of Christian bishops; the title he assumed was a classical one; his own real power rested on his achievements as a Teutonic warrior king.) But the coronation was more than a symbol; it was a precedent. The links between empire and papacy established by the ceremony of 800 helped to bind Europe into a cultural unity for centuries to come. Throughout the medieval period great Germanic kings claimed for themselves the title that Charlemagne had assumed. Their attempts to create a "Holy Roman Empire" (a later phrase) greatly influenced the political structure of Europe. They also influenced the whole medieval approach to the problem of church and state. Later emperors were inclined to assert that since they were legitimate rulers of Rome, they could appoint the bishop of Rome (as they often appointed bishops in their other territories). Popes were tempted to reply that, since they conferred the imperial dignity in the act of coronation, all power on earth, both temporal and spiritual, inhered in their office.

The historical consequences of the coronation are, then, literally incalculable but certainly very great indeed. This is the kind of supremely important event that a historian wants to understand as fully as possible. But to achieve such understanding proves to be very difficult. The problem is that there are only a few brief accounts of the coronation in contemporary sources (pp. 318–324), and each one tells a slightly different story. On these slender foundations historians have built a considerable edifice of speculation. Some, like Karl Heldmann (pp. 332–334) and Werner Ohnsorge (pp. 339–345), regard the whole coronation episode as the working out of a crafty plot by Pope Leo III to serve his own interests—though they disagree as to what particular interests he had in mind. The difficulty with this approach is that Pope Leo was utterly dependent on Charlemagne in 800. It is hard to suppose that he would have risked provoking the king's anger by imposing on him an unwanted title. Historians like Francis Ganshof (pp. 335–338), who argue that the initiative must have come from the Frankish side, can point out that the phrase "Christian empire" was current in Charlemagne's court circle before 800 (pp. 316–317). The problem for them is that one Frankish source declares plainly that Charlemagne had no knowledge of the pope's intention when he went to Mass on Christmas Day and that he viewed his new title with "aversion" (p. 321). It would be tempting to dismiss this as a merely conventional assertion of royal humility, without any basis in fact, but the charters issued by Charlemagne in the year 801 show that for several months after the coronation he refused to use the title that had been conferred on him in St. Peter's (pp. 323–324).

The whole affair remains something of a mystery. It has become one of the more famous of historians' detection problems. Who planned the coronation? Who had the best motive for doing so? Who had the opportunity to arrange the ceremony? Did Charlemagne want to be an emperor? If so, why was he displeased? If not, why did he retain the imperial title? What actually happened at Rome in the week before Christmas, 800?

1
CHARLEMAGNE AND CHRISTIAN CULTURE

Christopher Dawson treated the imperial coronation as an important stage in the emergence of "Western Christendom."

FROM The Making of Europe BY CHRISTOPHER DAWSON

The historical importance of the Carolingian age far transcends its material achievement. The unwieldy Empire of Charles the Great did not long survive the death of its founder, and it never really attained the economic and social organisation of a civilised state. But, for all that, it marks the first emergence of the European culture from the twilight of pre-natal existence into the consciousness of active life. Hitherto the barbarians had lived passively on the capital which they had inherited from the civilisation which they had plundered; now they began to co-operate with it in a creative social activity. The centre of mediaeval civilisation was not to be on the shores of the Mediterranean, but in the northern lands between the Loire and the Weser which were the heart of the Frankish dominions. This was the formative centre of the new culture, and it was there that the new conditions which were to govern the history of mediaeval culture find their origin. The ideal of the mediaeval Empire, the political position of the Papacy, the German hegemony in Italy and the expansion of Germany towards the East, the fundamental institutions of mediaeval society both in Church and State, and the incorporation of the classical tradition in mediaeval culture—all have their basis in the history of the Carolingian period.

From *The Making of Europe* by Christopher Dawson, pp. 169–171, 175–176, 226–227, published by Sheed & Ward Inc., New York. Reprinted by permission of The Society of Authors, London.

The essential feature of the new culture was its religious character. While the Merovingian state had been predominantly secular, the Carolingian Empire was a theocratic power—the political expression of a religious unity. This change in the character of the monarchy is shown by the actual circumstances of the installation of the new dynasty; for Pepin obtained Papal authority for the setting aside of the old royal house and was anointed king in the year 752 by St. Boniface according to the religious coronation rite which had grown up under ecclesiastical influence in Anglo-Saxon England and Visigothic Spain, but which had hitherto been unknown among the Franks. Thus the legitimation of the rule of the Carolingian house sealed the alliance between the Frankish monarchy and the Papacy which St. Boniface had done so much to bring about, and henceforward the Frankish monarchy was the recognised champion and protector of the Holy See. The Papacy had already been alienated from the Byzantine Empire by the Iconoclastic policy of the Isaurian emperors, and the extinction of the last survival of the Byzantine power at Ravenna by the Lombards in 751 forced the Pope to look for support elsewhere. In 754 Stephen II visited Pepin in his own dominions, and obtained from him a treaty which secured to the Papacy the Exarchate of Ravenna and the former Byzantine possessions in Italy, together with the duchies of Spoleto and Benevento. In return the Pope reconsecrated Pepin as King of the Franks, and also conferred on him the dignity of Patrician of the Romans. This was an epoch-making event, for it marked not only the foundation of the Papal State which was to endure until 1870, but also the protectorate of the Carolingians in Italy, and the beginning of their imperial mission as the leaders and organisers of Western Christendom.

The Carolingians were naturally fitted to undertake this mission since they were themselves the representatives of both sides of the European tradition. They traced their descent from Gallo-Roman bishops and saints as well as from Frankish warriors, and they combined the warlike prowess of a Charles Martel with a vein of religious idealism, which shows itself in Carloman's renunciation of his kingdom in order to enter the cloister, and Pepin's sincere devotion to the cause of the Church. But it is in Pepin's successor, Charles the Great, that both these elements find simultaneous expression. He was above all a soldier with a talent for war and military enterprise which made him the greatest conqueror of his time. But in spite of his ruthlessness and unscrupulous ambition he was no mere barbaric warrior; his policy was inspired by ideals and universal aims. His conquests were not only the fulfillment of the traditional Frankish policy of military expansion; they were also crusades for the protection and unity of Christendom. By his destruction of the Lombard Kingdom he freed the Papacy from the menace which had threatened its independence for two hundred years and brought Italy into the Frankish Empire. The long drawn out struggle with the Saxons was due to his determination to put an end to the last remains of Germanic heathenism as well as of Saxon independence. His conquest of the Avars in 793-794 destroyed the

Asiatic robber state which had terrorised the whole of Eastern Europe, and at the same time restored Christianity in the Danube provinces, while his war with the Saracens and his establishment of the Spanish March were the beginning of the Christian reaction to the victorious expansion of Islam. In the course of thirty years of incessant warfare he had extended the frontiers of the Frankish monarchy as far as the Elbe, the Mediterranean and the Lower Danube, and had united Western Christendom in a great imperial state.

The coronation of Charles as Roman Emperor and the restoration of the Western Empire in the year 800 marked the final stage in the reorganisation of Western Christendom and completed the union between the Frankish monarchy and the Roman Church which had been begun by the work of Boniface and Pepin.

* * *

As King, Charles had stood outside the Roman tradition; as Emperor, he entered into a definite juridical relationship with the head of the Church. His power was still as formidable as ever, but it was no longer indefinite and incalculable. Moreover, the idea of the Roman Empire was still indispensable to the Church. It was synonymous with Christian civilisation, while the rule of the barbarians was so identified with heathenism and war that the Liturgy couples together, "the enemies of the Roman name and the foes of the Catholic Faith." Consequently, it is by no means improbable that the Papacy as the representation of Roman universalism should have taken the initiative in the restoration of the Empire in 800, as it did once more seventy-five years later in the case of Charles the Bald.

However this may be, it is certain that the restoration of the Roman Empire, or rather the foundation of the new mediaeval Empire, had a religious and symbolic value which far outweighed its immediate importance from a political point of view. Charles used it, no doubt, as a diplomatic counter in his negotiations with the Eastern Empire, but his coronation made no difference in his life or government. He never attempted to ape the ways of a Roman or Byzantine Caesar, as did Otto III and other mediaeval emperors, but remained a thorough Frank, in dress and manners as well as in his political ideals. He even imperilled his whole work of imperial unification by dividing his dominions among his heirs in 806 according to the old Frankish custom, instead of following the Roman principle of indivisible political sovereignty; and the same tradition reasserted itself among his successors and proved fatal to the unity and continuity of the Carolingian Empire.

It was the churchmen and the men of letters, rather than the princes and statesmen, who cherished the ideal of the Holy Roman Empire. To them it meant the end of the centuries of barbarism and a return to civilised order. To Einhard, Charles is a new Augustus, and he views his achievement in the light of the Augustan ideal; while Modoin, the Bishop of Auxerre, writes of his age as the Renaissance of classical antiquity:

rursus in antiquos mutataque saecula mores;
aurea Roma iterum renovata renascitur orbe.

[*the changing ages turn to ancient ways;*
golden Rome is born again, the world renewed—B. T.]

In fact, though the learning of the Carolingian age may seem a poor thing to set by the side of that of the great Italian humanists, it was none the less a genuine Renaissance which had no less importance for the development of European culture than the more brilliant movement of the fifteenth century. The gathering together of the scattered elements of the classical and patristic traditions and their reorganisation as the basis of a new culture was the greatest of all the achievements of the Carolingian age.

* * *

Thus the culture that we regard as characteristically Western and European was confined in the main within the limits of the former Carolingian Empire, and found its centre in the old Frankish territories of Northern France and Western Germany. In the tenth century it was, as we have seen, hard pressed on every side and even tended to contract its frontiers. But the eleventh century saw the turn of the tide and the rapid expansion of this central continental culture in all directions. In the West the Norman Conquest took England out of the sphere of the Nordic culture that had threatened for two centuries to absorb it, and incorporated it into the continental society; in the North and East it gradually dominated the Western Slavs and penetrated Scandinavia by its cultural influence; while in the South it embarked with crusading energy on the great task of the reconquest of the Mediterranean from the power of Islam.

In this way the peoples of the Frankish Empire imposed their social hegemony and their ideals of culture on all the surrounding peoples, so that the Carolingian unity may be regarded without exaggeration as the foundation and starting-point of the whole development of mediaeval Western civilisation. It is true that the Carolingian Empire had long lost its unity, and France and Germany were becoming more and more conscious of their national differences. Nevertheless they both looked back to the same Carolingian tradition, and their culture was compounded of the same elements, though the proportions were different. They were still in essence the Western and East Frankish realms, though, like brothers who take after different sides of their family, they were often more conscious of their difference than of their resemblance. In both cases, however, the cultural leadership lay with the intermediate regions—the territories of the Empire that were most Latinised, and those in France where the Germanic element was strongest: Northern France, Lorraine and Burgundy, Flanders and the Rhineland. Above all, it was Normandy, where the Nordic and Latin elements stood in sharpest contrast and most immediate contact, that was the leader of the movement of expansion.

It was this middle territory, reaching from the Loire to the Rhine, that was the true homeland of mediaeval culture and the source of its creative and characteristic achievements. It was the cradle of Gothic architecture, of the great mediaeval schools, of the movement of monastic and ecclesiastical reform and of the crusading ideal. It was the centre of the typical development of the feudal state, of the North European communal movement and of the institution of knighthood. It was here that a complete synthesis was finally achieved between the Germanic North and the spiritual order of the Church and the traditions of the Latin culture.

2
CHARLEMAGNE AS SEEN BY HIS CONTEMPORARIES

This biography of Charlemagne was written by a member of the imperial court circle about ten years after the emperor's death.

FROM Life of Charlemagne BY EINHARD

Charles was large and strong, and of lofty stature, though not disproportionately tall (his height is well known to have been seven times the length of his foot); the upper part of his head was round, his eyes very large and animated, nose a little long, hair fair, and face laughing and merry. Thus his appearance was always stately and dignified, whether he was standing or sitting; although his neck was thick and somewhat short, and his belly rather prominent; but the symmetry of the rest of his body concealed these defects. His gait was firm, his whole carriage manly, and his voice clear, but not so strong as his size led one to expect. His health was excellent, except during the four years preceding his death, when he was subject to frequent fevers; at the last he even limped a little with one foot. Even in those years he consulted rather his own inclinations than the advice of physicians, who were almost hateful to him, because they wanted him to give up roasts, to which he was accustomed, and to eat boiled meat instead. In accordance with the national custom, he took frequent exercise on horseback and in the chase, accomplishments in which scarcely any people in the world can equal the Franks. He enjoyed the exhalations from natural warm springs, and often practiced swimming, in which he was such an adept that none could surpass him; and hence it was that he built his palace at Aix-la-Chapelle, and lived there con-

Einhard, *Life of Charlemagne* (1880), pp. 56–65, translated by Samuel Epes Turner.

stantly during his latter years until his death. He used not only to invite his sons to his bath, but his nobles and friends, and now and then a troop of his retinue or bodyguard, so that a hundred or more persons sometimes bathed with him.

He used to wear the national, that is to say, the Frank, dress—next his skin a linen shirt and linen breeches, and above these a tunic fringed with silk; while hose fastened by bands covered his lower limbs, and shoes his feet, and he protected his shoulders and chest in winter by a close-fitting coat of otter or marten skins. Over all he flung a blue cloak, and he always had a sword girt about him, usually one with a gold or silver hilt and belt; he sometimes carried a jeweled sword, but only on great feastdays or at the reception of ambassadors from foreign nations. He despised foreign costumes, however handsome, and never allowed himself to be robed in them, except twice in Rome, when he donned the Roman tunic, chlamys, and shoes; the first time at the request of Pope Hadrian, the second to gratify Leo, Hadrian's successor. On great feastdays he made use of embroidered clothes and shoes bedecked with precious stones, his cloak was fastened by a golden buckle, and he appeared crowned with a diadem of gold and gems, but on other days his dress varied little from the common dress of the people.

Charles was temperate in eating, and particularly so in drinking, for he abominated drunkenness in anybody, much more in himself and those of his household; but he could not easily abstain from food, and often complained that fasts injured his health. He very rarely gave entertainments, only on great feastdays, and then to large numbers of people. His meals ordinarily consisted of four courses, not counting the roast, which his huntsmen used to bring in on the spit; he was more fond of this than of any other dish. While at table, he listened to reading or music. The subjects of the readings were the stories and deeds of olden time: he was fond, too, of St. Augustine's books, and especially of the one entitled "The City of God." He was so moderate in the use of wine and all sorts of drink that he rarely allowed himself more than three cups in the course of a meal. In summer, after the midday meal, he would eat some fruit, drain a single cup, put off his clothes and shoes, just as he did for the night, and rest for two or three hours. He was in the habit of awaking and rising from bed four or five times during the night. While he was dressing and putting on his shoes, he not only gave audience to his friends, but if the Count of the Palace told him of any suit in which his judgment was necessary, he had the parties brought before him forthwith, took cognizance of the case, and gave his decision, just as if he were sitting on the judgment seat. This was not the only business that he transacted at this time, but he performed any duty of the day whatever, whether he had to attend to the matter himself, or to give commands concerning it to his officers.

Charles had the gift of ready and fluent speech, and could express whatever he had to say with the utmost clearness. He was not satisfied with command of his native language merely, but gave attention to the study of foreign ones, and in particular was such a master of Latin that he could speak it as well as his native tongue; but he could understand Greek better than he could speak it. He was so eloquent, indeed, that he might have passed for a teacher of eloquence. He most zealously cultivated the liberal arts, held those who taught them in great esteem, and conferred great honors upon them. He took lessons in grammar of the deacon Peter of Pisa, at that time an aged man. Another deacon, Albin of Britain, surnamed Alcuin, a man of Saxon extraction, who was the greatest scholar of the day, was his teacher in other branches of learning. The King spent much time and labor with him studying rhetoric, dialectics, and especially astronomy; he learned to reckon, and used to investigate the motions of the heavenly bodies most curiously, with an intelligent scrutiny. He also tried to write, and used to keep tablets and blanks in bed under his pillow, that at leisure hours he might accustom his hand to form the letters; however, as he did not begin his efforts in due season, but late in life, they met with ill success.

He cherished with the greatest fervor and devotion the principles of the Christian religion, which had been instilled into him from infancy. Hence it was that he built the beautiful basilica at Aix-la-Chapelle, which he adorned with gold and silver and lamps, and with rails and doors of solid brass. He had the columns and marbles for this structure brought from Rome and Ravenna, for he could not find such as were suitable elsewhere. He was a constant worshipper at this church as long as his health permitted, going morning and evening, even after nightfall, besides attending mass; and he took care that all the services there conducted should be administered with the utmost possible propriety, very often warning the sextons not to let any improper or unclean thing be brought into the building or remain in it. He provided it with a great number of sacred vessels of gold and silver and with such a quantity of clerical robes that not even the doorkeepers who fill the humblest office in the church were obliged to wear their everyday clothes when in the exercise of their duties. He was at great pains to improve the church reading and psalmody, for he was well skilled in both, although he neither read in public nor sang, except in a low tone and with others.

He was very forward in succoring the poor, and in that gratuitous generosity which the Greeks call alms, so much so that he not only made a point of giving in his own country and his own kingdom, but when he discovered that there were Christians living in poverty in Syria, Egypt, and Africa, at Jerusalem, Alexandria, and Carthage, he had compassion on their wants, and used to send money over the seas to them. The reason that he zealously strove to make friends with the kings beyond seas was that he might get help and relief to the Christians living under their rule. He cherished the Church of St. Peter the Apostle at Rome above all other holy and sacred places, and heaped its treasury with a vast wealth of gold, silver, and precious stones. He sent great and countless gifts to the popes, and throughout his whole reign the wish that he had nearest at heart was to re-establish the ancient authority of the city of Rome under his care and by his influence, and to defend and protect the Church of St. Peter, and to beautify and enrich it out of his own store above all other churches. Although he held it in such veneration, he only repaired to Rome to pay his vows and make his supplications four times during the whole forty-seven years that he reigned.

The writer of the following letters, Alcuin, was a leading member of the group of learned churchmen that Charlemagne brought together at his court. The letters were written in 799.

FROM Alcuin's Letters

Flaccus Albinus sends greetings to the peaceful Lord, King David [*Charlemagne—B. T.*].

. . . If I were present I should have used many words to persuade your venerable dignity, had you the opportunity to listen, or I the eloquence to speak. For the pen is often wont to stimulate the secrets of the love of my heart to write of your excellence, of the stability of the kingdom given to you by God, and of the progress of the holy Church of Christ. She is disturbed greatly by the manifold wickedness of evil men, and tainted by the audacious crimes of the worst of men, not only among low-born persons, but even among the greatest and highest. All this is greatly to be feared.

For three persons have hitherto been the highest in the world: that is, the apostolic sublimity, which is accustomed to rule the throne of St. Peter, the prince of the Apostles, as its vicar. Your venerable goodness has informed me of what should be done in the case of him, who was the ruler of the aforesaid seat. Another is the imperial dignity and secular power of the second Rome, whose governor was impiously deposed, not by foreigners, but by his own relatives and fellow-citizens, as the story was everywhere spread by rumor. The third is the royal dignity, in which the dispensation of our Lord Jesus Christ placed you, as ruler of the Christian people, more excellent in power than the others mentioned above, more renowned for your wisdom, more sublime in the dignity of your realm. Behold, on you alone rests the entire safety of the churches of Christ. You are the avenger of crimes, you are the guide of the erring, you are the consoler of the grieving, you are the exaltation of good men. . . .

Reprinted with permission of The Macmillan Company from Norman F. Cantor, *The Medieval World, 300–1300*, pp. 149–151. Copyright © Norman F. Cantor 1963.

Nothing can be concealed from your wisdom: for we know that you are exceedingly well-learned both in the holy Scriptures and in secular histories. In all these things you have been given full knowledge by God, so that through you the holy Church of God might be ruled, exalted, and preserved for the Christian people. Who can describe the magnitude of the reward which God will give you for your greatest devotion? For eye has not seen, nor ear heard, nor the heart of man conceived what God has prepared for those who love Him. . . .

Flaccus, the faithful orator, sends wishes for eternal blessedness in Christ to his most beloved lord of lords, King David.

. . . O most sweet [Charles], glory of the Christian people, O defense of the churches of Christ, consolation of this present life. Because of these virtues, it is necessary that all men should exalt your blessedness in their prayers and aid you by their intercessions, since it is through your prosperity that the Christian Empire may be protected, that the Catholic faith may be defended, and that the rule of justice may become known to all. . . .

And would that you, whenever divine grace grants you enough freedom from the wicked Saxon people, might travel on the roads, govern your realms, do justice, repair churches, discipline the people, decree laws for individual persons and classes, to defend the oppressed, to ordain laws, to comfort pilgrims, and to show the way of righteousness and heavenly life to everyone everywhere. Thus the arrival of your piety would be a consolation to all; and blessings would come to the most famous sons of your nobility through your copious blessings, just as it is read that through the sanctity of your namesake David alone, a king most pleasing to God, the power of the royal throne was preserved for all his descendants. In such exercises of this religion the exaltation of your sons, the felicity of your realm, the well-being of your people, the abundance of harvests, the delight of all good men, and the blessings which the heavenly kingdom holds in store for you shall increase and be augmented through all eternity, with the help of Christ the God, O most sweet David. . . .

3
THE
IMPERIAL
CORONATION

In 799 there was an attempted rebellion against Pope Leo III in Rome. This trouble was the immediate cause of Charlemagne's visit to the city in 800. Of the following five accounts the first three are by Frankish writers, the fourth by a member of the papal court, and the fifth by a Byzantine chronicler.

FROM Frankish Royal Annals

799

The Romans seized Pope Leo during a solemn procession and blinded him and cut out his tongue. [*It is evident from the following account that the chronicler exaggerated the pope's injuries—B. T.*] He was placed in custody but escaped over the wall and came to the legates of the lord king who were at St. Peter's basilica, namely abbot Wirindus and duke Winigis of Spoleto. He was then escorted to Spoleto. The lord king had set out for Saxony and, having crossed the Rhine near Lippeham, set up his camp at Paderborn . . . and there received Pope Leo honorably while he was waiting for the return of his son, Charles. The pope was sent away as honorably as he had been received and at once set out for Rome [with a Frankish escort] while the lord king returned to his palace at Aachen.

800

At the beginning of the month of August, when Charles came to Mainz, he announced a journey into Italy. Having arrived at Ravenna with his army he

---

Annales Laurissenses, in G. H. Pertz, ed., *Monumenta Germaniae Historiae, Scriptores,* I (1826), 184–189, translated by Brian Tierney.

set on foot a campaign against the Beneventans. He commanded his son, Pippin, to ravage their lands with the army while Charles, after seven days' delay, set out for Rome. As he drew near, Pope Leo, accompanied by Romans, went out to meet him at Nomentum which is twelve miles from the city and there received him with great humility and great honor. The pope dined with the king at this place and then at once returned to Rome. On the next day the pope stationed himself on the steps of the basilica of the blessed apostle Peter, with the standards of the city of Rome displayed and great crowds of pilgrims and citizens assembled there suitably grouped to shout the praises of him who was coming. Leo, with the clergy and bishops, welcomed the king when he dismounted from his horse and ascended the steps and then, having offered up a prayer, led him into the basilica of the blessed apostle Peter while all around chanted psalms. This happened on November 24.

Seven days later the king summoned a council and explained to all why he had come to Rome, and thenceforth he was daily occupied with the matters he had come to settle. He began with the most important of these, the investigation of the crimes of which the pontiff had been accused. Since no one would undertake to prove the crimes, Leo mounted into the pulpit of the basilica of the blessed apostle Peter before all the people with the Gospel in his hand and, invoking the name of the Holy Trinity, purged himself by oath of the crimes that had been imputed to him.

801

On the most holy day [*the chronicler reckons December 25 as the first day of the new year—B. T.*] of the nativity of the Lord, as the king rose from praying at Mass before the tomb of the blessed apostle Peter, Pope Leo placed a crown on his head and all the Roman people cried out, "To Charles Augustus, crowned by God, great and peace-giving emperor of the Romans, life and victory." And after the laudation he was adored by the pope in the manner of the ancient princes and, the title of patrician being set aside, he was called emperor and Augustus. A few days later he commanded the men who had deposed the pope the year before to be brought before him. They were examined according to Roman law on a charge of treason and condemned to death. However, the pope interceded for them with the emperor and they were spared in life and limb. Subsequently they were sent into exile for so great a crime.

FROM Annals of Lorsch

800

In the summer Charles gathered together his lords and faithful men in the city of Mainz. When he saw that there was peace throughout his dominions he called to mind the injuries that the Romans had inflicted on Pope Leo and, setting his face toward Rome, he journeyed there. After his arrival he summoned a great council of bishops and abbots, together with priests, deacons, counts and other Christian people. Those who wished to condemn the apostle Leo came before this assembly. When the king realised that they did not want to condemn the pope for the sake of justice but maliciously, it became clear to the most pious prince Charles and to all the bishops and holy fathers present that, if the pope wished it and requested it, he ought to clear himself, not by judgment of the council, but spontaneously, by his own will; and this was done. When the pope had taken the oath, the holy bishops, together with the clergy and prince Charles and the devoted Christian people, began the hymn, *Te Deum laudamus, te Dominum confitemur*. When this was finished the king and all the faithful people with him gave thanks to God who had preserved the apostle Leo sound in body and mind. And he passed the Winter in Rome.

Now since the title of emperor had become extinct among the Greeks and a woman claimed the imperial authority it seemed to the apostle Leo and to all the holy fathers who were present at the council and to the rest of the Christian people that Charles, king of the Franks, ought to be named emperor, for he held Rome itself where the Caesars were always wont to reside and also other cities in Italy, Gaul, and Germany. Since almighty God had put all these places in his power it seemed to them that, with the help of God, and in accordance with the request of all the Christian people, he should hold this title. King Charles did not wish to refuse their petition, and, humbly submitting himself to God and to the petition of all the Christian priests and people, he accepted the title of emperor on the day of the nativity of our Lord Jesus Christ and was consecrated by the lord Pope Leo.

Annales Laureshamenses, in G. H. Pertz, ed., *Monumenta Germaniae Historiae, Scriptores*, I (1826), 38, translated by Brian Tierney.

FROM Life of Charlemagne BY EINHARD

The Romans had inflicted many injuries upon the Pontiff Leo, tearing out his eyes and cutting out his tongue, so that he had been compelled to call

Nov. 24, 800   upon the King for help. Charles accordingly went to Rome, to set in order the affairs of the Church, which were in great confusion, and passed the whole winter there. It was then that

Dec. 25, 800   he received the titles of Emperor and Augustus, to which he at first had such an aversion that he declared that he would not have set foot in the Church the day that they were conferred, although it was a great feast-day, if he could have foreseen the design of the Pope. He bore very patiently with the jealousy which the Roman emperors showed upon his assuming these titles, for they took this step very ill; and by dint of frequent embassies and letters, in which he addressed them as brothers, he made their haughtiness yield to his magnanimity, a quality in which he was unquestionably much their superior.

It was after he had received the imperial name that, finding the laws of his people very defective (the Franks have two sets of laws, very different in many particulars), he determined to add what was wanting, to reconcile the discrepancies, and to correct what was vicious and wrongly cited in them. However, he went no further in this matter than to supplement the laws by a few capitularies, and those imperfect ones; but he caused the unwritten laws of all the tribes that came under his rule to be compiled and reduced to writing. He also had the old rude songs that celebrate the deeds and wars of the ancient kings written out for transmission to posterity.

Einhard, *Life of Charlemagne* (1880), pp. 65–66, translated by Samuel Epes Turner.

FROM Life of Leo III

The faithful envoys of Charlemagne who had returned with the pope to Rome . . . spent more than a week examining those most evil malefactors to discover what crimes they could impute to the pope. Neither Pascal nor Campulus nor their followers found anything to say against him; so the aforementioned envoys seized them and sent them to France.

After a time the great king joined them in the basilica of the blessed apostle Peter and was received with great honor. He called together a council of

---

Vita Leonis III, in L. Duchesne, ed., *Le Liber Pontificalis,* II (1892), 6–8. Translated by Brian Tierney by permission of Editions E. de Boccard, Paris.

archbishops, bishops, abbots and of all the Frankish and Roman nobility. The great king and likewise the most blessed pontiff took their seats and made the most holy archbishops and abbots seat themselves while all the other priests and the Frankish and Roman nobles remained standing. This council was to investigate all the charges that had been made against the holy pontiff. When all the archbishops, bishops and abbots heard this they declared unanimously, "We do not dare to judge the apostolic see which is the head of all the churches of God, for we are all judged by it and its vicar, but it may be judged by no one according to ancient custom. Whatever the supreme pontiff decrees we will obey canonically." The venerable pontiff said, "I follow the footsteps of the pontiffs who were my predecessors. I am ready to clear myself of the false charges that have been basely made against me."

On a later day, in the same church of the blessed apostle Peter, when all were present, namely the archbishops, bishops, abbots, all the Franks who were in the service of the great king and all the Romans, the venerable pontiff mounted to the altar holding the four Gospels of Christ and in a clear voice declared under oath, "I have no knowledge of these false crimes which the Romans who have persecuted me have basely charged me with, nor any knowledge of having done such things." When this was done all the archbishops, bishops, abbots and all the clergy chanted litanies and gave praise to God and to our lady the ever-virgin Mary, Mother of God, and to the blessed apostle Peter, prince of the apostles and of all the saints of God.

After this, on the day of the nativity of our Lord Jesus Christ, all were again gathered together in the basilica of the blessed apostle Peter. And then the venerable holy pontiff with his own hands crowned Charles with a most precious crown. Then all the faithful Romans, seeing how he loved the holy Roman church and its vicar and how he defended them, cried out with one voice by the will of God and of St. Peter, the key-bearer of the kingdom of Heaven, "To Charles, most pious Augustus, crowned by God, great and peace-giving emperor, life and victory." This was proclaimed three times before the tomb of blessed Peter the apostle, with the invocation of many saints, and he was instituted by all as the emperor of the Romans. Then on that same day of the nativity of our Lord Jesus Christ the most holy bishop and pontiff anointed Charlemagne's most excellent son, Charles, as king, with holy oil.

After the celebration of Mass, the most serene lord emperor presented a silver table weighing . . . pounds with its legs. Likewise, at the tomb of the apostle of God, the emperor and his kingly sons and his daughters presented various vases of pure gold . . .

Afterward those iniquitous malefactors, namely Pascal and Campulus, and their followers were brought into the presence of the most pious lord emperor, with all the noble Franks and Romans standing around, and everyone agreed about the evil words and deeds of those men. Campulus then rebuked Pascal and said, "It was an evil hour for me when I saw your face, for you have put me in this present danger." And so, each condemning the other they made manifest their own guilt. When the most pious emperor realized how cruel and wicked they were he sent them into exile in France.

FROM Annals of Theophanis

In the same year [801] partisans of the Roman pope, Hadrian, of blessed memory, started a riot against Pope Leo and injured his eyesight. The men who were selected to put out his eyes were moved by pity and spared him, so that he was not completely blinded. Leo immediately fled to Charles, king of the Franks. The king took vengeance on the enemies of the pope and restored him to his seat. Thus at this time Rome fell into the hands of the Franks and continued thus. Leo repaid Charles by anointing him from head to foot with oil in the church of the blessed apostle, and, having saluted him with the title of *Imperator,* he crowned him. He also clothed him with the imperial robes and insignia. This happened on the 25th day of the month of December, in the ninth indiction.

F. Duncalf and A. C. Krey, *Parallel Source Problems in Medieval History* (Harper & Brothers, 1912), pp. 18–19. Reprinted by permission of Harper & Row, Publishers.

Charlemagne's behavior after the coronation provides important evidence about his attitude toward the new dignity. The following formulas of greeting from his charters show how he chose to designate himself at different times during his reign.

Charlemagne's Royal and Imperial Titles

April 1, 772   Charles, by the grace of God king of the Franks . . .

June 5, 774   Charles, by the grace of God king of the Franks and of the Lombards . . .

July 16, 774   Charles, by the grace of God king of the Franks and of the Lombards and patrician of the Romans . . . (This last title was regularly used until after the imperial coronation on December 25, 800.)

E. Mühlbacher, *Diplomatum Karolinorum I, Monumenta Germaniae Historiae* (1906), pp. 95, 116, 264, 265; and E. Dümmler, *Epistolae Variorum I, Monumenta Germaniae Historiae* (1895), p. 556; both translated by Brian Tierney.

March 4, 801   Charles, by the grace of God king of the Franks and of the Lombards and patrician of the Romans . . .

May 29, 801   Charles, most serene Augustus, crowned by God, great and pacific emperor governing the Roman empire who also, through the mercy of God, is king of the Franks and of the Lombards . . .

813   Charles, by divine grace emperor and Augustus and king of the Franks and of the Lombards . . .

4
SOME MODERN
ACCOUNTS
OF THE
CORONATION

C. Delisle Burns presented the imperial coronation as the climax of a political policy deliberately pursued by Charlemagne and his predecessors.

FROM The First Europe BY C. DELISLE BURNS

On Christmas Day, A.D. 800, Charles the Great, the king of the Franks, was crowned as Emperor and Augustus in the basilica of St. Peter in the Vatican by Pope Leo III. Each of the chief actors in this episode was playing a part. And in view of the later history of the Holy Roman Empire, which was supposed by some historians to have then come into existence, the parts make the play almost a comedy. But that is from the point of view of a much later age. At the time and throughout the Middle Ages, the majority of men who thought at all on such subjects, no doubt, seriously believed that Charles was a successor of the Emperor Augustus, and that the successor of St. Peter had the power to make him so.

* * *

C. Delisle Burns, *The First Europe*, pp. 569, 580–581, 587–588, 599–603, 609–611. Reprinted by permission of George Allen & Unwin Ltd., London.

THE POLICY OF THE CAROLINGIANS

The steps taken by those in control of social power, which led eventually to the crowning of Charles the Great, may be shortly described as follows. They are all connected with the three names—Charles Martel, Pippin his son, and Charles the Great his grandson. It is the story of the conquest of supreme power by a Frankish family, of its entanglement in Italian rivalries and of the final acceptance of a theocratic authority, as a method of preserving and extending military conquests. Conscious policy was that of barbarian warriors who could extend their power by armed force but found, as all barbarians are surprised to find, that they could not hold their conquests except by acquiring some moral authority.

Charles Martel, the illegitimate son of Pippin of Herstal, made his first bid for power at the age of twenty-five, on the death of his father (A.D. 714). His father had secured, at the end of interminable and confused struggles and treacheries, the power to control, as chief of the Palace, the king of the Franks. Charles Martel had to fight battles and employ the traditional treachery, in order to secure his power. But, with the assistance of the Frankish warriors who held land in Austrasia, and of those from Neustria who were discontented with the recent efforts to restore power to the king's Court (*palatium*), he contrived eventually to secure the greatest military power in the kingdom for himself. His control of Neustria or northern France compelled him to take account of the advance of the Saracens northwards from Spain; and in A.D. 732 he defeated the Saracen raiders in a great battle near Poitiers. This battle has been given by some historians an exaggerated importance. It is even said to have saved western Europe from becoming Mohammedan. But it seems likely, in fact, that the Saracen raiders defeated by Charles Martel were only seeking for loot and not for permanent conquest; and besides, the Saracen leaders were already divided among themselves before meeting the Frankish forces. Their dissensions may have largely contributed to their defeat.

For the future policy of the Frankish leaders, however, what was generally believed was more important than what actually occurred. It was believed that Charles Martel had defended the whole of western Christendom and defeated its chief enemies. Thus he became the instrument of God's will and the protector of the Faith against "infidels."

* * *

THE FRANKS IN ITALY

The next step in the formation of the imperial idea was taken by Pippin, the son of Charles Martel. The expedition against the Lombards in Italy, which Gregory III had asked Charles to undertake, was eventually led into Italy by

Pippin in A.D. 754; but not before the Pope, Stephen II, had travelled North to make intercession himself with Pippin. By this time Pippin had been already crowned and anointed by St. Boniface as king of the Franks; and the Pope himself again anointed Pippin and his two sons at the monastery of St. Denis on January 6, 754. In the early summer after an assembly of the Franks, at which the policy was opposed by Frankish nobles, Pippin advanced into Italy and laid siege to Pavia, the Lombard capital. The Pope returned to Rome in October of that year; and from this time the king of the Franks was addressed in papal letters as *Patricius Romanorum*.

* * *

THE ROMAN EMPIRE

In the year following the Council of Frankfurt, Pope Hadrian died and was succeeded by Leo III (A.D. 795–816). The new Pope at once sent an embassy to Charles the Great to announce his election and to present to him the keys of the "Confession" of St. Peter and the banner of the city of Rome. Leo evidently intended to carry on the policy of Hadrian. But events in Constantinople drastically altered the situation, at any rate in the minds of Charles and his advisers. In A.D. 797 the Emperor, Constantine VI, was blinded by order of his mother, who thrust him from the imperial throne and assumed supreme authority herself. Irene favoured the worship of images and was supported by the monks and most of the clergy in the East. She might, therefore, have expected support for her policy in the West. But evidently the violent deposition of an Emperor by his own mother and the assumption by a woman, for the first time in history, of supreme authority in the Roman Empire, caused consternation among those who followed public policy.

Two years later a still greater shock to sentiment in the North affected the situation. Pope Leo III, going in procession at the Greater Litanies, April 25, 799, was set upon by officials of the Roman Church, relatives of the late Pope, who beat him to the ground and attempted to tear out his eyes and tongue. They left him for dead. But his own friends rescued him; and he fled as a suppliant to Charles the Great at Paderborn. Charles received him with honour; and an elaborate poem by Angilbert, abbot of St. Riquier, describes the procession of Charles and his beautiful daughters and the splendid feast prepared for the Pope. The impression made by these events, in so far as it affected policy, is well expressed in a letter from Alcuin to Charles the Great, containing the following passage.

"There have been until now three persons who were highest in the world. That is, the Apostolic Sublimity which rules as Vicar the seat of St. Peter, Prince of the Apostles. And what has happened to him who was the holder of that seat, your respected kindness has informed me. Another is the Imperial Dignity, the secular power of the second Rome (Constantinople). How impiously the governor of that Empire has been deposed, not by foreigners but by those of his own household and city, is everywhere increasingly narrated. The third is the Kingly Dignity in which the dispensation of Our Lord Jesus Christ has placed you as ruler of the Christian people—a ruler superior in power to the other above-mentioned dignities, more noble in wisdom and higher in the dignity of rule. Lo, now on you alone rests the whole safety of the Churches of Christ—you are the avenger of crime; you are the ruler of the sinful; you are the comforter of those who weep and the exaltation of the virtuous."

It will be noticed that Alcuin does not suggest any change in the status or function of the king of the Franks. Indeed, he definitely makes a distinction between the imperial and the regal power, and treats the second as the instrument for the assistance of the Church and the Christian people. The use of the word *imperium* in an earlier letter of Alcuin to Charles indicates only the same sort of indefinite, superior authority as was intended by Bede when he wrote that the king of Kent had an *imperium* over eastern England. For Alcuin, Charles is always "King David" and not the Emperor Augustus. Thus, in a letter of A.D. 789 to Charles the Great, Alcuin writes: "May God grant eternal salvation and the glory of empire (*decus imperii*) to you, beloved David." Clearly "imperium," in this use, has no definite reference to the Roman Empire.

The same vague use of titles drawn from the ancient tradition before the actual coronation of Charles by Pope Leo, is to be found in the poem of Angilbert, referred to above, which describes the meeting of Charles the Great and the fugitive Pope Leo. In that poem Charles is referred to as "king, ruler, revered chief, augustus"; and some lines farther down as "head of the world, chief of Europe, hero and augustus." When, in the poet's imagination, the Pope appears to Charles in a dream, the phrase from Lucan's *Pharsalia* is used—"cold fear held the limbs of the Augustus." Clearly "augustus" was not intended to imply in any exact sense the traditional imperial authority. It was to Charles, as the great *king,* that his followers turned.

A Pope suppliant at the Court of a Frankish king, asking to be restored to his authority over his rebellious subjects, created a new situation, of which Charles was evidently not unwilling to take advantage. He sent the Pope back to Rome under the protection of Frankish armed forces and himself followed with his Court and retainers, reaching Rome on November 24, 800. For some weeks consultations or discussions of policy were carried on in Rome. The opponents of the Pope had charged him with perjury, adultery and other crimes; and had excused their violence as a legitimate rebellion against tyranny. The king of the Franks, who had restored the Pope and was now in control of the city of Rome, evidently could not altogether disregard the charges brought against Leo. But there was no attempt to set up any public court or council for a decision of the case; and on December 23, 800, in St. Peter's, in the presence of Charles and his warriors, the Pope swore a solemn oath rebutting all the charges against him. The Greek historian,

Theophanes, was in no doubt about the political situation thus established. He writes that then "for the first time the city of Rome came under the power of the Franks." And according to Einhard, on the same day on which the Pope's oath was sworn, Charles received an embassy from the patriarch of Jerusalem which brought to him the keys of the Sepulchre, as well as the keys and the banner of the city itself, then in control of the Mohammedans.

THE CORONATION

The play at this point reaches the scene in St. Peter's when Charles was crowned by the Pope; but so many different interpretations have been placed upon what occurred, that it may be well to state explicitly what explanation will be given below. In the view here maintained the coronation was arranged beforehand between the Pope and Charles, and was probably the outcome of the policy, not of the Pope but of Charles himself. Secondly, the ceremony was intended by Charles to indicate the assumption of a *title,* and not the establishment of an *institution*—still less the claim to control an ancient institution already in existence, the Roman Empire. Thirdly, the title was intended to add prestige to the king of the Franks in all his territories indeed but primarily to express his new position in relation to the Pope. It implied the recognition of a higher status than that of Patrician; and from the Pope's point of view, it expressed the assumption that the king of the Franks was the official protector of the papal territories.

What actually occurred in St. Peter's on Christmas Day A.D. 800 is described in four different documents, of which two at least contain accounts amended in view of the political effects of the coronation in later years. These two accounts are in the *Annales Laureshamenses* of about A.D. 803 and in the *Life of Charles* by Einhard, composed about twenty-five years after the event. But even the two more reliable accounts, one in the *Liber Pontificalis,* the other in the *Annals of the Kingdom of the Franks (Annales Laurissenses),* are affected by two different points of view—the former that of the Roman clergy, the latter that of the Frankish Court. Allowance must, therefore, be made for the elements of what would now be called "propaganda" in all the documents now available. Each writer of these documents was affected by the policy current in his circle and by the atmosphere of his time. It is childish to treat any record, however contemporary, as a colourless scientific formula.

The record in the *Liber Pontificalis,* which was probably written at the death of Leo III in A.D. 816, runs as follows: "After this [that is, after the ceremony of Leo's oath] on Christmas Day in the same basilica of St. Peter all were again gathered. And then the venerable and kindly bishop with his own hands crowned him with a precious crown. Then all the Roman faithful, seeing the great protection and love which he had for the Holy Roman Church and its Vicar, unanimously with a loud voice, at a sign from God and St. Peter the key-bearer of the Kingdom of Heaven, cried out—'To

Charles, the devout, Augustus, crowned by God, great and pacific Emperor, life and victory!' Before the holy Confession of St. Peter, the Apostle, invoking many saints, it was three times said; and by all he was constituted Emperor of the Romans."

The account in the Frankish *Annals* runs as follows: "On the holy day of Christmas when the king, at Mass before the Confession of St. Peter, rose from prayer, Pope Leo placed a crown on his head and the cry was raised by the whole Roman people—'To Charles, Augustus, crowned by God, great and pacific Emperor of the Romans, life and victory!' And after acclamations, he was adored by the Pope in the manner of the ancient princes; and, dropping the title Patrician, he was called Emperor and Augustus."

It seems clear from these straightforward accounts, first, that Charles was quite well aware of what the Pope was going to do; secondly, that the crowd in the basilica, euphemistically called "the whole Roman people," knew beforehand what to call out; and thirdly, that the ceremony indicated the adoption of a title, not the assertion of new powers. It is extremely doubtful whether anyone in St. Peter's on that day was thinking of the Roman Empire which had its capital at Constantinople; and indeed the Greek historian, Theophanes, mentions the event in the short phrase—"In this year Charles, the king of the Franks, was crowned by Pope Leo"—as if crowning were a habit in the West, of not much importance.

*   *   *

If anything more were needed to show that Charles the Great did not establish an Empire, and was not in anything but name an Emperor, a brief review of the actual situation in which he left Europe would be conclusive. There was no capital or permanent centre of administration and law. The old barbarian custom continued of moving the king's officials and retinue from villa to villa. It made no difference in practice that a villa or country residence of a king might be called a "palace" (*palatium*). Indeed, this use of the word is merely another sign of make-believe by which the central offices of ancient Rome on the Palatine Hill gave their name to any of the scattered houses of a barbarian chieftain. Again there was no central administration. The king's agents (*missi dominici*) were quite unable to control the counts or other local landowners who had established themselves in almost independent power over different districts. Worse still, there was no permanent armed force, either for internal order or for defence against foreign enemies. Charles the Great followed the old practice of summoning for an expedition as many armed men as he could collect in the early summer, and of allowing them to return to their scattered homes in the autumn. He did, indeed, attempt to establish small permanent outposts on his north-eastern frontier, manned by counts and their armed retainers; but that there was no single defensive system is proved by the number of expeditions the king had to make, to help these outposts. Finally, in the system established or rather continued under Charles the Great, there was none of that "providence" (*providentia*) with which the Emperor was credited under the old Roman system. He made no roads. His system of government did not require them. He conceived a plan of a canal between the Main and Danube; but when the work was begun, it was abandoned because the sides fell in, owing to the lack of competent workers. He repaired the old Roman harbour at Boulogne, but seems never to have grasped the need for new harbours, as a protection against the raids of the Northmen. He did, indeed, give money and land for the building and maintenance of churches and monasteries—which may be taken to correspond to the building of temples and public baths by the Roman Emperors; but the administration of what would now be called "social services" was in the hands of the clergy and not of the king or his counts.

In short, Charles the Great, stripped of the romances which adorned "Charlemagne," was simply a barbarian warrior of great energy, limited intelligence, no education and great simplicity of mind. Like Clovis, three hundred years before him, he believed that he could promote Christianity in the form familiar to him by killing some of those who had never heard of it and compelling the others to be baptized. He was intelligent enough to appreciate the services of scholars and to support their efforts for the promotion of learning and music among the clergy. His ambitions and ideals were those of a barbarian chieftain; and his leisure was spent in hunting and swimming. He was frugal in food and drink and clothing, but somewhat expansive in his affections. The number of his concubines and illegitimate children is not known; and he enjoyed having about him all his daughters. But in an age in which savage cruelty and reckless treachery were not uncommon, even at the Court of the Roman Emperor, which claimed to be the centre of civilized life, Charles the Great was exceptional in attracting faithful supporters and in exciting admiration for the power of his personality.

He was a sincere Christian, in one of the many different meanings of that word. His correspondence shows that he was interested in the peculiar habits of the moon, in the status of the Holy Ghost, in the restriction of the use of religious pictures and in the correct method of administering Baptism. He was not interested in the more subtle moral issues which perhaps would have seemed important to Paulinus of Nola or to St. Boniface. He is said by Einhard to have listened with attention to the reading of St. Augustine's *City of God* and to have kept a writing tablet under his pillow at night, in order to practice writing the alphabet, which he never succeeded in doing. He spoke usually his own Germanic dialect but could speak Latin also fluently; and he understood Greek, although he could not speak it. He extended the dominions which Frankish warriors and churchmen controlled; but he left them so badly organized that soon after his death they were continually troubled by civil war and so badly defended that they were raided year after year by the Northmen and by the Saracens.

Karl Heldmann emphasized the role of Pope Leo III.

FROM The Empire of Charles the Great
BY KARL HELDMANN

Leo's oath of December 23, 800, had formally vindicated the pope—that meant that his opponents were placed formally in the wrong by virtue of his action. For every true son of the Church, and for Charles too, their guilt was thereby made clear in a legal sense. The tables were now turned: legal proceedings now not only could but indeed had to be directed against them. With these one could proceed properly only according to the precedents of the Roman law. Only now for the first time did the pope find himself in a position to raise a formal accusation against his opponents. This charge cited them as traitors.

In the writings concerning the problem the statement is often made that the sentencing of the opponents of Leo III followed immediately after the purification oath. But this is not correct. Between the two events lay the imperial coronation. And that is decisive. There can be no doubt about it. Since the imperial coronation cannot be explained in any other way, as my earlier investigations hoped to demonstrate, then it belongs organizationally to the sphere of this trial and is to be understood in the context of this trial.

The purification oath of Leo, in itself, had cleared the way for a criminal procedure against the conspirators. Any independent intervention of the pope or the king-*patricius* into such a procedure would—as things stood before December 25, 800—have signified not only a complete break with the legal traditions and order of Rome, would not only have upset the entire legal system of Rome, but also would have openly sharpened the political opposition and hatred against Leo to the extreme, and furthermore would have extended that feeling to Charles. Could either of them have allowed such a state of affairs to exist? According to the Roman law observed in Rome the urban prefect alone was able to conduct a legal criminal action. Of him, however, there is no mention in any source. Why not? This question has been answered in different ways . . . [and] none of these conjectures can be opposed or confirmed with certainty. But that is clearly not the point. For the essential consideration is something entirely different. . . .

A suitable pronouncement of judgment by the urban prefect—supposing

Karl Heldmann, *Das Kaisertum Karls des Grossen: Theorien und Wirklichkeit* (1928), translated by R. E. Sullivan in *The Coronation of Charlemagne* (1959), pp. 67–69. Reprinted by permission of D. C. Heath and Company and Hermann Böhlaus Nachfolger, Weimar.

the office was occupied at the time—would not necessarily have ended the struggle. For from his sentence the way was open for an appeal by the defeated party to the emperor: only the emperor's sentence was absolutely final. Furthermore: if the prefect refused [to judge the case in favor of the pope], if he himself perhaps belonged to the conspirators—which we do not know for certain—then only the direct judicial power of the emperor could intervene and the urban prefect himself could not be brought to account except by the emperor and his council of state, as was the case with all holders of the highest imperial offices. Thirdly, however, just at that time the legal organization not only of Rome but also of the empire in general was tottering, threatened most seriously at an unprecedented place in its basic structure, the emperorship, because after the overthrow and death of the Emperor Constantine VI (797), for the first time since the empire had arisen, a woman wielded the scepter of the Caesars with full sovereignty. It is of little consequence how Irene herself had laid her plans to cover up this political anomaly or to what extent the Eastern Empire under the pressure of force endured her overlordship as legitimate. But how did the West and especially Rome come to terms with the new situation? This is decisive for our question. . . . That the imperial urban prefect and the whole administration of justice in Rome could do without an emperor who was recognized on a sound basis, indeed, that anyone can doubt that an urban prefect was authorized to exercise his office at all without the authorization of the emperor needs no further argument after all the previous discussion.

As a result Leo III was in a difficult position. His purification oath had legally cleared him personally, but his position in Rome was still in no way "secure." From a juridical standpoint the possibility of a proper and final conclusion of the treason trial in his favor was completely uncertain as long as the question of the imperial throne, made acute by the *coup d'état* of Irene, appeared not to have been resolved beyond any doubt. From a political standpoint it was absolutely hazardous for the pope to appeal the decision of his dispute, from which the king-*patricius* Charles had to stand apart, to the imperial court in Constantinople which alone was competent to handle it, if on top of everything else, his enemies were in some way associated with the imperial party.

Out of this dilemma arose the new imperial project, built upon the *patricius* Charles. Who it was that brought the project up first we do not know. In any case its agent was none other than Leo III personally, and of him we shall speak as the father of the plan. It was the guarantee through which he could secure a proper and final settlement of the treason trial, favorable to his wishes; it was the political move by means of which he, after his own purification oath of December 23, intended to prepare an absolutely certain method in the form of a criminal procedure to bring about a quick and full defeat of his opponents in Rome, without first having to make juridically and politically precarious evasions with respect to Constantinople. The *patricius* Charles once established as emperor offered a way for the pope not merely to replace a sometimes lacking supreme judge, i.e., the imperial urban prefect, but also to place once again beyond a doubt and on a legitimate basis the whole legal system of Rome and imperial Italy, at least over against the doubtful right of Irene to rule.

This was the real motive which led to the coronation act of December 25, to the elevation of Charles, the king of the Franks and the Lombards and the *patricius* of the Romans, to the rank of emperor of the Romans. It was not the wish to sanction formally an outwardly already far developed separation of Rome from the Roman Empire and to establish in place of that Empire a legal supremacy of the Frankish king over Rome that supplied Leo with the imperial concept; rather it was the compelling need to bring into existence, at all costs as quickly and with as little risk as possible, a lord established on the basis of the Roman Empire and its legal organization who would have supreme authority over his opponents in Rome. Not the romantic spell of universal empire nor thankful respect for the truest son of the Roman Church created the emperorship of Charles the Great, but a sober political consideration of a purely local, yes, even purely personal kind.

Also the fact that such an intent fits in with actual historical events can be proved clearly. After the Mass Charles dedicated to St. Peter a silver table and along with his sons and daughters some golden vases, but this was not his first action in his official capacity as emperor: as simply *patricius*-king he would have brought his offerings there to the church too, especially after the (previously prepared for) coronation of his son Charles as king. The first official action of the new emperor and sovereign of Rome was not "an act of grace" but rather [his assumption of authority in seeing to] the continuation and the conclusion of the undecided quarrel between the pope and his opponents in the form of a criminal procedure against the latter. Whatever might have been the situation in that day with regard to the urban prefect, with an emperor at hand his powers no longer had any bearing on the question. The absolute and highest ranking court was now at hand. "A few days" after Christmas the new emperor took up the proceedings against Leo's opponents. They were subjected to "a severe questioning according to the Roman law" and "sentenced to death as traitors," but that sentence, on the request of the pope, was changed to exile into Francia. . . . Only after the death of their enemy Leo (May 25, 816) and the trip of his successor, Stephen IV (June 22, 816; died, Jan. 24, 817), to the imperial camp of Louis the Pious were they relieved from exile and their return to their homeland made possible.

Francis Ganshof maintained that the Frankish court, not Charlemagne himself or Pope Leo, planned the coronation.

FROM The Imperial Coronation of Charlemagne
BY FRANCIS GANSHOF

It seems to me that in order to understand Charlemagne's accession to the imperial dignity, we must go back to Alcuin's chief concern. The famous abbot of Saint-Martin de Tours, whose intimacy of thought with his royal protector is well known, was between 796 and 799 full of anxiety concerning the Church. The storm caused by the conflict about the worshipping of the sacred images had only just calmed down; abuses dishonoured the clergy; in Saxony resistance to Christianity was still active; hesitations and misunderstandings threatened to imperil the evangelisation of the Danubian countries and above all the adoptionist heresy preached by Elipand of Toledo and Felix of Urgel was gravely menacing the purity of faith in the West.

In May 799 arrived the news of the criminal attempt against pope Leo III: to Alcuin, deeply devoted to the Holy See, it was the scandal of scandals.

As has been noticed, it is in the midst of these anxious days that, about the year 798, the expression *Imperium Christianum*—"the Christian empire"—appears in Alcuin's correspondence; it was frequently used by him up to 801/802. He used it when writing to Charlemagne and to his friend Arn, archbishop of Salzburg.

That "Christian empire" is the whole of the territories submitted to Charlemagne's authority and inhabited by the *populus christianus,* which is the community of Christians spiritually dependent on Rome. Charles's task is to govern, defend and enlarge it and closely linked with these obligations is his duty to protect Faith and Church. It is in the letters where he most insistently implores Charlemagne to take measures against the adoptionist heresy or to re-establish the pope in his authority, that Alcuin uses these expressions.

It seems to me quite unquestionable that we are here in the presence of an obvious indication.

Charles is master of almost the whole Western Christendom and Rome itself is subject to his protectorate. He is more than a king; his states form a whole which may well deserve to be qualified "empire": the underlying idea is that Charlemagne must be emperor.

When Alcuin begs him to interfere in favour of Leo III he shows him the

Francis Ganshof, *The Imperial Coronation of Charlemagne* (1949), pp. 13–28. Reprinted by permission of Jackson Son and Co. (Booksellers) Ltd., Glasgow.

Holy See humiliated, the imperial throne in Byzantium vacant, and he proclaims that on Charles, the king of the Franks, chief of the "christian folk," rests the safeguarding of the Church's highest interests.

That character of guardian of the faith, protector of the church, was precisely the one which ecclesiastical tradition attributed—indeed quite arbitrarily —to the Roman emperor; Gregory the Great, in whose writings Alcuin had been steeped, is categorical in this respect. In the eyes of Alcuin it appeared a necessity for the sake of the Church that there should be an emperor, successor of the Christian Roman emperors, who would end the scandals and above all prevent new ones.

If Alcuin has expressed these ideas with particular force, he certainly was not the only one to think as he did. It would be strange if Arn, one of his most faithful correspondents, had had no notion of the kind. We have reason to believe that another of his correspondents, Angilbert, abbot of Saint-Riquier and familiar of Charlemagne as well as declared lover of one of his daughters, shared the same ideas.

We must also remember the insertion in certain liturgical prayers of the name of the king of the Franks next to that of the emperor, and of the *Regnum Francorum* next to the *Imperium Romanum,* and their association in the defence of the Christian world against pagans and in the maintenance of peace. In *Francia* towards the end of the VIIIth century these prayers must have familiarized many a cleric with the idea that the actual power of their king and the way in which he used it, fitted in rather well with the tasks appointed to the imperial institution.

Did Alcuin and the other "imperialists" succeed in convincing Charlemagne of their views? It certainly was a hard task. In the first place because other duties may have appeared to him more urgent than to go to Rome in order to settle the affairs of the papacy. It was difficult also because Charlemagne seems to have been prejudiced against the imperial title; he might even have felt some aversion from it. Finally because Charlemagne, in spite of his appetite for learning, lacked intellectual culture and most likely did not thoroughly grasp what Alcuin and his people meant by the imperial dignity —a notion which required some slight knowledge of history and theology, even if unsophisticated, and some capacity of abstraction.

And yet Charlemagne decided to go the way that, according to me, had been pointed to him.

At the end of the year 799, when Arn had imparted to Alcuin the charges levied against the pope and the anxiety then prevailing in Rome, the necessity for a personal intervention by Charles and for a restoration in Western Europe of the imperial power proved itself even more urgent than ever.

It is most likely during the stay of Charlemagne in Tours, in the spring of the year 800, and during his own stay at the palace of Aachen in June on the occasion of the council that compelled the heresiarch Felix to abjure adoptionism, that Alcuin managed to convince the king. Perhaps he succeeded by using the "hegemoniac" notion of the empire, the very vast kingdom which was not contained by rigorous frontiers: these notions were familiar to the Anglo-Saxon Alcuin and they might have been accessible to the realistic mind of Charlemagne, mostly impressed by reasons of power.

Charlemagne started for Italy some time after the assembly of Mainz, which took place in August. I think that I have shown elsewhere that at the end of summer or at the beginning of autumn, Alcuin knew that this expedition must lead to the restoration of the imperial dignity in favour of his master.

How did things happen in Rome?

The pope whom Charlemagne had re-established on his throne was surrounded by enemies and soon was compelled to clear himself publicly of the accusations brought forward against him. He was but a toy in the hands of the Frankish king and of his counsellors. He would certainly not have been in a position to oppose the realisation of a scheme which Charlemagne had adopted. His interests moreover were quite different: he might well believe that an emperor would efficiently protect him, and besides, he had always been compliant towards Charles. He might also have found pleasure in removing any suggestion of subordination to Byzantium. One must admit that Leo III showed himself quite willing to take his share in the events.

The leading part belongs, according to me, to a few Frankish clerics of the royal circle, namely, I take it, to Arn and to Alcuin's confidential agents, whom he had sent to Rome: Whitto-Candidus, Fridugisus-Nathanael and other monks of Saint-Martin de Tours. Thanks to their interference, the ideals of Alcuin and of the other "imperialist clerics" won the day.

They sat together in the council with other ecclesiastics; Frankish, Lombard and Roman. There were very strenuous debates, which resulted in the oath by which on December 23rd the pope justified himself. After this on the same day, the council and "the whole christian folk"—that is to say, the Franks and the Lombards as well as the Romans—decided that Charlemagne must be made emperor. Was not the imperial throne occupied by a criminal woman, vacant? Were not Rome—capital of the Caesars—Italy, Gaul and Germany in his possession? Charlemagne accepted.

The imperial dignity for Western Europe had been restored in his favour on that very day.

There only remained the ceremony at which this was to be celebrated.

On December 25th at St. Peter's, according to the rules that were known in Rome, but which the king and the Franks ignored and did not care about, Charles was regularly elected by the "Roman people" expressing their will by the way of ritual acclamations. But before these had sounded, the pope had himself crowned the new emperor. Like many weak characters, Leo III had played a crooked game. Through his gesture which could be understood as a symbolic livery—as a *traditio*—he had given the impression that it was he who had invested Charlemagne with the imperial dignity.

There lies, in my opinion, the reason of the great displeasure shown by Charlemagne, the reason for which he hesitated during several months to adorn himself with the imperial title in his diplomas and for which he refused to adopt the one which had appeared in the acclamations: *imperator Romanorum.*

He did not wish to seem as if he held his empire from the pope and especially not from a pope who owed him so much and had taken him now by a kind of treachery. When in the palace church of Aachen, on September 11th, 813, he himself crowned his son Louis emperor—or perhaps ordered him to take the crown from the altar and to put it on his head—without any interference of either pope or clergy, he showed how to his liking things should have taken place on December 25th, 800.

There is no doubt to me that Charlemagne has been considered, and has considered himself, as a Roman emperor, the successor of the Christian Roman emperors, of Constantine the Great and his heirs. His authority however, extended over territories of which some, like the greater part of his possessions beyond the Rhine, had not been part of the *Imperium Romanum.* Because it was for all the territories over which his power extended that he had become emperor, it is all his subjects that in the year 802 had to take an oath of allegiance to him in his capacity of emperor. This did not prevent him from keeping his titles of king of the Franks and of the Lombards; these titles alone were significant of a real political power.

Did he, in the year 800, also become emperor of the countries submitted to the Basileus of Byzantium? One might have admitted it all the more so as one of the reasons put forward in favour of his elevation to his new dignity was the vacancy in the imperial throne. Perhaps for a while in the East, such an attempt by him seemed possible. But he himself does not appear to have contemplated such a thing.

His empire was a Western Christian and Roman empire and on the day on which he could, in the year 812, constrain the emperor of Byzantium to recognise his new imperial dignity, the notion of empire ceased to be one of unique and universal authority.

Through most of the eighth century a theological dispute over "iconoclasm" divided the Greek and Roman churches. The iconoclasts at Constantinople rejected the practice of venerating images; the Roman church approved it. Charlemagne, in spite of his regard for the papacy, sympathised with the iconoclastic position. In 787 the queen regent at Constantinople, Irene, declared in favor of the Roman doctrine, and in 797 she deposed her son and illegitimately assumed sole power.

Emphasizing these circumstances, Werner Ohnsorge presented the coronation in Rome as an attempt by the papacy to free itself once and for all from Eastern Roman authority by making Charlemagne—against his own will—a "universal" Roman emperor.

FROM The Problem of Two Emperors in the Early Middle Ages BY WERNER OHNSORGE

Then the fact that Charles' wife died in the summer of 800 gave to the papacy the impulse to try an audacious secret plan to proclaim Charles as universal emperor of the Romans against his will and to establish through a marriage between Charles and Irene a new western emperorship in place of the existing eastern one. What strengthened the curia in its belief in its ability to carry through its project were certain tendencies in the Frankish court circle, which, because it was influenced by older Saxon and Anglo-Saxon concepts of sovereignty, was inclined to designate Charles in a rather perfunctory way [without bothering about legal formalities] as (Roman) world emperor. Furthermore, as already mentioned, there was the old religious tradition in the West of equating the "Imperium Romanum," the Roman Empire, with the "Imperium Christianum," the Christian world empire; by virtue of the Christian belief of Charles and his veneration for St. Peter this concept was of compelling importance. The papal curia could also understand from the fact that . . . Charles had adopted a gold seal modeled on the Byzantine style for his royal documents [to be used] along with the usual wax seal and that he had taken over the dating method of the so-called Greek indication for Frankish royal documents, that—in spite of the Franks' aversion in principle to the imperial concept—the Graeco-Roman court always stood as an object of comparison, an example, and a spur behind Charles' concept of kingship.

The papacy prepared its action in all secrecy. For the settlement of a conflict in the city of Rome, in which the pope was involved, Charles had in December, 800, come to Rome. . . . On Christmas day the son of Charles was to be anointed king according to previously arranged plans. Then before this anointment took place Leo III surprised Charles by placing on his head a crown and acclaiming him emperor. The world had a new Roman emperor who through the acclamation of the people, the Senate, and the warriors had been installed in a proper fashion in Irene's place, whose right to hold the imperial power was denied.

The coronation of Charles as emperor, i.e., the replacement of the Roman emperorship of the East with a new Roman emperorship in the West, was

Werner Ohnsorge, *Das Zweikaiserproblem in früheren Mittelalter* (1947), translated by R. E. Sullivan in *The Coronation of Charlemagne* (1959), pp. 84–89. Reprinted by permission of D. C. Heath and Company and August Lax, Hildesheim.

the consequence of a development dating back to the original empire. The political world up to this time had known merely one empire, the Roman Empire, whether it was officially designated as this or not. . . . Charles himself was on December 25, 800, called to be emperor and by virtue of that he was Roman emperor. There was no concept of emperor apart from Rome before 800 nor even before 812. . . .

It was completely clear to Charles that there were only two alternatives. The Roman emperorship could exist only as entity either if it were kept in Byzantium as at that time or if it were once again transferred from the East to the West, as it had at another time been transferred by Constantine the Great from the West to the East. But the papacy had taken this transferral into its own hands, from which it might be concluded that just as the transferral met the needs of the West, in view of the world political situation, so also had the curia at the same time made certain of its superiority over the new imperial regime which it had shaped. The coronation of Charles must appear as an organizational formalization of the . . . developing process of union between the Carolingians and the papacy, which had begun in 752 with papal approval of the transfer of the Frankish crown to Pepin.

The research of the last decades . . . has denied the universal character of the imperial coronation and has sought to explain it merely as the by-product of a particular historical moment in connection with the conflicts of the papacy in Roman politics. Certainly, reservations have rightly had to be raised against this modern position: it runs contrary to the line of development of papal policy, especially in the second half of the eighth century. In addition [*the argument raised against—B. T.*] the universalist position rests on a narrow interpretation almost always used in the last few years, yet a completely one-sided one, of the chief source concerning the coronation of the emperor, the *Vita Karoli* of Einhard, . . . an interpretation which says that although Charles actually denied the form in which Leo III had carried through the coronation on December 25, 800, he still did not stand unconditionally opposed to the imperial idea itself. It still is stated . . . clearly and unequivocally by Einhard, Charles' trusted biographer, that Charles so strongly disliked the "word," that is, the imperial title, that he would not have sought out the court of Peter, in spite of the great feast day, had he known beforehand that the pope planned his coronation as emperor. It accordingly remains certain, and this is reinforced by the surviving legal documents, chiefly the protocol of the diplomas of the winter of 800–801, that Charles did not want to be emperor on Christmas day 800; between the Charles of the *Libri karolini* and the Charles of December 25, 800, there was no difference; and in addition it is still certain that it was not just the form of the coronation as such that was extraordinarily painful and unacceptable to the great Frank.

Charles saw at once that the pope had played him against Irene and that this signified the end of the peaceful relations with Byzantium that had been established during the last years of the eighth century and could lead to unforeseen political developments. It signified further that the papal curia had forced him into the acceptance of a dignity which Charles in his whole inner course of development had proudly and consciously denied. He was the king of the Franks, filled with a sense of the greatness of his people, for whom he would provide a world position comparable to that possessed by the emperor in the East, who for all that was only a king as Charles himself was. Now this Roman imperial dignity had been imposed on him in a sanctified place which excluded any immediate resistance, by an act of the pope performed publicly and in a solemn fashion and not to be undone by subsequent protest; all of which he detested. Einhard knew why he designated his master only as king until his death, and it is not accidental that the chief wax seal of Charles, which bore only the inscription: "Christe, protege Carolum regem Francorum" [Christ, protect Charles, king of the Franks], was used from 772 to 813, even during the imperial period and was not replaced by a special imperial seal. Charles felt himself to be king of the Franks and wished only for the greatness of his Frankish people; all things Roman were indifferent to him, if not hated.

Step by step in the course of the winter of 800–801 the papal curia through tedious negotiations had subsequently won Charles over to its project. We can follow the steps. A few days passed [after the coronation] before Charles decided to make use of [his new power under] the Roman law in settling the difficulties in the city of Rome. With that step the papacy had already won a victory in principle: Charles had recognized on practical political grounds the necessity for assuming the Roman tradition. But still he thought it might be possible to champion Roman concepts without bearing the imperial title. For some months he had resisted the acceptance of the imperial title in his official documents; for a while in March 801 he believed that he had reached the same end [of exercising legal authority in Rome] when he consented to the honor of being named consul. For the first time in May 801 he finally acknowledged his acceptance of the imperial title through the suitable change of the protocol of his documents.

Very significant as a reflection of Charles' inner opposition is how this title [of May 801] was formed. In the first place he took over the words "Augustus . . . Imperator." So far this was the title of the Roman emperor, but Charles depreciated that title at the same moment to a certain extent by adding to it in a completely unusual way the words: "Romanum gubernans Imperium" [governing the Roman Empire]. The expression "Romanum gubernans Imperium" has, as has long been known, a double meaning. It can signify the Roman Empire as well as the territory of the city of Rome. Research has decided chiefly in favor of the last-named interpretation. But this is clearly not possible, since the words "Romanum gubernans Imperium" are absent in the last expression of Charles' title in the year 813. Charles had not at that time given up his authority over Rome, but rather, as will be shown, [had given up] the Roman emperorship. . . . The words "Romanum gubernans Imperium" thus mean "he who rules the Roman Empire." If this qualifying addition to the words: "Augustus . . . Imperator" in the imperial title, is not a senseless tautology, then at that time [May 801] Charles by this means instinctively distinguished an absolute emperorship from a Roman emperorship; on the basis of the latter he possessed the former. Then he added to the foregoing the title "King of the Franks and Lombards," so that the new title in its full expression with all additions read: "Karolus serenissimus augustus a Deo coronatus magnus pacificus imperator, Romanum gubernans imperium, qui et per misericordiam Dei rex Francorum et Langobardorum" [Charles, the most serene Augustus crowned by God the great pacific emperor, governing the Roman Empire, who through the mercy of God is king of the Franks and Lombards]. This imperial title of Charles was the product of intensive thought, built up, as can be proved, out of older title forms originating in the Frankish realm. It represented an attempt to de-romanize as far as possible the Roman imperial title, which Charles had had to accept under the pressure of the situation, and it already aimed toward shaping an imperial concept which would be independent of Rome without, however, actually being able to realize such a Roman-free imperial concept at this time. What we know about the political reforms made by Charles during the rest of his life is only further proof of the correctness of the explanation of the form of his title of 801 as we have expounded it. Also in the years during which Charles had to acknowledge the Roman emperorship against his will, he never denied his basically purely Frankish position.

Evidently the papal curia was able to convince Charles that at that time [in 801] the struggle for world prestige would be decided on the basis of the Roman imperial concept. The experiment of the *Libri karolini* had been an attempt [to raise the Franks to a supreme position] by unsuitable means. [The curia must have argued] that only by making the decision to continue the Roman tradition would Charles be able to obtain for his Franks the portion of universal power which they deserved.

Along with the political motive there was another one which up to now has not been recognized: a Christian-religious motive. . . . There was no reason why the curia should now hold back with the already noted marriage project . . . ; if in a sense the curia intended to replace the eastern emperorship with a new western one, in that case the change could have been brought to completion through a marriage of Charles with Irene. If from the following events the surprising fact emerges that this project found strong acceptance with Charles, still the motive of the Frank was quite different from that of the curia. A marriage was forbidden from Charles' viewpoint as long as Irene held fast to the worship of the idols. But was it not perhaps possible for Irene to return to her original iconoclastic position? Charles could consider himself a good servant of Christ if through his person he united the East and the West around a dogmatic position sanctioned by the Franks and accepted by them as the only correct one. That this concept did not coincide with papal ideas was for the curia provoking, but for the moment the papacy was willing on the whole to take it into the bargain considering what was at stake. The repeatedly disputed fact . . . that Charles after 801 embraced the universal imperial title merely to please the curia but against his own will, without in any way denying by that act his purely Frankish position, this fact is proved by Charles' position in the marriage affair.

When Charles departed in the spring of 801 from Rome, the pope could feel sure that he who had been newly crowned by the pope would not lay aside his crown. But Charles had declined to take any kind of initiative against the Eastern Romans. It was still in no way clear whether developments could really follow the direction wished by the papacy, and that a western emperorship could be established effectively in place of the eastern. There was the possibility that the East would simply overlook the development in the West; whereupon the imperial problem would become a problem of two emperors, especially inasmuch as Charles would not decide to proceed against Byzantium. First it had to be seen what attitude would be taken by the East. It has been maintained rightly that Charles after his return to Germany had given serious thought to the whole complex question: contrary to custom he remained in his imperial palace at Aachen and undertook no military expeditions. He demanded a new oath of loyalty from his subjects to him as emperor. He issued a new coin, stamped uniformly for his whole empire with a picture of his head. He introduced finally . . . a new form of imperial document, in which in place of the use of the actual signature of the ruler to complete the document there was employed the Eastern Roman form of imperial document in which the chancellor's signature, done in red ink, replaced the ruler's signature.

In 802 Irene's legates finally appeared at the Frankish court at Aachen, since Byzantium was interested in finding out how things stood with the new imperial usurper in the West, who now continued the line of earlier Roman emperors raised to power in the West, but who surprisingly made no threat to come to Constantinople and make good his rights with the sword. As a result of the wide reverberations of the political relationship of Charles with the caliph Harun-al-Rachid the political position of Charles had to be considered in the East at least as a cause for anxiety and especially was it to be feared that Charles would attack Sicily. The negotiations [of 802] must have been conducted in a friendly sense. The result was that an embassy of Charles, accompanied by papal legates, went to Constantinople and there set before Irene the marriage project. We know that this was synonymous with a demand for a change in the East from the veneration of the idols to iconoclasm. Also Charles would never have yielded to Eastern Roman custom in order to take up residence in Constantinople. . . . The movement of Irene to the West had to be accepted as the second condition for the marriage. It is very remarkable that in spite of these decisive stipulations . . . Irene reacted positively to the offer of the West. It seemed as if the papacy had comprehended the world political situation correctly, and that in the Roman emperorship it was as if its removal from the East could be brought about through the West.

It was, as far as we can establish, these two stipulations of Charles which brought about the fall of Irene. To the circle on which Irene had depended for protection after her return to the veneration of images, the thought of a reaction was intolerable. The western policy of Irene contained the seeds of her fall.

The Greek legates of her successor, the emperor Nicephorus, who appeared in 803 in Salz in Thuringia at the court of Charles in the company of the returning German negotiators, presented to the West a wholly new situation. Byzantium now had no intention of bowing before the West in any way. The new emperor in the East had been legally enthroned; he repudiated his western rival simply as a usurper. It has been pointed out correctly that the discussions at Salz as well as the letters which the Greeks brought with them must have been not very friendly. A completely changed position had developed: papal theories had been false, and the problem of two emperors had now arisen.

The question was now whether Charles would in the future force the course of events to follow the line desired by the curia, or whether this would be for him the occasion to take a course opposed to what the pope expected and so to seek now an independent political policy.

In the place of a universalist solution to the question of prominence [for the Franks in the] world Charles established a solution of equality, which basically corresponded to what he had stood for in the *Libri karolini* and had already striven for through the marriage of Rotrude. The path to a world emperorship [to be established] in the place of Eastern Rome, along which the papal curia had led him basically against his own will, had proved an impossible course. With a greater energy he now set himself to gain acceptance for his Franks as a power equal to Byzantium.

* * *

The first offer for a peaceful co-existence of the western and eastern emperors, which Charles had directed from Salz to Nicephorus, Byzantium passed over with disrespect. Years of war with Byzantium followed, fought in Italy by Charles' son Pepin. Political conditions in the East finally made it appear desirable for Constantinople to bring to an end the conflict in the West. A legate was sent to Pepin, who was no longer living, but the legate was sent on by the Franks to the court at Aachen. Charles himself was in no way inclined to war with Byzantium, but concerned himself only with striving for equality of rights in the realm of world politics. The leader of this Greek legation, Arsaphios, whose fitness was expressly attested by Charles, was a man of the greatest political capabilities. He recognized that Charles' emperorship had no universal, imperialistic tendencies, that Charles was in his way the king of the Franks and really wanted nothing more. . . . Charles' emperorship was only an "exalted kingship," an emperorship in title: that is what at that time became clear to the Greek negotiator. He reported in this sense to Byzantium. The result was that Constantinople decided in 812 to make a virtue of necessity, and through an official act the Byzantine legate in Aachen recognized

Charles as the spiritual "brother" of the Byzantines and of the emperor-basileus instead of the previously used "son"—he is the "emperor of the Franks," as [the Byzantine historian] Theophanes says. Political practice rendered necessary the introduction in Byzantium of a new imperial concept for Charles, which was in effect to consider him simply an exalted king. . . . While the eastern ruler up until 812 was designated sometimes simply as "emperor," and sometimes as "Roman emperor," henceforth "Roman emperor" always appeared on the coins and in all of the diplomatic designations, as a conscious expression of the claims of the East for its world emperorship —over against the new Frankish "emperor." Thus Byzantium had in no way departed from its ideology; it had merely introduced into the order of its designations for crowned rulers under the world emperor in Constantinople a special designation for the Frankish king.

Very much stronger was the ideological influence which Byzantium exercised on Charles in a reverse sense. We do not know what the decisive influential event had been for Charles . . . [but] in any case at the end of his life Charles recognized in the Byzantine emperorship a power which was in his eyes basically nothing more than an exalted kingship, whose rulers took the (Roman) imperial title only as a name, and which therefore could serve as a prototype and model for the creation of a native Frankish emperorship which in its internal characteristics had very little more to do with Roman concepts than it did with the Greek.

5
IMPERIAL
GOVERNMENT
AFTER THE
CORONATION

The General Capitulary of 802 was a decree regulating the government of Charlemagne's realm.

FROM General Capitulary of 802

1. Concerning the embassy sent out by the lord emperor. Therefore, the most serene and most Christian lord emperor Charles has chosen from his nobles the wisest and most prudent men, both archbishops and some of the other bishops also, and venerable abbots and pious laymen, and has sent them throughout his whole kingdom, and through them by all the following chapters has allowed men to live in accordance with the correct law. Moreover, where anything which is not right and just has been enacted in the law, he has ordered them to inquire into this most diligently and to inform him of it; he desires, God granting, to reform it. And let no one, through his cleverness or astuteness, dare to oppose or thwart the written law, as many are wont to do, or the judicial sentence passed upon him, or to do injury to the churches of God or the poor or the widows or the wards or any Christian. But all shall live entirely in accordance with God's precept, justly and under a just rule, and each one shall be admonished to live in harmony with his fellows in his business or profession; the canonical clergy ought to observe in every respect a canonical life without heeding base gain, nuns ought to keep diligent watch

University of Pennsylvania Translations and Reprints, VI, No. 5 (1900), 16–27, translated by D. C. Munro.

over their lives, laymen and the secular clergy ought rightly to observe their laws without malicious fraud, and all ought to live in mutual charity and perfect peace. And let the *missi* [*traveling agents of the king—B. T.*] themselves make a diligent investigation whenever any man claims that an injustice has been done to him by any one, just as they desire to deserve the grace of omnipotent God and to keep their fidelity promised to Him, so that entirely in all cases everywhere, in accordance with the will and fear of God, they shall administer the law fully and justly in the case of the holy churches of God and of the poor, of wards and widows and of the whole people. And if there shall be anything of such a nature that they, together with the provincial counts, are not able of themselves to correct it and to do justice concerning it, they shall, without any ambiguity, refer this, together with their reports, to the judgment of the emperor; and the straight path of justice shall not be impeded by any one on account of flattery or gifts from any one, or on account of any relationship, or from fear of the powerful.

2. Concerning the fidelity to be promised to the lord emperor. And he commanded that every man in his whole kingdom, whether ecclesiastic or layman, and each one according to his vow and occupation, should now promise to him as emperor the fidelity which he had previously promised to him as king; and all of those who had not yet made that promise should do likewise, down to those who were twelve years old. And that it shall be announced to all in public, so that each one might know, how great and how many things are comprehended in that oath; not merely, as many have thought hitherto, fidelity to the lord emperor as regards his life, and not introducing any enemy into his kingdom out of enmity, and not consenting to or concealing another's faithlessness to him; but that all may know that this oath contains in itself this meaning:

3. First, that each one voluntarily shall strive, in accordance with his knowledge and ability, to live wholly in the holy service of God in accordance with the precept of God and in accordance with his own promise, because the lord emperor is unable to give to all individually the necessary care and discipline.

4. Secondly, that no man, either through perjury or any other wile or fraud, on account of the flattery or gift of any one, shall refuse to give back or dare to abstract or conceal a serf of the lord emperor or a district or land or anything that belongs to him; and that no one shall presume, through perjury or other wile, to conceal or abstract his fugitive fiscaline serfs who unjustly and fraudulently say that they are free.

5. That no one shall presume to rob or do any injury fraudulently to the churches of God or widows or orphans or pilgrims; for the lord emperor himself, after God and His saints, has constituted himself their protector and defender.

6. That no one shall dare to lay waste a benefice of the lord emperor, or to make it his own property.

7. That no one shall presume to neglect a summons to war from the lord

emperor; and that no one of the counts shall be so presumptuous as to dare to dismiss thence any one of those who owe military service, either on account of relationship or flattery or gifts from any one.

8. That no one shall presume to impede at all in any way a ban or command of the lord emperor, or to dally with his work or to impede or to lessen or in any way to act contrary to his will or commands. And that no one shall dare to neglect to pay his dues or tax.

9. That no one, for any reason, shall make a practice in court of defending another unjustly, either from any desire of gain when the cause is weak, or by impeding a just judgment by his skill in reasoning, or by a desire of oppressing when the cause is weak. But each one shall answer for his own cause or tax or debt unless any one is infirm or ignorant of pleading; for these the *missi* or the chiefs who are in the court or the judge who knows the case in question shall plead before the court; or if it is necessary, such a person may be allowed as is acceptable to all and knows the case well; but this shall be done wholly according to the convenience of the chiefs or *missi* who are present. But in every case it shall be done in accordance with justice and the law; and that no one shall have the power to impede justice by a gift, reward, or any kind of evil flattery or from any hindrance of relationship. And that no one shall unjustly consent to another in anything, but that with all zeal and goodwill all shall be prepared to carry out justice.

For all the above mentioned ought to be observed by the imperial oath.

10. That bishops and priests shall live according to the canons and shall teach others to do the same.

11. That bishops, abbots, abbesses, who are in charge of others, with the greatest veneration shall strive to surpass their subjects in this diligence and shall not oppress their subjects with a harsh rule or tyranny, but with sincere love shall carefully guard the flock committed to them with mercy and charity or by the examples of good works.

[*Clauses 12–24 deal with points of ecclesiastical discipline—B. T.*]

* * *

25. That counts and *centenarii* [*subordinate officials—B. T.*] shall compel all to do justice in every respect, and shall have such assistants in their ministries as they can securely confide in, who will observe law and justice faithfully, who will oppress the poor in no manner, who will not dare under any pretext, on account of flattery or reward, to conceal thieves, robbers, murderers, adulterers, magicians, wizards or witches, and all sacrilegious men, but instead will give them up that they may be punished and chastised in accordance with the law, so that, God granting it, all of these evils may be removed from the Christian people.

26. That judges shall judge justly in accordance with the written law, and not according to their own will.

27. And we command that no one in our whole kingdom shall dare to deny hospitality to rich or poor or pilgrims, that is, no one shall deny shelter

and fire and water to pilgrims traversing our country in God's name, or to anyone travelling for the love of God or for the safety of his own soul. If, moreover, any one shall wish to serve them farther, let him expect the best reward from God, who Himself said: "And whoso shall receive one such little child in my name, receiveth me"; and elsewhere: "I was a stranger and ye took me in."

28. Concerning embassies coming from the lord emperor. That the counts and *centenarii* shall provide most carefully, as they desire the grace of the lord emperor, for the *missi* who are sent out, so that they may go through their departments without any delay; and he commands to all everywhere that they ought to see to it that no delay is encountered anywhere, but they shall cause them to go on their way in all haste and shall provide for them in such a manner as our *missi* may direct.

29. Concerning the poor to whom in his mercy the lord emperor has granted the ban which they ought to pay, that the judges, counts or our *missi* shall not, for their own advantage, have the power to compel them to pay the fine which has been granted to them.

30. Concerning those whom the lord emperor wishes, Christ being propitious, to enjoy peace and protection in his kingdom, namely, those who are hastening to his clemency, either Christians or pagans, because they desire to announce some news, or seeking his aid on account of their poverty or hunger, that no one shall dare to constrain them to serve him, or to seize them, or alienate or sell them; but wherever they may wish to remain voluntarily, there under the defence of the lord emperor they shall be aided in his mercy. If any one shall have presumed to act contrary to this, let him who has so presumptuously despised the commands of the lord emperor, know that he shall suffer the loss of his life for it.

31. And against those who announce the justice of the lord emperor, let no one presume to plot any injury or damage, or to stir up any enmity. But if any one shall have presumed, let him pay the imperial ban or, if he deserves a heavier punishment, it is commanded that he shall be brought to the emperor's presence.

32. Murders, by which a multitude of the Christian people perishes, we command in every way to be shunned and to be forbidden; God Himself forbade to His followers hatred and enmity, much more murder. For in what manner does any one trust to placate God, who has killed his son nearest to him? In what manner truly does he, who has killed his brother, think that the Lord Christ will be propitious to him? It is a great and terrible danger also with God the Father and Christ, Lord of heaven and earth, to stir up enmities among men: it is possible to escape for some time by remaining concealed, but nevertheless by accident at some time he falls into the hands of his enemies; moreover, where is it possible to flee from God, to whom all secrets are manifest? By what rashness does any one think to escape His anger? Wherefore, lest the people committed to us to be ruled over should perish from this evil, we have taken care to shun this by every

means of discipline; because he who shall not have dreaded the wrath of God, shall find us in no way propitious or to be placated; but we wish to inflict the most severe punishment upon any one who shall have dared to murder a man. Nevertheless, lest sin should also increase, in order that the greatest enmities may not arise among Christians, when by the persuasions of the devil murders happen, the criminal shall immediately hasten to make amends and with all celerity shall pay the fitting composition for the evil done to the relatives of the murdered man. And we forbid firmly, that the relatives of the murdered man shall dare in any way to continue their enmities on account of the evil done, or shall refuse to grant peace to him who asks it, but having given their pledges they shall receive the fitting composition and shall make a perpetual peace; moreover, the guilty one shall not delay to pay the composition. When, moreover, it shall have happened on account of sins that any one shall have killed his brethren or his neighbor, he shall immediately submit to the penance imposed upon him, and just as his bishop arranges for him, without any ambiguity; but by God's aid he shall desire to accomplish his atonement and he shall compound for the dead man in accordance with the law, and shall make peace in every way with his relatives; and the pledge being given, let no one dare thereafter to stir up enmity against him. But if any one shall have scorned to make the fitting composition, he shall be deprived of his property until we shall render our decision.

33. We prohibit in every way the crime of incest. But if any one shall have been contaminated by sinful fornication, he shall by no means be released without severe punishment, but for this he shall be corrected in such a manner that others shall fear to do likewise and that uncleanness shall be wholly removed from the Christian people, and that the guilty man shall fully atone for this by penance, just as his bishop shall arrange for him; and the woman shall be placed in the hands of her parents until we render our judgment. But if he shall have been unwilling to consent to the judgment of the bishops concerning his amendment, then he shall be brought to our presence, mindful of the example which was made concerning the incest which Fricco perpetrated with the nun of God.

34. That all shall be fully and well prepared, whenever our order or proclamation shall come. But if any one shall then say that he was unprepared and shall have neglected our command, he shall be brought to the palace; and not only he, but also all who dare to transgress our ban or command.

* * *

40. Lastly, therefore, we desire all our decrees to be known in our whole kingdom through our *missi* now sent out, either among the men of the church, bishops, abbots, priests, deacons, canons, all monks or nuns, so that each one in his ministry or profession may keep our ban or decree, or where it may be fitting to thank the citizens for their goodwill, or to furnish aid, or

where there may be need still of correcting anything. Likewise also to the laymen and in all places everywhere, whether they concern the guardianship of the holy churches or of widows and orphans and the weaker; or the robbing of them; or the arrangements for the assembling of the army; or any other matters; how they are to be obedient to our precept and will, or how they observe our ban, or how each one strives in all things to keep himself in the holy service of God; so that all these good things may be well done to the praise of omnipotent God, and we may return thanks where it is fitting. But where we believe there is anything unpunished, we shall so strive to correct it with all our zeal and will that with God's aid we may bring it to correction, both for our own eternal glory and that of all our faithful. Likewise we desire all the above to be fruitfully known by our counts or *centenarii*, our ministerials.

In 806 Charlemagne promulgated the following decree providing for an eventual division of his territories among his three sons.

Charlemagne's Division of the Kingdoms

In the name of the Father and Son and Holy Ghost. Charles most serene Augustus, great and pacific Emperor crowned by God, governing the Roman Empire, and also by the mercy of God King of the Franks and Lombards, to all the faithful of the holy church of God and to our subjects present and future.

As we believe it is known to all of you and hidden from none of you how the divine clemency, by whose will earthly tendencies to decay are checked through successive generations, has of His great mercy and kindness richly endowed us by giving to us three sons, because through them in accordance with our vows and our hopes He has strengthened the kingdom and has made the chance of oblivion in the future less; accordingly we wish to make this known to you, namely, that we desire to have these our sons by the grace of God as associates in the kingdom granted to us by God as long as we live, and after our departure from this life we desire to have them as heirs of the empire preserved and protected by God and our kingdom, if this is the will of the divine majesty. In order that we

University of Pennsylvania Translations and Reprints, VI, No. 5 (1900), 27–29, translated by D. C. Munro.

may not leave it to them in confusion and disorder or provoke strife and litigation by giving them the whole kingdom without division, we have caused to be described and designated the portion which each one of them ought to enjoy and rule; in this manner forsooth so that each one, content with his own portion in accordance with our ordination, may strive with the aid of God to defend the frontiers of his kingdom and preserve peace and charity with his brothers.

It has pleased us to divide the empire, preserved and protected by God, and our kingdom so that to our beloved son Louis we have assigned the whole of Aquitaine and Gascony, except the province of Tours, and whatever is beyond to the west and towards Spain and from the city Nevers, which is situated on the river Loire, with the province of Nevers, the province of Avallon and Auxois, Châlon, Mâcon, Lyons, Savoy, Maurienne, Tarantaise, Mont Cenis, the valley of Susa to the *Clusoe* and thence from the Italian mountains to the sea, these provinces with their cities and whatever is beyond these on the south and west as far as the sea or Spain, that is that portion of Burgundy and Provence and Septimania or Gothia.

To our beloved son Pippin, Italy, which is also called Lombardy and Bavaria, just as Tassilo held it, with the exception of the two villas of Ingolstadt and Lauterhofen which we formerly gave to Tassilo as a benefice and which belong to the district which is called the Northgau, and from Alemannia the part which is on the south bank of the river Danube, and from the source of the Danube in a direct line as far as the river Rhine on the boundary of the districts of Klettgau and Hegau at the place which is called Enge, and thence up the river Rhine to the Alps; whatever is within these limits and extending to the south or east together with the duchy of Chur and the canton of Thurgau.

To our beloved son Charles moreover we have granted all of our kingdom that is outside of these limits, that is France and Burgundy, except that part which we have given to Louis, and Alemannia, except the portion which we have assigned to Pippin, Austria and Neustria, Thüringen, Saxony, Friesland, and the part of Bavaria which is called the Northgau; so that Charles and Louis may be able to go into Italy to bear aid to their brother, if such a necessity should arise, Charles by the valley of the Aosta which is in his kingdom and Louis by the valley of the Susa; Pippin also has the means of ingress and exit by the Norican Alps and Chur.

In 813 Charles succeeded in obtaining recognition of his imperial title from the authorities in Constantinople. The first of the following extracts is from the *Annals of Lorsch,* the second from a letter of Charlemagne to the Byzantine emperor Michael.

FROM Annals of Lorsch

The emperor, Nicephorus, after winning many notable victories in Moesia, fell in battle against the Bulgarians, and his son-in-law Michael was made emperor. He received the ambassadors in Constantinople whom Karl had sent to Nicephorus and dismissed them, sending back to Karl with them his own ambassadors. Michael, a bishop, and Arsaphius and Theognostus, commanders of the imperial body-guard, to confirm the treaty which had been proposed in the time of Nicephorus. They came to the emperor at Aachen and received a copy of the treaty from him in the church of Aachen. In their address to him on this occasion, which they delivered in Greek, they called him emperor and *basileus.* They then proceeded to Rome on their way back, and received a copy of the treaty from the pope in the church of St. Peter, the apostle.

A Source Book for Mediaeval History (1905), pp. 58–59, translated by O. J. Thatcher and E. H. McNeal.

FROM Charlemagne's Letter to Emperor Michael

•

In the name of the Father, Son, and Holy Spirit. Karl, by the grace of God emperor and Augustus, king of the Franks and the Lombards, to his dear and honorable brother, Michael, glorious emperor and Augustus, eternal greeting in our Lord Jesus Christ. We bless and praise our Lord Jesus Christ with all our heart and strength for the ineffable gift of his kindness, with which he has enriched us. For he has deigned in our day to establish that peace between the east and the west, which we have long sought for and have always desired, and, in answer to the daily prayers which we have offered to him, has unified the holy immaculate catholic church throughout the whole world and given it peace. We speak of this peace as if it had been already brought about, for we have done our part, and we are sure you are willing to

A Source Book for Mediaeval History (1905), pp. 58–59, translated by O. J. Thatcher and E. H. McNeal.

do yours. We put our trust in God who has ordained that this matter, the making of peace between us, should be carried out; for he is faithful and true, giving his aid to all who are engaged in good works, and he will bring to perfection this work which we have begun. Desiring now to bring about this consummation, we have sent you our legates, Amalhar, venerable bishop of Trier, and Peter, abbot of the monastery of Nonantula, to receive from the holy altar by your hands a copy of the treaty of peace, bearing the signatures of your priests, patriarchs, and nobles, just as your legates, Michael, venerable metropolitan, and Arsaphius and Theognostus, commanders of the royal body-guard, received the copy from us, with our signature and the signatures of our priests and nobles.

After the agreement with Byzantium, Charles crowned his surviving son, Louis, emperor. The event is described by Einhard.

FROM Life of Charlemagne BY EINHARD

Toward the close of his life, when he was broken by ill-health and old age, he summoned Louis, King of Aquitania, his only surviving son by Hildegard, and gathered together all the chief men of the whole kingdom of the Franks in a solemn assembly. He appointed Louis, with their unanimous consent, to rule with himself over the whole kingdom, and constituted him heir to the imperial name; then, placing the diadem upon his son's head, he bade him be proclaimed Emperor and Augustus. This step was hailed by all present with great favor, for it really seemed as if God had prompted him to it for the kingdom's good; it increased the King's dignity, and struck no little terror into foreign nations.

Einhard, *Life of Charlemagne* (1880), pp. 58–59, translated by Samuel Epes Turner.

FEUDALISM—
CAUSE OR CURE OF ANARCHY?

CONTENTS

FROM The Making of the Middle Ages BY R. W. SOUTHERN
FROM Feudalism in Western Europe BY J. R. STRAYER

QUESTIONS FOR STUDY

1. *Explain the meaning of the terms "escheat," "relief," "aid," "counsel," "homage," "wardship."*

2. *Judging from the descriptions of Louis VI of France and William I of England, what qualities were most necessary in an effective feudal king?*

3. *What elments in feudalism, if any, were conducive to anarchy?*

4. *Magna Carta has been called a "reactionary feudal document." Which of the clauses given in this section do you consider "feudal"? Can you suggest any reasons why they might be called reactionary?*

5. *How does the scheme of government described in the Assizes of Romania resemble and differ from that defined in Magna Carta?*

6. *Compare the views of Calmette, Southern, and Strayer on feudalism as a system of government.*

Charlemagne's empire was short-lived. It was soon torn apart by civil wars and by incursions of pagan peoples from beyond its borders. During the ninth and tenth centuries a new pattern of social and political life emerged, which modern historians have called "the feudal system." Feudalism was really anything but systematic. There were all kinds of national and local variations. But most typically a feudal society displayed three main characteristics. First, the major cohesive force was a relationship of mutual loyalty between individual lords and their vassals—not a common loyalty of all citizens to the state. Second, a vassal held from his lord an estate of land called a "fief" (or "benefice") and rendered military service in exchange for it. Third, feudal tenure of land carried rights of government over it.

These aspects of feudalism are discussed in more detail in the reading from Carl Stephenson (pp. 359–363), and they are illustrated in the excerpts from medieval documents that follow (pp. 364–393). Many of these excerpts are fragmentary, but this reflects the nature of the source material itself. At the time that feudalism was coming into existence no one was consciously planning its development or writing treatises about its essential principles. A historian has to understand the changing reality as best he can from scattered references in chronicles, charters, and formularies. Things had changed by the thirteenth century. By then it had become possible to put together systematic compilations like the Assizes of Romania (pp. 382–384), in which feudal government was presented as an ordered structure of rights and obligations.

Early feudal society was decentralized and often torn by internal warfare. Some historians, like J. Calmette (pp. 394–397), have attributed this to the nature of feudalism itself and have concluded that the system was intrinsically anarchic. Others, like R. W. Southern (pp. 397–403) and J. R. Strayer (pp. 403–406), see feudalism as a constructive response to the difficult problems of the age that produced it. In considering the views of these scholars the student should realise that the apparently simple question "Feudalism—Cause or Cure of Anarchy?" conceals several ambiguities. We need to ask, for instance, what standard of comparison the different authors are using. It would be quite possible to maintain that the developed feudalism of the twelfth century was anarchic in comparison with the ancient Roman Empire or the modern nation-state but orderly in comparision with the near-chaos of the immediately preceding period.

Again, the word "anarchy" itself is highly charged. Instead of asking whether feudalism was a "cause of anarchy" we might just as well ask whether it was a "source of liberty." One man's anarchy is another man's liberty. This is well illustrated by Magna Carta (pp. 387–393). The barons of England resented King John's attempts to increase the power of the royal government and insisted that he continue to observe their feudal rights. To the king this may well have seemed a step toward anarchy. To the barons it was a defense of their liberty. Whether the barons' opposition to the king tended to enhance the liberty of all Englishmen at that time is a difficult question that historians still argue about.

Finally, it should be noted that some apparent disagreements arise because different historians are writing about different levels of government when they discuss feudalism. Perhaps feudalism promoted orderly government within particular baronies but impeded the growth of royal government over a whole kingdom. Certainly some feudal kings succeeded in establishing a strong royal authority while others failed to do so (pp. 384–386). The real problem here is to determine whether feudal institutions were, by their intrinsic nature, unsuited to the government of units larger and more complex than the individual baronial fiefs.

1
FEUDAL INSTITUTIONS— A MODERN DESCRIPTION

The following account describes the institutions and practices that were characteristic of medieval feudalism.

FROM Mediaeval Feudalism BY CARL STEPHENSON

By examining various customs of the Carolingian period we have necessarily concerned ourselves with the development of the institutions called feudal. Before we proceed further, it might be well to summarize the problem of that development through a series of questions and suggested answers.

What was the origin of vassalage? Since under the Carolingians, as in the later period, vassalage was an honorable relationship between members of the warrior class, to derive it from the Romans seems quite impossible. In spite of all the Latin words that came to be adopted by the Franks in Gaul, mediaeval vassalage remained essentially a barbarian custom, strikingly akin to that described by Tacitus as the *comitatus*. Originally this custom was shared by various Germanic peoples, notably the Anglo-Saxons. The peculiarity of Frankish vassalage resulted, in the main, from the governmental policy of the Carolingian kings.

What was the Carolingian policy with regard to vassalage? The Merovingian kingdom had been at most a pseudo-Roman sham. By the end of the seventh century it had utterly disintegrated. The Carolingian kingdom was a new unit created by the military genius of Charles Martel, Pepin, and Charlemagne. To preserve and strengthen their authority, these rulers depended less

Carl Stephenson, *Mediaeval Feudalism*, pp. 10–14, 24–31. Copyright 1942 by Cornell University. Used by permission of Cornell University Press.

on their theoretical sovereignty than on the fidelity of their personal retainers, now styled vassals. So the key positions in the army, as well as the more important offices in church and state, came to be held by royal vassals. Eventually the rule was adopted that every great official, if not already a royal vassal, had to become one. The Carolingian policy, as will be seen in the following pages, utterly failed; yet it established legal precedents that were observed for many centuries.

What was the origin of the fief? In Frankish times, as later, *beneficium* remained a vague term. Various kinds of persons were said to hold benefices, and in return for various kinds of service or rent. Since the benefice of a vassal was held on condition of military service, we may call it a military benefice. At first there was no technical Latin word for such a benefice, though in the Romance vernacular it became known as a *feos* or *fief*. This name, Latinized as *feodum* or *feudum*, ultimately came into official use and so provided the root for our adjective "feudal" (French *féodal*). Whether or not the military benefice existed before the eighth century is still disputed. In any case, it was the Carolingians who made that form of tenure into a common Frankish institution, and the best explanation of their policy is the one presented by Heinrich Brunner. According to his famous thesis, the old Frankish army had been largely made up of infantry—of ordinary freemen who provided their own weapons and served without pay. In the eighth century, as the experience of warfare proved the insufficiency of the traditional system, the Carolingians anxiously sought to enlarge their force of expert cavalry. And to do so they developed what we know as feudal tenure by associating vassalage with benefice-holding.

What was the nature of the fief? In its essence, we may say, a military benefice or fief was the special remuneration paid to a vassal for the rendering of special service. If the rulers had been able to hire mounted troops for cash, recourse to feudal tenure would have been unnecessary; for the Carolingian fief was primarily a unit of agrarian income. To call a fief a piece of land is inaccurate. What value would bare acres have for a professional warrior who considered the work of agriculture degrading? Being the possession of a gentleman, the fief included organized manors, worked by the native peasantry according to a customary routine of labor. Nor was this all. To hold a fief was also to enjoy the important privilege that the Carolingians knew as immunity. Within his own territory the royal vassal, like the clerical immunists of an earlier time, administered justice, collected fines and local taxes, raised military forces, and exacted services for the upkeep of roads, bridges, and fortifications. To some extent, therefore, he was a public official, a member of the hierarchy whose upper ranks included dukes, marquises, counts, and the greater ecclesiastics. As all these magnates came to be royal vassals, their offices, together with the attached estates, naturally appeared to be their fiefs. And as royal vassals passed on bits of their own privilege to subvassals, feudal tenure became inseparable from the exercise of political authority.

What, then, was the original feudalism? In this connection we can do no better than quote a shrewd observation by Ferdinand Lot: "It has become accepted usage to speak of 'feudalism,' rather than of 'vassalage,' from that point in history when, with rare exceptions, there were actually no vassals without fiefs." By "feudalism," in other words, we properly refer to the peculiar association of vassalage with fief-holding that was developed in the Carolingian Empire and thence spread to other parts of Europe.

* * *

In actual practice we know that, even before the close of the ninth century, it was customary for fiefs to pass from father to son; and that, within another hundred years or so, a fief was regularly described as hereditary. For reasons stated above, however, such inheritance is found to have been merely the renewal of a feudal contract, to which each of the parties, the lord and the vassal, had to give personal assent. When a vassal died, his fief reverted to the lord and really ceased to be a fief at all until another vassal had been invested with it. In case the vassal had no heir, the reversion was called escheat, and the lord was free to keep the dead man's estate or to regrant it to whomsoever he pleased. In case the vassal had an heir, the lord was legally obliged to accept him as the new holder. Yet even then a regrant was necessary through formal investiture; and in recognition of this fact the heir very commonly paid the lord a sum of money called relief.

Another striking peculiarity of feudal tenure was primogeniture, the rule that a fief should pass intact to the eldest son. No such form of inheritance was known either to Roman or to Germanic law, and allodial property continued to be shared by the children of a deceased owner. The fact that a fief was legally indivisible seems to prove that it was considered a public office rather than a piece of land. This was obviously true in the case of a duchy or county. But it was no less true, at least originally, in the case of an ordinary fief, where the income from agrarian estates combined with a territorial immunity provided remuneration for the service, military and political, of a vassal. It was greatly to the interest of a princely donor that responsibility for the needed service should be concentrated. To allow a fief to be indefinitely partitioned would nullify its value—would, in fact, contravene the very purpose of its establishment. On the other hand, the recipient of a fief might well be permitted to assign parts of it to his own vassals, for their default would remain his liability. Primogeniture thus came to be adopted as a very practical regulation for the continuance of feudal tenure, and with the latter spread widely throughout mediaeval Europe. The only significant modification of the rule for the benefit of younger children was the custom called parage. Under it a fief could be divided among a number of co-heirs if one of them rendered homage for all of it and so in a way guaranteed its integrity.

To introduce the subject of feudal inheritance it has been necessary to re-emphasize the fact that vassalage was always personal. A related fact also had important consequences—that vassalage was properly restricted to fighting-men. When a vassal died leaving an infant son as heir, the lord commonly enjoyed the right of wardship. That is to say, he took the fief into his own hands and, enjoying its revenue, supported the heir until such time as the latter attained majority. Then the youth, having been knighted and declared of age, performed homage to the lord and from him received investiture. This procedure logically solved the problem of a minority. But suppose the holder of a fief had only a daughter. If a girl could not be a vassal, how could she be recognized as an heiress? The answer, of course, was provided by the institution of marriage: a husband could render the necessary homage and acquire legal possession of the fief. Such a marriage required the lord's consent even during the lifetime of the girl's father. When he was dead, the lord as guardian took complete charge of the matter and, very generally, awarded the lady's hand to the noble suitor who bid the highest. True, the relatives of a young heir or heiress often objected to the lord's pretensions, and he was sometimes compelled to recognize one of them as guardian—on condition, however, that the latter became the lord's vassal for the duration of the minority.

Thus, by a series of legal devices, it was arranged that a fief should pass from one mature man to another; for the holder was normally required to perform military service. Although detailed records of the service actually rendered date only from the later Middle Ages, we may be sure that the principles then set forth were much older. Since at least the ninth century vassalage had implied a personal obligation to fight for the lord as a heavy-armed cavalryman, or knight. But, in addition, a royal vassal who had received a valuable fief was expected to bring with him a mounted troop of his own vassals, and the same requirement would apply to most men who held of a duke, a count, or some other magnate. It was in this way that the army of every feudal prince was regularly made up. At first, apparently, the size of each vassal's contingent and the length of his service were not precisely determined in advance. By the twelfth century, however, such determination had become usual in the better-organized states, especially those controlled by the Normans. According to the perfected scheme, the vassal took with him into the field enough knights to complete whatever quota was charged against his fief, but he was obliged to furnish the service at his own cost for no more than forty days once in the year.

* * *

That heavy expense was entailed by military service of this kind is apparent from the fact that it involved the finding, not only of trained men, but also of very superior horses, costly equipment, numerous servants, and enough food to supply the whole troop throughout the campaign. And the vassal's responsibility was by no means restricted to military service. On certain occasions he was required to pay his lord a contribution called aid. The northern French custom, taken by the Normans to England, specified three such occasions: the knighting of the lord's eldest son, the marriage of the lord's eldest daughter, and ransom of the lord when captured. In many regions, however, an aid could be exacted for the knighting of any son or the marriage of any daughter, and sometimes, as well, for a crusade, a journey to the royal court, or some other extraordinary undertaking. The vassal, furthermore, owed his lord hospitality. That is to say, whenever the lord came for a visit, the vassal was expected to provide free entertainment. And since every great lord was constantly moving about with a small army of mounted attendants, one could not afford to be too generous a host. As a consequence, the vassal's obligation in this respect often came to be strictly defined and was sometimes commuted into a money payment.

Every vassal, finally, was responsible for the important service called suit to court. When summoned to attend his lord, the vassal had to go in person and at his own expense. The reasons for the service were as varied as the meanings of the word "court." The occasion might be largely ceremonial, as in the case of a festival or the celebration of a wedding. Perhaps the lord wished to consult his men with regard to a war or a treaty. Very frequently they were asked to approve some act of government or to take part in a trial. For example, if the lord needed military service or financial aid beyond what was specifically owed by his vassals, his only recourse was to ask them for a voluntary grant. He had no right to tax or assess them arbitrarily, for his authority in such matters was determined by feudal contract. Nor did he have a discretionary power of legislation. Law was the unwritten custom of the country. To change or even to define it was the function, not of the lord, but of his court. It was the vassals themselves who declared the law under which they lived; and when one of them was accused of a misdeed, he was entitled to the judgment of his peers, i.e., his fellow vassals.

2
ORIGINS OF
FEUDALISM

Feudalism grew up in a society ravaged by incessant internal warfare and by frequent invasions from beyond the borders of Christendom. These conditions are illustrated in the following extracts from ninth-century sources.

FROM Annals of Fulda

841

The three brothers [*Lothaire, Louis, and Charles, grandsons of Charlemagne —B. T.*] met in Auxerre, near Fontenay. They could not agree to divide the Empire because Lothaire, who wished to be sole monarch, was opposed to it. So they agreed that the case should be decided by the power of the sword and so proved by the judgment of God. On the twenty-fifth of June a great battle was fought between them, and the blood shed on both sides was so great that the present age remembers no such carnage among the Frankish people before. On the same day Lothaire began a retreat to his city of Aix-la-Chapelle. Louis and Charles seized his camp and collected and buried the bodies of their slain. They then parted; Charles remained in the West and Louis went in the month of August to the royal town Salz.

Lothaire again collected his forces from all sides. He went to Mayence and ordered the Saxons, with his little son Lothaire, to meet him at Speyer. He himself crossed the Rhine, intending to pursue his brother Louis to the confines of the outlying nations. He returned to Worms, unsuccessful. He celebrated there the marriage of his daughter, and then marched toward Gaul to

Annals of Fulda, 841, in *Readings in European History,* I (1904), 156–157, translated by J. H. Robinson.

subdue Charles. He spent the whole winter in fruitless effort and strife and then returned to Aix. On the twenty-fifth of December a comet appeared in the sign of Aquarius.

FROM Annals of Xanten

845

Twice in the canton of Worms there was an earthquake; the first in the night following Palm Sunday, the second in the holy night of Christ's Resurrection. In the same year the heathen broke in upon the Christians at many points, but more than twelve thousand of them were killed by the Frisians. Another party of invaders devastated Gaul; of these more than six hundred men perished. Yet owing to his indolence Charles agreed to give them many thousand pounds of gold and silver if they would leave Gaul, and this they did. Nevertheless the cloisters of most of the saints were destroyed and many of the Christians were led away captive.

* * *

846

According to their custom the Northmen plundered Eastern and Western Frisia and burned the town of Dordrecht, with two other villages, before the eyes of Lothaire, who was then in the castle of Nimwegen, but could not punish the crime. The Northmen, with their boats filled with immense booty, including both men and goods, returned to their own country.

In the same year Louis sent an expedition from Saxony against the Wends across the Elbe. He personally, however, went with his army against the Bohemians, whom we called Beu-winitha, but with great risk. . . . Charles advanced against the Britons, but accomplished nothing.

At this same time, as no one can mention or hear without great sadness, the mother of all churches, the basilica of the apostle Peter, was taken and plundered by the Moors, or Saracens, who had already occupied the region of Beneventum. The Saracens, moreover, slaughtered all the Christians whom they found outside the walls of Rome, either within or without this church. They also carried men and women away prisoners. They tore down, among many others, the altar of the blessed Peter, and their crimes from day to day bring sorrow to Christians. Pope Sergius departed life this year.

Annals of Xanten, 845–854, in *Readings in European History*, I (1904), 158–162, translated by J. H. Robinson.

847

After the death of Sergius no mention of the apostolic see has come in any
way to our ears. Rabanus [Maurus], master and abbot of Fulda, was solemnly chosen archbishop as the successor of Bishop Otger, who had died.
Moreover the Northmen here and there plundered the Christians and engaged in a battle with the counts Sigir and Liuthar. They continued up the
Rhine as far as Dordrecht, and nine miles farther to Meginhard, when they
turned back, having taken their booty.

* * *

849

While King Louis was ill his army of Bavaria took its way against the Bohemians. Many of these were killed and the remainder withdrew, much humiliated, into their own country. The heathen from the North wrought havoc in
Christendom as usual and grew greater in strength; but it is revolting to say
more of this matter.

850

On January 1st of that season, in the octave of the Lord, towards evening, a
great deal of thunder was heard and a mighty flash of lightning seen; and an
overflow of water afflicted the human race during this winter. In the following summer an all too great heat of the sun burned the earth. Leo, pope of the
apostolic see, an extraordinary man, built a fortification round the church of
St. Peter the apostle. The Moors, however, devastated here and there the coast
towns in Italy. The Norman Rorik, brother of the above-mentioned younger
Heriold, who earlier had fled dishonored from Lothaire, again took Dordrecht and did much evil treacherously to the Christians. In the same year so
great a peace existed between the two brothers—Emperor Lothaire and King
Louis—that they spent many days together in Osning [Westphalia] and there
hunted, so that many were astonished thereat; and they went each his way in
peace.

851

The bodies of certain saints were sent from Rome to Saxony,—that of Alexander, one of seven brethren, and those of Romanus and Emerentiana. In the
same year the very noble empress, Irmingard by name, wife of the emperor

Lothaire, departed this world. The Normans inflicted much harm in Frisia and about the Rhine. A mighty army of them collected by the river Elbe against the Saxons, and some of the Saxon towns were besieged, others burned, and most terribly did they oppress the Christians. A meeting of our kings took place on the Maas.

852

The steel of the heathen glistened; excessive heat; a famine followed. There was not fodder enough for the animals. The pasturage for the swine was more than sufficient.

853

A great famine in Saxony so that many were forced to live on horse meat.

854

The Normans, in addition to the very many evils which they were everywhere inflicting upon the Christians, burned the church of St. Martin, bishop of Tours, where his body rests.

The various elements that were combined in feudalism—personal loyalty, vassalage, fief-holding—all existed separately before the ninth century. As early as the first century after Christ, Tacitus described the loyalty of Teutonic warriors to their chiefs.

FROM Germania BY TACITUS

They undertake no business whatever either of a public or a private character save they be armed. But it is not customary for any one to assume arms until the tribe has recognized his competence to use them. Then in a full assembly

Tacitus, *Germania,* American Philological Association Monograph No. 5 (1935), pp. 289–291, translated by R. P. Robinson. Reprinted by permission of the American Philological Association.

some one of the chiefs or the father or relatives of the youth invest him with the shield and spear. This has the same meaning as the assumption of the toga by Roman boys; it is their first honor. Before this he was only a member of a household, hereafter he is a member of the tribe. Distinguished rank or the great services of their parents secure even for mere striplings the claim to be ranked as chiefs. They attach themselves to certain more experienced chiefs of approved merit; nor are they ashamed to be looked upon as belonging to their followings. There are grades even within the train of followers assigned by the judgment of its leader. There is great rivalry among these companions as to who shall rank first with the chief, and among the chiefs as to who shall have the most and the bravest followers. It is an honor and a source of strength always to be surrounded by a great band of chosen youths, for they are an ornament in peace, a defence in war. It brings reputation and glory to a leader not only in his own tribe but also among the neighboring peoples if his following is superior in numbers and courage; for he is courted by embassies and honored by gifts, and often his very fame decides the issue of wars.

When they go into battle it is a disgrace for the chief to be outdone in deeds of valor and for the following not to match the courage of their chief; furthermore for any of the followers to have survived his chief and come unharmed out of a battle is life-long infamy and reproach. It is in accordance with their most sacred oath of allegiance to defend and protect him and to ascribe their bravest deeds to his renown. The chief fights for victory; the men of his following, for their chief. If the tribe to which they belong sinks into the lethargy of long peace and quiet, many of the noble youths voluntarily seek other tribes that are still carrying on war, because a quiet life is irksome to the Germans, and they gain renown more readily in the midst of perils, while a large following is not to be provided for except by violence and war. For they look to the liberality of their chief for their war-horse and their deadly and victorious spear; the feasts and entertainments, however, furnished them on a homely but liberal scale, fall to their lot as mere pay. The means for this bounty are acquired through war and plunder. Nor could you persuade them to till the soil and await the yearly produce so easily as you could induce them to stir up an enemy and earn glorious wounds. Nay even they think it tame and stupid to acquire by their sweat what they can purchase by their blood.

From the seventh century onward we have written formulas that show how a man commended himself to a lord. The following examples are from England and France respectively.

Feudal Oaths

Thus shall one take the oath of fidelity:

By the Lord before whom this sanctuary is holy, I will to N. be true and faithful, and love all which he loves and shun all which he shuns, according to the laws of God and the order of the world. Nor will I ever with will or action, through word or deed, do anything which is unpleasing to him, on condition that he will hold to me as I shall deserve it, and that he will perform everything as it was in our agreement when I submitted myself to him and chose his will.

* * *

It is right that those who offer to us unbroken fidelity should be protected by our aid. And since *such and such* a faithful one of ours, by the favor of God, coming here in our palace with his arms, has seen fit to swear trust and fidelity to us in our hand, therefore we decree and command by the present precept that for the future *such and such* above mentioned be counted with the number of the antrustions. And if anyone perchance should presume to kill him, let him know that he will be judged guilty of his wergild of 600 shillings.

University of Pennsylvania Translations and Reprints, IV, No. 3 (1897), 3–4, translated by E. P. Cheyney.

The first recorded example of the great noble accepting a status of "vassalage" dates from 757.

FROM Frankish Royal Annals

King Pepin held his court at Compiègne with the Franks. Tassilo, Duke of the Bavarians, came there and commended himself in vassalage by hand. He swore many, indeed innumerable oaths, laying his hand on relics of saints and promising to be faithful to King Pepin and his sons, the aforementioned lords Charles and Carloman, as by law a vassal should be toward his lords, sincerely and with devotion.

F. Kurze, ed., *Annales Regni Francorum* (1895), p. 14, translated by Brian Tierney.

From about the same period we have documents granting lands as *precaria* or *beneficia,* forms of land-holding that anticipated the later feudal tenure. The following document of 743, issued in France, required a church to lend out part of its lands for the support of royal warriors.

Capitulary of Lestinnes, 743

Because of the threats of war and the attacks of certain tribes on our borders, we have determined, with the consent of God and by the advice of our clergy and people, to appropriate for a time part of the ecclesiastical property for the support of our army. The lands are to be held as *precaria* for a fixed rent; one solidus, or twelve denarii, shall be paid annually to the church or monastery for each *casata* [farm]. When the holder dies the whole possession shall return to the church. If, however, the exigency of the time makes it necessary, the prince may require the *precarium* to be renewed and given out again. Care shall be taken, however, that the churches and monasteries do not incur suffering or poverty through the granting of *precaria*. If the poverty of the church makes it necessary, the whole possession shall be restored to the church.

A Source Book for Mediaeval History (1905), p. 357, translated by O. J. Thatcher and E. H. McNeal.

Sometimes royal grants conferred immunity from the jurisdiction of the king's local officers, as in the following example.

Grant of Immunity

Those who from their early youth have served us or our parents faithfully are justly rewarded by the gifts of our munificence. Know therefore that we have granted to that illustrious man (name), with greatest good will, the villa called (name), situated in the county of (name), with all its possessions and extent, in full as it was formerly held by him *or* by our treasury. Therefore by the present charter which we command to be observed forever, we decree that the said (name) shall possess the villa of (name), as has been said, in its entirety, with lands, houses, buildings, inhabitants, slaves, woods, pastures, meadows, streams, mills, and all its appurtenances and belongings, and with all the subjects of the royal treasure who dwell on the lands, and he shall hold it forever with full immunity from the entrance of any public official for the purpose of exacting the royal portion of the fines from cases arising there; to the extent finally that he shall have, hold, and possess it in full ownership, no one having the right to expect its transfer, and with the right of leaving it to his successors or to anyone whom he desires, and to do with it whatever else he wishes.

A Source Book for Mediaeval History (1905), pp. 352–353, translated by O. J. Thatcher and E. H. McNeal.

3
LORDS AND VASSALS

Vassals acquired fiefs in various ways. The manner in which the duchy of Normandy was established in 911 illustrates the endemic violence of the period. The following account was written about a century after the events it describes.

FROM The Customs and Acts of the First Dukes of Normandy

The Franks, not having the strength to resist the pagans and seeing all France brought to nothing, came to the king and said unanimously, "Why do you not aid the kingdom which you are bound by your scepter to care for and rule? Why is peace not made by negotiation since we cannot achieve it either by giving battle or by defensive fortifications? Royal honor and power is cast down; the insolence of the pagans is raised up. The land of France is almost a desert for its people are dying by famine or by the sword or are taken captive. Care for the kingdom, if not by arms then by taking counsel." . . .

Immediately Charles, having consulted with them, sent Franco, Archbishop of Rouen, to Rollo, Duke of the Pagans. Coming to him he began to speak with mild words. "Most exalted and distinguished of dukes, will you quarrel with the Franks as long as you live? Will you always wage war on them? What will become of you when you are seized by death? Whose creature are you? Do you think you are God? Are you not a man formed from filth? Are you not dust and ashes and food for worms? Remember what you are and will be and by whose judgment you will be condemned. You will experience Hell I think, and no longer injure anyone by your wars.

De Moribus et Actis Primorum Normanniae Ducum, Mémoires de la Société des Antiquaires de Normandie, 3è Série, III (1858), 165–169, translated by Brian Tierney.

If you are willing to become a Christian you will be able to enjoy peace in the present and the future and to dwell in this world with great riches. Charles, a long-suffering king, persuaded by the counsel of his men, is willing to give you this coastal province that you and Halstigno have grievously ravaged. He will also give you his daughter, Gisela, for a wife in order that peace and concord and a firm, stable and continuous friendship may endure for all time between you and him . . ."

At the agreed time Charles and Rollo came together at the place that had been decided on. . . . Looking on Rollo, the invader of France, the Franks said to one another, "This duke who has fought such battles against the warriors of this realm is a man of great power and great courage and prowess and good counsel and of great energy too." Then, persuaded by the words of the Franks, Rollo put his hands between the hands of the king, a thing which his father and grandfather and great-grandfather had never done; and so the king gave his daughter Gisela in marriage to the duke and conferred on him the agreed lands from the River Epte to the sea as his property in hereditary right, together with all Brittany from which he could live.

Rollo was not willing to kiss the foot of the king. The bishops said, "Anyone who receives such a gift ought to be eager to kiss the king's foot." He replied, "I have never bent my knees at anyone's knees, nor will I kiss anyone's foot." But, urged by the entreaties of the Franks, he commanded one of his warriors to kiss the foot of the king. The warrior promptly seized the king's foot, carried it to his mouth and kissed it standing up while the king was thrown flat on his back. At that there was a great outburst of laughter and great excitement among the people. Nevertheless King Charles, Duke Robert, the counts and nobles, the bishops and abbots swore by the Catholic faith and by their lives, limbs and the honor of the whole kingdom to the noble Rollo that he should hold and possess the land described above and pass it on to his heirs.

A more conventional ceremony, which took place in Flanders in 1127, is described in the next document.

FROM Chronicle of the Death of Charles the Good
BY GALBERT OF BRUGES

Through the whole remaining part of the day those who had been previously enfeoffed by the most pious count Charles, did homage to the count, taking up now again their fiefs and offices and whatever they had before rightfully and legitimately obtained. On Thursday the seventh of April, homages were again made to the count being completed in the following order of faith and security.

First they did their homage thus, the count asked if he was willing to become completely his man, and the other replied, "I am willing"; and with clasped hands, surrounded by the hands of the count, they were bound together by a kiss. Secondly, he who had done homage gave his fealty to the representative of the count in these words, "I promise on my faith that I will in future be faithful to count William, and will observe my homage to him completely against all persons in good faith and without deceit," and thirdly, he took his oath to this upon the relics of the saints. Afterward, with a little rod which the count held in his hand, he gave investitures to all who by this agreement had given their security and homage and accompanying oath.

University of Pennsylvania Translations and Reprints, IV, No. 3 (1897), 18, translated by E. P. Cheyney.

The following record of the grant of a fief in France (1200) illustrates some of the complexities that could arise when a vassal held land from several lords.

Grant of Fief, 1200

I, Thiebault, count palatine of Troyes, make known to those present and to come that I have given in fee to Jocelyn d'Avalon and his heirs the manor which is called Gillencourt, which is of the castellanerie of La Ferte sur Aube; and whatever the same Jocelyn shall be able to acquire in the same manor I have granted to him and his heirs in augmentation of that fief. I have granted, moreover, to him that in no free manor of mine will I retain men who are of this gift. The same Jocelyn, moreover, on account of this has become my liege man, saving however, his allegiance to Gerard d'Arcy, and to the lord duke of Burgundy, and to Peter, count of Auxerre. Done at Chouaude, by my own witness, in the year of the Incarnation of our Lord 1200 in the month of January. Given by the hand of Walter, my chancellor; note of Milo.

University of Pennsylvania Translations and Reprints, IV. No. 3 (1897), 15, translated by E. P. Cheyney.

The next group of documents explains in more detail the obligations of a vassal to his lord. The first extract refers to financial "aids."

FROM Le Grand Coutumier de Normandie

Next it is proper to see the chief aids of Normandy, which are called chief because they should be paid to the chief lords.

In Normandy there are three chief aids. One is to make the oldest son of his lord a knight; the second, to marry his oldest daughter; the third to ransom the body of his lord from prison when he is taken in the Duke's war.

University of Pennsylvania Translations and Reprints, IV, No. 3 (1897), 28, translated by E. P. Cheyney.

In 1270 King Louis IX of France defined the military service due from his vassals.

Definition of Knight Service BY LOUIS IX

The baron and all vassals of the king are bound to appear before him when he shall summon them, and to serve him at their own expense for forty days and forty nights, with as many knights as each one owes; and he is able to exact from them these services when he wishes and when he has need of them. And if the king wishes to keep them more than forty days at their own expense, they are not bound to remain if they do not wish it. And if the king wishes to keep them at his expense for the defence of the realm, they are bound to remain. And if the king wishes to lead them outside of the kingdom, they need not go unless they wish to, for they have already served their forty days and forty nights.

The following extract from the Exchequer Rolls of the medieval English government refers to feudal "reliefs."

FROM English Exchequer Rolls

Walter Hait renders an account of 5 marks of silver for the relief of the land of his father.

Walter Brito renders an account of £66, 13s. and 4d. for the relief of his land.

Richard of Estre renders an account of £15 for his relief for 3 knights' fees which he holds from the honor of Mortain.

Walter Fitz Thomas, of Newington, owes 28s. 4d. for having the fourth part of one knight's fee which had been seized into the hand of the king for default of relief.

John of Venetia renders an account of 300 marks for the fine of his land

University of Pennsylvania Translations and Reprints, IV, No. 3 (1897), 30, translated by E. P. Cheyney.

and for the relief of the land which was his father's and he does homage to the king against all mortals.

Ralph, son and heir of Ralph of Sullega renders an account of £100 for his relief for the lands which were Ralph his father's which he held from the king *in capite*.

John de Balliol owes £150 for the relief of 30 knights' fees which Hugh de Balliol his father held from the king *in capite,* that is 100s. for each fee.

Peter de Bruce renders an account of £100 for his relief for the barony which was of Peter his father.

The Exchequer Rolls also illustrate how the rights of wardship and marriage were exercised in a feudal society.

Roheisa de Doura renders account of £450 to have half of all the lands which belonged to Richard de Lucy, her grandfather, and which the brother of the same Roheisa had afterward as well in England as in Normandy, and for license to marry where she wishes so long as she does not marry herself to any of the enemies of the king.

Alice, countess of Warwick, renders account of £1000 and 10 palfreys to be allowed to remain a widow as long as she pleases, and not to be forced to marry by the king. And if perchance she should wish to marry, she shall not marry except with the assent and on the grant of the king, where the king shall be satisfied; and to have the custody of her sons whom she has from the earl of Warwick her late husband.

Hawisa, who was wife of William Fitz Robert renders account of 130 marks and 4 palfreys that she may have peace from Peter of Borough to whom the king has given permission to marry her; and that she may not be compelled to marry.

Geoffrey de Mandeville owes 20,000 marks to have as his wife Isabella, countess of Gloucester, with all the lands and tenements and fiefs which fall to her.

Thomas de Colville renders an account of 100 marks for having the custody of the sons of Roger Torpel and their land until they come of age.

William, bishop of Ely, owes 220 marks for having the custody of Stephen de Beauchamp with his inheritance and for marrying him where he wishes.

William of St. Mary's church, renders an account of 500 marks for having the custody of the heir of Robert Young, son of Robert Fitzharding, with all his inheritance and all its appurtenances and franchises; that is to say with the services of knights and gifts of churches and marriages of women, and to

University of Pennsylvania Translations and Reprints, IV, No. 3 (1897), 27, translated by E. P. Cheyney.

be allowed to marry him to whatever one of his relatives he wishes; and that all his land is to revert to him freely when he comes of age.

Bartholomew de Muleton renders an account of 100 marks for having the custody of the land the heiress of Lambert of Ibtoft, and for marrying the wife of the same Lambert to whomsoever he wishes where she shall not be disparaged and that he may be able to confer her (the heiress) upon whom he wishes.

The forfeiture of a fief for failure to render military service is described in the following extract.

FROM English Hundred Rolls

It is presented by the jurors above named that the manor of Chinnore along with the hamlet of Sydenham was held of old, from the time of the Conquest, from the lord king of England, by a certain man who was named Walter de Vernon, as one knight's fee; and because the said Walter de Vernon refused to perform his due service from the said manor to the lord king John in the time of the war which sprang up between the lord king John and the king of France, the lord king John with the advice of his council seized that same manor with its appurtenances and removed the said Walter de Vernon, on account of his ingratitude, from the possession of the aforesaid manor forever. And the lord king John granted that same manor with its appurtenances for the services that to the same lord king was due from it to Saer de Quincy formerly earl of Winchester, to hold to himself and his heirs *in capite* from the lord king as one knight's fee; and the heirs of the said Saer held the aforesaid manor in succession, and still hold it, except the hamlet of Sydenham, which the abbot of Thames holds as a gift from Roger de Quincy.

University of Pennsylvania Translations and Reprints, IV, No. 3 (1897), 36, translated by E. P. Cheyney.

4
FEUDAL KINGSHIP VERSUS FEUDAL CHAOS

It is generally agreed that feudal government worked differently in different countries and at different times. The following documents illustrate some of the problems and potentialities of feudal kingship. The first describes the pacification of the royal demesne in France by King Louis VI (1108–1135).

FROM Life of Louis VI BY SUGER

Guy Troussel, son of that violent man and troubler of the kingdom, Milo of Montlhéry, came back home from an expedition to the Holy Sepulcher, weakened by the hardships of the long journey and by many trials. He had been moved by exceeding great fear of Corbaran, and had descended from the wall of Antioch and left the army of God beleaguered within, and so he was forsaken by all. Fearing that his only daughter might in consequence be deprived of her heritage, he yielded to the desire and persuasions of Philip, the king, and of Louis, his son, who ardently longed for his castle, and gave his daughter in marriage to Philip, the king's younger son. . . .

When the castle of Montlhéry fell in this wise into their hands, the king and his son rejoiced as if they had plucked a straw from their eyes or had torn down bars by which they had been confined. And, indeed, we have heard the father say to his son Louis, "Go, son Louis, keep that tower with all vigilance, whose ravages have well-nigh made us grow old, and whose wiles and criminal frauds have never let me rest in good peace and quiet."

Suger, *Life of Louis VI*, in *Readings in European History*, I (1904), 201–204, translated by J. H. Robinson.

Indeed, its unfaithfulness made the faithful faithless, the faithless most faithless. It brought together the treacherous from far and near, and no ill was done in the whole kingdom without its support. And since the territory of Paris was commanded on the river Seine by Corbeil, midway by Montlhéry, on the right by Châteaufort, there resulted such confusion and chaos in the communications between the men of Paris and of Orleans that neither could go to visit the others without the consent of these faithless men, unless they traveled with a strong guard. But the marriage of which we have spoken tore down the barrier and made travel easy between the two cities. . . .

A king, when he takes the royal power, vows to put down with his strong right arm insolent tyrants whensoever he sees them vex the state with endless wars, rejoice in rapine, oppress the poor, destroy the churches, give themselves over to lawlessness which, and it be not checked, would flame out into ever greater madness; for the evil spirits who instigate them are wont cruelly to strike down those whom they fear to lose, but give free rein to those whom they hope to hold, while they add fuel to the flames which are to devour their victims to all eternity.

Such an utterly abandoned man was Thomas of Marle. While King Louis was busied with many wars, he laid waste the territories of Laon, Rheims, and Amiens, devouring like a raging wolf. He spared not the clergy—fearing not the vengeance of the Church—nor the people for humanity's sake. And the devil aided him, for the success of the foolish does ever lead them to perdition. Slaying all men, spoiling all things, he seized two manors, exceeding rich, from the abbey of the nuns of St. John of Laon. He fortified the two exceeding strong castles, Crécy and Nogent, with a marvelous wall and very high towers, as if they had been his own; and made them like to a den of dragons and a cave of robbers, whence he did waste almost the whole country with fire and pillage; and he had no pity.

The Church of France could no longer bear this great evil; wherefore the clergy, who had met together in a general synod at Beauvais, proceeded to pass sentence of condemnation upon the enemy of the Church's true spouse, Jesus Christ. The venerable Cono, bishop of Praeneste and legate of the holy Roman Church, troubled past endurance by the plaints of churches, of the orphans, of the poor, did smite this ruthless tyrant with the sword of the blessed Peter, which is general anathema. He did also ungird the knightly sword belt from him, though he was absent, and by the judgment of all declared him infamous, a scoundrel, unworthy the name of Christian.

And the king was moved by the plaints of this great council and led an army against him right quickly. He had the clergy, to whom he was ever humbly devoted, in his company, and marched straight against the castle of Crécy. Well fortified was it; yet he took it unprepared because his soldiers smote with an exceeding strong hand; or rather, because the hand of the Lord fought for him. He stormed the strongest tower as if it were the hut of a peasant, and put to confusion the wicked men and piously destroyed the impious. Because they had no pity upon other men, he cut them down without mercy. None could behold the castle tower flaming like the fires of hell and not exclaim, "The whole universe will fight for him against these madmen."

After he had won this victory, the king, who was ever swift to follow up his advantage, pushed forward toward the other castle, called Nogent. There came to him a man who said: "Oh, my lord king, it should be known to thy Serenity that in that wicked castle dwell exceeding wicked men who are worthy to lie in hell, and there only. Those are they who, when thou didst issue commands to destroy the commune of Laon, did burn with fire not only the city of Laon, but the noble church of the Mother of God, and many others beside. And well-nigh all the noble men of the city suffered martyrdom because they were true to their faith and defended their lord the bishop. And these evil men feared not to raise their hands against thy venerable Bishop Gaudin, the anointed of the Lord, defender of the church, but did him most cruelly to death, and exposed his naked body on the open road for beasts and birds of prey to feed upon; but first they cut off his finger with the pontifical ring. And they have agreed together, persuaded by the wicked Thomas, to attack and hold your tower."

The king was doubly animated by these words, and he attacked the wicked castle, broke open the abominable places of confinement, like prisons of hell, and set free the innocent; the guilty he punished with very heavy punishment. He alone avenged the injuries of many. Athirst for justice, he ordained that whatsoever murderous wretches he came upon should be fastened to a gibbet, and left as common food for the greed of kites, crows, and vultures. And this they deserved who had not feared to raise their hand against the Lord's anointed.

When he had taken these two adulterine castles and given back to the monastery of St. John the domains that had been seized, he returned to the city of Amiens and laid siege to a tower of that city which was held by a certain Adam, a cruel tyrant who was laying waste the churches and all the regions round about. He held the place besieged for hard upon two years, and at last forced those who defended it to give themselves up. When he had taken it he destroyed it utterly, and thus brought peace to the realm. He fulfilled most worthily the duty of a king who beareth not the sword in vain, and he deprived the wicked Thomas and his heirs forever of the lordship over that city.

Western Crusaders spread feudal practices to the eastern Mediterranean. These extracts from the *Assizes of Romania* deal with the operation of feudal jurisdiction in Greece in the thirteenth century.

FROM Feudal Institutions as Revealed in the Assizes of Romania BY P. W. TOPPING

HOW THE PRINCE CANNOT PUNISH ANY BARON OR VASSAL OF HIS WITHOUT THE CONSENT OF HIS LIEGEMEN

The Prince cannot punish any baron or vassal of his, either in civil or criminal action, nor injure him, nor place a penalty on him, without the counsel and consent of his liegemen or of the major part of them; nor render a decision concerning someone's fief or commission others to decide his actions at law; but he must render a decision through his liegemen. And the said lord or his officials cannot have any jurisdiction; but, in petty actions, like the matter of the vineyard of a fief or [the disposition] of a serf, the lord can entrust the judgment to his liegemen if the parties agree. And the lord cannot by force place any liegeman in any office against his will, nor punish him, nor retain his fief, unless it is with the judgment of his other liegemen.

HOW NO LIEGEMAN CAN BE HELD BY HIS LORD EXCEPT FOR TWO CAUSES

It has been ordered in the said Usages that no liegeman of the Principality can be detained in person by his lord for any reason except these two, to wit: for the causes of homicide and treason. And it is thus because his fief provides his security.

WHAT SHOULD BE DONE IF A LIEGEMAN COMMITS HOMICIDE OR TREASON?

If it should happen that a liegeman has committed homicide or treason, what should be done? To this the answer is, that according to the customs and usages aforesaid the lord cannot punish or detain him unless the homicide or

---

P. W. Topping, *Feudal Institutions as Revealed in the Assizes of Romania* (1949), pp. 25–31, 56. Reprinted by permission of University of Pennsylvania Press.

treason has first been proved and unless the judgment has been made in the case of the said liegeman by the other liegemen of the Principality. The lord can neither detain nor seize nor take his goods except by the judgment of the liegemen of the Principality.

AND IF IT HAPPENS THAT THE LORD HAS ONE OF HIS VASSALS, THAT IS, A FIEF OF ONE OF THEM, UNJUSTLY SEIZED, WHAT SHOULD BE DONE?

It is further asked, if the lord has the fief of one of his vassals seized unjustly, and this vassal of his has thrice asked for it in one year in the presence of his liegemen (if he can have such), demanding of him that he should return his fief and requesting the judgment of his court, and if the lord does not have the fief returned in full seizin when a year has passed, the homage for this fief passes to the nearest superior lord. And the vassal should first make a request for his fief within forty days, otherwise he shall lose the produce and revenues of that year. This same decision applies to others who have vassals subject to them if these vassals are liegemen. The man of simple homage has no court and can hold none. The liegeman or the man of simple homage shall be able to lodge a complaint before the overlord of his lord for the feudal goods which might have been taken from him unjustly by his lord; and he does this through a procurator appointed to this task.

When a criminal, civil, or feudal action arises between the Prince or another lord and one of his vassals, the Prince or the lord involved in the dispute must delegate one of his liegemen, or one not a liege, in his place. And the lord is required to rise, to give the delegate his baton and to leave the council, in accordance with the custom. And the delegate is to give the counsel of the liegemen of his court as much to the lord as to the party, retaining with him those liegemen who should appear to him most necessary in order to decide the question. And this is understood if the litigant is a liegeman.

* * *

By the Usage and Custom of the Empire of Romania, the Prince cannot place upon his vassals or freemen, or even on their serfs, any tallages or collections on any condition or under any name whatever, or anything, for the utility of the country, without the counsel and consent as well of the liegemen and vassals as of the other freemen. And in this case, those who consent are under obligation, and those who do not consent are under none. But in truth, if he wishes to marry his daughter or ransom himself from his enemies when he has been taken by them, in this case he can levy a collection only on the men of simple homage. Moreover, the lord should take care that no vassal, baron, or soldier allows straw, poultry, or any other thing to be taken by force from the serfs of his subjects.

* * *

If a liegeman has been injured in his fief or a part thereof by the Prince or by another lord, the said liegeman is bound to request his lord thrice in a year before some of his liegemen that he restore to him that in which he aggrieved him or reinstate him in his fief, demanding the judgment of his court. Moreover, he is not obliged to render service until he has been reinstated in his fief. And, if the lord is not willing to do him full justice, in this case he [the vassal] must summon his peers and together with them summon his lord also. And if the lord is negligent in doing what justice requires, in this case the other lieges who are with him are not bound to serve their lord until the fief in question is reinstated.

The next three readings deal with medieval England. The first, an extract from the *Anglo-Saxon Chronicle,* describes a highly successful feudal king, William the Conqueror (1066–1087).

FROM Anglo-Saxon Chronicle

If anyone wishes to know what sort of a man he was, or what dignity he had or of how many lands he was lord—then we will write of him even as we, who have looked upon him, and once lived at his court, have perceived him to be.

This King William of whom we speak was a very wise man, and very powerful and more worshipful and stronger than any predecessor of his had been. He was gentle to the good men who loved God, and stern beyond all measure to those people who resisted his will. In the same place where God permitted him to conquer England, he set up a famous monastery and appointed monks for it, and endowed it well. In his days the famous church at Canterbury was built, and also many another over all England. Also, this country was very full of monks and they lived their life under the rule of St. Benedict, and Christianity was such in his day that each man who wished followed out whatever concerned his order. Also, he was very dignified: three times every year he wore his crown, as often as he was in England. At Easter he wore it at Winchester, at Whitsuntide at Westminster, and at Christmas at Gloucester, and then there were with him all the powerful men over all

D. C. Douglas and G. Greenaway, *English Historical Documents 1042–1189* (1953), pp. 163–164. Reprinted by permission of Oxford University Press, Inc., and Eyre & Spottiswoode Ltd., London.

England, archbishops and bishops, abbots and earls, thegns and knights. Also, he was a very stern and violent man, so that no one dared do anything contrary to his will. He had earls in his fetters, who acted against his will. He expelled bishops from their sees, and abbots from their abbacies, and put thegns in prison, and finally he did not spare his own brother, who was called Odo; he was a very powerful bishop in Normandy (his cathedral church was at Bayeux)—and was the foremost man next the king, and had an earldom in England. And when the king was in Normandy, then he was master in this country: and he [the king] put *him* in prison. Amongst other things the good security he made in this country is not to be forgotten—so that any honest man could travel over his kingdom without injury with his bosom full of gold: and no one dared strike another, however much wrong he had done him. And if any man had intercourse with a woman against her will, he was forthwith castrated.

He ruled over England, and by his cunning it was so investigated that there was not one hide of land in England that he did not know who owned it, and what it was worth, and then set it down in his record. Wales was in his power, and he built castles there, and he entirely controlled that race. In the same way, he also subdued Scotland to himself, because of his great strength. The land of Normandy was his by natural inheritance, and he ruled over the county called Main: and if he could have lived two years more, he would have conquered Ireland by his prudence and without any weapons. Certainly in his time people had much oppression and very many injuries:

> He had castles built
> And poor men hard oppressed.
> The king was so very stark
> And deprived his underlings of many a mark
> Of gold and more hundreds of pounds of silver,
> That he took by weight and with great injustice
> From his people with little need for such a deed.
> Into avarice did he fall
> And loved greediness above all,
> He made great protection for the game
> And imposed laws for the same.
> That who so slew hart or hind
> Should be made blind.
>
> He preserved the harts and boars
> And loved the stags as much
> As if he were their father.
> Moreover, for the hare did he decree that they should go free.
> Powerful men complained of it and poor men lamented it
> But so fierce was he that he cared not for the rancour of them all
> But they had to follow out the king's will entirely

If they wished to live or hold their land,
Property or estate, or his favour great,
Alas! woe, that any man so proud should go,
And exalt himself and reckon himself above all men.
May Almighty God show mercy to his soul
And grant unto him forgiveness for his sins.

The *Anglo-Saxon Chronicle* also provides a picture of an unsuccessful feudal ruler, King Stephen (1135–1154).

When the traitors understood that he was a mild man, and gentle and good, and did not exact the full penalties of the law, they perpetrated every enormity. They had done him homage, and sworn oaths, but they kept no pledge; all of them were perjured and their pledges nullified, for every powerful man built his castles and held them against him and they filled the country full of castles. They oppressed the wretched people of the country severely with castle-building. When the castles were built, they filled them with devils and wicked men. Then, both by night and day they took those people that they thought had any goods—men and women—and put them in prison and tortured them with indescribable torture to extort gold and silver—for no martyrs were ever so tortured as they were. They were hung by the thumbs or by the head, and corselets were hung on their feet. Knotted ropes were put round their heads and twisted till they penetrated to the brains. They put them in prisons where there were adders and snakes and toads, and killed them like that. Some they put in a "torture-chamber"—that is in a chest that was short, narrow and shallow, and they put sharp stones in it and pressed the man in it so that he had all his limbs broken. In many of the castles was a "noose-and-trap"—consisting of chains of such a kind that two or three men had enough to do to carry one. It was so made that it was fastened to a beam, and they used to put a sharp iron around the man's throat and his neck, so that he could not in any direction either sit or lie or sleep, but had to carry all that iron. Many thousands they killed by starvation.

I have neither the ability nor the power to tell all the horrors nor all the torments they inflicted upon wretched people in this country: and that lasted the nineteen years Stephen was king, and it was always going from bad to worse. They levied taxes on the villages every so often, and called it "protection money." When the wretched people had no more to give, they robbed and burned all the villages, so that you could easily go a whole day's journey and never find anyone occupying a village, nor land tilled. Then corn was dear, and meat and butter and cheese, because there was none in the country.

Wretched people died of starvation; some lived by begging for alms, who had once been rich men; some fled the country.

There had never been till then greater misery in the country, nor had heathens ever done worse than then they did. For contrary to custom, they respected neither church nor churchyard, but took all the property that was inside, and then burnt the church and everything together. Neither did they respect bishops' land nor abbots' nor priests', but robbed monks and clerics, and everyone robbed somebody else if he had the greater power. If two or three men came riding to a village, all the villagers fled, because they expected they would be robbers. The bishops and learned men were always excommunicating them, but they thought nothing of it, because they were all utterly accursed and perjured and doomed to perdition.

Wherever cultivation was done, the ground produced no corn, because the land was all ruined by such doings, and they said openly that Christ and his saints were asleep. Such things, too much for us to describe, we suffered nineteen years for our sins.

The most famous constitutional document that survives from medieval England is *Magna Carta*—a "treaty of peace" between a feudal king and his barons (1215).

FROM Magna Carta

John, by the grace of God, king of England, lord of Ireland, duke of Normandy and Aquitaine, count of Anjou; to the archbishops, bishops, abbots, earls, barons, justiciars, foresters, sheriffs, reeves, servants, and all bailiffs and his faithful people greeting. . . .

1. In the first place we have granted to God and by this our present charter confirmed, for us and our heirs forever, that the English church shall be free, and shall hold its rights entire and its liberties uninjured; and we will that it thus be observed; which is shown by this, that the freedom of elections, which is considered to be most important and especially necessary to the English church, we, of our pure and spontaneous will, granted, and by our charter confirmed, before the contest between us and our barons had arisen; and obtained a confirmation of it by the lord Pope Innocent III; which we

University of Pennsylvania Translations and Reprints, I, No. 6 (1897), 6–17, translated by E. P. Cheyney.

will observe and which we will shall be observed in good faith by our heirs forever.

We have granted moreover to all free men of our kingdom for us and our heirs forever all the liberties written below, to be had and holden by themselves and their heirs from us and our heirs.

2. If any of our earls or barons, or others holding from us in chief by military service shall have died, and when he has died his heir shall be of full age and owe relief, he shall have his inheritance by the ancient relief; that is to say, the heir or heirs of an earl for the whole barony of an earl a hundred pounds; the heir or heirs of a baron for a whole barony a hundred pounds; the heir or heirs of a knight, for a whole knight's fee, a hundred shillings at most; and who owes less let him give less according to the ancient custom of fiefs.

3. If moreover the heir of any one of such shall be under age, and shall be in wardship, when he comes of age he shall have his inheritance without relief and without a fine.

4. The custodian of the land of such a minor heir shall not take from the land of the heir any except reasonable products, reasonable customary payments, and reasonable services, and this without destruction or waste of men or of property; and if we shall have committed the custody of the land of any such a one to the sheriff or to any other who is to be responsible to us for its proceeds, and that man shall have caused destruction or waste from his custody we will recover damages from him, and the land shall be committed to two legal and discreet men of that fief, who shall be responsible for its proceeds to us or to him to whom we have assigned them; and if we shall have given or sold to any one the custody of any such land, and he has caused destruction or waste there, he shall lose that custody, and it shall be handed over to two legal and discreet men of that fief who shall be in like manner responsible to us as is said above.

5. The custodian moreover, so long as he shall have the custody of the land, must keep up the houses, parks, warrens, fish ponds, mills, and other things pertaining to the land, from the proceeds of the land itself; and he must return to the heir, when he has come to full age, all his land, furnished with ploughs and implements of husbandry according as the time of wainage requires and as the proceeds of the land are able reasonably to sustain.

6. Heirs shall be married without disparity, so nevertheless that before the marriage is contracted, it shall be announced to the relatives by blood of the heir himself.

7. A widow, after the death of her husband, shall have her marriage portion and her inheritance immediately and without obstruction, nor shall she give anything for her dowry or for her marriage portion, or for her inheritance which inheritance her husband and she held on the day of the death of her husband; and she may remain in the house of her husband for forty days after his death, within which time her dowry shall be assigned to her.

8. No widow shall be compelled to marry so long as she prefers to live

without a husband, provided she gives security that she will not marry without our consent, if she holds from us, or without the consent of her lord from whom she holds, if she holds from another.

9. Neither we nor our bailiffs will seize any land or rent, for any debt, so long as the chattels of the debtor are sufficient for the payment of the debt; nor shall the pledges of a debtor be distrained so long as the principal debtor himself has enough for the payment of the debt; and if the principal debtor fails in the payment of the debt, not having the wherewithal to pay it, the pledges shall be responsible for the debt; and if they wish, they shall have the lands and the rents of the debtor until they shall have been satisfied for the debt which they have before paid for him, unless the principal debtor shall have shown himself to be quit in that respect towards those pledges.

10. If any one has taken anything from the Jews, by way of a loan, more or less, and dies before that debt is paid, the debt shall not draw interest so long as the heir is under age, from whomsoever he holds; and if that debt falls into our hands, we will take nothing except the chattel contained in the agreement.

11. And if anyone dies leaving a debt owing to the Jews, his wife shall have her dowry, and shall pay nothing of that debt; and if there remain minor children of the dead man, necessaries shall be provided for them corresponding to the holding of the dead man; and from the remainder shall be paid the debt, the service of the lords being retained. In the same way debts are to be treated which are owed to others than the Jews.

12. No scutage or aid shall be imposed in our kingdom except by the common council of our kingdom, except for the ransoming of our body, for the making of our oldest son a knight, and for once marrying our oldest daughter, and for these purposes it shall be only a reasonable aid; in the same way it shall be done concerning the aids of the city of London.

13. And the city of London shall have all its ancient liberties and free customs, as well by land as by water. Moreover, we will and grant that all other cities and boroughs and villages and ports shall have all their liberties and free customs.

14. And for holding a common council of the kingdom concerning the assessment of an aid otherwise than in the three cases mentioned above, or concerning the assessment of a scutage we shall cause to be summoned the archbishops, bishops, abbots, earls, and greater barons by our letters under seal; and besides we shall cause to be summoned generally, by our sheriffs and bailiffs all those who hold from us in chief, for a certain day, that is at the end of forty days at least, and for a certain place; and in all the letters of that summons, we will express the cause of the summons, and when the summons has thus been given the business shall proceed on the appointed day, on the advice of those who shall be present, even if not all of those who were summoned have come.

15. We will not grant to any one, moreover, that he shall take an aid from his free men, except for ransoming his body, for making his oldest son a

knight, and for once marrying his oldest daughter; and for these purposes only a reasonable aid shall be taken.

16. No one shall be compelled to perform any greater service for a knight's fee, or for any other free tenement than is owed from it.

17. The common pleas shall not follow our court, but shall be held in some certain place.

* * *

20. A free man shall not be fined for a small offence, except in proportion to the measure of the offence; and for a great offence he shall be fined in proportion to the magnitude of the offence, saving his freehold; and a merchant in the same way, saving his merchandise; and the villain shall be fined in the same way, saving his wainage, if he shall be at our mercy; and none of the above fines shall be imposed except by the oaths of honest men of the neighborhood.

21. Earls and barons shall only be fined by their peers, and only in proportion to their offence.

* * *

28. No constable or other bailiff of ours shall take anyone's grain or other chattels, without immediately paying for them in money, unless he is able to obtain a postponement at the good-will of the seller.

29. No constable shall require any knight to give money in place of his ward of a castle if he is willing to furnish that ward in his own person or through another honest man, if he himself is not able to do it for a reasonable cause; and if we shall lead or send him into the army he shall be free from ward in proportion to the amount of time by which he has been in the army through us.

30. No sheriff or bailiff of ours or any one else shall take horses or wagons of any free man for carrying purposes except on the permission of that free man.

31. Neither we nor our bailiffs will take the wood of another man for castles, or for anything else which we are doing, except by the permission of him to whom the wood belongs.

32. We will not hold the lands of those convicted of a felony for more than a year and a day, after which the lands shall be returned to the lords of the fiefs.

* * *

39. No free man shall be taken or imprisoned or dispossessed, or outlawed, or banished, or in any way destroyed, nor will we go upon him, nor send upon him, except by the legal judgment of his peers or by the law of the land.

40. To no one will we sell, to no one will we deny, or delay right or justice.

41. All merchants shall be safe and secure in going out from England and coming into England and in remaining and going through England, as well by land as by water, for buying and selling, free from all evil tolls, by the ancient and rightful customs, except in time of war, and if they are of a land at war with us; and if such are found in our land at the beginning of war, they shall be attached without injury to their bodies or goods, until it shall be known from us or from our principal justiciar in what way the merchants of our land are treated who shall be then found in the country which is at war with us; and if ours are safe there, the others shall be safe in our land.

42. It is allowed henceforth to anyone to go out from our kingdom, and to return, safely and securely, by land and by water, saving their fidelity to us, except in time of war for some short time, for the common good of the kingdom; excepting persons imprisoned and outlawed according to the law of the realm, and people of a land at war with us, and merchants, of whom it shall be done as is before said.

43. If anyone holds from any escheat, as from the honor of Wallingford, or Nottingham, or Boulogne, or Lancaster, or from other escheats which are in our hands and are baronies, and he dies, his heir shall not give any other relief, nor do to us any other service than he would do to the baron, if that barony was in the hands of the baron; and we will hold it in the same way as the baron held it.

* * *

54. No one shall be seized nor imprisoned on the appeal of a woman concerning the death of anyone except her husband.

55. All fines which have been imposed unjustly and against the law of the land, and all penalties imposed unjustly and against the law of the land are altogether excused, or will be on the judgment of the twenty-five barons of whom mention is made below in connection with the security of the peace, or on the judgment of the majority of them, along with the aforesaid Stephen, archbishop of Canterbury, if he is able to be present, and others whom he may wish to call for this purpose along with him. And if he should not be able to be present, nevertheless the business shall go on without him, provided that if any one or more of the aforesaid twenty-five barons are in a similar suit they should be removed as far as this particular judgment goes, and others who shall be chosen and put upon oath, by the remainder of the twenty-five shall be substituted for them for this purpose.

* * *

60. Moreover, all those customs and franchises mentioned above which we have conceded in our kingdom, and which are to be fulfilled, as far as pertains to us, in respect to our men; all men of our kingdom as well clergy as laymen, shall observe as far as pertains to them, in respect to their men.

61. Since, moreover, for the sake of God, and for the improvement of our

kingdom, and for the better quieting of the hostility sprung up lately between us and our barons, we have made all these concessions; wishing them to enjoy these in a complete and firm stability forever, we make and concede to them the security described below; that is to say, that they shall elect twenty-five barons of the kingdom, whom they will, who ought with all their power to observe, hold, and cause to be observed, the peace and liberties which we have conceded to them, and by this our present charter confirmed to them; in this manner, that if we or our justiciar, or our bailiffs, or any one of our servants shall have done wrong in any way toward any one, or shall have transgressed any of the articles of peace or security; and the wrong shall have been shown to four barons of the aforesaid twenty-five barons, let those four barons come to us to our justiciar, if we are out of the kingdom, laying before us the transgression, and let them ask that we cause that transgression to be corrected without delay. And if we shall not have corrected the transgression or, if we shall be out of the kingdom, if our justiciar shall not have corrected it within a period of forty days, counting from the time in which it has been shown to us or to our justiciar, if we are out of the kingdom; the aforesaid four barons shall refer the matter to the remainder of the twenty-five barons, and let these twenty-five barons with the whole community of the country distress and injure us in every way they can; that is to say by the seizure of our castles, lands, possessions, and in such other ways as they can until it shall have been corrected according to their judgment, saving our person and that of our queen, and those of our children; and when the correction has been made, let them devote themselves to us as they did before. And let whoever in the country wishes take an oath that in all the above-mentioned measures he will obey the orders of the aforesaid twenty-five barons, and that he will injure us as far as he is able with them, and we give permission to swear publicly and freely to each one who wishes to swear, and no one will we ever forbid to swear. All those, moreover, in the country who of themselves and their own will are unwilling to take an oath to the twenty-five barons as to distressing and injuring us along with them, we will compel to take the oath by our mandate, as before said. And if any one of the twenty-five barons shall have died or departed from the land or shall in any other way be prevented from taking the above-mentioned action, let the remainder of the aforesaid twenty-five barons choose another in his place, according to their judgment, who shall take an oath in the same way as the others. In all those things, moreover, which are committed to those five and twenty barons to carry out, if perhaps the twenty-five are present, and some disagreement arises among them about something, or if any of them when they have been summoned are not willing or are not able to be present, let that be considered valid and firm which the greater part of those who are present arrange or command, just as if the whole twenty-five had agreed in this; and let the aforesaid twenty-five swear that they will observe faithfully all the things which are said above, and with all their ability cause them to be observed. And we will obtain nothing from anyone, either by ourselves or by another by which any of these concessions and liberties shall be revoked or diminished; and if any such thing shall have been obtained, let it be invalid and void, and we will never use it by ourselves or by another.

5
FEUDALISM
AS A SYSTEM
OF
GOVERNMENT

The following readings present the views of three modern scholars on feudalism as a political system. J. Calmette saw feudalism as essentially a disintegrative force.

FROM The Feudal World BY J. CALMETTE

THE FEUDAL PRINCIPLE

Two fundamental ideas served as the bases of ancient society—the State and property. The feudal principle attacked these two ideas and so to speak disintegrated them. Properly speaking there was neither State nor property in feudalism. How could these two ideas which seem fundamental and solid have been dissolved? To explain it is to explain the emergence of feudalism.

DISSOLUTION OF PROPERTY

Property was undermined first. At the outset the early Middle Ages knew hardly any form of wealth except land, and land belonged chiefly to the great proprietors. These latter could not cultivate it themselves. Moreover, agricultural work could not be carried out, either by slave labor as in former times—

J. Calmette, *Le Monde Féodal* (1937), pp. 165–175. Translated by Brian Tierney by permission of Presses Universitaires de France, Paris.

slavery being condemned by the morals of the age—nor by paid workers as nowadays—the circulation of currency being insufficient to maintain a class of wage earners. Hence the problem was resolved by making grants of land by means of contracts. The land to be cultivated was partitioned into lots among tenants of divers conditions who, whatever their name or quality, were charged with labor services and rents while, for their part, they enjoyed a right to the use of the land. Words like *precarium, emphyteusis,* etc., refer merely to contractual variants of this system of grants. In the final reckoning, their common characteristic was that they were permanent and hereditary. . . . When possession was dissociated definitively from ownership the latter diminished to no more than an external right, purely and simply a capacity to exact certain services. Briefly, the right of property, being converted into a kind of eminent domain, had practically ceased to exist.

DISSOLUTION OF THE STATE

The State was eclipsed in the same way. On the morrow of the invasions it was personified in a barbarian king who fused together prerogatives of state and his own personal rights. A man governed, not an impersonal entity. This man bound other men to himself by personal oaths. The idea of personal loyalty dissolved the substance of the State just as the permanent and hereditary right of tenure dissolved property. The bond of dependence of man on man—that ancient custom that gave rise to the "clientage" of ancient law— acquired unprecedented importance from the fact of the invasions. Around the barbarian chief are his "companions," bound by oath and paid by booty, a band that forms an instrument of war and conquest. Now it is from his intimate circle derived from this band that the Frankish king usually draws his counts. Soon these, like the king, attach to themselves by oath men whom they intend to make use of or wish to dominate. It is "vassalage" which is taking root. If the word does not appear until the eighth century its rapid success manifests the force of the concept which it expresses.

LORDSHIP

Vassalage becomes combined with the granting of land. For, like the worker, the administrator cannot be paid in money in a society where currency is scarce and does not circulate. Hence the administrator, like the worker, is paid by a form of usufruct. In other words the king, who is the greatest of landlords, pays his agents in the same way that the landlord pays his peasants; he gives them the use of part of his domain. This right of use is at the same time payment for and conditional on the performing of formerly public service. This grant in exchange for service, above all military service on horseback, is called a "benefice" or "honor." Vassalage and benefice combined engender the fief. The fief, properly speaking, is a benefice that a vassal holds of his lord.

The lord or seigneur [senior—the oldest, the most exalted in dignity] receives the oath of the vassal and gives him the property whose revenues provide remuneration for the services implied by the oath. Thus, there is created between lord and vassal a contract. This is the feudal contract. But the services owed by virtue of this contract include those which formerly the subject was bound to render to the State from the very fact of his birth. A private right is thus substituted for a public right. Evidently the generalization of such a system impoverishes the State, which is no more than an idea or transcendental concept, deprived of concrete reality—just what has happened to property itself.

APPROPRIATION OF PUBLIC FUNCTIONS

However serious this transformation became the Carolingian regime would have continued as a semblance of a State if its functionaries had continued to obey it. But, on the contrary, they ceased little by little to be under the king's control and adopted the habit of exercising their powers, no longer on behalf of the State, but in their own name. The public function was absorbed into the lordship. The decline did not take place all at once but came about through insensible transitions. The kings did not react against it because they saw lordship as a means of administering. Moreover the struggles of prince against prince put loyalty on the auction block. The counts sell their support to the king. This support is paid for in benefices and the kingship is so thoroughly stripped of its lands that the descendants of Charlemagne will leave to their successors, the Capetians, a domain reduced almost to nothing. Each count, each holder of an immunity, in a word each lord, lives independently and this is the time when, to quote Quicherat, France—one might say all the West—"bristled with castles." . . .

FEUDAL PROTECTION

The success of this system would have been incomprehensible if it had not answered to a need. The need was for protection. Feudalism established itself because at a critical time it offered protection. We have already seen that insecurity worked in its favor. It was above all the Viking invasions—and to a lesser degree the Saracen and Magyar invasions—which brought about the victory of feudal principles in the ninth century. Faced with the peril of invasions in various localities, the central government proved incapable of finding any effective remedy. The royal failure betrayed the people, and local resistance was organized around the lord. The fortified castle was the center of resistance. Life was concentrated in the circle of the lord because the seigneury was a living cell, one in which the individual found relative security. . . .

PRIVATE WAR

The feudal nobility appears most of all as a military caste. The lord remains above all a soldier. Not all conflicts of law or fact are ended by means of a judgment of a feudal court. In case of discord there is war between lord and lord. Not only a clash of interests or personalities, but often sheer love of battle provokes these quarrels, which custom regulates, and which, once the gauntlet has been thrown down and accepted, unleash between two seigneuries all the horrors of steel, fire and blood. The Church, as a civilizing force, tried in vain to limit the evil. The Truce of God, the Peace of God, were palliatives of perceptible effect but insufficient and precarious in application. One might say that private war, the scourge of the feudal centuries, replaced the invasions against which men had sought to protect themselves by placing themselves under the protection of lords.

R. W. Southern saw the feudal principality as a constructive achievement.

FROM The Making of the Middle Ages
BY R. W. SOUTHERN

Politically, the great question in the tenth century, outside Germany, was how far the disintegration of authority would go. The immediate cause of the disintegration was lack of loyalty, and with lack of loyalty to persons went a decay and confusion of the ideas for which the persons stood. It was a time when claims of allegiance and duty, however well founded in law or in history, counted for nothing when they went beyond the bounds of effective personal power. It was easy for the Count of Anjou to throw off his obligations to the King of France. Would it prove equally possible for the lord of Loches or of any of the castles of the Loire to throw off the authority of the Count of Anjou? How far would the process go? The answer depended

R. W. Southern, *The Making of the Middle Ages* (1953), pp. 80–90. Reprinted by permission of Yale University Press and Hutchinson Publishing Group Ltd., London.

partly on the range of those small bodies of armoured, mounted soldiers who were growing up round the strong points of government. Partly it depended on the extent of the sacrifices people would be prepared to make for peace and security. It was no accident that after the confusion of the tenth century the strongest governmental units appeared where there was least in the way of marsh, mountain or forest to separate one community from another—in the open plains where the competition for power was most intense, and where the need for organization was consequently most keenly felt. But even in the most favourable geographical conditions, man's technical equipment was so primitive that this helplessness before Nature—which added to his misery in one way—saved him from the misery of organized tyranny. There was a mercifully large gap between the will to rule and the power to do so, and it may be that bad roads and an intractable soil contributed more to the fashioning of familiar liberties than any other factor at this time.

Perhaps more simply than anywhere else in Europe, the shaping of a new political order may be seen in the valley of the river Loire. There was here so clean a sweep of ancient institutions, title deeds and boundaries, that the emergence of new forms of loyalty and authority was facilitated. Elsewhere the same processes are to be observed, men have the same objects in view, but they work towards them less directly and less swiftly. We shall observe the ambitions, and the restraints imposed on the wills, of some of the most powerful personalities of their time, in studying the emergence of one of the strongest new political units of the eleventh century in the Loire valley.

THE COUNTY OF ANJOU [1]

The history of this county from the late tenth to the mid-twelfth century provides a rich portrait gallery of the makers of a medieval "state." Like other families, the counts took a great interest in their past; they were proud of it, and in the course of years they left a large collection of documents, which illuminate their history. Towards the end of the eleventh century, there was a historically minded Count, Fulk Rechin, who set himself to record the traditions of the family and his own recollections of his predecessors. Looking back from the eminence which the family had attained in his time, he could dimly perceive the origins of their good fortune in the career of an ancestor two hundred years earlier. Nothing was clearly reported about this ancestor except that his name was Ingelgarius, nor was much known about his de-

---

[1] For what follows, see L. Halphen, *Le Comté d'Anjou au XI Siècle* (Paris, 1906), J. Chartrou, *L'Anjou de 1109–1151* (Paris, 1928), and J. Boussard, *Le Comté d'Anjou sous Henri Plantegenêt et ses fils (1151–1204)* (Bibliothèque de l'école des Hautes Études, CLXXI, Paris, 1938). The chronicle sources are published in *Chroniques des Comtes d'Anjou et des seigneurs d'Amboise,* ed. L. Halphen and R. Poupardin (Collection des Textes pour servir à l'étude d'histoire, 1913).

cendants for nearly another hundred years; but the later panegyrists of the family were able to fill this gap by proclaiming that Ingelgarius was descended from an ancient Romano-British family of high rank. No amount of research or invention could discover how the family had lived in the intervening period since the fall of Rome, but it was concluded that "the matter is unimportant for we often read that senators have lived on the land and emperors have been snatched from the plough." This classical background was a twelfth-century addition to the history of the family—it reveals the romantic prejudices of that period—but in essentials the historians of the family were right. They saw that the effective origins of the family were to be sought in the later years of the ninth century—a time when, as one of them remarked, "the men in established positions relied on the merits of their ancestors and not on their own," and allowed themselves to be elbowed out of the way by new men pushing their way to the front by superior energy and military effectiveness.

The family of Ingelgarius were among these new men. War made them conspicuous, grants of land established their position, marriage consolidated it, and the acquisition of ancient titles of honour cloaked their usurpations. Ingelgarius gained the first foothold in the valley of the Loire, but it was his son Fulk the Red—with a name and physical characteristic which kept reappearing in his descendants—who made the family a power to be reckoned with in the neighbourhood: marriage added to his possessions, force held them together, and the comital rights (for what they were worth), which had previously been shared, were now acquired outright. Two more generations, covering the period from 941 to 987, gave the family a place in legend and in general repute, establishing them in a subtle way in men's minds as well as in their physical experience. The time of Fulk the Good (941 to c. 960) was looked back to as a period of growth, though it was not a time of territorial expansion: it was now that the unnatural fertility of the soil— the fruit of long years of depopulation—was discovered, and prodigious crops rewarded the labours of new settlers. The prize of the Loire valley, the capital city of Tours, still lay outside the range of the count's authority, but the family had great claims to the gratitude of the church in that city. It was said that Ingelgarius had restored to it by force of arms the relics of its patron saint, thus starting the family tradition of goodwill towards the church of Tours. Fulk's reputation in this respect was of a more scholarly kind. It was reported that he delighted to take part in the choir services with the canons and that he was the author of a famous rebuke to a king who ridiculed his clerical tastes. The story is exceedingly improbable, but it illustrates the way in which the family was adding to itself fame of a more than military kind. Fulk's son, Geoffrey Greymantle, who was Count from about 960 to 987, added to this legendary reputation: he was one of the select band of tenth-century heroes whose names were handed down to form part of the stock-in-trade of twelfth-century poetic memory. He was pictured as the standard

bearer of Charlemagne in the *Song of Roland,* and in his own right he was
the hero of various stories, in which his prowess and counsel saved the kingdom from its enemies.[2]

By 987 the family was ready to emerge from its legendary and epic age on
to the stage of history. At this moment there appeared one of those powerful
figures, who combined all the qualities and ferocity of his race and consolidated the achievements of the last four generations: Fulk Nerra, the Black,
Count of Anjou from 987 to 1040. We cannot do better than look at him
through the eyes of his grandson, Count Fulk Rechin. This is what he records of Fulk Nerra:

1 He built thirteen castles, which he can name, and many more besides.
2 He won two pitched battles, against his neighbours to East and West.
3 He built two abbeys, one at Angers and the other near Loches, the great
  outpost of his power in the South East.
4 He went twice to Jerusalem (this is an understatement: it is almost certain that he went three times); and he died on his way home during his
  last journey.

Each one of these items, properly considered, stamps him as a man of note:
taken together they convey a vivid impression of a pioneer in the art of
feudal government. In the first place, the castles: they were the guarantee
of the stability of the régime. Fulk was a pioneer in the building of stone
keeps, and one formidable example of his handiwork still survives at Langeais.
The inexpugnable fortresses solved at once the problem of defence and of
government—they made loyalty easy. The battles were more speculative—
brilliant gambles based on the solid capital of defensive positions. It was a
time when he who committed himself to open battle, committed his fortune
to the winds. But the reward of successful enterprise was great, as befitted
the uncertainty of the outcome; and the battle of Conquereuil in 992 against
the Count of Brittany was one of the foundations of Angevin greatness.

We pass to the expressions of Fulk Nerra's religious zeal. He and his contemporary the Duke of Normandy were the greatest of the pilgrims who set
on foot the movement to Jerusalem. In them the alternation of headlong
violence with abrupt acts of remorse and atonement, which characterises the
early feudal age, has its full play. Perhaps more than in anything else, the
nature of the man is revealed in the documents which recount his religious
benefactions. They breathe a vigorous and autocratic spirit, unencumbered by
any feeling after intangible things, yet accessible to a sense of guilt and stirred
by a sense of littleness before the miraculous disturbances of nature. These
documents deal with stark facts:

---

[2] For the place of Geoffrey Greymantle in epic tradition, see F. Lot, *Geoffroi Grisegonelle dans
l'Épopée* in Romania, 1890, XIX, 377–93, and *Traditions sur Geoffroi Grisegonelle et sur
Helgaud de Montreuil* in Romania, 1920, XLVI, 376–81.

I give them (says Fulk's charter to Beaulieu) the blood, the thieves and all evil deeds, of whatsoever kind they are (that is to say, jurisdiction over, and the profits arising from the punishment of, murderers, thieves and other criminals), between the rivulet *de Concere* and the oak of St. Hilary, and between the vegetable garden and the elm on which men are hanged. And wheresoever, on my land, the abbot does battle for anything, if his champion is beaten, he shall go free and pay no fine to my reeve or any official.[3]

So far as Fulk speaks to us at all, he speaks to us in words like these. Yet, when all is said, we are very far from understanding a man like Fulk Nerra. It is only occasionally that we are allowed to see behind the façade of ruthlessness and activity to the not overconfident humanity which guided arm and hand. It takes some extraordinary event to reveal these men in their more domestic moods. They must often have sat with their wives at the upper windows of their newly built castles, but it is not until a meteor falls into the garden below that we have a picture of Fulk's formidable son Geoffrey Martel and his wife Agnes (the mother of the Empress) racing down to the spot where it fell and vowing to found an abbey dedicated to the Holy Trinity, in memory of the three glowing fragments which had flashed before their awe-struck eyes. It was in the face of the miraculous that they became most human. When the Duke of Aquitaine heard that a rain of blood had fallen in his duchy, he did not reflect that he was hostile to the royal pretensions—he humbly wrote and asked the king if he had any learned men who could explain the event. And their answers were such as to make any man pause in a career of wrong-doing.[4] But, on the whole, the secular leaders of the early eleventh century must be judged by what they did, and not by what they thought or intended. Judged by this standard Fulk Nerra is the founder of the greatness of the County of Anjou.

His life-time brings us to an age of serious, expansive wars waged by well-organized and strongly fortified territorial lords. The confused warfare, haphazard battles and obscure acts of force of the first hundred years of the family's history had turned scattered and precarious rights into a complex, but geographically compact and militarily impregnable association, dependent on the Count. The process was directed by an instinctive feeling for strategic advantage, which perhaps lends to the history of these years an appearance of consistency greater than in fact it possessed. The methods were not refined, but they were practised with a consistency of purpose which inspires a certain respect. The swallowing of an important strong point might be preceded by many years of steady encroachment. It was necessary, first, to get established at some point within the territory to be threatened—an operation

---

[3] L. Halphen, *Le Comté d'Anjou au XI Siècle,* pp. 351–2.
[4] These letters were preserved among the correspondence of Fulbert of Chartres and they are printed in P. L. vol. 141, 239–40 and 935–8.

carried out by a careful marriage, a purchase which the documents represent as a gift, or an act of force or fraud. Then a castle was built as a base of operations. After that, watchfulness: a minority, the chance offered by the enemy's engagement elsewhere, or a lucky battle, might complete the circle. The town of Tours, for instance, was not swallowed until 1044, but in a sense the whole history of the family was a preparation for this event: the good relations with the church of the city seem to go back to the founder of the dynasty; the encircling of the town by a ring of castles at Langeais, Montbazon, Montrichard and Montboyau had been begun by Fulk Nerra fifty years before the final victory. How much was design and how much a kind of inspired opportunism it would be useless to enquire. Once started, the process went on as relentlessly as the operations of the Stock Exchange.

But by the middle of the eleventh century, easy progress by these familiar methods was no longer possible. The weak had been made dependent, the strongholds of intruding neighbours had been taken and, by the same token, distant claims of the Counts outside their own territory had been abandoned. To the west stood Brittany, to the east Blois, to the north—across the still debatable land of Maine—Normandy, to the south Poitou. They faced each others as equals. Although the armed peace was often broken, the chief interest of the next hundred and fifty years lies in the emergence of stable political institutions and the elaboration of a new system of law. The swashbuckling days were over, and the régimes which had emerged began to clothe themselves in habits of respectability. Up to this point, St. Augustine's dictum that secular governments are nothing but large-scale robbery seemed to be abundantly justified by the facts: but slowly something more complex, more sensitive to the positive merits of organized society, seemed to be required. Government became something more than a system of exactions from a conquered countryside, and there developed a routine for the peaceful exploitation of resources and for the administering of justice. For this, an expert and literate staff was needed, in addition to the menials and military leaders who had satisfied the requirements of a more primitive age. Government by means of the written word returned after a long silence. Until the time of Fulk Rechin, the Count seems not to have felt the need for having someone at hand who could write his letters. All the known comital documents were written by an outsider. It was quite natural that this should be so. The most frequent occasion for writing a document was to make a record of some act of generosity, by which the Count had endowed a religious house: it was the beneficiary who was interested in making the record, and to him fell the labour of making it. If on the other hand, as might sometimes happen, the Count wished to correspond with the Pope or the King of France, he called in some notable scholar for the occasion to write his letters for him. But slowly his needs outgrew this primitive expedient. The necessity for transmitting orders and preserving information became more pressing, and by the end of the eleventh century the Count was not only sealing or witnessing documents which had been written for him by those with whom he was in casual contact; he had men about him who could conduct his correspondence and were eager to manage his affairs. It is an important moment in history, not peculiar to Anjou but common to the governments of northwestern Europe. The continuity of government was re-established. The work required trained men, and the presence of trained men—by a process with which we are familiar—made more work for more trained men.

The rise of the great schools of Northern France and Norman England coincided with and forwarded this movement in government. Slowly the ruling households of Europe, at all levels from the Papal Court to the household of a minor baron, were penetrated by men calling themselves "Masters," men who had studied in the Schools—or as we should say university men. The flow of university men into the Civil Service and into technical positions from the 1870's to our own day is not more significant of the new part played by government in daily affairs, than the similar flow of "Masters" into official positions which began in the early twelfth century and, by the end of our period, had transformed the operations and outlook of secular government. The revolutions in thought which transformed the mainly monastic learning of the eleventh century on the one hand, and the mainly clerical education of the early nineteenth century on the other, had, both of them, wide repercussions in the sphere of government. The "Masters" of the twelfth century brought to government a training, a method and a breadth of vision which had been unknown in the previous century: they were only the instruments of government, but they were finer instruments than had been known before.

J. R. Strayer considered that feudalism provided a workable basis of government for the newly emerging European states.

FROM Feudalism in Western Europe BY J. R. STRAYER

We could hardly expect these early feudal governments to be well organized and efficient—they were improvised to meet a desperate situation and they bore all the signs of hasty construction. But they did have two great advantages which made them capable of further development. In the first place, feudalism forced men who had privileges to assume responsibility. In the late Roman Empire, the Frankish kingdom, and the Carolingian monarchy

J. R. Strayer, "Feudalism in Western Europe," in R. Coulborn, ed., *Feudalism in History*, pp. 22–25. Reprinted by permission of Princeton University Press, copyright, © 1956, by Princeton University Press.

wealthy landlords had assisted the central government as little as possible while using their position and influence to gain special advantages for themselves. Now they had to carry the whole load; if they shirked they lost everything. In the second place, feudalism simplified the structure of government to a point where it corresponded to existing social and economic conditions. For centuries rulers had been striving to preserve something of the Roman political system, at the very least to maintain their authority over relatively large areas through a hierarchy of appointed officials. These efforts had met little response from the great majority of people; large-scale government had given them few benefits and had forced them to carry heavy burdens. Always there had been a dangerous discrepancy between the wide interests of the rulers and the narrow, local interests of the ruled. Feudalism relieved this strain; it worked at a level which was comprehensible to the ordinary man and it made only minimum demands on him. It is probably true that early feudal governments did less than they should, but this was better than doing more than was wanted. When the abler feudal lords began to improve their governments they had the support of their people, who realized that new institutions were needed. The active demand for more and better government in the twelfth century offers a sharp contrast to the apathy with which the people of Western Europe watched the disintegration of the Roman and the Carolingian Empires.

Feudalism, in short, made a fairly clean sweep of obsolete institutions and replaced them with a rudimentary government which could be used as a basis for a fresh start. Early feudal government was informal and flexible. Contrary to common opinion, it was at first little bound by tradition. It is true that it followed local custom, but there were few written records, and oral tradition was neither very accurate nor very stable. Custom changed rapidly when circumstances changed; innovations were quickly accepted if they seemed to promise greater security. Important decisions were made by the lord and his vassals, meeting in informal councils which followed no strict rules of procedure. It was easy for an energetic lord to make experiments in government; for example, there was constant tinkering with the procedure of feudal courts in the eleventh and twelfth centuries in order to find better methods of proof. Temporary committees could be set up to do specific jobs; if they did their work well they might become permanent and form the nucleus of a department of government. It is true that many useful ideas came from the clergy, rather than from lay vassals, but if feudal governments had not been adaptable they could not have profited from the learning and skill of the clergy.

Feudalism produced its best results only in regions where it became the dominant form of government. France, for example, developed her first adequate governments in the feudal principalities of the north, Flanders, Normandy, Anjou and the king's own lordship of the Ile de France. The first great increase in the power of the French king came from enforcing his rights as feudal superior against his vassals. Many institutions of the French monarchy of the thirteenth century had already been tested in the feudal states of the late twelfth century; others grew out of the king's feudal court. By allowing newly annexed provinces to keep the laws and institutions developed in the feudal period, the king of France was able to unite the country with a minimum of ill-will. France later paid a high price for this provincial particularism, but the existence of local governments which could operate with little supervision immensely simplified the first stages of unification.

England in many ways was more like a single French province than the congeries of provinces which made up the kingdom of France. In fact, the first kings after the Conquest sometimes spoke of the kingdom as their "honor" or fief, just as a feudal lord might speak of his holding. As this example shows, England was thoroughly feudalized after the Conquest. While Anglo-Saxon law remained officially in force it became archaic and inapplicable; the law which grew into the common law of England was the law applied in the king's feudal court. The chief departments of the English government likewise grew out of this court. And when the combination of able kings and efficient institutions made the monarchy too strong, it was checked by the barons in the name of the feudal principles expressed in Magna Carta. Thus feudalism helped England to strike a happy balance between government which was too weak and government which was too strong.

The story was quite different in countries in which older political institutions prevented feudalism from reaching full development. Feudalism grew only slowly in Germany; it never included all fighting men or all lands. The German kings did not use feudalism as the chief support of their government; instead they relied on institutions inherited from the Carolingian period. This meant that the ruler acted as if local lords were still his officials and as if local courts were still under his control. In case of opposition, he turned to bishops and abbots for financial and military aid, instead of calling on his vassals. There was just enough vitality in this system to enable the king to interfere sporadically in political decisions all over Germany, and to prevent the growth of strong, feudal principalities. But while the German kings of the eleventh and twelfth centuries showed remarkable skill in using the old precedents, they failed to develop new institutions and ideas. Royal government became weaker, and Germany more disunited in every succeeding century. The most important provincial rulers, the dukes, were also unable to create effective governments. The kings were jealous of their power, and succeeded in destroying, or weakening, all the great duchies. The kings, however, were unable to profit from their success, because of their own lack of adequate institutions. Power eventually passed to rulers of the smaller principalities, not always by feudal arrangements, and only after the monarchy had been further weakened by a long conflict with the papacy. Thus the German kings of the later Middle Ages were unable to imitate the king of France, who had united his country through the use of his position as feudal superior. Germany remained disunited, and, on the whole, badly governed, throughout the rest of the Middle Ages and the early modern period.

Italy also suffered from competition among different types of government. The German emperor was traditionally king of (north) Italy. He could not govern this region effectively but he did intervene often enough to prevent the growth of large, native principalities. The Italian towns had never become depopulated, like those of the North, and the great economic revival of the late eleventh century made them wealthy and powerful. They were too strong to be fully controlled by any outside ruler, whether king or feudal lord, and too weak (at least in the early Middle Ages) to annex the rural districts outside their walls. The situation was further complicated by the existence of the papacy at Rome. The popes were usually on bad terms with the German emperors and wanted to rule directly a large part of central Italy. In defending themselves and their policies they encouraged the towns' claims to independence and opposed all efforts to unite the peninsula. Thus, while there was feudalism in Italy, it never had a clear field and was unable to develop as it did in France or England. Italy became more and more disunited; by the end of the Middle Ages the city-state, ruled by a "tyrant," was the dominant form of government in the peninsula. There was no justification for this type of government in medieval political theory, and this may be one reason why the Italians turned with such eagerness to the writings of the classical period. In any case, the Italian political system was a failure, and Italy was controlled by foreign states from the middle of the sixteenth to the middle of the nineteenth century.

There are certainly other factors, besides feudalism, which enabled France and England to set the pattern for political organization in Europe, and other weaknesses, besides the absence of fully developed feudalism, which condemned Germany and Italy to political sterility. At the same time, the basic institutions of France and England in the thirteenth century, which grew out of feudal customs, proved adaptable to changed conditions, while the basic institutions of Italy and Germany, which were largely non-feudal, had less vitality. Western feudalism was far from being an efficient form of government, but its very imperfections encouraged the experiments which kept it from being a stagnant form of government. It was far from being a just form of government, but the emphasis on personal relationships made it a source of persistent loyalties. And it was the flexibility of their institutions and the loyalty of their subjects which enabled the kings of the West to create the first modern states.

THE
MEDIEVAL
MIND

FAITH OR
REASON?

CONTENTS

FROM On Kingship BY THOMAS AQUINAS

FROM Aquinas BY F. C. COPLESTON

5 / AQUINAS AND THE EXISTENCE OF GOD

FROM Summa Theologiae BY THOMAS AQUINAS

FROM The Vindication of Religion BY A. E. TAYLOR

FROM The Existence of God BY W. I. MATSON

QUESTIONS FOR STUDY

1. *Abelard has been called an "orthodox skeptic." Do you think the description appropriate?*

2. *How did a medieval university resemble and how did it differ from a modern one?*

3. *Why did the study of Aristotle raise problems for thirteenth-century Christians? What do you think of the "double truth" theory as a solution to these problems?*

4. *Can you discern any significant differences between Bacon and Aquinas in their attitudes toward human knowledge and revealed truth?*

5. *Were Aquinas' arguments about the family and the state dependent on his theological presuppositions?*

6. *Could Aquinas have replied effectively to Ockham's assertion that in every proof for the existence of God "something doubtful or derived from faith is assumed"?*

The twelfth century saw a great revival of culture throughout Western Europe. In many centers of learning men began to study the legacy of the ancient world—Greek philosophy, Roman law, patristic theology—with new eagerness and new insight. Since virtually all medieval thinkers were sincere, believing Christians, the problem soon arose of defining the right relationship between rational inquiry and religious faith. This became a central issue of medieval intellectual life.

At the beginning of the twelfth century many theologians assumed that any question concerning the Christian faith could be answered by simply quoting an authoritative text from the Bible or the writings of the early church fathers. Peter Abelard (1079-1142) demonstrated that this approach was far too simplistic; he pointed out that one could cite respectable authorities to prove both sides of many controversial questions (pp. 412-416). Abelard never thought of abandoning the Scriptures or the church fathers, but he argued, in effect, that the citation of their texts had to be taken as only the starting point of a rational inquiry into the truth. Even this degree of rationalism was unacceptable to St. Bernard of Clairvaux, one of the greatest spiritual leaders of the age (pp. 416-417). Abelard was condemned during his lifetime, but his "dialectical method" of initiating an inquiry by juxtaposing apparently conflicting authorities came to be generally accepted after his death.

It is hard to understand the intellectual developments of the thirteenth century without some knowledge of the institutional context in which it took place. Following the selections describing the disputes of the twelfth century we have therefore presented a section of readings on the rise of the universities. The selection of C. H. Haskins describes the origins of these institutions (pp. 420-423), and the excerpts from medieval documents that follow illustrate their organization, discipline, and ways of teaching (pp. 423-430). The universities were self-governing corporations of scholars. They were ultimately subject to pope or king, but they exercised a great deal of freedom in regulating their own internal affairs, including their courses of study. This relative autonomy made possible the most important intellectual development of the thirteenth century—the widespread diffusion of a whole corpus of newly translated scientific and philosophical works of Aristotle. This diffusion took place in spite of the opposition of conservative bishops and even in the face of overt condemnations by the papacy (pp. 431-432).

The reception of Aristotelian philosophy posed the problem of reason and faith for medieval men in a new and more complicated form. At the time Abelard wrote, the main difficulty was that the body of received Christian writings seemed to contain certain internal inconsistencies. In the days of Thomas Aquinas a whole non-Christian philosophy had found wide acceptance in the universities. Moreover, at certain key points Aristotle's philosophy seemed to contradict Christian revelation. To take the simplest example: Aristotle taught that the universe had existed from all eternity; the Book of Genesis declared that God had created the universe at a particular point in past time. What was a Christian philosopher to believe? Some medieval approaches to this dilemma are discussed below in the reading from Etienne Gilson (pp. 436–439).

The medieval thinker who coped with the issue most successfully was Thomas Aquinas. Aquinas was serenely convinced that reason and faith could never contradict one another. He thought it possible to refute on rational, philosophical grounds the particular Aristotelian arguments that directly contradicted Christian revelation. But apart from these points he accepted virtually the whole of Aristotle's scientific explanations of the natural world as valid conclusions of human reason. Aquinas thought that Christian faith "perfected" the understanding of the world that natural reason could achieve; it did not destroy that understanding (pp. 440–452).

More than this, Aquinas believed that human reason, by employing Aristotelian modes of proof, could establish the validity of certain central truths of religion that were already known to the believer by faith alone. Above all, he thought that reason could establish the fact of God's existence (pp. 454–455). It should be noted that all Aquinas' proofs start out, in Aristotelian fashion, from man's experience of the external world and not from any mystical intuition of a divine being.

In conclusion we have presented two discussions of Aquinas' central argument by the modern philosophers A. E. Taylor (pp. 456–459) and W. I. Matson (pp. 460–463). The reader must expect to find these philosophical arguments complex and difficult. They may at least serve to remind him that some of the central problems of medieval intellectuals remain living issues for the thinkers of our own age.

1
PETER ABELARD

The problem of reason and faith was posed in striking fashion at the beginning of the twelfth century by the greatest teacher of the age, Peter Abelard (1079–1142). He pointed out, in a provocative work called *Sic et Non* (*Yes and No*), that a scholar could not simply accept all the writings of the early fathers of the church uncritically because the fathers often seemed to contradict themselves.

FROM Sic et Non BY PETER ABELARD

Among the multitudinous words of the holy Fathers some sayings seem not only to differ from one another but even to contradict one another. Hence it is not presumptuous to judge concerning those by whom the world itself will be judged, as it is written, "They shall judge nations" (Wisdom 3:8) and, again, "You shall sit and judge" (Luke 22:30). We do not presume to rebuke as untruthful or to denounce as erroneous those to whom the Lord said, "He who hears you hears me; he who despises you despises me" (Luke 10:26). Bearing in mind our foolishness we believe that our understanding is defective rather than the writing of those to whom the Truth Himself said, "It is not you who speak but the spirit of your Father who speaks in you" (Matthew 10:20). Why should it seem surprising if we, lacking the guidance of the Holy Spirit through whom those things were written and spoken, the Spirit impressing them on the writers, fail to understand them? Our achievement of full understanding is impeded especially by unusual modes of expression and by the different significances that can be attached to one and the same word, as a word is used now in one sense, now in another. Just as there are many meanings so there are many words. Tully says that sameness is the

J. P. Migne, ed., *Patrologia Latina*, CLXXVIII (1855), columns 1339–1354, translated by Brian Tierney.

mother of satiety in all things, that is to say it gives rise to fastidious distaste, and so it is appropriate to use a variety of words in discussing the same thing and not to express everything in common and vulgar words . . .

We must also take special care that we are not deceived by corruptions of the text or by false attributions when sayings of the Fathers are quoted that seem to differ from the truth or to be contrary to it; for many apocryphal writings are set down under names of saints to enhance their authority, and even the texts of divine Scripture are corrupted by the errors of scribes. That most faithful writer and true interpreter, Jerome, accordingly warned us, "Beware of apocryphal writings. . . ." Again, on the title of Psalm 77 which is "An Instruction of Asaph," he commented, "It is written according to Matthew that when the Lord had spoken in parables and they did not understand, he said, 'These things are done that it might be fulfilled which was written by the prophet Isaias, *I will open my mouth in parables.*' The Gospels still have it so. Yet it is not Isaias who says this but Asaph." Again, let us explain simply why in Matthew and John it is written that the Lord was crucified at the third hour but in Mark at the sixth hour. There was a scribal error, and in Mark too the sixth hour was mentioned, but many read the Greek *epismo* as *gamma.* So too there was a scribal error where "Isaias" was set down for "Asaph." We know that many churches were gathered together from among ignorant gentiles. When they read in the Gospel, "That it might be fulfilled which was written by the prophet Asaph," the one who first wrote down the Gospel began to say, "Who is this prophet Asaph?" for he was not known among the people. And what did he do? In seeking to amend an error he made an error. We would say the same of another text in Matthew. "He took," it says, "the thirty pieces of silver, the price of him that was prized, as was written by the prophet Jeremias." But we do not find this in Jeremias at all. Rather it is in Zacharias. You see then that here, as before, there was an error. If in the Gospels themselves some things are corrupted by the ignorance of scribes, we should not be surprised that the same thing has sometimes happened in the writings of later Fathers who are of much less authority . . .

It is no less important in my opinion to ascertain whether texts quoted from the Fathers may be ones that they themselves have retracted and corrected after they came to a better understanding of the truth as the blessed Augustine did on many occasions; or whether they are giving the opinion of another rather than their own opinion . . . or whether, in inquiring into certain matters, they left them open to question rather than settled them with a definitive solution . . .

In order that the way be not blocked and posterity deprived of the healthy labor of treating and debating difficult questions of language and style, a distinction must be drawn between the work of later authors and the supreme canonical authority of the Old and New Testaments. If, in Scripture, anything seems absurd you are not permitted to say, "The author of this book did not hold to the truth"—but rather that the codex is defective or that the interpreter erred or that you do not understand. But if anything seems contrary to truth in the works of later authors, which are contained in innumerable books, the reader or auditor is free to judge, so that he may approve what is pleasing and reject what gives offense, unless the matter is established by certain reason or by canonical authority (of the Scriptures) . . .

In view of these considerations we have undertaken to collect various sayings of the Fathers that give rise to questioning because of their apparent contradictions as they occur to our memory. This questioning excites young readers to the maximum of effort in inquiring into the truth, and such inquiry sharpens their minds. Assiduous and frequent questioning is indeed the first key to wisdom. Aristotle, that most perspicacious of all philosophers, exhorted the studious to practice it eagerly, saying, "Perhaps it is difficult to express oneself with confidence on such matters if they have not been much discussed. To entertain doubts on particular points will not be unprofitable." For by doubting we come to inquiry; through inquiring we perceive the truth, according to the Truth Himself. "Seek and you shall find," He says, "Knock and it shall be opened to you." In order to teach us by His example He chose to be found when He was about twelve years old sitting in the midst of the doctors and questioning them, presenting the appearance of a disciple by questioning rather than of a master by teaching, although there was in Him the complete and perfect wisdom of God. Where we have quoted texts of Scripture, the greater the authority attributed to Scripture, the more they should stimulate the reader and attract him to the search for truth. Hence I have prefixed to this my book, compiled in one volume from the saying of the saints, the decree of Pope Gelasius concerning authentic books, from which it may be known that I have cited nothing from apocryphal books. I have also added excerpts from the Retractations of St. Augustine, from which it will be clear that nothing is included which he later retracted and corrected.

[*Abelard then presented 156 questions dealing with such topics as these: "That God is one—and the contrary." "That the Son is without beginning— and the contrary." "That God can do all things—and the contrary." "That God knows all things—and the contrary." "That our first parents were created mortal—and the contrary." "That Adam was saved—and the contrary." "That Peter and Paul and all the apostles were equal—and the contrary." "That Christ alone is the foundation of the church—and the contrary." "That Peter did not deny Christ—and the contrary." "That without baptism of water no one can be saved—and the contrary." "That all are permitted to marry—and the contrary." "That saintly works do not justify man—and the contrary." "That it is permitted to kill men—and the contrary." The first question is given below—B. T.*]

THAT FAITH SHOULD BE BASED ON HUMAN REASON—AND THE CONTRARY

Gregory in Homily XXVI. We know that the works of the Lord would not excite wonder if they were understood by reason; nor is there any merit in faith where human reason offers proof.

Idem to Theodoric and Theudebert, Kings of the Franks. Faith and a good life are chosen by priests; if a good life is lacking so is faith.

Idem in Homily V. At one word of command Peter and Andrew left their nets and followed the Redeemer. They had seen him work no miracles; they had heard nothing from him about eternal retribution; and nevertheless, at one command of the Lord, they forgot what they had seemed to possess . . .

From the First Book of Augustine against Faustus. Faustus: It is a weak profession of faith if one does not believe in Christ without evidence and argument. You yourself are accustomed to say that Christian belief is simple and absolute and should not be inquired into too curiously. Why then are you destroying the simplicity of the faith by buttressing it with judgments and evidences?

From the Life of St. Sylvester, where, disputing with the Jews, he said to the Rabbi Roasus, "Faith is not submitted to human reason, and faith teaches us that this God, whom you confess to be one God, is Father, Son, and Holy Spirit."

Augustine, On the Morals of the Church against the Manicheans. The order of nature is such that, when we state anything, authority precedes reason for a reason might seem weak if, after it has been presented, authority is cited to confirm it . . .

Ambrose. If I am convinced by reason I give up faith . . .

Gregory to Bishop Dominicus. Although these things are so I wish that all heretics be held in check by Catholic priests vigorously and always by reasoning.

Idem in Pastoral Care. The wise of this world and the dull are to be admonished differently. The former are for the most part converted by the arguments of reason, the latter sometimes better by examples. Doubtless it profits the former to be defeated in their arguments; it is sometimes sufficient for the latter to know of the praiseworthy deeds of other men . . .

Hilary, On the Trinity, Book XII. It is fitting for those who preach Christ to the world to refute the irreligious and unsound doctrines of the world through their knowledge of omnipotent wisdom, according as the Apostle says, "Our weapons are not carnal but mighty before God for the destruction of strongholds and the destroying of arguments and of every obstacle raised up against the knowledge of God. . . ." (2 Corinthians 10:4.)

Augustine to Count Valerian, discussing marriage and concupiscence. While you satirize with a most robust faith it is good nevertheless that you

also know how to support what we believe by defending it; for the Apostle
Peter commanded us to be always ready to give satisfaction to anyone asking
us the reason for our faith and hope. . . . We should give an account of our
faith and hope to enquirers in a two-fold fashion. We should always explain
the just grounds of our faith and hope to questioners, whether they ask honestly or dishonestly, and we should hold fast to the pure profession of our
faith and hope even amid the pressures of our adversaries.

Abelard's technique of exposing the contradictions of the church fathers in
order to provide an intellectual exercise for his students aroused the indignation of St. Bernard of Clairvaux. Bernard attacked certain specific teachings
of Abelard and also his whole approach to sacred learning.

Bernard of Clairvaux's Letter to the Bishops and Cardinals

To the lords and reverend fathers, the Bishops and Cardinals in Curia, from
the child of their holiness.

No one has any doubt that it belongs especially to you to remove scandals
from the Kingdom of God, to cut back the growing thorns, to calm quarrels.
For this is what Moses commanded when he went up the mountain, saying:
"Wait here till we come back to you. You have Aaron and Hur with you; to
them refer all matters of dispute." I speak of that Moses who came through
water, and "not by water only, but by water and blood." And therefore he is
greater than Moses because he came through blood. And because by Aaron
and Hur the zeal and authority of the Roman Church are signified, I do well
to refer to her, not questions about the faith, but wounds to the faith, injuries
to Christ, insults and dishonours to the Fathers, the scandals of the present
generation and the dangers of those to come. The faith of the simple is being
held up to scorn, the secrets of God are being reft open, the most sacred
matters are being recklessly discussed, and the Fathers are being derided be-

The Letters of Bernard of Clairvaux (1953), pp. 315–317, translated by Bruno Scott James.
Reprinted by permission of Henry Regnery Co., Chicago.

cause they held that such matters are better allowed to rest than solved. Hence it comes about that, contrary to the law of God, the Paschal Lamb is either boiled or eaten raw, with bestial mouth and manners. And what is left over is not burned with fire, but trodden under foot. So mere human ingenuity is taking on itself to solve everything, and leave nothing to faith. It is trying for things above itself, prying into things too strong for it, rushing into divine things, and profaning rather than revealing what is holy. Things closed and sealed, it is not opening but tearing asunder, and what it is not able to force open, that it considers to be of no account and not worthy of belief.

Read, if you please, that book of Peter Abelard which he calls a book of Theology. You have it to hand since, as he boasts, it is read eagerly by many in the Curia. See what sort of things he says there about the Holy Trinity, about the generation of the Son, about the procession of the Holy Spirit, and much else that is very strange indeed to Catholic ears and minds. Read that other book which they call the *Book of Sentences,* and also the one entitled *Know Thyself,* and see how they too run riot with a whole crop of sacrileges and errors. See what he thinks about the soul of Christ, about the person of Christ, about his descent into hell, about the Sacrament of the Altar, about the power of binding and loosing, about original sin, about the sins of human weakness, about the sins of ignorance, about sinful action, and about sinful intention. And if you then consider that I am rightly disturbed, do you also bestir yourselves and, so as not to bestir yourselves in vain, act according to the position you hold, according to the dignity in which you are supreme, according to the power you have received, and let him who has scanned the heavens go down even into hell, and let the works of darkness that have braved the light be shown up by the light, so that while he who sins in public is publicly rebuked, others, who speak evil in their hearts and write it in their books, may restrain themselves from putting darkness for light, and disputing on divine matters at the crossroads. Thus shall the mouth that mutters wickedness be closed.

Although Bernard succeeded in obtaining a condemnation of various technical points in Abelard's theological writings, Abelard's "dialectical" method of juxtaposing conflicting authorities was widely adopted by the scholars of the next generation. They took more care than Abelard, however, to show how the apparently contradictory texts could be reconciled with one another. Abelard himself continued to fascinate and attract the students of Paris. He describes in his autobiography how, after the condemnation of his work at the Council of Soissons in 1121, he withdrew to a hermitage and the students of Paris followed him into the wilderness.

FROM Historia Calamitatum BY PETER ABELARD

And so I withdrew into a solitude in the district of Troyes already known to me. There on a plot which was given to me I built with the approval of the bishop of the diocese an oratory of reeds and thatch and called it the Holy Trinity. Secreted there with a certain cleric, I could sing the verse to the Lord: *Lo, I have gone far off flying away; and I abode in the wilderness.*

When my former students discovered my whereabouts, they began to leave the cities and towns and to flock there to dwell with me in my solitude. Instead of large houses, they built cottages; instead of delicate foods, they lived on wild herbs and coarse bread; instead of soft beds, they used thatch and straw and for tables they heaped up sods so that you would think they were imitating the philosophers of old . . .

* * *

Such a life also the sons of the Prophets who followed Eliseus are said to have lived. Jerome also speaks of them as the monks of that time when he writes to Rusticus the monk:

The sons of the Prophets, the monks of the Old Testament, built huts for themselves by the waters of the Jordan; and forsaking the crowded cities lived on pulse and wild herbs.

Such were our disciples, who building their huts there by the river Arduzon appeared to be hermits rather than students.

The more scholars flocked to me and the harder the life they endured, under my teaching, the greater the glory which my rivals thought accrued to me and the greater the ignominy to them. And when they had done everything they could against me, they were grieved that all things worked together to my good, and as Jerome says:

In hiding, as I was, far from the cities, the forum, the courts and crowds, as Quintilian says, envy discovered me.

Secretly complaining and bemoaning among themselves, they kept saying: "*Behold the whole world has gone after him,* we have got nowhere persecut-

The Story of Abelard's Adversities (1954), pp. 51–53, translated by J. T. Muckle. Reprinted by permission of Pontifical Institute of Mediaeval Studies, Toronto.

ing him and gained for him greater renown. We have tried to blot out his name and we have made it better known. Behold, students, who have at hand in the cities everything they need, despise the comforts of city life and flock to a solitude with its poverty, and of their own accord become wretched."

2
THE RISE
OF THE
UNIVERSITIES

The fame of Abelard's teaching helped to make Paris the leading center of learning north of the Alps. Around 1200 the masters who were teaching there organized themselves into a guild—in Latin, *universitas*. C. H. Haskins pointed out that this development marked the beginning of "university" education in Europe.

FROM The Renaissance of the Twelfth Century
BY C. H. HASKINS

Besides producing the earliest universities, the twelfth century also fixed their form of organization for succeeding ages. This was not a revival of some ancient model, for the Graeco-Roman world had no universities in the modern sense of the term. It had higher education, it is true, really superior instruction in law, rhetoric, and philosophy, but this was not organized into faculties and colleges with the mechanism of fixed curricula and academic degrees. Even when the state took on the responsibility of advanced instruction in the state-paid teachers and public law schools of the later Roman empire, it did not establish universities. These arise first in the twelfth century, and the modern university is derived in its fundamental features from them, from Salerno, Bologna, Paris, Montpellier, and Oxford. From these the continuity is direct to our own day, and there was no other source. The

Reprinted by permission of the publishers from Charles Homer Haskins, *The Renaissance of the Twelfth Century*, pp. 369–371, 377–379; 383–384. Cambridge, Mass.: Harvard University Press, Copyright, 1927, by the President and Fellows of Harvard College and, 1955, by Clare Allen Haskins.

university is a mediaeval contribution to civilization, and more specifically a contribution of the twelfth century.

The word university originally meant a corporation or gild in general, and the Middle Ages had many such forms of corporate life. Only gradually did the term become narrowed so as to denote exclusively a learned corporation or society of masters and scholars, *universitas societas magistrorum discipulorumque,* as it is expressed in the earliest and still the best definition of a university. In this general sense there might be several universities in the same town, just as there were several craft gilds, and these separate universities of law or of medicine were each jealous of their corporate life and were slow to coalesce into a single university with its special faculties. Speaking broadly, the nucleus of the new development was in Northern Europe a gild of masters and in the South a gild of students, but in both cases the point of chief importance centres about admission to the gild of masters or professors. Without such admission there could be no license to teach; until then one could be only a student, thereafter one was a master, in rank if not by occupation, and had passed out of the journeyman stage. In order to guard against favoritism and monopoly, such admission was determined by an examination, and ability to pass this examination was the natural test of academic attainment in the several subjects of study. This license to teach (*licentia docendi*) was thus the earliest form of academic degree. Historically, all degrees are in their origin teachers' certificates, as the names doctor and master still show us; a Master of Arts was a qualified teacher of arts, a Doctor of Laws or Medicine was a certified teacher of these subjects. Moreover the candidate regularly gave a specimen lecture, or, as it was said, incepted, and this inception is the origin of the modern commencement, which means commencing to teach. An examination presupposes a body of material upon which the candidate is examined, usually a set of standard textbooks, and this in turn implies systematic teaching and a minimum period of study. Curriculum, examinations, commencement, degrees, are all part of the same system; they are all inherited from the Middle Ages, and in some form they go back to the twelfth century.

* * *

At Paris the situation was complicated by the presence of three schools: that of the cathedral of Notre Dame, that of the canons regular of Saint-Victor, of which William of Champeaux at the beginning of this century was the first known master, and that of the collegiate church of Sainte-Geneviève, which passed into the hands of canons regular in 1147. Thus Abaelard began his studies and teaching at Notre Dame, where he seems to have become canon, later listened in the external schools of William of Champeaux at Saint-Victor, but in his maturer years taught on the Mount of Sainte-Geneviève where John of Salisbury heard him in the passage quoted above. The fame of Abaelard as an original and inspiring teacher, with a ready command of the ancient authorities and a quick perception of their inconsistencies, and

withal "able to move the minds of serious men to laughter," had much to do
with the resort of students to Paris, although Abaelard was for one reason or
another absent from Paris for long stretches of time and was followed by
large bodies of students to Melun and Corbeil and even into the desert. Still it
was in his day that Paris became the great centre of dialectic study, and if his
later teaching was associated only with Sainte-Geneviève and its direct influence suffered from the decline of this school, in a larger sense he contributed
powerfully to the habitual resort of students to Paris for advanced study. It is
true that our fullest description of his success as a teacher is given by himself,
but this receives general confirmation from unimpeachable witnesses like
John of Salisbury and Otto of Freising, as well as by more casual evidence. It
will be noted in John of Salisbury's account that Abaelard is only one of
many masters with whom he studied at Paris, so that already we see signs of
the change which Rashdall observes in the next generation, when "Paris became a city of teachers—the first city of teachers the medieval world had
known." The masters, like the students, came from many lands. John of
Salisbury had been preceded shortly by Otto, future bishop of Freising and
uncle of Frederick Barbarossa, and by Adalbert, the future archbishop of
Mainz; a list of masters ca. 1142 mentions not only Bretons like Abaelard and
Thierry of Chartres and a Norman like William of Conches, but Englishmen
such as Robert of Melun, Adam of the Little Bridge, and the future bishop of
Exeter, and an Italian in the person of Peter Lombard. A little later we hear
of students from still more remote countries, the nephews of the archbishop
of Lund in Sweden and an Hungarian friend of Walter Map who becomes
archbishop of Gran.

*   *   *

While the University of Paris thus originated of itself, it came to depend
upon royal and still more upon papal support, and with papal support came
papal control. The first specific document of the university's history belongs
to the year 1200, the famous charter of Philip Augustus from which the existence of a university is sometimes dated, though such an institution really
existed years earlier. There is here no suggestion of a new creation, but
merely the recognition of a body of students and teachers which already
exists: the *prévôt* and his men had attacked a hospice of German students and
killed some of their number, including the bishop-elect of Liége; the king
disciplines the *prévôt* severely and provides that students and their chattels
shall have justice and be exempt from the jurisdiction of lay courts. The
name university is not mentioned, but the assembly of scholars is recognized
as the body before which the royal officers shall take oath. In 1208 or 1209 the
earliest statutes deal with academic dress and funerals and with "the accustomed order in lectures and disputations," and the Pope recognizes the corporate character of this academic society, or university. Its right to self-
government is further extended by the papal legate in 1215 in a document
which gives the earliest outline of the course of study in arts. With the great

papal privilege of 1231, the result of another town and gown row and a prolonged cessation of lectures, the fundamental documents of the university are complete. Indeed, the chancellor has begun to complain that there is too much organization and too much time consumed with university business: "in the old days when each master taught for himself and the name of the university was unknown, lectures and disputations were more frequent and there was more zeal for study." Paris has already fallen from the traditions of the good old times!

The first detailed information that we have about the organization of studies at the University of Paris comes from a decree promulgated by a papal legate in 1215.

Rules of the University of Paris

Robert, servant of the cross of Christ by divine pity cardinal priest of the title, St. Stephen in Mons Caelius, legate of the apostolic see, to all the masters and scholars of Paris eternal greeting in the Lord. Let all know that, since we have had a special mandate from the pope to take effective measures to reform the state of the Parisian scholars for the better, wishing with the counsel of good men to provide for the tranquillity of the scholars in the future, we have decreed and ordained in this wise:

No one shall lecture in the arts at Paris before he is twenty-one years of age, and he shall have heard lectures for at least six years before he begins to lecture, and he shall promise to lecture for at least two years, unless a reasonable cause prevents, which he ought to prove publicly or before examiners. He shall not be stained by any infamy, and when he is ready to lecture, he shall be examined according to the form which is contained in the writing of the lord bishop of Paris, where is contained the peace confirmed between the chancellor and scholars by judges delegated by the pope, namely, by the bishop and dean of Troyes and by P. the bishop and J. the chancellor of Paris approved and confirmed. And they shall lecture on the books of Aristotle on dialectic old and new in the schools ordinarily and not *ad cursum*. They shall also lecture on both Priscians ordinarily, or at least on one. They shall not lecture on feast days except on philosophers and rhetoric and the quadrivium and *Barbarismus* and ethics, if it please them, and the fourth book of the

Lynn Thorndike, *University Records and Life in the Middle Ages* (1944), pp. 27–30. Reprinted by permission of Columbia University Press, New York.

Topics. They shall not lecture on the books of Aristotle on metaphysics and natural philosophy or on summaries of them or concerning the doctrine of master David of Dinant or the heretic Amaury or Mauritius of Spain.

In the *principia* and meetings of the masters and in the responsions or oppositions of the boys and youths there shall be no drinking. They may summon some friends or associates, but only a few. Donations of clothing or other things as has been customary, or more, we urge should be made, especially to the poor. None of the masters lecturing in arts shall have a cope except one round, black and reaching to the ankles, at least while it is new. Use of the pallium is permitted. No one shall wear with the round cope shoes that are ornamented or with elongated pointed toes. If any scholar in arts or theology dies, half of the masters of arts shall attend the funeral at one time, the other half the next time, and no one shall leave until the sepulture is finished, unless he has reasonable cause. If any master in arts or theology dies, all the masters shall keep vigils, each shall read or cause to be read the Psalter, each shall attend the church where is celebrated the watch until midnight or the greater part of the night, unless reasonable cause prevent. On the day when the master is buried, no one shall lecture or dispute.

We fully confirm to them the meadow of St. Germain in that condition in which it was adjudicated to them.

Each master shall have jurisdiction over his scholar. No one shall occupy a classroom or house without asking the consent of the tenant, provided one has a chance to ask it. No one shall receive the licentiate from the chancellor or another for money given or promise made or other condition agreed upon. Also, the masters and scholars can make both between themselves and with other persons obligations and constitutions supported by faith or penalty or oath in these cases: namely, the murder or mutilation of a scholar or atrocious injury done a scholar, if justice should not be forthcoming, arranging the prices of lodgings, costume, burial, lectures and disputations, so, however, that the university be not thereby dissolved or destroyed.

As to the status of the theologians, we decree that no one shall lecture at Paris before his thirty-fifth year and unless he has studied for eight years at least, and has heard the books faithfully and in classrooms, and has attended lectures in theology for five years before he gives lectures himself publicly. And none of these shall lecture before the third hour on days when masters lecture. No one shall be admitted at Paris to formal lectures or to preachings unless he shall be of approved life and science. No one shall be a scholar at Paris who has no definite master.

Moreover, that these decrees may be observed inviolate, we by virtue of our legatine authority have bound by the knot of excommunication all who shall contumaciously presume to go against these our statutes, unless within fifteen days after the offense they have taken care to emend their presumption before the university of masters and scholars or other persons constituted by the university. Done in the year of Grace 1215, the month of August.

Some of the difficulties that plague modern universities made their appearance very early. Student discipline was a problem from the beginning, as the following proclamation of 1269 indicates.

Proclamation of the Official of the Episcopal Court of Paris Against Clerks and Scholars Who Go About Paris Armed by Day and Night and Commit Crimes

The official of the court of Paris to all the rectors of churches, masters and scholars residing in the city and suburb of Paris, to whom the present letters may come, greeting in the Lord. A frequent and continual complaint has gone the rounds that there are in Paris some clerks and scholars, likewise their servants, trusting in the folly of the same clerks, unmindful of their salvation, not having God before their eyes, who, under pretense of leading the scholastic life, more and more often perpetrate unlawful and criminal acts, relying on their arms: namely, that by day and night they atrociously wound or kill many persons, rape women, oppress virgins, break into inns, also repeatedly committing robberies and many other enormities hateful to God. And since they attempt these and other crimes relying on their arms, we, having in mind the decree of the supreme pontiff in which it is warned that clerks bearing arms will be excommunicated, also having in mind that our predecessors sometimes excommunicated those who went about thus, and in view of the fact that this is so notorious and manifest that it cannot be concealed by any evasion and that their proclamation was not revoked, wishing to meet so great evils and to provide for the peace and tranquillity of students and others who wish to live at peace, at the instance of many good men and by their advice do excommunicate in writing clerks and scholars and their servants who go about Paris by day or night armed, unless by permission of the reverend bishop of Paris or ourselves. We also excommunicate in writing those who rape women, break into inns, oppress virgins, likewise all those who have banded together for this purpose. No less do we excommunicate all those who have known anything about the aforesaid, unless within seven days from the time of their information, after the proclamation issued against the aforesaid has come to their notice, they shall have revealed what they know to the said reverend bishop or ourselves and have submitted to fitting

Lynn Thorndike, *University Records and Life in the Middle Ages* (1944), pp. 78–80. Reprinted by permission of Columbia University Press, New York.

emendation. Nevertheless we specially reserve to the lord bishop or ourselves the right to absolve clerks excommunicated for the aforesaid reasons.

But inasmuch as some clerks and scholars and their servants have borne arms in Paris, coming there from their parts or returning to their parts, and likewise certain others, knowing that clerks, scholars and their servants have borne arms in Paris, fear that for the said reasons they have incurred the said penalty of excommunication, we do declare herewith that it neither is nor was our intention that those clerks, scholars and their servants should be liable to the said sentence who, coming to Paris for study and bearing arms on the way, on first entering the city bear the same to their lodgings, nor, further, those, wishing to return home or setting out on useful and honest business more than one day's journey from the city of Paris, who have borne such arms going and returning while they were outside the city. We further declare that in the clause in which it is said, "We excommunicate all those who have known anything about the aforesaid," etc., we do not understand that word, *aforesaid,* to refer to all and each of the aforesaid but to the clauses immediately preceding, namely, concerning those who rape women, break into inns, oppress virgins and those who band together for these ends. Moreover, you shall so observe the present mandate that you cannot be charged with or punished for disobedience. Given in the year 1268 A.D., the Friday following Epiphany.

Hazing of freshmen was forbidden in 1340.

Hazing of Freshmen Forbidden

This is the ordinance made by the deputies of the university as to the punishment of those hazing Freshmen. First, that no one, of whatever faculty he be, shall take any money from a Freshman because of his class or anything else, except from roommates with whom he lives or as a voluntary gift, under penalty of deprivation of any honor now held or to be held from the university, which deprivation from now as from then the said university brings upon any offending thus.

* * *

Fourth, the said university bids the said Freshmen, under penalty of deprivation of any honor from the said university, that if anyone does any wrong

Lynn Thorndike, *University Records and Life in the Middle Ages* (1944), pp. 192–193. Reprinted by permission of Columbia University Press, New York.

to them by word or deed on account of their class, they shall straightway secretly reveal this to the proctors and deans of the faculties who in general congregation shall be required to reveal the names of the offenders by their oaths.

Fifth, the said university enjoins all those renting lodgings to students that, as soon as they know that any corporal violence or threats have been made to a Freshman because of his class, they immediately reveal this, as above directed.

Sixth, the said university enjoins all who have taken its oaths that, if they know any person or persons to have inflicted bodily violence or insult, threats and any injury upon Freshmen because of their class, they reveal this by their oaths as quickly as they can, as has been said above.

Professors came in for some criticism too.

On the Vices of the Masters BY ALVARUS PELAGIUS

The first [*vice—B. T.*] is that, although they be unlearned and insufficiently prepared, they get themselves promoted to be masters by prayers and gifts. . . . And when they are called upon to examine others, they admit inept and ignorant persons to be masters.

Second, moved by envy, they scorn to admit well-prepared subordinates to professorial chairs, and, full of arrogance, they despise others and censure their utterances unreasonably. . . .

Third, they despise simple persons who know how to avoid faults of conduct better than those of words. . . .

Fourth, they teach useless, vain, and sometimes false doctrines, a most dangerous course in doctrine of faith and morals, yet one especially characteristic of doctors of theology. These are fountains without water and clouds driven by whirlwinds and darkening the landscape. . . .

Fifth, they are dumb dogs unable to bark, as Isaiah inveighs against them, 66:10. Seeing the faults of peoples and lords, they keep silent lest they displease them, when they ought to argue at least in secret—which they also sometimes omit to do because they are involved in like vices themselves. . . .

Sixth, they retain in their classes those who have been excommunicated, or do not reprove scholars who are undisciplined and practice turpitudes publicly. For they ought to impress morality along with science.

Lynn Thorndike, *University Records and Life in the Middle Ages* (1944), pp. 171–172. Reprinted by permission of Columbia University Press, New York.

Seventh, although receiving sufficient salaries, they avariciously demand beyond their due or refuse to teach the poor unless paid for it, and want pay whether they teach on feast days or not, or fail to lecture when they should, attending to other matters, or teach less diligently.

Eighth, they try to say what is subtle, not what is useful, so that they may be seen of men and called rabbis, which is especially reprehensible in masters of theology. And in this especially offend, remarks the aforesaid Alvarus, the masters of Paris and those in England at Oxford, secular as well as regular, Dominicans as well as Franciscans, and others, of whom the arrogance of some is inexplicable. In their classes not the prophets, nor the Mosaic law, nor the wisdom of the Father, nor the Gospel of Christ, nor the doctrine of the apostles and holy doctors are heard, but Reboat, the idolatrous philosopher, and his commentator, with other teachers of the liberal arts, so that in classes in theology not holy writ but philosophy is taught. Nay more, now doctors and bachelors do not even read the text of the *Sentences* in class but hurry on to curious questions which have no apparent connection with the text.

Teaching methods were debated; some techniques were approved and others condemned.

Method of Lecturing in the Liberal Arts Prescribed, Paris

In the name of the Lord, amen. Two methods of lecturing on books in the liberal arts having been tried, the former masters of philosophy uttering their words rapidly so that the mind of the hearer can take them in but the hand cannot keep up with them, the latter speaking slowly until their listeners can catch up with them with the pen; having compared these by diligent examination, the former method is found the better. Wherefore, the consensus of opinion warns us that we imitate it in our lectures. We, therefore, all and each, masters of the faculty of arts, teaching and not teaching, convoked for this specially by the venerable man, master Albert of Bohemia, then rector of the university, at St. Julien le Pauvre, have decreed in this wise, that all lecturers, whether masters or scholars of the same faculty, whenever and wherever they chance to lecture on any text ordinarily or cursorily in the same faculty, or to dispute any question concerning it, or anything else by way of

Lynn Thorndike, *University Records and Life in the Middle Ages* (1944), p. 237. Reprinted by permission of Columbia University Press, New York.

exposition, shall observe the former method of lecturing to the best of their ability, so speaking forsooth as if no one was taking notes before them, in the way that sermons and recommendations are made in the university and which the lectures in other faculties follow. Moreover, transgressors of this statute, if the lecturers are masters or scholars, we now deprive henceforth for a year from lecturing, honors, offices and other advantages of our faculty. Which if anyone violates, for the first relapse we double the penalty, for the second we quadruple it, and so on. Moreover, listeners who oppose the execution of this our statute by clamor, hissing, noise, throwing stones by themselves or by their servants and accomplices, or in any other way, we deprive of and cut off from our society for a year, and for each relapse we increase the penalty double and quadruple as above.

A distinguished law professor, Odofredus, explained *c.* 1250 his method of expounding the books of the *Corpus Iuris Civilis.*

Method of Expounding the Law BY ODOFREDUS

Concerning the method of teaching the following order was kept by ancient and modern doctors and especially by my own master, which method I shall observe: First, I shall give you summaries of each title before I proceed to the text; second, I shall give as clear and explicit a statement as I can of the purport of each law [included in the title]; third, I shall read the text with a view to correcting it; fourth, I shall briefly repeat the contents of the law; fifth, I shall solve apparent contradictions, adding any general principles of law [to be extracted from the passage], commonly called " 'Brocardica,' " and any distinctions or subtle and useful problems (*quaestiones*) arising out of the law with their solutions, as far as the Divine Providence shall enable me. And if any law shall seem deserving, by reason of its celebrity or difficulty, of a repetition, I shall reserve it for an evening repetition, for I shall dispute at least twice a year, once before Christmas and once before Easter, if you like.

I shall always begin the *Old Digest* on or about the octave of Michaelmas [6 October] and finish it entirely, by God's help, with everything ordinary and extraordinary, about the middle of August. The *Code* I shall always begin about a fortnight after Michaelmas and by God's help complete it, with

Reprinted by permission of the publishers from Charles Homer Haskins, *The Renaissance of the Twelfth Century,* pp. 203–204. Cambridge, Mass.: Harvard University Press, Copyright, 1927, by the President and Fellows of Harvard College and, 1955, by Clare Allen Haskins.

everything ordinary and extraordinary, about the first of August. Formerly the doctors did not lecture on the extraordinary portions; but with me all students can have profit, even the ignorant and the newcomers, for they will hear the whole book, nor will anything be omitted as was once the common practice here. For the ignorant can profit by the statement of the case and the exposition of the text, the more advanced can become more adept in the subtleties of questions and opposing opinions. And I shall read all the glosses, which was not the practice before my time.

[*Odofredus ended his course of lectures thus—B. T.*]

Now, gentlemen, we have begun and finished and gone through this book, as you know who have been in the class, for which we thank God and His Virgin Mother and all His Saints. It is an ancient custom in this city that when a book is finished mass should be sung to the Holy Ghost, and it is a good custom and hence should be observed. But since it is the practice that doctors on finishing a book should say something of their plans, I will tell you something, but not much. Next year I expect to give ordinary lectures well and lawfully as I always have, but no extraordinary lectures, for students are not good payers, wishing to learn but not to pay, as the saying is: All desire to know but none to pay the price. I have nothing more to say to you, beyond dismissing you with God's blessing and begging you to attend the mass.

The problem of dealing with subversive ideas arose soon after the establishment of the university at Paris. The subversive ideas in question were contained in various newly translated treatises of Aristotle on natural science. In 1210 a council of bishops banned these works.

Banning of Aristotle's Works

Neither the books of Aristotle on natural philosophy nor their commentaries are to be read at Paris in public or secret, and this we forbid under penalty of excommunication.

Lynn Thorndike, *University Records and Life in the Middle Ages* (1944), pp. 26–27. Reprinted by permission of Columbia University Press, New York.

In 1231 Pope Gregory IX promulgated a decretal modifying the foregoing condemnation and requiring that the offending books be expurgated.

Gregory IX on Books Offensive to the Catholic Faith

Since other sciences ought to render service to the wisdom of holy writ, they are to be in so far embraced by the faithful as they are known to conform to the good pleasure of the Giver, so that anything virulent or otherwise vicious, by which the purity of the Faith might be derogated from, be quite excluded, because a comely woman found in the number of captives is not permitted to be brought into the house unless shorn of superfluous hair and trimmed of sharp nails, and in order that the Hebrews might be enriched from the despoiled Egyptians they were bade to borrow precious gold and silver vessels, not ones of rusty copper or clay.

But since, as we have learned, the books on nature which were prohibited at Paris in provincial council are said to contain both useful and useless matter, lest the useful be vitiated by the useless, we command your discretion, in which we have full faith in the Lord, firmly bidding by apostolic writings under solemn adjuration of divine judgment, that, examining the same books as is convenient subtly and prudently, you entirely exclude what you shall find there erroneous or likely to give scandal or offense to readers, so that, what are suspect being removed, the rest may be studied without delay and without offense. Given at the Lateran, April 23, in the fifth year of our pontificate.

Lynn Thorndike, *University Records and Life in the Middle Ages* (1944), p. 40. Reprinted by permission of Columbia University Press, New York.

By 1255 all the condemned books—unexpurgated—were listed as required reading for the degree of Master of Arts at Paris.

Courses in Arts, Paris

In the year of the Lord 1254. Let all know that we, all and each, masters of arts by our common assent, no one contradicting, because of the new and incalculable peril which threatens in our faculty—some masters hurrying to finish their lectures sooner than the length and difficulty of the texts permits, for which reason both masters in lecturing and scholars in hearing make less progress—worrying over the ruin of our faculty and wishing to provide for our status, have decreed and ordained for the common utility and the reparation of our university to the honor of God and the church universal that all and single masters of our faculty in the future shall be required to finish the texts which they shall have begun on the feast of St. Remy at the times below noted, not before.

The Old Logic, namely the book of Porphyry, the *Praedicamenta, Periarmeniae, Divisions* and *Topics* of Boethius, except the fourth, on the feast of the Annunciation of the blessed Virgin or the last day for lectures preceding. *Priscian minor* and *major, Topics* and *Elenchi, Prior* and *Posterior Analytics* they must finish in the said or equal time. The *Ethics* through four books in twelve weeks, if they are read with another text; if *per se,* not with another, in half that time. Three short texts, namely *Sex principia, Barbarismus,* Priscian on accent, if read together and nothing else with them, in six weeks. The *Physics* of Aristotle, *Metaphysics,* and *De animalibus* on the feast of St. John the Baptist; *De celo et mundo,* first book of *Meteorology* with the fourth, on Ascension day; *De anima,* if read with the books on nature, on the feast of the Ascension, if with the logical texts, on the feast of the Annunciation of the blessed Virgin; *De generatione* on the feast of the Chair of St. Peter; *De causis* in seven weeks; *De sensu et sensato* in six weeks; *De sompno et vigilia* in five weeks; *De plantis* in five weeks; *De memoria et reminiscentia* in two weeks; *De differentia spiritus et animae* in two weeks; *De morte et vita* in one week. Moreover, if masters begin to read the said books at another time than the feast of St. Remy, they shall allow as much time for lecturing on them as is indicated above. Moreover, each of the said texts, if read by itself, not with another text, can be finished in half the time of lecturing assigned above. It will not be permitted anyone to finish the said texts in less time, but anyone may take more time.

Lynn Thorndike, *University Records and Life in the Middle Ages* (1944), pp. 64–65. Reprinted by permission of Columbia University Press, New York.

3
THE IMPACT
OF ARISTOTLE

The influence of Aristotle on medieval science is discussed in the following reading.

FROM A Sketch of Mediaeval Philosophy
BY D. J. B. HAWKINS

For us, nowadays, Aristotle is a philosopher, and still perhaps the greatest name in the history of philosophy, but until three centuries ago he was more even than that; his work covered the whole range of the natural sciences, and he was considered a grave authority there as well. His systematic scientific conceptions have been superseded, although he is still reckoned to have been an accurate observer. For us his philosophical fame alone remains, but we shall not appreciate his significance for the mediaevel thinkers unless we re-capture the idea of him as the master of those who know in every field of human speculation. The recovery of Aristotle was for the middle ages the acquisition not only of a philosophical system but of a whole encyclopaedia of scientific knowledge. To the men of that time he appeared almost as a personification of the human reason which they sought to integrate with the divine revelation acknowledged by them in Christian tradition. . . .

At a later period a rigid adherence to the details of Aristotelian physics was an obstacle to the development of modern science; on this account it must all the more be stressed that the introduction of Aristotelianism in the thirteenth century was a powerful reinforcement of the genuine scientific spirit, of the spirit of exact and dispassionate observation of what things are and how they behave. The superficial religious mind tends to disparage created things and

D. J. B. Hawkins, *A Sketch of Mediaeval Philosophy* (1946), pp. 49, 58–59. Reprinted by permission of Sheed & Ward Ltd., London.

thinks that thereby it does honour to their Creator. Some versions of Platonism strengthen this tendency with their view of the world of experience as a mere shadow of the world of essences, which, for Christian Platonism, was the Divine Word. The new Aristotelianism was a reminder that the things of experience had a being and an activity of their own, and deserved to be looked at for their own sake. The Christian Aristotelians were not slow to point out that it did more honour to God to recognize that he had created a world with its own value and interest than to suppose that men were expected to keep their gaze averted from it. In this way a sound religious philosophy was an encouragement to the spirit of humanism and of scientific investigation.

The medieval thinker who insisted most trenchantly on the need for observation and experiment in the pursuit of scientific knowledge was Roger Bacon. The following extract is from a work written for Pope Clement IV in 1266.

FROM Opus Maius BY ROGER BACON

Now there are four chief obstacles in grasping truth, which hinder every man, however learned, and scarcely allow any one to win a clear title to learning, namely, submission to faulty and unworthy authority, influence of custom, popular prejudice, and concealment of our own ignorance accompanied by an ostentatious display of our knowledge. Every man is entangled in these difficulties, every rank is beset. For people without distinction draw the same conclusion from three arguments, than which none could be worse, namely, for this the authority of our predecessors is adduced, this is the custom, this is the common belief; hence correct. But an opposite conclusion and a far better one should be drawn from the premises, as I shall abundantly show by authority, experience, and reason. Should, however, these three errors be refuted by the convincing force of reason, the fourth is always ready and on every one's lips for the excuse of his own ignorance, and although he has no knowledge worthy of the name, he may yet shamelessly magnify it, so that at least to the wretched satisfaction of his own folly he suppresses and evades the truth. Moreover, from these deadly banes come all the evils of the human race; for the most useful, the greatest, and most beautiful lessons of

The Opus Maius of Roger Bacon (1928), pp. 4, 584–585, translated by R. B. Burke. Reprinted by permission of University of Pennsylvania Press.

knowledge, as well as the secrets of all science and art, are unknown. But, still worse, men blinded in the fog of these four errors do not perceive their own ignorance, but with every precaution cloak and defend it so as not to find a remedy; and worst of all, although they are in the densest shadows of error, they think that they are in the full light of truth. For these reasons they reckon that truths most firmly established are at the extreme limits of false-hood, that our greatest blessings are of no moment, and our chief interests possess neither weight nor value. On the contrary, they proclaim what is most false, praise what is worst, extol what is most vile, blind to every gleam of wisdom and scorning what they can obtain with great ease.

* * *

He therefore who wishes to rejoice without doubt in regard to the truths underlying phenomena must know how to devote himself to experiment. For authors write many statements, and people believe them through reasoning which they formulate without experience. Their reasoning is wholly false. For it is generally believed that the diamond cannot be broken except by goat's blood, and philosophers and theologians misuse this idea. But fracture by means of blood of this kind has never been verified, although the effort has been made; and without that blood it can be broken easily. For I have seen this with my own eyes, and this is necessary, because gems cannot be carved except by fragments of this stone. . . . Moreover, it is generally believed that hot water freezes more quickly than cold water in vessels, and the argument in support of this is advanced that contrary is excited by contrary, just like enemies meeting each other. But it is certain that cold water freezes more quickly for any one who makes the experiment. People attribute this to Aris-totle in the second book of the Meteorologics; but he certainly does not make this statement, but he does make one like it, by which they have been de-ceived, namely, that if cold water and hot water are poured on a cold place, as upon ice, the hot water freezes more quickly, and this is true. But if hot water and cold are placed in two vessels, the cold will freeze more quickly. There-fore all things must be verified by experience.

But experience is of two kinds; one is gained through our external senses, and in this way we gain our experience of those things that are in the heavens by instruments made for this purpose, and of those things here below by means attested by our vision. Things that do not belong in our part of the world we know through other scientists who have had experience of them. As, for example, Aristotle on the authority of Alexander sent two thousand men through different parts of the world to gain experimental knowledge of all things that are on the surface of the earth, as Pliny bears witness in his Natural History. This experience is both human and philosophical, as far as man can act in accordance with the grace given him; but this experience does not suffice him, because it does not give full attestation in regard to things corporeal owing to its difficulty, and does not touch at all on things spiritual. It is necessary, therefore, that the intellect of man should be otherwise aided, and for this reason the holy patriarchs and prophets, who first gave sciences to the world, received illumination within and were not dependent on sense alone. The same is true of many believers since the time of Christ. For the grace of faith illuminates greatly, as also do divine inspirations, not only in things spiritual, but in things corporeal and in the sciences of philosophy; as Ptolemy states in the Centilogium, namely, and there are two roads by which we arrive at the knowledge of facts, one through the experience of philosophy, the other through divine inspiration, which is far the better way, as he says.

Roger Bacon evidently saw no conflict between science and religion. Other contemporary thinkers, however, were perplexed by new problems arising out of the fashionable Aristotelian studies. It seemed to them that the great Arab commentator on Aristotle, Averroës (1126–1198), had demonstrated that certain propositions that were incompatible with the Christian faith were nonetheless philosophically true. The problem of reason and faith thus arose in a new and more difficult form. Etienne Gilson discusses some thirteenth-century reactions to the situation in the following passage.

FROM Reason and Revelation in the Middle Ages
BY ETIENNE GILSON

In consequence of this, there was the rise of a new spiritual family: the Latin Averroists.

Among the many members of that family, I beg to distinguish a first variety, which I cannot help considering as entitled to our sincere sympathy. For indeed those poor people found themselves in sore straits. On the one side, they were good Christians and sincere believers. To them, it was beyond a doubt that Christian Revelation was, not only the truth, but the ultimate, supreme and absolute truth. This reason in itself was sufficient to make it impossible for them to be Averroists in identically the same way as Averroës himself. On the other side, and this time as philosophers, this group failed to see how any one of Averroës' philosophical doctrines could be refuted. What were they to do in the many instances where their faith and their reason were at odds? For instance, their philosophy proved by necessary reasons that the

Reprinted with the permission of Charles Scribner's Sons from Reason and Revelation in the Middle Ages, pp. 54–63, by Etienne Gilson. Copyright 1938 Charles Scribner's Sons.

world is eternal, perpetually moved by a self-thinking thought or mind, ruled from above by an intelligible necessity wholly indifferent to the destinies of individuals as such. In point of fact, the God of the Averroists does not even know that there are individuals, he knows only himself and that which is involved in his own necessity. Thus, knowing the human species, he is in no wise aware of the existence of those fleeting things, the individuals by which the eternal species is represented. Besides, as individuals, men have no intellect of their own; they do not think, they are merely thought into from above by a separate intellect, the same for the whole of mankind. Having no personal intellect, men can have no personal immortality, nor therefore can they hope for future rewards or fear eternal punishments in another life. Yet, at the same time when their reason was binding them to accept those conclusions, as philosophers, their faith was binding them to believe, as Christians, that the world has been freely created in time, by a God whose fatherly providence takes care of even the smallest among His Creatures; and if God so cares for every sparrow, what shall we say of man, who is of more value than many sparrows? Is not each of us endowed with a personal intellect of his own, responsible for each one of his thoughts as well as of his acts, and destined to live an immortal life of blessedness or of misery according to his own individual merits? In short, theology and philosophy were leading these men to conclusions that could neither be denied nor reconciled.

In order to free themselves from those contradictions, some among the Masters of Arts of the Parisian Faculty of Arts chose to declare that, having been appointed to teach philosophy, and nothing else, they would stick to their own job, which was to state the conclusions of philosophy such as necessarily follow from the principles of natural reason. True enough, their conclusions did not always agree with those of theology, but such was philosophy and they could not help it. Besides, it should be kept in mind that these professors would never tell their students, nor even think among themselves, that the conclusions of philosophy were true. They would say only this, that such conclusions were necessary from the point of view of natural reason; but what is human reason as compared with the wisdom and power of an infinite God? For instance, the very notion of a creation in time is a philosophical absurdity, but if we believe in God Almighty, why should not we also believe that, for such a God to create the world in time was not an impossibility? The same thing could be said everywhere. The conclusions of philosophy are at variance with the teaching of Revelation; let us therefore hold them as the *necessary* results of philosophical speculation, but, as Christians, let us believe that what Revelation says on such matters is *true;* thus, no contradiction will ever arise between philosophy and theology, or between Revelation and reason.

The doctrine of this first group of Latin Averroists is commonly called: the doctrine of the twofold truth. Philosophically justified as I think it is, such a designation is not an historically correct one. Not a single one among those men would have ever admitted that two sets of conclusions, the one in philosophy, the other in theology, could be, at one and the same time, both absolutely contradictory and absolutely true. There still are many medieval writings to be discovered, but with due reservation as to what could be found to the contrary in one of them, I can say that such a position was a most unlikely one, and that I have not yet been able to find a single medieval philosopher professing the doctrine of the twofold truth. Their actual position was a much less patently contradictory and a much less unthinkable one. As so many men who cannot reconcile their reason with their faith, and yet want them both, the Averroists were keeping both philosophy and Revelation, with a watertight separation between them. Why should not a man feel sure that Averroës cannot be refuted, and yet believe that the most necessary reasons fall short of the infinite wisdom of an all-powerful God? I would not say that it is a logically safe position, nor a philosophically brilliant one, but the combination of blind fideism in theology with scepticism in philosophy is by no means an uncommon phenomenon in the history of human thought. I seem to hear one of those divided minds saying to himself: here is all that philosophy can say about God, man and human destiny; it is not much; yet that at least is conclusively proven and I cannot make philosophy say anything else. Were we living in a non-Christian world, such conclusions would not be merely necessary, they would also be truth. But God has spoken. We now know that what appears as necessary in the light of a finite reason is not necessarily true. Let us therefore take philosophy for what it is: the knowledge of what man would hold as true, if absolute truth had not been given to him by the divine Revelation. There have been men of that type in the thirteenth-century University of Paris; to the best of my knowledge, there is no reason whatever to suppose that Siger of Brabant and Boethius of Dacia for instance, both of them Averroists in philosophy, were not also perfectly sincere in their religious faith. Such, at least, was the personal conviction of Dante concerning Siger, for had he entertained the least suspicion about the sincerity of Siger's faith, he would not have put him in the fourth heaven of the Sun, together with Albertus Magnus and Thomas Aquinas.

Besides that first group of Latin Averroists, there was another one, whose members were equally convinced that the philosophy of Averroës was the absolute truth, but felt no difficulty in reconciling it with their religious beliefs, because they had none. It is often said, and not without good reasons, that the civilization of the Middle Ages was an essentially religious one. Yet, even in the times of the Cathedrals and of the Crusades, not everybody was a saint; it would not even be correct to suppose that everybody was orthodox, and there are safe indications that confirmed unbelievers could be met on the streets of Paris and of Padua around the end of the thirteenth century. When such men were at the same time philosophers, the deism of Averroës was their natural philosophy. As to Revelation, they would profess, at least in words, absolute respect for its teachings, but none of them would ever miss an opportunity to demonstrate by necessary reasons the very reverse of what they were supposed to believe. Seen from without, the members of this second group were saying identically the same things as the members of the first one, but their tone was different and, cautious as they had to be, they usually found the way to make themselves understood.

One of the best specimens of that variety was undoubtedly the French philosopher John of Jaudun, better known to historians as the associate of Marsiglio di Padoa in his campaign against the temporal power of the Popes. Every time, in his commentaries upon Aristotle, he reached one of those critical points where his philosophy was at variance with the conclusions of Christian theology, John never failed to restate his complete submission to religious orthodoxy, but he usually did it in a rather strange way. In some cases he so obviously enjoys reminding us of all that which he merely believes, and cannot prove, that one wonders what interests him more about those points, that all of them should be believed, or that none of them can be proved. Here is one of those texts: "I believe and I firmly maintain that the substance of the soul is endowed with natural faculties whose activities are independent from all bodily organs. . . . Such faculties belong in a higher order than that of corporeal matter and far exceed its capacities. . . . And although the soul be united with matter, it nevertheless exercises an (intellectual) activity in which corporeal matter takes no part. All those properties of the soul belong to it truly, simply and absolutely, according to our own faith. And also that an immaterial soul can suffer from a material fire, and be reunited with its own body, after death, by order of the same God Who created it. On the other side, I would not undertake to demonstrate all that, but I think that such things should be believed by simple faith, as well as many others that are to be believed without demonstrative reasons, on the authority of Holy Writ and of miracles. Besides, this is why there is some merit in believing, for the theologians teach us, that there is no merit in believing that which reason can demonstrate." Most of the time, however, John of Jaudun would content himself with cracking some joke, which makes it difficult for his readers to take seriously his most formal professions of faith: "I do believe that that is true; but I cannot prove it. Good luck to those who can!" And again: "I say that God can do that, but how, I don't know; God knows." Another time, after proving at great length that the notion of creation is a philosophical impossibility, John naturally adds that we should nevertheless believe it. Of course, says he, no philosopher ever thought of it, "And no wonder, for it is impossible to reach the notion of creation from the consideration of empirical facts; nor is it possible to justify it by arguments borrowed from sensible experience. And this is why the Ancients, who used to draw their knowledge from rational arguments verified by sensible experience, never succeeded in conceiving such a mode of production." And here is the final stroke: "Let it be added, that creation very seldom happens; there has never been but one, and that was a very long time ago." There was a slight touch of Voltaire in John of Jaudun's irony; and yet, his carefully worded jokes represent only what could then be written; as is usually the case, much more could be said.

4
THOMAS AQUINAS ON FAITH AND REASON

Thomas Aquinas held that the anti-Christian tenets of Averroistic philosophy could not be definitively proved, while acknowledging that they could not always be disproved either. It is widely held nowadays that he achieved the most impressive medieval synthesis of Christian doctrine and Aristotelian philosophy. An older generation of scholars, however, was inclined to dismiss him as merely obscurantist. The following reading compares him with Roger Bacon.

FROM The Warfare of Science BY A. D. WHITE

More than three centuries before Francis Bacon advocated the experimental method, Roger Bacon practised it, and the results as now revealed are wonderful. He wrought with power in philosophy and in all sciences, and his knowledge was sound and exact. By him, more than by any other man of the middle ages, was the world put on the most fruitful paths of science—the paths which have led to the most precious inventions. Among them are clocks, lenses, burning specula, telescopes, which were given by him to the world, directly or indirectly. In his writings are found formulae for extracting phosphorus, manganese, and bismuth. It is even claimed, with much appearance of justice, that he investigated the power of steam. He seems to have very nearly reached also some of the principal doctrines of modern chemistry. But it should be borne in mind that his method of investigation was even

A. D. White, *The Warfare of Science* (1877), pp. 89–90, 79–81.

greater than these vast results. In the age when metaphysical subtilizing was alone thought to give the title of scholar, he insisted on *real* reasoning and the aid of natural science by mathematics. In an age when experimenting was sure to cost a man his reputation, and was likely to cost him his life, he insisted on experiment and braved all its risks. Few greater men have lived.

* * *

But the theological ecclesiastical spirit of the thirteenth century gained its greatest victory in the work of the most renowned of all thinkers of his time, St. Thomas Aquinas. In him was the theological spirit of his age incarnate. Although he yielded somewhat, at one period, to love of studies in natural science, it was he who finally made that great treaty or compromise which for ages subjected science entirely to theology. He it was whose thought reared the most enduring barrier against those who, in that age and in succeeding ages, labored to open for science the path by its own legitimate method toward its own noble ends.

Through the earlier systems of philosophy as they were then known, and through the earlier theologic thought, he had gone with great labor and vigor; he had been a pupil of Albert of Bollstadt, and from him had gained inspiration in science. All his mighty powers, thus disciplined and cultured, he brought to bear in making a treaty or truce, giving to theology the supremacy over science. The experimental method had already been practically initiated; Albert of Bollstadt and Roger Bacon had begun their work in accordance with its methods; but St. Thomas Aquinas gave all his thoughts to bringing science again under the sway of the theological bias, metaphysical methods, and ecclesiastical control. He gave to the world a striking example of what his method could be made to produce. In his commentary upon Aristotle's treatise upon "Heaven and Earth" he illustrates all the evils of such a combination of theological reasoning and literal interpretation of the Scriptural with scientific facts as then understood, and it remains to this day a prodigious monument to human genius and human folly. The ecclesiastical power of the time hailed him as a deliverer; it was claimed that striking miracles were vouchsafed, showing that the blessing of Heaven rested upon his labors. Among the legends embodying the Church spirit of that period is that given by the Bollandists and immortalized by a renowned painter. The great philosopher and saint is represented in the habit of his order, with book and pen in hand, kneeling before the image of Christ crucified; and as he kneels the image thus addresses him: "Thomas, thou hast written well concerning me; what price wilt thou receive for thy labor?" To this day, the greater ecclesiastical historians of the Roman Church, like the Abbé Rohrbacher, and the minor historians of science, who find it convenient to propitiate the Church, like Pouchet, dilate upon the glories of St. Thomas Aquinas in thus making a treaty of alliance between religious and scientific thought, and laying the foundations for a "sanctified science." But the unprejudiced historian cannot indulge in this enthusiastic view. The results both for the Church and for the

progress of science have been most unfortunate. It was a wretched step backward. The first result of this great man's great compromise was to close that
new path in science which alone leads to discoveries of value—the experimental method—and to reopen the old path of mixed theology and science,
which, as Hallam declares, "after three or four hundred years had not untied
a single knot, or added one unequivocal truth to the domain of philosophy";
the path which, as all modern history proves, has ever since led only to delu-
sion and evil.

A more recent account praises Aquinas for correctly distinguishing between
the spheres of faith and reason.

FROM The Evolution of Medieval Thought
BY DAVID KNOWLES

St Thomas Aquinas has been hailed by common consent in the modern
world as the prince of scholastics, not only the *doctor angelicus,* but also, as
he was acclaimed soon after his death, the *doctor communis.* To Thomists of
pure blood, as to many others besides, he appears as the authentic voice of
reason, interpreting and defending tradition, as the greatest medieval representative of the *philosophia perennis,* the way of thinking that is ever ancient
and ever new.
    The newcomer to Aquinas who is unacquainted with the language and
preoccupations of medieval theology, or whose reading in philosophy has lain
among the ancients or the moderns, will probably be dismayed or frustrated
by the form of his writings. He will find none of the literary charm that the
writer of a dialogue or treatise can diffuse; the great doctor goes remorselessly
forward through things great and small, following for the most part an invar-
iable sequence of objection, solution and argument; there is no emphasis, no
high-lighting, no difference between points that seem trivial or otiose and the
supreme problems of existence. All is settled by a personal assertion, with
little apparent distinction between what is substantial and of common belief,
and what is only a possibility or an opinion. It is this apparent lack of dis-
crimination that repels or confuses many readers of to-day, and it must be
admitted that some of the admirers and followers of St Thomas have done

Reprinted by permission of the publishers, Helicon Press, Inc., Baltimore, Maryland, and
Longmans, Green & Co., Ltd., Harlow, from David Knowles, *The Evolution of Medieval
Thought,* pp. 255–258, 261–262. Copyright © 1962 by David Knowles. All rights reserved.

him a real disservice by their failure to realize themselves, and to communicate to others, the fundamental characteristics of the spirit and doctrine of the master. A rigid and unspiritual Thomist can be the worst of guides to St Thomas.

For the greatness is there. The judgment of his contemporaries and posterity has not been false. As we read, with sympathy and a receptive mind, on and on in the two great *Summae,* the pattern unfolds and the cardinal principles of thought recur and are used, like keen knives, to separate the truth from all else. We come to expect, and never fail to find, a justice and lucidity of thought and expression that thrills and stimulates by the impression it creates that a veil has fallen away and that the pure light of reason and reality is streaming into our minds.

* * *

As a follower of Albert who outran his master, he accepted human reason as an adequate and self-sufficient instrument for attaining truth within the realm of man's natural experience, and in so doing gave, not only to abstract thought but to all scientific knowledge, rights of citizenship in a Christian world. He accepted in its main lines the system of Aristotle as a basis for his own interpretation of the visible universe, and this acceptance did not exclude the ethical and political teaching of the Philosopher. By so doing, and without a full realization of all the consequences, St Thomas admitted into the Christian purview all the natural values of human social activity and, by implication, a host of other activities such as art. All these activities were indeed subordinated by him to the supernatural vocation of man, and were raised to a higher power by the Christian's supernatural end of action, but they had their own reality and value, they were not mere shadows or vanities.

Aquinas did not merely adopt and "baptize" or "Christianize" Aristotle. He had, indeed, no hesitation in extending his thought, in filling gaps within it and in interpreting it in accord with Christian teaching. He also took many elements from elsewhere. But he did more than this: and Aristotle, had he been restored to life to read the *Summa contra Gentiles,* would have had difficulty in recognizing the thought as his. For indeed Aquinas stood the system of Aristotle on its head or, to speak more carefully, supplied the lack of higher metaphysics in Aristotle by framing a conception of the deity which was in part drawn from Judeo-Christian revelation and which, when proposed in Thomist terms, embodied all that was most valuable in the metaphysic of Platonism. While Aristotle, the empiricist, looked most carefully at the universe of being as it was displayed to the senses and intelligence, and explored in his *Metaphysics* the veins and sinews of substance, he became imprecise when he rose to consider mind and soul, and hesitant when he looked up towards the First Cause of all things. His God is a shadow, an unseen, unknown, uncaring force and reason necessary to give supreme unity to the universe. In the Aristotelian system reality, existential reality, is strongest in the world of everyday experience; the loftier the gaze, the weaker the reality. With Thomism, on the other hand, the infinitely rich, dynamic existential reality is God, the creator and source of all being, goodness and truth, present in all being by power and essence, holding and guiding and regarding every part of creation, while as the one subsistent Being, the uncaused cause, the *ens a se* in whom alone essence and existence are one, He takes the place of the Platonic forms and exemplars as the One of whose Being all created being, its essence perfected by its God-given existence, is a reflection and (according to its mode as creature) a participant. It is only on a lower level that the Aristotelian universe of being is found, but the two visions of reality are fused by Aquinas under the light of the unifying principles, first proposed by the Greeks, of cause, reason and order.

* * *

St Thomas followed his master, Albert, in a resolute separation of the spheres of reason and revelation, the natural and the supernatural. While on the one hand this recognized the autonomy of human reason in its own field, it also limited its competence severely. Pure mysteries, such as the Trinity and the Incarnation, were no longer susceptible of proof, of comprehension, or even of adequate explanation. The human mind was now bounded by its contacts with the external world, according to the axiom *nihil est in intellectu, nisi prius fuerit in sensu*.[1] It was from observation of external reality, not through the soul's direct consciousness of its own or of God's existence, that a proof of the First Cause could be found. It was from contact with external reality, not from a divine illumination or contact with the divine ideas, that a knowledge of truth came. This was in harmony with a key proposition of Aquinas: *quicquid recipitur, secundum modum recipientis recipitur,* which in the field of epistemology became: *cognitum est in cognoscente per modum cognoscentis*[2]—God is known from His works not in Himself—but it might well seem to theologians of the traditional Franciscan school a despiritualization of religious thought. Yet it gave a new dignity to the human reason by lending philosophical support to a conviction common to all men, viz., that our knowledge comes to us directly or indirectly from the universe of being around us, and that neither our senses nor our reason play us false when they function normally. In other words, the activity of the human mind is as much a factor in the dynamics of the universe as are purely material or mechanistic activities. The human reason is a perfectly adequate precision instrument for perceiving all truth in the world of matter and spirit around it, within the limits of its range. Aquinas thus set his face both against any kind of "double truth" and against the Platonic conception of the

---

[1] "The mind can perceive nothing that has not previously been perceived by the senses."

[2] "Whatever is received, is received according to the mode of being of the receiver," as for example, the sound of a clock striking is heard merely as a sound by an animal, but as a time-signal by a man. "What is known is in the mind of the knower according to his mode of being."

world as a mere shadow and symbol of true reality. The realms of reason and revelation became separate, and the bounds of theology and philosophy, faith and natural knowledge, stood out sharp and clear. There is only one truth, but there are realms of truth to which the unaided human mind cannot attain; there is only one truth, and we can recognize it when we see it; it is therefore not possible for a man to have faith and natural certainty about one and the same proposition, still less can faith and natural certainty be in opposition. Moreover, all being and therefore all truth comes from a single source; there is therefore an order and harmony in all the parts. In the celebrated and characteristic phrase of Aquinas: "Grace does not destroy nature; it perfects her."

Some of Aquinas' own comments on reason and faith are set out below. He held that the whole body of theological truth consisted of two parts. Some truths could be attained by natural human reason. Others were strictly "of faith" in that they could be grasped only through divine revelation. The first reading illustrates Aquinas' pattern of argumentation—a final, sophisticated development of Abelard's "dialectical" method.

FROM Summa Theologiae BY THOMAS AQUINAS

WHETHER, BESIDES PHILOSOPHY, ANY FURTHER DOCTRINE IS REQUIRED?

We proceed thus to the First Article:—

Objection 1. It seems that, besides philosophical science, we have no need of any further knowledge. Man should not seek to know what is above reason: *Seek not the things that are too high for thee* (Eccles. iii. 22). But whatever is not above reason is fully treated of in philosophical science. Therefore any other knowledge besides philosophical science is superfluous.

Objection 2. Further, knowledge can only be concerned with being, for nothing can be known, save what is true; and all that is, is true. But everything that is, is treated of in philosophical science—even God Himself; so

Quoted from *Summa Theologica,* I (1911), 1–3, translated by the Fathers of the English Dominican Province. Reprinted by permission of Benziger Brothers, New York, publishers and copyright owners, and Burns & Oates Ltd., London. The variations in the title arise from disagreement over the correct Latin original—B. T.

that there is a part of philosophy called Theology, or the Divine Science, as Aristotle has proved. Therefore, besides philosophical science, there is no need of any further knowledge.

On the contrary, It is said, *All Scripture inspired of God is profitable to teach, to reprove, to correct, to instruct in justice* (2 Tim. iii. 16). Scripture, inspired of God, is no part of philosophical science, which has been built up by human reason. Therefore it is useful that besides philosophical science there should be other knowledge—i.e., inspired of God.

I answer that, It was necessary for man's salvation that there should be a knowledge revealed by God, besides philosophical science built up by human reason. Firstly, indeed, because man is ordained to God, as to an end that surpasses the grasp of his reason; *The eye hath not seen, besides Thee, O God, what things Thou hast prepared for them that wait for Thee* (Isa. lxiv. 4). But the end must first be known by men who are to direct their thoughts and actions to the end. Hence it was necessary for the salvation of man that certain truths which exceed human reason should be made known to him by Divine Revelation. Even as regards those truths about God which human reason could have discovered, it was necessary that man should be taught by a Divine Revelation; because the Truth about God such as reason could discover, would only be known by a few, and that after a long time, and with the admixture of many errors. Whereas man's whole salvation, which is in God, depends upon the knowledge of this Truth. Therefore, in order that the salvation of men might be brought about more fitly and more surely, it was necessary that they should be taught Divine Truths by Divine Revelation. It was therefore necessary that, besides philosophical science built up by reason, there should be a sacred science learnt through Revelation.

The following extracts give the substance of Aquinas' conclusions on various relevant points.

Philosophical Extracts BY THOMAS AQUINAS

A man should remind himself that an object of faith is not scientifically demonstrable lest, presuming to demonstrate what is of faith, he should produce inconclusive reasons and offer occasion for unbelievers to scoff at a faith based on such grounds.

Summa Theologica, ia. xlvi. 2

St. Thomas Aquinas: Philosophical Texts (1951), pp. 29–31, translated by Thomas Gilby. Reprinted by permission of Oxford University Press, London.

There are two methods of argument, demonstrative and persuasive. Demonstrative, cogent, and intellectually convincing argument cannot lay hold of the truths of faith, though it may neutralize destructive criticism that would render faith untenable. Persuasive reasoning drawn from probabilities, however, does not weaken the merit of faith, for it implies no attempt to convert faith into sight by resolving what is believed into evident first principles.

Opusc. xvi, *de Trinitate,* ii. 1, *ad* 5

There is a double canon for the theological truths we profess. Some surpass the ingenuity of the human reason, for instance the Trinity. But others can be attained by the human reason, for instance the existence and unity of God, also similar truths demonstrated in the light of the philosophical reason.

1 *Contra Gentiles,* 3

* * *

Christian theology issues from the light of faith, philosophy from the natural light of reason. Philosophical truths cannot be opposed to the truths of faith, they fall short indeed, yet they also admit common analogies; and some moreover are foreshadowings, for nature is the preface to grace.

Opusc. xvi, Exposition, *de Trinitate,* ii. 3

From bare acquaintance with the commentary of Averroes it is strange how some have presumed to pronounce that his sentiments are shared by all philosophers, the western Christian philosophers excepted. It is an occasion of greater surprise, indeed of indignation, how any professing Christian can talk so irresponsibly about his faith as to contend that these westerners do not accept the doctrine of an unique intelligence because their religious belief happens to be against it.

Here two mischiefs are at work. First, that the repugnance of religious faith to such teachings should be left in doubt. Second, that their irrelevance to the creed should be alleged. Nor is another assertion less rash, namely that God himself could not produce a multitude of intelligences, for that implies a contradiction. More serious is a later statement, "Rationally I infer of necessity that intelligence must be numerically one, but by faith I firmly hold the opposite." This is tantamount to holding that belief can be about things whose contrary can be demonstrated. Since what can be so demonstrated is bound to be a necessary truth and its opposite false and impossible, the upshot would be that faith avows what is false and impossible. This is intolerable to our ears, for not even God could contrive such a situation.

. . . Opusc. vi, *de Unitate Intellectus contra Averroistas*

Although Aquinas held that there were certain mysteries of religion that had to be accepted by faith alone, he was exceptionally optimistic—for his age—about the capacity of reason to discern truth. He did not concern himself to any significant degree with natural science, but he wrote extensively about what we should call the "social sciences." In this sphere he sought to apply rational argumentation to topics that had usually been treated in the past simply as matters of religious doctrine. He argued, for example, for the "naturalness" of permanent marriage between men and women.

FROM Summa Theologiae BY THOMAS AQUINAS

WHETHER MATRIMONY IS OF NATURAL LAW?

We proceed thus to the First Article:—
Objection 1. It would seem that matrimony is not natural. Because the natural law is what nature has taught all animals. But in other animals the sexes are united without matrimony. Therefore matrimony is not of natural law.

I answer that, A thing is said to be natural in two ways. First, as resulting of necessity from the principles of nature; thus upward movement is natural to fire. In this way matrimony is not natural, nor are any of those things that come to pass at the intervention or motion of the free-will. Secondly, that is said to be natural to which nature inclines, although it comes to pass through the intervention of the free-will; thus acts of virtue and the virtues themselves are called natural; and in this way matrimony is natural, because natural reason inclines thereto in two ways. First, in relation to the principal end of matrimony, namely the good of the offspring. For nature intends not only the begetting of offspring, but also its education and development until it reach the perfect state of man as man, and that is the state of virtue. Hence, according to the Philosopher (*Ethic.* viii. 11, 12), we derive three things from our parents, namely *existence, nourishment,* and *education.* Now a child cannot be brought up and instructed unless it have certain and definite parents, and this would not be the case unless there were a tie between the man and a definite woman, and it is in this that matrimony consists. Secondly, in relation to the secondary end of matrimony, which is the mutual services which mar-

Quoted from *Summa Theologica,* XX (1922), 76–78, translated by the Fathers of the Englihs Dominican Province. Reprinted by permission of Benziger Brothers, New York, publishers and copyright owners, and Burns & Oates Ltd., London. The variations in the title arise from disagreement over the correct Latin original—B. T.

ried persons render one another in household matters. For just as natural reason dictates that men should live together, since one is not self-sufficient in all things concerning life, for which reason man is described as being naturally inclined to political society, so too among those works that are necessary for human life some are becoming to men, others to women. Wherefore nature inculcates that society of man and woman which consists in matrimony. These two reasons are given by the Philosopher (*Ethic.* viii., *loc. cit.*).

Reply Objection 1. Man's nature inclines to a thing in two ways. In one way, because that thing is becoming to the generic nature, and this is common to all animals; in another way because it is becoming to the nature of the difference, whereby the human species in so far as it is rational overflows the genus; such is an act of prudence or temperance. And just as the generic nature, though one in all animals, yet is not in all in the same way, so neither does it incline in the same way in all, but in a way befitting each one. Accordingly man's nature inclines to matrimony on the part of the difference, as regards the second reason given above; wherefore the Philosopher (*loc. cit.;* *Polit.* i.) gives this reason in men over other animals; but as regards the first reason it inclines on the part of the genus; wherefore he says that the begetting of children is common to all animals. Yet nature does not incline thereto in the same way in all animals; since there are animals whose offspring are able to seek food immediately after birth, or are sufficiently fed by their mother; and in these there is no tie between male and female; whereas in those whose offspring need the support of both parents, although for a short time, there is a certain tie, as may be seen in certain birds. In man, however, since the child needs the parents' care for a long time, there is a very great tie between male and female, to which tie even the generic nature inclines.

Aquinas thought that the state, as well as the family, was a proper subject for rational analysis.

FROM On Kingship BY THOMAS AQUINAS

In all things which are ordered towards an end wherein this or that course may be adopted, some directive principle is needed through which the due end may be reached by the most direct route. A ship, for example, which moves in different directions according to the impulse of the changing winds,

Thomas Aquinas, *On Kingship* (1949), pp. 3–7, 23–24, translated by G. B. Phelan and I T. Eschmann. Reprinted by permission of Pontifical Institute of Mediaeval Studies, Toronto.

would never reach its destination were it not brought to port by the skill of
the pilot. Now, man has an end to which his whole life and all his actions are
ordered; for man is an intelligent agent, and it is clearly the part of an intelligent agent to act in view of an end. Men also adopt different methods in
proceeding towards their proposed end, as the diversity of men's pursuits and
actions clearly indicates. Consequently man needs some directive principle to
guide him towards his end.

To be sure, the light of reason is placed by nature in every man, to guide
him in his acts towards his end. Wherefore, if man were intended to live
alone, as many animals do, he would require no other guide to his end. Each
man would be a king unto himself, under God, the highest King, inasmuch
as he would direct himself in his acts by the light of reason given him from
on high. Yet it is natural for man, more than for any other animal, to be a
social and political animal, to live in a group.

This is clearly a necessity of man's nature. For all other animals, nature has
prepared food, hair as a covering, teeth, horns, claws as means of defence or
at least speed in flight, while man alone was made without any natural provisions for these things. Instead of all these, man was endowed with reason, by
the use of which he could procure all these things for himself by the work of
his hands. Now, one man alone is not able to procure them all for himself, for
one man could not sufficiently provide for life, unassisted. It is therefore natural that man should live in the society of many. . . . This point is further and
most plainly evidenced by the fact that the use of speech is a prerogative
proper to man. . . .

If, then, it is natural for man to live in the society of many, it is necessary
that there exist among men some means by which the group may be governed. For where there are many men together and each one is looking after
his own interest, the multitude would be broken up and scattered unless there
were also an agency to take care of what appertains to the common-weal. In
like manner, the body of a man or any other animal would disintegrate unless there were a general ruling force within the body which watches over the
common good of all members. With this in mind, Solomon says: "Where
there is no governor, the people shall fall" (Proverbs 11:14).

Indeed it is reasonable that this should happen, for what is proper and
what is common are not identical. Things differ by what is proper to each:
they are united by what they have in common. But diversity of effects is due
to diversity of causes. Consequently, there must exist something which impels
towards the common good of the many, over and above that which impels
towards the particular good of each individual. Wherefore also in all things
that are ordained towards one end, one thing is found to rule the rest. Thus
in the corporeal universe, by the first body, i.e., the celestial body, the other
bodies are regulated according to the order of Divine Providence, and all
bodies are ruled by a rational creature. So, too, in the individual man, the soul
rules the body; and among the parts of the soul, the irascible and the con-
cupiscible parts are ruled by reason. Likewise, among the members of a body,

one, such as the heart or the head, is the principal and moves all the others. Therefore in every multitude there must be some governing power.

Therefore, since the rule of one man, which is the best, is to be preferred, and since it may happen that it be changed into a tyranny, which is the worst . . . a scheme should be carefully worked out which would prevent the multitude ruled by a king from falling into the hands of a tyrant.

First, it is necessary that the man who is raised up to be king by those whom it concerns should be of such condition that it is improbable that he should become a tyrant. Wherefore Daniel, commending the providence of God with respect to the institution of the king, says: "The Lord hath sought him a man according to his own heart and the Lord hath appointed him to be a prince over his people" (1 Kings 12:4). Then, once the king is established, the government of the kingdom must be so arranged that opportunity to tyrannize is removed. At the same time his power should be so tempered that he cannot easily fall into tyranny.

Aquinas' whole method of philosophizing within a framework of assumed religious truth is open to challenge. Some modern philosophers, like Bertrand Russell, have dismissed it as mere "special pleading." Another approach is suggested by F. C. Copleston.

FROM Aquinas BY F. C. COPLESTON

Some objections against medieval philosophy are connected with features which are more or less peculiar to the intellectual life of the Middle Ages. For example, the fact that most of the leading philosophers of the Middle Ages, including Aquinas, were theologians easily gives rise to the conviction that their philosophizing was improperly subordinated to theological beliefs and interests and that their metaphysical arguments were not infrequently instances of what we call "wishful thinking." But on this matter I must content myself with the observation that if we take any given line of argument in favour of some belief or position the relevant question from the philosophical point of view is whether the argument is sound rather than whether the writer wished to arrive at the conclusion at which he did in fact arrive or whether he already believed in that conclusion on other grounds. For example, it is possible for a man who has believed in God from childhood to

F. C. Copleston, *Aquinas* (1955), pp. 17–18. Reprinted by permission of Penguin Books, Ltd., Harmondsworth.

ask himself whether there is any rational evidence in favour of this belief. And if he offers what he considers to be rational evidence, it ought to be considered on its merits and not dismissed from the start on the ground that it cannot be anything more than an instance of wishful thinking. Whether or not we come to the conclusion that his arguments were in fact probably examples of wishful thinking, we should not assume that they were simply on the ground that the man already believed in God.

5

AQUINAS
AND THE
EXISTENCE
OF GOD

Aquinas was convinced that human reason, unaided by divine revelation, could prove the existence of God. His "proofs" represent a high-water mark of medieval rationalism.

The technical language in the first paragraph of Aquinas' first "proof" may be confusing, but the point Aquinas was seeking to make is not oversubtle. "Motion" throughout the argument means all change in general; "potentiality" means capacity to change. Aquinas was asserting simply that a thing could not change itself into something else without outside intervention. An acorn is thus potentially an oak tree, but it cannot become an actual oak tree without the play upon it of actually existing environmental factors.

Another problem is posed by the sentence "This cannot go on to infinity." Here the essential nature of the argument is obscured by extreme compression of statement. In other contexts Aquinas admitted that—as far as human reason could tell—the universe might well have existed from all eternity; and he explicitly acknowledged the possibility of their being an infinite series of events in time. The argument here must be taken to mean

---

Quoted from *Summa Theologica*, I (1911), 24–27, translated by the Fathers of the English Dominican Province. Reprinted by permission of Benziger Brothers, New York, publishers and copyright owners, and Burns & Oates Ltd., London. The variations in the title arise from disagreement over the correct Latin original—B. T.

that even if we postulate such an infinite series in time, it is still necessary to assume the existence of a first mover or first cause outside the series to account for the series as a whole.

FROM Summa Theologiae BY THOMAS AQUINAS

The existence of God can be proved in five ways.

The first and more manifest way is the argument from motion. It is certain and evident to our senses that some things are in motion. Whatever is in motion is moved by another, for nothing can be in motion except it have a potentiality for that towards which it is being moved; whereas a thing moves inasmuch as it is in act. By "motion" we mean nothing else than the reduction of something from a state of potentiality into a state of actuality. Nothing, however, can be reduced from a state of potentiality into a state of actuality unless by something already in a state of actuality. Thus that which is actually hot as fire, makes wood, which is potentially hot, to be actually hot, and thereby moves and changes it. It is not possible that the same thing should be at once in a state of actuality and potentiality from the same point of view, but only from different points of view. What is actually hot cannot simultaneously be only potentially hot; still, it is simultaneously potentially cold. It is therefore impossible that from the same point of view and in the same way anything should be both moved and mover, or that it should move itself. Therefore, whatever is in motion must be put in motion by another. If that by which it is put in motion be itself put in motion, then this also must needs be put in motion by another, and that by another again. This cannot go on to infinity, because then there would be no first mover, and, consequently, no other mover—seeing that subsequent movers only move inasmuch as they are put in motion by the first mover; as the staff only moves because it is put in motion by the hand. Therefore it is necessary to arrive at a First Mover, put in motion by no other; and this everyone understands to be God.

The second way is from the formality of efficient causation. In the world of sense we find there is an order of efficient causation. There is no case known (neither is it, indeed, possible) in which a thing is found to be the efficient cause of itself; for so it would be prior to itself, which is impossible. In efficient causes it is not possible to go on to infinity, because in all efficient causes following in order, the first is the cause of the intermediate cause, and the intermediate is the cause of the ultimate cause, whether the intermediate cause be several, or one only. To take away the cause is to take away the effect. Therefore, if there be no first cause among efficient causes, there will be no ultimate cause, nor any intermediate. If in efficient causes it is possible to go on to infinity, there will be no first efficient cause, neither will there be an ultimate effect, nor any intermediate efficient causes; all of which is plainly false. Therefore it is necessary to put forward a First Efficient Cause, to which everyone gives the name of God.

The third way is taken from possibility and necessity, and runs thus. We find in nature things that could either exist or not exist, since they are found to be generated, and then to corrupt; and, consequently, they can exist, and then not exist. It is impossible for these always to exist, for that which can one day cease to exist must at some time have not existed. Therefore, if everything could cease to exist, then at one time there could have been nothing in existence. If this were true, even now there would be nothing in existence, because that which does not exist only begins to exist by something already existing. Therefore, if at one time nothing was in existence, it would have been impossible for anything to have begun to exist; and thus even now nothing would be in existence—which is absurd. Therefore, not all beings are merely possible, but there must exist something the existence of which is necessary. Every necessary thing either has its necessity caused by another, or not. It is impossible to go on to infinity in necessary things which have their necessity caused by another, as has been already proved in regard to efficient causes. Therefore we cannot but postulate the existence of some being having of itself its own necessity, and not receiving it from another, but rather causing in others their necessity. This all men speak of as God.

The fourth way is taken from the gradation to be found in things. Among beings there are some more and some less good, true, noble, and the like. But "more" and "less" are predicated of different things, according as they resemble in their different ways something which is in the degree of "most," as a thing is said to be hotter according as it more nearly resembles that which is hottest; so that there is something which is truest, something best, something noblest, and, consequently, something which is uttermost being; for the truer things are, the more truly they exist. What is most complete in any genus is the cause of all in that genus; as fire, which is the most complete form of heat, is the cause whereby all things are made hot. Therefore there must also be something which is to all beings the cause of their being, goodness, and every other perfection; and this we call God.

The fifth way is taken from the governance of the world; for we see that things which lack intelligence, such as natural bodies, act for some purpose, which fact is evident from their acting always, or nearly always, in the same way, so as to obtain the best result. Hence it is plain that not fortuitously, but designedly, do they achieve their purpose. Whatever lacks intelligence cannot fulfil some purpose, unless it be directed by some being endowed with intelligence and knowledge; as the arrow is shot to its mark by the archer. Therefore some intelligent being exists by whom all natural things are ordained towards a definite purpose; and this being we call God.

Aquinas did not succeed in convincing all of the next generation of philosophers. William of Ockham, the most influential thinker of the fourteenth century, declared that in all arguments for the existence of God something doubtful or derived from faith was assumed. The Thomistic "proofs" continue to be argued by modern philosophers. The following discussion views them favorably.

FROM The Vindication of Religion
BY A. E. TAYLOR

The point of the argument about the necessity of an "unmoving source of motion" must not be missed. We shall grasp it better if we remember that "motion" in the vocabulary of Aristotle means change of every kind, so that what is being asserted is that there must be an unchanging cause or source of change. Also, we must not fancy that we have disposed of the argument by saying that there is no scientific presumption that the series of changes which make up the life of Nature may not have been without a beginning and destined to have no end. St. Thomas, whose famous five proofs of the existence of God are all of them variations on the argument from "motion," or, as we might say, the appeal to the principle of causality, was also the philosopher who created a sensation among the Christian thinkers of his day by insisting stiffly that, apart from the revelation given in Scripture, no reasons can be produced for holding that the world had a beginning or need have an end, as indeed Aristotle maintained that it has neither. The dependence meant in the argument has nothing to do with succession in time. What is really meant is that our knowledge of any event in Nature is not complete until we know the full reason for the event. So long as you only know that A is so because B is so, but cannot tell why B is so, your knowledge is incomplete. It only becomes complete when you are in a position to say that ultimately A is so because Z is so, Z being something which is its own *raison d'être*, and therefore such that it would be senseless to ask *why* Z is so. This at once leads to the conclusion that since we always have the right to ask about any event in Nature why that event is so, what are its conditions, the Z which is its own *raison d'être* cannot itself belong to Nature. The point of the reasoning is precisely that it is an argument from the fact that there is a "Na-

A. E. Taylor, "The Vindication of Religion," in G. Selwyn, ed., *Essays Catholic and Critical* (1926), pp. 49–55. Reprinted by permission of The Society for Promoting Christian Knowledge, London.

ture" to the reality of a "Supernature," and this point is unaffected by the question whether there ever was a beginning of time, or a time when there were no "events."

* * *

The nerve of the whole reasoning is that every explanation of given facts or events involves bringing in reference to further unexplained facts; a complete explanation of anything, if we could obtain one, would therefore require that we should trace the fact explained back to something which contains its own explanation within itself, a something which is and is what it is in its own right; such a something plainly is not an event or mere fact and therefore not included in "Nature," the complex of all events and facts, but "above" Nature. Any man has a right to say, if he pleases, that he personally does not care to spend his time in exercising this mode of thinking, but would rather occupy himself in discovering fresh facts or fresh and hitherto unsuspected relations between facts. We need not blame him for that; but we are entitled to ask those who are alive to the meaning of the old problem how they propose to deal with it, if they reject the inference from the unfinished and conditioned to the perfect and unconditioned. For my own part I can see only two alternatives.

1. One is to say, as Hume did in his "Dialogues on Natural Religion," that, though every "part" of Nature may be dependent on other parts for its explanation, the *whole* system of facts or events which we call Nature may as a whole be self-explanatory; the "world" itself may be that "necessary being" of which philosophers and divines have spoken. In other words, a complex system in which every member, taken singly, is temporal, may as a complex be eternal; every member may be incomplete, but the whole may be complete; every member mutable, but the whole unchanging. Thus, as many philosophers of yesterday and to-day have said, the "eternal" would just be the temporal fully understood; there would be no contrast between Nature and "Supernature," but only between "Nature apprehended as a whole" and Nature as we have to apprehend her fragmentarily. The thought is a pretty one, but I cannot believe that it will stand criticism. The very first question suggested by the sort of formula I have just quoted is whether it is not actually self-contradictory to call Nature a "whole" at all; if it is, there can clearly be no apprehending of Nature as something which she is not. And I think it quite clear that Nature, in the sense of the complex of events, is, in virtue of her very structure, something incomplete and not a true whole. I can explain the point best, perhaps, by an absurdly simplified example. Let us suppose that Nature consists of just four constituents, A, B, C, D. We are supposed to "explain" the behaviour of A by the structure of B, C, and D, and the interaction of B, C, and D with A, and similarly with each of the other three constituents. Obviously enough, with a set of "general laws" of some kind we can "explain" why A behaves as it does, if we know all about its structure and

the structures of B, C, and D. But it still remains entirely unexplained why A should be there at all, or why, if it is there, it should have B, C, and D as its neighbours rather than others with a totally different structure of their own. That this is so has to be accepted as a "brute" fact which is not explained nor yet self-explanatory. Thus no amount of knowledge of "natural laws" will explain the present actual state of Nature unless we also assume it as a brute fact that the distribution of "matter" and "energy" (or whatever else we take as the ultimates of our system of physics) a hundred millions of years ago was such and such. With the same "laws" and a different "initial" distribution the actual state of the world to-day would be very different. "Collocations," to use Mill's terminology, as well as "laws of causation" have to enter into all our scientific explanations. And though it is true that as our knowledge grows, we are continually learning to assign causes for particular "collocations" originally accepted as bare facts, we only succeed in doing so by falling back on other anterior "collocations" which we have equally to take as unexplained bare facts. As M. Meyerson puts it, we only get rid of the "inexplicable" at one point at the price of introducing it again somewhere else. Now any attempt to treat the complex of facts we call Nature as something which will be found to be more nearly self-explanatory the more of them we know, and would become quite self-explanatory if we only knew them all, amounts to an attempt to eliminate "bare fact" altogether, and reduce Nature simply to a complex of "laws." In other words, it is an attempt to manufacture particular existents out of mere universals, and therefore must end in failure. And the actual progress of science bears witness to this. The more we advance to the reduction of the visible face of Nature to "law," the more, not the less, complex and baffling become the mass of characters which we have to attribute as bare unexplained fact to our ultimate constituents. An electron is a much stiffer dose of "brute" fact than one of Newton's hard impenetrable corpuscles.

Thus we may fairly say that to surrender ourselves to the suggestion that Nature, if we only knew enough, would be seen to be a self-explanatory whole is to follow a will-of-the-wisp. The duality of "law" and "fact" cannot be eliminated from natural science, and this means that in the end either Nature is not explicable at all, or, if she is, the explanation has to be sought in something "outside" on which Nature depends.

2. Hence it is not surprising that both among men of science and among philosophers there is just now a strong tendency to give up the attempt to "explain" Nature completely and to fall back on an "ultimate pluralism." This means that we resign ourselves to the admission of the duality of "law" and "fact." We assume that there are a plurality of ultimately different constituents of Nature, each with its own specific character and way of behaving, and our business in explanation is simply to show how to account for the world as we find it by the fewest and simplest laws of interaction between these different constituents. In other words we give up altogether the at-

tempt to "explain Nature"; we are content to "explain" lesser "parts" of Nature in terms of their specific character and their relations to other "parts." This is clearly a completely justified mode of procedure for a man of science who is aiming at the solution of some particular problem such as, *e.g.,* the discovery of the conditions under which a permanent new "species" originates and maintains itself. But it is quite another question whether "ultimate pluralism" can be the last word of a "philosophy of Nature." If you take it so, it really means that in the end you have no reason to assign why there should be just so many ultimate constituents of "Nature" as you say there are, or why they should have the particular characters you say they have, except that "it happens to be the case." You are acquiescing in unexplained brute fact, not because in the present state of knowledge you do not see your way to do better, but on the plea that there is and can be no explanation. You are putting unintelligible mystery at the very heart of reality.

Perhaps it may be rejoined, "And why should we not acknowledge this, seeing that, whether we like it or not, we must come to this in the end?" Well, at least it may be retorted that to acquiesce in such a "final inexplicability" as final means that you have denied the validity of the very assumption on which all science is built. All through the history of scientific advance it has been taken for granted that we are not to acquiesce in inexplicable brute fact; whenever we come across what, with our present light, has to be accepted as merely fact, we have a right to ask for further explanation, and should be false to the spirit of science if we did not. Thus we inevitably reach the conclusion that either the very principles which inspire and guide scientific inquiry itself are an illusion, or Nature itself must be dependent on some reality which is self-explanatory, and therefore not Nature nor any part of Nature, but, in the strict sense of the words, "supernatural" or "transcendent" —transcendent, that is, in the sense that in it there is overcome that duality of "law" and "fact" which is characteristic of Nature and every part of Nature. It is not "brute" fact, and yet it is not an abstract universal law or complex of such laws, but a really existing self-luminous Being, such that you could see, if you only apprehended its true character, that to have that character and to be are the same thing. This is the way in which Nature, as it seems to me, inevitably points beyond itself as the temporal and mutable to an "other" which is eternal and immutable.

Another modern philosopher presents a more critical analysis.

FROM The Existence of God BY W. I. MATSON

Logicians warn us against a certain mistake in reasoning, which they call the fallacy of composition. This error consists in arguing that since every member of a collection has a certain property, therefore the collection itself (as a whole) must also have the same property. Stock examples: every player on the team has a mother, therefore the team has a mother; everything heavy falls if not supported, therefore the earth would fall if it were not held up by something. Is not this fallacy committed in arguing: There is a sufficient reason why everything that is, is so and not otherwise; therefore there is a sufficient reason why the universe (i.e., the collection of all things) is so and not otherwise?

But the WHOLE, you say, wants a cause. I answer, that the uniting of these parts into a whole, like the uniting of several distinct counties into one kingdom, or several distinct members into one body, is performed merely by an arbitrary act of the mind, and has no influence on the nature of things. Did I show you the particular causes of each individual in a collection of twenty particles of matter, I should think it very unreasonable, should you afterwards ask me, what was the cause of the whole twenty. This is sufficiently explained in explaining the cause of the parts. (David Hume)

But one must not lightly charge the great logician Leibniz—to say nothing of the Scholastics—with an elementary blunder. It is not always a matter of rote application of a simple rule to discover whether or not this fallacy has been committed. For instance, it is not committed in the following: Every resident of this community is wealthy; therefore this is a wealthy community. Besides, the argument explicitly states a reason for demanding an explanation of the universe: to wit, that it is not the only possible world. We must go somewhat more deeply into the matter. We must reopen our discussion of the nature of explanation.

The primary purpose of explanation of any sort is the elimination, or at least reduction, of puzzlement and uncertainty with their attendant fears. Let us consider first what kind of puzzlement causal explanation removes, and how.

Think of life as a game we play with nature. Success in this game, as in

Wallace I. Matson, *The Existence of God* (1965), pp. 78–83. Copyright © 1965 by Cornell University. Used by permission of Cornell University Press.

most others, depends on our being able to anticipate our opponent's next move—on the ability to tell from what is happening now what is likely to happen next. To do this we must discern patterns in the operations of nature, connecting events at one time with other events at other times. These patterns we call causal laws; they state that when, and only when, conditions of the kind C are fulfilled, events of the kind E will occur. A causal explanation is an argument of this form:

> E-events occur only in C-circumstances (causal law).
> E_0 is an E-event that has occurred (final condition).

Therefore conditions C_0 must have obtained (initial condition or inferred cause).

For example:

Only when the water supply is contaminated with the bacillus *Vibrio comma* does a cholera epidemic occur.
A cholera epidemic is now occurring in X.
Therefore the water supply in X is contaminated with *Vibrio comma*.

This last is only an expansion of what is contained in the statement "The citizens of X are suffering from cholera because their water supply is contaminated." Of course there is no warrant for calling it *the* explanation of the epidemic; we may want to know how the water supply got infected; or we may want to know more particulars of the process intervening between the contamination and the outbreak. That is to say, a causal chain of indefinitely many links is involved. But each link is expressible in the same form: causal law, final condition (report of observation, phenomenon to be explained), and inferred cause (initial condition, deduced from the preceding two statements).

Prediction differs in form from explanation only in that the minor premise of the argument states an initial rather than a final condition:

> In C-circumstances, E-events occur.
> Conditions C_0 are realized (initial condition).
> Therefore event E_0 will occur (final condition, prediction).

For example:

> Whenever war breaks out, the birth rate increases.
> X and Y have declared war on each other.
> Therefore the birth rates in X and Y will increase.

Every causal explanation requires two elements: a causal law, which as such mentions no particular occurrence at all; and a statement describing a particular occurrence (final condition, that which is to be explained). From these together we deduce a description of the initial condition (particular cause). But if every event has a cause, then the initial condition is itself the final condition in some other explanation, some other link in the causal chain. Hence causal explanation, by its very nature, always generates an infinite regress.

We have reached this conclusion in focusing our attention on the minor premises of explanatory arguments, the statements of particular conditions. But not only are events explained in terms of preceding events; laws themselves are explained in terms of more general laws. Inhalation of carbon monoxide causes death because the carbon monoxide combines with hemoglobin, rendering it incapable of absorbing oxygen. More formally:

Whenever hemoglobin is rendered incapable of absorbing oxygen, death ⎤ Laws
   ensues.   ⎟ of
When carbon monoxide is brought into contact with hemoglobin, the ⎬ Wider
   hemoglobin is rendered incapable of absorbing oxygen.   ⎦ Scope
Therefore when carbon monoxide is inhaled, death ensues (law of
   narrower scope, which was to be explained).

This procedure does not generate an infinite regress; theoretically, the end of the process comes when a law is enunciated broad enough in its scope to cover all lesser laws as particular instances. This condition is approximated in physics. If the supreme law were discovered, clearly it would be senseless to ask for an explanation of it—at least for an explanation in the sense just described.

We now see how causal explanation "eliminates alternative possibilities," how it shows us that such-and-such must be so and not otherwise. Here is E_0; might it not just as well have been F, or G, or . . . ? But now E_0 is explained: the explanation is to the effect that all C's are followed by E's, and there was C_0, therefore there had to be E_0 and not something else. The "must," then, is the "must" of logical necessity: it is logically impossible (literally inconceivable) for the explanatory premises to be true and the conclusion false. But this necessity is only relative to the premises, which are not in themselves necessary. The particular premise may be itself necessary relative to some other set of premises, but unconditional necessity is never attained. As for the major premise, the statement of a law of nature: might nature not have had some other law? No, because the law is explained, that is, deduced from a more inclusive law; and if that more inclusive law holds, then it is logically impossible for the restricted law not to hold. It logically cannot be the case that both (a) all interference with oxidation of hemoglobin results in death, and (b) carbon monoxide, when inhaled, interferes with oxidation of hemoglobin but does not cause death. But as in explaining events, so also in explaining laws we do not and cannot arrive at unconditional logical necessity. The most general law that we know is, by the very fact of its being the most general law, unexplained; and even in principle some law must

ultimately remain unexplained. And if it is unexplained, it has no kind of
necessity, and we may ask, if we like, why it should not have been otherwise.
But if we ask this, we ought not to be disappointed that no answer is forthcoming. This is no defect in causal explanation; it is not the case that causal
explanation is failing to do something that we might reasonably expect it to
do.

All this is to show more particularly why it is that causal explanations can
never yield a sufficient reason for the universe at large. To put it in a slightly
different way, the universe is the framework within which causal explanations operate. And although these explanations show the linkage of one part
of the universe to another, it is quite beyond their scope to link the universe
to anything else. To ask for the cause of the universe is to ask a question
similar to "When is time?" or "Where is space?"

* * *

Causal explanation and the prediction it facilitates alleviate puzzlement
and fear. If we know that conditions C lead to disaster, then, when we observe C_0, we can take to the hills; further, when we know that D leads to C,
and D is controllable by our efforts, we may eliminate D, if we have time.
Intellectual, or idle, curiosity may make us wonder what the causes of D are;
and if we have nothing better to do, we may investigate them. There is no
limit to the lengths to which we may push the inquiry. We shall never come
to a cause necessary in itself, but that does not disturb us, either practically or
theoretically—unless we are metaphysicians; in which case the proper remedy
for our puzzlement on this score is to get clear about why it is senseless to ask
for ultimate causal explanations.

RENAISSANCE MAN

MEDIEVAL OR MODERN?

CONTENTS

QUESTIONS FOR STUDY

1. *What characteristics of the Renaissance have been regarded as distinctively "modern"? Do you agree that these characteristics are in fact typical of the modern world?*

2. *How did political conditions in Renaissance Italy encourage the growth of individualism according to Burckhardt? Are his arguments convincing?*

3. *What do Petrarch, della Mirandola, Vasari, and Castiglione tell us about Renaissance attitudes toward nature and art?*

4. *Do you think that the qualities Castiglione praises in a Renaissance courtier would fit a man well to serve in the entourage of a modern head of state—as a White House aide, for instance?*

5. *Burckhardt held that the spirit of Italian humanism was "irreligious and pagan." What evidence can you find for and against this view?*

6. *Was the culture of the Renaissance essentially different from that of the Middle Ages? If so, in what ways?*

In its simplest literal meaning the term "Renaissance" refers to a "rebirth" of classical art and letters in Italy during the fourteenth, fifteenth, and sixteenth centuries. Many works of the ancient world had been known all through the Middle Ages, of course, but the Renaissance humanists studied them in a fresh spirit, with a new enthusiasm for the felicities of Latin style and the poetic values of Greek literature. Moreover, the revived classical studies inspired—or were inspired by—a changing attitude toward nature and toward man that expressed itself in a brilliant outburst of art and literature and also in new forms of political experimentation. Many historians have seen in this period a decisive break with the medieval tradition and the beginnings of a distinctively modern civilization. Others have reacted against this interpretation. The argument is still continuing.

Much of the modern writing on the Renaissance centers around the theses advanced by Jacob Burckhardt in his *Civilisation of the Renaissance in Italy*, first published in 1860 (pp. 470–477). Burckhardt very strongly emphasized the novelty and modernity of the Renaissance, arguing that Renaissance Italy produced the first fully self-aware, modern individual personalities. These first modern men deliberately created the modern state and embarked on new ways of exploring nature through science and art. Burckhardt attributed their emergence partly to a revival of "the influence of the ancient world" but mainly to "the genius of the Italian people."

Certainly Burckhardt was not wholly mistaken in his assertions. Many of the characteristics that he attributed to Renaissance Italy can be amply illustrated from the sources of that period—for example, the revival of classical studies (pp. 478–487), the existence of highly self-conscious individuals and of theorizing about the dignity of human nature (pp. 488–496), and the growth of secular ideas of the state (pp. 497–505). The criticism of Burckhardt's work is directed not so much against his delineation of such aspects of Renaissance life as against his whole periodization of Western history. Burckhardt seems to have regarded the medieval period as simply an irrelevant interruption in the development of modern society. For him, the Middle Ages were an era of "faith, illusion and childish prepossession." The modern world could grow into eixstence only when Renaissance men recovered the heritage of classical antiquity and turned their backs on the gloomy half-life of the medieval world.

Views like these still color some general histories of Western civilization, but many modern scholars find them quite unacceptable. Medievalists have pointed out with some warmth that the Middle Ages also produced passionate, fully self-aware individuals (pp. 506–508), coherent theories of the state (pp. 508–511), and great naturalistic art (pp. 511–514). They also argue that many features of the modern, twentieth-century world in which we live have their origins in the Middle Ages, not in classical antiquity or in the Renaissance period—for example, parliamentary government, university education, and the Anglo-American legal tradition. In the works of the most enthusiastic medievalists this argument is sometimes carried so far as to imply that no really significant changes occurred at all in the age of the Renaissance. But this is obviously an oversimplification, to say the least. A Renaissance church is very different from a Gothic cathedral; Machiavelli's political philosophy is very different from that of Thomas Aquinas.

It seems, then, that a new historical synthesis is required. In his article "Reinterpretation of the Renaissance" (pp. 515–518), W. K. Ferguson argues that early medieval culture was basically ecclesiastical, feudal, and rural. From the early twelfth century onward influences making for change were at work; but by 1300 they had not succeeded in changing the essential nature of medieval society. In the following two centuries their cumulative impact did have this effect. Ferguson discusses only economic history, but similar arguments might be advanced concerning the history of art, science, and politics. If this kind of interpretation proves acceptable, historians will be able to insist on the reality of decisive change during the age of the Renaissance without having to invent the fiction of a sudden break in the continuity of Western history at that time.

1
BURCKHARDT'S
RENAISSANCE

The most brilliant of the nineteenth-century works on the Renaissance was that of Jacob Burckhardt. In his view the Renaissance saw the beginning of both the modern state and modern man.

FROM The Civilisation of the Renaissance in Italy
BY JACOB BURCKHARDT

The struggle between the Popes and the Hohenstaufen left Italy in a political condition which differed essentially from that of other countries of the West. While in France, Spain and England the feudal system was so organized that, at the close of its existence, it was naturally transformed into a unified monarchy, and while in Germany it helped to maintain, at least outwardly, the unity of the empire, Italy had shaken it off almost entirely. The Emperors of the fourteenth century, even in the most favourable case, were no longer received and respected as feudal lords, but as possible leaders and supporters of powers already in existence; while the Papacy, with its creatures and allies, was strong enough to hinder national unity in the future, not strong enough itself to bring about that unity. Between the two lay a multitude of political units—republics and despots—in part of long standing, in part of recent origin, whose existence was founded simply on their power to maintain it. In them for the first time we detect the modern political spirit of Europe, surrendered freely to its own instincts, often displaying the worst features of an unbridled egotism, outraging every right, and killing every germ of a healthier culture. But, wherever this vicious tendency is overcome or in any way

Jacob Burckhardt, *The Civilisation of the Renaissance in Italy* (1921), pp. 4, 8–10, 61–62, 73–74, 83–84, 129–134, 171–172, translated by S. G. C. Middlemore. Reprinted by permission of George Allen & Unwin Ltd., London.

compensated, a new fact appears in history—the State as the outcome of reflection and calculation, the State as a work of art. . . .

The deliberate adaptation of means to ends, of which no prince out of Italy had at that time a conception, joined to almost absolute power within the limits of the State, produced among the despots both men and modes of life of a peculiar character. The chief secret of government in the hands of the prudent ruler lay in leaving the incidence of taxation so far as possible where he found it, or as he had first arranged it. The chief sources of income were: a land tax, based on a valuation; definite taxes on articles of consumption and duties on exported and imported goods; together with the private fortune of the ruling house. The only possible increase was derived from the growth of business and of general prosperity. Loans, such as we find in the free cities, were here unknown; a well-planned confiscation was held a preferable means of raising money, provided only that it left public credit unshaken—an end attained, for example, by the truly Oriental practice of deposing and plundering the director of the finances.

Out of this income the expenses of the little court, of the bodyguard, of the mercenary troops, and of the public buildings were met, as well as of the buffoons and men of talent who belonged to the personal attendants of the prince. The illegitimacy of his rule isolated the tyrant and surrounded him with constant danger; the most honourable alliance which he could form was with intellectual merit, without regard to its origin. The liberality of the northern princes of the thirteenth century was confined to the knights, to the nobility which served and sang. It was otherwise with the Italian despot. With his thirst for fame and his passion for monumental works, it was talent, not birth, which he needed. In the company of the poet and the scholar he felt himself in a new position, almost, indeed, in possession of a new legitimacy.

No prince was more famous in this respect than the ruler of Verona, Can Grande della Scala, who numbered among the illustrious exiles whom he entertained at his court representatives of the whole of Italy. The men of letters were not ungrateful. Petrarch, whose visits at the courts of such men have been so severely censured, sketched an ideal picture of a prince of the fourteenth century. He demands great things from his patron, the lord of Padua, but in a manner which shows that he holds him capable of them. "Thou must not be the master but the father of thy subjects, and must love them as thy children; yea, as members of thy body. Weapons, guards, and soldiers thou mayest employ against the enemy—with thy subjects goodwill is sufficient. By citizens, of course, I mean those who love the existing order; for those who daily desire change are rebels and traitors, and against such a stern justice may take its course."

Here follows, worked out in detail, the purely modern fiction of the omnipotence of the State. The prince is to take everything into his charge, to maintain and restore churches and public buildings, to keep up the municipal police, to drain the marshes, to look after the supply of wine and corn; so to distribute the taxes that the people can recognize their necessity; he is to support the sick and the helpless, and to give his protection and society to distinguished scholars, on whom his fame in after ages will depend.

But whatever might be the brighter sides of the system, and the merits of individual rulers, yet the men of the fourteenth century were not without a more or less distinct consciousness of the brief and uncertain tenure of most of these despotisms. Inasmuch as political institutions like these are naturally secure in proportion to the size of the territory in which they exist, the larger principalities were constantly tempted to swallow up the smaller. Whole hecatombs of petty rulers were sacrificed at this time to the Visconti alone. As a result of this outward danger an inward ferment was in ceaseless activity; and the effect of the situation on the character of the ruler was generally of the most sinister kind. Absolute power, with its temptations to luxury and unbridled selfishness, and the perils to which he was exposed from enemies and conspirators, turned him almost inevitably into a tyrant in the worst sense of the word. . . . The tyrants destroyed the freedom of most of the cities; here and there they were expelled, but not thoroughly, or only for a short time; and they were always restored, since the inward conditions were favourable to them, and the opposing forces were exhausted.

Among the cities which maintained their independence are two of deep significance for the history of the human race: Florence, the city of incessant movement, which has left us a record of the thoughts and aspirations of each and all who, for three centuries, took part in this movement, and Venice, the city of apparent stagnation and of political secrecy. . . .

The most elevated political thought and the most varied forms of human development are found united in the history of Florence, which in this sense deserves the name of the first modern State in the world. Here the whole people are busied with what in the despotic cities is the affair of a single family. That wondrous Florentine spirit, at once keenly critical and artistically creative, was incessantly transforming the social and political condition of the State, and as incessantly describing and judging the change. Florence thus became the home of political doctrines and theories, of experiments and sudden changes, but also, like Venice, the home of statistical science, and alone and above all other States in the world, the home of historical representation in the modern sense of the phrase. The spectacle of ancient Rome and a familiarity with its leading writers were not without influence; Giovanni Villani confesses that he received the first impulse to his great work at the jubilee of the year 1300, and began it immediately on his return home. Yet how many among the 200,000 pilgrims of that year may have been like him in gifts and tendencies and still did not write the history of their native cities! For not all of them could encourage themselves with the thought: "Rome is sinking; my native city is rising, and ready to achieve great things, and therefore I wish to relate its past history, and hope to continue the story to the present time, and as long as my life shall last." And besides the witness to its past, Florence obtained through its historians something further—a greater fame than fell to the lot of any other city of Italy.

* * *

In many of their chief merits the Florentines are the pattern and the earliest type of Italians and modern Europeans generally; they are so also in many of their defects. When Dante compares the city which was always mending its constitution with the sick man who is continually changing his posture to escape from pain, he touches with the comparison a permanent feature of the political life of Florence. The great modern fallacy that a constitution can be made, can be manufactured by a combination of existing forces and tendencies, was constantly cropping up in stormy times; even Machiavelli is not wholly free from it. Constitutional artists were never wanting who by an ingenious distribution and division of political power, by indirect elections of the most complicated kind, by the establishment of nominal offices, sought to found a lasting order of things, and to satisfy or to deceive the rich and the poor alike. They naïvely fetch their examples from classical antiquity, and borrow the party names "ottimati," "aristocrazia," as a matter of course. The world since then has become used to these expressions and given them a conventional European sense, whereas all former party names were purely national, and either characterized the cause at issue or sprang from the caprice of accident. But how a name colours or discolours a political cause!

But of all who thought it possible to construct a State, the greatest beyond all comparison was Machiavelli. He treats existing forces as living and active, takes a large and an accurate view of alternative possibilities, and seeks to mislead neither himself nor others. No man could be freer from vanity or ostentation; indeed, he does not write for the public, but either for princes and administrators or for personal friends. The danger for him does not lie in an affectation of genius or in a false order of ideas, but rather in a powerful imagination which he evidently controls with difficulty. The objectivity of his political judgement is sometimes appalling in its sincerity; but it is the sign of a time of no ordinary need and peril, when it was a hard matter to believe in right, or to credit others with just dealing. Virtuous indignation at his expense is thrown away upon us who have seen in what sense political morality is understood by the statesmen of our own century. Machiavelli was at all events able to forget himself in his cause. In truth, although his writings, with the exception of very few words, are altogether destitute of enthusiasm, and although the Florentines themselves treated him at last as a criminal, he was a patriot in the fullest meaning of the word. But free as he was, like most of his contemporaries, in speech and morals, the welfare of the State was yet his first and last thought.

* * *

In the character of these States, whether republics or despotisms, lies, not the only, but the chief reason for the early development of the Italian. To this it is due that he was the first-born among the sons of modern Europe.

In the Middle Ages both sides of human consciousness—that which was turned within as that which was turned without—lay dreaming or half awake beneath a common veil. The veil was woven of faith, illusion, and childish prepossession, through which the world and history were seen clad in strange hues. Man was conscious of himself only as a member of a race, people, party, family, or corporation—only through some general category. In Italy this veil first melted into air; an *objective* treatment and consideration of the State and of all the things of this world became possible. The *subjective* side at the same time asserted itself with corresponding emphasis; man became a spiritual *individual,* and recognized himself as such. In the same way the Greek had once distinguished himself from the barbarian, and the Arab had felt himself an individual at a time when other Asiatics knew themselves only as members of a race. It will not be difficult to show that this result was owing above all to the political circumstances of Italy.

In far earlier times we can here and there detect a development of free personality which in Northern Europe either did not occur at all, or could not display itself in the same manner. The band of audacious wrongdoers in the tenth century described to us by Liudprand, some of the contemporaries of Gregory VII (for example, Benzo of Alba), and a few of the opponents of the first Hohenstaufen, show us characters of this kind. But at the close of the thirteenth century Italy began to swarm with individuality; the ban laid upon human personality was dissolved; and a thousand figures meet us each in its own special shape and dress. Dante's great poem would have been impossible in any other country of Europe, if only for the reason that they all still lay under the spell of race. For Italy the august poet, through the wealth of individuality which he set forth, was the most national herald of his time. But this unfolding of the treasures of human nature in literature and art—this many-sided representation and criticism—will be discussed in separate chapters; here we have to deal only with the psychological fact itself. This fact appears in the most decisive and unmistakable form. The Italians of the fourteenth century knew little of false modesty or of hypocrisy in any shape; not one of them was afraid of singularity, of being and seeming unlike his neighbours.

Despotism, as we have already seen, fostered in the highest degree the individuality not only of the tyrant or Condottiere himself, but also of the men whom he protected or used as his tools—the secretary, minister, poet, and companion. These people were forced to know all the inward resources of their own nature, passing or permanent; and their enjoyment of life was enhanced and concentrated by the desire to obtain the greatest satisfaction from a possibly very brief period of power and influence.

But even the subjects whom they ruled over were not free from the same impulse. Leaving out of account those who wasted their lives in secret opposition and conspiracies, we speak of the majority who were content with a strictly private station, like most of the urban population of the Byzantine empire and the Mohammedan States. No doubt it was often hard for the subjects of a Visconti to maintain the dignity of their persons and families, and multitudes must have lost in moral character through the servitude they lived under. But this was not the case with regard to individuality; for political impotence does not hinder the different tendencies and manifestations of private life from thriving in the fullest vigour and variety. Wealth and culture, so far as display and rivalry were not forbidden to them, a municipal freedom which did not cease to be considerable, and a Church which, unlike that of the Byzantine or of the Mohammedan world, was not identical with the State—all these conditions undoubtedly favoured the growth of individual thought, for which the necessary leisure was furnished by the cessation of party conflicts. The private man, indifferent to politics, and busied partly with serious pursuits, partly with the interests of a *dilettante,* seems to have been first fully formed in these despotisms of the fourteenth century. Documentary evidence cannot, of course, be required on such a point. The novelists, from whom we might expect information, describe to us oddities in plenty, but only from one point of view and in so far as the needs of the story demand. Their scene, too, lies chiefly in the republican cities.

In the latter, circumstances were also, but in another way, favourable to the growth of individual character. The more frequently the governing party was changed, the more the individual was led to make the utmost of the exercise and enjoyment of power. The statesmen and popular leaders, especially in Florentine history, acquired so marked a personal character, that we can scarcely find, even exceptionally, a parallel to them in contemporary history, hardly even in Jacob van Artevelde.

The members of the defeated parties, on the other hand, often came into a position like that of the subjects of the despotic States, with the difference that the freedom or power already enjoyed, and in some cases the hope of recovering them, gave a higher energy to their individuality. Among these men of involuntary leisure we find, for instance, an Agnolo Pandolfini (d. 1446), whose work on domestic economy is the first complete programme of a developed private life. His estimate of the duties of the individual as against the dangers and thanklessness of public life is in its way a true monument of the age.

Banishment, too, has this effect above all, that it either wears the exile out or develops whatever is greatest in him. "In all our more populous cities," says Gioviano Pontano, "we see a crowd of people who have left their homes of their own free will; but a man takes his virtues with him wherever he goes." And, in fact, they were by no means only men who had been actually exiled, but thousands left their native place voluntarily, because they found its political or economical condition intolerable. The Florentine emigrants at Ferrara and the Lucchese in Venice formed whole colonies by themselves.

The cosmopolitanism which grew up in the most gifted circles is in itself a high stage of individualism. Dante, as we have already said, finds a new home in the language and culture of Italy, but goes beyond even this in the words, "My country is the whole world." And when his recall to Florence was offered him on unworthy conditions, he wrote back: "Can I not everywhere behold the light of the sun and the stars; everywhere meditate on the noblest truths, without appearing ingloriously and shamefully before the city and the people. Even my bread will not fail me." The artists exult no less defiantly in their freedom from the constraints of fixed residence. "Only he who has learned everything," says Ghiberti, "is nowhere a stranger; robbed of his fortune and without friends, he is yet the citizen of every country, and can fearlessly despise the changes of fortune." In the same strain an exiled humanist writes: "Wherever a learned man fixes his seat, there is home."

An acute and practised eye might be able to trace, step by step, the increase in the number of complete men during the fifteenth century. Whether they had before them as a conscious object the harmonious development of their spiritual and material existence, is hard to say; but several of them attained it, so far as is consistent with the imperfection of all that is earthly. It may be better to renounce the attempt at an estimate of the share which fortune, character, and talent had in the life of Lorenzo il Magnifico. But look at a personality like that of Ariosto, especially as shown in his satires. In what harmony are there expressed the pride of the man and the poet, the irony with which he treats his own enjoyments, the most delicate satire, and the deepest goodwill!

* * *

Now that this point in our historical view of Italian civilization has been reached, it is time to speak of the influence of antiquity, the "new birth" of which has been one-sidedly chosen as the name to sum up the whole period. The conditions which have been hitherto described would have sufficed, apart from antiquity, to upturn and to mature the national mind; and most of the intellectual tendencies which yet remain to be noticed would be conceivable without it. But both what has gone before and what we have still to discuss are coloured in a thousand ways by the influence of the ancient world; and though the essence of the phenomena might still have been the same without the classical revival, it is only with and through this revival that they are actually manifested to us. The Renaissance would not have been the process of world-wide significance which it is, if its elements could be so easily separated from one another. We must insist upon it, as one of the chief propositions of this book, that it was not the revival of antiquity alone, but its union with the genius of the Italian people, which achieved the conquest of the western world. The amount of independence which the national spirit maintained in this union varied according to circumstances. In the modern Latin literature of the period, it is very small, while in plastic art, as well as in other spheres, it is remarkably great; and hence the alliance between two distant epochs in the civilization of the same people, because concluded on equal terms, proved justifiable and fruitful. The rest of Europe was free either to repel or else partly or wholly to accept the mighty impulse which came forth from Italy. Where the latter was the case we may as well be spared the complaints over the early decay of mediaeval faith and civilization. Had these been strong enough to hold their ground, they would be alive to this day. If those elegiac natures which long to see them return could pass but one hour in the midst of them, they would gasp to be back in modern air. That in a great historical process of this kind flowers of exquisite beauty may perish, without being made immortal in poetry or tradition, is undoubtedly true; nevertheless, we cannot wish the process undone. The general result of it consists in this—that by the side of the Church which had hitherto held the countries of the West together (though it was unable to do so much longer) there arose a new spiritual influence which, spreading itself abroad from Italy, became the breath of life for all the more instructed minds in Europe.

2
THE CULT
OF THE
CLASSICS

Petrarch (1304–1374) was the first of the great Italian humanists. The following letter illustrates his devotion to Latin literature.

FROM Petrarch's Letters

Your Cicero has been in my possession four years and more. There is a good reason, though, for so long a delay; namely, the great scarcity of copyists who understand such work. It is a state of affairs that has resulted in an incredible loss to scholarship. Books that by their nature are a little hard to understand are no longer multiplied, and have ceased to be generally intelligible, and so have sunk into utter neglect, and in the end have perished. This age of ours consequently has let fall, bit by bit, some of the richest and sweetest fruits that the tree of knowledge has yielded; has thrown away the results of the vigils and labours of the most illustrious men of genius, things of more value, I am almost tempted to say, than anything else in the whole world. . . .

But I must return to your Cicero. I could not do without it, and the incompetence of the copyists would not let me possess it. What was left for me but to rely upon my own resources, and press these weary fingers and this worn and ragged pen into the service? The plan that I followed was this. I want you to know it, in case you should ever have to grapple with a similar task. Not a single word did I read except as I wrote. But how is that, I hear someone say; did you write without knowing what it was that you were

Epistolae, in *Petrarch, the First Modern Scholar and Man of Letters* (1899), pp. 275–278, translated by J. H. Robinson and H. W. Rolfe.

writing? Ah! but from the very first it was enough for me to know that it was a work of Tullius, and an extremely rare one too. And then as soon as I was fairly started I found at every step so much sweetness and charm, and felt so strong a desire to advance, that the only difficulty which I experienced in reading and writing at the same time came from the fact that my pen could not cover the ground so rapidly as I wanted it to, whereas my expectation had been rather that it would outstrip my eyes, and that my ardour for writing would be chilled by the slowness of my reading. So the pen held back the eye, and the eye drove on the pen, and I covered page after page, delighting in my task, and committing many and many a passage to memory as I wrote. For just in proportion as the writing is slower than the reading does the passage make a deep impression and cling to the mind.

And yet I must confess that I did finally reach a point in my copying where I was overcome by weariness; not mental, for how unlikely that would be where Cicero was concerned, but the sort of fatigue that springs from excessive manual labour. I began to feel doubtful about this plan that I was following, and to regret having undertaken a task for which I had not been trained; when suddenly I came across a place where Cicero tells how he himself copied the orations of—someone or other; just who it was I do not know, but certainly no Tullius, for there is but one such man, one such voice, one such mind. These are his words: "You say that you have been in the habit of reading the orations of Cassius in your idle moments. But I," he jestingly adds, with his customary disregard of his adversary's feelings, "have made a practice of *copying* them, so that I might *have* no idle moments." As I read this passage I grew hot with shame, like a modest young soldier who hears the voice of his beloved leader rebuking him. I said to myself, "So Cicero copied orations that another wrote, and you are not ready to copy his? What ardour! what scholarly devotion! what reverence for a man of godlike genius!" These thoughts were a spur to me, and I pushed on, with all my doubts dispelled. If ever from my darkness there shall come a single ray that can enhance the splendour of the reputation which his heavenly eloquence has won for him, it will proceed in no slight measure from the fact that I was so captivated by his ineffable sweetness that I did a thing in itself most irksome with such delight and eagerness that I scarcely knew I was doing it at all.

So then at last your Cicero has the happiness of returning to you, bearing you my thanks. And yet he also stays, very willingly, with me; a dear friend, to whom I give the credit of being almost the only man of letters for whose sake I would go to the length of spending my time, when the difficulties of life are pressing on me so sharply and inexorably and the cares pertaining to my literary labours make the longest life seem far too short, in transcribing compositions not my own. I may have done such things in former days, when I thought myself rich in time, and had not learned how stealthily it slips away: but I now know that this is of all our riches the most uncertain and fleeting; the years are closing in upon me now, and there is no longer any room for deviation from the beaten path. I am forced to practice strict economy; I only hope that I have not begun too late. But Cicero! he assuredly is worthy of a part of even the little that I still have left. Farewell.

Petrarch admired Greek literature too, but he had to read it in translation, as the next letter indicates. A century later any scholar of comparable eminence would have been trained in both Greek and Latin.

FROM Petrarch's Letters

You ask me finally to lend you the copy of Homer that was on sale at Padua, if, as you suppose, I have purchased it; since, you say, I have for a long time possessed another copy; so that our friend Leo may translate it from Greek into Latin for your benefit and for the benefit of our other studious compatriots. I saw this book, but neglected the opportunity of acquiring it, because it seemed inferior to my own. It can easily be had with the aid of the person to whom I owe my friendship with Leo; a letter from that source would be all-powerful in the matter, and I will myself write him.

If by chance the book escape us, which seems to me very unlikely, I will let you have mine. I have been always fond of this particular translation and of Greek literature in general, and if fortune had not frowned upon my beginnings, in the sad death of my excellent master, I should be perhaps today something more than a Greek still at his alphabet. I approve with all my heart and strength your enterprise, for I regret and am indignant that an ancient translation, presumably the work of Cicero, the commencement of which Horace inserted in his *Ars Poetica,* should have been lost to the Latin world, together with many other works. It angers me to see so much solicitude for the bad and so much neglect of the good. . . .

As for me, I wish the work to be done, whether well or ill. I am so famished for literature that just as he who is ravenously hungry is not inclined to quarrel with the cook's art, so I await with lively impatience whatever dishes are to be set before my soul. And in truth, the morsel in which the same Leo, translating into Latin prose the beginning of Homer, has given me a foretaste of the whole work, although it confirms the sentiment of St. Jerome, does not displease me. It possesses, in fact, a secret charm, as certain viands, which have failed to take a moulded shape, although they are lacking in form, neverthe-

Epistolae, in *A Literary Source Book of the Renaissance* (1900), pp. 13–15, translated by M. Whitcomb.

less preserve their taste and odor. May he continue with the aid of Heaven, and may he give us Homer, who has been lost to us!

In asking of me the volume of Plato which I have with me, and which escaped the fire at my trans-Alpine country house, you give me proof of your ardor, and I shall hold this book at your disposal, whenever the time shall come. I wish to aid with all my power such noble enterprises. But beware lest it should be unbecoming to unite in one bundle these two great princes of Greece, lest the weight of these two spirits should overwhelm mortal shoulders. Let your messenger undertake, with God's aid, one of the two, and first him who has written many centuries before the other. Farewell.

The mixture of introspection and sensitivity to natural beauty in the following passage has sometimes been taken as reflecting the "medieval" and "modern" elements in Petrarch's personality. The whole passage can be read as an allegory of "the ascent of the soul to God."

FROM Petrarch's Letters

To-day I made the ascent of the highest mountain in this region, which is not improperly called Ventosum [*i.e., windy—B. T.*]. My only motive was the wish to see what so great an elevation had to offer. I have had the expedition in mind for many years; for, as you know, I have lived in this region from infancy, having been cast here by that fate which determines the affairs of men. Consequently the mountain, which is visible from a great distance, was ever before my eyes, and I conceived the plan of some time doing what I have at last accomplished to-day. The idea took hold upon me with especial force when, in re-reading Livy's *History of Rome*, yesterday, I happened upon the place where Philip of Macedon, the same who waged war against the Romans, ascended Mount Haemus in Thessaly, from whose summit he was able, it is said, to see two seas, the Adriatic and the Euxine. Whether this be true or false I have not been able to determine, for the mountain is too far away, and writers disagree. Pomponius Mela, the cosmographer—not to mention others who have spoken of this occurrence—admits its truth without hesitation; Titus Livius, on the other hand, considers it false. I, assuredly, should not have left the question long in doubt, had that mountain been as easy to explore as this one. Let us leave this matter to one side, however, and

Epistolae, in *Petrarch, the First Modern Scholar and Man of Letters* (1899), pp. 307–317, translated by J. H. Robinson and H. W. Rolfe.

return to my mountain here,—it seems to me that a young man in private life may well be excused for attempting what an aged king could undertake without arousing criticism.

* * *

At the time fixed we left the house, and by evening reached Malaucène, which lies at the foot of the mountain, to the north. Having rested there a day, we finally made the ascent this morning, with no companions except two servants; and a most difficult task it was. The mountain is a very steep and almost inaccessible mass of stony soil. But, as the poet has well said, "Remorseless toil conquers all." It was a long day, the air fine. We enjoyed the advantages of vigour of mind and strength and agility of body, and everything else essential to those engaged in such an undertaking, and so had no other difficulties to face than those of the region itself. We found an old shepherd in one of the mountain dales, who tried, at great length, to dissuade us from the ascent, saying that some fifty years before he had, in the same ardour of youth, reached the summit, but had gotten for his pains nothing except fatigue and regret, and clothes and body torn by the rocks and briars. No one, so far as he or his companions knew, had ever tried the ascent before or after him. But his counsels increased rather than diminished our desire to proceed, since youth is suspicious of warnings. So the old man, finding that his efforts were in vain, went a little way with us, and pointed out a rough path among the rocks, uttering many admonitions, which he continued to send after us even after we had left him behind. Surrendering to him all such garments or other possessions as might prove burdensome to us, we made ready for the ascent, and started off at a good pace. But, as usually happens, fatigue quickly followed upon our excessive exertion, and we soon came to a halt at the top of a certain cliff. Upon starting on again we went more slowly, and I especially advanced along the rocky way with a more deliberate step. While my brother chose a direct path straight up the ridge, I weakly took an easier one which really descended. When I was called back, and the right road was shown me, I replied that I hoped to find a better way round on the other side, and that I did not mind going farther if the path were only less steep. This was just an excuse for my laziness; and when the others had already reached a considerable height I was still wandering in the valleys.

After being frequently misled in this way, I finally sat down in a valley and transferred my winged thoughts from things corporeal to the immaterial, addressing myself as follows:—"What thou hast repeatedly experienced to-day in the ascent of this mountain, happens to thee, as to many, in the journey toward the blessed life. But this is not so readily perceived by men, since the motions of the body are obvious and external while those of the soul are invisible and hidden. Yes, the life which we call blessed is to be sought for on a high eminence, and strait is the way that leads to it. Many, also, are the hills that lie between, and we must ascend, by a glorious stairway, from strength to strength. At the top is at once the end of our struggles and the goal for which we are bound. All wish to reach this goal, but, as Ovid says, 'To wish is little; we must long with the utmost eagerness to gain our end.' Thou certainly dost ardently desire, as well as simply wish, unless thou deceivest thyself in this matter, as in so many others. What, then, doth hold thee back? Nothing, assuredly, except that thou wouldst take a path which seems, at first thought, more easy, leading through low and worldly pleasures. But nevertheless in the end, after long wanderings, thou must perforce either climb the steeper path, under the burden of tasks foolishly deferred, to its blessed culmination, or lie down in the valley of thy sins, and (I shudder to think of it!), if the shadow of death overtake thee, spend an eternal night amid constant torments." These thoughts stimulated both body and mind in a wonderful degree for facing the difficulties which yet remained. . . .

One peak of the mountain, the highest of all, the country people call "Sonny," why, I do not know, unless by antiphrasis, as I have sometimes suspected in other instances; for the peak in question would seem to be the father of all the surrounding ones. On its top is a little level place, and here we could at last rest our tired bodies.

Now, my father, since you have followed the thoughts that spurred me on in my ascent, listen to the rest of the story, and devote one hour, I pray you, to reviewing the experiences of my entire day. At first, owing to the unaccustomed quality of the air and the effect of the great sweep of view spread out before me, I stood like one dazed. I beheld the clouds under our feet, and what I had read of Athos and Olympus seemed less incredible as I myself witnessed the same things from a mountain of less fame. I turned my eyes toward Italy, whither my heart most inclined. The Alps, rugged and snow-capped, seemed to rise close by, although they were really at a great distance; the very same Alps through which that fierce enemy of the Roman name once made his way, bursting the rocks, if we may believe the report, by the application of vinegar. I sighed, I must confess, for the skies of Italy, which I beheld rather with my mind than with my eyes.

* * *

The sinking sun and the lengthening shadows of the mountain were already warning us that the time was near at hand when we must go. As if suddenly wakened from sleep, I turned about and gazed toward the west. I was unable to discern the summits of the Pyrenees, which form the barrier between France and Spain; not because of any intervening obstacle that I know of but owing simply to the insufficiency of our mortal vision. But I could see with the utmost clearness, off to the right, the mountains of the region about Lyons, and to the left the bay of Marseilles and the waters that lash the shores of Aigues Mortes, altho' all these places were so distant that it would require a journey of several days to reach them. Under our very eyes flowed the Rhone.

While I was thus dividing my thoughts, now turning my attention to some terrestrial object that lay before me, now raising my soul, as I had done my body, to higher planes, it occurred to me to look into my copy of St. Augustine's *Confessions,* a gift that I owe to your love, and that I always have about me, in memory of both the author and the giver. I opened the compact little volume, small indeed in size, but of infinite charm, with the intention of reading whatever came to hand, for I could happen upon nothing that would be otherwise than edifying and devout. Now it chanced that the tenth book presented itself. My brother, waiting to hear something of St. Augustine's from my lips, stood attentively by. I call him, and God too, to witness that where I first fixed my eyes it was written: "And men go about to wonder at the heights of the mountains, and the mighty waves of the sea, and the wide sweep of rivers, and the circuit of the ocean, and the revolution of the stars, but themselves they consider not." I was abashed, and, asking my brother (who was anxious to hear more) not to annoy me, I closed the book, angry with myself that I should still be admiring earthly things who might long ago have learned from even the pagan philosophers that nothing is wonderful but the soul, which, when great itself, finds nothing great outside itself. Then, in truth, I was satisfied that I had seen enough of the mountain; I turned my inward eye upon myself, and from that time not a syllable fell from my lips until we reached the bottom again.

Many Renaissance men expressed a sense of affinity with classical civilization and of alienation from medieval culture. This attitude is apparent in the following comments by the sixteenth-century painter and art historian Giorgio Vasari.

FROM Lives of the Most Eminent Painters, Sculptors and Architects BY GIORGIO VASARI

It is without doubt a fixed opinion, common to almost all writers, that the arts of sculpture and painting were first discovered by the nations of Egypt, although there are some who attribute the first rude attempts in marble, and the first statues and relievi, to the Chaldeans, while they accord the invention of the pencil, and of colouring, to the Greeks. But I am myself convinced, that design, which is the foundation of both these arts, nay, rather the very soul of each, comprising and nourishing within itself all the essential parts of both, existed in its highest perfection from the first moment of creation, when

Giorgio Vasari, *Lives of the Most Eminent Painters, Sculptors and Architects* (1855), pp. 9–10, 12–13, 15–16, 20–22, 30–31, translated by Mrs. Jonathan Foster.

the Most High having formed the great body of the world, and adorned the heavens with their resplendent lights, descended by his spirit, through the limpidity of the air, and penetrating the solid mass of earth, created man; and thus unveiled, with the beauties of creation, the first form of sculpture and of painting. For from this man, as from a true model, were copied by slow degrees (we may not venture to affirm the contrary), statues and sculptures: the difficulties of varied attitude,—the flowing lines of contour—and in the first paintings, whatever these may have been, the softness, harmony, and that concord in discord, whence result light and shade. The first model, therefore, from which the first image of man arose, was a mass of earth; and not without significance, since the Divine Architect of time and nature, Himself all-perfect, designed to instruct us by the imperfection of the material, in the true method of attaining perfection, by repeatedly diminishing and adding to; as the best sculptors and painters are wont to do, for by perpetually taking from or adding to their models they conduct their work, from its first imperfect sketch, to that finish of perfection which they desire to attain. The Creator further adorned his model with the most vivid colours, and these same colours, being afterwards drawn by the painter from the mines of earth, enable him to imitate whatsoever object he may require for his picture. . . .

We find, then, that the art of sculpture was zealously cultivated by the Greeks, among whom many excellent artists appeared; those great masters, the Athenian Phidias, with Praxiteles and Polycletus, were of the number, while Lysippus and Pyrgoteles, worked successfully in intaglio, and Pygmalion produced admirable reliefs in ivory—nay, of him it was affirmed, that his prayers obtained life and soul for the statue of a virgin which he had formed. Painting was in like manner honoured, and those who practised it successfully were rewarded among the ancient Greeks and Romans; this is proved by their according the rights of citizenship, and the most exalted dignities, to such as attained high distinction in these arts, both of which flourished so greatly in Rome, that Fabius bequeathed fame to his posterity by subscribing his name to the pictures so admirably painted by him in the Temple of *Salus,* and calling himself Fabius Pictor. It was forbidden, by public decree, that slaves should exercise this art within the cities, and so much homage was paid by the nations to art and artists, that works of rare merit were sent to Rome and exhibited as something wonderful, among other trophies in the triumphal processions, while artists of extraordinary merit, if slaves, received their freedom, together with honours and rewards from the republics. . . .

I suggested above that the origin of these arts was Nature herself—the first image or model, the most beautiful fabric of the world—and the master, that divine light infused into us by special grace, and which has made us not only superior to all other animals, but has exalted us, if it be permitted so to speak, to the similitude of God Himself. This is my belief, and I think that every man who shall maturely consider the question, will be of my opinion. And if it has been seen in our times—as I hope to demonstrate presently by various examples—that simple children, rudely reared in the woods, have begun to practise the arts of design with no other model than those beautiful pictures and sculptures furnished by Nature, and no other teaching than their own genius—how much more easily may we believe that the first of mankind, in whom nature and intellect were all the more perfect in proportion as they were less removed from their first origin and divine parentage,—that these men, I say, having Nature for their guide, and the unsullied purity of their fresh intelligence for their master, with the beautiful model of the world for an exemplar, should have given birth to these most noble arts, and from a small beginning, ameliorating them by slow degrees, should have conducted them finally to perfection? . . .

But as fortune, when she has raised either persons or things to the summit of her wheel, very frequently casts them to the lowest point, whether in repentance or for her sport, so it chanced that, after these things, the barbarous nations of the world arose, in divers places, in rebellion against the Romans; whence there ensued, in no long time, not only the decline of that great empire, but the utter ruin of the whole and more especially of Rome herself, when all the best artists, sculptors, painters, and architects, were in like manner totally ruined, being submerged and buried, together with the arts themselves, beneath the miserable slaughters and ruins of that much renowned city. . . .

But infinitely more ruinous than all other enemies to the arts above named, was the fervent zeal of the new Christian religion, which, after long and sanguinary combats, had finally overcome and annihilated the ancient creeds of the pagan world, by the frequency of miracles exhibited, and by the earnest sincerity of the means adopted; and ardently devoted, with all diligence, to the extirpation of error, nay, to the removal of even the slightest temptation to heresy, it not only destroyed all the wondrous statues, paintings, sculptures, mosaics, and other ornaments of the false pagan deities, but at the same time extinguished the very memory, in casting down the honours, of numberless excellent ancients, to whom statues and other monuments had been erected, in public places, for their virtues, by the most virtuous times of antiquity. Nay, more than this, to build the churches of the Christian faith, this zeal not only destroyed the most renowned temples of the heathens, but, for the richer ornament of St. Peter's, and in addition to the many spoils previously bestowed on that building, the tomb of Adrian, now called the castle of St. Angelo, was deprived of its marble columns, to employ them for this church, many other buildings being in like manner despoiled, and which we now see wholly devastated. And although the Christian religion did not effect this from hatred to these works of art, but solely for the purpose of abasing and bringing into contempt the gods of the Gentiles, yet the result of this too ardent zeal did not fail to bring such total ruin over the noble arts, that their very form and existence was lost. . . .

In like manner, the best works in painting and sculpture, remaining buried under the ruins of Italy, were concealed during the same period, and continued wholly unknown to the rude men reared amidst the more modern usages of art, and by whom no other sculptures or pictures were produced, than such as were expected by the remnant of old Greek artists. They formed images of earth and stone, or painted monstrous figures, of which they traced the rude outline only in colour. These artists—the best as being the only ones —were conducted into Italy, whither they carried sculpture and painting, as well as mosaic, in such manner as they were themselves acquainted with them: these they taught, in their own coarse and rude style, to the Italians, who practised them, after such fashion, as I have said, and will further relate, down to a certain period. The men of those times, unaccustomed to works of greater perfection than those thus set before their eyes, admired them accordingly, and, barbarous as they were, yet imitated them as the most excellent models. It was only by slow degrees that those who came after, being aided in some places by the subtlety of the air around them, could begin to raise themselves from these depths; when, towards 1250, Heaven, moved to pity by the noble spirits which the Tuscan soil was producing every day, restored them to their primitive condition. It is true that those who lived in the times succeeding the ruin of Rome, had seen remnants of arches, colossi, statues, pillars, storied columns, and other works of art, not wholly destroyed by the fires and other devastations; yet they had not known how to avail themselves of this aid, nor had they derived any benefit from it, until the time specified above. When the minds then awakened, becoming capable of distinguishing the good from the worthless, and abandoning old methods, returned to the imitation of the antique, with all the force of their genius, and all the power of their industry.

3
RENAISSANCE MAN DESCRIBED

One characteristic of Renaissance humanism was a buoyant confidence in the dignity and capabilities of human nature itself. Pico della Mirandola (1463–1494) gave eloquent expression to this sentiment.

FROM Oration on the Dignity of Man
BY PICO DELLA MIRANDOLA

I have read in the records of the Arabians, reverend fathers, that Abdala the Saracen, when questioned as to what on this stage of the world, as it were, could be seen most worthy of wonder, replied: "There is nothing to be seen more wonderful than man." In agreement with this opinion is the saying of Hermes Trismegistus: "A great miracle, Asclepius, is man." But when I weighed the reason for these maxims, the many grounds for the excellence of human nature reported by many men failed to satisfy me—that man is the intermediary between creatures, the intimate of the gods, the king of the lower beings; by the acuteness of his senses, by the discernment of his reason, and by the light of his intelligence the interpreter of nature; the interval between fixed eternity and fleeting time, and (as the Persians say) the bond, nay, rather, the marriage song of the world, on David's testimony but little lower than the angels. Admittedly great though these reasons be, they are not the principal grounds, that is, those which may rightfully claim for them-

Pico della Mirandola, "Oration on the Dignity of Man." Reprinted from *The Renaissance Philosophy of Man,* pp. 223–225, edited by Ernst Cassirer, Paul Oskar Kristeller, and John Herman Randall, Jr., by permission of The University of Chicago Press. Copyright 1948 by The University of Chicago.

selves the privilege of the highest admiration. For why should we not admire more the angels themselves and the blessed choirs of heaven? At last it seems to me I have come to understand why man is the most fortunate of creatures and consequently worthy of all admiration and what precisely is that rank which is his lot in the universal chain of Being—a rank to be envied not only by brutes but even by the stars and by minds beyond this world. It is a matter past faith and a wondrous one. Why should it not be? For it is on this very account that man is rightly called and judged a great miracle and a wonderful creature indeed. But hear, Fathers, exactly what this rank is and, as friendly auditors, conformably to your kindness, do me this favor. God the Father, the supreme Architect, had already built this cosmic home we behold, the most sacred temple of His godhead, by the laws of His mysterious wisdom. The region above the heavens He had adorned with Intelligences, the heavenly spheres He had quickened with eternal souls, and the excrementary and filthy parts of the lower world He had filled with a multitude of animals of every kind. But, when the work was finished, the Craftsman kept wishing that there were someone to ponder the plan of so great a work, to love its beauty, and to wonder at its vastness. Therefore, when everything was done (as Moses and Timaeus bear witness), He finally took thought concerning the creation of man. But there was not among His archetypes that from which He could fashion a new offspring, nor was there in His treasure-houses anything which He might bestow on His new son as an inheritance, nor was there in the seats of all the world a place where the latter might sit to contemplate the universe. All was now complete; all things had been assigned to the highest, the middle, and the lowest orders. But in its final creation it was not the part of the Father's power to fail as though exhausted. It was not the part of His wisdom to waver in a needful matter through poverty of counsel. It was not the part of His kindly love that he who was to praise God's divine generosity in regard to others should be compelled to condemn it in regard to himself. At last the best of artisans ordained that that creature to whom He had been able to give nothing proper to himself should have joint possession of whatever had been peculiar to each of the different kinds of being. He therefore took man as a creature of indeterminate nature and, assigning him a place in the middle of the world, addressed him thus: "Neither a fixed abode nor a form that is thine alone nor any function peculiar to thyself have we given thee, Adam, to the end that according to thy longing and according to thy judgment thou mayest have and possess what abode, what form, and what functions thou thyself shalt desire. The nature of all other beings is limited and constrained within the bounds of laws prescribed by Us. Thou, constrained by no limits, in accordance with thine own free will, in whose hand We have placed thee, shalt ordain for thyself the limits of thy nature. We have set thee at the world's center that thou mayest from thence more easily observe whatever is in the world. We have made thee neither of heaven nor of earth, neither mortal nor immortal, so that with freedom of choice and with honor, as though the maker and molder of thyself, thou mayest fashion thyself in whatever shape thou shalt prefer. Thou shalt have the power to degenerate into the lower forms of life, which are brutish. Thou shalt have the power, out of thy soul's judgment, to be reborn into the higher forms, which are divine." O supreme generosity of God the Father, O highest and most marvelous felicity of man! To him it is granted to have whatever he chooses, to be whatever he wills.

Baldassare Castiglione (1478–1529) described the qualities of an ideal Renaissance courtier.

FROM The Book of the Courtier
BY BALDASSARE CASTIGLIONE

I wish, then, that this Courtier of ours should be nobly born and of gentle race; because it is far less unseemly for one of ignoble birth to fail in worthy deeds, than for one of noble birth, who, if he strays from the path of his predecessors, stains his family name, and not only fails to achieve but loses what has been achieved already; for noble birth is like a bright lamp that manifests and makes visible good and evil deeds, and kindles and stimulates to virtue both by fear of shame and by hope of praise. . . .

But to come to some details, I am of opinion that the principal and true profession of the Courtier ought to be that of arms; which I would have him follow actively above all else, and be known among others as bold and strong, and loyal to whomsoever he serves. And he will win a reputation for these good qualities by exercising them at all times and in all places, since one may never fail in this without severest censure. And just as among women, their fair fame once sullied never recovers its first lustre, so the reputation of a gentleman who bears arms, if once it be in the least tarnished with cowardice or other disgrace, remains forever infamous before the world and full of ignominy. Therefore the more our Courtier excels in this art, the more he will be worthy of praise; and yet I do not deem essential in him that perfect knowledge of things and those other qualities that befit a commander; since this would be too wide a sea, let us be content, as we have said, with perfect loyalty and unconquered courage, and that he be always seen to possess them. . . .

Not that we would have him look so fierce, or go about blustering, or say

Baldassare Castiglione, *The Book of the Courtier* (1903), pp. 22, 25–31, 59, 62–63, 65–66, 93–95, translated by Leonard E. Opdycke.

that he has taken his cuirass to wife, or threaten with those grim scowls that we have often seen in Berto, because to such men as this, one might justly say that which a brave lady jestingly said in gentle company to one whom I will not name at present; who, being invited by her out of compliment to dance, refused not only that, but to listen to the music, and many other entertainments proposed to him,—saying always that such silly trifles were not his business; so that at last the lady said, "What is your business, then?" He replied with a sour look, "To fight." Then the lady at once said, "Now that you are in no war and out of fighting trim, I should think it were a good thing to have yourself well oiled, and to stow yourself with all your battle harness in a closet until you be needed, lest you grow more rusty than you are"; and so, amid much laughter from the bystanders, she left the discomfited fellow to his silly presumption.

Therefore let the man we are seeking, be very bold, stern, and always among the first, where the enemy are to be seen; and in every other place, gentle, modest, reserved, above all things avoiding ostentation and that impudent self-praise by which men ever excite hatred and disgust in all who hear them. . . .

I say, however, that he, who in praising himself runs into no errour and incurs no annoyance or envy at the hands of those that hear him, is a very discreet man indeed and merits praise from others in addition to that which he bestows upon himself; because it is a very difficult matter. . . .

I would have our Courtier's aspect; not so soft and effeminate as is sought by many, who not only curl their hair and pluck their brows, but gloss their faces with all those arts employed by the most wanton and unchaste women in the world; and in their walk, posture and every act, they seem so limp and languid that their limbs are like to fall apart; and they pronounce their words so mournfully that they appear about to expire upon the spot: and the more they find themselves with men of rank, the more they affect such tricks. Since nature has not made them women, as they seem to wish to appear and be, they should be treated not as good women but as public harlots, and driven not merely from the courts of great lords but from the society of honest men.

Then coming to the bodily frame, I say it is enough if this be neither extremely short nor tall, for both of these conditions excite a certain contemptuous surprise, and men of either sort are gazed upon in much the same way that we gaze on monsters. Yet if we must offend in one of the two extremes, it is preferable to fall a little short of the just measure of height than to exceed it, for besides often being dull of intellect, men thus huge of body are also unfit for every exercise of agility, which thing I should much wish in the Courtier. And so I would have him well built and shapely of limb, and would have him show strength and lightness and suppleness, and know all bodily exercises that befit a man of war: whereof I think the first should be to handle every sort of weapon well on foot and on horse, to understand the advantages of each, and especially to be familiar with those weapons that are ordinarily used among gentlemen; for besides the use of them in war, where such subtlety in contrivance is perhaps not needful, there frequently arise differences between one gentleman and another, which afterwards result in duels often fought with such weapons as happen at the moment to be within reach: thus knowledge of this kind is a very safe thing.

* * *

There are also many other exercises, which although not immediately dependent upon arms, yet are closely connected therewith, and greatly foster manly sturdiness; and one of the chief among these seems to me to be the chase, because it bears a certain likeness to war: and truly it is an amusement for great lords and befitting a man at court, and furthermore it is seen to have been much cultivated among the ancients. It is fitting also to know how to swim, to leap, to run, to throw stones, for besides the use that may be made of this in war, a man often has occasion to show what he can do in such matters; whence good esteem is to be won, especially with the multitude, who must be taken into account withal. Another admirable exercise, and one very befitting a man at court, is the game of tennis, in which are well shown the disposition of the body, the quickness and suppleness of every member, and all those qualities that are seen in nearly every other exercise. Nor less highly do I esteem vaulting on horse, which although it be fatiguing and difficult, makes a man very light and dexterous more than any other thing; and besides its utility, if this lightness is accompanied by grace, it is to my thinking a finer show than any of the others.

* * *

I think that the conversation which the Courtier ought most to try in every way to make acceptable, is that which he holds with his prince; and although this word "conversation" implies a certain equality that seems impossible between a lord and his inferior, yet we will call it so for the present. Therefore, besides daily showing everyone that he possesses the worth we have already described, I would have the Courtier strive, with all the thoughts and forces of his mind, to love and almost to adore the prince whom he serves, above every other thing, and mould his wishes, habits and all his ways to his prince's liking. . . .

Moreover it is possible without flattery to obey and further the wishes of him we serve, for I am speaking of those wishes that are reasonable and right, or of those that in themselves are neither good nor evil, such as would be a liking for play or a devotion to one kind of exercise above another. And I would have the Courtier bend himself to this even if he be by nature alien to it, so that on seeing him his lord shall always feel that he will have something agreeable to say; which will come about if he has the good judgment to perceive what his prince likes, and the wit and prudence to bend himself thereto, and a deliberate purpose to like that which perhaps he by nature dislikes. . . . He will not be an idle or untruthful tattler, nor a boaster nor pointless flatterer, but modest and reserved, always and especially in public showing that reverence and respect which befit the servant towards the master. . . .

He will very rarely or almost never ask anything of his lord for himself, lest his lord, being reluctant to deny it to him directly, may sometimes grant it with an ill grace, which is much worse. Even in asking for others he will choose his time discreetly and ask proper and reasonable things; and he will so frame his request, by omitting what he knows may displease and by skilfully doing away with difficulties, that his lord shall always grant it, or shall not think him offended by refusal even if it be denied; for when lords have denied a favour to an importunate suitor, they often reflect that he who asked it with such eagerness, must have desired it greatly, and so having failed to obtain it, must feel ill will towards him who denied it; and believing this, they begin to hate the man and can never more look upon him with favour.

The autobiography of the artist Benvenuto Cellini (1500–1571) provides many vignettes of life in Renaissance Italy.

FROM Autobiography BY BENVENUTO CELLINI

[*Cellini has shown Pope Clement VII a model of a jeweled ornament—B. T.*] While we were waiting for the money, the Pope turned once more to gaze at leisure on the dexterous device I had employed for combining the diamond with the figure of God the Father. I had put the diamond exactly in the centre of the piece; and above it God the Father was shown seated, leaning nobly in a sideways attitude, which made a perfect composition, and did not interfere with the stone's effect. Lifting his right hand, he was in the act of giving the benediction. Below the diamond I had placed three children, who, with their arms upraised, were supporting the jewel. One of them, in the middle, was in full relief, the other two in half-relief. All round I set a crowd of cherubs, in divers attitudes, adapted to the other gems. A mantle undulated to the wind around the figure of the Father, from the folds of which cherubs peeped out; and there were other ornaments besides which made a very beautiful effect. The work was executed in white stucco on a black stone. When the money came, the Pope gave it me with his own hand, and begged me in the most winning terms to let him have it finished in his own days, adding that this should be to my advantage.

The Life of Benvenuto Cellini (1893), pp. 102, 114–119, translated by John Addington Symonds.

* * *

[*Cellini's brother was murdered at this time—B. T.*]

I went on applying myself with the utmost diligence upon the goldwork for Pope Clement's button. He was very eager to have it, and used to send for me two or three times a week, in order to inspect it; and his delight in the work always increased. Often would he rebuke and scold me, as it were, for the great grief in which my brother's loss had plunged me; and one day, observing me more downcast and out of trim than was proper, he cried aloud: "Benvenuto, oh! I did not know that you were mad. Have you only just learned that there is no remedy against death? One would think that you were trying to run after him." When I left the presence, I continued working at the jewel and the dies for the Mint; but I also took to watching the arquebusier who shot my brother, as though he had been a girl I was in love with. The man had formerly been in the light cavalry, but afterwards had joined the arquebusiers as one of the Bargello's corporals; and what increased my rage was that he had used these boastful words: "If it had not been for me, who killed that brave young man, the least trifle of delay would have resulted in his putting us all to flight with great disaster." When I saw that the fever caused by always seeing him about was depriving me of sleep and appetite, and was bringing me by degrees to sorry plight, I overcame my repugnance to so low and not quite praiseworthy an enterprise, and made my mind up one evening to rid myself of the torment. The fellow lived in a house near a place called Torre Sanguigua, next door to the lodging of one of the most fashionable courtesans in Rome, named Signora Antea. It had just struck twenty-four, and he was standing at the house-door, with his sword in hand, having risen from supper. With great address I stole up to him, holding a large Pistojan dagger, and dealt him a back-handed stroke, with which I meant to cut his head clean off; but as he turned round very suddenly, the blow fell upon the point of his left shoulder and broke the bone. He sprang up, dropped his sword, half-stunned with the great pain, and took to flight. I followed after, and in four steps caught him up, when I lifted my dagger above his head, which he was holding very low, and hit him in the back exactly at the junction of the nape-bone and the neck. The poniard entered this point so deep into the bone, that, though I used all my strength to pull it out, I was not able. For just at that moment four soldiers with drawn swords sprang out from Antea's lodging, and obliged me to set hand to my own sword to defend my life. Leaving the poniard then, I made off, and fearing I might be recognised, took refuge in the palace of Duke Alessandro, which was between Piazza Navona and the Rotunda. On my arrival, I asked to see the Duke, who told me that, if I was alone, I need only keep quiet and have no further anxiety, but go on working at the jewel which the Pope had set his heart on, and stay eight days indoors. . . .

More than eight days elapsed, and the Pope did not send for me according to his custom. Afterwards he summoned me through his chamberlain, the

Bolognese nobleman I have already mentioned, who let me, in his own modest manner, understand that his Holiness knew all, but was very well inclined toward me, and that I had only to mind my work and keep quiet. When we reached the presence, the Pope cast so menacing a glance towards me that the mere look of his eyes made me tremble. Afterwards, upon examining my work, his countenance cleared, and he began to praise me beyond measure, saying that I had done a vast amount in a short time. Then, looking me straight in the face, he added: "Now that you are cured, Benvenuto, take heed how you live." I, who understood his meaning, promised that I would. Immediately upon this, I opened a very fine shop in the Banchi, opposite Raffaello, and there I finished the jewel after the lapse of a few months.

The Pope had sent me all those precious stones, except the diamond, which was pawned to certain Genoese bankers for some pressing need he had of money. The rest were in my custody, together with a model of the diamond. I had five excellent journeymen, and in addition to the great piece, I was engaged on several jobs; so that my shop contained property of much value in jewels, gems, and gold and silver. I kept a shaggy dog, very big and handsome, which Duke Alessandro gave me; the beast was capital as a retriever, since he brought me every sort of birds and game I shot, but he also served most admirably for a watchdog. It happened, as was natural at the age of twenty-nine, that I had taken into my service a girl of great beauty and grace, whom I used as a model in my art, and who was also complaisant of her personal favours to me. Such being the case, I occupied an apartment far away from my workmen's room, as well as from the shop; and this communicated by a little dark passage with the maid's bedroom. I used frequently to pass the night with her; and though I sleep as lightly as ever yet did man upon this earth, yet, after indulgence in sexual pleasure, my slumber is sometimes very deep and heavy.

So it chanced one night: for I must say that a thief, under the pretext of being a goldsmith, had spied on me, and cast his eyes upon the precious stones, and made a plan to steal them. Well, then, this fellow broke into the shop, where he found a quantity of little things in gold and silver. He was engaged in bursting open certain boxes to get at the jewels he had noticed, when my dog jumped upon him, and put him to much trouble to defend himself with his sword. . . . [*The thief succeeded in escaping—B. T.*]

After sunrise my workmen went into the shop, and saw that it had been broken open and all the boxes smashed. They began to scream at the top of their voices: "Ah, woe is me! Ah, woe is me!" The clamour woke me, and I rushed out in a panic. Appearing thus before them, they cried out: "Alas to us! for we have been robbed by some one, who has broken and borne everything away!" These words wrought so forcibly upon my mind that I dared not go to my big chest and look if it still held the jewels of the Pope. So intense was the anxiety, that I seemed to lose my eyesight, and told them they themselves must unlock the chest, and see how many of the Pope's gems were missing. The fellows were all of them in their shirts; and when, on opening the chest, they saw the precious stones and my work with them, they took heart of joy and shouted: "There is no harm done; your piece and all the stones are here; but the thief has left us naked to the shirt, because last night, by reason of the burning heat, we took our clothes off in the shop and left them here." Recovering my senses, I thanked God, and said: "Go and get yourselves new suits of clothes; I will pay when I hear at leisure how the whole thing happened." What caused me the most pain, and made me lose my senses, and take fright—so contrary to my real nature—was the dread lest peradventure folk should fancy I had trumped a story of the robber up to steal the jewels. . . .

After telling the young men to provide themselves with fresh clothes, I took my piece, together with the gems, setting them as well as I could in their proper places, and went off at once with them to the Pope. Francesco del Nero had already told him something of the trouble in my shop, and had put suspicions in his head. So then, taking the thing rather ill than otherwise, he shot a furious glance upon me, and cried haughtily: "What have you come to do here? What is up?" "Here are all your precious stones, and not one of them is missing." At this the Pope's face cleared, and he said: "So then, you're welcome." I showed him the piece, and while he was inspecting it, I related to him the whole story of the thief and of my agony, and what had been my greatest trouble in the matter. During this speech, he often times turned round to look me sharply in the eyes; and Francesco del Nero being also in the presence, this seemed to make him half sorry that he had not guessed the truth. At last, breaking into laughter at the long tale I was telling, he sent me off with these words: "Go, and take heed to be an honest man, as indeed I know you are."

4
THE
RENAISSANCE
STATE

In the transitional period at the end of the Middle Ages, Marsilius of Padua produced a thoroughly secular theory of politics. Its distinctive characteristic was that the priesthood was treated as merely a constituent element of the state, fully subject to the state's authority.

FROM The Defender of the Peace
BY MARSILIUS OF PADUA

The state, according to Aristotle in the *Politics,* Book I, Chapter 1, is "the perfect community having the full limit of self-sufficiency, which came into existence for the sake of living, but exists for the sake of living well." This phrase of Aristotle—"came into existence for the sake of living, but exists for the sake of living well"—signifies the perfect final cause of the state, since those who live a civil life not only live, which beasts or slaves do too, but live well, having leisure for those liberal functions in which are exercised the virtues of both the practical and the theoretic soul.

* * *

But the living and living well which are appropriate to men fall into two kinds, of which one is temporal or earthly, while the other is usually called eternal or heavenly. However, this latter kind of living, the eternal, the whole body of philosophers were unable to prove by demonstration, nor was it self-

Marsilius of Padua, *The Defender of the Peace,* II (1956), pp. 12–13, 44–45, 61, 100, 174–175, 253, 258, 264–265, translated by A. Gewirth. Reprinted by permission of Columbia University Press, New York.

evident, and therefore they did not concern themselves with the means thereto. But as to the first kind of living and living well or good life, that is, the earthly, and its necessary means, this the glorious philosophers comprehended almost completely through demonstration. Hence, for its attainment they concluded the necessity of the civil community, without which this sufficient life cannot be obtained. Thus the foremost of the philosophers, Aristotle, said in his *Politics,* Book I, Chapter 1: "All men are driven toward such an association by a natural impulse." Although sense experience teaches this, we wish to bring out more distinctly that cause of it which we have indicated, as follows: Man is born composed of contrary elements, because of whose contrary actions and passions some of his substance is continually being destroyed; moreover, he is born "bare and unprotected" from excess of the surrounding air and other elements, capable of suffering and of destruction, as has been said in the science of nature. As a consequence, he needed arts of diverse genera and species to avoid the afore-mentioned harms. But since these arts can be exercised only by a large number of men, and can be had only through their association with one another, men had to assemble together in order to attain what was beneficial through these arts and to avoid what was harmful.

But since among men thus assembled there arise disputes and quarrels which, if not regulated by a norm of justice, would cause men to fight and separate and thus finally would bring about the destruction of the state, there had to be established in this association a standard of justice and a guardian or maker thereof. . . .

But it must be remembered that the true knowledge or discovery of the just and the beneficial, and of their opposites, is not law taken in its last and most proper sense, whereby it is the measure of human civil acts, unless there is given a coercive command as to its observance, or it is made by way of such a command, by someone through whose authority its transgressors must and can be punished. Hence, we must now say to whom belongs the authority to make such a command and to punish its transgressors. This, indeed, is to inquire into the legislator or the maker of the law.

Let us say, then, in accordance with the truth and the counsel of Aristotle in the *Politics,* Book III, Chapter 6, that the legislator, or the primary and proper efficient cause of the law, is the people or the whole body of citizens, or the weightier part thereof, through its election or will expressed by words in the general assembly of the citizens, commanding or determining that something be done or omitted with regard to human civil acts, under a temporal pain or punishment. By the "weightier part" I mean to take into consideration the quantity and the quality of the persons in that community over which the law is made. The aforesaid whole body of citizens or the weightier part thereof is the legislator regardless of whether it makes the law directly by itself or entrusts the making of it to some person or persons, who are not and cannot be the legislator in the absolute sense, but only in a relative sense and for a particular time and in accordance with the authority of the primary legislator. . . .

It now remains to show the efficient cause of the ruler, that is, the cause by which there is given to one or more persons the authority of rulership which is established through election. For it is by this authority that a person becomes a ruler in actuality, and not by his knowledge of the laws, his prudence, or moral virtue, although these are qualities of the perfect ruler. For it happens that many men have these qualities, but nevertheless, lacking this authority, they are not rulers, unless perhaps in proximate potentiality.

Taking up the question, then, let us say, in accordance with the truth and the doctrine of Aristotle in the *Politics,* Book III, Chapter 6, that the efficient power to establish or elect the ruler belongs to the legislator or the whole body of the citizens, just as does the power to make the laws, as we said in Chapter XII. And to the legislator similarly belongs the power to make any correction of the ruler and even to depose him, if this be expedient for the common benefit. . . . [*The holy canons—B. T.*] clearly demonstrate that the Roman bishop called pope, or any other priest or bishop, or spiritual minister, collectively or individually, as such, has and ought to have no coercive jurisdiction over the property or person of any priest or bishop, or deacon, or group of them, and still less over any secular ruler or government, community, group, or individual, of whatever condition they may be; unless, indeed, such jurisdiction shall have been granted to a priest or bishop or group of them by the human legislator of the province. . . . Since, then, the heretic, the schismatic, or any other infidel is a transgressor of divine law, if he persists in this crime he will be punished by that judge to whom it pertains to correct transgressors of divine law as such, when he will exercise his judicial authority. But this judge is Christ, who will judge the living, the dead, and the dying, but in the future world, not in this one. For he has mercifully allowed sinners to have the opportunity of becoming deserving and penitent up to the very time when they finally pass from this world at death. But the other judge, namely, the pastor, bishop or priest, must teach and exhort man in the present life, must censure and rebuke the sinner and frighten him by a judgment or prediction of future glory or eternal damnation; but he must not coerce, as is plain from the previous chapter.

Now if human law were to prohibit heretics or other infidels from dwelling in the region, and yet such a person were found there, he must be corrected in this world as a transgressor of human law, and the penalty fixed by that law for such transgression must be inflicted on him by the judge who is the guardian of human law by the authority of the legislator, as we demonstrated in Chapter XV of Discourse I. But if human law did not prohibit the heretic or other infidel from dwelling among the faithful in the same province, as heretics and Jews are now permitted to do by human laws even in these times of Christian peoples, rulers, and pontiffs, then I say that no one is allowed to judge or coerce a heretic or other infidel by any penalty in property or in person for the status of the present life. And the general reason for this is as follows: no one is punished in this world for sinning against theoretic or practical disciplines precisely as such, however much he may sin against them, but only for sinning against a command of human law.

* * *

But with reference to our main thesis, this must be noted most of all: that even though it may for some reasons seem fitting that certain men should be called the successors of St. Peter, because they are more reverent than the successors of the other apostles, and especially because they occupy the episcopal seat at Rome, yet the sacred Scripture shows no necessary reason why the successors of the other apostles should be regarded as subject to them in any power. And even if the apostles were unequal in authority, yet St. Peter or any other apostle did not, by virtue of the words of the Scripture, have the power to appoint or depose them, with reference either to the priestly dignity which we have called essential, or to their being sent or assigned to a certain place or people, or to the interpretation of the Scripture or of the catholic faith, or to coercive jurisdiction over anyone in this world; any more than, conversely, the other apostles had any such power over St. Peter or some other apostle.

* * *

And now I wish to show that after the time of the apostles and of the first fathers who succeeded them in office, and especially now when the communities of believers have become perfected, the immediate efficient cause of the assignment or appointment of a prelate (whether of the major one, called the "bishop," or of the minor ones, called "curate priests," and likewise of the other minor ones) is or ought to be the entire multitude of believers of that place through their election or expressed will, or else the person or persons to whom the aforesaid multitude has given the authority to make such appointments. And I also wish to show that it pertains to the same authority lawfully to remove each of the afore-mentioned officials from such office, and to compel him to exercise it, if it seems expedient.

* * *

As for the distribution of temporal things, usually called "ecclesiastic benefices," it must be remembered that these things are set aside for the support of ecclesiastic ministers and other poor persons (which we discussed in Chapters XIV and XV of this discourse) either by the legislator or by some individual person or group. Now if such temporal goods have been thus set aside by the gift and establishment of the legislator, then, I say, the legislator can lawfully, in accordance with divine law, entrust to whomever it wants, and at any time, the authority to distribute these goods, and can, for cause, when it so wishes, revoke such authority from the individual or group to whom it has entrusted it.

The Florentine diplomat Niccolò Machiavelli (1469-1527) startled his contemporaries by writing a book on politics that did not aim at instructing
rulers in the moral virtues but rather gave them pragmatic advice on how to
win and hold power.

FROM The Prince BY NICCOLÒ MACHIAVELLI

It now remains for us to consider what ought to be the conduct and bearing
of a Prince in relation to his subjects and friends. And since I know that
many have written on this subject, I fear it may be thought presumptuous in
me to write of it also: the more so, because in my treatment of it I depart
from the views that others have taken.

But since it is my object to write what shall be useful to whosoever understands it, it seems to me better to follow the real truth of things than an
imaginary view of them. For many Republics and Princedoms have been
imagined that were never seen or known to exist in reality. And the manner
in which we live, and that in which we ought to live, are things so wide
asunder, that he who quits the one to betake himself to the other is more
likely to destroy than to save himself; since any one who would act up to a
perfect standard of goodness in everything, must be ruined among so many
who are not good. It is essential, therefore, for a Prince who desires to maintain his position, to have learned how to be other than good, and to use or not
to use his goodness as necessity requires.

* * *

Beginning, then, with the first of the qualities above noticed, I say that it
may be a good thing to be reputed liberal, but, nevertheless, that liberality
without the reputation of it is hurtful; because, though it be worthily and
rightly used, still if it be not known, you escape not the reproach of its opposite vice. Hence, to have credit for liberality with the world at large, you must
neglect no circumstance of sumptuous display; the result being, that a Prince
of a liberal disposition will consume his whole substance in things of this
sort, and, after all, be obliged, if he would maintain his reputation for liberality, to burden his subjects with extraordinary taxes, and to resort to confiscations and all the other shifts whereby money is raised. But in this way he
becomes hateful to his subjects, and growing impoverished is held in little
esteem by any. So that in the end, having by his liberality offended many and

Niccolò Machiavelli, *The Prince* (1897), pp. 109-110, 113-115, 118-119, 125-130, translated
by N. H. Thompson. Reprinted by permission of The Clarendon Press, Oxford.

obliged few, he is worse off than when he began, and is exposed to all his original dangers. Recognizing this, and endeavouring to retrace his steps, he at once incurs the infamy of miserliness.

A Prince, therefore, since he cannot without injury to himself practise the virtue of liberality so that it may be known, will not, if he be wise, greatly concern himself though he be called miserly. Because in time he will come to be regarded as more and more liberal, when it is seen that through his parsimony his revenues are sufficient; that he is able to defend himself against any who make war on him; that he can engage in enterprises against others without burdening his subjects; and thus exercise liberality towards all from whom he does not take, whose number is infinite, while he is miserly in respect of those only to whom he does not give, whose number is few.

* * *

Passing to the other qualities above referred to, I say that every Prince should desire to be accounted merciful and not cruel. Nevertheless, he should be on his guard against the abuse of this quality of mercy. Cesare Borgia was reputed cruel, yet his cruelty restored Romagna, united it, and brought it to order and obedience; so that if we look at things in their true light, it will be seen that he was in reality far more merciful than the people of Florence, who, to avoid the imputation of cruelty, suffered Pistoja to be torn to pieces by factions.

A Prince should therefore disregard the reproach of being thought cruel where it enables him to keep his subjects united and obedient. For he who quells disorder by a very few signal examples will in the end be more merciful than he who from too great leniency permits things to take their course and so to result in rapine and bloodshed; for these hurt the whole State, whereas the severities of the Prince injure individuals only.

* * *

A Prince should, therefore, understand how to use well both the man and the beast. And this lesson has been covertly taught by the ancient writers, who relate how Achilles and many others of these old Princes were given over to be brought up and trained by Chiron the Centaur; since the only meaning of their having for instructor one who was half man and half beast is, that it is necessary for a Prince to know how to use both natures, and that the one without the other has no stability.

But since a Prince should know how to use the beast's nature wisely, he ought of beasts to choose both the lion and the fox; for the lion cannot guard himself from the toils, nor the fox from wolves. He must therefore be a fox to discern toils, and a lion to drive off wolves.

To rely wholly on the lion is unwise; and for this reason a prudent Prince neither can nor ought to keep his word when to keep it is hurtful to him and the causes which led him to pledge it are removed. If all men were good, this would not be good advice, but since they are dishonest and do not keep faith with you, you, in return, need not keep faith with them; and no Prince was ever at a loss for plausible reasons to cloak a breach of faith. Of this numberless recent instances could be given, and it might be shown how many solemn treaties and engagements have been rendered inoperative and idle through want of faith in Princes, and that he who has best known to play the fox has had the best success.

It is necessary, indeed, to put a good colour on this nature, and to be skilful in simulating and dissembling. But men are so simple, and governed so absolutely by their present needs, that he who wishes to deceive will never fail in finding willing dupes. One recent example I will not omit. Pope Alexander VI had no care or thought but how to deceive, and always found material to work on. No man ever had a more effective manner of asseverating, or made promises with more solemn protestations, or observed them less. And yet, because he understood this side of human nature, his frauds always succeeded.

It is not essential, then, that a Prince should have all the good qualities which I have enumerated above, but it is most essential that he should seem to have them; I will even venture to affirm that if he has and invariably practises them all, they are hurtful, whereas the appearance of having them is useful. Thus, it is well to seem merciful, faithful, humane, religious, and upright, and also to be so; but the mind should remain so balanced that were it needful not to be so, you should be able and know how to change to the contrary.

And you are to understand that a Prince, and most of all a new Prince, cannot observe all those rules of conduct in respect whereof men are accounted good, being often forced, in order to preserve his Princedom, to act in opposition to good faith, charity, humanity, and religion. He must therefore keep his mind ready to shift as the winds and tides of Fortune turn, and, as I have already said, he ought not to quit good courses if he can help it, but should know how to follow evil courses if he must.

A Prince should therefore be very careful that nothing ever escapes his lips which is not replete with the five qualities above named, so that to see and hear him, one would think him the embodiment of mercy, good faith, integrity, humanity, and religion. And there is no virtue which it is more necessary for him to seem to possess than this last; because men in general judge rather by the eye than by the hand, for every one can see but few can touch. Every one sees what you seem, but few know what you are, and these few dare not oppose themselves to the opinion of the many who have the majesty of the State to back them up.

Moreover, in the actions of all men, and most of all of Princes, where there is no tribunal to which we can appeal, we look to results. Wherefore if a Prince succeeds in establishing and maintaining his authority, the means will always be judged honourable and be approved by every one. For the vulgar are always taken by appearances and by results, and the world is made up of the vulgar, the few only finding room when the many have no longer ground to stand on.

A distinguished modern historian of the Renaissance has evaluated Machiavelli's work as follows.

FROM Machiavelli and the Renaissance BY F. CHABOD

The *leitmotiv* of Machiavelli's posthumous life was his great assertion as a thinker, representing his true and essential contribution to the history of human thought, namely, the clear recognition of the autonomy and the necessity of politics, "which lies outside the realm of what is morally good or evil." Machiavelli thereby rejected the mediaeval concept of "unity" and became one of the pioneers of the modern spirit.

However, in the generations that immediately followed the Florentine Secretary's death such a motif of spiritual enrichment could not be revived, developed and perfected. Amid the vacillation and the uncertainty of thought and feeling which characterizes all periods of transition it remained as a guide-post and no more. . . .

But it did remain; and—albeit almost surreptitiously, without appearing in all its theoretical potency—it also upheld the historical value of the work, and by its clarity made it possible for the European significance of the composition to emerge.

For Machiavelli accepted the political challenge in its entirety; he swept aside every criterion of action not suggested by the concept of *raison d'état*, i.e. by the exact evaluation of the historical moment and the constructive forces whch the Prince must employ in order to achieve his aim; and he held that the activities of rulers were limited only by their capacity and energy. Hence, he paved the way for absolute governments, which theoretically were completely untrammelled, both in their home and in their foreign policies.

If this was made possible by the Florentine Secretary's recognition of the autonomy of politics, it depended, conversely, on his own peculiar conception of the State, which he identified with the government, or rather with its personal Head. Accordingly, in *The Prince* all his attention was riveted on

Reprinted by permission of the publishers from Federico Chabod, *Machiavelli and the Renaissance*, pp. 116–118, 121–123, translated by David Moore. Cambridge, Mass.: Harvard University Press, Copyright, 1958, by Federico Chabod; and Bowes & Bowes Ltd., London.

the human figure of the man who held the reins of government and so epitomized in his person the whole of public life. Such a conception, determined directly by the historical experience which Machiavelli possessed in such outstanding measure and presupposing a sustained effort on the part of the central government, was essential to the success and pre-eminence of his doctrine.

This was a turning-point in the history of the Christian world. The minds of political theorists were no longer trammelled by Catholic dogma. The structure of the State was not yet threatened in other directions by any revolt of the individual conscience. An entire moral world, if it was not eclipsed, had at any rate receded into the shadows, nor was any other at once forthcoming to take its place and to inspire a new fervour of religious belief; hence, political thought could express itself without being confused by considerations of a different character. It was an era in which unitarian States were being created amid the ruins of the social and political order of the Middle Ages, an era in which it was necessary to place all the weapons of resistance in the hands of those who had still to combat the forces of feudalism and particularism. It was, in short, an era in which it was essential that the freedom and grandeur of political action and the strength and authority of central government should be clearly affirmed. Only thus was it possible to obliterate once and for all the traces of the past and to offer to the society of the future, in the guise of a precept, the weapons which would preserve the life of the united nation in face of disruptive elements old and new.

* * *

Thus by its unadorned and axiomatic pronouncements Machiavelli's work contributed to keep alive the memory of the greatness which Italy had achieved before the peninsula was obliged to submit to foreign sovereignty. The Seigneurs and the Princes had failed in their purpose; and in the end, overwhelmed by Powers that were wealthier, stronger, and more deeply versed in the arts of war and politics, they had had to yield, either taking to flight or resigning themselves to the idea of leaving the conduct of Italian life to others. Yet in the course of an effort twice repeated within a hundred years they had created something which was not destined to perish, even if it was only completely and successfully developed abroad. The wisdom and administrative ability which had enabled them gradually to establish their power; the clarity and preciseness of political vision which had led them to adopt a vigorous unitarian policy, at any rate within the borders of their domains; their stubborn fight to ensure the absolute supremacy of the sovereign authority and to unite the various elements of the State—all these things established a tradition of civic wisdom and political energy which was destined to survive even when it was left to others to bring about its ultimate triumph.

This was the course on which Western Europe had embarked. It was the unique good fortune of the Italian tradition to be seized upon and epitomized in a few pages by Machiavelli, so that it became a model for Europe.

5
THE REVOLT
OF THE
MEDIEVALISTS

W. K. Ferguson has described one modern trend in Renaissance histori-
ography as a "revolt of the medievalists." The following extract will serve to
illustrate the meaning of this phrase.

FROM Héloïse and Abélard BY ETIENNE GILSON

There is nothing quite comparable to the passion of the historians of the
Renaissance for its individualism, its independence of mind, its rebellion
against the principle of authority, unless perchance it is the docility with
which those same historians copy one another in dogmatizing about the
Middle Ages of which they know so little. We should not attach much importance to this attitude, save that those who speak thus of things they understand so poorly pretend to act in defense of reason and of personal observation. Their charge that all those who hold a different opinion are yielding to
prejudice would, indeed, be sad, were it not so comic. Indifference to facts,
distrust of direct observation and personal knowledge, the tendency to prune
their data to suit their hypotheses, the naïve and dogmatic tendency to charge
that those who would refute their position with self-evident facts lack a critical sense—these are the substance of their charge against the Middle Ages.
Certainly, the Middle Ages had its fair share of these limitations. But at the
same time these same limitations provide a perfect picture of the attitude of
these historians of the Renaissance. They themselves possess the weaknesses of
which they accuse the Middle Ages.

E. Gilson, *Héloïse and Abélard* (1951), pp. 124–128, translated by L. K. Shook. Reprinted by
permission of Henry Regnery Co., Chicago.

For Jacob Burckhardt, who only echoes the Preface to Volume VII of Michelet's *History of France,* the Renaissance is characterized by the discovery of the world and by the discovery of man. . . . . What he wishes to prove before everything else is that such strong individuals could only have appeared first in the tiny Italian tyrannies of the fourteenth century where men led so intense a personal life that they had to talk about it. And so we read that "Even autobiography (and not merely history) takes here and there in Italy a bold and vigorous flight, and puts before us, together with the most varied incidents of external life, striking revelations of the inner man. Among other nations, even in Germany, at the time of the Reformation, it deals only with outward experiences, and leaves us to guess at the spirit within. It seems as though Dante's *La Vita nuova,* with the inexorable truthfulness that runs through it, had shown his people the way." We can, moreover, find a reason for this absence of individuality among medieval folk. Need we speak it? It is to be found in the subjugation and standardization which Christianity forced upon them. "Once mistress, the Church does not tolerate the development of the individual. All must be resigned to becoming simple links in her long chain and to obeying the laws of her institutions."

A man lacking individuality, incapable of analyzing himself, without the taste for describing others in biography or himself in autobiography, such is the man Christianity produces. Let us cite, as an example, St. Augustine! But to confine ourselves to the twelfth century, and without asking from what unique mould we could fashion at the same time a Bernard of Clairvaux and a Pierre Abélard, let us make a simple comparison between the Renaissance of the professors and the facts which become manifest in the correspondence of Héloïse and Abélard.

If all we need for a Renaissance is to find individuals developed to the highest point, does not this pair suffice? To be sure, Abélard and Héloïse are not Italians. They were not born in some tiny Tuscan "tyranny" of the fourteenth century. They satisfy, in brief, none of the conditions which the theory demands except that they were just what they ought not to have been if the theory were true. One insists, however, upon persons capable of "freely describing the moral man," even as the great Italians could do it. Perhaps even here Abélard and Héloïse labored with some success! No one would be so foolish as to compare their correspondence with the *Vita nuova* as literature. But if it is just a matter of stating in which of the two works one finds the moral man more simply and more directly described, the tables are turned. It is the *Vita nuova* that can no longer bear the comparison. Historians still wonder whether Beatrice was a little Florentine or a symbol. But there is nothing symbolic about Héloïse, nor was her love for Abélard but the unfolding of allegorical remarks. This story of flesh and blood, carried along by a passion at once brutal and ardent to its celebrated conclusion, we know from within as, indeed, we know few others. Its heroes observe themselves, analyze themselves as only Christian consciences fallen prey to passions can do it. Nor do they merely analyze themselves, but they talk about themselves as well. What Renaissance autobiographies can be compared with the correspondence of Abélard and Héloïse? Perchance Benvenuto Cellini's? But even Burckhardt recognizes that this does not claim to be "founded on introspection." Moreover, the reader "often detects him bragging or lying." On the contrary, it is absolutely certain that it is their inmost selves about which Abélard and Héloïse instruct us; and if they sometimes lie to themselves, they never lie to us.

Before such disagreement between facts and theory, we might reasonably expect the theory to yield a little. But not a bit of it! . . . No fact, whatever it may be, no facts, however numerous they may be, can ever persuade those who hold this theory that it is false, because it is of its very essence and by definition that the Renaissance is the negation of the Middle Ages.

Gaines Post argued that the origins of the modern state are to be found in the twelfth and thirteenth centuries rather than in the age of the Renaissance.

FROM Studies in Medieval Legal Thought
BY GAINES POST

Almost forty years ago Charles Homer Haskins applied the word renaissance to the twelfth century. Whether or not it was a renaissance, the twelfth century was in fact a period of great creative activity. The revival of political, economic, and social life, along with the appearance of new learning, new schools and new literatures and styles of art and architecture, signified the beginnings, in the West, of modern European civilization. In the thirteenth century what had begun in the twelfth arrived at such maturity that it is safe to say that early modern Europe was coming into being.

Among the institutions and fields of knowledge created by medieval men, the university and the State and the legal science that aided in the creation of both were, as much as the rise of an active economy and the organization of towns, important manifestations of the new age. While accepting and respecting tradition and believing in the unchanging higher law of nature that came from God, kings, statesmen, and men of learning confidently applied reason and skill to the work of introducing order into society and societies, into feudal kingdoms, Italian communes, and lesser communities of the clergy and laity. Long before the recovery of Aristotle's *Politics,* the natural-

Gaines Post, *Studies in Medieval Legal Thought,* pp. 3–4, 20–24, 248–249. Reprinted by permission of the Princeton University Press. Copyright © 1964 by Princeton University Press.

ness of living in politically and legally organized communities of corporate guilds, chapters, towns, and States was recognized both in practice and in legal thought. Nature itself sanctioned the use of human reason and art to create new laws for the social and political life on earth—provided always, of course, that the new did not violate the will of God.

At the very time when merchants, artisans, townsmen, and schoolmen were forming their associations for mutual aid and protection, the study of the Roman and Canon law at Bologna introduced lawyers, jurists, and secular and ecclesiastical authorities to the legal thought of Rome on corporations. When kings were trying to overcome the anarchy of feudalism, the new legal science furnished those principles of public law that helped them convert their realms into States. . . .

The objection is often raised, however, that medieval kingdoms were not States because (1) they accepted the spiritual authority of the pope and the universal Church, (2) king and realm were under God and the law of nature, and (3) the royal government was poorly centralized. As for the first argument, it might be raised against the use of the term "State" for Eire and Spain today. Yet we assume that these two countries are States even though they are essentially Catholic and in some fashion recognize the spiritual authority of the Roman Church. With respect to other ideals of universalism, the United States and Italy, not to mention other nations, are sovereign States while belonging to the United Nations. As for the second argument, on subjection to God and a moral law, it must be replied that the official motto of the United States is "In God We Trust," and Americans take an oath of loyalty to "one nation indivisible under God." Furthermore, the sovereignty of the American people and their State is surely limited in fact by a moral law that belongs to the Judaeo-Christian tradition: it is not likely that the representatives of the people in Congress will ever think of making laws that violate the Ten Commandments, nor that the Supreme Court will approve them. It is therefore not absurd to call medieval kingdoms States despite limitations within which derived from the ideal of law and justice, and despite limitations from without (also within) from the universalism of Christianity and the Church. Papal arbitration of "international" disputes in the thirteenth century interfered with the sovereign right of kings to go to war (always the "just war" in defense of the *patria* and the *status regni*) no more and no less than international organizations do in the twentieth century. And "world opinion" was respected as much or as little.

In reply to the third argument, regarding the amount of centralization, one must ask, what degree of centralization is necessary for a State to exist? If the central government must be absolute in power, then the United States might not qualify, since a great many powers remain in the fifty states within. And did France become a State only with the more thorough centralization that resulted from the Revolution? Logically we might conclude that only a totalitarian State is a true State.

* * *

[*During the Middle Ages—B. T.*], in the emergency of a danger that threatened the safety of all, the ruler had a superior right to take such action as would ensure the public welfare or safety, that is, maintain the *status* or state of the realm. This emergency was a case of necessity—usually, as I have had occasion to say above, a just war of defense. Now the case of necessity, Meinecke has shown, was asserted by Machiavelli as a part of his theory of the State: the State is above all; and the prince, to assure the noble end of the State, has the right to use any means to meet the necessity and preserve the State. Necessity is Guicciardini's reason of State. But it had its medieval background—Meinecke finding the earliest statement in the maxim, "Necessity knows no law," in the late fourteenth century—in Gerson: Helene Wieruszowski finding it stated, along with public utility, in the time of Frederick II.

Actually it goes back farther—if not to the Greeks, at any rate to Mark 2, 25–26; and above all to the *Corpus Iuris Canonici* and the *Corpus Iuris Civilis*. A pseudo-Isidorian canon in Gratian (De cons., Dist. 1, c. 11) uses the very expression, "quoniam necessitas non habet legem"; decretists and decretalists from the late twelfth century on state the maxim and in their glosses explain its meaning in connection with the equitable interpretation of the law. For example, the necessity of hunger, says one, excuses theft; poverty, says another, knows no law; and the law ends, says a glossator, when necessity begins. Azo in his *Brocardica* discusses the rule and gives many citations *pro* and *con* to *Code* and *Digest*. To *D.* 9, 2, 4, where we find that it is lawful to kill a thief in the night (the correspondence to *Exod.* 22, 2–3, had been noted by St. Augustine and was discussed by the canonists) because "natural reason" permits one to defend oneself against danger, Accursius gives complete approval.

Here, "Necessity knows no law" was a principle of private law. But because of the theory of the just war, that is, the right of the kingdom to defend itself against the aggressor (St. Augustine stated it, as did the scholastic philosophers), the case of necessity became a principle of public laws in the thirteenth century; the equivalent of "just cause," "evident utility," and the common welfare, it was perforce connected with the preservation of the *status regni*. From the twelfth century on, the kings of France and England appealed to necessity as the justification for demanding extraordinary taxes. As we have seen, the Church had already recognized the validity of necessity in the lay taxation of the clergy. No wonder, then, that in the late thirteenth century French lawyers, not only Beaumanoir and Pierre Dubois, but royal councillors like Pierre Flot and William of Nogaret, were asserting that in a case of necessity the defense of the kingdom and all its members was a superior right of the *status regni;* and that if "what touched all must be approved of all," the king had the right to compel all, even the clergy, to consent to measures taken to meet the danger.

At the same time, the situation of "international wars," necessity, public welfare, and the rise of powerful monarchies broke down the corporate hierarchy of communities within the Empire. Each great kingdom, like England or France, by the middle of the thirteenth century was independent of the Empire in theory and practice alike. And at the end of the century each was independent of the Church—and even above the Church, except in purely spiritual matters.

* * *

On the foundation of the two laws and of the rise of feudal monarchies, the theory, and some practice, of public law and the State thus arose in the twelfth and thirteenth centuries. Private rights and privileges remained powerful and enjoyed a recrudescence in localism and privileged orders in the fourteenth century and later. At times, in periods of war and civil dissension, they weakened the public authority of kings and threatened the very survival of the State.[1] But the ideas and ideal of the State and public order, of a public and constitutional law, were constantly at hand to remind statesmen of their right to reconstitute the State.

Lynn Thorndike criticized Burckhardt's interpretation of the Renaissance from the standpoint of a historian of science.

FROM Renaissance or Prenaissance?
BY LYNN THORNDIKE

Michelet called the Renaissance "the discovery of the world and of man," and was followed in this lead by the very influential book of Burckhardt, in

Lynn Thorndike, "Renaissance or Prenaissance?" *Journal of the History of Ideas*, IV (1943), 69–74.

[1] Naturally I cannot attempt to outline the history of the failures of the public order of the State and of the public authority of the king in the fourteenth and fifteenth centuries. At times, in France for example, king and realm meant little except in the continuity of the ideas and ideal of the public law symbolized by the crown. As late as the eighteenth century, local and individual privileges and local resistance to the commands of the central government made the State weak. On this see in general the excellent book by R. R. Palmer, *The Age of the Democratic Revolution*. To return to the fourteenth century, in France, after the time of Philip IV, particularly in the period of the disasters of the Hundred Years' War and the Black Death, there was far less of a State than in the thirteenth century. *Plena potestas, quod omnes tangit*, and *status regni* apparently no longer manifested the power as well as the theoretical right of the king to obtain more than haphazard and sporadic consent, chiefly in local assemblies, to extraordinary taxes. In England the situation was different, but even there the legal thought I have investigated needs study in relation to the political events. For the situation in France see, besides C. H. Taylor in Strayer and Taylor, *Studies*, Fredric Cheyette, "Procurations by Large-Scale Communities in Fourteenth-Century France," *Speculum*, xxxvii (1962), 18–31.

which, on what seem too often to be dogmatic or imaginary grounds without sufficient presentation of facts as evidence, the Renaissance was no longer regarded as primarily a rebirth of classical learning and culture but rather as a prebirth or precursor of present society and of modern civilization—"a period," to quote the *Boston Transcript* (February 27, 1926) concerning Elizabethan England, "that witnessed the birth pangs of most that is worth while in modern civilization and government."

This made a well-calculated appeal to the average reader who is little interested to be told that Erasmus was a great Greek scholar or that Leonardo da Vinci copied from Albert of Saxony, but whose ego is titillated to be told that Leonardo was an individual like himself or that Erasmus's chief claim to fame is that he was the first modern man—the first one like you and me. All this was quite soothing and flattering and did much to compensate for one's inability to read Horace or to quote Euripides.

* * *

Was the individual freed and personality enhanced by the Renaissance or Prenaissance? Burckhardt affirmed that with it "man became a spiritual individual and recognized himself as such," whereas "in the middle ages both sides of human consciousness—that which was turned within as that which was turned without—lay dreaming or half awake beneath a common veil." It might be remarked that individualism may be a mark of decline rather than progress. The self-centered sage of the Stoics and Epicureans rang the knell of the Greek city-state. Basil, on the verge of the barbarian invasions, complained that men "for the greater part prefer individual and private life to the union of common life." Carl Nemann held that "true modern individualism has its roots in the strength of the barbarians, in the realism of the barbarians, and in the Christian middle ages." Cunningham believed that the Roman Empire "left little scope for individual aims and tended to check the energy of capitalists and laborers alike," whereas Christianity taught the supreme dignity of man and encouraged the individual and personal responsibility. Moreover, in the thirteenth century there were "fewer barriers to social intercourse than now." According to Schäfer, "So far as public life in the broadest sense, in church and state, city and country, law and society, is concerned, the middle ages are the time of most distinctive individuality and independent personality in volition and action." We may no longer think of the Gothic architects as anonymous, and de Mely discovered hundreds of signatures of miniaturists hidden in the initials and illuminations of medieval manuscripts. No period in the history of philosophy has discussed individuality and its problems more often or more subtly than did the medieval schoolmen. Vittorino da Feltre and other humanist educators may have suited their teaching to the individual pupil; at the medieval university the individual scholar suited himself. The humanists were imitative in their writing, not original. Vitruvius was the Bible of Renaissance architects who came to follow authority far more than their creative Gothic predecessors. For the middle ages loved variety; the Renaissance, uniformity.

Not only has it been demonstrated that the thirteenth and fourteenth centuries were more active and penetrating in natural science than was the quatrocento, but the notion that "appreciation of natural beauty" was "introduced into modern Europe by the Italian Renaissance" must also be abandoned. Burckhardt admitted that medieval literature displayed sympathy with nature, but nevertheless regarded Petrarch's ascent of Mount Ventoux (which is only 6260 feet high) in 1336 as epoch-making. Petrarch represented an old herdsman who had tried in vain to climb it fifty years before as beseeching him to turn back on the ground that he had received only torn clothes and broken bones for his pains and that no one had attempted the ascent since. As a matter of fact, Jean Buridan, the Parisian schoolman, had visited it between 1316 and 1334, had given details as to its altitude, and had waxed enthusiastic as to the Cevennes. So that all Petrarch's account proves is his capacity for story-telling and sentimental ability to make a mountain out of a molehill. Miss Stockmayer, in a book on feeling for nature in Germany in the tenth and eleventh centuries, has noted various ascents and descriptions of mountains from that period. In the closing years of his life archbishop Anno of Cologne climbed his beloved mountain oftener than usual.

As for the feeling for nature in medieval art, let me repeat what I have written elsewhere anent the interest displayed by the students of Albertus Magnus in particular herbs and trees.

This healthy interest in nature and commendable curiosity concerning real things was not confined to Albert's students nor to "rustic intelligences." One has only to examine the sculpture of the great thirteenth-century cathedrals to see that the craftsmen of the towns were close observers of the world of nature, and that every artist was a naturalist too. In the foliage that twines about the capitals of the columns in the French Gothic cathedrals it is easy to recognize, says M. Mâle, a large number of plants: "the plantain, arum, ranunculus, fern, clover, coladine, hepatica, columbine, cress, parsley, strawberry-plant, ivy, snapdragon, the flower of the broom, and the leaf of the oak, a typically French collection of flowers loved from childhood." *Mutatis mutandis,* the same statement could be made concerning the carved vegetation that runs riot in Lincoln cathedral. "The thirteenth-century sculptors sang their *chant de mai.* All the spring delights of the Middle Ages live again in their work—the exhilaration of Palm Sunday, the garlands of flowers, the bouquets fastened on the doors, the strewing of fresh herbs in the chapels, the magical flowers of the feast of Saint John—all the fleeting charm of those old-time springs and summers. The Middle Ages, so often said to have little love for nature, in point of fact gazed at every blade of grass with reverence."

It is not merely love of nature but scientific interest and accuracy that we see revealed in the sculptures of the cathedrals and in the note-books of the thirteenth-century architect, Villard de Honnecourt, with its sketches of insect as well as animal life, of a lobster, two parroquets on a perch, the spirals of a snail's shell, a fly, a dragonfly, and a grasshopper, as well as a bear and a lion from life, and more familiar animals such as the cat and the swan. The sculptors of gargoyles and chimeras were not content to reproduce existing animals but showed their command of animal anatomy by creating strange compound and hybrid monsters—one might almost say, evolving new species —which nevertheless have all the verisimilitude of copies from living forms. It was these breeders in stone, these Burbanks of the pencil, these Darwins with the chisel, who knew nature and had studied botany and zoology in a way superior to the scholar who simply pored over the works of Aristotle and Pliny. No wonder that Albert's students were curious about particular things.

* * *

The concept of the Italian Renaissance or Prenaissance has in my opinion done a great deal of harm in the past and may continue to do harm in the future. It is too suggestive of a sensational, miraculous, extraordinary, magical, human and intellectual development, like unto the phoenix rising from its ashes after five hundred years. It is contrary to the fact that human nature tends to remain much the same in all times. It has led to a chorus of rhapsodists as to freedom, breadth, soaring ideas, horizons, perspectives, out of fetters and swaddling clothes, and so on. It long discouraged the study of centuries of human development that preceded it, and blinded the French *philosophes* and revolutionists to the value of medieval political and economic institutions. It has kept men in general from recognizing that our life and thought is based more nearly and actually on the middle ages than on distant Greece and Rome, from whom our heritage is more indirect, bookish and sentimental, less institutional, social, religious, even less economic and experimental.

But what is the use of questioning the Renaissance? No one has ever proved its existence; no one has really tried to. So often as one phase of it or conception of it is disproved, or is shown to be equally characteristic of the preceding period, its defenders take up a new position and are just as happy, just as enthusiastic, just as complacent as ever.

6
A SUGGESTED SYNTHESIS

W. K. Ferguson has recently defended the older interpretation of the Renaissance as an age of brilliant innovation, while taking note of the criticisms of the medievalists.

FROM The Reinterpretation of the Renaissance
BY W. K. FERGUSON

It should be understood, of course, that recognition of the Renaissance as a period in history does not imply that it was completely different from what preceded and what followed it. Even in a dynamic view of history, periodization may prove a very useful instrument if properly handled. The gradual changes brought about by a continuous historical development may be in large part changes in degree, but when they have progressed far enough they become for all practical purposes changes in kind. To follow a good humanist precedent and argue from the analogy of the human body, the gradual growth of man from childhood to maturity is an unbroken process, yet there is a recognizable difference between the man and the child he has been. Perhaps the analogy, as applied to the Middle Ages and the Renaissance, is unfortunate in that it suggests a value judgment that might be regarded as invidious. However that may be, it is my contention that by about the beginning of the fourteenth century in Italy and somewhat later in the North those elements in society which had set the tone of medieval culture had perceptibly lost their dominant position and thereafter gradually gave way to more recently developed forces. These, while active in the earlier period, had not

Wallace K. Ferguson, "The Reinterpretation of the Renaissance," in W. H. Werkmeister, ed., *Facets of the Renaissance* (1959), pp. 13–17. Reprinted by permission of University of Southern California, Los Angeles.

been the determining factors in the creation of medieval culture but were to be the most influential in shaping the culture of the Renaissance.

That somewhat involved statement brings me to the hazardous question of what were the fundamental differences between medieval and Renaissance civilization, and to the approach to the problem which I have found most generally satisfactory. It is an approach suggested by the work of the recent economic historians who have called attention to the dynamic influence of the revival of trade, urban life, and money economy in the midst of the agrarian feudal society of the high Middle Ages. Unfortunately, economic historians have seldom spared much thought for the development of intellectual and aesthetic culture, having been content to leave that to the specialists, while, on the other hand, the historians whose special interest was religion, philosophy, literature, science, or art have all too frequently striven to explain the developments in these fields without correlating them with changes in the economic, social, and political structure of society. In the past few years, however, historians have become increasingly aware of the necessity of including all forms of human activity in any general synthesis, an awareness illustrated by Myron Gilmore's recent volume on *The World of Humanism*. Further, there has been a growing tendency to find the original motive forces of historical development in basic alterations of the economic, political, and social system, which in time exert a limiting and directing influence upon intellectual interests, religious attitudes, and cultural forms. As applied to the Renaissance, this tendency has been evident in the work of several historians, notably, Edward P. Cheyney, Ferdinand Schevill, Eugenio Garin, Hans Baron, and some of the contributors to the *Propyläen Weltgeschichte*.

To state my point as briefly as possible, and therefore more dogmatically than I could wish: let us begin with the axiomatic premise that the two essential elements in medieval civilization were the feudal system and the universal church. The latter represented an older tradition than feudalism, but in its external structure and in many of its ideals and ways of thought it had been forced to adapt itself to the conditions of feudal society. And feudalism in turn was shaped by the necessity of adapting all forms of social and political life to the limitations of an agrarian and relatively moneyless economy. Into this agrarian feudal society the revival of commerce and industry, accompanied by the growth of towns and money economy, introduced a new and alien element. The first effect of this was to stimulate the existing medieval civilization, freeing it from the economic, social, and cultural restrictions that an almost exclusive dependence upon agriculture had imposed upon it, and making possible a rapid development in every branch of social and cultural activity. That the twelfth and thirteenth centuries were marked by the growth of a very vigorous culture no longer needs to be asserted. They witnessed the recovery of much ancient learning, the creation of scholastic philosophy, the rise of vernacular literatures and of Gothic art, perhaps on the whole a greater advance than was achieved in the two following centuries. Nevertheless, it seems to me that, despite new elements and despite rapid development, the civilization of these two centuries remained in form and spirit predominantly feudal and ecclesiastical.

But medieval civilization, founded as it was upon a basis of land tenure and agriculture, could not continue indefinitely to absorb an expanding urban society and money economy without losing its essential character, without gradually changing into something recognizably different. The changes were most obvious in the political sphere, as feudalism gave way before the rise of city states or centralized territorial states under princes who were learning to utilize the power of money. The effect upon the church was almost equally great. Its universal authority was shaken by the growing power of the national states, while its internal organization was transformed by the evolution of a monetary fiscal system which had, for a time, disastrous effects upon its moral character and prestige. Meanwhile, within the cities the growth of capital was bringing significant changes in the whole character of urban economic and social organizations, of which not the least significant was the appearance of a growing class of urban laymen who had the leisure and means to secure a liberal education and to take an active part in every form of intellectual and aesthetic culture.

Taking all these factors together, the result was an essential change in the character of European civilization. The feudal and ecclesiastical elements, though still strong, no longer dominated, and they were themselves more or less transformed by the changing conditions. The culture of the period we call the Renaissance was predominantly and increasingly the product of the cities, created in major part by urban laymen whose social environment, personal habits, and professional interests were different from those of the feudal and clerical aristocracy who had largely dominated the culture of the Middle Ages. These urban laymen, and with them the churchmen who were recruited from their midst as the medieval clergy had been recruited from the landed classes, did not break suddenly or completely with their inherited traditions, but they introduced new materials and restated the old in ways that reflected a different manner of life. The Renaissance, it seems to me, was essentially an age of transition, containing much that was still medieval, much that was recognizably modern, and, also, much that, because of the mixture of medieval and modern elements, was peculiar to itself and was responsible for its contradictions and contrasts and its amazing vitality.

This interpretation of the Renaissance leaves many of the old controversial points unanswered, though a partial answer to most of them is implied in it. It may be as well not to attempt to answer all questions with a single formula. There was certainly enough variety in the changing culture of western Europe during both the Middle Ages and the Renaissance to provide historians with material to keep them happily engaged in controversy for some time to come. All that can be claimed for the approach I have suggested is that it seems to offer the broadest basis for periodization, that it points to the most fundamental differences between the civilization of the Renaissance and the Middle Ages, while recognizing the dynamic character of both. At the same time, by suggesting a broad theory of causation in the gradual transformation of the economic and social structure of western Europe, it tends to reduce the controversial questions regarding the primary influence of the classical revival, of the Italian genius, Germanic blood, medieval French culture, or Franciscan mysticism to a secondary, if not irrelevant, status. Finally, such an approach to the problem might make it possible to take what was genuinely illuminating in Burckhardt, without the exaggerations of the classical-rational-Hegelian tradition, and also without the necessity of attacking the Renaissance *per se* in attacking Burckhardtian orthodoxy.

MARTIN LUTHER

REFORMER OR REVOLUTION-ARY?

CONTENTS

QUESTIONS FOR STUDY

1. *What was Luther's position on the relation of God to man?*

2. *To what extent was Luther heretical before the indulgence controversy?*

3. *What, according to Luther, was the true liberty of a Christian?*

4. *What role in the making of the Reformation do the various historians cited assign to Luther?*

5. *Would there have been a Reformation if Martin Luther had never lived?*

The advent of the Protestant Reformation is generally taken to mark the end of the Middle Ages in northern Europe and the beginnings of the modern world. The unity of Western Christendom was destroyed and one of the most important medieval ideals—that of the unified, Christian, Catholic empire—was dealt a death blow. In its place emerged the idea of the nation-state in which, ultimately, the religion of the state became a question of national policy. The sixteenth-century formula *cujus regio, ejus religio* ("the religion of the ruler shall be the religion of the ruled") explicitly acknowledged the breakdown of the monopoly of religious truth and practice exercised by the Catholic Church for more than a millennium. From this breakdown was to emerge the emphasis upon individual conscience, religious tolerance, and awareness of cultural and national differences that marks the modern world.

The Reformation was a revolution of considerable magnitude. Moreover, all the aforementioned modern elements, except tolerance, were present in the "prerevolutionary" times. Martin Luther's individual conscience was what drove him into religious orders and ultimately into religious rebellion. Luther was intensely German in his outlook and was quite aware of the cultural gulf between Germany and Latin Christendom. The national question was also present in the Germany of the early sixteenth century. German gold flowed to Rome and the Germans resented it. The policies and politics of Rome influenced the German scene and some of the German princes resented this too. Finally, the ideal of Christian unity, which was to appeal so strongly to Charles V, elected Holy Roman Emperor in 1519, was a threat to the independence of these princes, and it has been argued that they protected Luther and embraced Protestantism less because of sincere religious belief than because of political expediency. All of this has led some historians to see the Protestant Reformation as both inevitable and impersonal. The Reformation, they argue, was the inevitable result of the economic, social, and political development of Germany in the fifteenth century. If it had not been initiated by Martin Luther, it would have been started by someone else. Luther just happened to be the one who threw down the challenge to the church.

It is, of course, impossible to answer the question "Would the Reformation have occurred if Luther had never lived?" since Luther did live and there is no way to alter that. We can, however, question the answer given by those who would make Luther a mere cipher in the coming of the Reformation. After all, the church had been corrupt in previous ages and had been successfully reformed. Other times had witnessed resentment of Rome and princes jealous of their powers without also undergoing irreparable schism. Might not the difference between these times and the early sixteenth century be precisely the presence of one man, Martin Luther? This is not to say that Luther, singlehandedly, made the Reformation. But it is to suggest that there were essential ingredients in the Reformation that owed their existence to the personal and unique experiences of Martin Luther. Not the least of these ingredients was Luther's determination to purify the faith. We can legitimately ask a number of questions about this aspect of the Reformation, and we may also expect to find historical evidence to permit us to draw some rather firm conclusions from it. For example, did Luther's initial hostility to Rome derive from any of the abovementioned social, economic, and political "sources" of the Reformation, or were they much more personal? Did the selling of indulgences trigger Luther's attack on corruption in Rome, or was this merely the occasion for Luther to launch a much more fundamental attack against theoretical theology rather than corrupt practice? Finally, did Luther really believe that he could *reform* the church? Certainly all the public issues were negotiable. What was not was Luther's private conviction that he had found the way to salvation and that this way, to put it mildly, appeared to conflict with the traditional way of the Catholic Church. It was this private conviction that sustained Luther in the years of battle that were to ensue. As historians we may legitimately ask its source from the historical evidence, and if we discover it, we may then attempt to understand how such a private conviction could receive such widespread public support.

The problem posed by the documents that follow is central to all historical investigation. It involves the question of the role of the individual in historical crises and, as a subsidiary issue, the question of whether an individual actually knows what he is doing. For even if we accept the thesis that Luther, the man, was essential to the Reformation, we must still ask to what extent Luther was merely the vehicle for the expression of more general social or psychological forces. The reader should be aware of the fact that no answer can be proven but that some answer must be given. How he decides will affect his interpretation of the past and his actions in the present.

1
THE ROAD
TO
REFORMATION

The English historian Gordon Rupp puts Luther and the problems facing him at the very outset of the Reformation in historical perspective.

FROM The Righteousness of God BY GORDON RUPP

It was a critical moment during the Leipzig Disputation (1519) when Martin Luther, out-manoeuvred by his opponent, Dr. Eck, was goaded into declaring that "among the articles of John Huss . . . which were condemned, are many which are truly Christian." The audience was horrified, and perhaps Luther himself was a little shocked. For he had grown to accept the judgment of contemporary opinion against the heretic of a former generation. "I used to abhor the very name of Huss. So zealous was I for the Pope that I would have helped to bring iron and fire to kill Huss, if not in very deed, at least with a consenting mind." In this verdict faith and party loyalty combined, for the Erfurt Augustinians were proud that a member of their own order, John Zachariae, had earned the title "Scourge of Huss" and his tomb bore in effigy the Golden Rose bestowed upon him by a grateful Pope. It was not until Luther himself entered a similar context of Papal condemnation that he turned to examine the writings of Huss, and to criticize this unexamined assumption. Then indeed he could cry to Spalatin, "We are all Hussites, without knowing it . . . even Paul and Augustine!"

Luther did not know that in later centuries, a similar weight of received opinion would lie against himself, and that faith and party loyalty, formi-

Gordon Rupp, *The Righteousness of God: Luther Studies* (1953), pp. 3–15. Reprinted by permission of Hodder & Stoughton Ltd., London.

dable vested interests of the mind, would come to obscure the truth about himself. To every age there belong mental patterns, involving assumptions about causes and persons, for the most part accepted without reference to the canons of historical criticism, and even the expert in one particular field of historical investigation is bound to take over certain general assumptions when he considers matters beyond his own exact knowledge. Yet it is needful for the soul's health of any culture that there should exist places where these assumptions may be roughly handled. Above all, it would seem that Universities might be centres of vigorous and unremitting self-criticism, where there are few closed questions, and where at any time a case may be heard afresh, if it can reasonably be shown that evidence has been ignored, or that new facts have been brought to light.

There are reasons why a good deal of received academic opinion should be unfriendly towards Martin Luther. There is the modern reaction against the judgments of the Victorian Age, not least among those who have shed the Protestantism of their fathers. The virile theological tradition deriving from the Oxford Movement has made great and positive theological contributions to English religion, but from the time of Hurrell Froude onwards, its "blind spot" has been a rigid, narrow and wooden hostility towards the Reformers and their works. Then there is the tradition of the liberal historians with their wistful preference for a Reformation "along Erasmian lines" which, they consider, might have been, but for the violent intervention of Luther and his friends. To the liberal historians and theologians, aloof from theology and dogma, Martin Luther could hardly be a congenial figure. The events of our generation have hardly disposed us to a sympathetic judgment of the course of German history, and made only too plausible the arguments of those who derive all our ills from the Reformation, and not a few from the influence of Martin Luther.

The case for the reconsideration of Luther is that all these judgments, good or ill, rest upon an insufficient consideration of facts. Of the many thousands of Luther's writings, hardly more than a score have been available in English throughout the greater part of four centuries. There has been little awareness of the problems and discoveries of modern Luther study which both in detail and in principle have been of a quality and intricacy high among historical disciplines, second only, it may be, to that of Biblical criticism.

Reconsideration must not prejudge the issue. It must be confessed that so much of the writing about Luther in four centuries has been polemical that it is very difficult not to be on the defensive, or offensive, about him. When Protestants admit faults, and Catholics virtues, in his character, these concessions are bound to be taken from their context and used for polemical purposes. Yet we have the soundest reasons for supposing that an infallible Luther is no part of any Protestant confession. It was a disciple of Melanchthon, Joachim Camerarius, who wrote, "Those who count it a reproach to great and famous people when anything blameworthy is found in them, have too soft a conception of the position of such people. For only God has this privilege, to be without a fault: human nature is not capable of it."

When we have confessed that loyalty and party judgment are inevitably involved, we must face more formidable difficulties. There is first, the vastness of the material to be mastered. . . . A sound historical background: familiarity with secular and ecclesiastical history, and with dogmatic theology, including a more than nodding acquaintance with late scholasticism: a knowledge of Protestant theology in its origin and development. These are essential preliminaries. Then, leaving out of account secondary studies (in half a dozen languages) which run into thousands, there remain the works of Luther himself.

We know that at the Diet of Worms, the Emperor Charles V and the Papal Nuncio, Alexander, were reluctant to believe that the pile of Luther's works heaped before them could have been the work of one man in a few months. Yet that man continued to produce something like a treatise a fortnight over the next twenty-five years. As the great Weimar edition with ninety-four folio volumes draws within sight of completion, we admire a feat of theological engineering, but we remember that such engineering achievements are never finished, always under repair, and that often the beginning is in need of amendment while the work is being finished. So it seems to be with the works of Luther. . . .

If the historian has a mass of material of undoubted authenticity, there is a penumbra which is his titillation and despair. There are many volumes of sermons and lectures by Luther which we possess only in their reported form, and some, like a great part of the Genesis commentary, were published only after Luther's death. The historian is constantly tempted to have his cake, and eat it. But if he rejects the "Sermon on Marriage" (1519) for the sound reason that it is a pirated version very strongly repudiated by Luther, then he has also to admit that Luther did not sponsor the most famous of all sayings attributed to him, the famous "Hier stehe ich: ich kann nicht anders." [*Here I stand: I cannot do otherwise—L. P. W.*]

Above all, there is the nice problem of the Table Talk. One hardly knows whether to be grateful or not for that hospitality of Luther which allowed a motley club of inferior Boswells to frequent his table, and that their garbled remembrances have, in sundry portions and in divers manners, been transmitted to posterity. We know how it irked Frau Luther to play Martha to half a dozen male Marys who made Luther talk while the food got cold. And we know how they intruded into the most domestic privacies, as in that solemn hour when Luther's beloved Magdalena lay dying in her father's arms. But they were all made welcome: the Wittenberg theologians as and when they could come: including, of course, the Melanchthons, though Frau Luther seldom could forget that while she was a Von Bora, Frau Melanchthon was the daughter of a small town mayor. There came travelling scholars and distinguished refugees, and the students. And then, from 1530 onwards, the reporters. Cordatus perhaps, seven years the senior of Luther, irascible and ungracious, a teutonic Crawley of Hogglestock: or the melancholy Schlaginhaufen, always in the dumps, but who softened Kate Luther's tongue because, really, he was wonderful with the children. And Mathesius, that enterprising young usher who smuggled some of his pupils to Luther's table until the master of the house decided that this was a little too much, even for Liberty Hall.

It is very tantalizing. Here is richly personal material, offering again and again to fill critical gaps in our knowledge. We are tempted to select what suits us, and to complain when others do the same. Moreover, while the conscious mind may reject testimony, or suspend judgment, the mind is subtly influenced by reading. Not that we need to be too sceptical. Enough of the real Luther has got into even the most dubious collections. But on the whole it is safer to use the Table Talk to confirm rather than to establish, and not to use it as a sufficient source for Luther's exact words or technical vocabulary. Modern research has established a pedigree of the sources, and brought to light some of the original note-books, so that the Weimar edition has a careful compilation in six volumes. But there it all is: letters, sermons, tracts, commentaries, polemic, Table Talk providing material so heterogeneous that select quotation can support the most varied and opposite interpretations.

Luther's method aggravates the difficulty. In a preface to the Book of Exodus Luther has words about Moses, and his apparent inconsistencies, which apply also to himself. "Moses writes as the case demands, so that his book is a picture and illustration of government and life. For this is what happens when things are moving . . . now this work has to be done, and now that . . . and a man must be ready every hour for anything, and do the first thing that comes to hand. The books of Moses are mixed up in just this way." Luther's writing is invariably called forth by a concrete, particular historical occasion: he had neither the leisure nor the talent to produce a systematized text-book, after the manner of the "Loci Communes" of Melanchthon, or the "Institutes" of Calvin. When we consider how for Luther, as for Moses, things were moving (between 1517 and 1546), we need not wonder that historians and theologians have found it hard to reconcile apparent differences, or driven wedges between various sections of his life.

Then there is the difficulty of Luther's personal character. When Frederick the Wise met Erasmus at Cologne in November 1520 and asked for a plain judgment on Luther, he got instead an enigmatic epigram which drove him to complain, "What a wonderful little man that is! You never know where you are with him." That kind of reticence was completely foreign to Luther, about whom even his enemy Duke George had to admit "those people at Wittenberg are at least not mealy-mouthed. They do say what they really mean, frankly and straightforwardly." The result is that for good and ill, what Luther thought came straight out, and his few attempts to be subtle, or to restrain himself, usually ended in tragi-comedy. Like St. Jerome, Luther had a physical excuse, especially in his last years, for his tantrums. But some of his best, as well as his worst, writing was done in the heat of righteous anger. When his blood was up, he would charge into battle, and when he did, his pen was not so much a sword as the spiked club with which Holbein pictures him as the Hercules Germanicus. And when the first impetus had spent itself, sheer pig-headedness might keep him going, while on such occasions he delighted to greet the scared expostulations of his timid friends with something really shocking. For he was a thorough polemic divine, and not Rabelais or Sir Thomas More had more violent and varied ways of calling a spade a spade. His sense of humour was elephantine, large and clumsy, and since it was often misunderstood by his contemporaries, it can be imagined what a mine of potential misconception it bequeathed to owl-like theologians fumbling with what is called "the jocular element in Luther."

There is a good deal in the controversial writings of Luther which repels and disgusts, and polemic has made the most of it. Yet to concentrate the muck in a few pages is to give a completely false impression. Certainly the Luther of the polemical writings is not the whole Luther. We must turn elsewhere to find the surprising reticences, the unexpected mildness, the swift contritions, and the melancholy so closely related to his fun. He had no sympathy with the obscenities of humanist literature.

Finally, there is the whole matter of the Reformation. We read our Luther according to our interpretation of the sixteenth century. "Luther apart from the Reformation would cease to be Luther," wrote Hare. "His work was not something external to him. . . . It was his own very self, that grew out of him, while he grew out of his work. Wherefore they who do not rightly estimate the Reformation cannot rightly understand Luther." But "rightly to understand the Reformation" is a great complexity.

The distinction is capital between the historical Luther—what Luther was, and did, and said; and the Luther myth—what men have believed he said, and did, and was. The historical Luther made an abiding impress on European history, and the story of the Western Church. But what men have believed about Luther throughout four centuries is itself a "factor in modern history." And the Luther of this creative tradition is a different Luther from the figure with whom a modern historian grapples from within an elaborate critical apparatus. The modern historian is confronted with the whole range of Luther's writings, but over most of four centuries very much of this material has been inert, dormant, unknown to more than a tiny band of scholars. Those early Latin commentaries, so precious to modern scholarship, were unheeded for many generations, and their influence on history has been far less than the garbled collection of Aurifaber's Table Talk, with its numerous editions and translations. Nobody can weigh imponderables, but it is possible that "Eyn feste Burg" and the little Catechism have influenced history more profoundly than all the rest of Luther's writings. And we have not only to ask what men read of Luther, but we have to remember what they neglected. We have to ask not only how well they understood him, but where they misunderstood him. Leaving on one side the perennial question whether

Melanchthon is the great expositor or perverter of the legacy of Martin Luther, there is much evidence that generations of Court chaplains expounded Luther's doctrine of "Obrigkeit" for the benefit of Protestant Princes and their subjects in a way which disastrously over-simplified Luther's profound and subtle teaching, and with far-reaching practical result. Thus the Luther myth, of legend and of caricature, many-sided, taking form and colour from the changing mental environment, has itself become a creative historical force. No interpretation of Luther can afford to ignore what Lutherans have believed about Martin Luther.

At the close of his great history of dogma, which he conceived to have been brought to an end by Luther, Adolf Harnack wrote, "Catholicism is not the Pope, neither is it the worship of saints, or the Mass, but it is the slavish dependence on tradition, and the false doctrines of sacrament, of repentance and of faith." But in Luther's own estimate of his work, the Pope occupied a more important place, to which the famous epitaph of the Reformer bears witness:

> Pestis eram vivus, moriens ero mors tua, papa.
> [Living I was thy plague, dying I shall be thy death, O Pope.]

If we are to understand Luther's violence against the Papacy we must treat this inscription seriously, and recognize that for the sixteenth century Lutherans, Luther and the Pope are "apocalyptic figures within the action of the history of salvation."

Luther prided himself on the fact that while others had attacked the manners and the morals of particular popes, or the abuses and corruptions of the Curia, he had begun with doctrine. We know that in its essentials Luther's theology existed before the opening of the Church struggle in 1517, and that it was not an improvization devised in the course of that conflict. Nevertheless, it was as the conflict developed out of the Indulgence controversy that he began to question the basis of the Papal power, and turned to the issues raised in a preceding generation by the theologians of the Conciliar movement, the question whether the Papacy were of divine or of human institution. Early in 1519 he could still write, "If unfortunately there are such things in Rome as might be improved, there neither is, nor can be, any reason that one should tear oneself away from the Church in schism. Rather, the worse things become, the more a man should help, and cling to her, for by schism and contempt nothing can be mended." In fateful weeks before the Leipzig Disputation, Luther studied church history and the Papal decretals. On 13th March 1519 he wrote to his friend Spalatin, "I do not know whether the Pope is Anti-Christ himself, or only his apostle, so grievously is Christ, i.e. Truth, manhandled and crucified by him in these decretals."

The Leipzig Disputation forced Luther to face the implications of his revolt, and made him realize that he could not come so far, without going further in repudiation of papal authority. Then, early in 1520, he read Hut-

ten's edition of Valla's exposure of the "Donation of Constantine," and he
wrote in disgust, "I have hardly any doubt left that the Pope is the very Anti-
Christ himself, whom the common report expects, so well do all the things he
lives, does, speaks, ordains, fit the picture."

In June 1520 he wrote solemn, final words, in a writing of exceptional
vehemence. "Farewell, unhappy, hopeless, blasphemous Rome! The wrath
of God is come upon thee, as thou deservest. . . . We have cared for Babylon, and she is not healed: let us leave her then, that she may be the habitation of dragons, spectres and witches, and true to her name of Babel, an
everlasting confusion, a new pantheon of wickedness."

There are battles of the mind which most men cannot go on fighting again
and again. We make up our minds, as we say, and the account is settled.
Thereafter we reopen that particular issue only with great reluctance. No
doubt this is a weakness of our spirit, though to be able to keep an open mind
requires perhaps detachment from the hurly-burly of decision, and is more
easily achieved in academic groves than in the battlefield or marketplace or
temple. Luther's words here perhaps show us the point at which he hardened
his mind with terrible finality against the Papacy, as later on he reached a
point at which Zwingli and Erasmus were to him as heathen men and publi-
cans. He had become convinced that the Papacy had become the tool of the
Devil, that it was blasphemous . . . "possessed and oppressed by Satan, the
damned seat of Anti-Christ."

The papacy which Luther attacked was not the Post-Tridentine papacy.
On the other hand, he meant something more when he called it "Anti-
Christ" than we mean by the adjective "Anti-Christian." Like many great
Christians from St. Cyprian to Lord Shaftesbury, Luther believed himself to
be living in the last age of the world, on the very edge of time. He believed
that the papacy was toppling to its doom, and that this fate was a merited
judgment upon a perversion of spiritual power to which there could be no
parallel in the temporal realm, and for which only one category would serve,
the Biblical category of Anti-Christ.

There are striking words in his "Of Good Works" (1520) which go to the
root of this conviction. "There is not such great danger in the temporal
power as in the spiritual, when it does wrong. For the temporal power can do
no harm, since it has nothing to do with preaching and faith, and the first
three commandments. But the spiritual power does harm not only when it
does wrong, but also when it neglects its duty and busies itself with other
things, even if they were better than the very best works of the temporal
power." For Luther the blessed thing for men and institutions is that they
should be where God intends them, doing what God has called them to do,
and the cursed thing for men and institutions is when they run amok in
God's ordered creation, going where God has not sent them, and occupied
with other things than their divine vocation.

The papacy had become entangled in diplomatic, juridical, political, financial pressure. Its crime was not that these things were necessarily bad in

themselves, but that for their sake the awful, supreme, God-given task of the pastoral care and the cure of souls had been neglected and forsaken. Two consequences had followed. In the first place, it had become a tyranny, like any other institution which succumbs before the temptation of power. In that exposition of the Magnificat, which was interrupted by the famous journey to Worms in 1521, Luther had profoundly diagnosed this corrupting effect of power upon institutions. The tract embodies Luther's reflections upon the fate of great Empires in the Bible and in secular history. It is not empire, but the abuse of it which is wrong. "For while the earth remains authority, rule, power . . . must needs remain. But God will not suffer men to abuse them. He puts down one kingdom, and exalts another: increases one people and destroys another: as he did with Assyria, Babylon, Persia, Greece and Rome, though they thought they should sit in their seats forever."

But when empire is abused, then power becomes an incentive to arrogance, and a terrible inflation begins. These institutions or individuals swell and stretch their authority with a curious bubble-like, balloon-like quality. Outwardly they seem omnipotent, and those who take them at their face value can be paralysed and brought into bondage to them. But in fact they are hollow shams, corroded from within, so that doom comes upon them, that swift collapse so often the fate of tyrants and empires. "When their bubble is full blown, and everyone supposes them to have won and overcome, and they feel themselves safe and secure, then God pricks the bubble . . . and it is all over . . . therefore their prosperity has its day, disappears like a bubble, and is as if it had never been." It is interesting that Shakespeare turns to the same metaphor when he describes the fall of Wolsey:

> I have ventured,
> Like little wanton boys that swim on bladders,
> This many summers in a sea of glory,
> But far beyond my depth: my high-blown pride
> At length broke under me.

Luther is fond of punning on the double meaning of the Latin word "Bulla," which means bubble, but also the papal bull.

It may well be that Luther's meditation on this quality of tyranny derives from his own experiences, 1517–20. The initial threat of excommunication, and the final promulgation of the papal bull had a deep significance for him. These were the challenge which focussed all his doubts and fears, and evoked his courage at a time when he had no reason to anticipate anything but the dire fate prophesied for him by friends and foes. But, in fact, these papal sanctions led to the revelation of the weakness of the papal authority, a revelation of immense significance, from which all over Christendom (not forgetting the England of Henry VIII) men could draw their own conclusions. It was not that a man could defy the papacy and get away with it. After all,

Wyclif had died in his bed, and throughout most of the Middle Ages there were parts of Europe where heresy flourished openly. But there was a new background which echoed and reverberated Luther's defiance, and a concentration of public attention on it which rallied great historical forces.

For centuries the papal sanctions had been as thunder and lightning, and there had been times and places when princes and peoples had cowered before them. Even now the sonorous phrases, the hallowed ritual, did not lack of menacing effect and struck deep into Luther's mind, always hypersensitive to words. The extraordinary agitation of his sermon, "On the Power of Excommunication" (1518), an utterance so outspoken that it was perhaps more effectual than the Ninety-five Theses in securing his impeachment, reveals the tension in his mind. It is noticeable that in the printed elaboration of this sermon he turns to the "bladder" motif. "They say . . . our Ban must be feared, right or wrong. With this saying they insolently comfort themselves, swell their chests, and puff themselves up like adders, and almost dare to defy heaven, and to threaten the whole world: with this bugaboo they have made a deep and mighty impression, imagining that there is more in these words than there really is. Therefore we would explain them more fully, and prick this bladder which with its three peas makes such a frightful noise." The publication of the Bull in 1520 evoked the same tension, and in his writings against it he affirms, "The Truth is asserting itself and will burst all the bladders of the Papists."

Only gradually did Luther and his friends realize how the world had changed since the days of Huss, that the Diet of Worms would not be as the Council of Constance, though the devout Charles V might be as anxious to dispose of heretics as any Emperor Sigismund. Now the accumulated weight of the past intervened, with paralysing effect. An enormous moral prestige had been frittered away, and the papal authority was revealed as a weak thing in comparison with the deep moving tide of anti-clericalism, nationalism and the fierce energies of a changing society.

But the papacy is for Luther not simply a tyranny, which can be described, as a liberal historian might describe it, in terms of the corrupting influence of power. Its tyranny is of a unique kind, for which there can only be one category, the demonic, Biblical category of Anti-Christ. By its entanglement with law and politics, the papacy has brought the souls of men and women into bondage, has confused disastrously the Law and Gospel, has become the antithesis of the Word of God which comes to free and liberate men's souls. Thus he cannot regard the papacy simply as a corrupt institution, as did the mediaeval moralists and the heretics. In Luther's later writings the papacy is included along with the Law, Sin and Death among the tyrants who beset the Christians, and is part of a view of salvation which demands an apocalyptic interpretation of history.

Two sets of Luther's writings are of special virulence: those against the Jews, the apostates of the Old Israel, and those against the Pope, the apostate of the New. Against what he considered the capital sin of blasphemy Luther turned all his invective. It is noticeable that like Ezekiel, he turned to an imagery of physical repulsion. Blasphemy and apostasy are not simply evil: they are filthy things, which must be described in language coarse enough and repulsive enough to nauseate the reader. That is not in any sense to excuse Luther's language, or to justify his reading of the papacy. But those' sadly over-simplify who see in these tracts the vapourings of a dirty mind.

Luther's epitaph was premature. He had indeed plagued the papacy. He could say, "While I slept or drank Wittenberg beer with my Philip and my Amsdorf, the Word so greatly weakened the Papacy that never Prince or Emperor inflicted such damage on it." He did not kill the papacy, but in strange partnership with Ignatius Loyola, the Popes of the Counter-Reformation, the Society of Jesus, not to mention the Anabaptists, he had provoked a new historical pattern which made an end, for good and all, of the peculiar perversions of the later Middle Ages. But I think we can understand how it seemed to him that the papacy was doomed and dying, how it seemed to him the engine of Satin, the embodiment of Anti-Christ in what he believed to be the closing act of the human drama.

If the papacy belongs to the dramatic, dualistic, apocalyptic view of history, the rôle of Luther himself belonged to the same setting. . . . It goes back to the moment when Melanchthon broke the news of Luther's death to the students at Wittenberg with "Alas, gone is the horseman and the chariots of Israel."

For this first generation (which included the first sketches of Luther's career by Melanchthon, Bugenhagen, Jonas, Mathesius), Luther is, as for Coelius, "a veritable Elijah and a John the Baptist, whom God has sent before the Great Day." Both Melanchthon and Mathesius drew upon Luther's own interpretation of history, the conception of the "Wundermann," the inspired hero, and the theme of the Word going forth conquering and to conquer. For Melanchthon, Luther stands within a long succession which began with the patriarchs and which includes the great Fathers of the Church, men sent by God, one after another, "just as those who fall in an order of battle, are replaced by others."

We should expect, that as the contemporaries of Luther passed from the scene, there should be a diminishing sense of the personality of the Reformer. The change was accelerated by the fact that the Lutheran Churches were now fighting for their existence, and finding a dogmatic norm in their great Confessional Documents (which included the Catechisms, and the Schmalkaldic Articles of Luther). The result was an emphasis upon those confessional documents and upon the pure doctrine to which they witnessed which led in the seventeenth century to a remarkable neglect of the writings of Luther himself. This was the period of fierce dogmatic strife between disparate elements within the Lutheran tradition, evoking Shakespeare's reference to "spleeny Lutherans," and reaching comedy when Cyriacus Spangenberg interpreted Luther's famous hymn:

Erhalt uns, Herr, bei deinem Wort,
Und steur des Papsts und Türken Mord

to mean "all our enemies are to be understood by these two titles (Papists and Turks) . . . Interimists, Adiaphorists, Sacramentarians, Anabaptists, Calvinists, Osiandrists, Schwenckfeldists, Stancarists, Servetianists, Sabbatarians, Davidists, Majorists, Synergists, etc., etc."! . . . Luther's teaching, reflected by the Confessions, became more important than Luther. "He acquired his own stereotyped work, which belonged to him, like the Wheel of St. Catherine, or the Dragon of St. George. . . . He lost his individual proportions and grew into the superhuman and mythical . . . the greatness of his work pushed him into the background."

The polemic of the Counter-Reformation did useful service in preventing the Luther myth from escaping altogether from its connection with history. A century after the beginning of the Reformation Johann Gerard disputed with Becanus and Bellarmine about the "Vocation of Luther" and had to admit the test of accuracy: "if Luther's writings can be shown to be lying, erroneous and false, then we shall at once recognize that Luther was no prophet."

2
LUTHER
BEFORE THE
CONTROVERSY
OVER
INDULGENCES

The Reuchlin case, to which Luther alludes in this letter, is one of considerable complexity, involving the place of Hebraic studies in Christian theology. This issue need not concern us here; what is important is Luther's attitude toward both Reuchlin's approach—which he was to imitate when he
proposed the Ninety-Five Theses for debate in 1517—and the importance of
Scripture.

Martin Luther's Letter to George Spalatin

Wittenberg (January or February, 1514).
Peace be with you, Reverend Spalatin! Brother John Lang has just asked me
what I think of the innocent and learned John Reuchlin and his prosecutors
at Cologne, and whether he is in danger of heresy. You know that I greatly
esteem and like the man, and perchance my judgment will be suspected,
because, as I say, I am not free and neutral; nevertheless as you wish it I will
give my opinion, namely that in all his writings there appears to me absolutely nothing dangerous.
I much wonder at the men of Cologne ferreting out such an obscure perplexity, worse tangled than the Gordian knot as they say, in a case as plain as
day. Reuchlin himself has often protested his innocence, and solemnly asserts
he is only proposing questions for debate, not laying down articles of faith,

Luther's Correspondence and other Contemporary Letters, I (1913), 28–29, translated and edited
by Preserved Smith. Reprinted by permission of Fortress Press.

which alone, in my opinion, absolves him, so that had he the dregs of all known heresies in his memorial, I should believe him sound and pure of faith. For if such protests and expressions of opinion are not free from danger, we must needs fear that these inquisitors, who strain at gnats though they swallow camels, should at their own pleasure pronounce the orthodox heretics, no matter how much the accused protested their innocence.

What shall I say? that they are trying to cast out Beelzebub but not by the finger of God. I often regret and deplore that we Christians have begun to be wise abroad and fools at home. A hundred times worse blasphemies than this exist in the very streets of Jerusalem, and the high places are filled with spiritual idols. We ought to show our excessive zeal in removing these offences which are our real, intestine enemies. Instead of which we abandon all that is really urgent and turn to foreign and external affairs, under the inspiration of the devil who intends that we should neglect our own business without helping that of others.

Pray can anything be imagined more foolish and imprudent than such zeal? Has unhappy Cologne no waste places nor turbulence in her own church, to which she could devote her knowledge, zeal and charity, that she must needs search out such cases as this in remote parts?

But what am I doing? My heart is fuller of these thoughts than my tongue can tell. I have come to the conclusion that the Jews will always curse and blaspheme God and his King Christ, as all the prophets have predicted. He who neither reads nor understands this, as yet knows no theology, in my opinion. And so I presume the men of Cologne cannot understand the Scripture, because it is necessary that such things take place to fulfill prophecy. If they are trying to stop the Jews blaspheming, they are working to prove the Bible and God liars.

But trust God to be true, even if a million men of Cologne sweat to make him false. Conversion of the Jews will be the work of God alone operating from within, and not of man working—or rather playing—from without. If these offences be taken away, worse will follow. For they are thus given over by the wrath of God to reprobation, that they may become incorrigible, as Ecclesiastes says, for every one who is incorrigible is rendered worse rather than better by correction.

Farewell in the Lord; pardon my words, and pray the Lord for my sinning soul.

Your brother,
Martin Luther

Spenlein was a fellow Augustinian brother to whom Luther could reveal his most intimate thoughts on theology and the relation of man to God. The date (April 8, 1516) is significant, a year and a half before Luther posted his Ninety-Five Theses.

Martin Luther's Letter to George Spenlein

Wittenberg, April 8, 1516.

Grace and peace to you from God the Father and the Lord Jesus Christ. Dear Brother George:

Now I would like to know whether your soul, tired of her own righteousness, would learn to breathe and confide in the righteousness of Christ. For in our age the temptation to presumption besets many, especially those who try to be just and good before all men, not knowing the righteousness of God, which is most bountifully and freely given us in Christ. Thus they long seek to do right by themselves, that they may have courage to stand before God as though fortified with their own virtues and merits, which is impossible. You yourself were of this opinion, or rather error, and so was I, who still fight against the error and have not yet conquered it.

Therefore, my sweet brother, learn Christ and him crucified; learn to pray to him despairing of yourself, saying: Thou, Lord Jesus, art my righteousness, but I am thy sin; thou hast taken on thyself what thou wast not, and hast given to me what I was not. Beware of aspiring to such purity that you will not wish to seem to yourself, or to be, a sinner. For Christ only dwells in sinners. For that reason he descended from heaven, where he dwelt among the righteous, that he might dwell among sinners. Consider that kindness of his, and you will see his sweetest consolation. . . .

If you firmly believe this (and he is accursed who does not believe it) then take up your untaught and erring brothers, patiently uphold them, make their sins yours, and, if you have any goodness, let it be theirs. Thus the apostle teaches: Receive one another even as Christ received you, for the glory of God, and again: Have this mind in you which was also in Christ Jesus, who, when he was in the form of God, humbled himself, &c. Thus do you, if you seem pretty good to yourself, not count it as booty, as though it were yours alone, but humble yourself, forget what you are, and be as one of them that you may carry them. . . . Do this, my brother, and the Lord be with you. Farewell in the Lord.

Your brother,
Martin Luther, Augustinian

Luther's Correspondence and other Contemporary Letters, I (1913), 33–35, translated and edited by Preserved Smith. Reprinted by permission of Fortress Press.

Luther, as a professor of theology, had been thoroughly grounded in the Scholastic philosophy of the Middle Ages. Of the three pillars upon which Scholastic theology rested—Scripture, the writings of the church fathers, and the philosophy of Aristotle—Scripture had become increasingly de-emphasized by Luther's time. It was to remind men that the central point of the scriptural message was not the achievement of philosophical distinctions but the salvation of man's soul that Luther composed his disputation against Scholastic theology in 1517.

Disputation Against Scholastic Theology
BY MARTIN LUTHER

It is therefore true that man, being a bad tree, can only will and do evil. [Cf. Matt. 7:17–18.]

It is false to state that man's inclination is free to choose between either of two opposites. Indeed, the inclination is not free, but captive. This is said in opposition to common opinion.

It is false to state that the will can by nature conform to correct precept. . . .

As a matter of fact, without the grace of God the will produces an act that is perverse and evil.

It does not, however, follow that the will is by nature evil, that is, essentially evil, as the Manichaeans maintain.

It is nevertheless innately and inevitably evil and corrupt.

* * *

No act is done according to nature that is not an act of concupiscence against God.

Every act of concupiscence against God is evil and a fornication of the spirit.

* * *

The best and infallible preparation for grace and the sole means of obtaining grace is the eternal election and predestination of God.

On the part of man, however, nothing precedes grace except ill will and even rebellion against grace.

* * *

Helmut T. Lehmann and Jaroslav Pelikan, general eds., *Luther's Works*, XXXI (1957), 9–12, edited by Harold J. Grimm. Reprinted by permission of Fortress Press.

In brief, man by nature has neither correct precept nor good will.

It is not true that an invincible ignorance excuses one completely (all scholastics notwithstanding);

For ignorance of God and oneself and good works is by nature always invincible.

Nature, moreover, inwardly and necessarily glories and takes pride in every work which is apparently and outwardly good.

There is no moral virtue without either pride or sorrow, that is, without sin.

We are never lords of our actions, but servants. This in opposition to the philosophers.

We do not become righteous by doing righteous deeds but, having been made righteous, we do righteous deeds. This in opposition to the philosophers.

Virtually the entire *Ethics* of Aristotle is the worst enemy of grace. This in opposition to the scholastics.

It is an error to maintain that Aristotle's statement concerning happiness does not contradict Catholic doctrine. This in opposition to the doctrine on morals.

It is an error to say that no man can become a theologian without Aristotle. This in opposition to common opinion.

Indeed, no one can become a theologian unless he becomes one without Aristotle.

To state that a theologian who is not a logician is a monstrous heretic—this is a monstrous and heretical statement. This in opposition to common opinion.

In vain does one fashion a logic of faith, a substitution brought about without regard for limit and measure. This in opposition to the new dialecticians.

No syllogistic form is valid when applied to divine terms. . . .

Nevertheless it does not for that reason follow that the truth of the doctrine of the Trinity contradicts syllogistic forms. . . .

If a syllogistic form of reasoning holds in divine matters, then the doctrine of the Trinity is demonstrable and not the object of faith.

Briefly, the whole Aristotle is to theology as darkness is to light. This in opposition to the scholastics.

3
LUTHER
AND THE BREAK
WITH ROME

The doctrine of indulgences had a long history before Luther posted his opposition to it on October 31, 1517. It was based on Matthew 16:18–19: "Thou art Peter, and upon this rock I will build my church; and the gates of hell shall not prevail against it. And I will give unto thee the keys of the kingdom of heaven: and whatsoever thou shalt bind on earth shall be bound in heaven: and whatsoever thou shalt loose on earth shall be loosed in heaven."

Thus Christ granted to St. Peter (and to his successors, the popes) the power to remit the penalties for sins. This power was eagerly exploited by the Renaissance popes, who found themselves in almost constant financial difficulties.

Luther's challenge to debate the doctrine of indulgences, however, was not restricted to a narrow issue. It ranged over many fundamental points of church doctrine. Did Luther really believe that such basic things could be reformed? Or, without really facing up to it, must he not have known that he was proposing nothing less than a revolution?

Ninety-Five Theses BY MARTIN LUTHER

Out of love and zeal for truth and the desire to bring it to light, the following theses will be publicly discussed at Wittenberg under the chairmanship of the

Helmut T. Lehmann and Jaroslav Pelikan, general eds., *Luther's Works*, XXXI (1957), 25–29, 33, edited by Harold J. Grimm. Reprinted by permission of Fortress Press.

reverend father Martin Luther, Master of Arts and Sacred Theology and regularly appointed Lecturer on these subjects at that place. He requests that those who cannot be present to debate orally with us will do so by letter.

In the Name of Our Lord Jesus Christ. Amen.

When our Lord and Master Jesus Christ said, "Repent" [Matt. 4:17], he willed the entire life of believers to be one of repentance.

This word cannot be understood as referring to the sacrament of penance, that is, confession and satisfaction, as administered by the clergy.

Yet it does not mean solely inner repentance; such inner repentance is worthless unless it produces various outward mortifications of the flesh.

The penalty of sin remains as long as the hatred of self, that is, true inner repentance, until our entrance into the kingdom of heaven.

The pope neither desires nor is able to remit any penalties except those imposed by his own authority or that of the canons.

The pope cannot remit any guilt, except by declaring and showing that it has been remitted by God; or, to be sure, by remitting guilt in cases reserved to his judgment. If his right to grant remission in these cases were disregarded, the guilt would certainly remain unforgiven.

* * *

The dying are freed by death from all penalties, are already dead as far as the canon laws are concerned, and have a right to be released from them.

Imperfect piety or love on the part of the dying person necessarily brings with it great fear; and the smaller the love, the greater the fear.

This fear or horror is sufficient in itself, to say nothing of other things, to constitute the penalty of purgatory, since it is very near the horror of despair.

Hell, purgatory, and heaven seem to differ the same as despair, fear, and assurance of salvation.

* * *

If remission of all penalties whatsoever could be granted to anyone at all, certainly it would be granted only to the most perfect, that is, to very few.

For this reason most people are necessarily deceived by that indiscriminate and high-sounding promise of release from penalty.

* * *

The pope does very well when he grants remission to souls in purgatory, not by the power of the keys, which he does not have, but by way of intercession for them.

They preach only human doctrines who say that as soon as the money clinks into the money chest, the soul flies out of purgatory.

It is certain that when money clinks in the money chest, greed and avarice can be increased; but when the church intercedes, the result is in the hands of God alone.

* * *

Any truly repentant Christian has a right to full remission of penalty and guilt, even without indulgence letters.

Any true Christian, whether living or dead, participates in all the blessings of Christ and the church; and this is granted him by God, even without indulgence letters.

* * *

If, therefore, indulgences were preached according to the spirit and intention of the pope, all these doubts would be readily resolved. Indeed, they would not exist.

Away then with all those prophets who say to the people of Christ, "Peace, peace," and there is no peace! [Jer. 6:14.]

Blessed be all those prophets who say to the people of Christ, "Cross, cross," and there is no cross!

Christians should be exhorted to be diligent in following Christ, their head, through penalties, death, and hell;

And thus be confident of entering into heaven through many tribulations rather than through the false security of peace [Acts 14:22].

That Luther's position as stated in the Ninety-Five Theses involved more than technical and abstruse questions of theology can be seen in the reaction of the Holy Roman Emperor to Luther's proposed debate.

Maximilian's Letter to Leo X

Augsburg, August 5, 1518.

Most blessed Father and most revered Lord! We have recently heard that a certain Augustinian Friar, Martin Luther by name, has published certain theses on indulgences to be discussed in the scholastic way, and that in these theses he has taught much on this subject and concerning the power of papal excommunication, part of which appears injurious and heretical, as has been noted by the Master of your sacred palace. This has displeased us the more because, as we are informed, the said friar obstinately adheres to his doctrine, and is said to have found several defenders of his errors among the great.

And as suspicious assertions and dangerous dogmas can be judged by no

Luther's Correspondence and other Contemporary Letters, I (1913), 98, translated and edited by Preserved Smith. Reprinted by permission of Fortress Press.

one better, more rightly and more truly than by your Holiness, who alone is able and ought to silence the authors of vain questions, sophisms and wordy quarrels, than which nothing more pestilent can happen to Christianity, for these men consider only how to magnify what they have taught, so your Holiness can maintain the sincere and solid doctrine approved by the consensus of the more learned opinion of the present age and of those who formerly died piously in Christ.

There is an ancient decree of the Pontifical College on the licensing of teachers, in which there is no provision whatever against sophistry, save in case the decretals are called in question, and whether it is right to teach that, the study of which has been disapproved by many and great authors.

Since, therefore, the authority of the Popes is disregarded, and doubtful, or rather erroneous opinions are alone received, it is bound to occur that those little fanciful and blind teachers should be led astray. And it is due to them that not only are many of the more solid doctors of the Church not only neglected, but even corrupted and mutilated.

We do not mention that these authors hatch many more heresies than were ever condemned. We do not mention that both Reuchlin's trial and the present most dangerous dispute about indulgences and papal censures have been brought forth by these pernicious authors. If the authority of your Holiness and of the most reverend fathers does not put an end to such doctrines, soon their authors will not only impose on the unlearned multitude, but will win the favor of princes, to their mutual destruction. If we shut our eyes and leave them the field open and free, it will happen, as they chiefly desire, that the whole world will be forced to look on their follies instead of on the best and most holy doctors.

Of our singular reverence for the Apostolic See, we have signified this to your Holiness, so that simple Christianity may not be injured and scandalized by these rash disputes and captious arguments. Whatever may be righteously decided upon in this our Empire, we will make all our subjects obey for the praise and honor of God Almighty and the salvation of Christians.

The reaction that followed the publication of his Ninety-Five Theses forced Luther to define and defend his position in some detail. This he did in 1520 in the two treatises from which the following selections are taken. After their publication a reconciliation with Rome appeared doubtful.

FROM Address to the Christian Nobility of the German Nation BY MARTIN LUTHER

Grace and power from God, Most Illustrious Majesty, and most gracious and dear Lords.

It is not out of sheer forwardness or rashness that I, a single, poor man, have undertaken to address your worships. The distress and oppression which weigh down all the Estates of Christendom, especially of Germany, and which move not me alone, but everyone to cry out time and again, and to pray for help, have forced me even now to cry aloud that God may inspire some one with His Spirit to lend this suffering nation a helping hand. Ofttimes the councils have made some pretense at reformation, but their attempts have been cleverly hindered by the guile of certain men and things have gone from bad to worse. I now intend, by the help of God, to throw some light upon the wiles and wickedness of these men, to the end that when they are known, they may not henceforth be so hurtful and so great a hindrance. God has given us a noble youth to be our head and thereby has awakened great hopes of good in many hearts, wherefore it is meet that we should do our part and profitably use this time of grace.

In this whole matter the first and most important thing is that we take earnest heed not to enter on it trusting in great might or in human reason, even though all power in the world were ours; for God cannot and will not suffer a good work to be begun with trust in our own power or reason. Such works He crushes ruthlessly to earth, as it is written in the Thirty-third Psalm, "There is no king saved by the multitude of an host; a mighty man is not delivered by much strength." On this account, I fear, it came to pass of old that the good Emperors Frederick I and II and many other German emperors were shamefully oppressed and trodden under foot by the popes, although all the world feared them. It may be that they relied on their own might more than on God, and therefore they had to fall. In our own times, too, what was it that raised the bloodthirsty Julius II to such heights? Nothing else, I fear, except that France, the Germans and Venice relied upon

Martin Luther, *Three Treatises* (1947), pp. 10–16, 20–25. Reprinted by permission of Fortress Press.

themselves. The children of Benjamin slew 42,000 Israelites because the latter relied on their own strength.

That it may not so fare with us and our noble young Emperor Charles, we must be sure that in this matter we are dealing not with men, but with the princes of hell, who can fill the world with war and bloodshed, but whom war and bloodshed do not overcome. We must go at this work despairing of physical force and humbly trusting God; we must seek God's help with earnest prayer, and fix our minds on nothing else than the misery and distress of suffering Christendom, without regard to the deserts of evil men. Otherwise we may start the game with great prospect of success, but when we get well into it the evil spirits will stir up such confusion that the whole world will swim in blood, and yet nothing will come of it. Let us act wisely, therefore, and in the fear of God. The more force we use, the greater our disaster if we do not act humbly and in God's fear. The popes and the Romans have hitherto been able, by the devil's help, to set kings at odds with one another, and they may well be able to do it again, if we proceed by our own might and cunning, without God's help.

THE THREE WALLS OF THE ROMANISTS

The Romanists, with great adroitness, have built three walls about them, behind which they have hitherto defended themselves in such wise that no one has been able to reform them and this has been the cause of terrible corruption throughout all Christendom.

First, when pressed by the temporal power, they have made decrees and said that the temporal power has no jurisdiction over them, but, on the other hand, that the spiritual is above the temporal power. Second, when the attempt is made to reprove them out of the Scriptures, they raise the objection that the interpretation of the Scriptures belongs to no one except the pope. Third, if threatened with a council, they answer with the fable that no one can call a council but the pope.

In this wise they have slyly stolen from us our three rods, that they may go unpunished, and have ensconced themselves within the safe stronghold of these three walls, that they may practice all the knavery and wickedness which we now see. Even when they have been compelled to hold a council they have weakened its power in advance by previously binding the princes with an oath to let them remain as they are. Moreover, they have given the pope full authority over all the decisions of the council, so that it is all one whether there are many councils or no councils—except that they deceive us with puppet-shows and sham battles. So terribly do they fear for their skin in a really free council! And they have intimidated kings and princes by making them believe it would be an offense against God not to obey them in all these knavish, crafty deceptions.

Now God help us, and give us one of the trumpets with which the walls of

Jericho were overthrown, that we may blow down these walls of straw and paper, and may set free the Christian rods of the punishment of sin, bringing to light the craft and deceit of the devil, to the end that through punishment we may reform ourselves, and once more attain God's favor.

Against the *first wall* we will direct our first attack.

It is pure invention that pope, bishops, priests and monks are to be called the "spiritual estate"; princes, lords, artisans and farmers the "temporal estate." That is indeed a fine bit of lying and hypocrisy. Yet no one should be frightened by it and for this reason—viz., that all Christians are truly of the "spiritual estate," and there is among them no difference at all but that of office, as Paul says in I Corinthians 12. We are all one body, yet every member has its own work, whereby it serves every other, all because we have one baptism, one Gospel, one faith, and are all alike Christians; for baptism, Gospel, and faith alone make us "spiritual" and a Christian people.

But that a pope or a bishop anoints, confers tonsures, ordains, consecrates, or prescribes dress unlike that of the laity—this may make hypocrites and graven images, but it never makes a Christian or "spiritual" man. Through baptism all of us are consecrated to the priesthood, as St. Peter says in I Peter 2, "Ye are a royal priesthood, a priestly kingdom," and the book of Revelation says, "Thou hast made us by thy blood to be priests and kings." For if we had no higher consecration than pope or bishop gives, the consecration by pope or bishop would never make a priest, nor might anyone either say mass or preach a sermon or give absolution. Therefore when the bishop consecrates it is the same thing as if he, in the place and stead of the whole congregation, all of whom have like power, were to take one out of their number and charge him to use this power for the others; just as though ten brothers, all king's sons and equal heirs, were to choose one of themselves to rule the inheritance for them all—they would all be kings and equal in power, though one of them would be charged with the duty of ruling.

To make it still clearer. If a little group of pious Christian laymen were taken captive and set down in a wilderness, and had among them no priest consecrated by a bishop, and if there in the wilderness they were to agree in choosing one of themselves, married or unmarried, and were to charge him with the office of baptizing, saying mass, absolving and preaching, such a man would be as truly a priest as though all bishops and popes had consecrated him. That is why in cases of necessity anyone can baptize and give absolution, which would be impossible unless we were all priests. This great grace and power of baptism and of the Christian Estate they have well-nigh destroyed and caused us to forget through the canon law. It was in the manner aforesaid that Christians in olden days chose from their number bishops and priests, who were afterwards confirmed by other bishops, without all the show which now obtains. It was thus that Sts. Augustine, Ambrose, and Cyprian became bishops.

Since, then, the temporal authorities are baptized with the same baptism and have the same faith and Gospel as we, we must grant that they are priests and bishops, and count their office one which has a proper and a useful place in the Christian community. For whoever comes out of the water of baptism can boast that he is already consecrated priest, bishop, and pope, though it is not seemly that everyone should exercise the office. Nay, just because we are all in like manner priests, no one must put himself forward and undertake, without our consent and election, to do what is in the power of all of us. For what is common to all, no one dare take upon himself without the will and the command of the community; and should it happen that one chosen for such an office were deposed for malfeasance, he would then be just what he was before he held office. Therefore a priest in Christendom is nothing else than an office-holder. While he is in office, he has precedence; when deposed, he is a peasant or a townsman like the rest. Beyond all doubt, then, a priest is no longer a priest when he is deposed. But now they have invented *characteres indelebiles,* and prate that a deposed priest is nevertheless something different from a mere layman. They even dream that a priest can never become a layman, or be anything else than a priest. All this is mere talk and man-made law.

From all this it follows that there is really no difference between laymen and priests, princes and bishops, "spirituals" and "temporals," as they call them, except that of office and work, but not of "estate"; for they are all of the same estate—true priests, bishops and popes—though they are not all engaged in the same work, just as all priests and monks have not the same work.

*   *   *

The *second wall* is still more flimsy and worthless. They wish to be the only Masters of the Holy Scriptures even though in all their lives they learn nothing from them. They assume for themselves sole authority, and with insolent juggling of words they would persuade us that the pope, whether he be a bad man or a good man, cannot err in matters of faith, and yet they cannot prove a single letter of it. Hence it comes that so many heretical and unchristian, nay, even unnatural ordinances have a place in the canon law, of which, however, there is no present need to speak. For since they think that the Holy Spirit never leaves them, be they never so unlearned and wicked, they make bold to decree whatever they will. And if it were true, where would be the need or use of the Holy Scriptures? Let us burn them, and be satisfied with the unlearned lords at Rome, who are possessed of the Holy Spirit—although He can possess only pious hearts! Unless I had read it myself, I could not have believed that the devil would make such clumsy pretensions at Rome, and find a following.

But not to fight them with mere words, we will quote the Scriptures. St. Paul says in I Corinthians 14: "If to anyone something better is revealed, though he be sitting and listening to another in God's Word, then the first, who is speaking, shall hold his peace and give place." What would be the use of this commandment, if we were only to believe him who does the talking or who has the highest seat? Christ also says in John 6 that all Christians shall be taught of God. Thus it may well happen that the pope and his followers are wicked men, and no true Christians, not taught of God, not having true understanding. On the other hand, an ordinary man may have true understanding; why then should we not follow him? Has not the pope erred many times? Who would help Christendom when the pope errs, if we were not to believe another, who had the Scriptures on his side, more than the pope?

Therefore it is a wickedly invented fable, and they cannot produce a letter in defense of it, that the interpretation of Scripture or the confirmation of its interpretation belongs to the pope alone. They have themselves usurped this power; and although they allege that this power was given to Peter when the keys were given to him, it is plain enough that the keys were not given to Peter alone, but to the whole community. Moreover, the keys were not ordained for doctrine or government, but only for the binding and loosing of sin, and whatever further power of the key they arrogate to themselves is mere invention. But Christ's word to Peter, "I have prayed for thee that thy faith fail not," cannot be applied to the pope, since the majority of the popes have been without faith, as they must themselves confess. Besides, it is not only for Peter that Christ prayed, but also for all Apostles and Christians, as he says in John 17: "Father, I pray for those whom thou hast given me, and not for these only, but for all who believe on me through their word." Is not this clear enough?

Only think of it yourself! They must confess that there are pious Christians among us, who have the true faith, Spirit, understanding, word, and mind of Christ. Why, then, should we reject their word and understanding and follow the pope, who has neither faith nor Spirit? That would be to deny the whole faith and the Christian Church. Moreover, it is not the pope alone who is always in the right, if the article of the Creed is correct: "I believe one holy Christian Church"; otherwise the prayer must run: "I believe in the pope at Rome," and so reduce the Christian Church to one man—which would be nothing else than a devilish and hellish error.

Besides, if we are all priests, as was said above, and all have one faith, one Gospel, one sacrament, why should we not also have the power to test and judge what is correct or incorrect in matters of faith? What becomes of the words of Paul in I Corinthians 2: "He that is spiritual judgeth all things, yet he himself is judged of no man," and II Corinthians 4: "We have all the same Spirit of faith"? Why, then, should not we perceive what squares with faith and what does not, as well as does an unbelieving pope?

All these and many other texts should make us bold and free, and we should not allow the Spirit of liberty, as Paul calls Him, to be frightened off by the fabrications of the popes, but we ought to go boldly forward to test all that they do or leave undone, according to our interpretation of the Scriptures, which rests on faith, and compel them to follow not their own interpretation, but the one that is better. In the olden days Abraham had to listen to his Sarah, although she was in more complete subjection to him than we are to anyone on earth. Balaam's ass, also, was wiser than the prophet himself. If

God then spoke by an ass against a prophet, why should He not be able even now to speak by a righteous man against the pope? In like manner St. Paul rebukes St. Peter as a man in error. Therefore it behooves every Christian to espouse the cause of the faith, to understand and defend it, and to rebuke all errors.

The *third wall* falls of itself when the first two are down. For when the pope acts contrary to the Scriptures, it is our duty to stand by the Scriptures, to reprove him, and to constrain him, according to the word of Christ in Matthew 18: "If thy brother sin against thee, go and tell it him between thee and him alone; if he hear thee not, then take with thee one or two more; if he hear them not, tell it to the Church; if he hear not the Church, consider him a heathen." Here every member is commanded to care for every other. How much rather should we do this when the member that does evil is a ruling member, and by his evil-doing is the cause of much harm and offense to the rest! But if I am to accuse him before the Church, I must bring the Church together.

They have no basis in Scripture for their contention that it belongs to the pope alone to call a council or confirm its actions; for this is based merely upon their own laws, which are valid only in so far as they are not injurious to Christendom or contrary to the laws of God. When the pope deserves punishment, such laws go out of force, since it is injurious to Christendom not to punish him by means of a council.

Thus we read in Acts 15 that it was not St. Peter who called the Apostolic Council, but the Apostles and elders. If, then, that right had belonged to St. Peter alone, the council would not have been a Christian council, but a heretical *conciliabulum*. Even the Council of Nicaea—the most famous of all— was neither called nor confirmed by the Bishop of Rome, but by the Emperor Constantine, and many other emperors after him did the like, yet these councils were the most Christian of all. But if the pope alone had the right to call councils, then all these councils must have been heretical. Moreover, if I consider the councils which the pope has created, I find that they have done nothing of special importance.

Therefore, when necessity demands, and the pope is an offense to Christendom, the first man who is able should, as a faithful member of the whole body, do what he can to bring about a truly free council. No one can do this so well as the temporal authorities, especially since now they also are fellow-Christians, fellow-priests, "fellow-spirituals," fellow-lords over all things, and whenever it is needful or profitable, they should give free course to the office and work in which God has put them above every man. Would it not be an unnatural thing, if a fire broke out in a city, and everybody were to stand by and let it burn on and on and consume everything that could burn, for the sole reason that nobody had the authority of the burgomaster, or because, perhaps, the fire broke out in the burgomaster's house? In such case is it not the duty of every citizen to arouse and call the rest? How much more should this be done in the spiritual city of Christ, if a fire of offense breaks out, whether in the papal government, or anywhere else? In the same way, if the enemy attacks a city, he who first rouses the others deserves honor and thanks; why then should he not deserve honor who makes known the presence of the enemy from hell, and awakens the Christians, and calls them together?

But all their boasts of an authority which dare not be opposed amount to nothing after all. No one in Christendom has authority to do injury, or to forbid the resisting of injury. There is no authority in the Church save for edification. Therefore, if the pope were to use his authority to prevent the calling of a free council, and thus became a hindrance to the edification of the Church, we should have regard neither for him nor for his authority; and if he were to hurl his bans and thunderbolts, we should despise his conduct as that of a madman, and relying on God, hurl back the ban on him, and coerce him as best we could. For this presumptuous authority of his is nothing; he has no such authority, and he is quickly overthrown by a text of Scripture; for Paul says to the Corinthians, "God has given us authority not for the destruction, but for the edification of Christendom." Who is ready to overlap this text? It is only the power of the devil and of Antichrist which resists the things that serve for the edification of Christendom; it is, therefore, in no wise to be obeyed, but is to be opposed with life and goods and all our strength.

FROM A Treatise on Christian Liberty
BY MARTIN LUTHER

Many have thought Christian faith to be an easy thing, and not a few have given it a place among the virtues. This they do because they have had no experience of it, and have never tasted what virtue there is in faith. For it is impossible that anyone should write well of it or well understand what is correctly written of it, unless he has at some time tasted the courage faith gives a man when trials oppress him. But he who has had even a faint taste of it can never write, speak, meditate, or hear enough concerning it. For it is a living fountain springing up into life everlasting, as Christ calls it in John 4. For my part, although I have no wealth of faith to boast of and know how scant my store is, yet I hope that, driven about by great and various temptations, I have attained to a little faith, and that I can speak of it, if not more elegantly, certainly more to the point, than those literalists and all too subtle disputants have hitherto done, who have not even understood what they have written.

That I may make the way easier for the unlearned—for only such do I

Martin Luther, *Three Treatises* (1947), pp. 251–255. Reprinted by permission of Fortress Press.

serve—I set down first these two propositions concerning the liberty and the bondage of the spirit:

A Christian man is a perfectly free lord of all, subject to none.
A Christian man is a perfectly dutiful servant of all, subject to all.

Although these two theses seem to contradict each other, yet, if they should be found to fit together they would serve our purpose beautifully. For they are both Paul's own, who says, in I Corinthians 9, "Whereas I was free, I made myself the servant of all," and Romans 8, "Owe no man anything, but to love one another." Now love by its very nature is ready to serve and to be subject to him who is loved. So Christ, although Lord of all, was made of a woman, made under the law, and hence was at the same time free and a servant, at the same time in the form of God and in the form of a servant.

Let us start, however, with something more remote from our subject, but more obvious. Man has a twofold nature, a spiritual and a bodily. According to the spiritual nature, which men call the soul, he is called a spiritual, or inner, or new man; according to the bodily nature, which men call the flesh, he is called a carnal, or outward, or old man, of whom the Apostle writes, in 2 Corinthians 4, "Though our outward man is corrupted, yet the inward man is renewed day by day." Because of this diversity of nature the Scriptures assert contradictory things of the same man, since these two men in the same man contradict each other, since the flesh lusteth against the spirit and the spirit against the flesh (Galatians 5).

First, let us contemplate the inward man, to see how a righteous, free, and truly Christian man, that is, a new, spiritual, inward man, comes into being. It is evident that no external thing, whatsoever it be, has any influence whatever in producing Christian righteousness or liberty, nor in producing unrighteousness or bondage. A simple argument will furnish the proof. What can it profit the soul if the body fare well, be free and active, eat, drink, and do as it pleases? For in these things even the most godless slaves of all the vices fare well. On the other hand, how will ill health or imprisonment or hunger or thirst or any other external misfortune hurt the soul? With these things even the most godly men are afflicted, and those who because of a clear conscience are most free. None of these things touch either the liberty or the bondage of the soul. The soul receives no benefit if the body is adorned with the sacred robes of the priesthood, or dwells in sacred places, or is occupied with sacred duties, or prays, fasts, abstains from certain kinds of food, or does any work whatsoever that can be done by the body and in the body. The righteousness and the freedom of the soul demand something far different, since the things which have been mentioned could be done by any wicked man, and such works produce nothing but hypocrites. On the other hand, it will not hurt the soul if the body is clothed in secular dress, dwells in unconsecrated places, eats and drinks as others do, does not pray aloud, and neglects to do all the things mentioned above, which hypocrites can do.

Further, to put aside all manner of works, even contemplation, meditation, and all that the soul can do, avail nothing. One thing and one only is necessary for Christian life, righteousness, and liberty. That one thing is the most holy Word of God, the Gospel of Christ, as he says, John 11, "I am the resurrection and the life: he that believeth in me shall not die forever"; and John 8, "If the Son shall make you free, you shall be free indeed"; and Matthew 4, "Not in bread alone doth man live; but in every word that proceedeth from the mouth of God." Let us then consider it certain and conclusively established that the soul can do without all things except the Word of God, and that where this is not there is no help for the soul in anything else whatever. But if it has the Word it is rich and lacks nothing, since this Word is the Word of life, of truth, of light, of peace, of righteousness, of salvation, of joy, of liberty, of wisdom, of power, of grace, of glory, and of every blessing beyond our power to estimate. This is why the prophet in the entire One Hundred and Nineteenth Psalm, and in many other places of Scripture, with so many sighs yearns after the Word of God and applies so many names to it. On the other hand, there is no more terrible plague with which the wrath of God can smite men than a famine of the hearing of His Word, as He says in Amos, just as there is no greater mercy than when He sends forth His Word, as we read in Psalm 107, "He sent His word and healed them, and delivered them from their destructions." Nor was Christ sent into the world for any other ministry but that of the Word, and the whole spiritual estate, apostles, bishops and all the priests, has been called and instituted only for the ministry of the Word.

You ask, "What then is this Word of God, and how shall it be used, since there are so many words of God?" I answer, the Apostle explains that in Romans 1. The Word is the Gospel of God concerning His Son, who was made flesh, suffered, rose from the dead, and was glorified through the Spirit who sanctifies. For to preach Christ means to feed the soul, to make it righteous, to set it free, and to save it, if it believe the preaching. For faith alone is the saving and efficacious use of the Word of God, Romans 10, "If thou confess with thy mouth that Jesus is Lord, and believe with thy heart that God hath raised Him up from the dead, thou shalt be saved"; and again, "The end of the law is Christ, unto righteousness to everyone that believeth"; and, in Romans 1, "The just shall live by his faith." The Word of God cannot be received and cherished by any works whatever, but only by faith. Hence it is clear that, as the soul needs only the Word for its life and righteousness, so it is justified by faith alone and not by any works; for if it could be justified by anything else, it would not need the Word, and therefore it would not need faith. But this faith cannot at all exist in connection with works, that is to say, if you at the same time claim to be justified by works, whatever their character; for that would be to halt between two sides, to worship Baal and to kiss the hand, which, as Job says, is a very great iniquity. Therefore the moment you begin to believe, you learn that all things in you are altogether blameworthy, sinful, and damnable, as Romans 3 says, "For all have sinned and lack the glory of God"; and again, "There is none just, there is none that doeth good, all have turned out of the way: they are become unprofitable together." When you have learned this, you will know that you need Christ, who suffered and rose again for you, that, believing in Him, you may through this faith become a new man, in that all your sins are forgiven, and you are justified by the merits of another, namely, of Christ alone.

Since, therefore, this faith can rule only in the inward man, as Romans 10 says, "With the heart we believe unto righteousness"; and since faith alone justifies, it is clear that the inward man cannot be justified, made free, and be saved by any outward work or dealing whatsoever, and that works, whatever their character, have nothing to do with this inward man. On the other hand, only ungodliness and unbelief of heart, and no outward work, make him guilty and a damnable servant of sin. Wherefore it ought to be the first concern of every Christian to lay aside all trust in works, and more and more to strengthen faith alone, and through faith to grow in the knowledge, not of works, but of Christ Jesus, who suffered and rose for him, as Peter teaches, in the last chapter of his first Epistle; since no other work makes a Christian. Thus when the Jews asked Christ, John 6, what they should do that they might work the works of God, He brushed aside the multitude of works in which He saw that they abounded, and enjoined upon them a single work, saying, "This is the work of God, that you believe in Him whom He hath sent. For Him hath God the Father sealed."

Luther's declaration of theological independence was made at Worms in 1521. He had been summoned there to appear before the emperor and appropriate members of the church hierarchy to defend himself against the charge of heresy. The break with Rome now became irrevocable.

Speech Before Emperor Charles BY MARTIN LUTHER

"Most serene emperor, most illustrious princes, most clement lords, obedient to the time set for me yesterday evening, I appear before you, beseeching you, by the mercy of God, that your most serene majesty and your most illustrious lordships may deign to listen graciously to this my cause—which is, as I hope, a cause of justice and of truth. If through my inexperience I have either not given the proper titles to some, or have offended in some manner against

Helmut T. Lehmann and Jaroslav Pelikan, general eds., *Luther's Works*, XXXII (1957), 109–112, edited by George W. Forell. Reprinted by permission of Fortress Press.

court customs and etiquette, I beseech you to kindly pardon me, as a man accustomed not to courts but to the cells of monks. I can bear no other witness about myself but that I have taught and written up to this time with simplicity of heart, as I had in view only the glory of God and the sound instruction of Christ's faithful.

"Most serene emperor, most illustrious princes, concerning those questions proposed to me yesterday on behalf of your serene majesty, whether I acknowledged as mine the books enumerated and published in my name and whether I wished to persevere in their defense or to retract them, I have given to the first question my full and complete answer, in which I still persist and shall persist forever. These books are mine and they have been published in my name by me, unless in the meantime, either through the craft or the mistaken wisdom of my emulators, something in them has been changed or wrongly cut out. For plainly I cannot acknowledge anything except what is mine alone and what has been written by me alone, to the exclusion of all interpretations of anyone at all.

"In replying to the second question, I ask that your most serene majesty and your lordships may deign to note that my books are not all of the same kind.

"For there are some in which I have discussed religious faith and morals simply and evangelically, so that even my enemies themselves are compelled to admit that these are useful, harmless, and clearly worthy to be read by Christians. Even the bull, although harsh and cruel, admits that some of my books are inoffensive, and yet allows these also to be condemned with a judgment which is utterly monstrous. Thus, if I should begin to disavow them, I ask you, what would I be doing? Would not I, alone of all men, be condemning the very truth upon which friends and enemies equally agree, striving alone against the harmonious confession of all?

"Another group of my books attacks the papacy and the affairs of the papists as those who both by their doctrines and very wicked examples have laid waste the Christian world with evil that affects the spirit and the body. For no one can deny or conceal this fact, when the experience of all and the complaints of everyone witness that through the decrees of the pope and the doctrines of men the consciences of the faithful have been most miserably entangled, tortured, and torn to pieces. Also, property and possessions, especially in this illustrious nation of Germany, have been devoured by an unbelievable tyranny and are being devoured to this time without letup and by unworthy means. [Yet the papists] by their own decrees (as in dist. 9 and 25; ques. 1 and 2) warn that the papal laws and doctrines which are contrary to the gospel or the opinions of the fathers are to be regarded as erroneous and reprehensible. If, therefore, I should have retracted these writings, I should have done nothing other than to have added strength to this [papal] tyranny and I should have opened not only windows but doors to such great godlessness. It would rage farther and more freely than ever it has dared up to this time. Yes, from the proof of such a revocation on my part, their wholly lawless and unrestrained kingdom of wickedness would become still more intolerable for the already wretched people; and their rule would be further strengthened and established, especially if it should be reported that this evil deed had been done by me by virtue of the authority of your most serene majesty and of the whole Roman Empire. Good God! What a cover for wickedness and tyranny I should have then become.

"I have written a third sort of book against some private and (as they say) distinguished individuals—those, namely, who strive to preserve the Roman tyranny and to destroy the godliness taught by me. Against these I confess I have been more violent than my religion or profession demands. But then, I do not set myself up as a saint; neither am I disputing about my life, but about the teaching of Christ. It is not proper for me to retract these works, because by this retraction it would again happen that tyranny and godlessness would, with my patronage, rule and rage among the people of God more violently than ever before.

"However, because I am a man and not God, I am not able to shield my books with any other protection than that which my Lord Jesus Christ himself offered for his teaching. When questioned before Annas about his teaching and struck by a servant, he said: 'If I have spoken wrongly, bear witness to the wrong' [John 18:19–23]. If the Lord himself, who knew that he could not err, did not refuse to hear testimony against his teaching, even from the lowliest servant, how much more ought I, who am the lowest scum and able to do nothing except err, desire and expect that somebody should want to offer testimony against my teaching! Therefore, I ask by the mercy of God, may your most serene majesty, most illustrious lordships, or anyone at all who is able, either high or low, bear witness, expose my errors, overthrowing them by the writings of the prophets and the evangelists. Once I have been taught I shall be quite ready to renounce every error, and I shall be the first to cast my books into the fire.

"From these remarks I think it is clear that I have sufficiently considered and weighed the hazards and dangers, as well as the excitement and dissensions aroused in the world as a result of any teachings, things about which I was gravely and forcefully warned yesterday. To see excitement and dissension arise because of the Word of God is to me clearly the most joyful aspect of all in these matters. For this is the way, the opportunity, and the result of the Word of God, just as He [Christ] said, 'I have not come to bring peace, but a sword. For I have come to set a man against his father, etc.' [Matt. 10:34–35]. Therefore, we ought to think how marvelous and terrible is our God in his counsels, lest by chance what is attempted for settling strife grows rather into an intolerable deluge of evils, if we begin by condemning the Word of God. And concern must be shown lest the reign of this most noble youth, Prince Charles (in whom after God is our great hope), become unhappy and inauspicious. I could illustrate this with abundant examples from Scripture—like Pharaoh, the king of Babylon, and the kings of Israel who, when they endeavored to pacify and strengthen their kingdoms by the wisest counsels, most surely destroyed themselves. For it is He who takes the wise in their own craftiness [Job 5:13] and overturns mountains before they know it [Job 9:5]. Therefore we must fear God. I do not say these things because there is a need of either my teachings or my warnings for such leaders as you, but because I must not withhold the allegiance which I owe my Germany. With these words I commend myself to your most serene majesty and to your lordships, humbly asking that I not be allowed through the agitation of my enemies, without cause, to be made hateful to you. I have finished."

When I had finished, the speaker for the emperor said, as if in reproach, that I had not answered the question, that I ought not call into question those things which had been condemned and defined in councils; therefore what was sought from me was not a horned response, but a simple one, whether or not I wished to retract.

Here I answered:

"Since then your serene majesty and your lordships seek a simple answer, I will give it in this manner, neither horned nor toothed: Unless I am convinced by the testimony of the Scriptures or by clear reason (for I do not trust either in the pope or in councils alone, since it is well known that they have often erred and contradicted themselves), I am bound by the Scriptures I have quoted and my conscience is captive to the Word of God. I cannot and I will not retract anything, since it is neither safe nor right to go against conscience.

"I cannot do otherwise, here I stand, may God help me, Amen."

4
THE PROBLEM
OF
MARTIN LUTHER

Erik Erikson of Harvard University is a leader of contemporary psychiatric thought. In his book *Young Man Luther* he attempts to account for Luther's actions in terms of modern depth psychology.

FROM Young Man Luther BY E. H. ERIKSON

I have called the major crisis of adolescence the *identity crisis;* it occurs in that period of the life cycle when each youth must forge for himself some central perspective and direction, some working unity, out of the effective remnants of his childhood and the hopes of his anticipated adulthood; he must detect some meaningful resemblance between what he has come to see in himself and what his sharpened awareness tells him others judge and expect him to be. This sounds dangerously like common sense; like all health, however, it is a matter of course only to those who possess it, and appears as a most complex achievement to those who have tasted its absence. Only in ill health does one realize the intricacy of the body; and only in a crisis, individual or historical, does it become obvious what a sensitive combination of interrelated factors the human personality is—a combination of capacities created in the distant past and of opportunities divined in the present; a combination of totally unconscious preconditions developed in individual growth and of social conditions created and re-created in the precarious interplay of generations. In some young people, in some classes, at some periods

Reprinted from *Young Man Luther: A Study in Psychoanalysis and History,* pp. 14–16, 20–21, 206–213, by Erik H. Erikson, by permission of W. W. Norton & Company, Inc., and Faber & Faber Ltd., London. Copyright © 1958, 1962 by Erik H. Erikson.

in history, this crisis will be minimal; in other people, classes, and periods, the crisis will be clearly marked off as a critical period, a kind of "second birth," apt to be aggravated either by widespread neuroticisms or by pervasive ideological unrest. Some young individuals will succumb to this crisis in all manner of neurotic, psychotic, or delinquent behavior; others will resolve it through participation in ideological movements passionately concerned with religion or politics, nature or art. Still others, although suffering and deviating dangerously through what appears to be a prolonged adolescence, eventually come to contribute an original bit to an emerging style of life: the very danger which they have sensed has forced them to mobilize capacities to see and say, to dream and plan, to design and construct, in new ways.

Luther, so it seems, at one time was a rather endangered young man, beset with a syndrome of conflicts whose outline we have learned to recognize, and whose components to analyse. He found a spiritual solution, not without the well-timed help of a therapeutically clever superior in the Augustinian order. His solution roughly bridged a political and psychological vacuum which history had created in a significant portion of Western Christendom. Such coincidence, if further coinciding with the deployment of highly specific personal gifts, makes for historical "greatness." We will follow Luther through the crisis of his youth, and the unfolding of his gifts, to the first manifestation of his originality as a thinker, namely, to the emergence of a new theology, apparently not immediately perceived as a radical innovation either by him or his listeners, in his first Lectures on the Psalms (1513). What happened to him after he had acquired a historical identity is more than another chapter; for even half of the man is too much for one book. The difference between the young and the old Luther is so marked, and the second, the sturdy orator, so exclusive a Luther-image to most readers, that I will speak of "Martin" when I report on Luther's early years, which according to common usage in the Luther literature include his twenties; and of "Luther" where and when he has become the leader of Lutherans, seduced by history into looking back on his past as upon a mythological autobiography

Kierkegaard's remark has a second part: ". . . of very great import for Christendom." This calls for an investigation of how the individual "case" became an important, an historic "event," and for formulations concerning the spiritual and political identity crisis of Northern Christendom in Luther's time. True, I could have avoided those methodological uncertainties and impurities which will undoubtedly occur by sticking to my accustomed job of writing a case history, and leaving the historical event to those who, in turn, would consider the case a mere accessory to the event. But we clinicians have learned in recent years that we cannot lift a case history out of history, even as we suspect that historians, when they try to separate the logic of the historic event from that of the life histories which intersect in it, leave a number of vital historical problems unattended. So we may have to risk that bit of impurity which is inherent in the hyphen of the psycho-historical as well as of all other hyphenated approaches. They are the compost heap of today's interdisciplinary efforts, which may help to fertilize new fields, and to produce future flowers of new methodological clarity.

* * *

We cannot leave history entirely to nonclinical observers and to professional historians who often all too nobly immerse themselves into the very disguises, rationalizations, and idealizations of the historical process from which it should be their business to separate themselves. Only when the relation of historical forces to the basic functions and stages of the mind has been jointly charted and understood can we begin a psychoanalytic critique of society as such without falling back into mystical or moralistic philosophizing.

Freud warned against the possible misuse of his work as an ideology, a *"Weltanschauung";* but as we shall see in Luther's life and work, a man who inspires new ideas has little power to restrict them to the area of his original intentions. And Freud himself did not refrain from interpreting other total approaches to man's condition, such as religion, as consequences of man's inability to shake off the bonds of his prolonged childhood, and thus comparable to collective neuroses. The psychological and historical study of the religious crisis of a young great man renews the opportunity to review this assertion in the light of ego-psychology and of theories of psychosocial development.

* * *

In what follows, themes from Luther's first lectures are discussed side by side with psychoanalytic insights. Theological readers will wonder whether Luther saved theology from philosophy only to have it exploited by psychology; while psychoanalysts may suspect me of trying to make space for a Lutheran God in the structure of the psyche. My purposes, however, are more modest: I intend to demonstrate that Luther's redefinition of man's condition —while part and parcel of his theology—has striking configurational parallels with inner dynamic shifts like those which clinicians recognize in the recovery of individuals from psychic distress. In brief, I will try to indicate that Luther, in laying the foundation for a "religiosity for the adult man," displayed the attributes of his own hard-won adulthood; his renaissance of faith portrays a vigorous recovery of his own ego-initiative. To indicate this I will focus on three ideas: the affirmation of voice and word as the instruments of faith; the new recognition of God's "face" in the passion of Christ; and the redefinition of a just life.

After 1505 Luther had made no bones about the pernicious influence which "rancid Aristotelianism" had had on theology. Scholasticism had made him lose faith, he said; through St. Paul he had recovered it. He put the problem in terms of organ modes, by describing scholastic disputations as *dentes* and *linguae:* the teeth are hard and sinister, and form words in anger and fury; the tongue is soft and suavely persuasive. Using these modes, the devil can evoke purely intellectual mirages (*mira potest suggere in intellectu*). But the organ through which the word enters to replenish the heart is the ear (*natura enim verbi est audiri*), for it is in the nature of the word that it should be heard. On the other hand, faith comes from listening, not from looking (*quia est auditu fides, non ex visu*). Therefore, the greatest thing one can say about Christ, and about all Christians, is that they have *aures perfectas et perfossas:* good and open ears. But only what is perceived at the same time as a matter *affectionalis* and *moralis* as well as intellectual can be a matter sacred and divine: one must, therefore, hear before one sees, believe before one understands, be captivated before one captures. *Fides est "locus" animae:* faith is the seat, the organ of the soul. This had certainly been said before; but Luther's emphasis is not on Augustinian "infusion," or on a nominalist "obedience," but, in a truly Renaissance approach, on a self-verification through a God-given inner "apparatus." This *locus,* this apparatus, has its own way of seeking and searching—and it succeeds insofar as it develops its own *passivity.*

Paradoxically, many a young man (and son of a stubborn one) becomes a great man in his own sphere only by learning that deep passivity which permits him to let the data of his competency speak to him. As Freud said in a letter to Fliess, "I must wait until it moves in me so that I can perceive it: *bis es sich in mir ruehrt und ich davon erfahre."* This may sound feminine, and, indeed, Luther bluntly spoke of an attitude of womanly conception—*sicut mulier in conceptu.* Yet it is clear that men call such attitudes and modes feminine only because the strain of paternalism has alienated us from them; for these modes are any organism's birthright, and all our partial as well as our total functioning is based on a metabolism of passivity and activity. Mannish man always wants to pretend that he made himself, or at any rate, that no simple woman bore him, and many puberty rites (consider the rebirth from a kiva in the American Southwest) dramatize a new birth from a spiritual mother of a kind that only men understand.

The theology as well as the psychology of Luther's passivity is that of man in the *state of prayer,* a state in which he fully means what he can say only to God: *Tibi soli peccavi,* I have sinned, not in relation to any person or institution, but in relation only to God, to *my* God.

In two ways, then, rebirth by prayer is passive: it means surrender to God the Father; but it also means to be reborn *ex matrice scripturae nati:* out of the matrix of the scriptures. "Matrix" is as close as such a man's man will come to saying "mater." But he cannot remember and will not acknowledge that long before he had developed those wilful modes which were specifically suppressed and paradoxically aggravated by a challenging father, a mother had taught him to touch the world with his searching mouth and his probing senses. What to a man's man, in the course of his development, seems like a passivity hard to acquire, is only a regained ability to be active with his oldest and most neglected modes. Is it coincidence that Luther, now that he was explicitly teaching passivity, should come to the conclusion that a lecturer should feed his audience as a mother suckles her child? Intrinsic to the kind of passivity we speak of is not only the memory of having been given, but also the identification with the maternal giver: "the glory of a good thing is that it flows out to others." I think that in the Bible Luther at last found a mother whom he could acknowledge: he could attribute to the Bible a generosity to which he could open himself, and which he could pass on to others, at last a mother's son.

Luther did use the words *passiva* and *passivus* when he spoke Latin, and the translation *passive* must be accepted as correct. But in German he often used the word *passivisch,* which is more actively passive, as passific would be. I think that the difference between the old modalities of *passive* and *active* is really that between *erleben* and *handeln,* of being in the state of *experiencing* or of *acting.* Meaningful implications are lost in the flat word *passivity*— among them the total attitude of living receptively and through the senses, of willingly "suffering" the voice of one's intuition and of living a *Passion:* that total passivity in which man regains, through considered self-sacrifice and self-transcendence, his active position in the face of nothingness, and thus is saved. Could this be one of the psychological riddles in the wisdom of the "foolishness of the cross"?

To Luther, the preaching and the praying man, the measure in depth of the perceived presence of the Word was the reaction with a total affect which leaves no doubt that one "means it." It may seem paradoxical to speak of an affect that one could not thus mean; yet it is obvious that rituals, observances, and performances do evoke transitory affects which can be put on for the occasion and afterward hung in the closet with one's Sunday clothes. Man is able to ceremonialize, as he can "automatize" psychologically, the signs and behaviors that are born of the deepest reverence or despair; however, for an affect to have a deep and lasting effect, or, as Luther would say, be *affectionalis* and *moralis,* it must not only be experienced as nearly overwhelming, but it must also in some way be affirmed by the ego as valid, almost as chosen: one means the affect, it signifies something meaningful, it is significant. Such is the relative nature of our ego and of our conscience that when the ego regains its composure after the auditory condemnation of the absolutist voice of conscience we mean what we have learned to believe, and our affects become those of positive conscience: faith, conviction, authority, indignation— all subjective states which are attributes of a strong sense of identity and, incidentally, are indispensable tools for strengthening identity in others. Luther speaks of matters of faith as experiences from which one will profit to the degree to which they were intensive and expressive (*quanto expressius et intensius*). If they are more *frigidus,* however, they are not merely a profit missed, they are a terrible deficit confirmed: for man without intense convictions is a robot with destructive techniques.

It is easy to see that these formulations, once revolutionary, are the commonplaces of today's pulpits. They are the bases of that most inflated of all oratorial currency, credal protestation in church and lecture hall, in political propaganda and in oral advertisement: the protestation, made to order for the occasion, that truth is only that which one means with one's whole being, and lives every moment. We, the heirs of Protestantism, have made convention and pretense out of the very sound of meaning it. What started with the German *Brustton der Ueberzeugung,* the manly chestiness of conviction, took many forms of authoritative appeal, the most recent one being the cute sincerity of our TV announcers. All this only indicates that Luther was a pioneer on one of our eternal inner frontiers, and that his struggle must continue (as any great man's must) exactly at that point where his word is perverted in his own name.

Psychotherapists, professional listeners and talkers in the sphere of affectivity and morality know only too well that man seldom really knows what he really means; he as often lies by telling the truth as he reveals the truth when he tries to lie. This is a psychological statement; and the psychoanalytic method, when it does not pretend to deliver complete honesty, over a period of time reveals approximately what somebody really means. But the center of the problem is simply this: in truly significant matters people, and especially children, have a devastatingly clear if mostly unconscious perception of what other people really mean, and sooner or later royally reward real love or take well-aimed revenge for implicit hate. Families in which each member is separated from the others by asbestos walls of verbal propriety, overt sweetness, cheap frankness, and rectitude tell one another off and talk back to each other with minute and unconscious displays of affect—not to mention physical complaints and bodily ailments—with which they worry, accuse, undermine, and murder one another.

Meaning it, then, is not a matter of credal protestation; verbal explicitness is not a sign of faith. Meaning it, means to be at one with an ideology in the process of rejuvenation; it implies a successful sublimation of one's libidinal strivings; and it manifests itself in a liberated craftsmanship.

When Luther listened to the scriptures he did not do so with an unprejudiced ear. His method of making an unprejudiced approach consisted of listening both ways—to the Word coming from the book and to the echo in himself. "Whatever is in your disposition," he said, "that the word of God will be unto you." Disposition here means the inner configuration of your most meant meanings. He knew that he meant it when he could say it: the spoken Word was the activity appropriate for his kind of passivity. Here "faith and word become one, an invincible whole." *"Der Glaub und das Worth wirth gantz ein Ding und ein unuberwintlich ding."*

Twenty-five times in the Lectures on the Psalms, against once in the Lectures on the Romans, Luther quotes two corresponding passages from Paul's first Epistle to the Corinthians. The first passage:

22. For the Jews require a sign, and the Greeks seek after wisdom;
23. But we preach Christ crucified, unto the Jews a stumblingblock, and unto the Greeks foolishness;

25. Because the foolishness of God is wiser than men; and the weakness of God is stronger than men.

This paradoxical foolishness and weakness of God became a theological absolute for Luther: there is not a word in the Bible, he exclaimed, which is *extra crucem*, which can be understood without reference to the cross; and this is all that shall and can be understood, as Paul had said in the other passage:

1. And I, brethren, when I came to you, came not with excellency of speech or of wisdom, declaring unto you the testimony of God.
2. For I determined not to know any thing among you, save Jesus Christ, and him crucified.
3. And I was with you in weakness, and in fear, and in much trembling.

Thus Luther abandoned any theological quibbling about the cross. He did not share St. Augustine's opinion that when Christ on the cross exclaimed *Deus meus, quare me derelequisti,* He had not been really abandoned, for as God's son and as God's word, He *was* God. Luther could not help feeling that St. Paul came closer to the truth when he assumed an existential paradox rather than a platonic fusion of essences; he insists on Christ's complete sense of abandonment and on his sincere and active premeditation in visiting hell. Luther spoke here in passionate terms very different from those of medieval adoration. He spoke of a man who was unique in all creation, yet lives in each man; and who is dying *in* everyone even as he died *for* everyone. It is clear that Luther rejected all arrangements by which an assortment of saints made it unnecessary for man to embrace the maximum of his own existential suffering. What he had tried, so desperately and for so long, to counteract and overcome he now accepted as his divine gift—the sense of utter abandonment, *sicut jam damnatus,* as if already in hell. The worst temptation, he now says, is not to have any; one can be sure that God is most angry when He does not seem angry at all. Luther warns of all those well-meaning (*bone intentionarii*) religionists who encourage man "to do what he can": to forestall sinning by clever planning; to seek redemption by observing all occasions for rituals, not forgetting to bring cash along to the limit of their means; and to be secure in the feeling that they are as humble and as peaceful as "it is in them to be." Luther, instead, made a virtue out of what his superiors had considered a vice in him (and we, a symptom), namely, the determined search for the rock bottom of his sinfulness: only thus, he says, can man judge himself as God would: *conformis deo est et verax et justus.* One could consider such conformity utter passivity in the face of God's judgment; but note that it really is an active self-observation, which scans the frontier of conscience for the genuine sense of guilt. Instead of accepting some impersonal and mechanical absolution, it insists on dealing with sincere guilt, perceiving as "God's judgment" what in fact is the individual's own truly meant self-judgment.

Is all this an aspect of personal adjustment to be interpreted as a set of unconscious tricks? Martin the son, who on a personal level had suffered deeply because he could not coerce his father into approving his religiosity as genuine, and who had borne with him the words of this father with an unduly prolonged filial obedience, assumes now on a religious level a volitional role toward filial suffering, perhaps making out of his protracted sonhood the victory of his Christlikeness. In his first Mass, facing the altar—the Father in heaven—and at the same time waiting to face his angry earthly father, Martin had "overlooked" a passage concerning Christ's mediatorship. Yet now, in finding Christ in himself, he establishes an inner position which goes beyond that of a neurotic compromise identification. He finds the core of a praying man's identity, and advances Christian ideology by an important step. It is clear that Luther abandoned the appreciation of Christ as a substitute who has died "for"—in the sense of "instead of"—us; he also abandoned the concept of Christ as an ideal figure to be imitated, or abjectly venerated, or ceremonially remembered as an event in the past. Christ now becomes the core of the Christian's identity: *quotidianus Christi adventus,* Christ is today here, in me. The affirmed passivity of suffering becomes the daily Passion and the Passion is the substitution of the primitive sacrifice of others with a most active, most masterly, affirmation of man's nothingness—which, by his own masterly choice, becomes his existential identity.

The men revered by mankind as saviors face and describe in lasting words insights which the ordinary man must avoid with all possible self-deception and exploitation of others. These men prove their point by the magic of their voices which radiate to the farthest corner of their world and out into the millennia. Their passion contains elements of choice, mastery, and victory, and sooner or later earns them the name of King of Kings; their crown of thorns later becomes their successor's tiara. For a little while Luther, this first revolutionary individualist, saved the Saviour from the tiaras and the ceremonies, the hierarchies and the thought-police, and put him back where he arose: in each man's soul.

Is this not the counterpart, on the level of conscience, to Renaissance anthropocentrism? Luther left the heavens to science and restricted himself to what he could know of his own suffering and faith, that is, to what he could mean. He who had sought to dispel the angry cloud that darkened the face of the fathers and of The Father now said that Christ's life *is* God's face: *qui est facies patris.* The Passion is all that man can know of God: his conflicts, duly faced, are all that he can know of himself. The last judgment is the always present self-judgment. Christ did not live and die in order to make man poorer in the fear of his future judgment, but in order to make him abundant today: *nam judicia sunt ipsae passiones Christi quae in nobis abundant.* Look, Luther said at one point in these lectures (IV, 87), how everywhere painters depict Christ's passion as if they agreed with St. Paul that we know nothing but Christ crucified. The artist closest to Luther in spirit was Dürer, who etched his own face into Christ's countenance.

Gordon Rupp's discussion of the critical psychological period in Luther's life provides a historical counterweight to Erikson's reading of Luther's psychology.

FROM The Righteousness of God BY GORDON RUPP

We do not know when Luther began to study the Bible, though he must have begun his novitiate by learning portions of scripture which he would recite in the divine offices. It is certain that it became for him an all-important and absorbing study, until his mind was impregnated with the words and themes of the Bible, and he could handle the Biblical material with a facility which was the envy of his enemies, and with a frequent penetration into the exactness of Biblical vocabulary which modern Biblical scholarship has confirmed. But if the Bible was soon to become paramount with him, beyond Augustine and the Fathers, it was initially the meeting-place of all his problems, concentrated in one word. Here is his testimony, in the autobiographical preface which he wrote, at the end of his life (1545), before the Wittenberg edition of his Latin works. After rehearsing his career down to the year 1519, he pauses, and there follows this statement:

"Meanwhile then, in that year (1519), I turned once more to interpret the Psalms, relying on the fact that I was the more expert after I had handled in the schools the letters of St. Paul to the Romans and the Galatians, and that which is to the Hebrews. Certainly I had been seized with a greater ardour to understand Paul in the Epistle to the Romans (captus fueram cognoscendi), but as Virgil says, it was not 'coldness of the blood' which held me up until now, but one word (unicum vocabulum), that is, chapter 1. 'The Justice of God is revealed in it' (Justitia Dei). For I hated this word (vocabulum istud) 'Justitia Dei' which by the use and consent of all doctors I was taught (usu et consuetudine omnium doctorum doctus eram) to understand philosophically of that formal or active justice (as they call it) with which God is just, and punishes unjust sinners.

"For, however irreproachably I lived as a monk, I felt myself in the presence of God (coram Deo) to be a sinner with a most unquiet conscience nor could I trust that I had pleased him with my satisfaction. I did not love, nay, rather I hated this just God who punished sinners and if not with 'open blasphemy' certainly with huge murmuring I was angry with God, saying: 'As though it really were not enough that miserable sinners should be eter-

Gordon Rupp, *The Righteousness of God: Luther Studies* (1953), pp. 121–127. Reprinted by permission of Hodder & Stoughton Ltd., London.

nally damned with original sin, and have all kinds of calamities laid upon them by the law of the ten commandments, God must go and add sorrow upon sorrow and even through the Gospel itself bring his Justice and his Wrath to bear!' I raged in this way with a fierce and disturbed conscience, and yet I knocked importunately at Paul in this place, thirsting most ardently to know what St. Paul meant.

"At last, God being merciful, as I meditated day and night on the connection of the words, namely, 'the Justice of God is revealed in it, as it is written, "the Just shall live by Faith," ' there I began to understand the Justice of God as that by which the just lives by the gift of God, namely by faith, and this sentence, 'the Justice of God is revealed in the gospel,' to be that passive justice, with which the merciful God justifies us, by faith, as it is written 'The just lives by faith.'

"This straightway made me feel as though reborn, and as though I had entered through open gates into paradise itself. From then on, the whole face of scripture appeared different. I ran through the scriptures then, as memory served, and found the same analogy in other words, as the Work of God (opus) that which God works in us, Power of God (virtus Dei) with which he makes us strong, wisdom of God (sapientia Dei) with which he makes us wise, fortitude of God, salvation of God, glory of God.

"And now, as much as I had hated this word 'Justice of God' before, so much the more sweetly I extolled this word to myself now, so that this place in Paul was to me as a real gate of paradise. Afterwards, I read Augustine, 'On the Spirit and the Letter,' where beyond hope I found that he also similarly interpreted the Justice of God: that with which God endues us, when he justifies us. And although this were said imperfectly, and he does not clearly explain about 'imputation,' yet it pleased me that he should teach a Justice of God with which we are justified.

"Armed with these cogitations I began to interpret the Psalms again."

The narrative is in the main straightforward, and most of it can be checked against quotations already cited in these pages. But there are certain problems which must be faced. In the first place, to what period of his career does Luther refer when he speaks of his discovery about "Justitia Dei"? A superficial reading might suggest that he refers to the year (1519), when "armed with these cogitations" he began the second course of lectures on the Psalms. But it can be demonstrated that Luther had developed his teaching on this subject in these terms, at least by the time of his lectures on Romans (1515–16). The notion of a dislocation of the text, that refuge of desperate scholars, put forward by A. V. Müller, has no documentary evidence to support it, and as K. Holl pointed out, would make Luther commit grammatical solecisms. The suggestion that Luther in his old age made a slip of memory and confused his first and second lectures on the Psalms is hardly more convincing. Stracke has made a careful examination of the whole of this autobiographical fragment, and Luther emerges surprisingly well from the test. After thirty years, he is not unnaturally a month or two out here and there, gets a detail misplaced now and again, but when we remember that famous edition of the letters of Erasmus, which had more than half the dates wrong, and some of them years out, we can count this preface yet another disproof of the legend of Luther's anecdotage.

In fact, as Stracke pointed out, Luther's use of the phrase "captus fueram" makes perfectly tenable the interpretation that Luther has gone back in his reflection to an earlier period. Before attempting to identify this date more precisely, we must discuss the authenticity of the statement as a whole.

To impugn this was intended as a crowning demonstration of Denifle's "Luther und Luthertum." Denifle brought forward, in an appendix, a catena of 360 pages, giving the exposition of Rom. 1:17 by sixty doctors of the Western Church, which, he said, demonstrated beyond a doubt "not a single writer from the time of Ambrosiaster to the time of Luther understood this passage (Rom. 1:17) in the sense of the justice of God which punishes, of an angry God. All, on the contrary, have understood it of the God who justifies, the justice obtained by faith." Here, then, is the dilemma. Either Luther was a fool, or he was a liar. Either he was a bragging incompetent, boasting in his senility, or he was adding the last untruth to a long series of lying inventions. For Denifle, the two conclusions were not mutually exclusive.

Denifle included in the demonstration passages from the recently rediscovered lectures of Luther on Romans. This was intended as proof that Luther himself had used the supposed newly discovered meaning at a time anterior to 1515.

That part of his argument falls to the ground if we suppose Luther in fact to have spoken of a period before 1515. We may, therefore, re-sharpen Denifle's usefulness as an advocatus diaboli at this point, and present polemic with an argument here which, as far as we know, has been little noticed. In the Sentences of Peter Lombard, on which Luther lectured in 1509, and in the famous Dist. XVII of Book 1, to which, as we have seen, Luther paid special attention, there is imbedded a quotation from St. Augustine's "Spirit and Letter" which gives the so-called "passive" interpretation of "Justitia Dei":

"The love of God is said to be shed abroad in our hearts, not because he loves us, but because he makes us his lovers: just as the justice of God (Justitia Dei) is that by which we are made just by his gift (justi ejus munere efficimur): and 'salvation of the Lord' by which he saves us: and 'faith of Jesus Christ' that which makes us believers (fideles)."

The words are glossed by the Master of the Sentences, "And this is called the Justice of God, not with which he is just, but because with it he makes us just." At any rate, it seems clear that although in 1509 Luther had not read Augustine's "Spirit and the Letter," he had read an extract concerning this interpretation of the "Justitia Dei" during his study of Peter Lombard.

Denifle's tour de force was impressive, and like most polemic of this kind, got a good start of its pursuers. Among many replies the most notable were the essays by Karl Holl and Emmanuel Hirsch.

In the first place, it was pointed out that Luther in speaking of the "use and consent of all doctors" was referring not to Rom. 1:17, but to the "unicum vocabulum" of "Justitia Dei." The distinction is important, for, if granted, it means that the doctors in question were not the exegetes but the systematic theologians, and their views are to be found, not in the commentaries on the Epistles of St. Paul, but in those passages which concerned the conception of divine justice in Commentaries on the Sentences, and the like. Denifle's enormous collection of documents attested a wrong indictment.

Denifle, it is true, could appeal to a passage in Luther's lectures on Genesis, in which he referred to "hunc locum," i.e. Rom. 1:17, as the centre of his difficulties. But these lectures were not published until after Luther's death, and then only in the form in which they were reported. If there is glossing to be done, the 1545 fragment is primary, and Denifle, in his argument, showed some embarrassment at this point. As Holl was not slow to point out, nobody could say how many of Denifle's sixty doctors of the West could have been known, at first- or second-hand, to Luther, or whether he had studied the exegesis concerning Rom. 1:17. Holl proceeded thoroughly to analyse Denifle's authorities and disentangled two main streams of mediaeval exegesis, going back to Ambrosiaster and to Augustine. He showed that Ambrosiaster keeps in mind the problem of the Divine integrity, how the just God can receive sinners, and that while stressing the merciful promises of God, he keeps also the conception of retributive justice. Augustine is less concerned with justice as a divine property than with that bestowed righteousness, the work of grace infused within the human soul, on the ground of which sinners are made just in the presence of God. But Holl pointed out that neither of these expositions, nor all the permutations and combinations of them made thereafter, really met Luther's problem. "That from the time of St. Augustine the Western Church spoke of justifying grace, and that the later schoolmen strengthened this conception by their teaching about an 'habitus' is something known to all, and it is quite certain that Luther was not unaware of it." Emmanuel Hirsch dealt with a notable and fundamental omission from Denifle's authorities, namely, the Nominalist doctors whom Luther knew, and whom he had in mind when he said, "I was taught." He showed that Gabriel Biel, though admitting, even stressing the need for grace, and for the divine "Misericordia," normally preferred to reserve "Justitia" for the retributive justice of God which punishes sinners. This interpretation, which Hirsch based on Biel's commentary on the Sentences, seems confirmed by an examination of some scores of sermons by Biel upon the feasts of the Christian year.

Even more important than these arguments is the abundant testimony of Luther's good faith in this matter which is yielded by writings of other years, many of which, since they had never been published, might well have been completely forgotten by Luther. It is quite certain that, whatever the truth about his statement, it was no later invention, made up at the end of his life. Thus, in 1515:

"Wherefore, if I may speak personally, the word 'Justitia' so nauseated me to hear, that I would hardly have been sorry if somebody had made away with me."

In 1531 (published 1538):

"For thus the Holy Fathers who wrote about the Psalms were wont to expound the 'justus deus' as that in which he vindicates and punishes, not as that which justifies. So it happened to me as a young man, and even today I am as though terrified when I hear God called 'the just.'

"Justice, i.e. grace. This word I learned with much sweat. They used to expound justice as the truth of God which punishes the damned, mercy as that which saves believers. A dangerous opinion which arouses a secret hatred of the heart against God, so that it is terrified when he is so much as named. Justice is that which the Father does when he favours us, with which he justifies, or the gift with which he takes away our sin."

There are three passages in the Table Talk which must embody some core of truth. These suggest that Luther met his difficulty, before he came to the Epistle to the Romans, and in the interpretation of Psalm 31:1. "In justitia tua libera me." But the difficulty, "Justitia Dei" understood as retributive justice, is the same.

Two facts seem clear. First, that in his early career Luther found the conception of the "Justitia Dei" a stumbling block. Second, that this rock of offence did become for him the very corner-stone of his theology. The doctrine of Justification by Faith came to hold, in consequence, for him and for subsequent Protestant theology an altogether more important place than in the Catholic and mediaeval framework. In the sixteenth century men like Sir Thomas More and Stephen Gardiner found it hard to understand what all the Protestant fuss was about, and some striking parallels might be cited among modern Anglican scholars. Thus, even if we had not Luther's explicit testimony in the fragment under consideration, it would be necessary to invent something very like it to account for the remarkable and fundamental transformation in his thought. Denifle's demonstration may be held to have failed in so far as he attempted to show that Luther had wittingly perverted mediaeval teaching, and to have failed, too, in the more fundamental charge that Luther had in fact made no theological discoveries at all.

Thus in his narrative Luther explains simply and clearly why Rom. 1:17 was the climax of his difficulties. Luther already knew and believed that God condemned sinners through the Law. Now, in Rom. 1:17, he found that through the Gospel also was revealed the "Justitia Dei," which he took to mean the strict, retributive justice of God.

If the reader, having absorbed the academic roughage of this critical discussion, will turn back to the autobiographical fragment, he will find it tolerably plain. We can understand how, in the presence of a God who weighted everything against the sinner, Luther was filled with that "huge murmuring" which he elsewhere often and eloquently described, but which a man dared hardly admit to himself, so closely did it approximate to "open blasphemy." This inward ferment added to the outward practices of devotion and penitence an element of strain and unreality, and enforced hypocrisy which in turn aggravated the spiritual conflict. This was not merely an academic affair, though we need not shrink from admitting the theological enquiry of a theological professor into such a category. What he learned and taught about the Justice of God became for him a "carnifex theologistria," however, by reason of the unquiet conscience within. It was this fifth column, within the citadel of the soul, which betrayed him. Miegge's judgment is valid: "In the case of Luther, the religious crisis and the theological crisis are not to be separated."

Henri Daniel-Rops is a member of the French Academy and has written a number of popular works on the history of the church. The following selection gives a view of Luther's evolution toward heresy from a Catholic vantage point.

FROM The Protestant Reformation
BY HENRI DANIEL-ROPS

THE AFFAIR OF THE INDULGENCES

It was 31st October 1517. In the little town of Wittenberg, a part of the Elector of Saxony's possessions, the crush and animation were at their height. Every year the Feast of All Saints attracted countless pious folk, who came to see the precious relics which His Highness the Elector, Frederick the Wise, had collected at great expense, and which were brought out for the occasion from the storerooms of the Schlosskirche. There were plenty of them—several thousand—and they were of the most varied kind: they included not only the complete corpses of various saints, nails from the Passion and rods from the Flagellation, but part of the Child Jesus' swaddling-clothes and some wood from His crib, and even a few drops of His Blessed Mother's milk! Large numbers of most valuable indulgences were attached to the veneration of these distinguished treasures.

That same morning a manifesto, written in scholastic Latin and consisting of ninety-five theses, was found nailed to the door of the castle's chapel. Its author was an Augustinian monk who was extremely well known in the town, and he declared his intention of defending its contents against any

From the book *The Protestant Reformation*, I, 9–26, by Henri Daniel-Rops, translated by Audrey Butler. Translation Copyright, ©, 1961 by E. P. Dutton & Co., Inc., and J. M. Dent & Sons Ltd. Reprinted by permission of the publishers.

opponent prepared to stand up and argue with him. In fact, the document concerned those very indulgences which honest folk were even then showing such eagerness to obtain by praying before the relics and slipping their guilders into the offertory boxes. The pilgrims assembled outside the church heard the more knowledgeable among them translate its words: "Those preaching in favour of indulgences err when they say such indulgences can deliver man and grant him salvation. The man who gives to the poor performs a better action than the one who buys indulgences." There were three hundred yet more bitter lines in this strain. And the worthy pilgrims wondered what could be the purpose of this monk in thus shaking one of the pillars of the Church.

For this was what indulgences seemed to have become: a pillar of the faith. Palz, Master of Erfurt, actually taught that they were "the modern way of preaching the Gospel." Was there anything intrinsically reprehensible about them? A rereading of the treatise which the learned Johann Pfeffer had devoted to the subject a quarter of a century earlier, in that same town of Wittenberg, or a glance at the sermons of the celebrated Johann Geiler of Kayserberg, makes the real meaning of indulgences clear beyond any shadow of a doubt. What the Church understood by *indulgence* was the total or partial remission of the penalties of sin—to which everyone was liable, either on earth or in Purgatory—after the Sacrament of Penance had afforded him absolution from his fault and remission of eternal punishment. But the state of grace was indispensable for the obtaining of such temporal remission; good works, in the shape of prayers, fasting, pilgrimages, visits to churches and almsgiving, were only an incidental, or, to put it another way, a contributory factor. Where there was no firm resolve or inward glow there was no remission. In strict doctrine an indulgence was certainly not an automatic means of gaining a cheap discharge from penalties that were justly deserved. In 1476 a bull of Sixtus IV had recognized that indulgences could be applied to the souls of the departed, whose sufferings in the next world would be alleviated thereby; and the declaration of this principle had contributed to the success of the jubilee of 1500.

It was not of recent origin. As early as the eleventh century crusaders had reaped the benefits of the plenary indulgence. Since then it had been awarded more generally and bestowed on less heroic occasions. It had had a number of happy results, and countless works of religious or social utility had been financed by the money collected in this way; churches too, hospitals, pawn-shops, even dikes and bridges. Thanks to indulgences the Church in France had been materially restored on the morrow of the Hundred Years War. Nor had the spiritual results been insignificant: when proclaimed by special preachers the grant of an indulgence provided a spiritual jolt rather like the "missions" of modern times, and was the means of bringing numerous penitents to the confessional.

But it was not these excellent reasons alone which caused the institution to become so widespread, particularly from the fourteenth century onwards. For close on two centuries years of indulgence had been granted with unrestrained liberality in return for the briefest visit to a church, or the least meritorious of pilgrimages. In a period of twelve months the pious Elector Frederick the Wise laid up no fewer than 127,799 years, sufficient to empty a whole province of Purgatory and ensure himself more than one heaven. It is not difficult to imagine the kind of excesses which found their way into this practice, and they had already been condemned in 1312 by the decretal *Abusionibus*. Simony discovered some splendid material here and it is open to doubt whether preachers of indulgences, with their attendant collectors stationed at the foot of the pulpit, were primarily interested in saving souls or in collecting ducats. All too often the grant of an indulgence was part and parcel of some shady deal, and sometimes the right to collect for it was actually sold at auction. Pope Leo X himself once empowered the Fuggers, a celebrated firm of bankers at Augsburg, to preach an indulgence by way of security for a loan. The climate of the age was only too favourable to this type of proceedings. In 1514, when the Hohenzollern Albert of Brandenberg secured his election as Archbishop of Mainz, the heavy chancellery dues of 14,000 ducats, plus a "voluntary settlement" of a further 10,000 intended to ease the scruples of the Curia, were financed by the Fuggers, who were guaranteed in return one-third of the revenues from the great papal indulgence.

Misconduct such as this was not the only menace to the institution; the doctrine itself was affected by something even worse. Far too many preachers taught that an indulgence possessed a kind of magical quality, and that by spending money to obtain it men were taking out a mortgage on Heaven. One popular jingle ran:

> Sobald das Geld im Kasten klingt
> Die Seele aus dem Fegfeuer springt!

> [*As soon as the money in the collection box rings
> The soul from out of hellfire springs—L. P. W.*]

Moreover Germany was not the only country where such rubbish was taught. In 1482 the Sorbonne had condemned one preacher who recited it from the pulpit; at Besançon, in 1486, a certain Franciscan swore that provided a man wore the habit of his Order, St Francis would come in person to collect him from Purgatory. Naturally enough there were lively reactions to these specious claims. As early as 1484 a priest named Lallier had publicly rejected the view that the Pope had the power to remit the pains of another world by means of indulgence, and despite objections from the theological faculty, the Bishop of Paris had absolved him. In 1498 the Franciscan Vitrier had been hauled before the Sorbonne for having declared that "money must not be given in order to obtain forgiveness." His disciple Erasmus had lately written: "Any trader, mercenary soldier or judge has but to put down his money, however nefariously acquired, and he imagines that he has purged the whole

Lemean Marsh of his life." Views of this sort were taught in the University of
Wittenberg, which considered itself the rival of Leipzig and Erfurt; and
trenchancy of tone helped to further the renown of that centre, where, during
1516, statements such as the following had been heard: "It is an absurdity to
preach that the souls in Purgatory are ransomed by indulgences."

In 1517 the most important indulgence preached in Germany was that
which the popes had twice accorded to generous Christians donating money
for the new basilica of St. Peter's: Julius II in 1506, in order that building
might begin, and Leo X in 1514, to enable it to continue. It was the fruits of
this indulgence which had been the object of that extraordinary share-out
which we have already noticed on the occasion of the Mainz election. The
archbishop had entrusted the task of preaching the indulgence to the Dominicans, and this had provoked a fraternal but somewhat bitter jealousy among
the Augustinians.

At the head of these preachers was a certain Brother Tetzel, a burly, vol-
uble fellow, who pleaded his case with extreme enthusiasm. He was a well-
intentioned man, whose own moral conduct was perfectly honourable, and
he did not deserve the calumnies with which his opponents were to befoul
him; but his theology was highly questionable. His method of procedure
merely increased the public belief that an indulgence was a mere financial
transaction. He visited the whole area dependent on Mainz, and would arrive
with a vast retinue, preceded by the bull which was carried on a velvet cush-
ion embroidered with gold. The people would come out in procession to meet
him, accompanied by the ringing of bells and waving of banners; and Tetzel
would then mount the pulpit, or stand in the town square, offering "pass-
ports to cross the sea of wrath and go direct to Paradise." This was indeed a
splendid opportunity to make certain of escaping the seven years of suffering
—which, as all agreed, any forgiven sin still required in the Beyond—by obtaining the plenary indulgence accorded by a confessor of Tetzel's choice.
Besides, here also was an opportunity to snatch some friend or loved one
from the fires of Purgatory. Nor was the price extortionate. The penitent
must go to confession, visit seven churches, recite five *Paters* and five *Aves,*
and place an offering in the indulgence box. The offering demanded was a
modest one, scaled to the resources of each individual believer: for the poorest
a quarter of a florin was sufficient.

It was against such practices and such teaching that the manifesto nailed to
the door of the Schlosskirche protested so strongly. Tetzel had not preached
in Wittenberg, which was Saxon territory, but all recognized the target of
this attack. It was all very well for the author to maintain discretion by advis-
ing his readers to receive "the Apostolic Commissioners with respect"; his
theses rejected not only the Dominican's interpretation of the indulgence, but
protested against the institution itself. He denounced its financial side. "The
indulgences so extolled by preachers have only one merit, that of bringing in
money." Or again: "Nowadays the Pope's money-bag is fatter than those of
the richest capitalists; why does he not build this basilica with his own re-

sources rather than with the offerings of the poor?" These somewhat clumsy arguments made a deep impression among the common people. He also criticized the theological bases of the institution, suggesting that the indulgences caused men to lose their sense of penitence. "True contrition gladly accepts the penalties and seeks them out; indulgence remits them and inspires us with aversion for them. When a Christian is truly penitent he has the right to plenary remission, even without an ecclesiastical indulgence. The grace of Jesus Christ remits the penalties of sin, not the Pope. Man can hope to receive this grace by experiencing a hatred of self and of his sin, and not by the accomplishment of a few acts or the sacrifice of a little money." Although, in so far as they contain authentic Catholic doctrine, these theses are acceptable in many respects, they deviate from orthodoxy to the extent that they deny the Pope's power to remit penalties and refer implicitly to a theory of grace according to which man's merits are almost worthless.

What motive had impelled the author of this document to defy the official teaching of the Church? Indignation against traffickers in sacred things? Undoubtedly. Hatred of the Pope and contempt for the simoniacal Roman Curia? No. There was something deeper, more decisive, and it is revealed in the very last sentence of his ninety-five theses. Tetzel was trying to persuade the faithful that salvation was easily effected through works; he was concealing from his hapless listeners that it is necessary "to enter Heaven by way of many tribulations," as the Acts of the Apostles makes quite clear; he was encouraging them to "rest in false security." Here was the crux of the matter. It was against "this appalling error" that the professor of Wittenberg entered the lists; and he entered them with all the violence of a man for whom this theological dispute represented a drama played out in his own life, and whom false security had brought very close indeed to total despair and unbelief. His name was *Martin Luther*.

A BRILLIANT YOUNG MONK

At this date Luther was a tall, lean, bony man with powerful expressive hands. They were never still: they were forever pointing at an enemy or punctuating an argument. Everything about him indicated a passion, unease and a latent violence that was always on the verge of erupting to produce total destruction. The eyes in the rough-hewn face, with its high cheekbones, square chin and lined cheeks, often sparkled with anger or intelligence, but no less frequently they allowed a glimpse of uncontrollable anguish. It is difficult to escape the fascination which this monk in his simple Augustinian robe exerted on everyone who saw him. In 1517 he was thirty-four years old.

What had Luther's life been like up to this time? What events and reasoning had led him to quarrel openly with official conformity and make the gesture which, by setting him in the forefront of world affairs, was to turn him into the living symbol of contradiction? The *Rückblick*, that rapid and superficial glance which he threw back to his youth in 1545, a year before his death, is hardly an adequate answer to these questions; when old people evoke their memories they very often amend both truth and falsehood.

As for the traditional account, still widely believed, it seems best to retain here only the bare outline of the facts and not their substance. The explanation of Martin Luther's attitude must not be sought in his allegedly unhappy childhood and adolescence, nor, as the psychoanalysts would have it, in the crisis of a monk beset by temptations of the flesh, nor even in the scandalized indignation he is supposed to have felt during a brief visit to Rome. It is to be found rather in an inner conflict, something like those experienced by St Paul, St Augustine and Pascal—a conflict through which Luther lived in keen spiritual agony and uncertainty, and from which he unhappily emerged along a path which was no longer that approved by Mother Church.

Martin Luther was born on 10th November 1483, at Eisleben in Saxony, the second of eight children. He was brought up at Mansfeld, where Hans, his father, had settled six months after the boy's birth. His early years were no more and no less happy than that of many sons of ordinary folk. The harsh realities of life brutalized this class of persons, and in a large family there was no time for emotional refinement. Hans was a devout, stern man whose morals were irreproachable but who was easily roused to anger. He was striving with all his might to rise from artisan to foreman, and finally to become a small foundry owner on his own account, and his sole desire was that his entire household should behave with absolute propriety. Hans Luther's hardworking wife, Margaret, *née* Ziegler, was a stolid Franconian. She did not find it difficult to share her husband's ideas and she directed her family with a firm hand which her children occasionally found too heavy.

Martin's parents sent him to school at Mansfeld when he was six years old. There he received the customary education of the age, consisting of the old *trivium* and the catechism, instilled by the pedagogic methods which were then in current use and in which the cane played a large part. When it became apparent that he was an exceptionally gifted boy, his father decided that he should continue his studies with a view to the law. He spent a year in the Cathedral School at Magdeburg, which was excellently conducted by the Brethren of the Common Life, and there he acquired an unhappily all too brief experience of genuine spirituality: it was most probably here that he made his first real contact with the Bible. Then, because his great-uncle was sacristan of St Nicholas's, Luther was drawn back to Eisenach, and there he developed his innate talents for music. Finally, at the age of eighteen, he entered Erfurt University—his father, who was now more comfortably off, was henceforth able to pay him an allowance—where he obtained an outstanding degree and greatly improved his powers of self-expression and reasoning. His teachers, Fathers Usingen and Palz, trained him in their methods, which were those of Ockhamist scholasticism. His fellow students regarded him as an honourable, devout, but merry companion. So far everything about Luther's life had been utterly normal and ordinary. Then, just as he had begun his legal studies, an unforeseen event completely altered his destiny.

On 2nd July 1505, while he was returning alone from Mansfeld to Erfurt, a thunderstorm of unusual violence suddenly broke upon him. The lightning flashed so close that he believed himself lost. In the midst of this danger he invoked St Anne according to custom, and promised: "If you come to my aid I will become a monk." This was perhaps a rash vow, but it was certainly not spontaneous. Various other incidents had preceded this spiritual decision. Legend has embroidered upon them so much that their detail has become obscured, but their meaning is abundantly plain. A serious illness during adolescence, the sudden death of a friend, a sword wound acquired in a student's duel and which had bled for a long time—all these had brought Luther face to face with the one great fact that youth tends to ignore—the fact of death. The episode of the thunderstorm set the seal on this revelation. Luther's impressionable nature and naturally vivid sensibility responded urgently to that mortal fear which the thunderclap had inspired in his soul. He remembered the good Brethren of the Common Life, the Anhalt ruler in the Franciscan habit whom he had known at Magdeburg, and dedicated young Carthusians he often saw at Erfurt. He thought of all the people he knew who seemed to have found peace of heart, and the answer to the most dreadful of all questions beneath the homespun of the monastic robe. This vow of his was undoubtedly forced from his soul by terror, but the terror was not caused by the thunderstorm alone. Neither his family nor his friends could prevent him from remaining faithful to his promise. Fifteen days after the incident on the Erfurt road he set off to knock on the door of the Augustinian monastery there.

In 1517 then, when he nailed his theses on the door of the Schlosskirche in Wittenberg, he was a monk—and a monk of some importance in his Order—and he was moreover a monk who had not the slightest desire to renounce his vows. "I have been a pious monk for twenty years," he was to say; "I have said a Mass every day; I have worn myself out in prayer and fasting." Witnesses have described him as a good monk, "certainly not without sin, but above serious reproach." In 1507 he was ordained priest. Luther mounted the altar steps for the first time with an ardour mingled with fear, as befitted one who was about to hold the living God in his own hands. Theology had made him increasingly fervent; Duns Scotus and St Thomas, Pierre d'Ailly and Gerson, William of Ockham and others in the same tradition, notable Gabriel Biel, had been the object of his voracious reading, together with the Bible, and St Augustine, and all the mystics from St Bernard to Master Eckhart. In 1508, by order of Staupitz, the wise Vicar-General for Germany, who was much interested in this brilliant young man, Luther was transferred to Wittenberg, there to teach philosophy and acquire the title of Bachelor of Arts. He enjoyed a high reputation in his Order.

This was made very clear when, during the winter of 1510-11, he was chosen to go to Rome to submit the dispute between the Augustinians of the strict and conventual observances to the superiors of the Order. Legend has it that what he saw in the Eternal City so upset the young monk that he resolved to undertake the reform of the Church. This is a convenient story, but all the evidence is against it. Luther stayed in Rome for four short weeks, behaving like any other pious pilgrim. He was most anxious to see as many churches as possible, to win the indulgences attached to these visits and to climb the "scala sancta" on his knees; in short, as he himself recalled, he was filled with "holy madness." All he saw of the Papal Court were the usual glimpses that any humble visiting German cleric might expect to obtain. He obviously heard a good deal of gossip, but this did not have much immediate effect upon him. It was not until much later on, when he had been condemned by the Catholic Church, that he sought to justify his own attitude by reviving his memories of Rome. So great was men's ignorance in the capital of Christendom, he recalled, that he had been unable to find a confessor there; in St Sebastian's he had seen seven priests hurry through the Mass within the hour at a single altar; and he himself had witnessed the shameless behaviour of women in church. Perhaps; but he did not pronounce these strictures until twenty-five years after the incidents concerned—very much *a posteriori.*

On his return to Germany Luther was assigned to the Augustinian house in Wittenberg; in the following year, having been made doctor of theology, he was awarded the chair of Holy Scripture at the university. His lectures were outstandingly successful: he spoke on the Psalms and the Pauline Epistles; he was also a celebrated preacher, highly regarded by his congregations. Staupitz, his immediate superior, had a very exalted opinion of him; he made him "district vicar," in other words, provincial, with jurisdiction over eleven of the Order's houses; and he even went so far as to tell Luther: "God speaks through your mouth." Thus Luther's importance and prestige added considerable weight to his stand against the preachers of indulgences on All Saints' Eve 1517.

THE DRAMA OF A SOUL

In order to understand Luther's reasons for acting as he did we must penetrate his soul and reach into those dark and dangerous recesses of the mind wherein each man worthy of the name seeks, amid suffering and contradiction, to give a meaning to his own destiny. Because the light which he himself sheds upon the drama of his youth was given long after the period concerned, a number of critics have treated it all as legend. The aged Luther, they allege, invented the background of a Pascalian debate in order to provide his rebellion with fundamentally lofty and mystical origins. But an impartial study of the documents covering the decisive years—for example, his commentary on the Epistle to the Romans—is sufficient to convince the reader that their author could have adopted certain attitudes at the end of a secret and painful effort to find the answer to the gravest of man's problems. Anyone who refuses to believe that Luther was fundamentally one of those individuals for whom life and belief are serious matters is guilty of traducing historical and psychological truth. He was essentially a protagonist in great spiritual battles. The Augustinian monk who seemed to be making for himself such a brilliant career was inwardly tormented by that peculiarly religious anxiety which it is easier to feel than to define.

Luther had entered the monastery hoping to discover peace of mind, but he had not found it. He was very much a son of his age and of his native land—of Germany, where man's struggle against the powers of darkness was translated into a multitude of terrible or sublime legends; of Christianity at the crossroads, where morbid sermons and dances of death caused the faithful to be haunted with thoughts of their ultimate destiny. He had not been able to get rid of these phantoms merely by donning the monastic robe. "I know a man," he wrote in 1518, "who declared he has experienced such mortal terror that no words can describe it; he who has not suffered the like would never believe him. But it is a fact that if anyone were obliged to endure for long, for half an hour or even the tenth part of an hour, he would perish utterly, and his very bones would be reduced to ashes." Luther was in the grip of terrible anguish, and his friend Melanchthon relates that during the whole of his monastic life he was never able to throw it off. "My heart bled when I said the Canon of the Mass," Luther confesses, in reference to his years as a young priest. These are words that no one can read without emotion.

Whence came this anguish? Certain authors have suggested that it was caused by hereditary neurosis, but there is no real proof of this. It is perfectly clear to anyone reading many of his own confessions that Luther was not so much a sick man as one burdened with the tragic sense of sin in all its intensity. But of what sin? It is futile to pretend to find an answer in the stirrings of his flesh. Some have seen Luther as a monk in the grip of secret lusts, a familiar of the *delectatio morosa,* unable to quell the beast within him and revolting against the discipline of the Church in order to satisfy his craving. Yet if this were a true picture, if he had acted on the strength of such contemptible motives, his influence would scarcely have been so far-reaching, and would scarcely have inflicted so much suffering upon the Church. Besides, Luther himself frequently emphasized that the worst temptations were not carnal: "evil thoughts, hatred of God, blasphemy, despair and unbelief— these are the main temptations." The concupiscence which he had to conquer was not primarily that which draws male to female, but an irresistible craving of both body and soul that urges man to embrace all that is terrestrial and manifest—in a word, human—deflecting him from the invisible and divine.

In the monastery he had hoped to be delivered from these monsters. He was a mystical personality in many ways, and he dreamed of a warm, consoling presence which would shield him from evil and from himself, but he had discovered nothing in the monastic routine to provide such comfort. Was this because he lacked true humility, or because he had not the spirit of prayer?

Only God, who has already judged the soul of Martin Luther, can supply an answer. One obstacle, however, certainly prevented him from running like the Prodigal Son to the arms of his Father, for whenever the least flicker of impurity, violence or doubt crossed his mind he believed himself damned. He tried prayer, asceticism, and even daily confession, but none of them could rid him of this ever-present obsession with hell, which continually threatened to overwhelm him. "I did penance," Luther says, "but despair did not leave me."

The obstacle which barred Luther's way to the path of peace and love was his concept of God. He insists that this was the picture shown him in religious life. "We paled at the mere mention of Christ's Name, for He was always depicted as a stern judge who was angry with us." Was it necessary to work oneself to death in prayer, fasting and mortifications from fear of a Master wielding the rod of chastisement, a Divine Executioner? What was the good of it all, since one could not even be sure of melting His wrath? "When will you do enough to obtain God's mercy?" he asked himself in anguish. In that age of misery the message of Christ's love seemed sterile; there remained only the atrocious doctrine of inevitable punishment meted out by an inexorable judge.

It has not been difficult for Catholic critics to show that this doctrine has never been that of Holy Church. In a book of no fewer than 378 pages, Father Denifle has conclusively demonstrated that the "justice of God" mentioned in a famous passage of the Epistle to the Romans (1:17), and which Luther took to be the supreme spiritual reality, was intended to signify something far more than *justitia puniens,* divine wrath punishing the sins of men; the words were used rather of sanctifying grace, of the omnipotent mercy lavished by God on all who believe in Him and submit to His ordinances. Luther's interpretation of the phrase reveals a surprising failure to understand the philosophy of such writers as St Augustine and St Bernard, with whose works he was undoubtedly well acquainted. To explain the spiritual drama of the young Augustinian monk, however, it is sufficient to acknowledge that he himself regarded this erroneous doctrine as valid, and as that which his own professors had taught him.

The fact may have been due to the imperfect theological training offered by the representations of decadent scholasticism who filled all the university chairs. Moreover the teaching then in fashion contained one feature calculated to impel a restless soul along the downward slope. To such a man as Luther, obsessed with the desire to appease his terrible God, and deriving not the slightest comfort from his prayers and mortifications, one system in particular provided a kind of answer: Ockhamist Nominalism, in which, as we have seen, he had been brought up. Luther had discovered from the writings of this school not only that man could overcome sin by will alone, but also that no human action became meritorious unless God acknowledged it and willed it to be so. But if man's will failed it had no means of recovery, for reason was unavailing and grace was not conceived as a supernatural principle raising man's spiritual forces to the level of Divine Justice. Thus nothing was left save a capricious God, granting or withholding His grace and forgiveness for motives that defied all the rules of logic. Before Him stood a defenceless man, inert and passive in relation to the work of salvation. Destiny appeared to be regulated by the cold mechanics of a despot in whose eyes nothing had any merit. Luther strove hard to find confirmation of these theories in certain passages of St Paul and St Augustine, for they corresponded all too well with his fundamental and powerful belief in the futility of all human . effort. In several respects he remained an Ockhamist all his life; but he rejected the voluntarism taught by Ockham's disciples, he denied the human liberty which they recognized, and he gave it a ring of predestinationism which was absent from the master's philosophy. None of this did anything to grant him peace of mind.

But a number of more peaceful influences were at work. Luther had read all the mystics, especially the German writers of the late Middle Ages, notably Tauler. Here too he had found elements that tended to deny the importance of external works, to discard free will and to exalt the part played by faith in Christ the Redeemer. Man must lay himself open to God's action, submit to it and do nothing to resist it. This was one of the fundamental ideas of the *Theologica Germanica*. Furthermore Staupitz, anxious to heal this ravaged soul, had gone a long way in the same direction by showing Luther the gentleness of God's love and the need for supreme surrender to Providence. Neither the subtleties of the schools more ritual practices would give him the divine life to which he aspired, but only the impulse of a believing soul, and the piety which sprang from the most secret recesses of the heart. "True repentance begins with love of justice and of God." Once the young monk felt that part of his burden had been lifted, that he was on the way to a new enlightenment; and it seemed that ideas, arguments and biblical references poured in from all sides to confirm this doctrine "and dance a jig around it."

It was now that there happened the "discovery of mercy," a wholly spiritual event to which Luther's disciples afterwards traced the origins of the Reformation. The date and place of this occurrence are the subject of some dispute. He may have had his first glimpse of it in Rome, while making the pious pilgrimage on his knees up the "Scala sancta." It may, on the other hand, be necessary to advance the date to 1518 or 1519; if so he can have had only a kind of presentiment of his doctrine on the day when he nailed his theses to the chapel door. Its main features, however, are already apparent in the university lectures which he gave between 1514 and 1517. The most probable truth is that the "discovery" took place in his mind by gradual stages, before imposing itself on his soul with such force that all arguments and reservations became as nothing in the blinding clarity of what seemed to him to be incontrovertible evidence.

In the preface to the 1545 edition of his *Works* Luther describes in detail this "sudden illumination of the Holy Spirit." He was pondering once again the terrible seventeenth verse in the first chapter of the Epistle to the Romans when the true meaning—that is to say, the meaning he henceforth considered to be true—was revealed to him. "While I pursued my meditations day and night, examining the import of these words, 'The justice of God is revealed in the Gospel, as it is written, the just live by faith,' I began to understand that the justice of God signifies that justice whereby the just live through the gift of God, namely, through faith. Therefore the meaning of the sentence is as follows: "the Gospel shows us the justice of God, but it is a passive justice, through which, by means of faith, the God of mercy justifies us." To the young monk, tortured by fear and anguish, this was indeed a prodigious discovery! The hangman God, armed with His whip, faded away, yielding place to Him towards whom the soul could turn with perfect trust and confidence. . . .

At this juncture, as always happens where great minds are concerned, all kinds of reflections and arguments crystallized around this one apparently quite straightforward idea. It became the basis of a system. "System" is perhaps the wrong word here; for Luther there was no question of dry doctrine or paper thesis, but of a vital experience, the answer to all his own terrible problems. But he saw the answer so clearly that he was able to express it in the form of categorical principles. Man is a sinner, incapable of making himself just (i.e. righteous) and condemned to impotence by the enemy he bears within himself. Even though he conforms outwardly to the law, he remains in a state of sin. Even though he tries to behave righteously and hopes to acquire merit, he is unable to do so, for at the root of his very being there is a deadly germ. There must therefore be, and indeed there is, a justice exterior to man, which alone will save him. Through the grace of Jesus Christ all the soul's blemishes are, as it were, covered by a cloak of light. Thus the one means and only hope of salvation is to entrust oneself to Christ, as it were, to cling to Him. "The faith that justifies is that which seizes Jesus Christ." Compared with this saving reality all man's miserable efforts towards repentance and self-improvement were ridiculous and worthless. "The just live by faith."

It must be admitted that this view was perfectly adapted to set an anguished soul at rest. Where did it deviate from the orthodox? The Church teaches that God is "just" in the simplest sense of the term, that is to say, He distributes His graces to us all in an equitable manner, and not by virtue of a kind of incomprehensible caprice. She teaches that salvation and eternal bliss are earned in the world through positive effort and good works. She affirms the importance of sin, but she refuses to admit that man can do nothing to combat it. She does indeed proclaim the indispensability of the love of God and union with Christ, but she asserts that they demand from man a positive effort to acquire a supernatural resemblance. Faith is but the beginning of justification. It is completed by reception of the sacrament, in the act of contribution or the act of charity. Salvation demands much more than mere belief.

Luther, however, was so intoxicated by his discovery, so exalted by the joy of escaping at last from the vice which had held him in its grip, that he would consider no argument advanced against his theory. "I felt suddenly born anew," he said, "and it seemed that the doors of Paradise itself were flung wide open to me, and I entered in." He was saved! He knew he was a sinner, but Christ had taken upon His shoulders the sins of the whole world. It was distasteful to realize that all the pious exercises and all the theological reasoning to which he had recourse were of no effect, but in the blinding light of the Redemption all human things were nothing but dry dust. The dialectic of sin and grace contained the answer to everything. The exultant professor of Wittenberg announced his discovery at all his lectures even before his own philosophy had been fully defined, before it had been crowned with the maxim (not formulated until after 1518) that in order to be saved all that one needed was the inner certainty of one's own salvation. He set out his thesis at Easter 1517, at the beginning of a series of lectures on the Epistle to the Hebrews. "Man is incapable of obtaining relief from any sin by his own efforts alone. In the sight of God all human virtues are sin." He also directed one of his pupils, Bernhardi, to take "Grace and Free Will" as the subject of his thesis for the doctorate; it was to conform in all respects with the principles of Luther, who later admitted that at this period he felt "divinely possessed."

The preaching of indulgences offered Luther a splendid opportunity to make the truth blindingly clear to everyone. He was disgusted most of all by this computation of so-called merits shamefully acquired, in order to escape the just pains of the after-life. He himself enjoyed true security in that prodigious wager upon Christ which he intended to maintain from now onwards. The false, pitiable thing which these wretched folk believed that they acquired, by kneeling in front of some relics and throwing their money into a box provided by someone like Tetzel, was no true security. As for the authority of the Pope, who guaranteed the value of such practices, the Ockhamist in Luther recalled what the leaders of that school had had to say, their reservations on papal infallibility and indeed on the function of the Papacy in general. He remembered Gabriel Biel's declaration that every Catholic was competent to reform the Church. He had, of course, not the slightest idea that in adopting positions of this kind he was going to set in motion the gravest crisis which Christianity had ever experienced. He was, in his own words, "a blind wretch who set off without knowing where he was going." Spiritual argument did not really interest him. He was fundamentally interested only in making the world hear and understand Heaven's response to his *De Profundis;* but "the voice of Germany, restless and secretly trembling with unrestrained passion," was not slow to answer his cry, and the drama of one soul unleashed a revolution.